Captain T. E. ADLAM, V.C.

Second-Lieut. J. HARRISON, V.C., M.C.
Killed in action, May 3rd, 1917.

Second-Lieut. D. S. BELL, V.C.
Killed in action, July 10th, 1916.

MEMBERS OF THE UNION.

National Union of Teachers
WAR RECORD
1914 — 1919

A SHORT ACCOUNT
OF DUTY AND WORK
ACCOMPLISHED
DURING THE WAR.

LONDON:
HAMILTON HOUSE, MABLEDON PLACE, W.C.1.
1920

PER PIETATEM

I

Into the mystery, not of death only,
    Into strange life they went, learners anew;
School, home, and love they left, into a labyrinth
    Vanishing perilous, dead to our view.
Dark over Flanders death waited their coming,
    Mirk lay the North Sea, pulsing with death;
Even the Orient darkly received them:
    We darkly watching, holding our breath.

II

Out of the trench labyrinthine, the stifle,
    The bellowing and crashing, the hurtle of lead,
Back to love, home, and school came they, triumphant,
    All of them, all of them, even the dead.
Our dead and our quick are returned to us, hallowed,
    Our living respire again, breathing our air,
And there, by the blackboard, our dead—see, diaphanous!
    Singing the hymn again, part of the prayer.

III

We shall go on to the end never knowing
    What to the end of their days they must know
In dreaming, in waking—the brunt of the burden,
    The gore of the horror, the gasp of the woe.
Yet we too remember: the zeal sacrificial,
    The endurance, the courage, our rampart and shield;
To the dead and the living this book of remembrance
    As if for an altar we frame and upyield.

CONTENTS

CHAPTER I

INTRODUCTORY

PAGE
9

CHAPTER II

RELIEF FUNDS RAISED BY TEACHERS

Prince of Wales' National Relief Fund.—Local Relief Funds.—Belgian Funds.—Book Fund.—Fund for Clothing Serbian Children.—Donation by the Union to Serbian Teachers.—Thank-Offering and War Aid Funds 11

CHAPTER III

THE BELGIAN REFUGEE QUESTION AND REPATRIATION OF RUSSIAN TEACHERS

Action of N.U.T. and Refugee Teachers.—Benevolent and Orphan Council.—Local Education Authorities and Belgian Children.—Belgian Technical School Teachers.—Repatriation of Russian Teachers 16

CHAPTER IV

THE UNION'S ACTION ON MATTERS OF PUBLIC INTEREST IN CONNECTION WITH THE WAR

Scales of Pensions to Soldiers and Sailors in His Majesty's Forces.—National War Savings Campaign 20

CHAPTER V

THE UNION'S ACTION ON MATTERS OF PUBLIC INTEREST IN CONNECTION WITH THE WAR (*continued*)

Employment of Children and their Demobilisation after the War.—Cost of Living.—Education in the Army.—Jack Cornwell, V.C. 24

CONTENTS

CHAPTER VI
Union Action Concerning Teachers

War Service (Superannuation) Act.—Salaries of Teachers who joined the Forces.—Action of the Teachers' Provident Society.—Subscription to the Union.—Military Service and Facilities for Training College Students.—Teachers Exempt from Service.—Retired Teachers and School work.—Clergy in the Schools.—Committee of Appeal against Decisions by Local Tribunals.—Training of Disabled Soldiers as Teachers.—Enlistment and Demobilisation of Teachers.—Attestation of Pensioners' Declarations 29

CHAPTER VII
Services Rendered by Teachers who were unable to Join the Forces

Women and the War.—Teachers as Drill Instructors, in Volunteer Training Corps and as Special Constables.— War Transfers.—Services in connection with the National Register and on Relief Committees.—War Lecturing and Literature.—National Service 37

Teachers Killed in the War 43

Teachers Honoured for Gallant Services 79

Teachers who Joined the Forces 93

Staff of the Central Offices of the N.U.T. who Joined the Forces 207

CHAPTER I

INTRODUCTORY

THE close of the great European struggle, with all its tragedy of life and death, presents a fitting opportunity for reviewing the past few years in their relation to the primary school teachers of this country, and for placing on record some particulars of the splendid work accomplished by them. The story, incomplete and unadorned as it undoubtedly appears, is given in the hope that it may be of interest to teachers generally, and perhaps incidentally to pupils who have passed through their hands, as well as to relatives of the fallen.

It is shown by the following records that many thousands of teachers joined his Majesty's Forces, that many made the last and greatest sacrifice, and that many were honoured for their bravery and devotion; while those who remained in the schools gave such patriotic help as they could, by monetary assistance, service in organising and directing the multitudinous local efforts demanded by the war, benevolent love, pity, admiration and devotion. The tribute to the teachers in the Board of Education Report for 1916 was that : "When peace is restored the teachers of England need have no fear if anyone asks them what they did in the war. They offered themselves freely, and whether they stayed in the schools or carried arms, they did their duty, and the service of education is the richer for their practice and exemplification of those principles of civic duty and patriotism which in times of peace they taught, and not in vain, by precept and exhortation." The Bishop of Lichfield remarked, in an address to the Staffordshire County Association of the Union, that : "It is a mistake to suppose the war had created the fine spirit of self-sacrifice and service predominant to-day. War did not create such things ; it brought them to the front and developed them, turning something potential into something actual. Unless the boys and girls had learnt somewhere that spirit of service and self-sacrifice we should not have seen it when war brought it to the test."

N.U.T. WAR RECORD

The gracious tribute sent by their Majesties the King and Queen to the President of the Board of Education in 1918 is perhaps a fitting note on which to open up the record contained in the next chapters. The letter was as follows:

"Windsor Castle,
"*6th April*, 1918.

"Dear Mr. Fisher,

"It has given the King and Queen much pleasure to visit recently the schools of various types and thus gain an insight into the daily life of the rising generation at work and at play.

"Their Majesties are aware of the magnificent response which the Educational Service throughout the country has made to the demands of the present time, not only in its contribution to the fighting forces, but also in the assistance which it has rendered in many kinds of important war work.

"Above all, they wish to express their admiration of the self-denial and devotion of the teachers, who it is evident, while training the mind and body of their pupils, recognise the importance of formation of character.

"These visits have brought home to the King and Queen the keenness and patriotism of the youth of the country.

"They realise the unselfishness and hearty manner in which boys and girls, inspired by the example of their teachers, have formed War Savings Associations, subscribed money for charitable purposes, and by their handiwork contributed to the personal needs and comforts of the troops.

"Their Majesties feel that the nation can be proud of its young sons and daughters whose example during this great war augurs well for the future of our race.

"I am commanded to request you to convey to the School Authorities and teachers the hearty congratulations of the King and Queen upon the admirable manner in which the public service of education is being maintained, the progress of which their Majesties will ever watch with interest and sympathy.

"Believe me, yours very truly,
"(Signed) Stamfordham."

The Rt. Honble. H. A. L. Fisher, M.P.,
President, Board of Education.

CHAPTER II

RELIEF FUNDS RAISED BY TEACHERS

Prince of Wales' National Relief Fund.—Local Relief Funds.—Belgian Relief Funds.—Book Fund.—Belgian and Serbian Children's Clothing Fund.—Thank-Offering Fund.—War Aid Fund.

Prince of Wales' National Relief Fund

The opening of the columns of the *Schoolmaster* for subscriptions to the Prince of Wales' National Relief Fund called forth a generous response from teachers, the amount when the list was closed in January, 1916, having reached a total of £16,470 2s. 9d. A donation from the Sierra Leone Association was accompanied by the following letter:—

"The members feel that their loyalty to the throne of England and the protection they enjoy through the British nation are sufficient reasons to identify themselves with the National Union of Teachers in particular, and other British subjects in general, and in this time of stress and danger, to contribute towards the fund. Although the amount is indeed inadequate, the members trust it may be regarded as a token of hearts big with sympathy, gratitude and devotion. They pray that British arms may continue to prevail ('Thrice-armed is he who hath his quarrel just') until ruthless Germany acknowledges that the fighting qualities of England have not impaired since 1814, but enhanced and developed only too happily—and especially for the Germans—in a refined and humane degree."

Local Relief Funds

Local Associations of the Union and individual schools and teachers also contributed freely to Local Relief Funds, and though it would be quite impossible to give any adequate idea of the amounts so raised, yet from definite information which reached the Union from time to time it was known that about £50,000 was received, and it would be safe to assume that that amount was

N.U.T. WAR RECORD

finally quite if not more than doubled. It may here be mentioned that at the beginning of the war a circular was sent by the Union to all Local Associations advising them to co-operate with the various agencies throughout the country in all efforts to secure :—

(a) The administration of War Relief Funds in such manner that employment rather than monetary aid should be given where possible and desirable ;

(b) The maximum amount of employment in all industries during the continuance of the war.

Belgian Relief Funds

A fund for the relief of Belgian refugee teachers was raised by the Union, and £2,674 11s. 5d. was expended on their maintenance during the war ; this was exclusive of a similar fund provided by the teachers of London, which finally totalled £2,022 1s. 2d. Over £600 was sent to the Dutch teachers in Holland, who had established a branch of the Teachers' International Bureau for the relief of Belgian teachers. £200 of this amount was forwarded direct from the teachers of Birmingham to the Bureau.

Book Fund

The great body of teachers who kindle the love of books and who teach the comfort and companionship that can be derived from them, looked upon the supply of reading matter for the troops as a special duty. A Book Fund was therefore inaugurated and many hundreds of books were supplied to the troops in the field as well as to prisoners of war in Germany. The *Schoolmaster* co-operated with the British Red Cross War Library and other acknowledged institutions in the choice of volumes and other matters connected with the administration of the fund. The amount subscribed was about £116. A certificate was prepared containing the names of the head teacher and of the scholars who acted as collectors, and a copy was sent to each school which helped the fund. The following is a typical letter of thanks received from a soldier teacher :—

> "It was kind of you to send me posies from the home garden ; but what did me most good were the primroses and violets which you sent me in the shape of a parcel of books. These are imperishable flowers. I handed them round from bed to bed, and they did not lose one bit of their fragrance.

RELIEF FUNDS RAISED BY TEACHERS

In fact, their sweet breath seems to be sweeter and richer in these moments when we are away from our loved ones and on beds of suffering."

Belgian and Serbian Children's Clothing Fund

Again, there was a fund raised for the purpose of supplying clothing to the Belgian and Serbian children, the total sum collected in the schools of London for this purpose having amounted to nearly £4,300. The number of kits supplied was about 10,000, each kit consisting of five garments.

The Union also sent a £50 donation towards the relief of Serbian teachers.

Thank-Offering Fund

The Thank-Offering Fund is indirectly an outcome of war conditions, and was inaugurated as a token of gratitude on the part of teachers for the Superannuation Act of 1918. The object of the fund is to augment the pensions or other allowances of codal pensioners under the old Minutes of 1847 and 1851, and of members of the Union who retired prior to 1912 under the Teachers' Superannuation Act, 1898.

By the terms which govern the disposal of the fund the Executive of the Union is, in addition, empowered to grant assistance in certain cases to post-1912 teachers, after making due provision for the claims of codal pensioners and teachers who retired prior to 1912.

That the appeal was gladly and gratefully welcomed is shown by the fact that at the end of December, 1919, £45,235 9s. 2d. had been contributed to the fund. At that date £25,310 had been expended on grants, the total number of such grants being 2,828. The gratitude expressed by the recipients shows how great has been their need, and the Union, encouraged by the results, is proceeding with the work of dispensing grants on lines satisfactory both to the subscribers and to the teachers who are receiving aid.

War Aid Fund

Of all the organised efforts of the Union during the war, the greatest was the raising of the War Aid Fund for the alleviation of distress in the families of fallen and disabled teachers. The fund was inaugurated by the Union early in 1915 for the purpose of augmenting pensions and allowances from the National Exchequer, so that the widows and orphans of teachers killed in the war might be enabled to live in circumstances of comfort comparable to those which existed before the teachers joined the colours. Soon after its inauguration the scope of the fund was extended to include all dependents, a trust deed being executed which prescribed that the fund was "to be used for the benefit of teachers in State-aided schools serving as soldiers, sailors, or nurses, or in other capacities in the defence of the realm, and of their dependents in the case of death, disablement, or exceptional cases of need arising through the war." Thus membership of the Union is not a condition for assistance, the benefits being open to all service teachers in State-aided schools and their proved dependents. It was estimated that a capital sum of at least £100,000 would have to be raised, and that this sum might be expected to bear interest at the rate of $3\frac{1}{2}$ per cent. per annum, and thus yield a yearly revenue of £3,500. It was further agreed that if any surplus remained after administering the fund, the Executive should be empowered to use it for some charitable purpose for the benefit of teachers and their dependents in such a way as the Executive might decide. Measured by the numbers in the Union and by the average pay of teachers, the subscribing of the £100,000 was an unprecedented thing, and this amount was raised after two and a half years of war. It must be remembered that there are no wealthy members of the N.U.T.—the Union consists of men and women the majority of whom are dependent on their salaries for a livelihood—and the sum mentioned was collected in addition to, and hardly to any extent at the cost of, the Union's Benevolent and Orphan Fund. It was found, however, that even these generous donations were not enough. The fund was initiated at a time when there were only some 4,000 teachers with the forces, and in 1917 the numbers had risen to more than 20,000. The Executive therefore decided to ask the Local Associations to continue their efforts for the duration of the war, seeing that the amount originally agreed upon would not be sufficient to meet the anticipated demand.

The fund is administered by a special Committee of twelve persons appointed annually by the Executive and consisting of six members of the Executive, not London members, three members nominated by the Central Council of the Benevolent and Orphan Fund, and three members of the Union nominated by the Joint Committee of the National Union of Teachers and the London Teachers' Association.

Each application for relief is treated on its merits, grants being made subject to revision annually or whenever other circumstances alter. One feature of the administration of the fund is probably

RELIEF FUNDS RAISED BY TEACHERS

unique ; not one penny subscribed has been used for management, the whole cost of which is borne by the General Fund of the Union.

The relief given by the fund has assumed various forms. In the majority of cases a monthly grant has been made to the widows and children, or to the aged mothers of teachers whose lives have been sacrificed. Special grants have been made to some dependents to meet special liabilities. Many incapacitated teachers have received, in addition sometimes to continued monthly grants, hospital or sanatorium treatment, or have been provided with mechanical appliances rendered necessary by their disablement. Before the decision of the Ministry of Pensions to supply duplicate limbs, these were provided in amputation cases at the cost of the War Aid Fund.

From the inauguration of the fund to the end of 1919 the Committee had spent in relief the sum of £30,339 16s. 11d. At that time 633 applications for assistance had been received. This had been granted in all but a few cases, and monthly grants were still being paid in 330 cases at the rate of about £1,100 per month.

The appeal for subscriptions was withdrawn shortly after the close of hostilities, and by the 31st December, 1919, the amount of the fund was :—Subscriptions, £153,775 15s. 9d. Interest, £22,581 4s. 11d. Total, £176,357 0s. 8d.

CHAPTER III

THE BELGIAN REFUGEE QUESTION AND REPATRIATION OF RUSSIAN TEACHERS

Action of N.U.T. and Refugee Teachers.—Benevolent and Orphan Council.—Local Education Authorities and Belgian Children.—Belgian Technical School Teachers.

Action of N.U.T. and Refugee Teachers

At the beginning of September, 1914, correspondence was received at the central office of the Union from the Belgian Teachers' Federation telling of the plight of the Belgian Teachers owing to the outbreak of war, and asking what assistance the teachers of England could render in the event of the necessity arising for them to seek refuge in this country. A reply was immediately sent that the Executive would do all that was possible to relieve the distress, and should any of the Belgian teachers be forced to come to England, the members of the Union would be willing to receive them into their homes. Between two hundred and three hundred Belgian teachers were helped or advised by the Union as an outcome of this action. About £2,026 was expended in maintenance grants for them, which were continued until they were either able to support themselves or to return to their own country, while a portion of the money was used to defray the expenses of travelling from one part of the country to the other to take advantage of the hospitality offered and for hotel accommodation. In some cases homes were provided by N.U.T. Local Associations, while in others the teachers acted independently of the Association and clubbed together to obtain a certain amount of relief for their Belgian colleagues. In other instances hospitality was provided through local relief committees, though the majority of the offers were received from individual teachers prepared in many cases to take the refugees into their own homes without repayment of any kind.

The following are some typical letters of thanks and appreciation from Belgian teachers for whom homes were found :—

" Allow me to take this opportunity of expressing all our gratitude for the great kindness on your part of which we have been the

THE BELGIAN REFUGEE QUESTION

recipients. We say this, that the remembrance of the care with which we have been surrounded in our dreadful plight will never be effaced from our minds. Also we feel that we are accomplishing our first duty in reiterating our thanks, which, be sure, come from the bottom of our hearts. If not asking too much, would you be so good as to convey to the National Union of Teachers our great gratitude for what they have done for us in this time of stress. When the happy time comes that we are able to return to our own country we shall never cease to proclaim the cordial hospitality that we have received from the English people in such trying circumstances. While waiting the time when we shall be able to witness our admiration of England in other than words, we say again thank you—a thousand times thank you."

"I should like to express my gratitude for the help that you have given me in obtaining for myself and family such generous and gracious hospitality. We are more than touched by so much kindness, and we should like to be able to return it in some way. I put myself entirely at your service and at the service of your Union. We would also thank the ladies who received and helped us with such delicacy."

"The welcome we have received has touched us profoundly. We cannot find words to express our gratitude. Many, many thanks and long life to England who is protecting and sustaining poor little Belgium."

"We have been received at Hoddesdon most heartily, and are moved beyond expression by the cordial welcome which has been accorded to us. The ladies of the committee have placed us in a most comfortable home, and are doing all that is possible to help us to forget the miseries through which we have passed. The family who accompanied us join in expressing their deep thanks. The cottage placed at our disposal is beautifully situated in a most picturesque part. We have found here among these devoted hearts some repose after our sad experiences. We shall never forget what the English nation has so generously done for us. We shall be glad indeed if you will convey our deep thanks to the members of the National Union of Teachers who have helped us in our difficulties."

"I have much pleasure in telling you that I am very happy indeed with Mrs. H—— B——, in whose tender care you have placed me. I am truly touched at the attention and delicate feeling with which I am surrounded."

"I feel I should like to thank you for your cordial welcome. Our hosts could not do more for us. We shall try, but we know that we can never repay you for what you have done. Our debt will exist for ever. Through you our parents have been sheltered from the horrors of the war, and we thank you a thousand times over for it."

" Please accept our sincere thanks for placing us with Mr. and Mrs. H——, who are treating us almost like brother and sister. Their hospitality has softened our miseries and helped us to forget somewhat the troubles through which we have passed. What can we do when we return ? We should like to express our deep gratitude to you and to the two ladies of your staff concerned."

" We have pleasure in thanking you for the great help you have given us. Through your care we are now enjoying calm after the troubled time in Antwerp."

In connection with the above, Mrs. C——, at whose house Mesdames —— and —— stayed, wrote as follows :—" I think we all esteem it a duty, as well as a privilege, to do anything in our power to help the gallant little nation who preferred disaster to dishonour. My four Belgian ladies are extremely nice, and, I am glad to say, they seem to be very well pleased with their quarters. We are all busy now in preparing three houses for the reception of more refugees."

" We hasten to express our gratitude to you for procuring such a comfortable home for us. What you have done for the Belgian refugees is truly enormous. It is a great solace in our misfortune."

" The War Committee having made arrangements for us, we regret that we are unable to profit by your generous offer. We are not the less grateful for all the care with which you have come to our aid. Will you kindly convey to the members of your powerful English Union our warmest thanks for their sympathetic welcome ? "

" We had to start immediately for Oxford, and that hindered us from coming to thank you for all your kindness. We hope, however, to be able to visit you before our return. We thank you infinitely. We assure you of our strong affection for great England, and in particular for the brotherly help which has drawn in closer bonds the union of our two countries."

" We thank you all deeply for your generous help. We are very happily installed here, and the rector of the parish is treating us in a truly brotherly fashion. We are happy because we are together in our exile. We shall have imperishable remembrances of the hospitality of England.

THE BELGIAN REFUGEE QUESTION

Benevolent and Orphan Council

With the influx of the Belgians in 1914 the Benevolent and Orphan Council agreed to give hospitality to eight Belgian boys, sons of teachers, in the Boys' Orphanage at Sydenham, thus filling the home to its fullest capacity. In most cases the sorrows of these refugees had been too intense for them to think of the possibility of parting with their children, though definite arrangements were finally made in the case of two Belgian boys, one of whom remained in residence at the Orphanage for four and a half years.

Local Education Authorities and Belgian Children

Many Local Education Authorities allowed Belgian children who were able to benefit to enter their Secondary Schools without payment of fees. Some authorities also provided the necessary textbooks free of charge, and others formed classes and appointed a special Belgian teacher. The travelling expenses of such children were sometimes paid by the authority, and facilities were offered in many cases for the learning of the English language.

Belgian Technical School Teachers

The English Association of Teachers in Technical Institutions undertook the relief of Belgian refugee teachers of the same class and opened a fund for the purpose.

REPATRIATION OF RUSSIAN TEACHERS.—Shortly after the war broke out a party of 134 Russian teachers who had been on a visit to this country, found on reaching Paris that they would be unable to use their return tickets through Germany. They accordingly came back to England and applied to the Union for assistance. The Russian Consul gave an undertaking to be responsible for their food and lodging in London so long as it was impossible for them to leave England. Inquiries were made of the various authorities concerned, and in a few days the party was accompanied by an official of the Union to Newcastle where they embarked for Bergen. The fares were advanced by the Union, and also a sum to enable them to travel from Bergen to Stockholm. The total amount of the expenses of the party while detained in London and Newcastle was £1,181 19s. 10d. The Russian Consul repaid £122 4s. 10d., the cost of housing and feeding the party while in London, and a further £550 was received in repayment of the amount advanced for the travelling, etc. Before the party left London they deposited with the Union 3,000 roubles which were later exchanged at the proper recognised rate.

CHAPTER IV

THE UNION'S ACTION ON MATTERS OF PUBLIC INTEREST IN CONNECTION WITH THE WAR

Scales of Pensions to Soldiers and Sailors in His Majesty's Forces.—National War Savings Campaign.

SCALES OF PENSIONS TO SOLDIERS AND SAILORS IN HIS MAJESTY'S FORCES

Soon after the outbreak of war the attention of the Union was directed to the necessity of endeavouring to obtain improved pensions for disabled soldiers and for the widows and dependents of those killed in the war. It was strongly felt that the pensions then being granted would not meet the accustomed needs of the relatives of teachers in the case of death or disablement, and various communications, memoranda, etc., were sent to Cabinet Ministers urging the necessity for immediate action and setting out the minimum amounts which, in the opinion of the Union, ought to be granted. These views were submitted to the Pensions and Grants Select Committee, and certain improvements were made in March, 1915. The following Table shows the recommendations of the Pensions and Grants Select Committee which were adopted, together with the old scale and the scale suggested by the Union :—

	Old Scale.	Scale adopted by the Pensions and Grants Committee in 1915.	Scale suggested by the Union.
Total Disablement	14/- (minimum 16/6 if married with no children) up to maximum of 23/-, in addition to any payments for disablement beneft under Insurance Act.	25/-, with an additional allowance of 2/6 for each child.	£1 per week, plus 5/- for each child.

The Union's Action on Matters of Public Interest

	Old Scale.	Scale adopted by the Pensions and Grants Committee in 1915.	Scale suggested by the Union.
Widow without children	7/6, discretionary increase by 5/-.	10/-; 12/6 at 35; 15/- at 45.	£1 per week.
Widow with 1 child	12/6	15/- (or more if the mother is over 35).	25/-
,, ,, 2 children	15/-	18/6 (or more if the mother is over 35).	30/-
,, ,, 3 ,,	17/6	20/6 (or more if the mother is over 35).	35/-
,, ,, 4 ,,	20/-	22/6 (or more if the mother is over 35).	40/-

In February, 1917, the Government War Emergency Committee, on which the Union was represented, suggested further improvements in view of the fact that food prices were shown to have increased 71 per cent. since the previous settlement had been made. These recommendations were forwarded to the members of the Cabinet and to the Pensions Minister, together with certain suggested conditions which it was felt should govern payment of the pensions. It is probable that partly as an outcome of this action, certain important changes were made in March, 1917. According to this new scale the minimum for complete disablement was fixed at 27s. 6d., an increase of 2s. 6d. on the then existing scale, together with additional allowances for children under sixteen, which might in certain cases be extended beyond that age. These were as follows: First child, 5s.; Second, 4s. 2d.; Third, 3s. 4d.; each other child, 2s. 6d.; the pensions of widows were generally to be one-half of that which, with children's allowances, would have been awarded to the deceased husband had he been totally disabled. In May, 1918, the rates for children were further raised to: First child, 6s. 8d.; Second, 5s.; each other child, 4s. 2d. Substantial improvements were also made in separation allowances in October of the same year.

In addition to the action set out above, a Fund was opened by the Union for the purpose of augmenting the Government provision of pensions for the widows and orphans of teachers particulars of which are given in a preceding chapter.

N.U.T. WAR RECORD

NATIONAL WAR SAVINGS CAMPAIGN

At the beginning of 1916 a national economy campaign was inaugurated in official circles, and the Union was asked to co-operate. The first meeting took place at the Guildhall, London, when the Chancellor of the Exchequer, the late Lord Kitchener, and Mr. G. N. Barnes, M.P., emphasised the bearing of thrift on the war. The National War Savings Committee was the first outcome of the movement, and it was then decided that local committees should be formed, and that it should be left to them to adapt the general scheme of War Savings to their particular area. Local Authorities were encouraged to co-opt representative teachers on their local central committees, and many took the advice and asked the Local Associations of the Union to nominate members. Early in June, 1916, more than 500 of these War Savings Associations were in being, and applications for affiliation to the National Committee were being received from all parts of the country at a rate which increased daily. A model scheme, specially suitable for the formation of school associations, was prepared by the National War Savings Committee, and under this scheme the teachers were able to form a committee in their own schools and to provide from their number a secretary and a treasurer; all the scholars might become members of the association. The money subscribed was invested in 15s. 6d. War Savings Certificates. The Board of Education was requested by the National War Savings Committee to ask for the assistance of Local Education Authorities in making known through the public elementary schools the increased facilities that existed for saving by persons of small incomes. For this purpose the Committee prepared a leaflet, and it was suggested that this leaflet should form the basis of a lesson by the teacher, and that copies should subsequently be taken home by the children. Any necessary deviation from the approved time-table for the purpose of giving instruction on the subject could be made without formal application to the inspector or the Board. As a result of the enterprise the number of War Savings Associations formed in the different schools of the country, and the amount of money collected, was one of the real wonders of the War Savings Campaign, for in September, 1917, we find that the total number of such associations in the whole country was 36,316, over one-third of them being school associations, and that in 1918 this number had risen to over 14,000. In London a Committee of Teachers (the London Schools War Savings Committee) undertook the organisation and control of War Savings in the schools of London, and formed nearly 500 associations.

The UNION'S ACTION on MATTERS of PUBLIC INTEREST

The success of the movement may be gauged by the following typical instances :—

In a Welsh county, where the schools had been the centre of the War Savings work, thirty-two schools received subscriptions ranging from £3,000 to £10,000 each. One school in a Midland county invested £11,217 in War Savings Certificates, an average of over £100 a week, while a very large number of schools in the country raised over £1,000. In addition, the schools took a prominent part in the local special efforts. For example, a South Wales school sold 3,000 certificates during " Tank Week," and a school in a South-Eastern county invested £2,105 during the local " War Weapons Week." The teachers indeed had had a great opportunity for utilising the patriotic feeling engendered in the children, and the harvest matured beyond the wildest expectations. It may here be mentioned that at the end of December, 1919, the Union itself had purchased War Stock to the following amounts :—Provident Society, £573,000 ; War Aid Fund, £142,900 ; N.U.T., £41,097 5s.

CHAPTER V

THE UNION'S ACTION ON MATTERS OF PUBLIC INTEREST IN CONNECTION WITH THE WAR (*continued*)

Employment of Children and their Demobilisation after the War.—Cost of Living.—Education in the Army.—Jack Cornwell, V.C.

EMPLOYMENT OF CHILDREN AND THEIR DEMOBILISATION AFTER THE WAR

The claim of the farmer which has been successfully made in spite of the law on more than one occasion for the use of children in agriculture, was again put forward at the beginning of the war. A deputation from the Workers' War Emergency National Committee was received by the President of the Board of Education early in 1915, and Lord Gainford was informed of the revelations made to the Committee concerning the way in which child labour was being employed on farms, and of the proposal of a section of agriculturists to proceed further with this reprehensible practice. The Union was represented on the deputation by its President, Mr. W. B. Steer. In reply, Lord Gainford promised that the efforts of the Board should be directed to bringing pressure to bear upon Local Authorities to maintain the integrity of the bye-laws in their relation to the elementary school child, and the attention of the authorities was directed to the conditions which in the view of the Government should be satisfied before any children were specially exempted. These conditions were:—

(1) That the employment of children of school age must be exceptional.

(2) That the Education Authority must be sure that all reasonable efforts to secure adult labour had been made.

(3) Every case to be considered on its merits, and no general relaxation of the bye-laws allowed.

(4) The employment to be slight in character; and

(5) That the permission, if given, was to be for a definite period only.

The UNION'S ACTION on MATTERS of PUBLIC INTEREST

Many heard these decisions with extreme apprehension, which appears to have been justified. The promises were given in March, 1915. In March, 1916, over 8,000 withdrawals had been made throughout the country, and this not of children who might legally leave school, but of children who were under a statutory obligation to attend. But this was apparently only the beginning, for six months later, in October, 1916, a summary of the returns supplied by Local Education Authorities of children excused from school for employment in agriculture showed a total of 15,000—a most striking increase. This return, however, by no means accounted for the thousands of boys and girls under fourteen years of age who were employed as wage-earners in the United Kingdom. Even before the outbreak of war the number was over 500,000, and this number was probably doubled during the two or three following years. The question was raised in Parliament, when some forceful arguments for the abolition of child labour were advanced by the General Secretary of the Union, for while it was true that the Board of Education had laid down certain safeguards, yet no action had been taken to see that those safeguards were put into operation.

Of the amount of labour, thought and money which the Union expended on this vital question no adequate idea can be formed, and, finally, when the Government Committee was appointed to consider what steps should be taken to make provision for the education and instruction of children and young persons after the war, a prominent official of the Union, Captain F. W. Goldstone, was nominated as a member. Special regard was to be given, among other matters, to the interests of those children who had been abnormally employed during the war. The Final Report of the Committee, issued about the end of March, 1917, recommended a uniform leaving age of fourteen and the establishment of obligatory day continuation classes for children between fourteen and eighteen, the obligation to attend such classes to extend to children under fourteen when the Act came into operation though they might already have left the day school. The Education Act of 1918 followed out these recommendations, and in addition entirely abolished the objectionable half-time system.

At the end of the war, to meet the demobilisation of the great number of children who had been employed on war work of various kinds, centres of instruction were provided, and the Chancellor of the Exchequer agreed to defray the cost of these centres in large towns for a period of six months, and longer if necessary, pending the operation of the new Education Act granting 50 per cent. of the expenditure.

N.U.T. WAR RECORD

Cost of Living

The question of the continued rise in the price of food and other necessaries of life was viewed with the gravest concern by the Union, especially in view of the fact that the increase did not, in the early days of the war, appear to be the result of natural causes. It was felt that in some quarters the nation's needs were being exploited for private profit. The teachers had a peculiar charge and a peculiar experience, inasmuch as they came into daily contact with the children of the men and women more directly affected by the increase, and they were in a position to know the untold miseries and suffering entailed upon these little ones through want of food and clothing. Big manufacturers of war material were redoubling their profits, as also were the shipping firms, and, finally, the farmers were taking the work of little children at a cheap rate in order to enhance their profits. It was agreed that all representative bodies ought to take advantage of any opportunity for voicing their opinions with regard to the conditions, and in February, 1915, therefore, the Government was asked by the Union to take immediate steps to prevent the nation being exploited for the purposes of private profit. Copies of the communication were sent to the Prime Minister, the Chancellor of the Exchequer, and the President of the Board of Trade; the Local Associations of the Union were urged to take similar action in their areas. The expenditure on food in the standard working class budget—which was reckoned at 22s. 6d. in 1904—the estimate being based on 1,944 family budgets collected by a Board of Trade inquiry—rose to 25s. in July, 1914. From that time to May, 1918, it had risen in the large centres of population to 52s. 9d., an increase of 111 per cent. The purchasing power of the sovereign spent on food declined as shown in the following table:—

	s.	d.
1914—July	20	0
1915—January	16	10
1916—January	13	6
1917—January	10	5
1918—January	9	6
July	9	5
October	8	6

The decline represented the 111 per cent. increase in the cost of food to May, 1918. The action of the Union had no political bias, but it was very keenly felt that an effort should be made to circumscribe the amount of the profits which those who were dealing in war

The UNION'S ACTION on MATTERS of PUBLIC INTEREST

materials or in articles greatly affected by the war might be able to exact owing to the existence of abnormal conditions.

Education in the Army

The desire evinced by many of the men in the forces for something more than the amusements which were provided was met for a time by lectures and classes, and later, as the demand became greater, by definitely educational studies. Such work was undertaken, as far as the military exigencies permitted, with the strong encouragement of the military authorities. The Y.M.C.A. Universities Committee, on which the Union was represented by Miss Conway, M.A., Sir James Yoxall, M.A., and Mr. T. H. J. Underdown, M.A., did splendid work in the organisation of systematic teaching, provision of libraries, etc.; but although abundant enthusiasm was shown and remarkable results obtained, it was not until September, 1918, that official authorisation was given to the work.

The decision of the Army Council to set up a department specially to direct and co-ordinate education in the army was received with enthusiasm, and an Inter-Departmental Committee, to which the President of the Board of Education and the Ministers of Labour, Reconstruction and Pensions were nominated representatives, was appointed to advise upon general principles. Captain F. W. Goldstone, the Secretary of the Organisation Department of the Union, served as a member of the Directorate of Staff Duties in connection with this work. The Army Order was the outcome of what was termed the "remarkable demand among all ranks" for such an arrangement, it being recognised that the mental diversion which such education provided raised the spirits of the men and improved their military efficiency and moral.

Jack Cornwell, V.C.

Probably no incident in the war roused the public spirit more than the heroic conduct of the sailor boy, Jack Travers Cornwell, when mortally wounded in the battle of Jutland. Admiral Beatty's report stated :—" Boy (1st class) John Travers Cornwell, of Chester, was mortally wounded in the action. He nevertheless remained standing alone at a most exposed place, quietly awaiting orders till the end of the action with the gun's crew dead and wounded all round him. His age was under sixteen and a half years. I regret that he has since died, but I recommend his case for special recognition in justice to his memory, and as an example of the high example set by him."

N.U.T. WAR RECORD

So strong was the feeling aroused that a movement was initiated by a small committee, on which the National Union of Teachers was represented by Sir James Yoxall, and it was agreed that an appeal should be made to the schools for the raising of a memorial. On February 12th, 1917, remittances had been received through 28,400 schools and 485 individual subscribers, which with the sale of books, etc., amounted to £22,009 8s. 2d. The first instalment of £18,000 was presented to Her Majesty the Queen for the endowment of beds at the Star and Garter Hospital, and a second instalment of £4,600 was forwarded later. In addition, a certain sum was set aside from the fund to provide an increase in the income of the boy's mother during her lifetime. On account of the further publicity of Mrs. Cornwell's case this was increased in 1919. The picture of Jack Cornwell, which was placed in the contributing schools, will serve to remind future generations of British children of the heroism of a British boy, and his exploit will go down to history, and will be an inspiration for generations to come. Jack Cornwell is a type of the product of our elementary schools and a type of our British Army. The bulk of this army, and their fathers and mothers before them, passed through the primary schools, and the outcome has surely vindicated the work of the teachers, and has shown that they have to a very great extent succeeded in their aims.

CHAPTER VI

UNION ACTION CONCERNING TEACHERS

War Service (Superannuation) Act.—Salaries of Teachers who joined the Forces.—Action of Teachers' Provident Society.—Subscription to the Union.—Military Service and Facilities for Training College Students.—Teachers exempt from Service.—Retired Teachers and School Work.—Clergy in the Schools.—Committee of Appeal against Decisions by Local Tribunals.—Training of Disabled Soldiers as Teachers.—Enlistment and Demobilisation of Teachers.—Attestation of Pensioners' Declarations.

WAR SERVICE (SUPERANNUATION) ACT

An Act of Parliament to enable certificated teachers to reckon service in connection with the war as "recorded service" for the purpose of the Acts relating to Elementary School Teachers' Superannuation was placed on the Statute Book early in September, 1914, as a result of representation made by the Union to the President of the Board of Education.

SALARIES OF TEACHERS WHO JOINED THE FORCES—TEACHER OFFICERS

In cases where it was known that equitable rates of salary were not being paid to teachers who had joined the forces, the Union put itself into communication with the Local Education Authorities concerned with a view to raising the standard in such cases. In addition, an appeal was submitted asking that all teachers should be treated alike in the matter of salaries, irrespective of whether they had or had not obtained commissions—in short, that the deduction from salary should be no greater in the case of commissioned officers than in the case of privates. In the majority of cases it had been shown that teachers were for the most part much worse off as officers than as privates owing to the heavy expenses which the holding of the commission entailed.

ACTION OF THE TEACHERS' PROVIDENT SOCIETY.

1. *Concessions to Teachers with the Forces.*—In September, 1914, the following proposals were adopted by the Teachers' Provident

Society in respect to their members who left school for service at home or abroad in the Regular, Naval, or Territorial Forces, and in Red Cross Societies :—

(a) To excuse all contributions during the period that the member was engaged on active service.

(b) To accept and pay all death claims that might arise in consequence of the war, even though the contributions had been excused during the continuance of the war.

(c) To pay all sickness claims arising from the war to members of the Deposit or Ordinary (Table 1) Sections when the member was within the limits of the United Kingdom (in the case of members injured abroad and invalided home, from the day they landed in the United Kingdom they were eligible to receive sickness benefit).

The concessions applied to members who were in the Sick Pay and Life Assurance Branches prior to August, 1914, and the contributions excused were paid from the surplus funds of the Society. Closely connected with this was the question of the position of deposit members for sick pay, and later a grant was made from the surplus funds to the Common Sick Fund of such amounts as would be due from the members on active service necessary to pay their proportion of the amount due for sickness benefit payable to that fund. About twelve months after these concessions had been granted, viz., in September, 1915, a limit was placed on the privileges extended to those who joined within a reasonable period of the commencement of the war, and it was decided that the resolutions should then apply only to those members qualified under the resolutions who voluntarily enlisted on or before October 31st, 1915.

In March, 1916, a further arrangement was made whereby full bonuses were allowed to Life Assurance branches (as in the case of other members) for all those on active service whose contributions were being paid by the Society. It was also agreed at this time that no interim bonuses should be paid on any policy which became a claim or matured prior to the next valuation, and such payments were therefore suspended until the actual rate of bonus had been declared.

2. *Applications from Teachers Eligible for Enlistment.*—The question of applications from teachers eligible for enlistment occupied the attention of the Board of Management in the early part of 1916, and as a result a proviso was inserted in the policy of such members declaring that in the event of the member joining

UNION ACTION CONCERNING TEACHERS

the forces the policy should become void, and that all premiums paid under the policy, less a small charge for death risk during the time such member was assured, should be returned to the member, his nominee, or executors. By the insertion of this proviso the applicant was under no disability if he were not called up for service, whilst in the event of such a contingency the Society would be safeguarded under the conditions set out.

In the case of applicants for sick pay under similar conditions, a proviso was inserted arranging that membership should cease, and that all amounts standing to the member's credit in the Rest and Deposit accounts should be returned in full.

The number of death claims paid through the Life Assurance Branch on account of members who actually died in the war was 226, amounting to £28,206; whilst £5,624 was expended on 597 similar claims through the Deposit Branch of the Society. Sick pay to members on active service during the war amounted to £11,000. In addition, a sum of £23,000 was paid from the Surplus Fund on account of contributions of members with the forces.

3. *War Loan.*—In February, 1917, the Teachers' Provident Society took up £400,000 worth of the great War Loan for the benefit of its members, and also for the members of the N.U.T. Teachers who bought shares were allowed to extend their payments over a period of ten years. Shares were also taken in the Victory Loan of 1919 to the extent of £250,000.

Subscription to the N.U.T. of Members Engaged with the Forces

The conditions set out below were made applicable to all members who enlisted and returned to school work:—The member to pay a year's subscription which should cover the year in which he enlisted, the period of his service with the forces, and the year in which he recommenced school duty.

Military Service and Facilities for Training College Students

Through the efforts of the Union, facilities were afforded to Training College students in 1914 as follows:—

(1) Students who were in their second year of training when called up for service were allowed to return and complete their course after the war. Alternately, any such students who served with the colours for a year were granted temporary

N.U.T. WAR RECORD

recognition as certificated teachers without further training or examination, such recognition being made permanent under certain conditions.

(2) A certificate examination was provided at Easter, 1915, which students of the second year who were anxious to enlist were able to take instead of waiting for the summer examination.

(3) Students in the first year were allowed the option of returning to college or receiving temporary, and subsequently permanent, recognition upon the same conditions as set out in number (1).

The Board undertook that the interests of such students should be safeguarded, and at the end of the war those who elected to return to college for the purpose of completing their training were accorded a special grant of an amount which would (when added to the grant of £35, or £20 payable in respect of maintenance in college) make up a total of £104 for each year of training.

Teachers Exempt from Service

In June, 1916, arrangements were made with the military authorities that teachers medically unfit for active service should be permitted to continue their work in the schools, and should not again be called up without reference to the Board of Education. About eight months later, however, this arrangement was modified in view of the urgent need for men, and all teachers medically classified as A or B1, unless in the latter case they were over thirty-one years of age, were called up for service. The Army Council realised to a certain extent the difficulties caused to the education service by the calling up of these teachers, and they therefore agreed to release from the army, where practicable, teachers classed below B1, on condition that they returned to the teaching service.

Again, in 1918, further modifications were made, the net result of which was that all Grade I. men over forty-five on the 1st January, 1918, all Grade II. men over the age of thirty-six on the same date, and all Grade III. were not called up for military service. Grade I. men under forty-five and Grade II. under thirty-six were called up unless a special application were made by the Board of Education showing that their retention in school work was absolutely essential to the efficiency of the particular school concerned.

Retired Teachers and School Work

As a result of representations made by the Union, Local Education Authorities were allowed to employ retired teachers in receipt

UNION ACTION CONCERNING TEACHERS

of a deferred annuity and superannuation allowance under the Elementary School Teachers' (Superannuation) Acts, provided that such teachers were approved by His Majesty's Inspector. This was a purely emergency measure which terminated on the restoration of normal conditions at the conclusion of the war. During their employment in the schools these teachers continued to receive their deferred annuities and superannuation allowances.

Clergy in the Schools

In March, 1917, the Education Department decided to allow ministers of religion to give secular instruction as assistant teachers in elementary schools for the duration of the war, where it was impossible to obtain the services of teachers qualified under the ordinary provisions of the code. In order to safeguard the interests of children and teachers, the Executive agreed that where a teacher refused to work in a school in which a clergyman or minister of religion of military age and fitness had been substituted for a teacher withdrawn for military service, sustentation should be granted by the Union on the usual terms.

Committee of Appeal against Decisions by Local Tribunals

It was largely due to the action taken by the Union that a Central Committee of Appeal against decisions by Local Tribunals was formed.

Training of Disabled Soldiers as Teachers

In 1917 the National Union of Teachers was given facilities for expressing its opinion on the proposal to consider applications from discharged soldiers for training as teachers, and an Advisory Committee of the Board of Education was ultimately set up to deal with the question. Two prominent members of the Executive represented the Union on this Committee, and the principle was emphasised by them that selected candidates should go through a course of training similar to that required for other teachers, and should pass a qualifying examination equal to that required for the ordinary certificated teacher. Questions as to superannuation and other points were left to be solved later.

Enlistment and Demobilisation of Teachers

From August 1914 onwards, advice and assistance were given in hundreds of cases on the various questions which arose consequent on the change from civil to military life and vice versa. The rapid enlistment at the beginning of the war, the Derby Scheme, the Military Service Acts, the calling up of low category teachers, the release of unfit teachers and, finally, demobilisation, all brought fresh problems and new points to be elucidated. War allowances were secured from Local Education Authorities, applications for commissions supported, members advised as to appeals for exemption, and prisoners of war aided. Hundreds of cases respecting the release of teachers in a low medical category and similar matters were taken up, and the Union was able in most cases to secure satisfaction for its members. The following are one or two typical cases. A letter was sent to the Board of Education stating :—

" Sergt. ——— was mobilised in August, 1914. As he suffers from cardiac trouble, he has never been fit for service overseas, and about a month ago was placed by a medical board in category B2. Before mobilisation he was a teacher at the ——— school under the ——— Education Authority. I understand that the headmaster of the school is the only man now on the staff, and it would appear that Sergt. ———'s services would be of greater value, nationally, if he were back in school. As you know, the ——— Education Committee does not see its way to apply in any of these cases for a man's release, though any teacher who returns is most welcome. I hope, under the circumstances, the Board will bring the case to the notice of the military authorities as one where release might very well be granted."

A few weeks later the teacher was back in school, and he regarded his release as " one more example of the power of an organised professional association."

One member released under this arrangement received instructions to rejoin his regiment. He wrote to Hamilton House, the attention of the Board of Education was drawn to the matter, and the notice was immediately cancelled. Cases of wrongful calling up were not infrequent. After an issue of one of the circulars dealing with the medical examination of teachers, quite a number who were really exempt from its provisions were summoned for examination. In all these cases members were told to return the documents, call attention to the terms of the circular, and ask that the notices might be cancelled. Where necessary, this advice was followed up by communications by wire or post to National Service representatives. The wisdom of the course followed may be

UNION ACTION CONCERNING TEACHERS

judged from the following extract from a letter from one of the teachers who benefited :—

"I wish to express my gratitude for the way you have worked with untiring zeal on my behalf, and with marked success. The results have been real and valuable, not only to myself, but to several other members of the profession in this district."

A teacher, forty-six years of age, took advantage of the option offered by the Government of enrolling as a war agricultural volunteer, but the Local Education Authority's War Allowance Sub-Committee decided that he had not joined the forces, and declined to pay any part of his salary. A few days later the calling up of teachers over forty-five was stopped, and the teacher desired to return to school. The Union communicated with the Board of Education on the matter, and shortly afterwards the teacher's enrolment as a war agricultural volunteer was cancelled.

Members with the forces wrote to Hamilton House on an infinite variety of subjects. In one case a teacher wrote respecting his reversion from the rank of regimental quarter-mastersergeant to that of corporal on the reduction of the establishment of a cavalry depot. The War Office was asked to institute inquiries, when it was found that a mistake had been made, and that the teacher should not have been reduced below the rank of acting sergeant.

Towards the end of 1915 a local secretary reported the receipt of a letter from a member who was a prisoner of war in Germany, and had been in confinement six weeks on a charge of inciting other prisoners to mutiny while working on coke ovens. He added that if he could get a fair trial he could prove his innocence. Inquiries were at once made of the Foreign Office as to the best way to deal with the matter, and eventually the case was placed in the hands of the American Ambassador. On two occasions representations were made to the German Government, and, after long delays, the matter was dealt with, the teacher being tried, acquitted and released from prison. Writing to Hamilton House, his brother, also a teacher-soldier, expressed his extreme gratitude for what had been done.

Throughout the period of the war the Union refrained from asking for any special treatment of teachers serving with the forces, but in the national interest, and more especially in view of the State programme of educational reconstruction, it was felt desirable that their speedy demobilisation after the war was essential to the efficient carrying out of that programme. It would not be possible to give an account of the negotiations step by step which took place on this question, but an announcement appeared in January, 1919, to the effect that instructions for the demobilisation of teachers had been sent to the forces, and that the Board of Education had asked Local Education Authorities to supply them with a list of teachers serving in the Army or Navy with a view to hastening their return to school work. It was understood also that Authorities had been asked to give facilities to teachers who responded to the invitation of the War Office to remain for a year longer in the forces as teachers under the Army Education Scheme which had been inaugurated.

Attestation of Pensioners' Declarations

In 1918 the Union secured that head teachers of public elementary schools might be authorised to attest forms of the kind in question. By the new order, schoolmasters might attest declarations for half-pay or Army, Navy or civil non-effective service.

CHAPTER VII

SERVICES RENDERED BY TEACHERS WHO WERE UNABLE TO JOIN THE FORCES

Women and the War.—Teachers as Drill Instructors, in Volunteer Training Corps, and as Special Constables.—War Transfers.—Services in connection with the National Register and on Relief Committees.—War Lecturing and Literature.—National Service.

In civil life the task of the teachers who for reasons of age or infirmity were not mobilised, was almost as arduous as that of the fighting forces, while the splendid work rendered by women during the crisis was of paramount importance. Inspired by a zeal to serve their country, the teachers at home contributed materially to the stability of the nation.

WOMEN AND THE WAR

The work of the women teachers during the war was extremely difficult, but through it all they bravely continued to meet the varied calls upon their time, patience and monetary resources. The depletion of staff owing to enlistment occasioned much dislocation for the time, though this was in great measure met by the return of women teachers who had left the profession. It is estimated in this connection that approximately 17,500 women teachers were directly replacing men in July, 1916, of whom 1,400 were in London alone. About 200 women members of the Union gave up school duties to undertake work as nurses, while many others gave part-time service, as well as service out of school hours. Membership of Relief and Maternity Committees, the investigation of cases, care of refugees, free services in connection with the National Register, the provision of material for garment making, knitting and needlework generally for the benefit of the forces and refugees, as well as work for furthering the National War Savings Campaign, came within the scope of their labours.

Again, many women teachers spent their mid-summer vacations in farm work, fruit picking, and voluntary clerical work. Among the records of their labour also was the provision of appliances for the wounded; for instance, the women teachers of London gave from time to time such useful and expensive gifts as ambulance cars for the wounded, invalid chairs, spinal carriages, surgical microscopes, etc. Cookery teachers in different parts of the country gave material assistance to the Ministry of Food by conducting demonstrations of economical methods of cooking, and to the Navy and Army Canteens Board, under which they served as cooks or undertook the management of canteens. Others worked as V.A.D. cooks or as military cooks in hospitals and nursing homes, while a certain number acted as superintendents and cooks in national kitchens and restaurants, or as inspectors of these kitchens under the Ministry of Food.

Besides all these services, an enormous amount of relief work was quietly performed by the women teachers in the different localities, their continual contact with the children enabling them to ascertain where help was really needed, and in which particular direction it might be applied to the greatest advantage. When the scheme of voluntary national service was adopted early in 1917, considerable unrest was caused. Many of the women teachers felt that they would be rendering better service to the country by going into other occupations. However, something in the way of an official pronouncement was made by Mr. Fisher, the Minister of Education, to the effect that " women training for the high profession of teaching were in a very real sense equipping themselves for a valuable and expert branch of national service." This indicated the course which women teachers should take and satisfied the disquiet which had existed. In June, 1918, Mr. Fisher emphasised the point that women teachers would be best serving their country's interest by remaining at their posts.

Four women teachers lost their lives on war service, and several women were honoured for bravery and devotion to duty. Two were awarded the Military Medal, while three London women teachers obtained the O.B.E. for bravery when bombs were falling on their school while the children were assembled; there were other cases of the award of the O.B.E. to women teachers as well as that of the Royal Red Cross, and of women mentioned in despatches.

Teachers as Drill Instructors

As the result of a request from the Army Council, the Board of Education in 1914 sent to the Local Education Authorities asking that teachers in their service, under thirty-five years of age, who had experience in giving instruction in physical exercises and drill, and who possessed the personal qualities necessary for maintaining

SERVICES RENDERED BY TEACHERS

discipline, should be given every facility for enlisting in the Army. Any school teacher under thirty-five, who was able to produce a certificate of efficiency issued by a Local Education Authority that he was competent to act as an instructor in physical exercises and drill, and who had attained the physical standard in force, might be enlisted for the duration of the war, or such less period as his services might be required, as a private and be given the acting rank of corporal. Teachers who, on account of age or some slight physical disability, were not able to enlist also came within the scope of the Army Council's appeal. Many teachers patriotically responded both as regards enlistment and in undertaking to give instruction in a temporary civilian capacity under the terms of the circular. The Army Council expressed approval, the teachers' knowledge of the official handbook having proved of great advantage.

TEACHERS IN VOLUNTEER TRAINING CORPS

In response to an appeal from the Board of Education in December, 1914, many teachers enrolled in Volunteer Training Corps. The appeal was drafted to meet the needs of teachers who could not be spared from their posts without substantial detriment to the teaching service, but who were willing to place their services at the disposal of the military authorities in case of emergency. It was, however, stipulated that any teacher, who, being of military age, enrolled himself in a Volunteer Training Corps, would be subject to the condition that he must subsequently enlist if specially called upon by the War Office to do so.

SPECIAL CONSTABLES

Many hundreds of teachers at the outbreak of war undertook work as special constables in addition to their ordinary school duties.

WAR TRANSFERS

On account of the lack of men teachers in certain boys' schools caused by the absence of the members of the staff serving with the forces, the London County Council asked for volunteers from among the men serving in the schools less affected by such absence, to serve on the staffs of those schools which had suffered more than ordinary depletion.

The services of these teachers were temporarily transferred, and on return to duty of the teachers who had joined the forces and whom they had replaced, the volunteers were transferred to

N.U.T. WAR RECORD

their original schools. It is probable that many Authorities adopted the same course.

Free Services in Connection with the National Register and with the Issue of Food Control Cards

The teaching profession with great enthusiasm volunteered to assist the Local Authorities in carrying out work in connection with the compilation of the National Register in 1915. In London, Manchester, York, and many other boroughs the teachers practically made themselves entirely responsible for the distribution and collection of the forms, whilst in many cases they volunteered to undertake the tabulation of the forms when collected. That this assistance was warmly appreciated by the Authorities was very evident. In York, for instance, where the reopening of the schools after holidays overlapped the registration period, an extra week's holiday was given, so that the teachers could devote their time uninterruptedly to the work. The teachers also came to the assistance of the Food Control Department in connection with the issue of food tickets early in 1918.

Teachers on Relief Committees

In many places a point was made of electing teachers on Relief Committees owing to their special knowledge of the circumstances of the children and parents. In London, in particular, as the result of a letter which was sent out by the London Teachers' Association offering the assistance and co-operation of teachers in the work of local distress, a great many of the boroughs arranged that one teacher from each school should be co-opted upon the Relief Committees.

War Lecturing and Literature by Teachers

In face of many difficulties and in the midst of duties and preoccupations arising out of the war, many teachers, especially those more used to public speaking, felt it their duty in the national crisis to spread by means of lectures, sound and sane ideas on the causes, origin, and purposes of the war. An article appeared in the *Schoolmaster* dealing generally with the methods which might be adopted. Also, the attention of the Local Associations of the Union was drawn to the fact that where meetings were held, advantage might well be taken of the opportunity by arranging in the programme for a recruiting speech, and members of the Executive from time to time included points on recruiting in their speeches when attending Association meetings.

SERVICES RENDERED BY TEACHERS

Many pamphlets and writings by teachers and educationists influenced public feeling during the war. Among these were:—

"To My Colleagues in the National Service of Education," a memorandum from Lord Gainford, the President of the Board of Education, written in 1914, to the teachers of Great Britain.

"Britain's Duty To-day," by Dr. E. Lyttleton, Headmaster of Eton.

Leaflet by Mr. J. H. L. Ridley, President of the London Teachers' Association, putting into conversational form a pamphlet by Sir Edward Cook on "Why Britain is at War."

Leaflet by Mr. W. J. Pincombe, Secretary to the London Teachers' Association, putting into conversational form a pamphlet by Sir Edward Cook called "Britain and Gallant Belgium—a Talk to the School Children of Britain." This pamphlet was reprinted in English and Dutch by the Transvaal Government under the name of "The British Empire and Gallant Belgium," for free distribution to the scholars of the schools in the Transvaal. In the preface the Government express their indebtedness to Mr. Pincombe, the author of the original pamphlet.

"Modern Germany and the Modern World," by Dr. Michael Sadler.

"Why Britain went to War—to the Boys and Girls of the British Empire," by Sir James Yoxall.

"A Memorandum to all Teachers in Public Elementary Schools in London," by Sir Robert Blair, Education Officer of the London County Council.

"Who is Responsible?" by Mr. Cloudesley Brereton.

"How the War came about," by Dr. Holland Rose, Reader in Modern History at the Cambridge University.

"A Talk to Children on the Causes of the War," by Mr. J. H. L. Ridley, issued by the Victoria League. The Lancashire Education Committee circulated 30,000 copies of this pamphlet, as well as copies of the letter issued by the President of the Board of Education.

The London Education Committee sent out three detailed memoranda of suggestions to its head teachers—one concerning the teaching of History and English as affected by the European War; the second dealing with the economic aspect of the early stages of the war; and the third, relating to geography as affected by the war.

N.U.T. WAR RECORD

An illustrated booklet, entitled "St. David's Day, 1915," was published by the Welsh Department of the Board of Education. The pamphlet was of a commemorative and patriotic character, and was designed to assist the celebration of the national anniversary during a time of war.

"To My Fellow Teachers," a memorandum by Mr. Fisher, President of the Board of Education, to the teachers of Great Britain.

"Marching Away," Sir James Yoxall.

National Service

The position of teachers under the scheme of Voluntary National Service inaugurated in February, 1917, was not defined. Under the Board of Education Regulations only men fit for active military service were called upon to join the Army, and as far as other teachers were concerned, it was considered that they were serving their country better in the class-room than in taking up other occupations. In view of the serious depletion in the staffs of schools, the Board therefore deprecated volunteering by teachers for full-time work under that scheme. It was understood, however, that in exceptional cases the special qualifications of individual teachers for other work might justify their volunteering, and the Board was prepared to advise in these cases.

The Gallant Dead

Note.—The names are arranged alphabetically under Local Associations.

Name.	Rank.	Regiment.	School.
Aberdare.			
Howells, J. E.	2nd Lieutenant	Tank Corps	Cardiff St. N.S.
Watkins, W. M.	Bombardier	R.G.A.	Aman C.S.
Abertillery.			
Davies, A. I.	Private	Welsh	Crumlin C.S.
Evans, E.	Sergeant	S.W.B.	Six Bells C.S.
Reed, C. S.	2nd Lieutenant	Monmouth	Intermediate S.
Rumsey, C. G.	Lieutenant	S.W.B.	Brynhytrydd C.S.
Thomas, H. R.	Private	S.W.B.	Six Bells C.S.
Accrington.			
Duckworth, W.	Lieutenant	Lancs Fusiliers	St. Mary Magdalene Ch.S.
Rushworth, H.	Lieutenant	K.R.R.	St. Peter's Ch.S.
Acton.			
Wood, W. J.	2nd Lieutenant	Middlesex	Acton C.S.
Aldershot.			
Ross, D.	Sergeant	Q.V.R.	West End C.S.
Shanks, C. W.	Lance-Corporal	Hants	West End C.S.
Ampthill and North Bedfordshire.			
Apthorpe, H. W.	Lance-Corporal	R. Warwick	Cople C.S.
Lowndes, C. A.	2nd Lieutenant	N. Staffs	Up End C.S., Kempton.
Andover.			
Baines, G. E.	Corporal	R. Sussex	Braintree C.S.
Anglesey.			
Owen, H.	Private	R.W.F.	Park C.S., Holyhead.
Thomas, G. A.	Private	N. Wales	Cybi C.S., Holyhead.
Ashford (Kent).			
Maynard, H. C.	Private	Q.R.W.S.	S.E. & C.R. S.
Ashton-under-Lyne.			
Eller, C.	Lieutenant	Manchester	Old Road, Dukinfield.
Jones, F.	2nd Lieutenant	Manchester	West End C.S.
Stringer, A. E.	2nd Lieutenant	Manchester	Sec.S.
Atherton, etc.			
Stringer, A. O.	Sergeant	R. Scots	Astley Ch.S.
Aylesbury.			
Clarke, C. G.	Lieutenant	E. Yorks	Aylesbury C.S.
Barking.			
Beal, J. W.	Corporal	Essex	Church S.
Barkston Ash.			
Firth, A.	Private	K.O.S.B.	Garforth C.S.
Hepworth, J. S.	Private	W. Riding	Tadcaster C.S.

N.U.T. WAR RECORD

Name.	Rank.	Regiment.	School.
Barnard Castle.			
Chambers, N. W.	Private	D.L.I.	Cockfield C.S.
Harrison, T. R. S.	Gunner	D.L.I.	Woodland C.S., Darlington.
Robson, R. R.	Corporal	D.L.I.	Church S., Barnard Castle.
Barnes and Mortlake.			
London, R. H.	Private	R.A.M.C.	Westfields C.S.
Ridout, F. S.	Lance-Corporal	London Scottish	Mortlake C.S.
Barnet.			
Woods, J. W. (M.C.)	Captain	K.O.Y.L.I.	Christ Ch.S.
Barnsley.			
Bayliss, L.	Private	York and Lancs	Worsbro' Dale N.S.
Dalgoutte, G. C.	2nd Lieutenant	Rifle Brigade	Mapplewell C.S.
Downend, J. M.	Captain	N.F.	Cross Hill, Hemsworth.
Haynes, C. S.	2nd Lieutenant	D.L.I.	Darfield C.S.
Heathcote, A.	Q.M. Sergeant	York and Lancs	Oaks C.S., Ardsley.
Hirst, J.			Wombwell.
Kellett, G. W.	Private	York and Lancs	Brampton Bierlow C.S.
Nicolson, F.	2nd Lieutenant	H.L.I.	Doncaster Road C.S.
Barrow-in-Furness.			
Addison, F.	2nd Lieutenant	R. Sussex	Oxford St. C.S.
Gross, W. H. B.	2nd Lieutenant	Q.R.W.S.	Vickerstown C.S.
Rutherford, N. E.	2nd Lieutenant	K.O.R.L.	Barrow Island C.S.
Wenham, F. C.	Private	K.O.R.L.	Vickerstown C.S.
Barry.			
Evans, G. R.	Lieutenant	S.W.B.	Crogan Hill.
Harris, D. J.	Private	R.W.F.	Holton Rd. C.S.
Phillips, A.	2nd Lieutenant	R.W.F.	Romilley Rd. C.S.
Basingstoke.			
Dyer, F. P.	Private	R. Warwick	Bursledon, Southampton.
Bath.			
Gunning, W. T.	Sergeant	Somerset L.I.	West Tiverton C.S.
Humphris, E. G.	Bombardier	R.G.A.	Englishcombe C.S.
Strong, G.	Lieutenant	Nigerian	St. Saviour's N.S.
Bedford Borough.			
Harper, H. S.	Lance-Corporal	London Scottish	9, St. Mary's St.
Heeps, F. B.	Gunner	R.G.A.	Goldington Rd. C.S.
Parsons, E. O.	Petty Offr. Mech.	Naval Armoured Cars	Emberton, Newport Pagnell.
Tompkinson, P. A.	Lieutenant	Sherwood Foresters	Ampthill Rd. C.S.
Belper and Crich.			
Arnold, H.	Sergeant	Sherwood Foresters	Belper N.S.
Raistrick, J. W.	Lieutenant	W. Yorks	" Herbert Strutt " Sec.S.
Wright, —	Lieutenant	Middlesex	" Herbert Strutt " Sec.S.
Berkshire (North).			
Lupton, F. W.	2nd Lieutenant	R. Fusiliers	9, Bostock Av., Abingdon.
Biggleswade.			
Maltby, A. P.	Sergeant	Middlesex	Arlesey Siding C.S.
Bingley.			
Crowther, J.	Private	K.O.Y.L.I.	Great Houghton C.S., Barnsley.

THE GALLANT DEAD

Name.	Rank.	Regiment.	School.
Birkenhead.			
Beverley, C. A.	Private	R.A.M.C.	Higher Elementary S.
Concannon, J. H.	Private	King's Liverpool	St. Anne's R.C.S., Rock Ferry.
Jones, W. H.	Q.M. Sergeant	S. Lancs	Rock Ferry C.S.
McGuinness, G.	Private	King's Liverpool	St. Lawrence R.C.S.
McNaught, T.	Private	Liverpool Scottish	Rock Ferry C.S.
Palmer, H.	Private	King's Liverpool	Higher Elementary S.
Pearson, C. T.	2nd Lieutenant	R.G.A.	Woodchurch Rd. C.S.
Skinner, R. H.	Private	King's Liverpool	Brassey St. C.S.
Birmingham.			
Allan, S.	Private	R.A.M.C.	Boulton Rd. C.S.
Barratt, J. F.	Private	R. Warwick	Moor End C.S.
Bateson, H. S.	Bombardier	R.G.A.	Edgbaston Ch.S.
Beddoes, C. J.	Corporal	R. Warwick	Arden Rd. C.S.
Bennett, J. E. F. T. (M.M.)	Lieutenant	R. Warwick	Steward St. C.S.
Bennett, J. W.	Private	R. Warwick	Golden Hillock Rd. C.S.
Benson, W.	Private	R. Warwick	Raddle Barn C.S.
Brindle, H. (M.M.)	Private	R.A.M.C.	Mary St. C.S.
Clare, F. C.	Private	R. Warwick	Oratory S.
Clarke, H.	Lance-Corporal	Gloucester	"Eboracum," Willow Av., Edgbaston.
Daniels, F. (M.C.)	2nd Lieutenant	R. Warwick	Hope St. C.S.
Dobson, W. G.	Private	D.L.I.	Brookfields C.S.
Dugard, P. W.	Private	R. Fusiliers	Canterbury Rd. C.S.
Eldridge, J. T.	Lieutenant	R. Worcester	St. George's N.S.
Evans, A. W.	Driver	R.A.S.C.	King's Heath C.S.
Farmer, G. H.	Private	R. Warwick	Saltley Training College.
Harcourt, W.	Private	R.W.F.	Arden Rd. C.S.
Hostler, A. C.	Private	R.A.M.C.	Selly Park C.S.
Jelleyman, H. W.	Rifleman	Q.V.R.	Handsworth New Rd. C.S.
Jephson, H.	Lieutenant	S. Staffs	Wattville Rd. C.S.
Kaye, A. E.	Corporal	Worcester	Highfield Rd. C.S.
Moon, S. H.	Sergeant	R. Warwick	St. Mary's N.S.
Moore, V. W.	Bombardier	R.G.A.	Garrison Lane C.S.
Morgan, J. H.	Sergeant	R. Warwick	St. David's N.S.
Osborn, A. G.	Captain	S.W.B.	King's Norton C.S.
Pickering, F. S.	Lance-Corporal	Wilts	St. Mark's N.S.
Piper, H.	Private	R. Warwick	Floodgate St. C.S.
Randall, H. A.	Private	R. Warwick	Elkington St. C.S.
Richardson, T. J.	Private	M.G.C.	Windsor St. C.S.
Robinson, A. G.	2nd Lieutenant	R.E.	Birchfield Rd. C.S.
Sedgley, J. P.	Sergeant	R.A.M.C.	Allcock St. C.S.
Shiel, B. R. (D.C.M.)	Sergeant	R. Warwick	HolyTrinity Ch.S., Handsworth.
Slade, W. J.	Corporal	R.G.A.	Bristol St. C.S.
Smith, B.	Corporal	R.A.M.C.	Colmore Rd. C.S.
Stevens, H.	Lance-Corporal	R. Warwick	Loxton St. C.S.
Stone, J. H.	Gunner	R.G.A.	Icknield St. C.S.
Strickley, W.	Corporal	O. & B.L.I.	Cherrywood Rd. C.S.
Styler, F. W.	Sergeant	R. Warwick	Boulton Rd. C.S.
Summers, O. (D.C.M.)	Sergeant	R. Warwick	Bloomsbury C.S.
Trevar, J. O.	Lance-Corporal	E. Surrey	St. Michael's Ch.S.
Tongue, J. W. C.	Captain	Gloucester	Station Rd. C.S., Aston.
Warriner, T. A. L.	Lieutenant	Worcester	St. Paul's N.S., Vincent St.
Watkin, A. C.	Lieutenant	R. Warwick	Conway Rd. C.S.
Whatmore, L. W.	Signaller	Worcester	Clifton Rd. C.S.
Willis, O. P.	Corporal	R. Warwick	Floodgate St. C.S.
Bishop Auckland.			
Atkinson, J. H.	Private	D.L.I.	Cockton Hill C.S.
Pybus, R.	2nd Lieutenant	D.L.I.	New Shildon C.S.
Blackburn.			
Beardsworth, J.	Lieutenant	R.G.A.	St. Stephen's Ch.S.
Cox, E.	Corporal	Dublin Fusiliers	St. Albans R.C.S.

N.U.T. WAR RECORD

Name.	Rank.	Regiment.	School.
Blackburn—*continued.*			
Mashiter, E.	Sergeant	E. Lancs	St. Luke's Ch.S.
Pemberton, W.	Sergeant	E. Lancs	Audley Range C.S.
Blackpool.			
Haworth, H.	Lieutenant	L.N.L.	Claremont C.S.
Blaydon.			
Axtell, A. J.	Corporal	N.F.	Whickham C.S.
Bradley, W. H.	Sergeant-Major	R.A.M.C.	Emmaville C.S.
Minks, T.	Private	D.L.I.	Highfield C.S.
Noon, G.	2nd Lieutenant	Sherwood Foresters	Dunstan C.S.
Prudham, T. P.	2nd Lieutenant	N.F.	Marley Hill C.S.
Robertson, A. H.	Sergeant	D.L.I.	High Spen C.S.
Stockdale, W. H.	Sergeant	D.L.I.	Blaydon C.S.
Bletchley.			
Gillam, J. G.	Sergeant	Northants	Bletchley Rd. C.S.
Blyth.			
Cottrell, L. S. J.	Lieutenant	Cyclists' Battalion	Morpeth Rd. C.S.
Crosby, T.	Lance-Sergeant	N.F.	Crofton C.S.
Mitchell, W.	2nd Lieutenant	N.F.	Bebside C.S.
Bodmin.			
Knight, J.	Naval Schoolmaster	R.N.	Port Isaac C.S.
Bolton Borough.			
Hunt, G. N.	Corporal	L.N.L.	Clarence St. C.S.
Whyman, J. W.	Private	R.E.	Wolfenden St. C.S.
Wood, J.	2nd Lieutenant	L.N.L.	St. James' N.S.
Wood, R. J.	Lance-Corporal	London	Eden's Orphanage.
Bolton District.			
Ashton, J.	Private	R.N.	Christ Ch.S., Pendlebury.
Freeman, J.	2nd Lieutenant	R.G.A.	Chequerbent Ch.S.
Morris, T.	Lance-Corporal	R. Fusiliers	Wingate's St. John Ch.S., Westhoughton.
Bootle.			
Bell, J. C.	Private	King's Liverpool	St. Mary's Ch.S.
Large, H.	Gunner	R.F.A.	Christ Ch.S.
Rowland, A. I.	Gunner	R.G.A.	Hawthorne Rd. C.S.
Boston.			
Comer, T.	Gunner	Lincoln	Alvey's S., Sleaford.
Bournemouth.			
Taylor, J. R. N.	2nd Lieutenant	E. Yorks	St. Paul's Ch.S.
Brackley and Woodford.			
Bilclough, S.	Sergeant	N.F.	Woodford Halse N.S.
Bradford.			
Forryan, W. C.	Pioneer	R.E.	St. Jude's N.S.
Lintott, E.	Lieutenant	W. Yorks	Dudley Hill C.S.
Manley, W.	Private	Q.R.W.S.	Lorne St. C.S.
Mitchell, R. (M.M.)	Sergeant	R.E.	Carr Lane N.S.
Pendlebury, R.	Corporal	City Volunteers	Belle Vue Sec.S.
Schofield, H.	Lance-Corporal	K.O.Y.L.I.	Usher St. C.S.
Tindle, J. W.	Private	W. Yorks	Great Horton N.S.
Brentford.			
Belsten. W. H.	Sergeant	London	St. Paul's N.S.
Dark, M. V.	Corporal	Civil Service Rifles	Clifton Rd. C.S., Southall.
Kelly, P. E.	2nd Lieutenant	Middlesex	Clifton Rd. C.S., Southall.
Whitney, C. W.	Corporal	K.R.R.	Featherstone Rd. C.S., Southall.

THE GALLANT DEAD

Name.	Rank.	Regiment.	School.
Bridgend.			
Jacques, F.	Private	Worcester	Oldcastle C.S.
Jones, B. J.	Sergeant	Gloucester	Penybont C.S.
Bridgnorth.			
Wightman, C. N.	Private	R. Warwick	Listley St., Bridgnorth.
Bridgwater.			
Ferguson, J. F. C.	Corporal	O. & B.L.I.	Bishop's Lydeard C.S., Taunton.
Reynolds, N. J.	Sergeant	Somerset L.I.	Huntspill C.S.
Smith, E. J.	Acting Captain	W. Riding	Sexey's Sec.S., Blackford.
Brierley Hill.			
Davis, D.	Private	S. Staffs	Robert St. C.S.
Brighouse.			
Sladdin, E. A.	Private	W. Riding	St. Andrew's Ch.S.
Temperton, B. S.	Private	W. Riding	St. Andrew's Ch.S.
Brighton and Hove District.			
Banks, R.	Private	R.A.M.C.	Park St. C.S.
Chard, T. N.	2nd Lieutenant	D.C.L.I.	Municipal Sec.S.
Feest, E. L.	Private	Q.R.W.S.	Coombe Rd. C.S.
Meaton, H. J.	C.Q.M. Sergeant	R.A.S.C.	East Hove C.S.
Norman, W. S.	Private	London	St. Stephen's N.S.
Pile, E. H.	Private	Middlesex	St. Stephen's N.S.
Salvage, G.	Private	R. Sussex	Coombe Rd. C.S.
Saunders, C. H.	Private	R. Sussex	Coombe Rd. C.S.
Warne, A. H.	Private	Hants	Burgess Hill C.S.
Bristol.			
Bickell, A. W.	Sergeant-Major	Gloucester	Moorfields S.
Barnidge, J.	Lieutenant	Manchester	St. Mary's-on-the-Quay.
Gold, H.	Lance-Corporal	Somerset L.I.	St. Simon's N.S.
Hansford, J. S.	Captain	King's Liverpool	Merrywood Sec.S.
Jennings, W.	Sergeant	R.A.O.C.	Moorfields Man. Cent.
Joyce, A. J.	Private	London	St. Luke's S.
Rundle, J. G.	Private	R.A.M.C.	Fairfield Man. Cent.
Slade, E. M.	Private	Gloucester	Ashley Down C.S.
Smallcombe, A. G.	Private	R.E.	Merrywood Sec.S.
Bromley.			
Cuss, F. E. (D.C.M.)	Lance-Corporal	London Rifles	107, Wordsworth Rd., Penge.
Vivash, J. B.	Sergeant	R.W. Kent	Aylesbury Rd. C.S.
Bromsgrove.			
Wainwright, F.	Private	N.F.	Droitwich N.S.
Brynmawr.			
Williams, D. J.	2nd Lieutenant	Shropshire L.I.	County S.
Builth Wells.			
Jones, H. V.	Lieutenant	R.W.F.	The Pines, Builth.
Burnley.			
Allen, F.	Private	R. Fusiliers	Heasandford C.S.
Dagg, T. (M.M.)	Sergeant	R.G.A.	St. Mary's R.C.S.
Greenwood, E.	Private	King's Liverpool	Red Lion St. W.S.
Nutter, H.	Gunner	R.H.A.	St. Andrew's Ch.S.
Openshaw, T. W.	Lance-Corporal	King's Liverpool	Abel C.S.
Spencer, A.	2nd Air Mechanic	R.F.C.	St. Paul's Ch. S.
Stanworth, P.	Corporal	L.N.L.	St. Stephen's Ch.S.
Sutcliffe, H.	Bombardier	R.G.A.	Claremont C.S.

N.U.T. WAR RECORD

Name.	Rank.	Regiment.	School.
Burton-on-Trent.			
Fisher, R.	Private	N. Staffs	9, Needwood Street.
Slater, R. J.	Private	W. Yorks	Broadway C.S.
Bury.			
Lowe, R. C.	Lieutenant	King's Liverpool	Municipal Sec.S.
Bury St. Edmunds.			
Palmer, F. A.	Private	London	Guildhall Feoffment U.S.
Calder Valley.			
Rothwell, G.	Lance-Corporal	K.R.R.	Central C.S., Hebden Bridge.
Cambridge Borough.			
Boucher, A. E. (M.C.)	Lieutenant	R. Warwick	East Rd. Ch.S.
Clarke, E. R.	Captain	Connaught Rangers	Higher Grade C.S.
Davies, J. Ll.	Major	Essex	Perse Gr.S.
Dyson, S. G.	Lieutenant	R.A.F.	Milton Rd. C.S.
Lilley, G.	Corporal	Northants	Romsey C.S.
Mountford, E. H.	Corporal	Gloucester	New St. C.S.
Nelder, G. C. A.	2nd Lieutenant	Hants	Higher Grade C.S.
Watson, R. (M.M.)	Lance-Corporal	R.A.M.C.	St. Paul's Ch.S.
Cambridgeshire.			
Goose, P. A.	Lance-Corporal	Suffolk	Willingham C.S.
Sadler, W. H.	2nd Lieutenant	London	Harston C.S.
Canterbury.			
Cook, F. W.	Corporal	Bedford Yeo.	City C.S., Northgate.
Moore, —	2nd Lieutenant	W. Yorks	St. Dunstan's N.S.
Pudney, H. W.	Sergeant	M.G.C.	Chilham Ch.S.
Sharp, R. A.	2nd Lieutenant	R.G.A.	Wickhambreaux N.S.
Cardiff.			
Cottrell, F. O.	Private	Welsh	Ninian Park C.S.
Hartland, G. H.	Private	R. Fusiliers	Municipal Sec.S.
Hickey, R.	Private	Welsh	Kitchener Rd. C.S.
Moore, A. H.	Lieutenant	S.W.B.	Kitchener Rd. C.S.
Morgan, F. R.	Corporal	Welsh Guards	Tredegarville C.S.
Smith, C. H. (M.C.)	2nd Lieutenant	R.G.A.	Grange N.S.
Young, Miss A. E.	Nurse	V.A.D.	Lansdowne C.S.
Carlisle.			
Bolt, H. J. R.	Corporal	R.A.S.C.	Lowther St. C.S.
Clementson, G.	Sergeant	Border	Brook St. C.S.
Henderson, W.	2nd Lieutenant	Argyle & Suth'd Highrs.	Fawcett Ch.S.
Thwaites, R.	Captain	D.L.I.	Powis Cottage, Long Marton.
Carnarvon.			
Jones, R.	Lieutenant	S. Lancs	Bontnewydd C.S.
Carnarvon (South).			
Jones, W.	Lance-Corporal	R.W.F	Criccieth C.S.
Castleford and Pontefract.			
Briscoe, E. W.	Lance-Corporal	R. Fusiliers	Brackenhill C.S., Pontefract.
Garlick, J. P.	Sergeant	R.E.	Featherstone C.S.
Chatham and Rochester.			
Andrews, H. G.	Captain	York and Lancs	St. Peter's Ch. S., Rochester.
Claxton, S. H.	Private	H.A.C.	Snodland B.S., Kent.

THE GALLANT DEAD

Name.	Rank.	Regiment.	School.
Chatham and Rochester—*continued*.			
Greenhalgh, H. F.	2nd Lieutenant	R.A.O.C.	Rainham C.S., Gillingham.
Little, J. C. H.	Sergeant	Lincoln	St. Peter's Ch.S., Rochester.
Payne, S. T.	Private	R.A.S.C.	Halling C.S.
Cheltenham.			
Dunn, R.	Sergeant	Gloucester	St. Mark's N.S.
Price, A. J.	Sergeant	R.G.A.	Naunton Park C.S.
Wright, S.	Sergeant	R. Berks	Parish Ch.S.
Chester.			
Bevan, G. E.	Corporal	King's Liverpool	Holy Trinity Ch.S.
Bishop, F. (M.C.)	Captain	Cheshire	College S.
Chester-le-Street.			
Ashworth, J. F. G.	2nd Lieutenant	D.L.I.	Fatfield C.S.
Brock, A. L.	Acting Captain	D.L.I.	Council S.
Buffham, H. A.	Corporal	D.L.I.	Pelton Fell C.S.
Clark, J. G. (M.M.)	Private	Public Schs. Batt.	Birtley Lane C.S.
Fullerton, M.	Private	D.L.I.	Pelton Fell C.S.
Heslop, J. G.	Private	D.L.I.	Pelton C.S.
Metcalfe, A. J.	Lance-Corporal	D.L.I.	Fatfield C.S.
Richardson, A. L.	Private	D.L.I.	Fence Houses C.S.
Rivers, G. S.	Private	D.L.I.	Birtley Lane C.S.
Robson, T.	Sergeant	D.L.I.	3, Hawthorn Terrace.
Stobbs, H.	2nd Lieutenant	N.F.	Fence Houses C.S.
Waud, E. H.	Lieutenant	R.A.F.	Eighton Banks Ch.S.
Chippenham.			
Atlay, J. K.	Sergeant	Wilts.	Melksham Ch.S.
Chorley.			
Renwick, W.	Private	L.N.L.	Brinscall W.S.
Coalville.			
Thomson, J.	2nd Lieutenant	King's Liverpool	Measham C.S.
Colchester and East Essex.			
Gardner, E. H.	Pioneer	R.E.	Canterbury Rd. C.S.
Colwyn Bay.			
Bevan, G. E.	Sergeant	Manchester	Abergele N.S.
Cornwall (East).			
James, V. G.	Lieutenant	R.W.F.	Callington County S.
Sargent, O. A.	Sergeant	D.C.L.I.	Pensilva Ch.S.
Cornwall (Mid).			
Hunkin, F.	Corporal	D.C.L.I.	Carclaze C.S.
Trerise, W. T. L.	2nd Lieutenant	R. Warwick	St. Columb Major C.S.
Cornwall (West).			
Oates, J. S.	Captain	D.C.L.I.	St. Agnes' C.S.
Smitham, W.	Sergeant	D.C.L.I.	Barncoose C.S.
Ceseley.			
Phillips, J. J.	Sergeant	R. Warwick	Daisy Bank C.S.
Coventry.			
Jolly, F. W.	Private	R. Warwick	" John Gulson " C.S.
Mascord, A. E.	2nd Lieutenant	R. Warwick	Centaur Rd. C.S.
Suddens, A. J.	Company Sgt.-Maj.	O. & B.L.I.	" Frederick Bird " C.S.
Toms, W.	Sergeant	O. & B.L.I.	Cheylesmore C.S.
Yardley, F.	2nd Lieutenant	R. Warwick	Stoke C.S.

N.U.T. WAR RECORD

Name.	Rank.	Regiment.	School.
Crewe.			
Bostock, —	Lieutenant	Cheshire	Bedford St. C.S.
Parberry, W.	Gunner	R.F.A.	Edleston Rd. C.S.
Sparrow, G. W.	Corporal	R.E.	St. Paul's Ch.S.
Crompton and Royton.			
Mellor, J. G.	Lance-Corporal	Devon	St. Paul's Ch.S., Royton.
Crook.			
Groves, R. L.	Private	E. Yorks	Hunwick Ch.S.
Rigg, T. (M.M.)	Sergeant	Durham	Stanley C.S.
Stanfield, T. W. (M.M.)	Lieutenant	E. Yorks	Peases West C.S.
Croydon.			
Airriss, G. F.	Private	Middlesex	Mitcham Road C.S.
Babbage, J. C.	2nd Lieutenant	Manchester	"Woodside," Moreland Rd. C.S.
Beaumont, S. (M.C.)	2nd Lieutenant	E. Lancs	Oval Rd. C.S.
Byrne, E.	2nd Lieutenant	D.C.L.I.	Brighton Rd. C.S.
Creek, S. A.	Sergeant	London	Oval Rd. C.S.
Crittenden, F.	2nd Lieutenant	R.G.A.	Ingram Rd. C.S.
Foster, G. C.	Private	M.G.C.	Winterbourne Rd. C.S.
Marshall, C. S.	2nd Lieutenant	R. Worcester	Winterbourne Rd. C.S.
Rothen, F.	Lance-Corporal	Queen's Westminster	Borough Sec.S.
Shaw, E. B.	Private	R. Fusiliers	Christ Ch.S.
Smith, F. H.	Lieutenant	London	Dering Place C.S.
Cumberland (West).			
Wedgwood, J. (M.M.)	Private	Border	Bookwell C.S.
Darlington.			
Dixon, C. G.	Sergeant	D.L.I.	Reed St. C.S.
Howell, A.	Sergeant	D.L.I.	St. John's N.S.
Mais, W.	Sergeant	D.L.I.	Beaumont St. C.S.
Robson, H.	Private	K.R.R.	115, Craig Street.
Ward, T.	Sergeant-Inst.	A.G.S.	Corporation Rd. C.S.
Darwen.			
Kay, H.	Lance-Corporal	R.W.F.	Sudell Rd. C.S.
Daventry.			
Muddiman, J. E.	Private	R. Fusiliers	Barby N.S.
Boyson, M. (M.M.)	Private	Northants	Weedon N.S.
Deal and Sandwich.			
George, S. O.	Sergeant	Bedford	Parochial S.
Deptford and Greenwich.			
Brooker, G.	Sergeant	London	Morden Tce. L.C.C.S.
Burrows, W. A.	2nd Lieutenant	London	Creed Place L.C.C.S.
Challis, C.	Private	Devon	Alverton St. L.C.C.S.
Fell, W. J.	Private	R. Fusiliers	Royal Hill L.C.C.S.
Fox, C. J.	2nd Lieutenant	R.W. Kent	Clifton Rd. L.C.C.S.
Legg, W. A.	Lance-Corporal	Civil Service Rifles	Old Woolwich Rd.L.C.C.S.
Nevey, F.	Lieutenant	W. Riding	The "Charlton" Central S.
Palmer, L.	Private	London	Frankham St. L.C.C.S.
Pert, L. H.	Private	L.R.B.	Nynehead Rd. L.C.C.S.
Shrewsbury, J.	Sergeant	K.R.R.	Glenister Rd. L.C.C.S.
Simons, L. (M.C.)	Captain	R. Fusiliers	The "Charlton" Central S.
Trask, S. R.	2nd Lieutenant	Suffolk	45, Manor Rd., Brockley, S.E.
Derby.			
Sephton, R. T.	Private	R. Fusiliers	St. James's Ch.S.
Thompson, A. M.	Signaller	Sherwood Foresters	Kedleston Rd. C.S.

THE GALLANT DEAD

Name.	Rank.	Regiment.	School.
Derbyshire (East).			
Clarke, R. E.	Sergeant	Sherwood Foresters	Newbold Ch.S.
Durrant, J.	Lieutenant	Sherwood Foresters	North Wingfield C.S.
Hargreaves, J. H.	Private	H.A.C.	Hipper St. C.S.
Lister, E.	Sergeant	York and Lancs	Beighton C.S.
Mellor, J.	Private	R. Fusiliers	Chester Training College.
Rushton, G.	Private	Sherwood Foresters	Grassmoor N.S.
Wright, R. T.	2nd Lieutenant	Sherwood Foresters	Beighton C.S.
Devizes.			
Paget, C.	Lieutenant	Warwick	Wargrave Ch.S.
Devon (North).			
Carter, W. J. C.	2nd Lieutenant	Devon	Ilfracombe N.S.
Sanders, C.	Private	Devon	Pilton N.S.
Dewsbury and Batley.			
Hinchliffe, F. B.	Lieutenant	W. Riding	Boothroyd Lane C.S.
Hinchliffe, J. R.	Private	York and Lancs	Grimethorpe C.S.
Kitson, T. A. B.	Gunner	R.G.A.	Savile Town N.S.
Wood, J.	Private	Coldstream Guards	43, Purlwell Hall Rd. Batley.
Doncaster.			
Ball, D.	Corporal	K.R.R.	Bentley New Village C.S.
Batley, E.	Private	York and Lancs	Askern C.S.
Cook, P.	Lance-Corporal	W. Yorks	New Edlington C.S.
Holmes, H. (M.M.)	Sergeant	Welsh	Hyde Park C.S.
Marks, H. T.	Sergeant-Instr.	Suffolk	Chequer Rd. C.S.
Ogley, G. Y.	Sergeant	K.O.Y.L.I.	Bentley New Village C.S.
Richardson, R. E.	Private	R.W.F.	Bentley Rd. C.S.
Slack, C. A.	Lance-Corporal	R.E.	Highfields C.S.
Slater, A.	Petty Officer	R.N.R.	South Elmsall C.S.
Street, A.	Private	W. Yorks	South Kirkby C.S.
Watson, F. J.	2nd Lieutenant	D.C.L.I.	Highfields C.S.
Dorking.			
Carpenter, H. W.	Lance-Corporal	Queen's	Abinger Upper C.S.
Dorset (East).			
Bogart, W. G.	Gunner	R.G.A.	St. Aldhelm's Ch.S., Branksome.
Hart, E. F. C.	Private	Hants	Oak Cottage, Broadstone.
Lovell, E. R.	Sergeant	Hants	Oakdale C.S.
Dorset (North).			
Falla, M. B.	Private	London Irish Rifles	Bishops Caundle Ch.S.
Haynes, A. E.	Lance-Corporal	Middlesex	Sturminster Newton C.S.
Palmer, F. R.	2nd Lieutenant	Dorset	Sherborne C.S.
Dorset (South).			
Ashton, A. E.	Gunner	Trench Mortar Battery	Dorchester Ch.S.
Betts, E.	Private	Dorset	Holy Trinity Ch.S., Weymouth.
Dorset (West).			
Smallshaw, W.	Private	Devon	Woodhouse, Uplyme, Lyme Regis.
Dover.			
Eaves, A. T.	Captain	R.W. Surrey	St. Martin's C.S.
Driffield and Bridlington.			
Smart, W.	Sergeant	K.R.R.	Bempton C.S.
Dudley.			
Brown, A. T.	Gunner	R.G.A.	Parson's Charity S.
Higginson, F.	Private	S. Staffs	Baylies' Charity S.

N.U.T. WAR RECORD

Name.	Rank.	Regiment.	School.
Durham.			
Armstrong, J.	Private	D.L.I.	Browney Colliery C.S.
Brown, C.	Sergeant	D.L.I.	Waterhouses C.S.
Brown, W. H.	Lieutenant	D.L.I.	Witton Gilbert Ch.S.
Chipchase, H.	Private	D.L.I.	East Hetton C.S.
Chrisp, T.	Sergeant-Major	D.L.I.	St. Margaret's Ch.S.
Cook, J. E.	Private	D.L.I.	Thornley C.S.
Cook, P.	Private	D.L.I.	Thornley C.S.
Corker, R. R.	Sergeant	D.L.I.	Waterhouses C.S.
Cosgrove, A. B.	2nd Lieutenant	Tyneside Scottish	Kimblesworth C.S.
Forrest, W.	Sergeant-Major	D.L.I.	New Brancepeth C.S.
Gibson, M.	Corporal	D.L.I.	Castle Eden Ch.S.
Hauxwell, G. W.	Private	D.L.I.	4, Atherton St.
Martindale, S.	Private	D.L.I.	New Shildon C.S.
Moore, J.	Lieutenant	D.L.I.	Kimblesworth C.S.
Prickett, J. E.	Private	D.L.I.	St. Oswald's Ch.S.
Shortridge, L.	Private	D.L.I.	Castle Eden Ch.S.
Ealing.			
Best,	Private	E. Kent	Drayton C.S.
Bevan, E.	Private	R. Fusiliers	Little Ealing C.S.
Bonshor, W. J.	Lieutenant	S. Staffs	St. John's N.S.
Cleaver, C. H.	Private	R.A.M.C.	Northfields C.S.
Cowley, H. W.	Lance-Corporal	O.T.C.	Central C.S., Isleworth.
Hancock, G. E.	Sergeant	Middlesex	St. Stephen's N.S.
Jones, E.	Sergeant	London Scottish	Northfields C.S.
Klein, F.	Sergeant	Middlesex	St. John's N.S
Palmer, H. J.	Lieutenant	R.E.	Grove Rd. C.S., Hounslow.
Paynter, G. A.	Sergeant	R. Fusiliers	Lammas C.S.
Easington.			
Beardmore, N.	Corporal	R.E.	Shotton C.S.
Hedger, W. S.		London	Wheatley Hill C.S.
Eastbourne.			
Goodwin, F. C. P.	Private	R.W. Kent	East St. C.S.
Green, H. W.	2nd Lieutenant	R. Sussex	St. Mary's Ch.S.
North, S. F.	2nd Lieutenant	Lancs Fusiliers	Christ Ch.S.
Slidel, S. R.	2nd Lieutenant	Lincoln	Warbleton, Heathfield.
East Cleveland.			
Barker, A.	Private	D.L.I.	Brotton Ch.S.
Parsons, M. J.	Private	Yorks	Margrove Park C.S.
Shepherd, W. J.	Private	D.L.I.	Saltburn C.S.
East Dereham.			
Payne, A. C.	Private	Bedford	Mileham C.S.
East Ham.			
Foreman, D. J.	Private	London	Walton Rd. C.S.
Gill, H. H.	Private	K.O. Lancs	Kensington Av. C.S.
Graham, W. T.	Lance-Corporal	Queen's Westminster	Kensington Rd. C.S.
Green, F. C.	2nd Lieutenant	Lincoln	Vicarage Lane C.S.
Packer, B. F.	2nd Lieutenant	Suffolk	Central Park C.S.
East Lambeth.			
Allen, J. D.	Lance-Corporal	London	Crawford St. L.C.C.S.
Baker, B. R.	2nd Lieutenant	R. Fusiliers	Crampton St. L.C.C.S.
Bilcliffe, B. L.	Private	Civil Service Rifles	Rockingham St. L.C.C.S.
Cook, S.	Lieutenant	D.L.I.	Reddins Rd. L.C.C.S.
Gatehouse, H. C.	Sergeant	R.A.M.C.	"Paragon" L.C.C.S.
Gleadall, J.	Private	Middlesex	Kennington Rd. L.C.C.S.
Hard, W. T.	2nd Lieutenant	London	Surrey Square L.C.C.S.
Harden, W. F.	Able Seaman	H.M.S. *Glatton*	Christ Ch.S., Cancell Rd.
Hattam, H. C.	Lieutenant	Suffolk	Choumert Rd. L.C.C.S.
Hatton, F. J.	Corporal	Deptford Gun Brigade	Gloucester Rd. L.C.C.S.

THE GALLANT DEAD

Name.	Rank.	Regiment.	School.
East Lambeth—*continued.*			
Huddart, A.	Private	Sherwood Foresters	Leo St. L.C.C.S.
Lewis, E.	Lance-Corporal	London	Sumner Rd. L.C.C.S.
Long, W. E.	Corporal	London	Grove Vale L.C.C.S.
Mallpress, V. K.	Private	London	Settle St. L.C.C.S.
Morton, C.	Private	Civil Service Rifles	Lomond Grove L.C.C.S.
Pugh, H. G.	Private	London	Sussex Rd. L.C.C.S.
Rees, H. G.	Private	Civil Service Rifles	Holy Trinity N.S.
Richardson, H. B.	Sergeant	H.L.I.	Sumner Rd. L.C.C.S.
Rose, A. G.	Lance-Corporal	Civil Service Rifles	Rockingham St. L.C.C.S.
Rose, T.	Bombardier	R.F.A.	" John Ruskin " L.C.C.S.
Saunders, F. J. B.	Private	Civil Service Rifles	St. Mary's N.S.
Stannard, W. G.	Corporal	Grenadier Guards	Gloucester Rd. L.C.C.S.
Wardley, M. E.	2nd Lieutenant	R. Fusiliers	Westmoreland Rd.L.C.C.S
Williams, D. J.	2nd Lieutenant	M.G.C.	Cator St. L.C.C.S.
Williams, S. M.	2nd Lieutenant	London	Adys Rd. L.C.C.S.
Woodhouse, F. C.	Q.M. Sergeant	R. Berks	St. John's N.S., Brixton.
East Ward (Westmorland).			
Humphris, H. W.	Sergeant	Border	Great Asby End.S.
Eccles.			
Jolley, V.	Private	R.A.M.C.	Green Lane C.S.
Murdock, F. A.	Private	R. Fusiliers	Lewes St. C.S.
Parker, G. W.	2nd Lieutenant	Lancs Fusiliers	Beech St. C.S.
Thompson, C.	2nd Lieutenant	Lancs Fusiliers	St. Mary's R.C.S.
Edmonton.			
Cardell, E. J.	Lance-Bombardier	R.G.A.	Silver St. C.S.
Roderick, P.	Corporal	H.A.C.	Croyland Rd. C.S.
Sexton, R.	Corporal	Civil Service Rifles	Houndsfield Rd. C.S.
Enfield.			
Dodderidge, R. W.	Signaller	R.N.	George Spicer C.S.
Jope, R.	Corporal	E. Kent	St. James' N.S.
Powell, J. H.	2nd Lieutenant	S. Staffs	St. Andrew's N.S.
Light, S. T.	Batty. Sergt.-Maj.	R.G.A.	Bush Hill Pk. C.S.
Searle, W. G.	Corporal	Middlesex	Bush Hill Pk. C.S.
Score, W.	2nd Lieutenant	E. Kent	Chesterfield Rd. C.S.
Taylor, F. A.	Private	Middlesex	Alma Rd. C.S.
Epsom and Sutton.			
Walker, W. H.	2nd Lieutenant	Middlesex	Newtown C.S.
Erewash Valley.			
Pearce, H. (M.M.)	Lance-Corporal	R.W.F.	Stonebroom C.S.
Erith.			
Bond, E.	Lieutenant	W. Riding	Belvedere C.S.
Edwards, W. M.	Sergeant	K.R.R.	St. Augustine's Rd. C.S.
Playle, W. E. G.	Corporal	London	Manor Rd. C.S.
Webley, C. E.	Lieutenant	R.W. Kent	West St. C.S.
Essex (Mid).			
Dixon, L. F.	2nd Lieutenant	S.W.B.	Trinity Rd. C.S., Chelmsford.
Evesham.			
Lewis, R. C.	Corporal	Gloucester	Badsey C.S.
Stanton, R. W.	Private	Warwick	Evesham C.S.
Exeter City.			
Brewer, A. K.	Company Sgt.-Maj.	Devon	Ladysmith Rd. C.S.
Jones, E.	Sergeant	Devon	St. Sidwell's N.S.
Warner, P. S.	2nd Lieutenant	Devon	St. Sidwell's N.S.

N.U.T. WAR RECORD

Name.	Rank.	Regiment.	School.
Exeter District.			
Nicholls, F. W. T.	Corporal	Devon	Topsham C.S.
Ninnis, J.	Private	Devon	Bradninch.
Farnham.			
Garner, R. L.	2nd Lieutenant	London	West St. C.S.
Phillips, E. J.	Private	R.W. Kent	Tilford Ch.S.
Faversham.			
Curling, E. T.	Lieutenant	London	Hernhill Ch.S.
Felling.			
Scott, F. E.	2nd Lieutenant	R.G.A.	Bill Quay C.S.
Festiniog.			
Williams, E. R.	Private	R.W.F.	Rhyl C.S.
Finsbury and City.			
Adam, J. G. S.	Company Sgt.-Maj.	London	Drayton Park L.C.C.S.
Bence, S. (M.C.)	Sergeant	R. Fusiliers	St. Mark's Ch.S.
Boughton, W. C. R.	Private	L.R.B.	Hungerford Rd. L.C.C.S.
Carpenter, E. S.	Corporal	R. Fusiliers	St. Paul's Ch.S.
Cleall, C. P.	Lieutenant	Essex	Church St. L.C.C.S.
Cook, A.	Private	L.R.B.	" Hugh Myddelton " L.C.C.S.
Cotter, C. J.	Sergeant	Middlesex	St. Peter's Italian R.C.S.
Downes, B.	2nd Lieutenant	London Irish	Princess May Rd. L.C.C.S.
Ferguson, H. H. E.	Captain	H.L.I.	Moreland St. L.C.C.S.
Fisher, J.	Sapper	R.E.	Amwell St. L.C.C.S.
Hammond, A.J.	Private	London	Vittoria Place L.C.C.S.
Hancock, J. L.	Corporal	R. Fusiliers	Canonbury Rd. L.C.C.S.
Haselden, E. A.	Captain	W. Yorks	Queen's Head St. L.C.C.S.
Hornsby, W.	2nd Lieutenant	Somerset L.I.	Montem St. L.C.C.S.
Hymans, L. H.			147, Nevill Rd., Stoke Newington, N.
Lewin, H. C.	Private	York and Lancs	St. Mary Magdalene Ch.S.
Morgan, E. T.	Lieutenant	W. Fusiliers	Station Rd. L.C.C.S.
Ore, J. F.	Lance-Corporal	Middlesex	" Hugh Myddelton " L.C.C.S.
Pearson, G. P.	Corporal	L.R.B.	Hanover St. L.C.C.S.
Pearson, W.	Private	H.A.C.	Cottenham Rd. L.C.C.S.
Wholey, F.	Corporal	Middlesex	Hanover St. L.C.C.S.
Worner, P.	Lieutenant	Devon	St. John's Ch.S., Red Lion Square.
Fishguard.			
Lewis, W. Bowen	Private	Welsh	Mathry N.S.
Flint County.			
Hughes, E. J. (M.C., M.M.)	2nd Lieutenant	R.W.F.	Sea View, Aston, Hawarden.
Trickett, W. E.	Major	R.W.F.	Mold Ch.S.
Folkestone.			
Clay, W.	Lance-Corporal	R. Fusiliers	Dover Rd. C.S.
Dennett, W. A. H.	Sergeant	R.W. Kent	Hythe N.S.
Forest of Dean.			
James, G. H.	Private	Gloucester	Pillowell C.S.
Turner, D.	Gunner	R.F.A.	Parkend C.S.
Furness.			
Burrows, J.	Sergeant	K.O.R.L.	Dalton-in-Furness N.S.
Gainsborough.			
Taylor, J.	Sergeant	Lincoln	Kirton Lindsey C.S.

THE GALLANT DEAD

Name.	Rank.	Regiment.	School.
Gateshead.			
Bamborough, J. M.	Lance-Corporal	Yorks	St. Wilfred's R.C.S.
Birney, T.	Sergeant	N.F.	Blessed Sacrament R.C.S.
Davidson, W.	Gunner	R.G.A.	Shipcote C.S.
Hadden, E. C.	2nd Lieutenant	D.L.I.	Windmill Hills C.S.
Russell, R.	Private	E. Yorks	Oakwellgate C.S.
Smith, F. G.	2nd Lieutenant	D.L.I.	St. Mary's Ch.S.
Gelligaer.			
Curtis, J. H.	2nd Lieutenant	Welsh	Ystrad Mynach C.S.
Davies, E. T.	Lieutenant	R.G.A.	Hengoed C.S.
Gillingham (Kent).			
Andrews, F.	Sergeant	R.W. Kent	Byron Rd. C.S.
Burt, G. H.	Sergeant	Middlesex	Byron Rd. C.S.
Dier, F.	Private	R.E.K. Mounted Rifles	Napier Rd. C.S.
Hammans, H.	Corporal	Middlesex	Church S.
Reid, G. H. S.	Lance-Corporal	E. Kent	Napier Rd. C.S.
Stevens, G. A.	Sapper	R.E.	Barnsole Rd. C.S.
Tucker, A.	Sergeant	R.W. Kent	Church S.
Glamorgan (Mid).			
Nicholas, J. A.	Captain	R.F.A. (Welsh)	Crediton Gr.S.
Owen, E. E.	Corporal	R.E.	Port Talbot Cent. C.S.
Thomas, Morgan	Lieutenant	S.W.B.	Cwmavon C.S.
Wheeler, L. E.	Sergeant	R.A.S.C.	Cwmavon C.S.
Glamorgan (West).			
Andrews, G. L.	Captain	Welsh	Penllergaer C.S.
Dennis, H. J.	Private	Welsh	Glais C.S.
Thomas, L. J.	Private	R.W.F.	Glais C.S.
Gloucester.			
Hill, R.	Corporal	Gloucester	Northgate St. C.S.
Murray, W.	Company Sgt.-Maj.	Gloucester	Archdeacon St. C.S.
Russell, A. C.	Lieutenant	Rifle Brigade	Widden St. C.S.
Smith, F. G.	C.Q.M. Sergeant	Gloucester	Widden St. C.S.
Gloucester (North).			
Hale, F. E.	2nd Lieutenant	K.R.R.	Tewkesbury C.S.
Goole.			
Burnitt, A.	Corporal	K.R.R.	Old Goole C.S.
Grantham.			
Harris, F.	Sergeant	Lincoln	National S.
Gravesend.			
Ashenden, H. E.	Sergeant	R.W. Kent	Cecil Rd. C.S.
Deakin, E.	Private	R. Sussex	Dover Rd. C.S.
Hemsley, M.	Private	R.W. Kent	Dover Rd. C.S.
Johnson, H. E.	Sergeant	R.W. Kent	St. James's N.S.
Great Yarmouth.			
Bagge, W. J.	Sergeant	R.W. Kent	E. Anglian Inst. for Blind.
Legrice, S.	Sub-Conductor	R.A.O.C.	Church Rd. C.S., Gorleston.
Grimsby.			
Bland, R.	Sergeant	W. Yorks	Little Coates C.S.
Branfoot, C.	Lieutenant	Lincoln	Mun. College.
Coates, H.	Captain	Lincoln	Elliston St. C.S.
Hill, E.	Private	M.G.C.	Bursar St. C.S.
Phillips, R.	Corporal	R. Sussex	Hilda C.S.
Richmond, R.	Bombardier	W. Yorks	Harold St. C.S

N.U.T. WAR RECORD

Name.	Rank.	Regiment.	School.
Guernsey.			
Binley, P. A. (M.C.)	2nd Lieutenant	R. Essex	Melrose P.S.
Molteno, L. C.	Lance-Corporal	Gloucester	37, Hauteville, St. Peter Port.
Hackney.			
Ayles, G.	Lance-Corporal	R.A.M.C.	Sigdon Rd. L.C.C.S.
Belben, H. J.	Corporal	Hants	Daniel St. L.C.C.S.
Carne, J. R.	2nd Lieutenant	R. Sussex	"Shacklewell" L.C.C.S.
Curtis, W. S.	Private	London	Mandeville St. L.C.C.S.
Davis, E.	Private	R. Fusiliers	Hackney Par.S.
Dibble, T. H.	Private	London	Settles St. L.C.C.S.
Edwards, J. E.	Private	R.A.F.	Queen's Rd. L.C.C.S.
Gordon, G. H.	Gunner	R.F.A.	Sidney Rd. L.C.C.S.
Greenwood, A. G.	Lance-Corporal	Middlesex	Daubeney Rd. L.C.C.S.
Groves, L.	Private	Civil Service Rifles	Tottenham Rd. L.C.CS.
Jeynes, T. G.	Corporal	R. Warwick	Curtain Rd. L.C.C.S.
Kirkwood, J.	Lance-Corporal	L.R.B.	Bay St. L.C.C.S.
Martin, W. E.	Corporal	R. Scots	Wolverley St. L.C.C.S.
Perry, E. J.	Sergeant	London	Greencoat S.
Potter, W. J.	Rifleman	K.R.R.	Chatham Gdns. L.C.C.S.
Pragnell, A. G.	2nd Lieutenant	London	Gopsall St. L.C.C.S.
Salmon, V. E. T.	Private	H.A.C.	Scawfell St. L.C.C.S.
Siebert, S. P.	2nd Lieutenant	K.R.R.	Berkshire Rd. L.C.C.S.
Steven, A.	Lieutenant	Gloucester	Wolverley St. L.C.C.S.
Stevenson, J. C. (M.C.)	Acting Captain	R.W. Surrey	"Shacklewell" L.C.C.S.
Sturtridge, F.	Sergeant	London	Queen's Rd. L.C.C.S.
Taylor, F. H, H.	Private	E. Kent	Rushmore Rd. L.C.C.S.
Truman, T. C.	Sergeant	R.G.A.	Chisenhale Rd. L.C.C.S.
Wale, S. J.	Sergeant	London	St. Phillip's N.S.
Whiteley, F. J.	Sergeant	L.R.B.	"Avoca," Highview Av., Grays, Essex.
Wilkinson, W. A.	2nd Lieutenant	R.F.A.	Northwold Rd. L.C.C.S.
Winbush, E. T.	2nd Lieutenant	R.F.A.	Canal Rd. L.C.C.S.
Halifax.			
Ashworth, E. L.	Lance-Corporal	W. Riding	Trinity Ch.S.
Noone, J.	Private	W. Riding	St. Marie's R.C.S.
Wilson, S.	Lance-Corporal	W. Riding	Sunnyside C.S.
Harrogate.			
Bell, D. S. (V.C.)	2nd Lieutenant	Yorks	Starbeck C.S.
Harrow.			
Davies, J.	Sergeant	M.G.C.	Roxeth Hill C.S.
Demmery, J.	Private	Gloucester	Graham Rd. C.S.
Jennings, R. J.	Lance-Corporal	Middlesex	Bridge C.S.
Mitchley, S.	2nd Lieutenant	Norfolk	Greenhill C.S.
Owen, W. H.	Sapper	R.E.	High St. C.S., Wealdstone.
Webb, C.S.	Company Sgt.-Maj.	London	Park Lane C.S.
Hartlepools.			
Dyer, H.	Corporal	D.L.I.	Lynnfield C.S.
Jobling, J. W.	Bombardier	R.F.A.	Brougham C.S.
Jones, T.	Private	D.L.I.	St. Aidan's N.S.
Vickers, A. D. L.	Lance-Corporal	D.L.I.	Trimdon Grange C.S.
Hastings.			
Willis, —.	2nd Lieutenant	R. Sussex	Clive Vale C.S.
Hemel Hempstead.			
Blaber, T. M.	Lance-Corporal	London	N.S., Berkhampstead.
Hendon.			
Alford, E. N.	Captain	Bedford	Garden Suburb C.S.
Beare, C. E.	Lance-Corporal	Q.V.R.	The Hyde C.S.

THE GALLANT DEAD

Name.	Rank.	Regiment.	School.
Hendon—*continued*.			
Caton, J. L.	Lance-Corporal	Border	Childs Hill C.S.
Chick, A. G.	Sergeant	London	Bell St. C.S.
Clough, W.	Sergeant	London	The Hyde C.S.
Jackson, A. F.	2nd Lieutenant	London	The Hyde C.S.
Hereford.			
Rimmer, G.	Private	King's Liverpool	Norton Canon N.S.
Horler, E.	2nd Lieutenant	M.G.C.	Dymock S., Gloucester.
Hertford.			
Cawley, H.	Private	Suffolk	Cowper N.S.
May, W. J.	Lance-Corporal	R.E.	33, Barclay Rd., Fulham, S.W.
Veysey, S.	2nd Lieutenant	R.G.A.	St. Mary's N.S., Ware.
Hexham.			
Southern, M.	2nd Lieutenant	E. Yorks	Shaftoe Trust C.S.
Heywood.			
Bridge, W.	Rifleman	K.R.R.	St. Luke's C.S.
Hinckley.			
Walker, H.	Private	Leicester	Church S.
Hitchin.			
Osborne, W. J.	Private	R. Fusiliers	Stotfold C.S., Baldock.
Hornsey.			
Andrew, A. A.	2nd Lieutenant	London	Mattison Rd. C.S.
Canby, T. B.	Rifleman	Q.V.R.	Stroud Green C.S.
Dunn, W.	2nd Lieutenant	Lincoln	Mattison Rd. C.S.
Lucas, E.	Private	R.A.M.C.	Mattison Rd. C.S.
Peet, J. T.	Company Sgt.-Maj.	O. & B.L.I.	St. James's N.S.
Stace, A. W.	Lance-Corporal	Queen's Westminster	Mattison Rd. C.S.
Horsham.			
Adams, H.	Lance-Corporal	Suffolk	Rusper C.S.
Hart, G. J.	Private	R. Fusiliers	Shoreham C.S.
Houghton-le-Spring.			
Crawford, G.	Private	King's Liverpool	New Penshaw C.S.
Duke, J.	Sergeant	D.L.I.	Dubmire C.S.
Francis, T.	Private	D.L.I.	Houghton-le-Spring C.S.
Pyburn, T. B.	Private	King's Liverpool	Lyons C.S.
Robson, J. W.	Corporal	D.L.I.	Houghton-le-Spring C.S.
Sanderson, J. J.	Sergeant	D.L.I.	Barrington C.S.
Huddersfield.			
Johnson, B. C.	2nd Lieutenant	W. Riding	Holmfirth N.S.
Wilkinson, P.	Lieutenant	Lancs Fusiliers	Nields C.S.
Hull.			
Collett, C. H.	Private	E. Yorks	Newland Av. C.S.
Dickens, C. E.	Private	E. Yorks	Blenkin St. C.S.
Gibson, A.	Private	E. Yorks	South Myton C.S.
Harrison, J. (V.C., M.C.)	2nd Lieutenant	E. Yorks	Lime St. C.S.
Hicks, H.	Private	E. Yorks	South Myton C.S.
Jackson, W. J.	Private	E. Yorks	St. George's Rd. C.S.
Johnson, F.	Private	E. Yorks	Christ Ch.S.
Johnson, J. A.	Sergeant	E. Yorks	Mersey St. C.S.
Jones, R. P.	Sergeant	E. Yorks	Hessle Ch.S.
Keal, R.	Private	E. Yorks	Crowle St. C.S.
Millard, T. P.	Private	E. Yorks	Blenkin St. C.S.
Powell, T. A.	Private	E. Yorks	Scarborough St. C.S.
Reeder, E. E.	Lieutenant	E. Yorks	Courtney St. C.S.

N.U.T. WAR RECORD

Name.	Rank.	Regiment.	School.
Hull—*continued.*			
Richardson, R. W.	Private	R.W.F.	Estcourt St. C.S.
Robinson, W.	Private	E. Yorks	Charterhouse Lane C.S.
Stainforth, G.	2nd Lieutenant	Liverpool	Selby St. West C.S.
Thorp, A.	Sergeant	R.G.A.	Craven St. Manual Centre.
Tomkins, E.	Private	E. Yorks	Chiltern St. C.S.
Wardle, J. G.	Private	E. Yorks	Park Rd. C.S.
Watmough, F. T.	Gunner	R.G.A.	Newland Av. C.S.
West, G. A.	2nd Lieutenant	E. Lancs	Thomas Stratten C.S.
Witty, E.	Private	E. Yorks	West Dock Av. C.S.
Huntingdonshire.			
Harrison, R.	2nd Lieutenant	Black Watch	Filsert Walk, St. Ives.
Hyndburn.			
Hesketh, R. C.	Private	E. Lancs	St. Paul's C.S.
Sagar, F.	Sergeant	E. Lancs	Holy Trinity Ch.S., Oswaldtwistle.
Woods, E.	Lieutenant	E. Lancs	Gt. Harwood N.S.
Ilford.			
Benson, I.	Captain	Border	Goodmayes C.S.
Cole, H.	2nd Air Mechanic	R.F.C.	Goodmayes C.S.
Dines, J.	2nd Lieutenant	Liverpool	Highlands C.S.
Foot, F. W.	Gunner	R.G.A.	Church S.
Gussin, F. G.	Private	R.A.M.C.	Cleveland Rd. C.S.
Holmes, E. F.	Corporal	R. Fusiliers	South Park C.S.
Porter, S.	Lieutenant	York and Lancs	Sec.S., Belper.
Ilkeston.			
Dann, S.	Private	R.A.M.C.	Chaucer St. C.S.
Rollason, H.	Private	R.F.A.	Stapleford C.S.
Shaw, C. G.	Lieutenant	Lincoln	Bennerley Av. C.S.
Ingleborough.			
Bennett, C. D.	Captain	W. Riding	Langcliffe C.S.
Ward, W.	Lance-Corporal	W. Yorks	Long Preston End.S.
Ipswich.			
Sadler, G.	Private	Northampton	St. Margaret's N.S.
Isle of Ely.			
Law, E.	Lieutenant	Northampton	Broad St. C.S., Whittlesey.
Wordingham, V. R.	Lieutenant	Intelligence Corps	South District C.S.
Isle of Wight.			
Glover, J. W. E.	Gunner	R.G.A.	Newport Sec.S.
Itchen.			
Hackett, E. F.	Private	Hants	Ludlow Rd. C.S.
Neville, C.	Captain	Sherwood Foresters	Swaythling C.S.
Penney, F. G.	Lance-Corporal	Hants	Swaythling C.S.
Jarrow.			
Bruce, R.	Driver	R.F.A.	Croft Terrace C.S.
Newsam, H.	2nd Lieutenant	Tank Corps	Ellison N.S.
Spencer, J.	Private	D.L.I.	Dunn St. C.S.
Jersey.			
Penny, H. E.	Private	Middlesex	Orphan S., Haverstock Hill, London.
Purkis, H. S.	Private	Hants	Don St. C.S.
Stent, E. C.	Private	R.F.A.	Don St. C.S.

THE GALLANT DEAD

NAME.	RANK.	REGIMENT.	SCHOOL.
Keighley.			
Craven, A.	2nd Lieutenant	Black Watch	Laurieknowe, Maxwelltown, Dumfries.
Hollings, P.	Sergeant	R.G.A.	Ingrow C.S.
Wilkinson, V. A. S.	2nd Lieutenant	Middlesex	Oakworth C.S.
Kendal.			
Bell, S. J.	Corporal	Border	Central Ch.S.
Kent (West).			
Hicks, W. G.	Lieutenant	R.G.A.	Lady Boswell's U.D.S., Sevenoaks.
Kettering.			
Smith, A. R.	2nd Lieutenant	Gloucester	31, Eskdaill St., Kettering.
Kidderminster.			
Buckley, E.	Rifleman	K.R.R.	Foley Park C.S.
Perkins, W. E.	Private	Artists Rifles	Grammar S., Penistone, Sheffield.
Talbot, R. S.	2nd Lieutenant	R.F.A.	Stourport N.S.
Kingston and Surbiton.			
Fincher, E. F.	Company Sgt.-Maj.	O. & B.L.I.	Tolworth C.S.
Saunders, P. A.		L.R.B.	Richmond Rd. C.S.
Kiveton Park.			
Froggatt, A.	Private	W. Riding	Wales C.S.
Warren, W. S.	2nd Lieutenant	Border	Dinnington C.S.
Lancaster.			
Brash, W.	2nd Lieutenant	K.O.R.L.	National S.
Bullough, F. W.	2nd Lieutenant	R.G.A.	Over Kellett C.S.
Irving, R.	2nd Lieutenant	K.O.R.L.	Greaves C.S.
Kirkbride, R. W.	Sergeant	City of London	National S.
Pinch, W.	2nd Lieutenant	K.O.R.L.	National S.
Leeds.			
Arnold, J.	2nd Lieutenant	Manchester	St. Joseph's R.C.S.
Blakey, J. H.	Able Seaman	H.M.S. *Tipperary*	Parish Ch.S.
Blackburn, E.	Rifleman	K.R.R.	Upper Wortley C.S.
Calder, E. G.	Private	London	Castleton C.S.
Duckett, J. E.	Rifleman	K.R.R.	Farnley C.S.
Hall, M. A.	2nd Lieutenant	M.G.C.	Kirkstall N.S.
Harrison, E.	2nd Lieutenant	R.G.A.	City of Leeds Training College.
Hawley, J.	Rifleman	K.R.R.	Blenheim C.S.
Hemingway, W. M.	Gunner	R.G.A.	Hunslet N.S.
Liversedge, A. E.	2nd Lieutenant	W. Yorks	Hunslett Moor C.S.
McCubbin, P. G.	2nd Lieutenant	Rifle Brigade	Quarry Mount C.S.
Mossop, M. H.	Sergeant	W. Yorks	Bramley N.S.
Mountain, J. W.	Corporal	W. Yorks	Cockburn High S.
Perry, R.	Company Sgt.-Maj.	W. Yorks	Whitehall Rd. C.S.
Smith, H.	Private	R.A.M.C.	Whitehall Rd. C.S.
Stockwell, A. E.	Private	W. Yorks	Manston N.S.
Teale, N. D.	Private	Coldstream Guards	St. Hilda's N.S.
Walker, J. C.	2nd Lieutenant	W. Yorks	Buslingthorpe N.S.
Ward, A. B.	2nd Lieutenant	E. Yorks	St. Hilda's N.S.
Watkins, T. G.	Regtl. Sgt.-Maj.	R.A.M.C.	Cowper St. C.S.
Wilde, W. J.	Private	W. Yorks	Jack Lane C.S.
Leicester.			
Ashby, T. P.	Lieutenant	R. Sussex	Overton Rd. C.S.
Burgess, G. G.	Private	R.G.A.	King Richard's Rd. C.S.
Cramp, G. H.	2nd Lieutenant	R.G.A.	St. John the Baptist Ch.S
Harle, F.	Private	R. Fusiliers	Medway St. C.S.
Langton, J. T.	Private	R.F.C.	Elbow Lane C.S.

N.U.T. WAR RECORD

Name.	Rank.	Regiment.	School.
Leicestershire (Mid).			
Handford, J.	Lieutenant	Cheshire	Quorn N.S.
Neale, J. H.	Private	Leicester	Whetstone N.S.
Leigh.			
Spencer, F.	Corporal	R. Fusiliers	St. Peter's Ch.S.
Lewes.			
Markwick, H.	Corporal	R. Sussex	Lindfield N.S.
Lewisham.			
Bright, A. J.	Sergeant	London	Hither Green L.C.C.S.
Brown, L. F.	Lieutenant	M.G.C.	Brownhill Rd. Central L.C.C.S.
Moore, J.	Captain	Border	East London Indl.S.
Reed, W. J.	2nd Lieutenant	Devon	Mina Rd. L.C.C.S.
Taylor, W. F.	Lieutenant	E. Kent	20, Effingham Rd., Lee.
Leyton.			
Alger, G.	Sergeant	L.R.B.	KirkdaleRd. C.S.
Calder, J. S. (M.C. and Bar)	Captain	L.R.B.	Canterbury Rd. C.S.
Cody, V. M. W.	Private	Essex	Church Rd. C.S.
Hudson, H. E.	2nd Lieutenant	Essex	Church Rd. C.S.
Lydamore, W. F.	Rifleman	L.R.B.	Davies Lane C.S.
Perrier, W. S.	2nd Lieutenant	R. Fusiliers	Canterbury Rd. C.S.
Pitts, H. B.	Sergeant-Major	H.A.C.	Harrow Green C.S.
Purcell, W. F.	Private	Queen's Westminster	Ruckholt Rd. C.S.
Vincent, R.	Lance-Corporal	Essex	Canterbury Rd. C.S.
Lincoln.			
Elvin,	Lance-Corporal	Lincoln	Sincil Bank C.S.
Walker, F.	Company Sgt.-Maj.	Lincoln	St. Swithin's Ch.S.
Wroe, W. D.	Lieutenant	Lincoln	North District N.S.
Liverpool.			
Auger, P. J.	Dispatch Rider	Infantry Brigade	Holt Sec.S.
Ashplant, W.	Gunner	Tank Corps	Park Hill C.S.
Baker, E. T.	2nd Lieutenant	R.F.C.	15, Albert Drive, Orrell Park, Liverpool.
Bottomley, F.	2nd Lieutenant	R.W.F.	St. Alphonsus Back Gt. R.C.S.
Bretland, H.	Private	King's Liverpool	Anfield Rd. C.S.
Brown, G. P. S.	Private	King's Liverpool	Westminster Rd. C.S.
Carr, J. S.	Lieutenant	L.N.L.	Gwladys St. C.S.
Cornish, A. J.	Corporal	King's Liverpool	40, Church Rd., Stanley.
Cunningham, S. H.	Corporal	Northumbrian C.C.	51, Kelso Rd.
Davies, P.	Lieutenant		Birchfield Rd. C.S.
Duffy, W.	Private	King's Liverpool	Our Lady R.C.S.,Eldon St.
Edwards, J.	Private	Staffs	Hey Green Rd. C.S.
Hague, J.	2nd Lieutenant	Manchester	Birchfield Rd. C.S.
Hickling, A. E.	Lance-Corporal	King's Liverpool	St. Lawrence N.S., Kirkdale.
Isaac, G. W.	Company Sgt.-Maj.	R.A.M.C.	Mersey St. R.C.S.
Lewin, C.C.H. (M.C.)	2nd Lieutenant	Somerset L.I.	Queens Rd. C.S.
Light, G.	Lieutenant	L.N.L.	Our Lady Immaculate R.C.S.
Maddrell, J. K.	Lieutenant	M.G.C.	Sec.S., Bootle.
Mogridge, L.	Lieutenant	R.F.C.	Loraine St. C.S.
Pearson, A.	Private	King's Liverpool	Booler St. C.S.
Tickle, A. B.	Lieutenant	King's Liverpool	St. Margaret's H.G.S.
Tolson, H.	2nd Lieutenant	R. Warwick	The "Morrison" C.S.
Wedlake, F. H.	Private	King's Liverpool	St. Margaret's N.S., Anfield.
Weights, J. H.	2nd Lieutenant	Tank Corps	54, Coltart Rd.
Whittle, E. T.	2nd Lieutenant	Manchester	Birchfield Rd. C.S.
Wilkinson, A.	Corporal	R.E.	St. Francis Xavier's S.
Williams, J. G.	Lieutenant	R.W.F.	Normal College, Bangor.
Williams, J. L.	Sergeant	Liverpool Rifles	Seaman's Orphanage.

THE GALLANT DEAD

Name.	Rank.	Regiment.	School.
Llandudno.			
Hughes, J. E.	Lieutenant	R.W.F.	Central S.
Llanidloes.			
Burford, W.	Lance-Corporal	O. & B.L.I.	Llanidloes N.S.
London (East).			
Bonshor, I. H.	Private	R.G.A.	Trafalgar Square L.C.C.S.
Boxall, G. T.	Lance-Corporal	London	Broad St. L.C.C.S.
Cameron, H. S.	Captain	Norfolk	Broad St. L.C.C.S.
Doughty, H. J.	Private	R.A.M.C.	"Ben Jonson" L.C.C.S.
Dunford, H. J.	Private	H.A.C.	Alton St. L.C.C.S.
Hart, E.	Sergeant	Norfolk	St. Paul's L.C.C.S., Bow.
Horn, C. B.	Private	R.A.M.C.	Senrab St. L.C.C.S.
Kelly, J.	Private	Civil Service Rifles	Holy Trinity L.C.C.S., Bow.
Morris, A. E.	Lance-Corporal	R.W.F.	High St. L.C.C.S., Bow.
Parry, T. E.	2nd Lieutenant	Lancs Fusiliers	Essex St. L.C.C.S.
Pope, T. C.	Lieutenant	London	St. Mark's Ch.S., Whitechapel.
Procter, A. D. G.	2nd Lieutenant	R. Fusiliers	"Ben Jonson" L.C.C.S.
Simmons, R. E.	2nd Lieutenant	R.G.A.	Senrab St. L.C.C.S.
Sizeland, C.	2nd Lieutenant	Norfolk	Red Coat S.
Thomas, J. G.	Batty. Sgt.-Maj.	R.G.A.	Monteith Rd. L.C.C.S.
Thornton, H. V.	Lieutenant	R.A.F.	Heckford St. L.C.C.S.
Timpson, W. M.	Private	R.A.M.C.	Old Montague St. L.C.C.S.
Warren, A. F.	Private	Middlesex	Underwood St. L.C.C.S.
London (North-West).			
Bissley, W. H.	Lieutenant	R. Berks	Essendine Rd. L.C.C.S.
Carson, F. M.	Private	London	The "Moberley" L.C.C.S.
Clark, C. W.	2nd Lieutenant	Rifle Brigade	Carlton Rd. L.C.C.S.
Cross, G.	Sergeant	O. & B.L.I.	St. Anne's Ch.S., Chester Rd.
Dearing, C. (M.M.)	Sergeant	L.R.B.	Cosway St. L.C.C.S.
Durban, A. E.	Sergeant	Middlesex	Islip St. L.C.C.S.
Green, L.	Pioneer	R.E.	Bayswater Jewish S.
Haward, A. E.	Private	L.R.B.	Rhyl St. L.C.C.S.
Holloway, F.	Lance-Corporal	L.R.B.	37, Alexandra Rd. N.
Johnson, J. W.	Lieutenant	Middlesex	Amberley Rd. L.C.C.S.
Knight, H. A. W.	Private	London	St. Augustine's Ch.S.
McAllister, H. P.	Sergeant-Major	L.R.B.	Camden St. L.C.C.S.
Westaway, L. J.	2nd Lieutenant	R. Fusiliers	120, Melrose Av., N.W.
Wynne, J. A.	Private	London	Haverstock Hill L.C.C.S.
London (West).			
Brown, H.	Corporal	Middlesex	Halford Rd. L.C.C.S.
Bryant, B. T.	Captain	Lincoln	Addison Gardens L.C.C.S.
Denly, C. J.	Gunner	R.F.A.	St. John's Ch.S., Walham Green.
Drury, M. W.	C.Q.M.S.	R.E.	Islington Trg. College.
Elliott, B.	Sergeant	O. & B.L.I.	"Peterboro'" L.C.C.S.
Foley, J.	Captain	N.F.	Addison Gardens L.C.C.S.
Freeland, H. W.	R.Q.M. Sergeant	Kensington	"The Bousfield" L.C.C.S.
Froome, C. W. (D.C.M.)	Company Sgt.-Maj.	London	Oxford Gardens L.C.C.S.
Hamer, W. H.	Lance-Corporal	R. Fusiliers	Everington St. L.C.C.S.
King, H. A.	2nd Lieutenant	R.G.A.	Middle Row L.C.C.S.
Maidment, E. A.	Corporal	R.G.A.	Brook Green Spec.L.C.C.S.
Maley, R. J. H.	Private	London	Childerley St. L.C.C.S.
Newbold, R. H.	Sergeant	R. Fusiliers	Middle Row L.C.C.S.
Stanton, R. M.	Lieutenant	York and Lancs	Sawley Rd. L.C.C.S.
Tremeer, S. C.	2nd Lieutenant	Bedford	William St. L.C.C.S.
Walker, J. A.	Private	R.A.M.C.	Lillie Rd. L.C.C.S.
Warren, H.	2nd Lieutenant	Hants	St. John's Ch.S., Hammersmith.
Watson, S. T.	Company Sgt.-Maj.	London	Park Walk L.C.C.S.
Loughborough.			
Gibson, J.	Lieutenant	R.D.C.	Woodhouse Eaves N.S.
Pepper, B.	2nd Lieutenant	R.A.F.	Ashby Parva, Lutterworth.

N.U.T. WAR RECORD

Name.	Rank.	Regiment.	School.
Louth.			
Harrison, L. P.	Sergeant	E. Yorks	Butterwick, Doncaster.
Lowestoft.			
Francis, S. G.	Lance-Corporal	Essex	Roman Hill C.S.
Ludlow.			
Davies, W. E.	Sergeant	Shropshire L.I.	Abdon Ch.S., Munslow.
Maidstone.			
Leigh, W. B.	Lieutenant	L.N.L.	Borough Green C.S.
Martin, J. A. W.	Sergeant-Major	City of London Rifles	York Rd. C.S., Dartford.
Welton, W. N.	Sapper	R.E.	Wallington, Surrey.
Makerfield.			
Anderton, W. N.	Q.M. Sergeant	Gloucester	Glazebury Ch.S.
Haselden, H. E.	Corporal	R.A.M.C.	Manor Ch.S., Earlstown.
Moss, S. F. (M.M.)	2nd Lieutenant	R.E.	District Ch.S., Earlstown.
Pickett, J.	Corporal	R.G.A.	Central C.S., Earlstown.
Stevenson, W. (M.C.)	Lieutenant	R.G.A.	St. James's Ch.S., Haydock.
Maldon and Southminster.			
Hore, W. E.	Private	H.A.C.	C.S., Tollesbury.
Malton.			
Essex, J.	Sergeant	Yorks	Nunnington N.S.
Manchester.			
Allen, R. H.	Private	Manchester	Alfred St. C.S.
Armstrong, S. J.	2nd Lieutenant	N.F.	Grammar S., Wigan.
Ashton, T. J.	Private	R.N.D.	Christ Ch.S., Pendlebury.
Bramwell, F.	Pioneer	R.E.	Burgess St. C.S.
Brownjohn, L. C.	Sergeant	Manchester	St. Luke's N.S.
Byrne, J. F.	Private	Irish Guards	St. Augustine's R.C.S.
Charlton, J.	2nd Lieutenant	R. Scots Fusiliers	St. George's C.S.
Clarke, J.	Private	R.W.F.	Birley St. C.S.
Cleary, J.	Sergeant	K.O.R.L.	St. Joseph's R.C.S.
Collinson, J.	Private	Manchester	Bradford Mem. S.
Crewe, P.	Private	Manchester	Holy Trinity Ch.S.
Crofts, W.	Captain	Manchester	St. Mark's Ch.S., Cheetham.
Daniels, G.	2nd Lieutenant	Manchester	Hyde Rd. C.S.
Dawes, C. E.	2nd Lieutenant	L.N.L.	Princess Rd. C.S.
Duddle, W. K.	2nd Lieutenant	Lancs Fusiliers	Cavendish C.S., C.-on-M.
Dyson, J.	Corporal	Manchester	St. Jude's Ch.S.
Edwards, F.	Lance-Corporal	Manchester	124, Crossliffe St.
Hallworth, T.	Bombardier	R.G.A.	St. Thomas' Ch.S.
Hanley, A.	2nd Lieutenant	D.L.I.	School for Deaf and Dumb.
Hayes, G. W.	Corporal	Manchester	Upper Jackson St. C.S.
Heald, E. J.	Private	Manchester	Ducie Av. C.S.
Heywood, T.	Private	Manchester	St. Oswald's C.S.
Higgins, L. T.	Private	K.S.L.I.	St. Agnes Ch.S., Manchester.
Hinde, G. H.	Sub-Lieutenant	R.N.V.R.	Manley Park Mun. S.
Hollinshead, C.	Private	R.N.D.	St. Peter's Ch.S.
Kirkpatrick, J.	Corporal	Labour Battalion	Collyhurst Mun. S.
Lally, J.	Private	Manchester	St. Albans R.C.S.
Lea, H.	Corporal	Gloucester	St. Clement's Ch.S., West Park St.
Leigh, F.	Lance-Corporal	Manchester	Queen St. C.S.
Lomas, H.	Private	Cheshire	Plymouth Grove C.S.
Lowther, C.	2nd Lieutenant	Manchester	Devonshire St. C.S.
Marsden, J. W.	2nd Lieutenant	Lancs Fusiliers	Upper Jackson St. C.S.
Marshall, H.	Lieutenant	Lancs Fusiliers	St. John's Ch.S.
Mason, R.	Acting Captain	Yorks	Birley St. C.S.
Mathieu, J.	Private	Manchester	Varna St. C.S.

THE GALLANT DEAD

NAME.	RANK.	REGIMENT.	SCHOOL.
Manchester—*continued.*			
McIntyre, D.	Private	Manchester	St. Chad's R.C.S.
Melem, E.	Private	Manchester	Queen St. C.S.
Metcalfe, F. E.	Sergeant	Manchester	St. Francis' R.C.S.
Norris, J. H.	Private	R. Fusiliers	Chethams Hospital S.
Ormerod, J.	2nd Lieutenant	Manchester	St. Bridget's R.C.S.
Parker, J.	Private	Liverpool Yeomanry	St. Chad's R.C.S.
Ravenscroft, S.	Lance-Corporal	Manchester	Armitage St. C.S.
Riley, J. L.	Lieutenant	King's Liverpool	St. Chad's R.C.S.
Scully, B.	Company Sgt.-Maj.	R. Munster Fusiliers	Old Hall Drive C.S.
Sedgwick, J.	2nd Lieutenant	Manchester	St. Bridget's R.C.S.
Smith, A. G.	Captain	Manchester	Bank Meadow C.S.
Smith, R. F.	Private	R.A.M.C.	Holy Trinity Ch.S.
Taylforth, W.	Sergeant	Manchester	St. Mark's Ch.S.
Upton, J. S.	Sergeant	Manchester	Atherton St. C.S.
Valentine, C. K.	Sergeant	Manchester	St. John the Baptist Ch.S.
Vernon, N.	Private	King's Liverpool	St. Wilfred's Ch.S.
Whittaker, G.	Private	Manchester	St. Wilfred's Ch.S.
Williams, R. H.	Lance-Corporal	Pals Battalion	St. Jude's Ch.S.
Willott, H.	Private	R. Fusiliers	Southall St. C.S.
Witham, H.	Private	D.L.I.	Chain Bar, Moston.
Wood, C. P.	2nd Lieutenant	E. Lancs	St. Augustine's Ch.S.
Woods, G.	Sergeant	Manchester	Christ Ch.S.
Maryport.			
Pattinson, W.	Sergeant	D.L.I.	Church S.
Matlock and Bakewell.			
Stubbs, F. W. A. (M.C.)	Lieutenant	Sherwood Foresters	Woodville Ch.S., Burton-on-Trent.
Menai.			
Evans, R. P.	2nd Lieutenant	Welsh	Llanfairfechan C.S.
Jones, C. O.	2nd Lieutenant	Welsh	St. Paul's C.S., Bangor.
Merthyr Tydfil.			
Connolly, D.	Private	Welsh	Dowlais C.S.
Evans, R. D.	Private	Welsh	Dowlais C.S.
Hopkins, T.	Lieutenant	Welsh	Twynyrodyn C.S.
Pugh, M. J.	Corporal	Training Reserve	Pantyglais C.S.
Wightman, J. M. (M.C.)	Colonel	Munster	Troedyrhiw C.S.
Williams, J. E.	Private	Welsh	Merthyr Vale C.S.
Mexborough.			
Crowther, J.	Private	York and Lancs	Grimethorpe C.S.
Douglas, R. R.	Private	R.A.M.C.	Goldthorpe C.S.
Jones, F. W.	Corporal	York and Lancs	Balby St. C.S.
Smith, E. W.	Private	Cameron Highlanders	Swinton Bridge C.S.
Middlesbrough (late Tees-Side).			
Brogden, I.	Sergeant	Yorks	The "Lawson" C.S., Cargo Fleet.
Callan, H.	Signaller	R.F.A.	St. Mary's R.C.S.
Carruthers, A. J. (M.M.)	Private	R. Fusiliers	Marton Rd. C.S.
Coulson, J. W.	Private	Durham	Stockton St. C.S.
Green, W. W.	Lance-Corporal	Yorks	Crescent Rd. C.S.
Myers, R. W.	Sergeant	R.E.	The "Lawson" C.S., Cargo Fleet.
Nichols, J. A.	Private	Durham	Southend C.S.
Richards, H.	Private	Durham	Fleetham St. C.S.
Richardson, H.	Lance-Corporal	R. Fusiliers	The "Lawson" C.S., Cargo Fleet.
Selkirk, W. O.	Gunner	R.G.A.	Victoria Rd. C.S.
Witham, H.	Private	D.L.I.	Hugh Bell C.S.
Wood, C. W.	Private	Durham	St. Paul's N.S.
Morley.			
Midwood, H.	2nd Lieutenant	York and Lancs	Victoria Rd. C.S.

N.U.T. WAR RECORD

Name.	Rank.	Regiment.	School.
Mountain Ash.			
Davies, D. B.	Sergeant	R.G.A.	Miskin C.S.
Fryer, G. (M.M)	Bombardier	R.F.A.	York St. C.S.
Harris, E.	Lance-Corporal	Welsh	Abertaf C.S.
Lloyd, I.	Private	R.A.S.C.	Abertaf C.S.
Masters, T.	Private	R.A.M.C.	Pengeulan C.S.
Pugh, A.	Private	R.W.F.	Darran Las C.S.
Rogers, T.	2nd Lieutenant	Welsh	Ynysybwl C.S.
Thomas, B.(M.M.)	Private	London	Caegarw C.S.
Nelson, Colne, etc.			
Ashworth, F.	Private	Liverpool Scottish	West St. C.S.
Hartley, E.	Lance-Corporal	E. Lancs	Bradley C.S.
Long, F. P.	Corporal	R.E.	Bradshaw St. C.S.
Walsh, A. (M.C.)	Captain	L.N.L.	Secondary S.
Newbury.			
Chalmers, F.	2nd Lieutenant	E. Yorks	Newbury C.S.
Rose, .	2nd Lieutenant	W. Yorks	Newbury C.S.
Newcastle-upon-Tyne.			
Bell, J.	Private	N.F.	Ouseburn C.S.
Collin, R.	Corporal	Yorks	Westgate Hill C.S.
Cox, P. E.	Captain	N.F.	Walker (East) C.S.
Elliott, C. W.	Pioneer	R.E.	Rutherford College Sec.S.
Hancock, W.	2nd Lieutenant	N.F.	Walker R.C.S.
Henderson, J. L.	Captain	N.F.	Welbeck Rd. C.S.
Hudspith, A.	2nd Lieutenant	D.L.I.	Westgate Hill C.S.
Hughes, J.	Lance-Corporal	N.F.	West Walker C.S.
Morgan, C. J.	2nd Lieutenant	M.G.C.	St. Mary's R.C.S.
Mouboussin, V.	Lieutenant	French Army	Rutherford College Sec.S.
Ogg, Miss K. E.	Nurse	V.A.D.	Wingrove C.S.
Roan, W. T.	2nd Lieutenant	D.L.I.	Walker Gate C.S.
Rowland, E. C.	Private	N.F.	St. Peter's C.S.
Sibbitt, G. B.	Lieutenant	N.F.	St. Paul's Ch.S.
Sibbitt, H.	Major	N.F.	West Jesmond C.S.
Watson, E. G.	2nd Lieutenant	S. Lincs	Ouseburn C.S.
Wright, F. H.	R.Q.M. Sergeant	N.F.	Canning St. C.S.
New Forest.			
Wing, T. A.	Corporal	Devon	Boldre (East) Ch.S.
Newport (Mon.).			
Davies, E.	Major	R.W.F.	Maindee C.S.
Downing, H. H.	Sapper	R.E.	Church Rd. C.S.
Gardner, H.	Company Sgt.-Maj.	Monmouthshire	Church Rd. C.S.
Troakes, W. J.	Corporal	R.W.F.	Alexander Rd. C.S.
Newport Pagnell.			
Billingham, J. A.	2nd Air Mechanic	R.A.F.	Bradwell C.S.
Lloyd, A. L.	Private	R.A.M.C.	39, Victoria St., Wolverton, Bucks.
Nidderdale.			
Burrell, G. O.	Rifleman	K.R.R.	N.S., Knaresborough.
Northampton.			
Shaw, J. W. (M.C.)	2nd Lieutenant	K.R.R.	Stimpson Av. C.S.
North Cleveland.			
Hermiston, F.	Lieutenant	Yorks	Princess St. C.S.
Serginson, J.	Captain	Yorks	W. Dyke C.S., Redcar.
Northumberland (East).			
Barker, J.	Gunner	R.G.A.	Murton C.S.
Locke, A.	Private	D.L.I.	Newbiggin West C.S.

THE GALLANT DEAD

NAME.	RANK.	REGIMENT.	SCHOOL.
Northumberland (East)—*continued.*			
Marshall, W. E.	Lance-Corporal	D.L.I.	Hirst East C.S.
Patterson, J.	Corporal	D.L.I.	Bedlington C.S.
Ross, A.	Lieutenant	R.F.A.	Bothal Ch.S.
Rutherford, R.	Captain	D.L.I.	Forest Hall C.S.
Smith, W. D.	Corporal	R.A.M.C.	Hirst North Sen. S.
Smyth, T.	Sergeant-Major	N.F.	Whitley Mem. S.
Tait, H.	Corporal	D.L.I.	3, Sixth Row, Ashington.
Wilson, A.	Private	D.L.I.	Hontington, Cambo.
Wright, S. A.	Sergeant	Scots Guards	Morpeth Grammar S.
Northumberland (North).			
Clements, R. C.	Lieutenant	N.F.	Spittal C.S.
Hunter, R. H.	Private	K.R.R.	Spittal C.S.
Tate, J. M.	Captain	N.F.	Spittal C.S.
Northumberland (South).			
Ash, W. B.	Captain	N.F.	Gosforth Cent. C.S.
Clothier, H. W.	Bombardier	R.G.A.	Belford C.S.
Dodds, T. G.	Private	N.F.	Dudley C.S.
Pritchard, S. G.	Corporal	R.A.S.C.	Whorlton C.S.
Northwich.			
Brocklehurst, J.	Sergeant	Manchester	Brunner C.S.
Roberts, H. S.	Sergeant	Cheshire	Wharton Ch.S., Northwich.
Norwich City.			
Booty, W.	Sergeant	R.F.	Avenue Rd. C.S.
Hadingham, B.G.	Private	Essex	Holywood, nr. Westcliff-on-Sea.
Huson, E. A.	Sergeant-Major	Norfolk	Aylsham N.P.S.
Ong, C. S. B.	Private	Essex	" George White " C.S.
Ormiston, A.	Sergeant	Middlesex	Northwold, Stoke Ferry.
Sizer, E. J.	Private	R.A.S.C.	St. Mark's N.S.
Williams, R.	Lance-Corporal	R.W.F.	City of Norwich Sec. S.
Norwich District.			
Warby, A. S.	Private	R.A.M.C.	Melton Constable C.S.
Nottingham.			
Coe, H.	Lance-Corporal	Sherwood Foresters	Kimberley Undenl. S.
Currie, G. H. N.	Sergeant	Wilts	St. Andrew's Trust S.
Drew, F. W.	2nd Lieutenant	E. Yorks	University College.
Dyson, W.	Sergeant	Sherwood Foresters	Ropewalk C.S.
Hayes, J. J.	2nd Lieutenant	R.W.F.	Acourt St. C.S.
Jackson, A. S.	2nd Lieutenant	K.O.Y.L.I.	Holme Pierrepont N.S.
Kent, P. J.	2nd Lieutenant	Sherwood Foresters	Forest Fields Tech. Cent.
Laws, B. C.	Lieutenant	York and Lancs	Trent Bridge C.S.
Peek, T. A.	Bombardier	R.G.A.	Redcliffe-on-Trent N.S.
Roadley, T.	Flt.-Commander	R.A.F.	Haydn Rd. C.S.
Sharp, T. B.	Private	Civil Service Rifles	St. Andrew's Trust S.
Toon, H. R.	2nd Lieutenant	D.L.I.	Kirkby Upper Standard S.
White, A.	Bombardier	R.G.A.	Haydn Rd. C.S.
Nuneaton.			
Rogers, A. H.	Private	R.A.M.C.	Vicarage St. Ch.S.
Tayton, W. E.	2nd Lieutenant	Northants	Attleborough Ch.S.
Thacker, A. C.	Private	Grenadier Guards	Vicarage St. Ch.S.
Tite, K. G. W.	Air Mechanic	R.A.F.	Stockingford C.S.
Ogmore, &c.			
Bowen, R.	Pioneer	R.E.	Aber C.S.
Cole, A. W.	Private	R.W.F.	Tynewydd C.S.
Evans, G. R.	2nd Lieutenant	S. Staffs	Ffaldau C.S., Pontycymmer.

N.U.T. WAR RECORD

Name.	Rank.	Regiment.	School.
Ogmore, &c.—*continued.*			
Roberts, I. C.	2nd Lieutenant	M.G.C.	Ffaldau C.S., Pontycymmer.
Williams, A.	Private	R.W.F.	Aber C.S.
Oldbury.			
Sadler, J. J.	Private	R. Warwick	St. Michael's N.S.
Oldham.			
Davenport, H.	Lieutenant	R.G.A.	St. Stephen's Ch.S.
Doyne, W. L.	Private	L.N.L.	Roundthorne C.S.
Jackson, C. E.	Gunner	R.G.A.	Grange St. C.S.
Lees, F.	Private	R.W.F.	Alexandra Rd. C.S.
Newton, J. E.	Private	London	Richmond St. C.S.
Slater, J. H.	Private	Manchester	Coldhurst Ch.S.
Walmsley, E. L.	Private	R.A.M.C.	Higginshaw C.S.
Ormskirk.			
Taylor, H.	2nd Lieutenant	Lancs Fusiliers	United Charity S.
Oxford and District.			
Brooks, E. W.	2nd Lieutenant	O. & B.L.I.	Central C.S.
Mitchell, J. M. G.	2nd Lieutenant	O. & B.L.I.	St. Barnabas' N.S.
Preston, A. J.	2nd Lieutenant	R. Berks	Burford, Oxford.
Oxfordshire (South).			
Potter, F. G.	2nd Lieutenant	Worcester	N.S., Henley-on-Thames.
Pembrokeshire (Mid).			
Jones, G. R.	Lieutenant	R.W.F.	Hook C.S.
Thomas, W.	Private	R.A.M.C.	Llanddewi Velfrey C.S.
Webb, J. G. (M.C.)	Lieutenant	R.W.F.	Neyland C.S.
Pembrokeshire (South).			
Davies, G. P.	2nd Lieutenant	R.W.F.	Coronation S., Pembroke Dock.
Thomas, B. S. B. (M.C.)	Captain	R.A.F.	71, Gwyther St., Pembroke Dock.
Penarth.			
Hooper, H. C.	Private	R.A.M.C.	Albert Rd. C.S.
Penrith.			
Sowerby, I.	2nd Lieutenant	R. Warwick	National S.
Peterborough.			
Clamp, L. P.	Corporal	R. W. Kent	Gt. Gidding S.
Fitzjohn, H.	Private	R.A.M.C.	St. Mark's Ch.S.
Swift, W.	2nd Lieutenant	Lincoln	H.G.C.S., Cambridge.
Tuke, W. S.	Sergeant	Gloucester	St. Mark's Ch.S.
Plymouth.			
Bidgood, W. H.	Lance-Corporal	Warwick	St. Mary's N.S., Devonport.
Burt, G. A.	Sergeant	Devon	St. Andrew's N.S.
Charleston, E.	2nd Lieutenant	K.R.R.	Camel's Head C.S.
Dusting, J.	Private	Devon	St. Boniface R.C.S.
Isaac, W. G.	Private	R. Fusiliers	St. Mary's N.S., Devonport.
Lake, W. E. R.	Private	Devon	Public S. for Boys.
Mahoney, B. J.	Private	R. Fusiliers	Holy Cross R.C.S.
McNamee, G.	N. Schoolmaster		H.M.S. *Queen Mary.*
Stribling, L. J.	2nd Lieutenant	R.G.A.	High St. C.S.
Thomas, T. J.	N. Schoolmaster		H.M.S. *Impregnable.*
Wakeley, H. E.	1st Air Mechanic	R.A.F.	Stuart Rd. C.S., Devonport.

THE GALLANT DEAD

Name.	Rank.	Regiment.	School.
Pontypool.			
Herbert, J. H.	Sergeant	O. & B.L.I.	Griffithstown C.S.
Portsmouth.			
Barrell, H. J.	Lance-Corporal	Hants	Portsmouth Town C.S.
Iggleden, J. H. F.	Private	Hants	Wellington Place C.S.
Mulligan, P.	Private	Hants	Drayton Rd. C.S.
Scarbrough, H. T.	Sergeant	London Scottish	9, Alverstone Rd.
Stilwell, A. P.	Corporal	R.A.O.C.	New Rd. C.S.
Summers, E. H.	Corporal	Hants	Fratton C.S.
Tuite, P.	Sapper	R.E.	St. John's R.C.S.
Wager, B. E. S.	Lance-Corporal	R. Fusiliers	Portsmouth Town C.S.
Wills, W. T.	Sergeant	R.A.S.C.	Drayton Rd. Metalwork Centre.
Williamson, F. H.	Corporal	Hants	Omega St. C.S.
Winter, T. R.		Friends' Ambulance	Church St. C.S.
Woods, F. H.	Lieutenant	Devon	Penhale Rd. C.S.
Preston Borough.			
Hodgson, G.	Private	L.N.L.	Moor Park W.S.
Preston District.			
Green, J. L.	Private	K.O.R.L.	Brownedge R.C.S.
Iddon, H.	2nd Lieutenant	R.F.A.	Baines' Grammar S., Poulton-le-Fylde.
Radstock.			
Brewer, W. A.	Lieutenant	Sherwood Foresters	Crewkerne Ch.S.
Reading.			
Andrews, E. G.	Private	R.F.A.	St. Mary's N.S., Mortimer.
Cowles, R. P.	Sergeant	Middlesex	Binfield Ch.S., Bracknell.
Davies, E. L. (M.M.)	Corporal	Berks	Wokingham Rd. C.S.
Drake, W. W.	Lieutenant	Devon	Oxford Rd. C.S.
Hole, M.	2nd Lieutenant	K.R.R.	Central C.S.
Johnson, V. R.	2nd Lieutenant	Wilts	41, Addington Rd.
Leake, G.E.A.(D.S.O.)	Captain	London	Taplow S., Bucks.
Paget, C.	Lieutenant	R. Warwick	Wargrave N.S.
Reynolds, F. L.	2nd Lieutenant	Sherwood Foresters	Sunning Hill N.S.
Sheldon, F. G.	Sergeant	R.A.O.C.	George Palmer C.S.
Vickers, H. J.	Sergeant	R.G.A.	Wescott Rd. C.S.
Webster, A. E.	Air Mechanic	R.A.F.	St. Giles' Ch.S.
White, P.	Private	R.A.S.C.	Caversham C.S.
Redditch.			
Denny, E.	2nd Lieutenant	Artists Rifles	196, Mount Pleasant.
Dobbins, W. F.	Private	R. Warwick	Headless Cross Ch.S.
Pullen, E. H.	Lance-Corporal	R. Gloucester	Bridge St. C.S.
Reigate.			
Hewitt, W.	Sergeant	London	St. Mary's Rd.
Retford.			
Atkinson, W. E.	2nd Lieutenant	Tank Corps	Ordsall C.S.
Rhondda.			
Evans, R. G.	Lieutenant	S.W.B.	Penyrenglyn C.S.
Gorvet, H.			Hendrefadog C.S., Tylorstown.
Hughes, B. T.	2nd Lieutenant	Welsh	Ynyswen C.S.
Jenkins, W. E.	Private	R.W.F.	Park C.S.
Jones. D. J.	Lance-Corporal	W. Yorks	Bronllwyn C.S.
Jones, G.	Lieutenant	Lincolns	Porth C.S.
Jones, G. T.	Private	Welsh	Trealaw C.S.
Lewis, R. H.	Corporal	R.W.F.	Treorchy, S.
Sullivan, W. E.(M.C.)	Lieutenant	Welsh	Cymmer C.S.

N.U.T. WAR RECORD

Name.	Rank.	Regiment.	School.
Rhondda—*continued.*			
Tanner, D. T.	Captain	R.W.F.	Cilfynydd C.S.
Thomas, I. J.	Private	Welsh	Trealaw C.S.
Williams, E.	2nd Lieutenant	York and Lancs	Pontrhondda C.S.
Williams, J.	Major	R.W.F.	Ton Pentre C.S.
Williams, T. J.	Lance-Corporal	Welsh	Hawthorne C.S., Pontypridd.
Rhymney Valley.			
Tanner, O. B. (M.M.)	Corporal	Shropshire L.I.	Abertysswg C.S., Cardiff.
Richmond (Surrey).			
Figg, H. H.	Sergt.-Instructor	Gymnastic Staff	King's Ch.S., Kew.
Hopkinson, W. E.	Lance-Corporal	London	Darell Rd. C.S.
Southwick, C. T.	Sergeant	Kensington	Vineyard C.S.
Ripon.			
Illingworth, E. A.	Bombardier	R.G.A.	North Stainley Ch.S.
Rochdale.			
Holt, W.	2nd Lieutenant	W. Yorks	Heybrook C.S.
Hunsworth, H.	Lance-Corporal	Lancs Fusiliers	Secondary S.
Wood, E. B.	Company Sgt.-Maj.	Lancs Fusiliers	Spotland C.S.
Romford.			
Carr, L.	Rifleman	London	St. Edward's N.S.
Parker, F.	Sergeant	R.E.	Training Ship *Exmouth*.
Rotherham.			
Baker, G. A. (C.deG.; Chev. de la Couronne, Belgium)	2nd Lieutenant	R.G.A.	Thrybergh C.S.
Cundliffe, C.	Sergeant	York and Lancs	Doncaster Rd. C.S.
Damms, H.	Private	York and Lancs	St. Ann's R.C.S.
Drury, C. W.	Corporal	N.F.	Parkgate Central S.
Sugden, T.	Lance-Corporal	K.R.R.	Eastwood N.S.
Wilson, H. D.	Private	York and Lancs	St. Ann's C.S.
Rugby.			
Chirgwin, J. C.	Corporal	R. Warwick	St. Matthew's N.S.
Wolfe, S. G.	Lieutenant	Lancs Fusiliers	Elborow End S.
Runcorn.			
Fowles, W.	Bombardier	R.G.A.	Balfour Rd. Higher Std. C.S.
Newport, R.	Sergeant	Cheshire	Parish Ch.S.
Yearsley, H. A.	2nd Lieutenant	R.E.	16, Leinster Gdns.
St. Davids.			
Lawrence, E. E.	Private	Artists Rifles	Hayscastle C.S.
St. Helens.			
Holt, J.	Sergeant	R.F.A.	Allanson St. C.S.
Thornton, F. H.	Sergeant	R.E.	Robin's Lane C.S.
Sale.			
Robinson, J.	Private	R. Fusiliers	Springfield C.S.
Salford.			
Barratt, H.	Private	Manchester	Wesleyan S.
Brown, A.	Sergeant	R.A.M.C.	St. Bartholomew's Ch.S
Carlisle, T.	Lance-Corporal	Border	Langworthy Rd. C.S.
Carruthers, G.	Lance-Corporal	Manchester	St. John's R.C.S.
Cash, —.	2nd Lieutenant	D.L.I.	St. Matthias' Ch.S.
Cormack, W.	Lance-Corporal	Black Watch	Trafford Rd. C.S.
Dobson,	Sergeant	R. Fusiliers	Langworthy Rd. C.S.
Grayson, A.	Sergeant	R. Sussex	St. Cyprian's Ch.S.

THE GALLANT DEAD

Name.	Rank.	Regiment.	School.
Salford—*continued.*			
Irlam, L. J.	Sergeant	R.A.M.C.	Trafford Rd. C.S.
Marlow, G.	2nd Lieutenant	Manchester	St. Luke's Ch.S.
Nicholls, L. H.	2nd Lieutenant	Manchester	St. John's Ch.S.
Purcell, F.	Sergeant	Lancs Fusiliers	St. Joseph's R.C.S.
Shaw, R.	2nd Lieutenant	S. Lancs	St. Stephen's Ch.S.
Butters, W. H.	Corporal	E. Lancs	Marlborough Rd. C.S.
Scarborough.			
Horsman, S. B.	Sergeant	K.R.R.	Falsgrave C.S.
Wright, W. C.	2nd Lieutenant	R.W.F.	Norton C.S.
Sheffield.			
Anneley, E. G.	Lieutenant	W. Yorks	Abbeydale C.S.
Beever, T.	Private	K.O.Y.L.I.	Darnall Rd. Ch.S.
Bower, E.	Corporal	R.G.A.	Darnall Rd. C.S.
Brook, H. (M.S.M.)	Corporal	R.A.M.C.	Attercliffe Ch.S.
Busby, R. G. C.	2nd Lieutenant	D.L.I.	Bow St. C.S.
Carpenter, H. A. S.	Lieutenant	R. Scots	Woodside Rd. C.S.
Charlesworth, F.	2nd Lieutenant	Duke of Wellington's	Duchess Rd. C.S.
Crapper, W.	Lance-Corporal	K.O.Y.L.I.	Owler Lane C.S.
Crozier, H. C. (M.M.)	Sergeant	York and Lancs	Sharrow Lane C.S.
Flear, T. E.	Private	R. Warwick	Norton Lees C.S.
Fletcher, H.	Private	K.O.Y.L.I.	Abbeydale C.S.
Gill, E. J.	Sergeant-Major	York and Lancs	Firshill C.S.
Gould, J. W.	2nd Lieutenant	York and Lancs	Newhall C.S.
Hughes, W.	2nd Lieutenant	K.O.Y.L.I.	Carlisle St. C.S.
Jones, L. S.			
Knighton, J. B.	Private	York and Lancs	Ellesmere Rd. C.S.
Mear, E.	Private	York and Lancs	Cathedral Ch.S.
Morley, J. D.	Sergeant	E. Yorks	Springfield C.S.
Morris, W.	Lance-Corporal	Cameron Highlanders	Coleridge Rd. Sen. C.S.
Mountford, T.	Gunner	R.F.A.	Brightside C.S.
Nock, F. T.	2nd Lieutenant	K.O.Y.L.I.	Carbrook C.S.
Philbey, G.	Sergeant	York and Lancs	St. Stephen's Ch.S.
Pickersgill, R. M.	Gunner	R.G.A.	Attercliffe C.S.
Register, B. J.	Sergeant	York and Lancs	Hunters Bar C.S.
Scarborough, H.	Lieutenant	W. Yorks	Hammerton St. C.S.
Schofield, J.	Gunner	R.F.A.	Woodside Lane C.S.
Shiell, A.W.	Private	York and Lancs	Woodseats C.S.
Shooter, J. H. (M.C.)	Lieutenant	R.A.F.	Lancasterian C.S.
Townsend, J. W.	2nd Lieutenant	W. Yorks	Whitby Rd. C.S.
Unwin, G. E.	2nd Lieutenant	Labour Corps	Sharrow Lane C.S.
Watling, H.	Lance-Corporal	K.O.Y.L.I.	Brightside C.S.
Wholley, C. M. G.	Lance-Corporal	K.R.R.	Darnall Rd. C.S.
Wilford, C.	Lance-Corporal	York and Lancs	Woodside Lane C.S.
Wood, C. C.	Private	R.F.A.	St. John's C.S.
Wright, J. R.	Lance-Corporal	York and Lancs	Upperthorpe C.S.
Shrewsbury.			
Ashton, W. T.	Private	Warwick	Saltley College.
Goodwin, F. R.	Private	Shropshire	St. Chad's N.S.
Newbold, H. G.	Lieutenant	R.F.A.	Abbey N.S.
Shropshire (East).			
Bailey, A. E.	Sergeant	S. Staffs	Malins Lee, Ch.S., Dawley
Sittingbourne.			
Morris, F.	Sergeant	R.F.A.	Holy Trinity N.S.
Skipton.			
Bailey, H. M.	Private	London	New Rd. C.S.
Bushby, J.	2nd Lieutenant	Staffs	Brougham St. C.S.
Carruthers, G.	2nd Lieutenant	W. Riding	Glusburn C.S.
Slough.			
Leat, E. J.	2nd Lieutenant	Dorset	Chalvey Ch.S.

N.U.T. WAR RECORD

Name.	Rank.	Regiment.	School.
Smethwick.			
Candlin, W. C.	Private	Lancs Fusiliers	Central S.
Hipkins, N.	Captain	N. Staffs	191, High St.
James, E. B.	Private	R. Warwick	Smethwick Hall C.S.
Summerton, L. H.	Lieutenant	S. Staffs	Brasshouse Lane C.S.
Thompson, C. H.	Lance-Corporal	R.E.	Oldbury Rd. C.S.
Solihull.			
Bird, W. A. J.	Lance-Corporal	R.W. Kent	Knowle S., Birmingham.
Somerset (North).			
Fairchild, E. S.	Lance-Corporal	Somerset L.I.	26, Whitecross Rd., Weston-super-Mare.
Radford, G.E. (M.M.)	Sergeant	R.G.A.	Central C.S., Weston-super-Mare.
Somerset (South-West).			
Hill, W.	Captain	D.C.L.I.	High St. C.S., Chard.
Southampton.			
Hallum, H. G. (M.C.)	Lieutenant	Hants	Foundry Lane C.S.
Hewitt, G. S.	Bombardier	R.G.A.	Foundry Lane C.S.
Pescod, W. F.	Sergeant	R.A.M.C.	Freemantle Ch.S.
Wilde, F. E.	Sergeant	D.L.I.	Taunton's Sec.S.
Wrenn, W. A. E.	Gunner	R.G.A.	Mount Pleasant C.S.
Southend-on-Sea.			
Griffiths, O.	Lieutenant	R.F.A.	Westborough Rd. C.S.
Hobbs, R. G.	Lieutenant	K.R.R.	North St. C.S.
Stanley, A.	2nd Lieutenant	R. Fusiliers	Rochford C.S.
Walford, H.	Sergeant	Essex	Brewery Rd. C.S.
Southgate.			
Evans, P. L.	Sergeant	Middlesex	Holly Pk. C.S.
Fraser, H. D.	Sergeant	Queen's Westminster	Bowes Rd. C.S.
Fuge, F. H.	Lieutenant	Somerset L.I.	Bowes Rd. C.S.
Tripp, H.	Private	L.R.B.	Hazelwood Lane C.S.
Southport.			
Loveridge, F. W.	Sergeant	King's Liverpool	Holy Trinity N.S.
South Shields.			
Armstrong, J. W.	2nd Lieutenant	D.L.I.	Laygate Lane C.S.
Bright, S.	Private	R.A.M.C.	Westoe C.S.
Daniels, A. V.	Private	E. Yorks	Westoe C.S.
Hogg, R.	Private	D.L.I.	St. Stephen's C.S.
Keedy, E. N.	Sergeant	D.L.I.	Westoe C.S.
Kennedy, J.L. (M.M.)	Corporal	R.E.	Dean Rd. C.S.
Napier, J. C.	2nd Lieutenant	N.F.	Laygate Lane C.S.
Ohlson, A.	Private	D.L.I.	Westoe C.S.
Ward, T.	Lieutenant	N.F.	High School.
Watmough, J. C.	2nd Lieutenant	N.F.	Barnes C.S.
Winter, J. C.	Private	D.L.I.	Mortimer Rd. C.S.
Wylie, W. S.	Lieutenant	E. Yorks	Dean Rd. C.S.
Southwark.			
Boden, S. S.	2nd Lieutenant	D.L.I.	East Lane L.C.C.S.
Brown, S. A.	2nd Lieutenant	R. Berks	Alexis St. L.C.C.S.
Heard, E.	Corporal	London	Pages Walk L.C.C.S.
Hutson, F. W.	Gunner	Howitzer Brigade	Southwark Pk. L.C.C.S.
Jones, H. F. C.	Lance-Corporal	L.R.B.	Holy Trinity S.
Lang, S. D.	2nd Lieutenant	K.O.Y.L.I.	St. James's N.S.
McKimmie, A. J.	Lieutenant	R.F.C.	Pages Walk L.C.C.S.
Springbett, G. T.	Sergeant	R.W. Kent	Keetons Rd. L.C.C.S
Terrell, V. J.	Private	London	St. Mary's N.S.

THE GALLANT DEAD

Name.	Rank.	Regiment.	School.
Spalding.			
Bristow, R. C.	Private	Lincoln	Crowland C.S.
Porter, J. J.	Sergeant	London Scottish	Clough C.S., Gosberton.
Spennymoor.			
Arnett, W.	Private	D.L.I.	Dean Bank C.S.
Bailes, H.	Private	D.L.I.	Dean Bank C.S.
Corner, A. H.	Private	D.L.I.	Tudhoe Colliery C.S.
Fairless, E.	Private	D.L.I.	Tudhoe Colliery C.S.
Fergurson, T.	Private	D.L.I.	Cornforth C.S.
Macpherson, G.	Sergeant	D.L.I.	Coxhoe Ch.S.
Moore, H.	Reg.-Sergt.-Maj.	N.F.	Cassop C.S.
Robinson, F.	Lieutenant	D.L.I.	Tudhoe Colliery C.S.
Sanderson,C.(D.S.O.) Order of St.George, Russia)	Lieutenant	Gordon Highlanders	North Rd. C.S.
Turner, A.	Private	D.L.I.	Coxhoe Ch.S.
Spen Valley.			
Hopkinson, W. E.	Corporal	Queen's Rifles	Boath St., Cleckheaton.
Lister, R. (D.C.M.)	Corporal	R.E.	Birstall Central S.
Stafford and District.			
Cartledge, A.	Private	N. Staffs	Corporation St. C.S.
Staffordshire (North).			
Arrowsmith, E.	Sergeant	N. Staffs	Baddeley Green C.S.
Booth, J. C.	Sergeant	Nigerian	Cheadle N.S.
Challinor, F. W.	2nd Lieutenant	N. Staffs	High St. C.S., Longton.
Forse, C. R.	Corporal	R.G.A.	Trentham N.S.
Greenhill, E. O.	Sergeant	N. Staffs	National S., Leigh.
Leese, E.	Private	L.N.L.	Heron Cross C.S., Fenton.
Moakler, R. J.(M.M.)	Company Sgt.-Maj.	Warwick	Tunstall R.C.S.
Roughan, E.	Private	R. Dublin Fusiliers	St.Mary's R.C.S., Tunstall.
Udall, M. V.	Private	N. Staffs	Northwood N.S., Hanley.
Whitehurst, A. P.	2nd Lieutenant	Worcester	Longport C.S.
Staines.			
Baker, H. J.	Private	London	Sunbury Par.S.
Hedgeland, C. S.	Lieutenant	Worcester	"Peterborough" L.C.C.S., Fulham.
Rix, F.E.	Rifleman	London	Sunbury Par.S.
Stockport.			
Goodier, T.	Lance-Corporal	Public Sch. and Univers. Corp.	Banks Lane C.S.
Powner, F.	Private	R.A.	Brentnall St. W.S.
Stockton.			
Caux, H. de	Lieutenant	D.L.I.	Hartburn C.S.
Featherstone, T. R.	Private	Yorks	Holy Trinity N.S.
Hetherington, A.	Lieutenant	K.O.Y.L.I.	Haverton Hill C.S.
Reed, W. O.	Private	Seaforth Highlanders	Bowesfield Lane C.S.
Wilson, S. J.	Private	W. Yorks	Bowesfield Lane C.S.
Stroud.			
Ricketts, G. H.	Corporal	Gloucester	Woodchester End.S.
Sunderland.			
Coleman, A.	2nd Lieutenant	N.F.	St. Joseph's R.C.S.
Hoole, W. D.	Lance-Corporal	D.L.I.	St. Columbas N.S.
Parker, A. E. L.	Sergeant	R.W. Kent	Southwick Cent.S.
Pattison, C. L.	Private	D.L.I.	Pallion C.S.
Robson, J. T.	Private	D.L.I.	Stansfield St. C.S.
Rowell, J. F.	Gunner	R.G.A.	Seaham Harbour N.S.
Stafford, R. H.	Private	D.L.I.	Simpson St. C.S.
Tweedie D. S.(M.M.)	Company Sgt.-Maj.	Tyneside Scottish	Redby C.S.

N.U.T. WAR RECORD

Name.	Rank.	Regiment.	School.
Surrey (North-West).			
Bowring, W. J.	2nd Lieutenant	R.W. Surrey	Brookwood C.S.
Butler, F. C.	Act. Sergeant-Maj.	London	Oakleigh, Guildford Rd., Bagshot.
Collins, F. F.	2nd Lieutenant	R.A.F.	Shaftesbury S., Bisley.
Moulding, S. D.	Lieutenant	R. Inniskilling	Thursley Ch.S.
Rodwell, C. A.	Rifleman	Queen's Westminster	Walton Central S.
Vokes, B.	2nd Lieutenant	O. & B.L.I.	Weybridge Ch.S.
Waller, J. G.	Sergeant	R.W. Surrey	Haselmere Ch.S.
Wise, F. V.	Able Seaman	H.M.S. *Invincible*	Bagshot C.S.
Wootton, G. N.	Private	Hants	Weybridge Ch.S.
Surrey (South-East).			
Davis, H. C.	Lance-Corporal	L.R.B.	Caterham Hill C.S.
Merrett, A.	2nd Lieutenant	Hants	Coulsdon Smitham C.S.
Smith, M.	Private	R. Fusiliers	Lingfield C.S.
Swansea.			
Beynon, W. C.	Lieutenant	R.W.F.	Brynmill C.S.
George, H. G.	Sergeant	Tank Corps	Plasmarl C.S.
Jenkins, A. E.	2nd Lieutenant	Welsh	Hafod C.S.
Liddicott, G.	Corporal	R.G.A.	Morriston C.S.
Meecham, D. J.	Lieutenant	R.W.F.	Pentrepoth C.S.
Murphy, C.	Lieutenant	R.W.F.	St. Thomas' C.S.
Rees, H. T.	Sergeant	R.W.F.	Waunwen C.S.
Tyler, H. J.	Private	R.W.F.	Manselton C.S.
Swindon.			
Beales, E. N.	Private	R.A.M.C.	Clarence St. C.S.
Fell, C.	Private	Worcester	King William St. Ch.S.
Fricker, A. C.	Lieutenant	E. Yorks	Rodbourne Green.
Lynes, N.	Private	Middlesex	St. Paul's S., Canonbury, London.
Smith, F. W.	Private	Wilts	Upper Stratton C.S.
Williams, H. H.	Captain	Wilts	Ferndale Rd. C.S.
Tamworth.			
Farmer, G. H.	Private	R. Welsh	Pract. S., Saltley College.
Jenkins, A.	2nd Lieutenant	R.A.F.	Fazeley C.S.
Taunton and West Somerset.			
Goss, C. L.	Bombardier	R.F.A.	Courtland Rd. C.S., Wellington.
Seed, J. R.	Lance-Corporal	W. Riding	Memorial S.
Teddington.			
Brown, B. J.	Corporal	R. Fusiliers	Hampton C.S.
Brown, W. J.	Private	Middlesex	Stanley Rd. C.S.
Ketcher, P. T.	Private	London Cyclists	Waterworks, Hampton.
Teign and Dart.			
Billing, O. S.	Gunner	R.F.A.	3, Ebenezer Place, Paignton.
Thornaby-on-Tees.			
Cross, F.	Sergeant	R. Fusiliers	" Arthur Head " C.S.
Perrin, J.	Private	R. Fusiliers	Handicraft Centre.
Torridge.			
Buckler, A. R.	Private	R.A.M.C.	Hartland C.S., Bideford.
Tottenham.			
Barton, F. H.		London	Trade S., Ponders End.
Billen, S. J.	Sergeant	M.G.C.	Belmont Rd. C.S.
Brewin, T. B.	Private	London	Belmont Rd. C.S.
Carter, I. G.	Private	London Scottish	Seven Sisters C.S.

THE GALLANT DEAD

Name.	Rank.	Regiment.	School.
Tottenham—*continued.*			
Cowherd, T.	Private	Civil Service Rifles	Parkhurst Rd. N.S.
Curtis, R. H.	2nd Lieutenant	W. Surrey	Parkhurst Rd. N.S.
Farnham, R.	Captain	Lancs Fusiliers	Bruce Grove C.S.
Freeman, B. H. J.	Private	London	Culvert Rd. C.S.
Glockler, S. A.	Private	London	Downhills C.S.
Hall, A. H.	Private	London	Risley Avenue C.S.
Head, P. T.	Sergeant	R. Fusiliers	Lancasterian C.S.
Jeffries, C. W.	Sergeant	R. Fusiliers	Lancasterian C.S.
Martin, P. H.	Private	R. Fusiliers	Woodlands Pk. C.S.
Rowlatt, J. J.	Private	Middlesex	Lancasterian C.S.
Swan, S. H.	Corporal	R. Fusiliers	Bruce Grove C.S.
Townsend, A. G. C.	Private	London	Downhills C.S.
Tredegar.			
Bowen, W. L. (M.C.)	Lieutenant	Monmouthshire	Sirhowy C.S.
Hogan, W. I.	Private	Monmouthshire	Sirhowy C.S.
Onions, W.	2nd Lieutenant	Monmouthshire	Georgetown C.S.
Williams, E. D.	Private	Monmouthshire	Earl St. C.S.
Tunbridge Wells.			
Stubbs, A. J.	2nd Lieutenant	R.W. Kent	St. Peter's Ch.S.
Twickenham.			
Banks, F. W.	Sergeant	Middlesex	Archdeacon Cambridge's Ch.S.
Burt, C. S.	Corporal	Hants	Whitton Ch.S.
Cooper, H. M.	2nd Lieutenant	Middlesex	Archdeacon Cambridge's Ch.S.
Tynemouth.			
Forsyth, R.	Pioneer	R.E.	Aberhill Public S., Fife.
Marley, F. G.	Lance-Corporal	R. Fusiliers	Eastern C.S.
Standen, J. W.	Lance-Corporal	N.F.	St. Joseph's R.C.S.
Wallace, D. S.	2nd Lieutenant	S. Lincoln	Royal Jubilee C.S.
Uxbridge.			
Hankins, J. F.	Sergeant	R. Berks	Harlington N.S.
Leake, H.	Private	R. Fusiliers	St. Margaret's N.S.
Partridge, A. F.	Private	O. & B.L.I.	Cowley Rd. C.S.
Vale of Clwyd.			
Roberts, W.	2nd Lieutenant	S.W.B.	8, Clifton Tce., Denbigh.
Vale of Derwent.			
Allen, F.	Private	R. Fusiliers	Benfieldside C.S.
Clark, P.	Lance-Corporal	D.L.I.	Consett C.S.
Ford, B.	Sergeant-Major	N.F.	Leadgate Ch.S.
Smith, T. H.	Private	London Scottish	Burnhope Colliery C.S.
Werry, H. S.	C.Q.M. Sergeant	D.L.I.	Consett C.S.
Wakefield.			
Day, H.	Signaller	K.O.Y.L.I.	Cathedral N.S.
Howes, A.	Private	D.L.I.	Crofton C.S.
Jackson, H.	Signaller	K.O.Y.L.I.	Lofthouse Gate C.S.
Lees, L.	Company Sgt.-Maj.	K.O.Y.L.I.	Normanton Cent. S.
Noble, B.	Bombardier	R.G.A.	Altofts Ch.S.
Roper, W. L.	Private	D.L.I.	Woodhouse C.S.
Shippam, S. P.	Sergeant	K.O.Y.L.I.	Lawefield Lane C.S.
Teale, J. A.	2nd Lieutenant	N.F.	Ryhill N.S.
Wallasey.			
Cannell, A. E.	Private	King's L'pool Scottish	St. Mary's Ch.S.
Chandler, A. P.	Private	Cheshire	Riverside C.S.
Coleman, G.	Lance-Corporal	King's L'pool Scottish	Poulton C.S.
Dunn, C. F.	Private	Leinster	Somerville C.S.

N.U.T. WAR RECORD

Name.	Rank.	Regiment.	School.
Wallasey—*continued*.			
Harding, W. E.	Private	King's L'pool Scottish	St. Mary's Ch.S.
Morris, W. G.	Private	King's L'pool Scottish	Wesleyan S.
Rowe, F. W.	Private	King's L'pool Scottish	Manor Rd. C.S.
Wilson, P. S.	2nd Lieutenant	R.W.F.	Somerville C.S.
Walsall.			
Allen, B.	Lieutenant	S. Staffs	Chuckery C.S.
Bytheway, Miss G.	Nurse	Red Cross	Palfrey C.S.
Davis, S. J.	2nd Lieutenant	S. Staffs	Whitehall C.S.
Harriman, H. W. (M.C.)	Captain	W. Riding	Palfrey C.S.
Sanders, H. S.	Private	R. Warwick	Field St. C.S.
Sanger, R.	Lieutenant	S. Staffs	St. Mary's R.C.S.
Smith, W. P.	Private	R.A.M.C.	North Walsall C.S.
Wilks, C.	Captain	S. Staffs	North Walsall C.S.
Wise, F.	Private	S. Staffs	Centenary W.S.
Wallsend.			
Graham, W. G.	Captain	N.F.	Stephenson Mem. S.
Moffatt, T.	Lance-Corporal	N.F.	Stephenson Mem. S.
Smith, H.	Sergeant	R. Fusiliers	St. Aidan's R.C.S.
Walthamstow.			
Goddard, F. W.	Private	R.A.M.C.	Selwyn Av. C.S.
Went, A. G.	Q.M. Sergeant	Cyclists' Corps	Coppermill Rd. C.S.
Wood, A. J.	Private	London	"W. E. Whittingham" C.S.
Warrington.			
Foulkes, J. H.	Pioneer	R.E.	Evelyn St. C.S.
Glover, M. J.	Warrant Officer	R.N.	Parochial S.
Westwell, Miss	Asst. Adminstr.	Q.M.A.A.C.	Evelyn St. C.S.
Whitfield, G. A.	Lance-Corporal	W. Riding	Arpley St. U.S.
Warwickshire (North).			
McIntosh, —.	Lieutenant	Lancs Fusiliers	Glascote C.S.
Watford.			
Collis, A. D.	Private	London Scottish	Berkhampstead N.S.
Flavin, P. C.	Private	R. Fusiliers	The "Chater" C.S.
Russell, F.	Private	Middlesex	Pulteney S., Soho.
Waveney Valley.			
Chambers, H.	2nd Lieutenant	Cambs	Wrentham R.C.S.
Weardale.			
Horn, J. H.	2nd Lieutenant	York and Lancs	Wolsingham C.S.
Wellingborough.			
Bagnall, H.	Lance-Corporal	E. Kent	Park St. C.S.
Bayes, G.	Lance-Corporal	Northants	Harrowden N.S.
Fox, S. T.	2nd Lieutenant	R.G.A.	Rushden N.S.
French, J. L.	Lieutenant	R.A.S.C.	Stanwick.
Wensleydale.			
Bargh, G.	2nd Lieutenant	King's Liverpool	Hawes C.S.
West Bromwich.			
Roberts, W.	2nd Lieutenant	M.G.C.	Lodge Estate C.S.
Walters, H.	Private	R. Warwick	Christ Ch.S.
West Ham.			
Beardmore, W.	Q.M. Sergeant	R. Munster Fusiliers	Grange Rd. C.S.
Bengough, C. W.	2nd Lieutenant	R.G.A.	Water Lane H.E.S.
Bennett, W.	Lance-Corporal	R. Fusiliers	North St. C.S.
Church, C.	W'less Telegraphist	R.N.	Waltham Abbey C.S.

THE GALLANT DEAD

Name.	Rank.	Regiment.	School.
West Ham—*continued.*			
Coakley, N. F.	Private	Civil Service Rifles	South Hallsville C.S.
Crocker, H. H.	Rifleman	London	Shipman Rd. C.S.
Gilbert, H. J.	2nd Lieutenant	K.R.R.	Russell Rd. C.S.
Grice, P. S.	Lieutenant	London	Abbey Rd. C.S.
Holt, T.	Rifleman	L.R.B.	St. James's Ch.S.
Hotten, H. J.	Private	L.R.B.	Gainsborough Rd. C.S.
Lenz, W. A. P.	2nd Lieutenant	R.G.A.	Custom House C.S.
Millar, E.	Lance-Corporal	R. Fusiliers	St. Antony's R.C.S.
Norcross, W. H.	Private	R.A.M.C.	Whitehall Place C.S.
Oliver, A. C.	Private	Civil Service Rifles	Shipman Rd. C.S.
Pett, J.	Lieutenant	O. & B.L.I.	St. Andrew's N.S.
Pollock, W.			25, Liverpool Rd.
Poulain, H. R.	Private	H.A.C.	Russell Rd. C.S.
Shandley, R. N.	2nd Lieutenant	Essex	New City Rd. C.S.
Shaw, W. T.	Private	Essex	Credon Rd. C.S.
Shean, P. C.	Private	London	Russell Rd. C.S.
Tarlton, R. T.	Sergeant	R. Fusiliers	New City Rd. C.S.
Taylor, D.	Lance-Corporal	London	New City Rd. C.S.
Taylor, G. J. (M.M.)	Company Sgt.-Maj.	London	South Hallsville C.S.
Tindale, E.	Corporal	R.E.	Holy Trinity C.S.
Turner, A. T. (M.M.)	Lance-Corporal	O. & B.L.I.	Russell Rd. C.S.
Webb, A. H. W.	Corporal	Civil Service Rifles	South Hallsville C.S.
Wingfield, H.	Sergeant	R. Sussex	Custom House C.S.
West Lambeth.			
Bonfield, S. M.	Sergeant-Inst.	R.E.	Sudbourne Rd. L.C.C.S.
Buxton, R. P.	Captain	O. & B.L.I.	Lavender Hill L.C.C.S.
Cæsar, H. J.	Private	R.A.M.C.	The " Earlsfield " L.C.C.S.
Chamberlain, C. J.	Lieutenant	L.R.B.	St. Andrew's Par.S.
Churcher, E.	2nd Lieutenant	Rifle Brigade	31, Meadow Rd., S.W. 8.
Dancer, A. C. (M.C.)	Captain	Dorset	Larkhall Lane L.C.C.S.
Davis, W. H.	Lieutenant	Sherwood Foresters	Marylebone Cent. S.
Elliott, V. M.	Sergeant	O. & B.L.I.	Eltringham St. L.C.C.S.
Field, W. J.	Lieutenant	R. Fusiliers	West Hill L.C.C.S.
Hart, A. K.	Lance-Corporal	Middlesex	Fountain Rd. L.C.C.S.
Jefcoate, F.	Captain	R.A.F.	St. Mary's Ch.S., Putney.
Jessop, R.	Private	Middlesex	Lavender Hill L.C.C.S.
Keys, W. H.	Lance-Sergeant	Seaforth Highlanders	Swaffield Rd. L.C.C.S.
Lord, E. W.	Acting Sergeant	Gloucester	Priory Grove L.C.C.S.
Monkhouse, J. A.	Lieutenant	R.A.M.C.	All Saints' Ch.S., Wandsworth.
Palmer, G. R.	2nd Lieutenant	W. Riding	Merchant Venturers' Sec. S., Bristol.
Pearson, J. A.	Captain	R. Fusiliers	Walthamstow Gram.S.
Roberts, C. H. H. (M.C.)	Captain	Surrey Rifles	Waldron Rd. L.C.C.S.
Roberts, T.	Lieutenant	Cheshire	The Nurseries, Swansea Rd., Llanelly.
Shea, W. D.	Private	Artists Rifles	Old Battersea R.C.S.
Smith, F. W.	Private	R. Sussex	St. Andrew's St. L.C.C.S.
Stanfield, W. A.	Acting Sergeant	R.A.M.C.	Santley St. L.C.C.S.
Waterland, D.	Private	London	4, Brussels Rd., Wandsworth.
West, C. E.	Private	London Scottish	Derington Rd. S. (Temp.).
Wheatcroft, F. G.	2nd Lieutenant	E. Surrey	Swaffield Rd. L.C.C.S.
Willis, W. F. B.	Lieutenant	D.C.L.I.	16, Stanton Rd., Wimbledon, S.W.
Wilson, C. F.	Lieutenant	Hants	Rosendale Rd. L.C.C.S.
Westminster.			
Despicht, T. L.(M.C.)	Lieut. (Act. Adjt.)	Bedford	St. Mary's Ch.S.
Duprès, E. C.	Captain	R. Fusiliers	Westminster Cathedral R.C.S.
Hatcher, E. W.	Private	London	St. Gabriel's Ch.S.
Hill, J.	Corporal	Queen's Westminster	St. Barnabas' Ch.S.
Wareham, F. W.	Lieutenant	R. Warwick	St. Matthew's Ch.S.
Wrigley, J.	2nd Lieutenant	R.G.A.	St. Peter's Ch.S.

N.U.T. WAR RECORD

Name.	Rank.	Regiment.	School.
West Stanley.			
Peadon, H.	2nd Lieutenant	Welsh	Annfield Plain C.S.
Seed, F.	Wireless Operator	Dover Drifter	Greenland C.S.
Wharfedale.			
Leyland, H.	Sergeant	W. Riding	Ilkley N.S.
Lockwood, A.	2nd Lieutenant	R.F.A.	Lofthouse C.S.
Whitby.			
Skilbeck, H.	Corporal	R.F.A.	St. Michael's C.S.
Whitehaven.			
Cowen, J.	Private	Seaforth Highlanders	Crosthwaite Mem. S.
Wilson, W. J.	Lieutenant	Devon	Irish St. C.S.
Widnes.			
Ireland, A.	Rifleman	King's Liverpool	Warrington Rd. C.S.
Wigan.			
Heaton, F. V.	Private	King's Liverpool	St. Thomas' Ch.S.
Jones, J. B.	Private	Warwick	St. Catherine's Ch.S.
McGrath, W. E.	Corporal	R. Fusiliers	St. William's R.C.S.
Willenhall.			
Carter, G.	Gunner	R.F.A.	Holy Trinity Ch.S., Short Heath.
Willesden.			
Brawn, M. (D.C.M.)	Lieut. and Q.M.	Q.V.R.	St. Andrew's Ch.S.
Brewer, H. G.	Sergeant	K.R.R.	Chamberlayne Wood Rd. C.S.
Hawkins, W.	Private	L.R.B.	Keble Mem. S.
James, S. H.	Sapper	R.E.	21, Bolton Gdns., N.W.
Nicholls, W.	Corporal	Middlesex	St. Andrew's Ch.S.
Pepper, J. W.	Private	L.R.B.	Bridge Rd. C.S.
Pipe, P. D.	Private	O. & B.L.I.	Acton Lane C.S.
Sanders, W. F.	Private	L.R.B.	Bridge Rd. C.S.
Smee, P. G. F.	Gunner	R.G.A.	Dudding Hill C.S.
Warne,	Private	London	Holy Trinity Ch.S.
Wiltshire (West).			
Collings, H. C.	2nd Lieutenant	R.G.A.	Holy Trinity Ch.S., Trowbridge.
Wimbledon.			
Bartlett, A. O.	Lieut. and Q.M.	Camel Corps	Haydon's Rd. Ch.S.
Betts, W. E.	Corporal	E. Surrey	Upper Mitcham C.S.
Dawson, H.	2nd Lieutenant	London	Durnsford Rd. C.S.
Hull, H. B.	Corporal	Queen's Westminster	Durnsford Rd. C.S.
Ponsford, E. H.	Leading Seaman	R.N.	Dundonald C.S.
Tucker, P.	Sergeant	R. Fusiliers	Dundonald C.S.
Winchester.			
Bogie, A. W.	C.S.M.	Hants	St. Thomas' N.S.
Everest, H. R.	Private	K.R.R.	St. Bartholomew's C.S.
Leach, W. F.	Reg. Sergt.-Maj.	Hants	St. Thomas' N.S.
Seeviour, S.H. (M.M.)	Private	Hants	St. Bartholomew's C.S.
Windermere.			
Abraham, C. R.	Sergeant	W.L.C.C.S.	Crosthwaite End.S., Kendal.
Windsor.			
Dowell, W.	Private	Somerset L.I.	Cranborne Ranelagh S.

THE GALLANT DEAD

Name.	Rank.	Regiment.	School.
Wolverhampton.			
Astle, L.	Lance-Sergeant	S. Staffs	Walsall St. C.S.
Piper, R. C.	Captain	S. Staffs	St. Andrew's Ch.S.
Smith, W.	Gunner	R.G.A.	Walsall St. C.S.
Walters, T.	Private	S. Staffs	St. Jude's Ch.S.
Walters, T. H.	Private	S. Staffs	Dudley Rd. C.S.
Wood Green.			
Deeson, L. A.	Petty Officer	R.N.	Alexandra C.S.
Jones, H.	Lieutenant	London	Higher Grade S.
Matthews, E. S.	Lieutenant	Middlesex	Noel Park C.S.
Morris, S. H.	Private	London	Lordship Lane C.S.
Salmon, —...	Lieutenant	R.E.	Higher Grade S.
Woolwich.			
Davis, W.	2nd Lieutenant	Essex	Elizabeth St. L.C.C.S.
Dimond, S.	Sergeant	L.R.B.	Ch. Manorway L.C.C.S.
Erwood, C. M. W.	Lance-Corporal	Bedford	High St. L.C.C.S.
Miles, F. J.	Lieutenant	R.F.A.	Ancona Rd. L.C.C.S.
Pearse, C. G.	Lieutenant	R.F.A.	Conway Rd. L.C.C.S.
Worcester City.			
Gladwell, J. H.	2nd Lieutenant	R.W. Kent	Stanley Rd. C.S.
Harris, R. W. J.	Private	R.A.S.C.	Stourbridge Rd. C.S., Bromsgrove.
Redler, H.	Private	R.W. Kent	Stanley Rd. C.S.
Worcester District.			
Warren, A. J. T.	Bombardier	R.F.A.	Abberley N.S.
Workington.			
Gorton, W.	Lance-Corporal	R.E.	Higher Standard C.S.
Worksop.			
Knight, C. E.	Corporal	Leicester	St. John's Ch.S.
Worsley, &c.			
Taylor, H.	2nd Lieutenant	Manchester	Cadishead C.S.
Wrexham.			
Evans, J.	Private	R.W.F.	Ponkey C.S.
Harris, P. G.	Lieutenant	R.A.F.	Wrexham N.S.
York.			
Appleby, R. B.	Bombardier	R.G.A.	Poppleton Rd. C.S.
Hawthorne, E.	Sergeant-Major	R.N.	Scarcroft Rd. C.S.
Hunsley, F.	Private	R. Fusiliers	Minster Boys' S., Beverley.
Joy, D.	Sergeant	Yorks	Sand Hutton C.S.
Kew, R. G.	Corporal	R.E.	St. Barnabas' Ch.S.
March, R. E.	Bombardier	R.G.A.	Micklegate C.S.
Molyneux, C.	Sergeant	R.G.A.	St. Paul's S.
Waring, G.	Private	T.R. Batt.	Sheriff Hutton W.S.
Yoxford.			
Hurren, H.M. (M.M.)	Sergeant	Warwick	Yoxford.

Military Honours.

1. Where honours have been gained in addition to that under which the name of the teacher appears, this is shown by letters after the name indicative of the particular additional honour or honours conferred.

    V.C. = Victoria Cross.
    D.S.O. = Distinguished Service Order.
    D.S.C. = Distinguished Service Cross. (Naval).
    M.C. = Military Cross.
    D.F.C. = Distinguished Flying Cross.
    D.C.M. = Distinguished Conduct Medal.
    D.S.M. = Distinguished Service Medal. (Naval).
    M.M. = Military Medal.
    M.S.M. = Meritorious Service Medal.
    C. de G. = Croix de Guerre (France, Belgium, and Italy).

2. An asterisk (*) indicates the addition of a Bar to the award under which the name of the teacher appears.

Name.	Rank.	Regiment.	School.	Association.
VICTORIA CROSS.				
Adlam, T. E.	Capt.	Bedford	Brook St. C.S.	Basingstoke.
Bell, D. S.	2nd Lt.	Yorks	Starbeck C.S.	Harrogate.
Harrison, J. (M.C.)	2nd Lt.	E. Yorks	Lime St. C.S.	Hull.
DISTINGUISHED SERVICE ORDER.				
*Buckle, A. W. (3 Bars)	Lt.-Com.	R.N.V.R.	St. Augustine's Ch.S.	London (N.W.).
Church, A. G. (M.C.) (Order of St. Vladimir)	Major	R.G.A.	Morpeth St. Cent.S.	London (E.).
Dick, H. W. (M.C.)	Major	E. Yorks	Southcoates LaneC.S.	Hull.
Edwards, J.	Major	R.W.F.	Central Foundation S., CityRd., London	Aberdare.
Leake, G. E. A.	Capt.	London	Taplow (Bucks) S.	Reading.
Muir, A.W. (M.C. and Bar)	Capt.	N.F.	Seaton Delaval C.S.	Northumberland (E.).
Pring, B.V. (M.C. and Bar)	Capt.	K.O.Y.L.I.	Boston Rd. C.S.	Croydon.
Read, H.S. (M.C. and Bar)	Major	London	Tamworth Rd. C.S.	Croydon.
Reade, A. (M.C.)	Lieut.	S. Lancs	Monmouth N. Pr.S.	Monmouth.
Reay, T.	Major	N.F.	Bothal Ch.S., Ashington.	Northumberland (E.).
Rees, E. T. (M.C.)	Lt.-Col.	S.W.B.	Cadoxton C.S.	Barry.
Rowlands, H. (M.C. and Bar) (C. de G. with Palm, France)	Capt.	London	Llaniestyn C.S.	Carnarvon (S.).
Sanderson, C. (Order of St. George, Russia)	Lieut.	Gordon Hdrs.	North Rd. C.S.	Spennymoor.
Slater, H. A.	Lieut.	Shrwd. For.	41, Tichfield St., Hucknall Torkard	Nottingham.
Whitmarsh, A. J. (M.C.)	Capt.	E. Kent	Smarden C.S.	Weald of Kent.
DISTINGUISHED SERVICE CROSS (NAVAL).				
Barnes, F. W.	Warrant Officer.	Skipper(Mine-Sweeper).	School for Fishermen.	Hull.

N.U.T. WAR RECORD

MILITARY CROSS.

Name.	Rank.	Regiment.	School.	Association.
Adamson, A. J.	2nd Lt.	Shrwd. For.	Mundella Sec.S.	Nottingham.
Adshead, H. J.	Capt.	Lincoln	Batley Ch.S.	Dewsbury and Batley
Albon, H.	Capt.	R.F.A.	Mitcham Rd. C.S.	Croydon.
Allen, C. A.	Major	R. Sussex	Christ Ch.S.	Folkestone.
Ames, G.	Major	R.H.A.	St. Mary's S.	East Lambeth.
Anderson, H. R.	2nd Lt.	M.G.C.	St. Thomas' Ch.S.	Waterloo.
*Andrew, R. B.	Major	London	Darell Rd. C.S.	Richmond (Surrey)
Angel, A. A.	Lieut.	M.G.C.	Westminster R.C.S.	Westminster.
Arrowsmith, C. F. (Order d'Avez, Portugal).	Lieut.	King's L'pool	St. Francis Xavier's College.	Liverpool.
Aston, A. A.	Capt.	R.G.A.	Eldon Rd. C.S.	Edmonton.
*Attewell, O. P.	Major	R. Fuslrs.	Welford Rd. C.S.	Newbury.
Backhouse, G. E.	Lieut.	M.G.C.	Stanhope Barrington Ch.S.	Weardale.
Balls, E. G.	Lieut.	R.E.	Bruce Grove C.S.	Tottenham, etc.
Bathurst, W. J.	Capt.	Cheshire	Tantarra St. C.S.	Walsall.
Bardsley, J.	Lieut.	R. Fuslrs.	St. Peter's Ch.S.	Burnley.
Barker, G. H.	Lieut.	Hants	Holy Trinity N.S.	Winchester.
Barkworth, S. J. (M.M.)	2nd Lt.	R. Fuslrs.	E. London Indl.S.	Lewisham.
Barron, F. J.	C.S.M.	R.W.F.	Courtney St. C.S.	Hull.
Baxenden, J.	C.S.M.	Cameronians	Beaufort St. C.S.	Liverpool.
Beaumont, H. S.	Tem.Capt.	L.N.L.	St. John's Ch.S.	Blackpool.
Beaumont, S.	2nd Lt.	E. Lancs.	Oval Rd. C.S.	Croydon.
Bebbington, B.	Lieut.	R.F.A.	Elysian St. C.S.	Manchester.
Beckett, J. R.	Capt.	L.N.L.	Westminster Rd.C.S.	Liverpool.
Beckley, R. F.	C.S.M.	K.R.R.	Central C.S., Aylesbury.	Chesham.
Beedham, N. H.	Capt.	Shrwd. For.	Trent Bridge C.S.	Nottingham.
Bell, G. B.	Lieut.		Raby St. C.S.	Newcastle.
Bell, H. G. (C. de G. with Palm, France).	Major	R.G.A.	Omega St. C.S.	Portsmouth.
Bence, S.	Sgt.	R. Fuslrs.	St. Mark's S., Holloway.	Finsbury, etc.
Best, D. A.	Lieut.	Manchester	Boughton-under-Blane W.S.	Faversham.
Binley, P. A.	2nd Lt.	R. Essex	Melrose S.	Guernsey.
Bishop, F.	Capt.	Cheshire	College S.	Chester.
Blowers, A. H.	Capt.	Tank Corps.	Leiston C.S.	Yoxford.
Borradale, J. F.	Lieut.	N.F.	West Jesmond C.S.	Newcastle-on-Tyne.
Boucher, A. E.	Lieut.	R. Warwick	East Rd. Ch.S.	Cambridge Borough.
Bowen, W. L.	Lieut.	Monmouth	Sirbowy C.S.	Tredegar.
Boyes, R. J.	2nd Lt.	R. Sussex	Crampton St.L.C.C.S.	East Lambeth.
Brace, R. B.	Capt.	Shrwd. For.	Craven Pk. L.C.C.S.	Hackney.
Bridge, J. T. (M.M.)	Capt.	Warwick	Rock C.S., near Bewdley.	Stourbridge.
Broadhurst, T.	2nd Lt.	R.W.F.	St. George's Ch.S.	Stockport.
Brook, G. H.	Capt.	Yorks L.I.	Ryan St. C.S.	Bradford.
Buckley, J.	Capt.	W. Riding	St. Luke's Ch.S.	Chadderton.
Buckley, J. W.	Major	R.F.A.	Wellgate C.S.	Rotherham.
Burnett, A. W. K.	Capt.	R.F.A.	LombardWall L.C.C.S	Woolwich.
Burrows, H. R. (C. de G. with Palm, France).	Capt.	W. Yorks	Hornsea C.S.	Hull.
Butcher, A. G.	Lieut.	M.G.C.	St. Paul's N.S.	Brentford.
*Calder, J. S.	Capt.	L.R.B.	Canterbury Rd. C.S.	Leyton.
Campion, W. J.	Capt.	Bedford	Gopsall St. L.C.C.S.	Hackney.
Carter, H. W.	2nd Lt.	W. Riding	St. Augustine's N.S.	Bradford.
Carter, J. A.	Lieut.	M.G.C.	L'pool Collegiate S.	Liverpool.
Chandler, F. E.	Lieut.	R.E.	All Saints Ch.S.	Manchester.
Chivers, S. N.	Lieut.	R.G.A.	Twyn C.S.	Caerphilly.
Church, A. G. (D.S.O.) (Order of St. Vladimir)	Major	R.G.A.	Morpeth St. L.C.C.S	London (E.).
Clark, F. C. C.	Major	R.G.A.	Moorside C.S.	Halifax.
Clarke, H. C.	Lieut.	Shrwd. For.	St. Peter's Ch.S.	Mansfield Borough.
Clist, L. F.	Lieut.	Cheshire	Stanford Rd. C.S.	Brighton, etc.

MILITARY HONOURS

MILITARY CROSS—cont.

Name.	Rank.	Regiment.	School.	Association.
Coe, A.	2nd Lt.	Worcester	Rochford Ch.S.	Rock and Tenbury.
Collins, S. H.	Capt.	Hants	Portswood C.S.	Southampton.
Connell, J. W.	Lieut.	R.W.F.	Connahs Quay	Flint County.
Cowls, J. M.	2nd Lt.	D.C.L.I.	Herland Cross C.S.	Cornwall (W.).
Craig, J.	Capt.	E. Yorks	St. Dominic's R.C.S.	Newcastle-on-Tyne.
*Crandon, G. L.	Capt.	Suffolk	Windmill Hill C.S.	Bristol.
Crowder, A. E.	Capt.	S.W.B.	Boys' N.S.	Grantham.
Dalziel, J. (Order of Redeemer, Greece)	Lieut.	R.G.A.	Montreal Ch.S., Cleator Moor.	Cumberland (W.).
Dancer, A. C.	Capt.	Dorset	Larkhall Lane L.C.C.S.	West Lambeth.
Daniels, F.	C.S.M.	R. Warwick	Hope St. C.S.	Birmingham.
Davies, D.	Lieut.	R.G.A.	Ynyslwyd C.S.	Aberdare.
Davies, D. J.	Lieut.	R.W.F.	Holy Trinity S.	West Lambeth.
Davies, H. R.	Lieut.	R.W.F.	Church Rd. C.S.	Newport (Mon.).
Davies, T.	C.S.M.	R.W.F.	Higher Elem.S.	Newport (Mon.).
Davis, G. H.	2nd Lt.	R.F.A.	St. Peter's Ch.S.	Bexhill.
Dawson, J.	Capt.	Border	Old Hall Drive C.S.	Manchester.
Deal, W. J.	Lieut.	R.G.A.	West Leigh C.S.	Southend-on-Sea.
Despicht, T. L.	Lt.(Actg. Adj.).	Bedford	St. Mary's Ch.S.	Westminster.
Dick, H. W. (D.S.O.)	Major	E. Yorks	Southcoates LaneC.S.	Hull.
Edgar, J. G.	Capt.	D.L.I.	Laygate Lane C.S.	South Shields.
Edwards, T. A.	Lieut.	R.N.D.	Christ Ch.S.	East Lambeth.
*Ellis, A. G.	2nd Lt.	R.F.A.	St. Mary's Ch.S.	Teign and Dart.
Eva, W. H.	Capt.	R.G.A.	St. George's N.S.	Bolton Borough.
Evans, Llew.	Capt.	R.W.F.	Pentre Sec.S.	Maesteg.
Evans, M.	Lieut.	Welsh	Bodringallt Boys' S.	Rhondda.
Exton, W.	Capt.	Devon	St. Mary's H.G.S.	Folkestone.
Fawkes, —.	Capt.	M.G.C.	Winshill C.S.	Burton-on-Trent.
Fielding, J. W. S.	Lieut.	R.F.A.	Whitfield Ch.S.	Glossop.
Fisher, G. H.	2nd Lt.	R.F.A.	Underwood St. C.S.	London (E.).
Fisher, H. W.	Lieut.	Middlesex	Surrey SquareL.C.C.S	East Lambeth.
Fleming, W. A. J.	Lieut.	R.G.A.	St. Patrick's S.	Oldham.
Flint, H. H.	Capt.	Middlesex	Garratt LaneL.C.C.S.	West Lambeth.
*Ford, H. C.	Lieut.	R.W.F.	Woods Rd. L.C.C.S.	East Lambeth.
Foulkes, J.	Lieut.	Manchester	Hamilton St. C.S.	Warrington.
Fox, J.	Lieut.	Manchester	Milnrow Moorhouse C.S.	Roch Valley.
Franks, E.	Lieut.	R.F.A.	Southend C.S.	Middlesbrough.
Fraser, J.	2nd Lt.	R.G.A.	Municipal Sec.S.	Ipswich.
French, W. E.	Major	Cyclist Batt.	Wornington Road. L.C.C.S.	London (W.).
Garner, F. B.	Major	R.F.A.	Queen's Rd. C.S.	Wimbledon.
Gibbs, F. J.	Capt.	R.A.F.	Handsworth New Rd. C.S.	Birmingham.
Gibson, E. S.	Capt.	D.L.I.	Upper Stand. S.	Sunderland.
Goacher, F.	Capt.	Artists Rifles	Bridge Rd. C.S.	Willesden.
Godwin, J.	Lieut.	King's L'pool	Cherry Rd. C.S.	Chester.
Gowland, S. J.	Major	Lancs Fuslrs.	Littleborough Ch.S.	Roch Valley.
Gravelle, H. L.	Lieut.	Tank Corps.	Lansdowne Rd. C.S.	Cardiff.
Greensmith, E. B.	Capt.	Shrwd. For.	St. John's S.	East Lambeth.
Guest, G.	Lieut.	R.E.	Secondary S.	Haslingden.
Hacking, W. T.	Lieut.	R.F.A.	138, Latham Tce.	Darwen.
Hacon, C. R.	2nd Lt.	M.G.C.	St. Mary Stoke N.S.	Ipswich.
Hallett, H. H. L.	Capt.	Hants	Chacewater C.S.	Falmouth and Truro.
Halliday, B. J. (M.M.)	Lieut.	Lincoln	Shodfriars C.S.	Boston.
Hallum, H. G.	Lieut.	Hants	Foundry Lane C.S.	Southampton.
Haney, F. J. (D.F.C.)	Capt.	R.F.A.	Our Lady Mount Carmel R.C.S.	Liverpool.
†Hankins, J. W.	Lieut.	R.F.A.	Clowne C.S.	Derbyshire (E.).
Harding, C.	Capt.	R. Warwick	Grove Lane C.S.	Birmingham.
Harker, T. R.	Capt.	D.L.I.	Upper Standard Sch., Annfield Plain.	Chester-le-Street.

N.U.T. WAR RECORD

Name.	Rank.	Regiment.	School.	Association.
MILITARY CROSS—*cont.*				
Harriman, H. W.	Capt.	W. Riding	Palfrey C.S.	Walsall.
Harrison, J. (V.C.)	2nd Lt.	E. Yorks	Lime St. C.S.	Hull.
Harrison, R. F.	Capt.	Norfolk	St. Lawrence's S.	Waveney Valley.
Harvey, E. A.	Capt.	Rifle Brigade	Christ Ch.S.	Banbury.
Hayes, F.	Capt.	L.N.L.	St. Andrew's Ch. S.	Accrington.
Hayward, W. H. (M.M.)	Lieut.	Tank Corps.	Acocks Green C.S.	Birmingham.
Hogg, G. E.	2nd Lt.	R.E.	Western C.S.	Tynemouth.
Hogg, J. C.	Lieut.	M.G.C.	Welbeck Rd. C.S., Bolsover.	Derbyshire (E.).
Holt, G.	Capt.	Welsh	Alder Grange C.S.	Rossendale.
Hopkinson, E.	Lieut.	Shrwd. For.	Newslead Colliery S.	Notts West.
Hughes, E. J. (M.M.)	2nd Lt.	R.W.F.	Sea View, Aston Hawarden.	Flint County.
Jaggard, F. W.	Capt.	Seaforth Hdrs	St. Mary's Ch.S.	Hornsey.
Jenkins, W. E.	Lieut.	Monmouth	Georgetown C.S.	Tredegar.
Jenks, F. A.	Capt.	S.L.I.	Church School	Barking.
Johns, F. T.	2nd Lt.	R.E.	Queen's Park C.S.	Bedford Borough.
Jones, G. H.	Lieut.	Worcester	East St. C.S.	Eastbourne.
Jones, J. Glynne	Capt.	R.W.F.	Corporation St. C.S.	Stafford and District.
*Jones, R. W.	Capt.	King's L'pool	Tiber St. C.S.	Liverpool.
Keevil, F. G.	Capt.	N. Staffs	Hooley C.S.	Reigate.
Kelsey, L. J.	Capt.	N. Staffs.	Centaur Rd. C.S.	Coventry.
Lamb, C. W.	Lieut.	Yorks	Lavender Hill L.C.C.S	West Lambeth.
Lanceley, T.	2nd Lt.	Liverpool	Love St. C.S.	Chester.
Levy, J.	2nd Lt.	R. Fuslrs.	Jews' Free S.	London (E.).
Lewin, C. C. H.	2nd Lt.	King's L'pool	Queen's Rd. C.S.	Liverpool.
Lindsay, D.	2nd Lt.	Worcester	St. Paul's N.S.	Worcester City.
Lintern, E. C.	Capt.	R.F.A.	Surrey St. C.S.	Luton.
Lloyd, E. E.	Lieut.	W. Yorks.	Belle Vue Rd. C.S.	Leeds.
Lofthouse, L. F.	Capt.	Tank Corps	St. Bridget's R.C.S.	Manchester.
Lord, A.	Act. Capt.	R.G.A.	Warley Rd. C.S.	Halifax.
Lovering, P. W.	Capt.	R. Sussex	St. Paul's Ch. S.	Chatham, etc.
Lowery, H. E. S.	Capt.	R. Scots	Irish Sch. C.S.	Whitehaven.
Mansell, C. J.	Lieut.	R. Warwick	Little Green Lane C.S.	Birmingham.
Marsden, F. K.	2nd Lt.	W. Riding	St. Andrew's Ch.S.	Brighouse.
*Marshall, F. J.	2nd Lt.	Devon	Barlby Rd. S.	London (W.).
Meakin, H. M.	Lieut.	Indian	Crown St. Sen. C.S.	Worksop.
Merry, T. A.	Capt.	York & Lancs.	S. Normanton C.S.	Erewash Valley, etc.
Miles, R. W. (D.C.M.)	Staff-Capt.	R.F.A.	Birley House S.	Woolwich.
Mollett, E. B.	Capt.	Middlesex	Sydenham Rd. C.S.	Croydon.
Morgan, T.	Lieut.	R.G.A.	Pontygof C.S.	Ebbw Vale.
*Muir, A.W. (D.S.O.)	Capt.	N.F.	Seaton Delaval C.S.	Northumberland (E.).
Neave, J. R.	Lieut.	Lincoln	Orleans C.S.	Twickenham.
Nevitt, A.	Capt.	R.W.F.	Talybont C.S.	Llandudno.
Nicholls, L.	Capt.	R.A.	St. Mary Magdalene S.	East Lambeth.
Norton, P. O.	2nd Lt.	Gloucester	St. Dominic's S.	London (N.W.).
*Ogden, B. D.	Capt.	E. Surrey	Pelham Rd. C.S.	Wimbledon.
Ogle, H.	Lieut.	K.O.R.L.	Bridge St. C.S.	Redditch.
Page, C. A.	2nd Lt.	R.G.A.	Elbow Lane C.S.	Leicester.
Painting, A. A.	Capt.	M.G.C.	Stanley Rd. C.S.	Worcester City.
Parke, E. A.	Capt.	D.L.I.	St. Andrew's Ch.S.	Newcastle-on-Tyne.
Parsons, E. H.	Lieut.	Lancs Fuslrs.	Townsend Lane C.S.	Liverpool.
Payne, H.	Capt.	York & Lancs	Treeton C.S., Rotherham.	Sheffield.
Perry, R. C.	Lieut.	Gloucester	Powell's End.S.	Cirencester.
Pewtress, A. W.	Capt.	R.F.A.	Goodshaw C.S.	Rossendale.
Phillips, C. A.	2nd Lt.	R.F.A.	Christ Ch. S.	Waterloo.
Phillips, W. H.	Lieut.	Welsh	HamletCourtRd.C.S.	Southend-on-Sea.
Philpotts, S. J.	Act. Capt.	R.G.A.	Lyham Rd. L.C.C.S.	East Lambeth.
Pitcher, W. H.	Capt.	Coldstm.Gds.	Rainham C.S.	Chatham, etc.
*Porter, G. E.	Capt.	Tank Corps.	Penrose St. L.C.C.S.	East Lambeth.
Powell, P. W. (D.C.M.)	Capt.	London	Council S.	Hinckley.
Pratt, B.	Major	M.G.C.	Nelson St. C.S.	Birmingham.

MILITARY HONOURS

Name.	Rank.	Regiment.	School.	Association.

MILITARY CROSS—cont.

Name.	Rank.	Regiment.	School.	Association.
*Pring, B.V. (D.S.O.)	Capt.	K.O.Y.L.I.	Boston Rd. C.S.	Croydon.
Pugh, G. H.	Capt.	R.G.A.	Mina Rd. C.S.	Bristol.
Pugh, R. H. (M.M.)	2nd Lt.	Welsh	Pontrhondda C.S.	Rhondda.
Radford, C. G.	Lieut.	Shrwd. For.	Broomhill C.S.	Mansfield.
*Read, H. S. (D.S.O.)	Major	London	Tamworth Rd. C.S.	Croydon.
Reade, A. (D.S.O.)	Lieut.	S. Lancs	Monmouth Boys' S.	Monmouth.
Rees, E. T. (D.S.O.)	Lt.-Col.	S.W.B.	Cadoxton C.S.	Barry.
Rickaby, J. D.	Capt.	D.L.I.	Todd's Nook C.S.	Newcastle-on-Tyne.
Riley, W. H.	2nd Lt.	Lancs Fuslrs.	St. Martin's S.	Sale.
Rimington, E.	Lieut.	R.E.	Technical S., Portadown, Ireland.	Hull.
Roberts, C. H. H.	Capt.	Surrey Rifles	Waldron Rd. L.C.C.S.	West Lambeth.
Roberts, J. A.	2nd Lt.	Welsh	Cwmaber C.S.	Caerphilly.
Roberts, T.	Lieut.	M.G.C.	Council S., Connah's Quay.	Flint County.
Roberton, W. H.	Capt.	D.L.I.	Lower Place C.S.	Willesden.
*Rothfield, A.	Lieut.	D.L.I.	Jews' Hosp. and Orphan Asylum.	West Lambeth.
*Rowlands, H. (D.S.O.) (C. de G. with Palm, France)	Capt.	London	Llaniestyn C.S.	Carnarvon (S.).
Salt, A.	2nd Lt.	R.W.F.	Simms Cross C. S.	Widnes.
Shaw, J. W.	2nd Lt.	K.R.R.	Stimpson Av. C.S.	Northampton.
Shooter, J. H.	2nd Lt.	R.A.F.	Lancasterian C.S.	Sheffield.
Simons, L.	Capt.	R. Fuslrs.	"Charlton" Cent. C.S.	Deptford and Greenwich.
Sizeland, R.	Lieut.	R.G.A.	Church S., Witney.	London (N.W.).
Skuse, S. C.	Lieut.	R.W.F.	Crumlin C.S.	Tredegar.
Smart, J. E. (C. de G., Belgium).	Capt.	Manchester	Manchester Univ.	Makerfield.
Smith, C.	Lieut.	London	Percy Rd. C.S., Hampton.	Teddington.
Smith, C. H.	2nd Lt.	R.G.A.	Grange N.S.	Cardiff.
Smith, P. J.	2nd Lt.	Naval Bde.	Goodrich Rd. L.C.C.S.	East Lambeth.
*Snell, J. E.	Capt.&Adj.	Devon	"John Gulson" C.S.	Coventry.
Spencer, L. K.	Capt.	London	Gopsall St. L.C.C.S.	Hackney.
Spink, H. M.	Lieut.	N.F.	St. Clement's Ch.S.	Liverpool.
Stevenson, J. C.	Act. Capt.	R.W. Surrey	"Shacklewell" L.C.C.S.	Hackney.
Stevenson, W.	Lieut.	R.G.A.	St. James Ch.S., Haydock.	Makerfield.
Storey, S. O.	Lieut.	R.G.A.	Oxbridge Lane C.S.	Stockton.
Stott, L. R.	Lieut.	Leeds Pals Batt.	Central S., Birstall.	Morley.
Streets, A. H.	Capt.	London	High St. C.S., Wealdstone.	Harrow.
Stubbs, F. W. A.	Lieut.	Shrwd. For.	Woodville Ch.S.	Matlock & Bakewell.
Sullivan, W. E.	Lieut.	Welsh	Cymmer C.S.	Rhondda.
*Sykes, H. C.	Lieut.	Border	Parish Ch.S.	Bradford.
Taylor, J. W. A.	Lieut.	R.E.	Arnot St. C.S.	Liverpool.
Taylor, R. A.	Lt.& Q.M.	Manchester	Christ Ch.S.	Manchester.
Telford, W. T.	Capt.	London	Langley Cent. C.S.	Slough.
Thomas, B. S. B.	Capt.	R.A.F.	71, Gwyther St., Pembroke Dock.	Pembrokeshire (S.).
Thomas, H. E.	Capt.	R.E.	Linacre C.S.	Bootle.
Thomas, T. (C. de G., Italy).	Lieut.	R.G.A.	Town C.S.	Aberdare.
Thompson, J.	2nd Lt.	W. Yorks	St. Thomas' Ch.S.	Oldham.
Tomlinson, A.	Capt.	Middlesex	Furness Rd. C.S.	Willesden.
Tossell, I. G.	Capt.	Welsh	N.Pr.S., Letterston	St. Davids.
Townsend, H. E. R.	Lieut.	R.G.A.	Green Lane C.S.	Sutton Coldfield.
Trigg, G.	2nd Lt.	E. Yorks	Boston Spa End.S.	Barkston Ash.
Trump, R. W.	Lieut.	R.E.	Loxton St. C.S.	Birmingham.
Turner, T.	Lieut.	Hants	County S.	Finchley.
Vincent, H. C.	2nd Lt.	L.N.L.	Balliol Rd. C.S.	Bootle.

N.U.T. WAR RECORD

Name.	Rank.	Regiment.	School.	Association.
MILITARY CROSS—*cont.*				
Wake, T. H.	Capt.	Inf. Brigade	Rutherford Coll.S.	Newcastle-on-Tyne.
Wallace, T.	Capt.	Border	Whitley Bay North C.S.	Northumberland (S.).
Walsh, A.	Capt.	L.N.L.	Sec.S.	Nelson, Colne, etc.
Waters, H. G.	C.S.M.	K.R.R.	St. Clement's Ch.S.	York.
Watt, G. R.	Lieut.	R.F.A.	Ancona Rd. L.C.C.S.	Woolwich.
Webb, J. G.	Lieut.	R.W.F.	Neyland C.S.	Pembrokeshire (Mid.)
Welch, T.	Capt.	D.L.I.	Higher Elem.S.	Spennymoor.
Whitmarsh, A.J. (D.S.O.)	Capt.	E. Kent	Smarden C.S.	Weald of Kent.
Wightman, J. M.	Colonel	Munster	Troedyrhiw C.S.	Merthyr Tydfil.
Williams, H.	Lieut.	M.G.C.	St. Augustine's Rd. C.S.	Erith.
*Wilson, J.	Act. Capt.	York & Lancs	Shipley Cent.S.	Shipley.
Wilson, S. J.	Capt.	Manchester	Central C.S., Denton	Hyde.
*Wintle, G. H.	Capt.	Gloucester	Double View C.S.	Forest of Dean.
Wood, E.	Lieut.	W. Riding	Lowfields C.S.	Sheffield.
Woods, J. W.	Capt.	K.O.Y.L.I.	Christ Ch.S.	Barnet.
Wright, W.	2nd Lt.	M.G.C.	Elwick Rd. C.S.	Hartlepools.
Yates, W.	Lieut.	W. Riding	C.S., Settle, Yorks.	Ingleborough.
Young, J. W.	Lieut.	D.L.I.	Hirst North C.S.	Northumberland(E.)
DISTINGUISHED FLYING CROSS.				
Haney, F. J. (M.C.)	Capt.	R.F.A.	Our Lady Mount Carmel R.C.S.	Liverpool.
Parke, J.(C. de G., France)	Lieut.	D.L.I.	East Walker C.S.	Newcastle-on-Tyne.
DISTINGUISHED FLYING MEDAL.				
Chapman, R. C.	Sgt. Obs.	R.A.F.	Central Park C.S.	East Ham.
DISTINGUISHED CONDUCT MEDAL.				
Allen, E. (C. de G. with Palm, France).	2nd Lt.	Hants	Bordon C.S.	Andover.
Archdeacon, J.	C.S.M.	London	Johnson St. R.C.S.	London (E.).
Bear, H. C. (M.S.M.)	C.S.M.	Middlesex	Bandon Hill C.S.	Epsom.
Bird, F. W.	Sgt.	C. of London Yeomanry.	Stanley St. L.C.C.S.	Deptford and Greenwich.
Bond, E. E.	C.S.M.	K. Ed. Horse	Clint Rd. C.S.	Liverpool.
Bowkett, E. C.	Pte.	E. Lancs Fld. Ambulance	All Saints S., C-on-M.	Manchester.
Brawn, M.	Lt. & Q.M.	Q.V.R.	St. Andrew's Ch.S.	Willesden.
Caiger, A. C.	Sgt.	O. & B.L.I.	St. Margaret's C.S.	Uxbridge.
*Cairns, J. C.	S.M.	O. & B.L.I.	Lyham Rd. L.C.C.S.	East Lambeth.
Carr, J. V. (Order of St. George, Russia)	C.S.M.	King's L'pool	St. Bede's R.C.S.	Widnes.
Clark, H. A.	Sgt.	Oxon	Springfield Rd. C.S.	Wolverhampton.
Clarke, V. C.	L.-Cpl.	M.G.C.	District S.	Faversham.
Cleghorn, R.	Pte.	W. Riding	Rose St. C.S.	Gateshead.
Cooke, H. A.	Pte.	R.A.M.C.	Pleasant St. C.S.	Liverpool.
Cooper, A. G.	Wnt. Offr.	Somerset	East Brent N.S.	Somerset (N.).
Cuss, F. E.	L.-Cpl.	C.of Lon.Rfls.	107, Wordsworth Rd., Penge.	Bromley.
Dare, E. C.	Sgt.	L.R.B.	Redmans Rd.L.C.C.S.	London (E.).
Dawes, A. E.	C.S.M.	London	Cooks Ground C.S.	Brentford.
Diplock, F. H.	2nd Lt.	R. Sussex	Bagillt C.S.	Flint County.
*Drury, S. C. (Médaille Militaire)	C.S.M.	R.E.	Old Oak Estate C.S.	Barnes and Mortlake.
Fairley, R. E.	S.M.	London	Middle Row L.C.C.S.	London (W.).
Field, W.	Sgt.	Black Watch	Netherton C.S.	Wakefield.
Fretwell, C. M.	Sgt.	Yorks	Jack Lane C.S.	Leeds.
Froome, C. W.	Col. S.M.	Q. Westmns.	Oxford Gdns.L.C.C.S.	London (W.).
Gastall, W. H.	B.S.M.	R.F.A.	Sec.S.	Blackpool.
Graham, M.	Lieut.	R.A.F.	Gamelsby Mill, Wigton.	Carlisle.

MILITARY HONOURS

Name.	Rank.	Regiment.	School.	Association.
\multicolumn{5}{c}{DISTINGUISHED CONDUCT MEDAL—cont.}				
Hales, B. C.	C.S.M.	London	WoodlandRd.L.C.C.S.	East Lambeth.
Hall, C. W.	C.S.M.	Lancs Fuslrs.	Higher Elem.S.	Birkenhead.
Harris, L.	Sgt.	M.G.C.	St. Augustine's S.	Wrexham.
Harvey, E. C.	Sgt.	Hants	Stamshaw C.S.	Portsmouth.
Heath, W. L.	R.S.M.	R.G.A.	Churchfields C.S.	West Ham.
Higham, E.	R.S.M.	Border	St. John's Ch.S.	Denton & Failsworth.
Hockridge, J. R.	C.S.M.	H.A.C.	Palace Court C.S.	Plymouth.
Landon, L. A.	2nd Lt.	L.N.L.	Caulden Rd. C.S.	Staffs (N.).
Lister Rhodes	Cpl.	R.E.	Birstall Cent.S.	Spen Valley.
Manning, J.	Sgt.	London	St. Michael's R.C.S.	Liverpool.
Mapham, N.	Sgt.	O. & B.L.I.	KingwoodRd.L.C.C.S.	London (W.).
Martin, D. G.	Lieut.	R.A.M.C.	Venice Rd. C.S.	Liverpool.
Martin, R. R. S.	Sgt.	R.A.M.C.	Amble Ch.S.	Alnwick.
McNamara, J.	Sgt.	Manchester	St. Wilfred's S.	Manchester.
Miles, R. W. (M.C.)	Staff-Capt.	R.F.A.	Birley House S.	Woolwich.
Mundy, F. G.	Sgt.	Wilts.	86, Trowbridge Rd., Bradford-on-Avon.	Warminster.
Neville, L.	C.Q.M.S.	Middlesex	C.S., Teddington	Teddington.
O'Nions, R.	Staff-Sgt.	R.A.M.C.	Lonsdale Rd. C.S.	Barnes and Mortlake.
Payne, E. G.	B'dier	R.F.A.	St. Luke's N.S.	Cheltenham.
Peake, F.	L.-Sgt.	London Irish	Greenhill C.S.	Harrow.
Pearce, W. (M.M.)	Sgt.	R.A.M.C.	Wolborough N.S.	Teign and Dart.
Phillips, A. J. (Médaille Militaire).	2nd Lt.	R.A.S.C.	Aristotle Rd.Cent.S.	West Lambeth.
Phillips, E. M.	Sgt.	R.E.	Broadway C.S.	Burton-on-Trent.
Pinkney, M. R.	2nd Lt.	D.L.I.	Greenside C.S.	Blaydon.
Potter, A. C.	2nd Lt.	K.R.R.	Park Lane C.S., Hornchurch.	Romford, etc.
Powell, P. W. (M.C.)	Capt.	London	Council S.	Hinckley.
Preston, T. J.	Sgt.	R.E.	Old Palace L.C.C.S.	London (E.).
Price, W. J.	S.M.	R.F.A.	St. Joseph's R.C.S.	Southwark.
Ramsden, T. V.	Act. Sgt.	W. Riding	Wyke C.S.	Bradford.
Rathbone, H. L.	Cpl.	R.G.A.	Fisher St. C.S.	West Bromwich.
Rayment, F.	Q.M.S.	Herts	Boreham C.S.	Hertford.
Shiel, B. R.	Sgt.	R. Warwick	Holy Trinity C.S.	Birmingham.
Summers, O.	Sgt.	R. Warwick	Bloomfield C.S.	Birmingham.
Thomas, W. I. (Croix de Guerre, France)	L.-Cpl.	M.G.C.	Cwmaman C.S.	Aberdare.
Tilson, J. H. (M.M.)	C.S.M.	Hants	Mawney Rd. C.S.	Romford, etc.
Ward, W. W.	Pte.	R.A.M.C.	Danygraig C.S.	Swansea.
Warren, W. N.	L.-Cpl.	R.A.M.C.	Clive Rd. C.S.	Barry.
White, R. H.	R.S.M.	R.W.F.	Llangwnadl Ch.S.	Carnarvon (S.).
Whitehouse, J.	Lieut.	R.A.S.C.	Bolton C.S.	Warrington.
Wignall, A.	Sgt.	Manchester	" Russell Scott " Memorial S., Denton	Hyde.
\multicolumn{5}{c}{DISTINGUISHED SERVICE MEDAL (NAVAL).}				
Caldwell, T. J.	Ord. Tel.	R.N.V.R.	Waunllywd C.S.	Ebbw Vale.
\multicolumn{5}{c}{MILITARY MEDAL.}				
Abba, A. C.	Capt.	Manchester	Park Rd. C.S.	Hull.
Adkins, G. W.	Cpl.	O. & B.L.I.	Churchfields C.S.	West Ham.
Ambrose, W.	Lieut.	R.E.	Lander Rd. C.S.	Litherland, etc.
Armstrong, F.	2nd Lt.	R.F.A.	Barnes C.S.	Sunderland.
Aspinall, J.	Pte.	Border	St. Joseph's R.C.S.	Leigh.
Bailey, C.	Spr.	R.E.	Nelson C.S.	Gt. Yarmouth.
Ball, E.	C.S.M.	Lancs. Fuslrs.	Regent St. C.S.	Heywood.
Ballantyne, T.	Cpl.	R.E.	Priory Ch.S.	Gt. Yarmouth.
Banks, R. W.	Q.M.S.	Field Amb.	Stoke Cent. N.S.	Staffs (N.).
Barker, W. D.	Lieut.	K.R.R.	Christ Church S.	Cheltenham.
Barkworth, S. J. (M.C.)	2nd Lt.	R. Fuslrs.	E. London Indl.S.	Lewisham.
Barrass, C.	Pte.	E. Yorks	Dean Rd. C.S.	South Shields.

N.U.T. WAR RECORD

Name.	Rank.	Regiment.	School.	Association.
MILITARY MEDAL—cont.				
Bassadona, S. H.	Sgt.	W. Lancs Fld. Ambulance	St. Saviour's S.	Liverpool.
Bennett, J. E. F. T.	2nd L.	R. Warwick	Stewart St. C.S.	Birmingham.
Best, E.	Lieut.	E. Yorks	Riddings Ch.S.	Erewash Valley and Ripley.
Bevan, A. E.	Cpl.	R.A.M.C.	Newbury Park C.S.	Ilford.
Billam, J. W. A.	Sgt.	R.A.M.C.	Bruce Grove C.S.	Tottenham, etc.
Binns, A.	Pte.	W. Yorks	Thurnscoe C.S.	Mexborough.
Bowden, J.	Cpl.	N. Hussars	Sheriff Hill C.S.	Gateshead.
Bowes, G. R.	Pte.	Civ. Serv. Rfls.	Crescent Rd. C.S.	Middlesbrough.
Boyce, F. J. (M.S.M.)	C.Q.M.S.	W. Yorks	Park C.S.	Sheffield.
Boyson, M.	Pte.	Northants	Weedon N.S.	Daventry.
Brereton, A. E.	Cpl.	O. & B.L.I.	Cator St. L.C.C.S.	East Lambeth.
Bridge, J. T. (M.C.)	Capt.	Warwick	Rock C.S., near Bewdley.	Stourbridge.
Brindle, H.	Pte.	R.A.M.C.	Mary St. S.	Birmingham.
Bristow, R.	Pte.	R.A.M.C.	St. John's Rd. C.S.	Hackney.
Buchan, C. M.	2nd Lt.	Shrwd. For.	Cowan Terr. S.	Sunderland.
Buckley, J. C.	Pte.	R.A.M.C.	Settles St. L.C.C.S.	London (E.).
Butler, E. H.	Sgt.	R. Warwick	Church Rd. C.S.	Birmingham.
Campion, E.	Pte.	R.A.M.C.	Ashburnham L.C.C.S.	London (W.).
Carruthers, A. J.	Pte.	R. Fuslrs.	Marton Rd. C.S.	Middlesbrough.
Chaytor, R. G. (Order of Leopold II. and C. de G., Belgium).	Cpl.	R.A.M.C.	Medomsley C.S.	Vale of Derwent.
Clark, J. G.	Pte.	Public Schs. Batt.	Birtley Lane C.S.	Chester-le-Street.
Claughton, W.	Pte.	R.F.A.	Richmond St. C.S.	Oldham.
Clegg, A. B.	L.-Cpl.	R.G.A.	Medomsley Ch.S.	Vale of Derwent.
Cogan, A.	Sgt.	R.E.	St. Joseph's R.C.S.	Leeds.
Cohen, P.	Sgt.	R.E.	Tilery Rd. C.S.	Stockton.
Cooper, T. B.	Capt.	London	Isleworth Blue N.S.	Ealing.
Crabtree, P.	L.-Cpl.	E. Lancs	Bradley C.S.	Nelson, Colne, etc.
Crookes, R. B.	Capt.	M.G.C.	Neensend C.S.	Sheffield.
Crozier, H. C.	Sgt.	York & Lancs	Sharrow Lane C.S.	Sheffield.
Dagg, T.	Sgt.	R.G.A.	St. Mary's R.C.S.	Burnley.
Dale, P.	Sgt.	R.G.A.	Brindley Ford C.S.	Staffs (N.).
Davies, E. L.	Cpl.	Berks	Wokingham Rd.C.S.	Reading.
Davies, J. E.	Lieut.	R.G.A.	Cwmaman C.S.	Aberdare.
Davison, W. R.	Lieut.	R.E.	St. Stephen's C.S.	South Shields.
Dearing, C.	Sgt.	L.R.B.	Cosway St. L.C.C.S.	London (N.W.).
Downing, R.	2nd Lt.	N. Staffs.	Goldenhill Ch.S.	Staffs (N.).
Dyer, P. T.	Lieut.	L.R.B.	Downsell Rd. C.S.	Leyton.
Ebbetts, R. F.	Sgt.	L.R.B.	Acton Wells C.S.	Acton.
Edgar, W. G. (Italian Medal)	Lieut.	N.F.	Dean Rd. C.S.	South Shields.
Eeles, F. T.	Pte.	Yorks	'Edward Kitching''C.S.	Stokesley.
Emery, W. J.	L.-Cpl.	London	Beech Hill C.S.	Luton.
Ensell, E. E. E.	L.-Cpl.	N.F.	Windmill Hill C.S.	Gateshead.
Enstone, A.	Q.M.S.	O. & B.L.I.	NorthNewingtonN.S.	Banbury.
Farmer, F.	Pte.	R. Warwick	Leicester St. C.S.	Leamington.
Farrer, W. (C. de G., France).	B'dier.	R.F.A.	Sacraston C.S.	Durham.
Finch, R. A.	Pte.	R.A.M.C.	St. Anne's Ch.S.	Liverpool.
Francis, H. W.	Cpl.	London	Chislehurst S.	Chatham, etc.
Fryer, G.	B'dier.	R.F.A.	York St. C.S.	Mountain Ash.
Germaney, W. T.	Cpl.	R.A.M.C.	St. Matthew's Ch S.	Westminster.
Gibson, S.	L.-Cpl.	D.L.I.	Barrington Ch.S.	Bishop Auckland.
Gill, N.	Cpl.	R.E.	Central C.S., Weston-super-Mare.	Somerset (N.).
Grant, W. P.	Sgt.	R.G.A.	Rosherville Ch.S.	Dartford.
Green, E.	Sgt.	W. Yorks	Kirkstall Rd. C.S.	Leeds.
Gutteridge, E. N.	2nd Lt.	R.F.A.	Christ Ch.S.	Croydon.
Gwynne, G. D.	Sgt.	Welsh	Elliot Town C.S., Cardiff.	Rhymney Valley.

MILITARY HONOURS

MILITARY MEDAL—cont.

Name.	Rank.	Regiment.	School.	Association.
Halliday, B. J. (M.C.)	Lieut.	Lincoln	Shodfriars C.S.	Boston.
Hammond, S. H.	Sgt.	L.R.B.	Droop St. L.C.C.S.	London (N.W.).
Hampton, R.	Cpl.	Hants	Bolton-on-DearneC.S.	Mexborough.
Hardwick, R.	Sgt.	R. Warwick	Garrison Lane C.S.	Birmingham.
Harmsworth, H. J.	C.Q.M.S.	O. & B.L.I.	Deddington N.S.	Banbury.
Harper, J. R.	Pte.	R.A.M.C.	Park C.S.	Dudley.
Haworth, J. B.	2nd Lt.	R. Fuslrs.	Holy Trinity S.	Denton and Failsworth
Hayward, W. H. (M.C.)	Lieut.	Tank Corps	Acocks Green C.S.	Birmingham.
Helmer, B.	2nd Lt.	R.E.	Garrison Lane C.S.	Birmingham.
Hermiston, R. N.	C.S.M.	Yorks	Fleetham St. C.S.	Middlesbrough.
Holmes, H.	Sgt.	Welsh	Hyde Park C.S.	Doncaster.
Hooson, H. B.	Sgt.	L.R.B.	Canal Rd. C.S.	Hackney.
Hopkins, F.	Cpl.	L.R.B.	Croyland Rd. C.S.	Edmonton.
Hopkinson, O.	Cpl.	R.E.	Mill St. C.S.	Crewe.
Horn, H.	C.S.M.	London	Edward St. S.	Grimsby.
Houseley, P. B.	Pte.	O. & B.L.I.	Shirebrook C.S.	Derbyshire (E.).
Howard, G. R.	Cpl.	R.E.	Priory Ch.S.	Gt. Yarmouth.
Hughes, E. J. (M.C.)	2nd Lt.	R.W.F.	Sea View, Aston, Hawarden.	Flint County.
Hughes, G.	Gnr.	R.G.A.	Aberystwyth Tr.Coll.	Mountain Ash.
Humphreys, E. W.	Sigl.	R.F.A.	Manor Park C.S.	East Ham.
*Humphreys, W. A.	Sgt.	R.E.	Mandeville St.L.C.C.S.	Hackney.
Hunt, J. S.	Sgt.	Coldstm.Gds.	Sandringham Rd.C.S.	East Ham.
Hunter, R. E.	Sgt.	R.E.	Westoe Sec.S.	South Shields.
Hurren, H. M.	Sgt.	R. Warwicks	Yoxford	Yoxford.
Hyslop, M.	Gnr.	R.G.A.	Rutherford Coll. Sec.	Newcastle-on-Tyne.
Irwin, J. E.	Pte.	R. Warwick	Cowper St. C.S.	Birmingham.
Jay, A.	C.Q.M.S.	R. Warwick	Bushbury Lane C.S., Wolverhampton.	Willenhall.
Johnson, J. R.	Cpl. Sigl.	R.F.A.	St. John's N.S.	Sunderland.
Jones, D. J.	Pnr.	R.E.	Bargoed C.S.	Gelligaer.
Joss, E. J.	Lieut.	Black Watch	Eppleton C.S.	Houghton-le-Spring.
*Kay, S. T.	Sgt.	R.A.M.C.	Broad Green Rd. C.S.	Liverpool.
Keen, J. W.	Sgt.	London	The Bridge C.S., Wealdstone.	Harrow.
Kennedy, J. L.	Cpl.	R.E.	Dean Rd. C.S.	South Shields.
Kent, H. G.	B'dier	R.F.A.	Connaught Rd. C.S.	Brighton, etc.
King, F.	Sgt.	R.A.M.C.	Broad Green Rd. C.S.	Liverpool.
King, M. P.	Sgt.	CameronHdrs	The "Fox" L.C.C.S.	London (W.).
Leavis, T.	Sgt.	L.N.L.	St. John's N.S.	Bolton Borough.
Leeds, G. J.	L.-Cpl.	R. Fuslrs.	West Leigh C.S.	Southend-on-Sea.
Lishman, T. B.	Pte.	Border	Walkden Wes.S., Little Hulton.	Bolton District.
*Lisle, J. R.	Sgt.	N.F.	New Delaval C.S.	Blyth.
Llewellyn, T.	Sgt.	R.W.F.	Gelli Pentre C.S.	Rhondda.
Locker, A. C.	Sgt. Inst.	R. Warwick	Colmore Rd. C.S.	Birmingham.
McHugh, R.	L.-Cpl.	R.E.	Baring St. C.S.	South Shields.
Mellers, W.	Pnr.	R.E.	Wellgate C.S.	Rotherham.
Miller, F. J.	2nd Lt.	M.G.C.	Churchtown C.S.	Southport.
Millett, F.	Lieut.	C. of Lon.Rfls.	Churchfield Rd. S.	Bromley.
Mitchell, R.	Sgt.	R.E.	Carr Lane N.S.	Bradford.
Moakler, R. J.	C.S.M.	R. Warwick	Tunstall R.C.S.	Staffs (N.).
Moore, H.	Sgt.	R.G.A.	Westwood C.S.	Vale of Derwent.
Mosley, E.	L.-Cpl.	Dorset	St. Edmund's Ch.S.	Salisbury.
Moss, S. F.	2nd Lt.	R.E.	DistrictCh.S.,Earlestown.	Makerfield.
Munnings, H.	Act.R.S.M.	Q.V.R.	Hyde C.S., Hendon	Hendon.
Nash, W. H.	Cpl.	O. & B.L.I.	Cator St. L.C.C.S.	East Lambeth.
Newcombe, F.	L.-Cpl.	D.L.I.	Whitton C.S., Carlton Ironworks, Durham.	Stockton.
Newis, H. T.	Sgt.	R.G.A.	Brookdale Pk. C.S.	Manchester.
Nicholson, W. P.	Pte.	D.L.I.	Fatfield C.S.	Chester-le-Street.

N.U.T. WAR RECORD

Name.	Rank.	Regiment.	School.	Association.
MILITARY MEDAL—*cont.*				
North, H.	Sgt.	M.G.C.	St. John's Ch.S.	Worksop.
Odams, F.	Rflman.	L.R.B.	Oldfield Rd. C.S.	Willesden.
*Page, F. G.	Sgt.	E. Yorks	Somerset St. C.S.	Hull.
Patterson, S. B.	Sgt.	R. Warwick	Palfrey C.S.	Walsall.
Pearce, H.	L.-Cpl.	R.W.F.	Stonebroom C.S.	Erewash Valley, etc.
Pearce, W. (D.C.M.)	Sgt.	R.A.M.C.	Wolborough N.S.	Teign and Dart.
Pearson, A.	Sgt.	Dk.of Well...	Bearpark C.S.	Durham.
Pepler, F. C.	2nd Lt.	K.R.R.	Grammar S., Nantwich.	London (E.).
Philipson, T.	Pte.	N. Hussars	Rosa St. C.S.	Spennymoor.
Pollard, P. J.	Q.M.S.	Bedford	High St. L.C.C.S.	Woolwich.
Precious, H. P.	Sgt.	London	High Rd. C.S.	Leyton.
Prentice, A.	Sgt.	O. & B.L.I.	Smallwood Rd.L.C.C.S.	West Lambeth.
Pringle, L.	Sgt.	Div. Sig. Co.	Bolam St. C.S.	Newcastle-on-Tyne.
Pugh, R. H. (M.C.)	2nd Lt.	Welsh	Pontrhondda C.S.	Rhondda.
Radford, G. E.	Sgt.	R.G.A.	Central C.S., Weston-super-Mare.	Somerset (N.).
Ranner, C. E.	Sgt.	R.E.	Tiber St. C.S.	Liverpool.
Raper, D. A.	Sgt.	Yorks	Oxbridge Lane C.S.	Stockton.
Read, —.	Pte.	R. Sussex	Staplecross N.S.	Hastings.
Rigg, T.	Sgt.	Durham	Stanley C.S.	Crook.
Sainty, J. E.	L.-Cpl.	R.E.	City of Norwich Sec. Sch.	Norwich City.
Sampson, R. W. K.	Lieut.	Devon	Bosoigo C.S.	Falmouth and Truro.
Seeviour, S. H.	Pte.	Hants	St. Bartholomew's Ch.S.	Winchester.
Shambrook, R. J.	Cpl.	R.A.M.C.	Millwall Cent. S.	East Lambeth.
Sheldrick, H. L.	2nd Lt.	R. Sussex	St. Mary's S.	Chatham, etc.
Sherry, L. R.	Cpl.	London	Cricklade Ch.S.	Swindon.
Simcock, F. W.	Sgt.		Bolton C.S.	Warrington.
Smith, A. E.	Pte.	R.A.M.C.	Cobham S., Surrey	Kingston and Surbiton.
Smith, S. W.	Sgt.	R.W. Surrey	Blackhall Mill C.S.	Vale of Derwent.
Snook, A. G.	Sigl.	Cheshire	26, Chesterfield St.	Barry.
Sockett, J. W.	Pte.	R.A.M.C.	Gower St. C.S.	Birmingham.
Spencer, A.	Sgt.	W. Yorks	Parish Ch.S.	Bradford.
Sperring, A. H.	Act. Sgt.	R.A.S.C.	Arundel St. C.S., Landport.	Portsmouth.
Stancliffe, W.	Pte.	W. Yorks	Mount Pleasant C.S.	Huddersfield.
Stanfield, T. W.	Lieut.	E. Yorks	Peases West C.S.	Crook.
Stanners, H.	2nd Lt.	R.Muns.Fslrs.	Featherstone Rd. C.S., Southall.	Brentford.
Stockley, P. H.	2nd Lt.	York & Lancs	Abbeydale C.S.	Sheffield.
Sturdey, O.	Cpl.	Welsh	Eleanor St. C.S.	Cardiff.
Sweeting, E.	Q.M.S.	R.A.M.C.	Crindan C.S.	Newport (Mon.).
Swithinbank, W.	L.-Cpl.	R.A.M.C.	Whitefield Rd. W.S.	Liverpool.
Tanner, O. B.	Cpl.	K. Shrops.L.I.	Abertysswg C.S., Cardiff.	Rhymney Valley.
Taylor, G. J.	C.S.M.	London	S. Hallsville C.S.	West Ham.
*Thomas, B.	Staff Sgt.	Field Amb.	Caergawr C.S.	Mountain Ash.
*Thómas, E. B.	Sgt.	Field Amb.	Carnetown C.S.	Mountain Ash.
Thomas, S.	Cpl.	Manchester	Castle Hill C.S.	Todmorden.
Tidswell, S.	B'dier	R.G.A.	Salterhebble C.S.	Halifax.
Tilson, J. H. (D.C.M.)	C.S.M.	Hants	Mawney Rd. C.S.	Romford, etc.
*Titley, W.	Sgt.	R.N.D.	Chillingham Rd. C.S.	Newcastle-on-Tyne.
Turner, A. T.	L.-Cpl.	O. & B.L.I.	Russell Rd. C.S.	West Ham.
Tweedie, D. S.	C.S.M.	Tyneside Scot.	Redby C.S.	Sunderland.
Vardy, W. H.	L.-Cpl.	Shrwd. For.	Broomhill C.S.	Mansfield Borough.
Varley, W.	Spr.	Div. Sig. Co.	St. Barnabas Ch.S.	York.
Vaughan, J. D.	Sgt.	R.E.	Marshfield C.S.	Bradford.
Walsh, E.	Pte.	R.A.M.C.	St. Bede's R.C.S.	South Shields.
Walsh, F.	Pte.	R.A.M.C.	St. Bede's R.C.S.	South Shields.
Ward, W. C. J.	Cpl.	R.G.A.	Squires Lane C.S.	Finchley.
Ward, W. P.	Sgt.	M.G.C.	Colmore Rd. C.S.	Birmingham.

MILITARY HONOURS

Name.	Rank.	Regiment.	School.	Association.
MILITARY MEDAL—*cont.*				
Watson, H.	Sgt.	W. Lancs. Fld. Ambulance.	Aigburth N.S.	Liverpool.
Watson, R.	L.-Cpl.	R.A.M.C.	St. Paul's Ch.S.	Cambridge Borough.
Weaver, A. A.	Sgt.	R.A.M.C.	Lonsdale Rd. C.S.	Barnes and Mortlake.
Wedgwood, J.	Pte.	Border	Bookwell C.S.	Cumberland (W.).
Whittles, W.	Sgt.	R.A.M.C.	Rookery Rd. C.S.	Birmingham.
Williams, H. T.	Sgt.	R.G.A.	St. Mary's Ch.S.	Dover.
Winchester, C. F.	Gnr.	R.F.A.	Upland C.S., Bexley Heath.	Dartford.
Windmill, J. W.	C.S.M.	R. Warwick	Pensnett Ch.S., Dudley.	Brierley Hill.
Woodcock, T.	Pte.	H.A.C.	Parish Ch.S.	Doncaster.
Youngs, A. L.	Pte.	R.A.M.C.	Bruce Grove C.S.	Tottenham, etc.
MERITORIOUS SERVICE MEDAL.				
Bakewell, G.	Cpl.	R.F.A.	Newhall C.S.	Burton-on-Trent.
Balcombe, H. R.	R.S.M.	R.G.A.	Hampden Park C.S.	Eastbourne.
Beach, W. W.	Q.M.S.	Som. R.H.A.	Walton Ch.S.	Somerset (E.C.).
Bear, H. C. (D.C.M.)	C.S.M.	Middlesex	Bandon Hill C.S.	Epsom.
Bell, M. C.	C.Q.M.S.	York & Lancs	Sacriston C.S.	Durham.
Boyce, F. J. (M.M.)	C.Q.M.S.	W. Yorks	Park C.S.	Sheffield.
Brook, H.	Cpl.	R.A.M.C.	Attercliffe Ch.S.	Sheffield.
Burkett, G. P. W.	S.M.	R.A.	"Peckham Park" L.C.C.S.	East Lambeth.
Charlton, W. R.	Sgt.	R.A.F.	Christ Church C.S.	Tynemouth.
Clarke, A. E.	2nd Lt.	R.G.A.	Christ Church Rd.S.	Ilford.
Claxton, E.	Cpl.	R.A.F.	Earith C.S.	Huntingdonshire.
Clough, T. (C. de G., Italy).	Sgt.	A. & S. Hdrs.	King St. C.S.	Spennymoor.
Collett, H. F.	Sgt.	R.A.S.C.	Kirkdale Rd. C.S.	Leyton.
Dalby, J.	Cpl.	R.A.M.C.	West Slaithwaite C.S.	Huddersfield.
Denney, A. W.	Sgt.	R.A.M.C.	Kensington Av. C.S.	East Ham.
Dennis, C. C.	Sgt.	R. Warwicks	National S.	Ludlow.
Dow, F. W.	C.Q.M.S.	R. Warwick	Leigh Rd. C.S.	Birmingham.
Duckworth, E. E.	Staff Sgt.	R. Marines	Wolfenden St. C.S.	Bolton Borough.
Essam, W.	C.S.M.	Q.W.R.	Westgate C.S.	Warwick.
Evans, E.	Q.M.S.	R.A.M.C.	Rectory Park C.S.	Sunderland.
Everitt, W. A.	Q.M.S.Inst.	Arm.Gym.Stf.	Boulton Rd. C.S.	Birmingham.
Farnish, J.	Sgt.	W. Riding	Holmfirth C.S.	Bradford.
Foster, D.	S.M.	R.F.A.	Church St. S.	West Lambeth.
Golland, A. R.	C.Q.M.S.	Gym. Staff	Borough Rd. C.S.	Darlington.
Goodland, P. H. E.	Sgt.	Coldstm.Gds.	All Saints N.S., Walworth.	East Lambeth.
Goodwin, J. T.	Sgt.	R.A.M.C.	Shildon, C.S.	Bishop Auckland.
Grattridge, A. W.	Cpl.	R.A.M.C.	Green Lane C.S.	Leicester.
Hares, J.	Sgt.	R.E.	Radnor Rd. C.S.	Cardiff.
Haynes, J. W.	Pte.	R. Marines (Submarine Miners).	Christ Ch.S.	Tynemouth.
Hewitt, R. G.	Sgt.	R.E.	Hill Lane H.E.S.	Huddersfield.
Hooper, J. W.	Sgt.	R. Warwick	Alexis St. L.C.C.S.	Southwark.
Hudson, F. M.	S.M.	R.A.M.C.	Westoe Sen. S.	South Shields.
Hurrell, H. R. W.	S.M.	R.A.O.C.	Bedfont Parish S.	Staines.
Iliffe, J.	Sgt.	Middlesex	North Harringay C.S.	Hornsey.
Jenkinson, S. R.	Pte.	Border	Irish St. C.S.	Whitehaven.
Kilburn, P.	Pte.	R.A.M.C.	Adwick Rd. C.S.	Mexborough.
Kirtley, R. W.	Cpl.	R.A.M.C.	Cone St. C.S.	South Shields.
Lloyd, E. A.	Q.M.S.	R.W.F.	Battersea Park Rd. L.C.C.S.	West Lambeth.
Lloyd, W. H.	L.-Cpl.	O. & B.L.I.	High St. C.S., Wealdstone.	Harrow.
Longbottom, E.	Sgt.	R.A.M.C.	Camden St. C.S.	Birmingham.
Marples, H.	C.S.M.	K.O.Y.L.I.	Park C.S.	Sheffield.

N.U.T. WAR RECORD

Name.	Rank.	Regiment.	School.	Association.
\multicolumn{5}{c}{MERITORIOUS SERVICE MEDAL—*cont.*}				

Name.	Rank.	Regiment.	School.	Association.
Martin, A. F.	Sgt.	R.W. Surrey	Lincoln Rd. C.S.	Peterborough.
Martin, S.	Q.M.S.	Field Ambl.	Highweek C.S.	Teign and Dart.
Morris, W.	Lieut.	R.E.	"Palmer" Trade S.	Reading.
Murch, T. A.	R.Q.M.S.	London	St. Agnes' N.S.	East Lambeth.
Murray, R.	S.-S.M.	R.A.S.C.	St. John's Ch.S.	Bootle.
Oliphant, L.	R.Q.M.S.	D.L.I.	Church S.	Maryport.
Oliver, M. F.	Act. Sgt.	Emplmt. Coy.	South Church C.S.	Bishop Auckland.
Parkinson, G. H.	Sgt.	R.F.A.	Linacre C.S.	Bootle.
Reid, J.	Cpl.	R.E.	Lepton C.S.	Huddersfield.
Rodwell, E.	C.Q.M.S.	London	"The Latchmere" L.C.C.S.	West Lambeth.
Slater, T.	Sgt.	N.F.	Seaton Delaval C.S.	Northumberland (E.).
Sleath, C. G.	Pte.	R. Warwick	Higher Grade C.S.	Wolverhampton.
Smith, F.	Sgt.	W. Riding	Siddal C.S.	Halifax.
Smith, H.	Q.M.S.	R.W.F.	Goodall Rd. C.S.	Leyton.
Stackhouse, P. C.	C.S.M.Inst	Arm.Gym.Stf.	Benson Rd. C.S.	Birmingham.
Steele, A.	Colr. Sgt.	D.L.I.	St. Stephens C.S.	South Shields.
Straw, J. W. (Medaille d'Honneur)	Sgt.	R.A.M.C.	Pelton Ch.S.	Chester-le-Street.
Sumner, R.	C.Q.M.S.	R.A.S.C.	St. Mary's N.S.	Liverpool.
Turner, J.	C.Q.M.S.	Manchester	St. Wilfred's Ch.S.	Manchester.
Viner, H.	Pte.	R.A.S.C.	St. Mary's Ch.S.	Liverpool.
White, H. C.	Sgt.	R.A.M.C.	St. Paul's N.S.	Hastings.
Wilson, D.	W.O.	R.A.S.C.	Barnes C.S.	Sunderland.
Wilson, J.	Staff Sgt.	R.A.S.C.	St. Hilda's N.S.	South Shields.

ROYAL RED CROSS.

Name.	Rank.	Regiment.	School.	Association.
Bishop, Miss K.	Nursing Sister.	St. John Ambl.	Bedlington Colliery C.S.	Northumberland (E.).
Woods, Mrs. R.	Supt.	V.A.D. Hosp.	Frant Ch.S.	Heathfield.

CROIX DE GUERRE.

Name.	Rank.	Regiment.	School.	Association.
Allen, E. (with Palm, France) (D.C.M.).	2nd Lt.	Hants	Bordon C.S.	Andover.
Baker, G. A. (Belgium) (Chev. de la Couronne)	2nd Lt.	R.G.A.	Thrybergh C.S.	Rotherham.
Bell, H. G. (with Palm, France) (M.C.).	Major	R.G.A.	Omega St. C.S.	Portsmouth.
Benson, C. G. (France)	Cpl.	R.G.A.	Southwick Cent.S.	Sunderland.
Burrows, H. R. (with Palm, France). (M.C.).	Capt.	W. Yorks	Hornsea C.S.	Hull.
Chaytor, R. G. (Belgium) (M.M. and Order of Leopold II.).	Cpl.	R.A.M.C.	Medomsley C.S.	Vale of Derwent.
Clough, T. (Italy) (M.S.M.).	Sgt.	A. & S. Hdrs.	King St. C.S.	Spennymoor.
Ellwood, A. (Belgium)	Cpl.	R.G.A.	Varna St. C.S.	Manchester.
Farrer, W. (France) (M.M.).	B'dier.	R.F.A.	Sacriston C.S.	Durham.
Goodman, S. F. (with Palm, France).	2nd Lt.	R.F.A.	Somerville C.S.	Wallasey.
Hamby, A. (Belgium)	2nd Lt.	R.F.A.	Greenmoor Prov.S., Wortley, Sheffield.	Penistone.
Jackson, R. G. (Belgium).	Sgt.	R.A.M.C.	Childs Hill C.S.	Hendon.
Morgan, A. L. (Belgium)	Sgt.	R.W.F.	Pontrhondda C.S.	Rhondda.
Palmer, F. (Belgium)	B'dier	R.G.A.	Winterbourne Rd. C.S.	Croydon.
Parke, J. (France) (D.F.C.)	Lieut.	D.L.I.	East Walker C.S.	Newcastle-on-Tyne.
Parkes, C. H. (Belgium)	Q.M.S.	R.A.M.C.	Christ Ch.S.	Bradford.
Perkins, W. (France)	Sgt.	R.G.A.	Avenue Rd. C.S.	Leicester.

MILITARY HONOURS

Name.	Rank.	Regiment.	School.	Association.
CROIX DE GUERRE—*cont.*				
Rowlands, H. (with Palm, France) (D.S.O.) (M.C. with Bar).	Capt.	London	Llaniestyn C.S.	Carnarvon (S.).
Smart, J. E. (Belgium) (M.C.).	Capt.	Manchester	Manchester Univ.	Makerfield.
Smith, F. C. (Belgium)	Sgt.	R.A.M.C.	Daubeney Rd. L.C.C.S.	Hackney.
Stott, S. (France)	Cpl.	R.A.M.C.	Marsden N.S.	Huddersfield.
Thomas, T. (Italy) (M.C.)	Lieut.	R.G.A.	Town C.S.	Aberdare.
Thomas, W. I. (France) (D.C.M.)	L.-Cpl.	M.G.C.	Cwmaman C.S.	Aberdare.
Vassiere, H. J. (with Palm, France).	2nd Lt.	Tank Corps	Queens Rd. C.S.	Walthamstow.
FOREIGN AWARDS (excluding the Croix de Guerre).				
ORDER D'AVEZ (PORTUGAL).				
Arrowsmith, C. F. (M.C.)	Lieut.	King's L'pool	St. Francis Xavier's College.	Liverpool.
CHEVALIER DE LA COURONNE (BELGIUM).				
Baker, G. A. (C. de G., Belgium).	2nd Lt.	R.G.A.	Thrybergh C.S.	Rotherham.
SERBIAN MEDAL.				
Appleton, H.	Capt.	Lancs. Fuslrs.	Edmondsley C.S.	Chester-le-Street.
Bates, T. C.	Sgt.	R.A.S.C.	Lister Drive C.S.	Liverpool.
Webb, C.	Capt.	Dorset	Newbury C.S.	Newbury.
ORDER OF LEOPOLD II (BELGIUM).				
Chaytor, R. G. (M.M. and C. de G., Belgium.)	Cpl.	R.A.M.C.	Medomsley C.S.	Vale of Derwent.
ITALIAN MEDAL.				
Edgar, W. G. (M.M.)	Lieut.	N.F.	Dean Rd. C.S.	South Shields.
Milner, F.	Q.M.S.	R.A.M.C.	St. George-the-Martyr's N.S.	Bolton Borough.
MÉDAILLE MILITAIRE (FRANCE).				
Belshaw, C. H.	C.S.M.	O. & B.L.I.	National S.	Atherton, etc.
Drury, S. C. (D.C.M.)	C.S.M.	R.E.	Old Oak Estate C.S.	Barnes and Mortlake.
Gempton, A. G.	Sgt.	Devon	Wolborough N.S.	Teign and Dart.
Phillips, A. J. (D.C.M.)	2nd Lt.	R.A.S.C.	Aristotle Rd. Central C.S.	West Lambeth.
ORDER OF ST. ANNE (RUSSIA).				
Maxey, H. R.	Capt.	Tyneside Scot.	Princess Louise C.S.	Blyth.
ORDER OF ST. GEORGE (RUSSIA).				
Carr, J. V. (D.C.M.)	C.S.M.	King's L'pool	St. Bede's R.C.S.	Widnes.
Sanderson, C. (D.S.O.)	Lieut.	Gordon Hrs.	North Rd. C.S.	Spennymoor.

N.U.T. WAR RECORD

Name.	Rank.	Regiment.	School.	Association.
ORDER OF REDEEMER (GREECE).				
Dalziel, J. (M.C.)	Lieut.	R.G.A.	Montreal Ch.S., Cleator Moor.	Cumberland (W.).
MÉDAILLE D'HONNEUR.				
Straw, J. W. (M.S.M.)	Sgt.	R.A.M.C.	Pelton Ch.S.	Chester-le-Street.
ORDER OF ST. VLADIMIR (RUSSIA) WITH CROSSED SWORDS AND BOW.				
Church, A. G. (D.S.O.) (M.C.).	Major	R.G.A.	Morpeth St. Cent. S.	London (E.).
Holder, A. E.	Capt.	R.A.S.C.	Somerville Rd. C.S.	Birmingham.
CHEVALIER OF THE ORDER OF THE CROWN OF ROUMANIA.				
Taylor, H. G.	Capt.	R.N.D. Lab. Corps.	Ford C.S.	Plymouth.
RECONNAISANCE FRANCAISE.				
Ashton, Miss E. M.	Cook	V.A.D., Scottish Hospital France.	Laygate Lane C.S.	South Shields.
ORDER OF THE NILE (EGYPT).				
Powell, A. T.	Lt.-Col.	R.F.A.	Grammar School	Nantwich.

Teachers who joined the Forces.

The following list contains the names of all members of the National Union of Teachers who joined his Majesty's Forces (Army or Navy), including women members who acted as nurses, together with their Local Associations. The names are arranged alphabetically, and an asterisk distinguishes those who were honoured for gallant services, while the names of those teachers who were killed or who died as a result of war conditions appear in heavy type. The list does not, of course, contain the names of all primary school teachers who joined the Forces. There were, in addition, non-members of the Union, certificated and uncertificated teachers, student teachers and others who enlisted in one or other of the above classes, bringing the total up to about 23,000.

More detailed information including rank, regiment and school of those teacher members of the Union who were killed or who died in the war, and similar particulars respecting teachers honoured for gallant services appear on pages 43 to 77 and pages 79 to 92 respectively.

NOTES.

(1) **The names of those teachers who were killed or who died as a result of war conditions appear in this type.**

(2) Where an asterisk (*) is placed against a name, this denotes that the teacher has been honoured for gallant services.

NAME.	ASSOCIATION.	NAME.	ASSOCIATION.
Aarons, W. P.	East Ham.	Abigail, —.	Norwich City.
*Abba, A. C.	Hull.	Ablett, H.	Hull.
Abba, C. L.	Hull.	Ablitt, W. V.	Ipswich.
Abba, J. K.	Penrith.	**Abraham, O. R.**	Windermere.
Abbott, —.	Southend-on-Sea.	Abrahams, —.	Leyton.
Abbott, B.	Southwark.	Abrahams, S.	Liverpool.
Abbott, S.	West Ham.	Abram, Mrs.	Carlisle.
Abbott, W. H.	Oundle.	Abrams, C.	Leeds.
Abel, F.	Tottenham, etc.	Abrams, F. S.	Leeds.
Abell, R. A.	Nottingham.	Abrams, W.	Canterbury.
Abell, E. I.	Lincoln.	Acaster, H.	Nelson, Colne, etc.
Abelson, I.	Finsbury, etc.	Ackerley, G. H.	Crewe.

N.U.T. WAR RECORD

Name.	Association.
Ackland, A. T.	Tottenham, etc.
Ackroyd, J. E.	Mexborough.
Ackroyd, R. G.	Shipley.
Acton, P.	Manchester.
Acton, W. C.	Gillingham.
Acutt, B. L. A.	Lewisham.
Adam, J. G. S.	Finsbury, etc.
Adams, A. G.	Abercarn.
Adams, A. S.	London (W.).
Adams, B. C.	East Ham.
Adams, C.	Finsbury, etc.
Adams, C.	West Wilts.
Adams, D.	Plymouth.
Adams, D. S.	Portsmouth.
Adams, E. C.	Birmingham.
Adams, E. C.	Reading.
Adams, E. F.	West Lambeth.
Adams, E. P.	Harrow.
Adams, H.	Horsham.
Adams, H. A.	Halstead.
Adams, J. F.	Hull.
Adams, J. S.	Epsom and Sutton.
Adams, J. T.	Shrewsbury.
Adams, P.	Hackney.
Adams, P. F.	Gillingham.
Adams, R. J.	Bristol.
Adams, S.	Rowley Regis.
Adams, S.	Walthamstow.
Adams, T. R.	Cheltenham.
Adams, W. J.	Birmingham.
Adamson, A.	Bury.
*Adamson, A. J.	Nottingham.
Adamson, C. W.	Castleford, etc.
Adamson (Miss) E.	Willesden.
Adamson, R. W.	South Shields.
Adderley, A.	Gravesend, etc.
Adderley, A.	Romford, etc.
Addinall, C. R.	Dewsbury and Batley.
Addis, A. J.	Hartlepools.
Addison, F.	Barrow.
Addison, F.	West Lambeth.
Addy, A. R.	Sheffield.
Addyman, F. R.	Plymouth.
Adey, F. C.	Portsmouth.
Adkins, F. J.	Sheffield.
*Adkins, G. W.	West Ham.
Adkins, T. F.	West Lambeth.
Adkins, W.	Tottenham, etc.
Adlam, G.	East Ham.
Adlam, L. W.	West Ham.
*Adlam, T. E.	Basingstoke.
*Adshead, H. J.	Dewsbury, etc.
Agar, —.	Leicester.
Ager, B. N.	Norfolk (W.).
Ager, J. A.	Weald of Kent.
Agerskow, S. G.	Hull.
Agland, E.	Dorset (S.).
Aiano, H.	Isle of Thanet.
Ainscough, Miss	Preston District.
Ainsworth, J. S.	Folkestone.
Aireton, F. A.	Finsbury, etc.
Airey, W. C.	Chester-le-Street.
Akriss, G. F.	Croydon.
Aisbett, J.	Gateshead.
Aitchison, —.	Reading.
Aitchison, G. L.	London (W.).
Aitchison, W.	West Stanley.
Aitkin, A.	Wallasey.
Akester, A.	Hull.
Albert, C. H.	Kidderminster.
Albon, A. J.	Hendon.
*Albon, H.	Croydon.
Alcock, C. A.	Lowestoft.
Alcock, R.	Sheffield.
Alcott, E. A.	Coventry.
Alder, P. W.	Birmingham.
Aldersley, E. P.	Clitheroe.
Alderson, J.	Hartlepools.
Alderson, J. W.	Sheffield.
Alderson, S. E.	Sunderland.
Alderson, T. E.	Carlisle.
Alderthay, B.	Smethwick.
Alderton G. H.	Harrow.
Alderton, W. G.	St. Albans.
Aldred, H.	Cardiff.
Aldred, H.	Ilkeston.
Aldrich, H. C.	Radnor.
Alen, L. W.	Colchester, etc.
Alexander, A. C.	Castleford, etc.
Alexander, C. W.	Stourbridge.
Alexander, F.	Enfield.
Alexander, J.	Hull.
Alexander, W. B.	Norfolk (S.).
Alford, E. N.	Hendon.
Alford, R. A.	Uxbridge.
Algate, E. W.	Plymouth.
Alger, G.	Leyton.
Allan, A. J.	West Lambeth.
Allan, G. A.	Manchester.
Allan, S.	Birmingham.
Allanson, W.	Darwen.
Allard, E. G.	Woolwich.
Allard, G. N.	Sunderland.
Allason, J. G.	Tottenham, etc.
Allaway, A. E.	Isle of Thanet.
Allchurch, S. A.	Birmingham.
Allcoat, E. J.	Maidstone.
Allcock, F.	Manchester.
Allcock, S.	Matlock, etc.
Allcott, A.	Somerset (S.E.).
Allden, H. A.	Hackney.
Allen, Miss	Leyton.
Allen, A.	Tottenham, etc.
Allen, A.	Waterloo-with-Seaforth.
Allen, A. F.	Deptford and Greenwich.
Allen, A. F.	Mansfield.
Allen, B.	Walsall.
Allen, C.	Nottingham.
Allen, C.	South Shields.
*Allen, C. A.	Folkestone.
*Allen, E.	Andover.
Allen, E.	Burnley.
Allen, E. H.	Walthamstow.
Allen, E. J. C.	Portsmouth.
Allen, F.	Burnley.
Allen, F.	Sheffield.
Allen, F.	Sheffield.
Allen, F.	Vale of Derwent.
Allen, F. W.	Castleford, etc.
Allen, F. W.	Kingston and Surbiton.
Allen, G.	Portsmouth.
Allen, G. F.	Finsbury, etc.
Allen, H.	Northampton.
Allen, H. J.	Leeds.
Allen, I.	Deptford and Greenwich.
Allen, J.	Wellingborough.
Allen, J. D.	East Lambeth.
Allen, J. G.	Jersey.
Allen, J. H.	Birmingham.
Allen, R.	Ipswich.

TEACHERS WHO JOINED THE FORCES

Name.	Association.	Name.	Association.
Allen, R. H.	Manchester.	Andrews, N. J.	Birmingham.
Allen, R. S.	Kingston and Surbiton.	Andrews, S. J.	Liverpool.
Allen, S. H.	West Bromwich.	Andrews, S. T.	London (E.).
Allen, T.	Leeds.	Andrews, W. A.	Leeds.
Allen, T. H.	Cardiff.	Andrews, W. H.	West Ham.
Allen, W. C.	Manchester.	Andrews-Bligh,L.P.	Southgate.
Allen, W. H. E.	Finsbury, etc.	*Angell, A. A.	Westminster.
Allenby, S.	Finsbury, etc.	Angell, C. B.	Easington.
Allerton, C. B.	Peterborough.	Angell, C. W.	Birmingham.
Allford, W.	Somerset (S.E.).	Angold, H.	Hull.
Allgrove, A. A.	Richmond (Surrey).	Angus, H. F.	Newcastle-on-Tyne.
Allison, J. E.	Liverpool.	Angwin, A.	Cornwall (W.).
Allison, R. G.	Manchester.	Ann, E. D.	Gloucester.
Allman, F. J.	West Lambeth.	Annear, J.	Harwich.
Allott, C. H.	Birkenhead.	**Anneley, E. G.**	Sheffield.
Allpress, A.	East Lambeth.	Annett, E. C.	Doncaster.
Allsop(Miss),E. A.	Bradford.	Anniss, F.	London (W.).
Allsop, F. J.	Norfolk (W.).	Ansell, A. E.	Birmingham.
Allsop, J. H.	Leek.	Ansell, C. G.	Erith.
Almond, J. W.	Salford.	Ansell, F.	Coventry.
Alsop, W. P.	Pontypool.	Anson, W. C. F.	London (W.).
Alston, E. J.	Birmingham.	Anstead, F.	London (N.W.).
Althouse, P.	London (W.).	Anstey, E. J.	Wimbledon.
Alvey, F. H.	West Lambeth.	Anstis, C.	Downham.
Alway, W.	Plymouth.	Anstis, H. J.	Abertillery.
Ambler, F.	Barnsley.	Anstis, P.	Doncaster.
Ambler, G. O.	Edmonton.	Anthony, C.	Hackney.
*Ambrose, W.	Litherland, etc.	Anthony, C. A.	London (W.).
*Ames, G.	East Lambeth.	Anthony, D.	Birmingham.
Amess, N. S.	Woolwich.	Anthony, W. T.	Khondda, etc.
Amis, N. P.	Wolverhampton.	Applebee, F. J.	Liverpool.
Amos, A. D.	Leicester.	Appleby, R.	Bishop Auckland.
Amos, F. E.	Evesham.	**Appleby, R. S.**	York.
Amos, J.	West Ham.	Appleby, S. E.	Grantham.
Amos, L.	Erewash Valley.	Appleby, T.	Blyth.
Amos, T.	Carlisle.	Appleby, W. L.	Grantham.
Amos, T. D.	Warrington.	Appleby, W. P.	London (W.).
Amos, V. A.	Chippenham.	Appleford H. M.	West Lambeth.
Amplett, E.	Hackney.	Appleford, J.	West Ham.
Amstell, S.	London (E.).	Appleton, G.	Stockton.
Anderson, A.	Swindon.	*Appleton, H.	Chester-le-Street.
Anderson, G. K.	Ogmore, etc.	Appleton, H. N.	Sunderland.
*Anderson, H. R.	Waterloo-with-Seaforth.	Appleton, J. B.	Maldon, etc.
Anderson, J.	West Stanley.	Appleton, J. W.	Makerfield.
Anderson, J. J.	Bournemouth.	Appleton, R.	Lewisham.
Anderson, J. T.	Spennymoor.	Appleyard, H.	Sheffield.
Anderson, R.	East Lambeth.	Appleyard, J.H.R.	Halifax.
Anderson, R.	Newcastle-on-Tyne.	Appleyard, W. E.	Goole.
Anderson, T.	Wallsend.	Applin, R.	Southampton.
Anderson, W.	Lincoln.	**Apthorpe, H. W.**	Ampthill, etc.
Anderson, W. J.	Surrey (N.W.).	Arber, F. C.	Kettering.
Anderson, W. N.	Newcastle-on-Tyne.	Arch, A.	Worcester City.
Anderton, J. D.	Fleetwood.	Archard, V. S.	Winchester.
Anderton, T.	St Helens.	Archbold, J. E.	Northumberland (E.).
Anderton, W. N.	Makerfield.	*Archdeacon, J.	London (E.).
Andrew, J.	Barry.	Archer, C.	Walsall.
Andrew, J. E.	Castleford, etc.	Archer, G. S.	West Ham.
*Andrew, R. B.	Richmond (Surrey).	Archer, H. J.	Norwich.
Andrews, A. A.	Hornsey.	Archer, J. H.	Sheffield.
Andrews, A.	Exeter District.	Archer, W.	Grantham.
Andrews, A. J.	Colchester, etc.	Arden, J. E.	Makerfield.
Andrews, C. H.	Liverpool.	Ardern, G. P.	Flint County.
Andrews, E. G.	Reading.	Ardley, J.	Durham.
Andrews, F.	Gillingham (Kent).	Arkless, F. C.	Stockton-on-Tees.
Andrews, G. L.	Glamorgan (W.).	Arkwright, H.	London (E.).
Andrews, H.	Hackney.	Armett, H. T.	East Lambeth.
Andrews, H.	Willesden.	Armistead, F. E.	Lancaster.
Andrews, H. G.	Chatham, etc.	Armitage, D. W.	Richmond (Surrey).
Andrews, J. W.	Birkenhead.	Armitage, F.	Huddersfield.

N.U.T. WAR RECORD

Name.	Association.
Armitage, J. L.	Stratford.
Armitage, L.	Huddersfield.
Armitstead, J.	West Lambeth.
Armour, G. C.	Liverpool.
Armstrong, A.	East Lambeth.
Armstrong, A. J. C.	Lichfield.
Armstrong, E. S.	Newcastle-on-Tyne.
*Armstrong, F.	Sunderland.
Armstrong, H.H.R.	London (N.W.).
Armstrong, J.	Durham.
Armstrong, J. K.	Hereford.
Armstrong, J. W.	South Shields.
Armstrong, P.	Workington.
Armstrong, R.	Cheltenham.
Armstrong, R.	West Stanley.
Armstrong, S. J.	Manchester.
Armytage, J.	Rotherham.
Arnall, J. A. E.	Plymouth.
Arnall, S. J.	Preston Borough.
Arnell, J.	Runcorn.
Arnett, M. G.	Oxford.
Arnett, W.	Spennymoor.
Arnfield, W.	Stockport.
Arnison, J. H.	Sunderland.
Arnold, —.	Bala.
Arnold, A. J.	Cambridgeshire.
Arnold, C. R.	Brentford.
Arnold, E. H.	Ripon.
Arnold, F. H.	Keighley.
Arnold, H.	Belper and Crich.
Arnold, H.	West Lambeth.
Arnold, J.	Leeds.
Arnold, T. H.	Sunderland.
Arnold, W. R.	Tottenham, etc.
Arrowsmith, —.	Stafford.
*Arrowsmith, C. F.	Liverpool.
Arrowsmith, E.	Staffs. (N.).
Arthrell, H. J.	Croydon.
Arthur, H. F. R.	Bournemouth.
Arthur, J. F.	Bristol.
Arthur, S. B.	Bournemouth.
Arthur, S. E.	Kingsbridge.
Arthurson, E.	Runcorn.
Ascroft, A. G.	Liverpool.
Ash, C. L.	Wellingborough.
Ash, E. W.	Middlesbrough.
Ash, F.	Eastbourne.
Ash, J.	Yoxford.
Ash, L.	East Lambeth.
Ash, W.	Willenhall.
Ash, W. B.	Northumberland (S.).
Ashbery, E. H.	Andover.
Ashby, T. P.	Leicester.
Ashby, W. J.	Ashford.
Ashdown, E. G.	Barnes and Mortlake.
Ashdown, H.	Lewisham.
Ashdown, V. W. F.	Tonbridge.
Ashenden, H. E.	Gravesend.
Ashley, A. P.	Durham.
Ashley, E.	Manchester.
Ashley, E. W.	Aylesbury.
Ashley, F.	Widnes.
Ashley, J.	Rhondda, etc.
Ashley, W.	Manchester.
Ashman, E. T.	Southgate.
Ashmore, J.	Rock and Tenbury.
Ashmore, J. W.	Derbyshire (E.).
Ashplant, W.	Liverpool.
Ashton, —.	Cambridge Borough.

Name.	Association.
Ashton, A. E.	Dorset (S.).
*Ashton (Miss), E.M.	South Shields.
Ashton, D. P. H.	Cardiganshire (N.).
Ashton, F.	Liverpool.
Ashton, H.	Barnsley.
Ashton, I. J.	Liverpool.
Ashton, J.	Bolton District.
Ashton, J. H.	Farnworth.
Ashton, J. W.	Hartlepools.
Ashton, R.	Epsom, etc.
Ashton, R.	Rhondda.
Ashton, T. J.	Manchester.
Ashton, W.	Blackburn.
Ashton, W. T.	Shrewsbury.
Ashwell, F.	Bedford.
Ashworth, A. E.	West Lambeth.
Ashworth, E. L.	Halifax.
Ashworth, F.	Nelson, Colne, etc.
Ashworth, H.	Pendle Forest.
Ashworth, H.W.W.	Gloucester (N.).
Ashworth, J. F.	Rochdale.
Ashworth, J. F.	Chester-le-Street.
Ashworth, J. W.	West Lambeth.
Ashworth, N.	Leeds.
Askew, G.	Erewash Valley, etc.
Askew, G. C.	Sunderland.
Askew, H. C.	Liverpool.
Askew, H. C.	Spennymoor.
Aspden, J. A.	Tottington, etc.
Aspin, J. H.	Blackburn.
Aspin, T	Liverpool.
Aspinall, A.	Makerfield.
*Aspinall, J.	Leigh.
Aspinall, R.	Staffs. (N.).
Aspinall, T.	Atherton, etc.
Aspinwall, J.	Hebburn.
Aspinwall, W.	Waterloo-with-Seaforth.
Astle, L.	Wolverhampton.
*Aston, A. A.	Edmonton.
Aston, J. B.	Peterborough.
Atack, W. B.	Manchester.
Atchison, F.	Sunderland.
Atha, I.	Doncaster.
Atherfold, H. C.	Eastbourne.
Atherton, H.	Wirral.
Atherton, P.	Wirral.
Athey, J. W.	Halifax.
Atkin, A. F.	Liverpool.
Atkin, J.	Swadlincote.
Atkins, F. H.	Doncaster.
Atkins, F. J.	Woolwich.
Atkins, F. W.	Leicester.
Atkins, G. L.	Grantham.
Atkins, M. H.	Brentford.
Atkins, S.	Halifax.
Atkins, W. T.	Woolwich.
Atkinson, Mrs.	Birmingham.
Atkinson, A.	Northumberland (E.).
Atkinson, A. C.	Brighton, etc.
Atkinson, A. W.	London (E.).
Atkinson, F.	Blackburn.
Atkinson, F.	Leeds.
Atkinson, G.	Gateshead.
Atkinson, G. R.	Hull.
Atkinson, H.	Manchester.
Atkinson, H.	Manchester.
Atkinson, J. G.	Newark.
Atkinson, J. H.	Bishop Auckland.
Atkinson, J. H.	East Lambeth.

TEACHERS WHO JOINED THE FORCES

Name.	Association.
Atkinson, J. M.	Halifax.
Atkinson, J. W.	North Cleveland.
Atkinson, J. W.	Whitehaven.
Atkinson, M.	Hexham.
Atkinson, T.	Vale of Derwent.
Atkinson, T.	Sheffield.
Atkinson, V. H.	York.
Atkinson, W. E.	Preston Borough.
Atkinson, W. E.	Retford.
Atlay, J. K.	Chippenham.
Atlay, T.	Sunderland.
Attewell, C. J.	Nottingham.
*Attewell, O. P.	Newbury.
Attewell, T.	Newcastle-on-Tyne.
Attfield, G. W.	Rhondda, etc.
Atton, H.	East Ham.
Attrill, S. C.	Easington.
Attwell, P.	Willesden.
Attwood, H.	Hackney.
Attwooll, H.	Southwark.
Atwell, C.	Reading.
Atwill, H. F.	West Lambeth.
Aubrey, F. E.	West Lambeth.
Audus, A. R.	London (N.W.).
Auger, P. J.	Liverpool.
August, C. G. W.	London (E.).
Austin, A.	Cambridgeshire.
Austin, A. H.	St. Helens.
Austin, A. H.	Southport.
Austin, A. J.	Isle of Wight.
Austin, C. F.	London (N.W.).
Austin, G. H.	Hull.
Austin, H. R.	Croydon.
Austin, J.	Liverpool.
Austin, J. E.	Wolverhampton.
Austin, T. H.	Birkenhead.
Auty, A. W.	Croydon.
Auty, E.	Dewsbury, etc.
Avery, F.	London (N.W.).
Avery, H.	Aylesbury.
Avery, H.	Derby.
Avery, H. W.	Dorset (E.).
Axford, W. H.	Northampton.
Axon, W. T.	Northumberland (E.).
Axtell, A. J.	Blaydon.
Ayling, C. A.	Tottenham, etc.
Ayling, R. H.	East Lambeth.
Ayles, G.	Hackney.
Aylwin, R. H.	Croydon.
Aynsley, G.	Sunderland.
Ayre, W.	Spennymoor.
Ayres, D.	East Lambeth.
Ayres, D.	West Lambeth.
Ayres, H. B.	Southwark.
Babbage, J. O.	Croydon.
Baber, G.	West Ham.
Baber, W. A.	East Ham.
Backhouse, —.	Castleford, etc.
*Backhouse, G. E.	Weardale.
Backhouse, J. B.	Gainsborough.
Bacon, —.	Derby.
Bacon, A. C.	Birmingham.
Bacon, A. D.	Petworth, etc.
Bacon, J. H.	North Cleveland.
Bacon, L.	Leeds.
Bacon, P.	Sale.
Badcock, E.	Cornwall (W.).
Baddeley, G. H.	Staffordshire (N.).
Badman, C. J.	Lewisham.

Name.	Association.
Badman, L. D.	London (N.W.).
Bagg, G.	Willesden.
Baggallay, W. R.	East Lambeth.
Bagge, W. J.	Great Yarmouth.
Baggott, G. W.	Crook.
Baggott, J. J.	Rhondda, etc.
Baggs, —.	Bodmin.
Baggs, F. H.	West Lambeth.
Bagley, —.	Shrewsbury.
Bagley, A. A.	Hornsey.
Bagley, B. W.	Durham (N.E.).
Bagley, R.	Stratford-on-Avon.
Bagley, T. E.	Tottenham, etc.
Bagnall, A. T.	Liverpool.
Bagnall, E. C.	Birmingham.
Bagnall, H.	Wellingborough.
Bagnall, J. H.	Manchester.
Bagnall, T.	Castleford, etc.
Bagnell, R. E.	Northwich.
Bagshaw, G.	Bournemouth.
Bailes, H.	Spennymoor.
Bailey, —.	Cannock.
Bailey, A. E.	Birmingham.
Bailey, A. E.	Windsor.
Bailey, A. E.	Shropshire (E.).
Bailey, B.	Kiveton Park.
*Bailey, C.	Great Yarmouth.
Bailey, (Miss) D.	Manchester.
Bailey, F.	Sheffield.
Bailey, F.	Woolwich.
Bailey, F. W.	Hackney.
Bailey, F. W.	Southend-on-Sea.
Bailey, H.	Hull.
Bailey, H. H.	Sheffield.
Bailey, H. M.	Skipton.
Bailey, J. S.	East Lambeth.
Bailey, R. N.	Chippenham.
Bailey, T.	Bingley.
Bailie, J.	Ormskirk.
Bain, G.	Bristol.
Bainbridge, R.	Hull.
Baines, G. E.	Andover.
Baines, S.	Birmingham.
Baird, —.	Ipswich.
Baker, —.	Hereford.
Baker, A.	Farnham.
Baker, A.	Tavistock.
Baker, A. A.	Jarrow.
Baker, A. E.	St. Albans.
Baker, A. G.	Manchester.
Baker, B. R.	East Lambeth.
Baker, B. W.	Mexborough.
Baker, C. H.	Worcester District.
Baker, E. J.	Hackney.
Baker, E. T.	Liverpool.
*Baker, G. A.	Rotherham.
Baker, G. J.	High Wycombe.
Baker, G. W.	Ilford.
Baker, H.	Dudley.
Baker, H.	Norwich City.
Baker, H. A.	Somerset (E.C.).
Baker, H. A.	Woolwich.
Baker, H. J.	Staines.
Baker, H. R.	Brighton, etc.
Baker, H. R.	West Lambeth.
Baker, J.	Hornsey.
Baker, J.	Surrey (S.E.).
Baker, J.	Brierley Hill, etc.
Baker, J. E.	West Lambeth.
Baker, J. R.	Brierley Hill, etc.

N.U.T. WAR RECORD

Name.	Association.
Baker, R. A. L.	Brierley Hill, etc.
Baker, W. S.	Leicestershire (Mid.).
*Bakewell, G.	Burton-on-Trent.
*Balcombe, H. R.	Eastbourne.
Balding, C.	West Ham.
Baldry, J. W.	Exeter District.
Baldwin, —.	St. Helens.
Baldwin, A. H.	Norwich City.
Baldwin, A. V.	Birmingham.
Baldwin, C.	Dover.
Bale, J.	Harrow.
Bales, E. W.	Norwich District.
Ball, A.	Leicester.
Ball, A. W.	London (E).
Ball, B. C.	Northampton.
Ball, C. H.	Liverpool.
Ball, C. W.	Peterborough.
Ball, D.	Doncaster.
*Ball, E.	Heywood.
Ball, E.	Hinckley.
Ball, E.	Leyton.
Ball, E. A.	Manchester.
Ball, E. H.	Staffordshire (North).
Ball, G. T.	Manchester.
Ball, H. F.	Leicester.
Ball, H. J.	Northampton.
Ball, R.	Hereford.
Ball, R. H.	Finsbury, etc.
Ball, S. S.	Cardiff.
Ball, T.	Ilkeston.
Ball, W.	Shropshire (E.).
Ball, W. E.	Staffordshire (N.).
Ballan, J. F.	Blaydon.
Ballantine, J. H.	West Lambeth.
Ballantyne, J. D.	Finsbury, etc.
*Ballantyne, T.	Great Yarmouth.
Ballard, A.	Gelligaer.
Ballinger, A.	Walsall.
Ballisatt, R.	West Lambeth.
*Balls, E. G.	Tottenham, etc.
Balls, J.	Sunderland.
Bamber, H.	Peterborough.
Bamborough, J. M.	Gateshead.
Bambridge, E.	West Ham.
Bambrough, M.	Newcastle-on-Tyne.
Bamford, J. R.	Manchester.
Bamforth, J. W.	Makerfield.
Bamphfylde, H.	Sheffield.
Bamsey, G. T.	Wiltshire (W.).
Bamsey, G. T.	Wimbledon.
Band, C.	Surrey (N.W.).
Banfield, A. D.	Bristol.
Banham, T. J. H.	Nottingham.
Banks, F. W.	Twickenham.
Banks, G.	Wirral.
Banks, (Miss) P.	Louth.
Banks, H. W.	Sheffield.
Banks, J. A.	Spen Valley.
Banks, R.	Brighton, etc.
*Banks, R. W.	Staffordshire (N.).
Banks, T.	Hackney.
Bannell, A. S.	Salisbury.
Banner, W.	Woolwich.
Bannerman, W.	Darlington.
Bannister, (Miss) E.	Leicester.
Bantoft, E. H.	Willesden.
Baple, W. H.	Exeter District.
Baraclough, A. V.	Leyton.
Barber, C.	Surrey (S.E.).

Name.	Association.
Barber, C. P.	Manchester.
Barber, E. H.	Croydon.
Barber, F.	Bournemouth.
Barber, T.	Stockton-on-Tees.
Barber, W. J.	Lichfield.
Barcham, C. A.	Wiltshire (W.).
Barclay, J.	Bishop Auckland.
Bardsley, F.	Crewe.
*Bardsley, J.	Burnley.
Bardsley, J.	Manchester.
Bardwell, R.	Norwich City.
Barford, W.	Leeds.
Bargh, G.	Wensleydale.
Barham, A. R.	Hackney.
Barkas, F. G.	Crook.
Barkas, L.	Hartlepools.
Barkell, J. H.	Tavistock.
Barker, A.	East Cleveland.
Barker, A. G.	Birmingham.
Barker, A. J.	Hertford.
Barker, A. S.	Rotherham.
Barker, A. T.	Newport Pagnell.
Barker, E.	West Lambeth.
Barker, E. H.	Wellingborough.
Barker, F.	Essex (Mid).
Barker, F.	Manchester.
Barker, G. F.	West Ham.
Barker, G. H.	Walthamstow.
*Barker, G. H.	Winchester.
Barker, G. T.	Tottenham, etc.
Barker, H.	Birmingham.
Barker, H.	Leeds.
Barker, H. F.	Portsmouth.
Barker, J.	Mexborough.
Barker, J.	Northumberland (S.).
Barker, J.	Northumberland (E.).
Barker, J. E.	Rossendale.
Barker, J. F.	Crook.
Barker, J. S.	Leeds.
Barker, J. W.	Knutsford.
Barker, R.	Liverpool.
Barker, S. T.	Gravesend, etc.
Barker, V.	Walsall.
Barker, W.	Driffield, etc.
*Barker, W. D.	Cheltenham.
Barkus, B.	Blaydon.
Barkway, R. C.	Woolwich.
*Barkworth, S. J.	Lewisham.
Barlow, A.	Manchester.
Barlow, C.	Sandbach.
Barlow, E.	Sheffield.
Barlow, E.	Rotherham.
Barlow, F. A.	Manchester.
Barlow, F. M.	Sheffield.
Barlow, H. S.	Nottingham.
Barlow, J.	Staffordshire (N.).
Barlow, J. J.	Blackpool.
Barlow, S. H.	Nottinghamshire (W.).
Barnaby, H.	Hull.
Barnacle, (Miss) F.	Erith.
Barnard, W. C.	Newport Pagnell, etc.
Barnes, A.	Burnley.
Barnes, A.	Ilford.
Barnes, A. B.	Willesden.
Barnes, B. F.	Ilford.
Barnes, C.	Southampton.
Barnes, E. A.	Hackney.
Barnes, E. B.	Enfield.
Barnes, F. A.	Liverpool.

TEACHERS WHO JOINED THE FORCES

Name	Association
*Barnes, F. W.	Hull.
Barnes, H.	Morley.
Barnes, H. C.	Radstock.
Barnes, H. J.	Norfolk (N.E.).
Barnes, J. O.	West Lambeth.
Barnes, L. E.	Northampton.
Barnes, T. L.	Liverpool.
Barnes, W.	Workington.
Barnes, W. H.	Devon (E.).
Barnett, G. H.	York.
Barnett, H. H.	Hackney.
Barnett, J. C. D.	Middlesbrough.
Barnett, R. T. F.	Belper, etc.
Barnett, T.	Knutsford.
Barnfather, F.	Northumberland (E.).
Barnicoat, E. J.	Teign and Dart.
Barnidge, J.	Bristol.
Barnwell, J. D.	Maidstone.
Barnwell, W. F.	Colwyn Bay.
Barons, P. A.	London (E.).
Barr, H.	Brighton, etc.
Barr, J. L.	Farnham.
Barr, R.	Sheffield.
Barraclough, S.	Leeds.
*Barrass, C.	South Shields.
Barrass, J.	Leicester.
Barrass, J. W.	Loughborough.
Barratt, C. W.	Burton-on-Trent.
Barratt, J. F.	Birmingham.
Barrel, L.	Portsmouth.
Barrell, H. J.	Portsmouth.
Barrett, E. J.	Birmingham.
Barrett, G. H.	Spennymoor.
Barrett, H.	Salford.
Barrett, J.	Keighley.
Barrett, R.	Devon (N.).
Barrett, R.	East Lambeth.
Barrett, W. W.	Great Yarmouth.
Barringer, —.	Guildford.
Barrington, G.	South Shields.
*Barron, F. J.	Hull.
Barron, W.	Sandbach.
Barrow, E.	Burnley.
Barrowclough, P.	Huddersfield.
Barrs, W. A.	Birmingham.
Barry, G. T.	East Lambeth.
Barsby, F.	Hendon.
Barter, H. W.	East Lambeth.
Bartle, T. R.	West Lambeth.
Bartlett, A. O.	Wimbledon.
Bartlett, F. E.	Teign and Dart.
Bartlett, H.	Twickenham.
Bartlett, H.	West Lambeth.
Bartlett, H. A. D.	Reading.
Bartlett, H. S.	Cheltenham.
Bartlett, J. W.	Derbyshire (E.).
Bartlett, P.	Bodmin.
Bartlett, R. W.	Birmingham.
Bartlett, W. J. G.	Gelligaer.
Bartlett, W. S.	East Lambeth.
Bartley, G. H.	Finsbury, etc.
Bartley, H. S.	Liverpool.
Barton, A.	Tottenham, etc.
Barton, B.	Manchester.
Barton, F. H.	Sheffield.
Barton, G. F.	East Lambeth.
Barton, H. T.	Worsley, etc.
Barton, J. C. S.	Isle of Wight.
Barton, J. E.	Chipping Norton, etc.
Barton, J. H.	Northampton.
Barton, L.	Liverpool.
Barton, W. H.	Liverpool.
Barton, W. M.	Burnley.
Bartram, C. W.	East Ham.
Bartrop, H.	Walsall.
Bartter, A. S.	Folkestone.
Barwell, W.	Sheffield.
Basford, H.	Birmingham.
Basley, E.	Ealing.
Basnett, J. W. C.	Staffordshire (N.).
Bass, L.	London (N.W.).
*Bassadona, S. H.	Liverpool.
Bassett, D. B.	Barry.
Bassett, H.	Erewash Valley, etc.
Bassett, J.	Finsbury, etc.
Bassett, R. E.	Dorset (E.).
Bassett, T. R.	Teign and Dart.
Bassett, W. P.	Stroud.
Bassingthwaighte, H. G.	Norwich City.
Bastian, J.	Hackney.
Bastian, W. W.	Cornwall (W.).
Bastick, A. J. H.	Leicester.
Bastiman, A. C.	Doncaster.
Bastow, —.	Reading.
Bastow, J.	Wakefield.
Batchelor, A. J.	Guildford.
Batchelor, R. O. F.	Willesden.
Batchelor, W. G.	Southampton.
Bate, C.	Stourbridge.
Bateman, A. L.	Finsbury, etc.
Bateman, H.	Liverpool.
Bateman, J.	Manchester.
Bateman, J. W.	Leeds.
Bateman, T. A.	Abercarn.
Bateman, W. G.	Birmingham.
Bates, A. D.	East Dereham.
Bates. A. W.	Hereford.
Bates, J.	Kidderminster.
Bates, (Miss) N. M.	Ashford (Kent).
*Bates, T. C.	Liverpool.
Bateson, C.	Brackley, etc.
Bateson, H. S.	Birmingham.
Bateson, W. A.	Leeds.
Batey, D.	Durham.
Bath, F. E.	Middlesbrough.
Batho, W. S.	East Lambeth.
*Bathurst, W. J.	Walsall.
Batkin, L. W.	Lichfield.
Batley, E.	Doncaster.
Batley, J.	Swindon.
Batson, —.	Bury St. Edmunds.
Batson, —.	Northampton.
Batson, A. W.	London (E.).
Batstone, H.	Liverpool.
Batt, —.	Ogmore, etc.
Batten, H.	Castleford, etc.
Batten, T.	Ebbw Vale.
Batterley, G. F. W.	Manchester.
Battersby, A. H.	Southport.
Battersby, G.	Blackburn.
Batting, S.	West Ham.
Battison, —.	Birmingham.
Batty, G. W.	Hull.
Baty, A.	Houghton-le-Spring.
Baty, T.	Tottenham, etc.
Baughn, A. P. de	Brighton, etc.
Baughn, W. J. de	Brighton, etc.

99

N.U.T. WAR RECORD

Name.	Association.
Baume, F. H.	Huddersfield.
Bavidge, G. G.	Tynemouth.
Bawden, G. C.	Dorset (S.).
Baxendale, —.	Hindley.
Baxendale, F.	Calder Valley.
Baxendall, E.	Woolwich.
Baxendall, V. H.	Woolwich.
*Baxenden, J.	Liverpool.
Baxter, A.	Chorley.
Baxter, A. J.	Great Yarmouth.
Baxter, B.	Doncaster.
Baxter, E. T.	Southend-on-Sea.
Baxter, F.	Bradford.
Baxter, (Miss) S.	Watford.
Baxter, T. D.	East Ham.
Bayes, G.	Wellingboro'.
Bayley, F.	Walsall.
Bayley, G. S.	London (E.).
Bayley, T. H. L.	Birmingham.
Baylis, V.	Waveney Valley
Bayliss, C. E.	Brighton, etc.
Bayliss, L.	Barnsley.
Bayliss, W.	Birmingham.
Baynes Smith, W.	Harwich.
Beach, E. B.	Rhondda, etc.
Beach, J.	Oldbury.
Beach, W. J.	London (W.).
*Beach, W. W.	Somerset (E.C.).
Beagley, H. W.	Brentford.
Beahan, J. P.	Leeds.
Beal, B.	Alnwick.
Beal, C. E.	Manchester.
Beal, J. W.	Barking.
Beal, W. H.	Sunderland.
Beale, W. J.	Hailsham.
Beales, E. N.	Swindon.
Beamish, —.	Salford.
Beams, R. H.	Dorset (W.).
Bean, —.	Folkestone.
Bean, H.	East Lambeth.
*Bear, H. C.	Epsom, etc.
Beard, —.	Ealing.
Beard, A. E.	Barking.
Beard, F. A.	Plymouth.
Beard, J.	Mansfield.
Beard, L. J.	Finsbury, etc.
Beard, W.	Dudley.
Beardmore, C. A.	Preston Borough.
Beardmore, N.	Easington.
Beardmore, W.	West Ham.
Beards, E.	Wolverhampton.
Beardsley, —.	Derby.
Beardsmore, J. H.	Brierley Hill, etc.
Beardsworth, J.	Blackburn.
Beare, A. J.	Chatham, etc.
Beare, C. E.	Hendon.
Beatson, J. H.	Manchester.
Beattie, (Miss) C.	West Ham.
Beattie, F.	Manchester.
Beattie, T.	Northumberland (E.).
Beaumont, A. E.	Ilford.
Beaumont, B. T.	Chatham, etc.
Beaumont, F. W.	Windsor.
Beaumont, G.	Huddersfield
Beaumont, H.	Hull.
*Beaumont, H. S.	Blackpool.
Beaumont, H. W.	Manchester.
Beaumont, S.	Croydon.
Beavan, —.	Bromley.

Name.	Association.
Beaven, E. D.	Rhondda, etc.
*Bebbington, B.	Manchester.
Bechervaise, A.	Gloucestershire (S.).
Beck, G. C.	Chester-le-Street.
Beck, R. F.	Hackney.
Beckett, C.	Plymouth.
*Beckett, J. R.	Liverpool.
Beckett, W.	Cardiff.
*Beckley, R. F.	Chesham.
Beddoes, G. J.	Birmingham.
Beddous, —.	East Lambeth.
Bedford, A. E.	Exeter City.
Bedford, A. G.	Lincoln.
Bedford, F.	Castleford, etc.
Bedford, W.	West Lambeth.
Bedford, W.	West Lambeth.
Bee, C.	West Lambeth.
Beech, H.	Warrington.
*Beedham, N. H.	Nottingham.
Boeken, G. W.	Swansea.
Beeken, J. W.	Hull.
Beer, A.	Exeter City.
Beer, F.	Plymouth.
Beer, L. B.	Plymouth.
Beesley, C.	London (W.).
Beesley, W. C.	Finsbury, etc.
Beeson, —.	Derby.
Beeson, W.	Croydon.
Beeston, J. H.	Rye.
Beeston, P. W.	Walsall.
Beeston, W.	Walsall.
Beever, T.	Sheffield.
Beevers C. E.	Leeds.
Belben, H. J.	Hackney.
Belcher, F. C. E.	Hackney.
Belcher, L. J.	Southend-on-Sea.
Belfield, H. W.	Birmingham.
Bell, —.	Grimsby.
Bell, —.	Willesden.
Bell, —.	Yoxford.
Bell, A.	Bolton Borough.
Bell, A.	Hull.
Bell. A. C.	York.
Bell, C. F.	Manchester.
Bell, D. J.	Kettering.
Bell, D. S.	Harrogate.
Bell, E.	Stockport.
Bell, F. E.	Bridgwater.
*Bell, G. B.	Newcastle-on-Tyne.
Bell, H.	Gainsborough.
Bell, H.	London (W.).
*Bell, H. G.	Portsmouth.
Bell, H. W.	Liverpool.
Bell, J.	Gateshead.
Bell, J.	Newcastle-on-Tyne.
Bell, J. O.	Bootle.
Bell, M.	Middlesbrough.
*Bell, M. C.	Durham.
Bell, R	Chester-le-Street.
Bell, R	Manchester.
Bell, S. H.	Great Yarmouth.
Bell, S. J.	Kendal.
Bell, 1.	Furness District.
Bell, T. A.	Hexham, etc.
Bell, T. M.	Northumberland (S.).
Bell, V. A.	East Lambeth.
Bell, W.	Sunderland.
Bell, W.	Whitby.
Bell, W. H.	Portsmouth.

TEACHERS WHO JOINED THE FORCES

Name.	Association.
Bellamy, —.	Brentford.
Bellamy, B. M.	Sheffield.
Bellamy, F.	Dartford.
Bellerby, —.	Blaydon.
Bellis, S. I.	Wrexham.
Bellman, L. F.	Exeter District
Belsham, W. F.	East Lambeth.
Belsham, R.	Chesham.
*Belshaw, C. H.	Atherton, etc.
Belshaw, H.	Durham.
Belsten, L. C.	Lewisham.
Belsten, W. H.	Brentford.
Belton, —.	Ipswich.
***Bence, S.** ..	Finsbury, etc.
Bending, —.	Radstock.
Bending, P. E.	Plymouth.
Bengough, O. W.	West Ham.
Benison, —.	Belper and Crich.
Benjafield, H. W.	Isle-of-Ely.
Benjamin, J.	Leeds.
Benjamin, J.	London (E.).
Benjamin, J.	Rhondda, etc.
Benn, H.	Bradford.
Bennett, —.	St. Helens.
Bennett, A.	Bristol.
Bennett, A. E.	Stroud.
Bennett, A. R.	Isle-of-Ely.
Bennett, O. D.	Ingleborough.
Bennett, C. H.	Hailsham.
Bennett, C. J.	Tottenham, etc.
Bennett, D. T.	Rugby.
Bennett, E.	Staffordshire (N.).
Bennett, E. M.	Rotherham.
Bennett, G.	Merthyr Tydfil.
Bennett, G. M.	Southwark.
Bennett, G. W.	London (E.).
Bennett, H.	Manchester.
Bennett, H.	Runcorn.
Bennett, H. E.	Canterbury.
Bennett, H. S.	West Lambeth.
Bennett, J.	Stockport.
***Bennett, J. E. F. T.**	Birmingham.
Bennett, J. W.	Birmingham.
Bennett, L. T.	Finsbury, etc.
Bennett, P.	Itchen.
Bennett, P.	York.
Bennett, P. F.	Surrey (N.W.).
Bennett, R. G.	Surrey (N.W.).
Bennett, T. D.	Deptford and Greenwich.
Bennett, T. H.	Bolton District.
Bennett, W.	West Ham.
Bennett, W.	Stratford-on-Avon.
Bennett, W. W.	Lowestoft.
Benney, A. E.	Ampthill, etc.
Benney, W. E.	Cornwall (W.).
Bennison, —.	Birmingham.
Bennison, W.	Darwen.
Benson, —.	Stockport.
*Benson, C. G.	Sunderland.
Benson, C. O.	Southend-on-Sea.
Benson, E.	Rhondda, etc.
Benson, E. C.	Bromley.
Benson, F. W.	Folkestone.
Benson, I.	Ilford.
Benson, J.	Worsley, etc.
Benson, T. S.	Hull.
Benson, W.	Birmingham.
Bentley, C. A. J. A.	Attleborough.
Bentley, H.	Barking.
Bentley, J.	Todmorden.
Bentley, J. G.	Barnsley.
Bentliff, H. D.	West Lambeth.
Beraet, —.	Willesden.
Berdinner, H. F.	Woolwich.
Berends, J. F.	Tottenham, etc.
Bernthall, J. C.	Chatham, etc.
Berry, C.	Barnet.
Berry, C.	Finchley.
Berry, F. G.	West Ham.
Berry, G.	Huddersfield.
Berry, H. G.	Barking.
Berry, J. R.	Manchester.
Berry, (Miss) L.	Leyton.
Berryman, A.	Vale of Derwent.
Berryman, J. S.	Darwen.
Berryman, L.	Birmingham.
Berryman, P.	Cornwall (W.).
Besant, C. T.	Southgate.
Best, —. ..	Ealing.
Best, A. A.	Brighton, etc.
*Best, D. A.	Faversham.
*Best, E.	Erewash Valley, etc.
Best, H.	Surrey (S.E.).
Best, J.	London (E.).
Best, J. H.	Vale of Derwent.
Best, N. W.	East Lambeth.
Best, W.	Hull.
Beswick, F.	Bromley.
Bethel, V. C.	Birkenhead.
Bethell, W. W.	Deptford and Greenwich.
Bett, A.	Hull.
Bettany, —.	Hastings.
Bettess, J. P.	Finsbury, etc.
Betts, —.	East Lambeth.
Betts, —.	Leyton.
Betts, A. E.	Norwich City.
Betts, C. G.	Nottingham.
Betts, C. J.	Norwich City.
Betts, E. ..	Dorset (S.).
Betts, E. H.	West Lambeth.
Betts, E. W.	Wimbledon.
Betts, F. A.	Bromley.
Betts, G.	Enfield.
*Bevan, A. E.	Ilford.
Bevan, E.	Ealing.
Bevan, E. G.	Pembrokeshire (Mid.).
Bevan, E. W.	Selby.
Bevan, G. E.	Colwyn Bay.
Bevan, G. E.	Chester.
Bevan, P. A.	Rhondda, etc.
Bevan, S.	Swansea.
Bevan, W.	Mountain Ash.
Bevan, W.	Swansea.
Beveridge, (Miss) H.	Abergavenny.
Beverley, C. A.	Birkenhead.
Beverley, G. R.	Hackney.
Beverley, J.	Blackpool.
Bevington, H.	Manchester.
Bewick, J.	Sunderland.
Bex, —.	Gravesend, etc.
Beynon, —.	Ogmore, etc.
Beynon, G. W.	Glamorgan (W.).
Beynon, W. O.	Swansea.
Bezant, E. E.	Newport (Mon.).
Bibby, E.	Darwen.
Bichard, H. N.	Hackney.
Bicheno, E.	Maidstone.
Bickell, —...	Dorset (E.).

101

N.U.T. WAR RECORD

Name.	Association.
Bickell, A. W.	Bristol.
Bickell, E. G.	Bristol.
Bickle, F.	Teign and Dart.
Bickley, D. P.	Wimbledon.
Bicknell, F.	Croydon.
Bidgood, —.	Bodmin.
Bidgood, E.	Forest of Dean.
Bidgood, (Miss) G. B.	Finchley.
Bidgood, O.	Finsbury, etc.
Bidgood, W. H.	Plymouth.
Bidnell, H. J.	Watford.
Bidwell, W. H.	London (W.).
Bielby, P.	Leeds.
Biggs (Mrs.)	London (W.).
Biggs, —.	Dover.
Biggs, A. L.	Leicestershire (Mid).
Biggs, J. J.	West Lambeth.
Bilcliffe, B. L.	East Lambeth.
Bilclough, S.	Brackley, etc.
Biles, A. C.	Kingston and Surbiton.
Bilham, A. L.	Finchley.
Bill, J. H.	Dudley.
*Billam, J. W. A.	Tottenham, etc.
Billen, S. J.	Tottenham, etc.
Billett, A. W.	Swindon.
Billing, E.	Cardiff.
Billing, O. S.	Teign and Dart.
Billing, W. J.	Tonbridge.
Billingham, J. A.	Newport Pagnell.
[Billings, W. L.	Birmingham.
Billington, A.	Wirral.
Billington, E.	Manchester.
Billington, H. C.	Manchester.
Billowes, H.	Portsmouth.
Billson, F.	Nottingham.
Binger, F. H. E.	Southwark.
Bingham, (Miss) J.	Barrow-in-Furness.
Bingham, J. E.	Lewes.
Binks, W.	Macclesfield Boro'.
*Binley, P. A.	Guernsey.
*Binns, A.	Mexborough.
Binns, F. G.	Wakefield.
Binns, J.	Derbyshire (E.).
Bint, C. W.	Birmingham.
Birbeck, A. H.	Teign and Dart.
Birch, E.	Eccles.
Birch, B. H.	Hackney.
Birch, H. E.	Castleford, etc.
Birch, R. K. N.	Dorset (N.).
Birch, W. K.	Cambridge Borough.
Birchall, C. H.	Staffordshire (N.).
Birchall, H. H.	Staffordshire (N.).
Birchall, P.	Wallasey.
Bircher, A.	Birmingham.
Bird, B.	Finsbury, etc.
Bird, B. V.	Oldbury.
Bird, C. B.	Jersey.
Bird, D. H.	Reading.
*Bird, F. W.	Deptford and Greenwich.
Bird, J. E.	Bromley.
Bird, M.	Hull.
Bird, R.	Leicester.
Bird, W. A. J.	Solihull.
Bird, W. J.	Richmond (Surrey).
Birkenhead, P. W.	Edmonton.
Birkett, F.	East Ham.
Birkett, J.	Burnley.
Birkett, W. S.	London (N.W.).
Birkinshaw, J. R.	Wakefield.
Birks, —.	Crewe.
Birks, S.	Staffordshire (N.).
Birney, T.	Gateshead.
Birtchnell, A. A.	Croydon.
Birtley, —.	Salford.
Birtwistle, A.	Blackburn.
Birtwistle, P. J.	Rossendale.
Bishop, —.	Ipswich.
Bishop, —.	Exeter District.
Bishop, —.	Epsom, etc.
Bishop, A. F.	London (N.W.).
Bishop, E.	Tonbridge.
B shop, E. W.	Birmingham.
*Bishop, F.	Chester.
Bishop, F. C.	Hull.
Bishop, H. E.	Woolwich.
Bishop, J.	Daventry.
*Bishop, (Miss) K.	Northumberland (E.).
Bishop, L.	Woolwich.
Bishop, W. J.	Cardiff.
Bispham, J. W.	West Lambeth.
Bissley, W. H.	London (N.W.).
Blaber, T. M.	Hemel Hempstead.
Black, A.	West Stanley.
Black, A. E.	Cornwall (E.).
Black, J. J.	East Ham.
Black, J. T.	Sunderland.
Blackburn, E.	Leeds.
Blackburn, H.	Dewsbury, etc.
Blackburn, J.	Northumberland (E.).
Blackburn, V.	Morley.
Blackburn, W.	Folkestone.
Blackburn, W. B.	Barnsley.
Blacker, C. W.	Wakefield.
Blackett, J. D.	West Lambeth.
Blackford, C. H.	Birmingham.
Blackford, M. B.	Plymouth.
Blackledge, —.	St. Helens.
Blacklee, J. H.	Woolwich.
Blackman, —.	Epsom, etc.
Blackman, G.	Aldershot.
Blackman, H.	Lewisham.
Blackmore, P. T.	Petworth, etc.
Blackmore, W. O.	Sittingbourne.
Blackshaw, F. C.	Wakefield.
Blackshaw, S. C.	Saddleworth.
Blackwell, A. T.	Sheffield.
Blackwell, E. W.	Birmingham.
Blackwell, F.	Gloucester.
Blackwell, H. J.	London (N.W.).
Blackwell, T. H.	West Bromwich.
Blackwell, W.	Makerfield.
Blackwell, W.	Wilmslow.
Blackwell, W. H.	Worsley.
Blackwood, J.	Birmingham.
Blade, E. C.	East Ham.
Blagg, H.	York.
Blagrove, —.	Ealing.
Blair, E.	Spennymoor.
Blair, G. H.	Cornwall (W.).
Blair, J.	Stockton-on-Tees.
Blake, B.	Doncaster.
Blake, C. H.	Hackney.
Blake, C. W.	Coventry.
Blake, C. W.	Teign and Dart.
Blake, H. A.	Portsmouth.
Blake, H. A.	Portsmouth.
Blake, P. J.	Lowestoft.
Blake, T. H.	Harrow.

TEACHERS WHO JOINED THE FORCES

Name.	Association.	Name.	Association.
Blakemore, T.	Wigan.	**Bolt, H. J. R.**	Carlisle.
Blaker, W. C.	Worthing.	Bolt, L. G.	Southwark.
Blakey, J. H.	Leeds.	Bolton, —.	St. Helens.
Blakey, S. J.	Birmingham.	Bolton, A. A.	East Ham.
Blamire, F.	Blackpool.	Bolton, G. V. N.	Warwick.
Blamire, J.	Windermere.	Bolton, H.	Manchester.
Blanchard, R. A.	Uxbridge.	Bolton, J. E.	Liverpool.
Blanchard, W. J.	Leicester.	Bolton, J. H.	West Lambeth.
Blanchett, H.	Wakefield.	Bolton, T. S.	Blackburn.
Blanchflower, J.	South Shields.	Boltwood, H. G.	Hornsey.
Bland, H.	Birmingham.	Bolwell, E. J.	Horsham, etc.
Bland, L.	Wharfedale.	**Bond, E.**	Erith.
Bland, R.	Grimsby.	*Bond, E. E.	Liverpool.
Bland, W. E.	Westminster.	Bond, J. R.	Hackney.
Blatchley, L.	Ilford.	Bond, O.	Waveney Valley.
Blaxland, W.	Surrey (N.W.).	Bond, S. J.	Cornwall (Mid).
Blayney, H.	Essex (N.).	Bond, S. J.	Romford, etc.
Blea, —.	Newbury.	Bond, W.	Macclesfield Borough.
Blench, G. H.	Middlesbrough.	Boneham, H.	Bromley.
Blewett, —.	Bodmin.	**Benfield, S. M.**	West Lambeth.
Blewett, S. C.	Cornwall (W.).	Bonnar, J. E.	Plymouth.
Blewitt, —.	Birmingham.	Bonner, A. W.	Woolwich.
Blewitt, A.	Middlesbrough.	Bonner, J. E.	Liverpool.
Blewitt, R. T.	West Lambeth.	Bonner, T.	Ipswich.
Bliaux, A. R.	Aldershot.	**Benshor, I. H.**	London (E.).
Blight, —.	Teign and Dart.	**Benshor, W. J.**	Ealing.
Blight, F. S.	Plymouth.	Boobyer, J. E.	Ogmore, etc.
Blight, W.	Plymouth.	Boodson, D.	Manchester.
Blincoe, G. B.	Middlesbrough.	Booker, H.	Tottenham, etc.
Blizzard, (Miss) B.	Wolverhampton.	Booker, H. E.	Deal, etc.
Blomeley, H.	Wolverhampton.	Bookman, J.	Leeds.
Bloodworth, J.	Burton-on-Trent.	Bool, —.	London (W.).
Bloom, E. J.	Lewisham.	Boome, (Miss) C.	Reigate.
Bloom, P. W.	Lewisham.	Boon, R. P.	Stafford.
Bloomfield, C. W.	Hartlepools.	Boore, W. A.	Ebbw Vale.
Bloomfield, F. H.	Deptford and Greenwich.	Boorer, J. T.	East Lambeth.
Bloomfield, H. B.	East Lambeth.	Boorman, A.	Woolwich.
Blount, A.	Brentford.	Boot, P.	Cannock.
Blount, E.	Swindon.	Bootes, A. B.	Southwark.
Blower, G.	Leamington.	Booth, A.	Leeds.
*Blowers, A. H.	Yoxford.	Booth, A.	Market Rasen.
Bloxham, H. W.	Derbyshire (E.).	Booth, E. A.	Swindon.
Bloyce, E. J.	Surrey (N.W.).	Booth, G. F.	Northwich.
Bloye, W. C.	Plymouth.	Booth, H.	Rotherham.
Blundell, J. W.	Oldbury.	**Booth, J. C.**	Staffordshire (N.).
Blundell, W. H.	Portsmouth.	Booth-Hampson, F.	Ashbourne, etc.
Blunden, —.	Avon Valley.	Booth-Williams, W.	Rhondda, etc.
Blunden, D. P.	Bishops Waltham.	**Booty, W.**	Norwich City.
Blunden, S. A. W.	West Lambeth.	Booy, R. H.	Brentford.
Blunsdon, T.	Woolwich.	Borash, H.	Southwark.
Blunt, C. G.	Folkestone.	Bore, G. V.	Southend-on-Sea.
Blyth, T. H.	Sunderland.	Borland, A. F.	Salford.
Boam, F. E.	Erewash Valley, etc.	Borland, H.	Salford.
Boardman, —.	Salford.	Borradale, C.	Newcastle-on-Tyne.
Boardman, C.	Staffordshire (N.).	*Borradale, J. F.	Newcastle-on-Tyne.
Boardman, F. C.	Bootle.	Borrell, A.	Alnwick.
Bockin, C. L.	Rugby.	Borrell, A.	Sunderland.
Boddy, G. H.	Blackburn.	Borrett, H. J.	Norwich City.
Boddy, J.	Plymouth.	Borrow, I.	Portsmouth.
Boden, S. S.	Southwark.	**Bestock, —.**	Crewe.
Bodenham, B.	Abertillery.	Bostock, A. H.	Loughborough.
Bodley, C. A.	Exeter City.	Bosworth, —.	London (W.).
Boeree, A. R.	West Ham.	Bosworth, A.	Wirral.
Bogart, W. G.	Dorset (E.).	Bosworth, F.	Nuneaton.
Bogle, A. W.	Winchester.	Bosworth,(Miss)M.E.	Rugby.
Bolam, W.	West Stanley.	Botcherby, F.	Spennymoor.
Bolingbroke, A.	London (W.).	Botham, (Miss) M.A.	Manchester.
Bolitho, J. R.	Tottenham, etc.	Bott, (Miss)	Hinckley.
Boll, G. W.	Hartlepools.	Bott, A.	Sheffield.

103

N.U.T. WAR RECORD

Name.	Association.
Bott, E. H.	Birmingham.
Bott, F. B.	Birmingham.
Botterill, P.	York.
Bottomley, —.	Deptford and Greenwich.
Bottomley, A. W.	London (W.).
Bottomley, F.	Liverpool.
Bottoms, F.	Oldham.
Bouch, J. R.	Stockton-on-Tees.
Bouch, T. J.	Leeds.
*****Boucher, A. E.**	Cambridge Borough.
Boucher, T. L.	Bradford.
Boughey, J.	Manchester.
Boughton, W. C. R.	Finsbury, etc.
Bould, —.	Derby.
Bould, W. E.	Willenhall.
Boulter, S. G.	Romford, etc.
Boulter, W. E.	Leicester.
Boundy, —.	Devon (N.).
Boundy, J.	Northumberland (E.).
Bourne, C. H.	Chester-le-Street.
Bourne, H. S.	Tottenham, etc.
Bourne, R. H.	Flint County.
Bournes, A.	Canterbury.
Boustead, R. L.	Liverpool.
Boutcher, —.	Liverpool.
Bouttell, (Miss) L. M.	Watford.
Bowden, —.	East Dereham.
Bowden, A. V.	Staffordshire (N.).
Bowden, F.	Itchen.
Bowden, H. Y.	Isle of Thanet.
Bowden, J.	Exeter City.
*Bowden, J.	Gateshead.
Bowe, E.	Cockermouth, etc.
Bowen, A.	Swansea.
Bowen, E. B.	Tredegar.
Bowen, F.	Bolton Borough.
Bowen, F. W.	London (W.).
Bowen, L.	Stockton-on-Tees.
Bowen, R.	Ogmore, etc.
Bowen, T. J.	Rhondda, etc.
Bowen, T. R.	Maesteg.
Bowen, W. H.	Cardiff.
*****Bowen, W. L.**	Tredegar.
Bowen, W. L.	Tredegar.
Bower, E.	Sheffield.
Bower, H. J.	Huddersfield.
Bowers, A. H.	Manchester.
Bowers, G. J.	Stockport.
Bowers, H.	Bradford.
*Bowes, G. R.	Middlesbrough.
Bowes, R. S.	East Ward (Westmorland.
Bowesman, E. B.	Tottenham, etc.
Bowey, J. W.	Newcastle-on-Tyne.
Bowie, S.	Newcastle-on-Tyne.
*Bowkett, E. C.	Manchester.
Bowler, J. H.	Epsom.
Bowles, T.	Great Yarmouth.
Bowles, W. F.	Birmingham.
Bowling, —.	Stourbridge.
Bowling, J.	Ilford.
Bowling, W. H.	Finsbury, etc.
Bown, G.	Leicester.
Bown, H.	Salford.
Bowness, G.	Hackney.
Bowrah, F.	Leicester.
Bowring, E. H. W.	Dorset (S.).
Bowring, S.	Surrey (N.W.).
Bowring, W. J.	Surrey (N.W).

Name.	Association.
Bowstead, —.	Ross.
Bowyer, A. E.	West Lambeth.
Bowyer, G. H.	Abercarn and District.
Box, A. W.	Abertillery.
Box, D.	Durham.
Box, D.	West Lambeth.
Box, J. W.	Liverpool.
Boxall, C. W.	Chatham, etc.
Boxall, G. T.	London (E.).
Boxall, W.	West Ham.
Boyce, A. J.	Worthing.
Boyce, C. B.	Blaydon.
Boyce, E. K. A.	Southampton.
*Boyce, F. J.	Sheffield.
Boyce, H. W.	Sheffield.
Boyce, T.	Blackburn.
Boyd, E.	Hull.
Boyd, H. C.	Liverpool.
Boyd, T. G.	Durham.
Boyden, C. J.	Teddington.
Boyes, J.	Surrey (N.W.).
Boyes, J. W.	Leeds.
*Boyes, R. J.	East Lambeth.
Boyle, T.	Farnworth.
Boyson, M.	Daventry.
Brabin, H.	Manchester.
*Brace, R. B.	Hackney.
Bracewell, W.	Todmorden.
Bracewell-Smith, M.	London (E.).
Bracher, J.	Harrow.
Brackenbury, J. R.	Hartlepools.
Brackley, C. H.	Barnes and Mortlake.
Bradbeer, W.	Bridgwater.
Bradbrook, C.	Surrey (N.W.).
Bradbury, —.	Salford.
Bradbury, F. C.	Herts (W.).
Bradbury, H. D.	Bradford.
Bradbury, J.	Manchester.
Braddock, E. S.	Birmingham.
Bradfield, F. W. J.	Cornwall (W.).
Bradfield, J.	Chippenham.
Bradford, —.	Deptford and Greenwich.
Bradford, —.	Reading.
Bradford, H.	Brighton, etc.
Bradford, H. C.	Swadlincote.
Bradford, T. J.	Eastbourne.
Brading, A. E.	Bournemouth.
Bradley, —.	Birmingham.
Bradley, F.	Melton Mowbray.
Bradley, G.	Flint County.
Bradley, H.	Huddersfield.
Bradley, H. L.	Bolton Borough.
Bradley, J.	Surrey (S.E.).
Bradley, J.	Bradford.
Bradley, T.	Rotherham.
Bradley, W.	Hackney.
Bradley, W. H.	Blaydon.
Bradley, W. J.	Nottingham.
Bradney, H.	Dudley.
Bradshaw, —.	Liverpool.
Bradshaw, A.	Blackburn.
Bradshaw, E.	Wirral.
Bradshaw, H.	Manchester.
Bradshaw, H. C.	Manchester.
Bradshaw, J.	Westminster.
Bradwell, C.	Sheffield.
Bradwell, E.	Sheffield.
Braham, —.	Ealing.
Braham, W. H.	Barnsley.

104

TEACHERS WHO JOINED THE FORCES

Name.	Association.
Braid, J.	Hebburn.
Braik, —.	Derby.
Braim, C. H.	Vale of Derwent.
Braim, F. W.	Vale of Derwent.
Brain, —.	Northampton.
Brain, —.	Dover.
Brain, L. J.	Coventry.
Brain, V. H.	Kingston and Surbiton.
Braithwaite, —.	Nottingham.
Braithwaite —.	Leeds.
Braithwaite, T. J.	Ripon.
Bramble, T.	East Lambeth.
Bramford, G. H.	Birmingham.
Bramley, C.	Isle of Axholme.
Bramley, J. W.	Barnes and Mortlake.
Brammer, C. T.	Sheffield.
Bramwell, F.	Manchester.
Bramwell, P.	Durham.
Brand, B.	Hitchin.
Brand, H.	Wallsend.
Brander, A. A.	Staffordshire (N.).
Brandwood, G. A.	Liverpool.
Branfield, N.	Bridgwater.
Branfoot, O.	Grimsby.
Branford, G. R.	Goole.
Brangwyn, C.	West Ham.
Bransden, A. E.	Staines.
Bransden, W. J.	Romford, etc.
Brant, —.	Reading.
Brash, W.	Lancaster.
Brasier, J.	Manchester.
Brass, J.	Chester-le-Street.
Brass, R.	Durham.
Brassington, S.	Crompton, etc.
Braund, T. S.	Newcastle-on-Tyne.
Brawn, C. J.	London (W.).
*Brawn, M.	Willesden.
Brawn, W.	London (W.).
Bray, F. C.	East Lambeth.
Bray, H. E.	Dorset (S.).
Bray, H. H.	East Lambeth.
Bray, P.	Bristol.
Bray, W. S.	Leeds.
Braybrook, W.	Hackney.
Brayley, C. E. W.	Leeds.
Breach, W. G.	East Lambeth.
Breakall, C.	Preston Borough.
Bream, W. H.	Chippenham.
Brears, P.	East Ham.
Brebner, G.	Brighton, etc.
Breddon, H. S.	Barnsley.
Breeze, —.	Sutton Coldfield.
Breeze, S. M.	Rhondda, etc.
Brennan, M. J.	Jarrow.
Brenton, T. H.	West Lambeth.
*Brereton, A. E.	West Lambeth.
Bretland, G. F.	Liverpool.
Bretland, H.	Liverpool.
Brett, H. J.	Gravesend.
Bretton, A. H.	Wakefield.
Bretton, W.	Barnsley.
Brew, G. I.	Leeds.
Brew, S.	Birmingham.
Brewer, A. K.	Exeter City.
Brewer, E. J.	Teign and Dart.
Brewer, H. G.	Willesden.
Brewer, L. G. T.	Barnes and Mortlake.
Brewer, O. J.	Liverpool.
Brewer, T. E.	East Grinstead.
Brewer, W. A.	Radstock.
Brewin, T. B.	Tottenham, etc.
Brewster, A. W.	Lowestoft.
Brickell, H. E. C.	Dorset (S.).
Brickles, H.	Bolton Borough.
Bricknell, E.	Ross.
Brideaux, W. E.	Leek.
*Bridge, J. T.	Stourbridge.
Bridge, W.	Heywood.
Bridgeland, —.	Maidstone.
Bridgeman, C.	Isle of Ely.
Bridges, C. E.	Finchley.
Bridgin, S. R.	Oxford.
Bridgman, A. J.	Evesham.
Bridle, E. C.	West Lambeth.
Brien, —.	St. Helens.
Briggs, A.	Bexhill.
Briggs, A. J. B.	Manchester.
Briggs, F.	Notts (W.).
Briggs, H.	Sheffield.
Briggs, S.	Dartford.
Briggs, S. J.	Nuneaton.
Bright, A. J.	Lewisham.
Bright, G.	Wakefield.
Bright, S.	South Shields.
Brightman, P.	London (E.).
Brighton, J. A.	Bilston.
Brightwell, E. L.	Wellingborough.
Brignall, W. A.	Newcastle-on-Tyne.
Brigstocke, J. M.	Cardiff.
Brill, —.	Uxbridge.
Brill, C.	Tottenham, etc.
Brimelow, P.	Sittingbourne.
Brimicombe, M. H.	Hackney.
*Brindle, H.	Birmingham.
Brine, C.	Jersey.
Brinkworth, R.	Swindon.
Brinkworth, W. H.	London (E.).
Briscoe, E. W.	Castleford, etc.
Brister, F. S.	Leicester.
Brister, H. W.	London (W.).
Bristow, —.	Surrey (S.E.).
Bristow, —.	Wimbledon.
Bristow, E. F.	Surrey (N.W.).
Bristow, J. G.	Hackney.
*Bristow, R.	Hackney.
Bristow, R. O.	Spalding, etc.
Bristow, W. P.	Deptford and Greenwich.
Brittain, H. B.	Houghton-le-Spring.
Brittain, T. J.	Walsall.
Britton, —.	Hastings.
Britton, A.	East Lambeth.
Britton, A.	Manchester.
Britton, H.	West Lambeth.
Britton, J.	Rhymney Valley.
Britton, R.	Southend-on-Sea.
Brixey, —.	Willesden.
Broad, H. B.	East Lambeth.
Broad, W.	Launceston.
Broadbent, H.	Isle of Ely.
*Broadhurst, T.	Stockport.
Broadley, T. W.	East Ham.
Broadway, A. E.	Southampton.
Brock, A. L.	Chester-le-Street.
Brockbank, F.	Wharfedale.
Brockis, C.	Tottenham, etc.
Brocklebank, R.	Hull.
Brocklehurst, E.	Wallasey.
Brocklehurst, J.	Northwich.

N.U.T. WAR RECORD

Name.	Association.
Brocklehurst, W.	Macclesfield Borough.
Brocksom, S.	Grimsby.
Broderick, A. R. J.	Surrey (N.W.).
Brodrick, F.	Spennymoor.
Brogden, G.	Hull.
Brogden, I.	Middlesbrough.
Brokensha, A. C.	Glamorgan (Mid.).
Bromley, B.	Somerset, (S.W.).
Bromley, J. T.	Manchester.
Brommage, A. G.	Westminster.
Bromwich, W. T.	Walsall.
Brook, F.	Isle of Thanet.
Brook, F.	Dewsbury, etc.
Brook, F.	Widnes.
*Brook, G. H.	Bradford.
*__Brook, H.__	Sheffield.
Brook, H. A.	Coventry.
Brook, W. H.	Hereford.
Brooke, H. J.	Walthamstow.
Brooke, J.	Crook.
Brooke, W.	Gainsborough.
Brooker, A.	London (W.).
Brooker, G.	Deptford and Greenwich.
Brooker, H. E.	Deal, etc.
Brookes, S.	Birmingham.
Brookes, T.	Brierley Hill.
Brookhouse, W.	Staffordshire (N.).
Brooks, —.	Mexborough.
Brooks, —.	Somerset (N.).
Brooks, A.	Hendon.
Brooks, E. J.	Bishop Auckland.
Brooks, E. W.	Oxford.
Brooks, F.	Bromley.
Brooks, F.	Manchester.
Brooks, F. J.	Hertford.
Brooks, F. W.	Bromley.
Brooks, G.	Derbyshire (E.).
Brooks, G. W.	Staines.
Brooks, J. D.	Birmingham.
Brooks, J. H.	Sheffield.
Brooks, W. H.	Hereford.
Brooks, W. H.	West Bromwich.
Brooksbank, I.M.M.	Wensleydale.
Broome, J. J.	Buckingham.
Broome, W. F.	Southwark.
Broome, W. J.	Bristol.
Brosman, T.	London (E.).
Brothers, H. J.	Acton.
Brough, —.	Willesden.
Brougham (Miss), L. A.	Stretford.
Broughton, A. M.	Louth.
Broughton, E.	Derby.
Broughton, E.	Dewsbury, etc.
Broughton, H.	Woolwich.
Broughton, W.	Rutland.
Browell, C. W.	Bellingham.
Brown (Miss),	Dorset (S.).
Brown, —.	Hitchen.
Brown, A.	Dartford.
Brown, A.	Salford.
Brown, A. C. O.	Portsmouth.
Brown, A. T.	Dudley.
Brown, B.	East Cleveland.
Brown, B. J.	Teddington.
Brown, C.	Durham.
Brown, C. H.	Lincoln.
Brown, D.	Brighton, etc.
Brown, D.	Northumberland (S.).
Brown, D.	West Lambeth.
Brown, E.	Jarrow.
Brown, E.	Vale of Derwent.
Brown, F.	Louth.
Brown, F.	Hull.
Brown, F.	Nuneaton.
Brown, F.	Blaydon.
Brown, F.	Southport.
Brown, F.	Nantwich.
Brown, F. C.	Worthing.
Brown, F. H.	Deptford and Greenwich.
Brown, F. J.	Wimbledon.
Brown, F. L.	Colchester.
Brown, G.	Lowestoft.
Brown, G.	Felling.
Brown, G. A.	Doncaster.
Brown, G. A. D.	Plymouth.
Brown, G. F.	Spalding, etc.
Brown, G. L.	Flint County.
Brown, G. L.	Brighton, etc.
Brown, G. P. S.	Liverpool.
Brown, G. V.	Colchester.
Brown, H.	Darlington.
Brown, H.	Flint County.
Brown, H.	London (W.).
Brown, H.	Accrington.
Brown, H.	Mexborough.
Brown, H. E.	Bury.
Brown, H. H.	Tottenham, etc.
Brown, H. J.	Birmingham.
Brown, H. T.	Manchester.
Brown, H. W.	Ilford.
Brown, J.	Alnwick.
Brown, J.	Leeds.
Brown, J.	Surrey (S.E.).
Brown, J.	Wallasey.
Brown, J.	Staffordshire (N.).
Brown, J.	Salford.
Brown, J.	Warrington.
Brown, J. A.	Kingston and Surbiton.
Brown, J. H.	Hull.
Brown, J. H.	Crook.
Brown, (Miss), J.I.C.	Newcastle-on-Tyne.
Brown, L. F.	Lewisham.
Brown, N.	Portsmouth.
Brown, N.	Grimsby.
Brown, O. T.	Maidstone.
Brown, P. S.	Kidderminster.
Brown, P. W.	London (N.W.).
Brown, R.	Middlesbrough.
Brown, R. A.	Hull.
Brown, R. C. C.	West Lambeth.
Brown, R. H.	Barking.
Brown, R. R.	Crook.
Brown, S. A.	Southwark.
Brown, T.	Lincoln.
Brown, T.	Durham.
Brown, T.	Salford.
Brown, V. J.	Kingston and Surbiton.
Brown, W.	Willesden.
Brown, W. A.	Nottingham.
Brown, W. B.	Hull.
Brown, W. E.	Finsbury, etc.
Brown, W. G.	Nelson.
Brown, W. H.	Durham.
Brown, W. J.	Teddington.
Brown, W. R.	St. Helens.
Brown, W. S.	Manchester.
Brown, W. S.	Southwark.

TEACHERS WHO JOINED THE FORCES

Name.	Association.
Browne, —.	Newbury.
Browne, C. L.	Leyton.
Browne, C. S.	West Lambeth.
Browne, F.	Chatham, etc.
Browne, F. J.	Lowestoft.
Browne, H.	Hendon.
Browne, J. D.	Surrey (N.W.).
Browne, L.	Tottenham, etc.
Browne, W. A.	Watford.
Browning, J. M.	Coventry.
Browning, R. G.	Isle of Thanet.
Brownjohn, L. C.	Manchester.
Bruce, C.	West Stanley.
Bruce, F.	South Shields.
Bruce, F.	Blackburn.
Bruce, R.	Jarrow.
Bruce, R. S.	South Shields.
Bruckel, V. A.	Gloucester.
Brunker, W. G.	Carmarthen.
Brunner, U.	Northampton.
Brunswick, R.	London (W.).
Brunt, C.	Sheffield.
Brunton, F.	Derby.
Brunyee, H.	Goole.
Bruton, J. E.	London (N.W.).
Bryan, C. F.	Willenhall.
Bryant, A. D.	Richmond (Surrey).
Bryant, B. T.	London (W.).
Bryant, C. W.	Cornwall (W.).
Bryant, E. H.	Colchester, etc.
Bryant, G.	Bath.
Bryant, L.	Norwich District.
Bryant, P. L.	Finsbury, etc.
Bryant, T.	Tredegar.
Bryant, T. H.	Ipswich.
Bryce, J. M.	Manchester.
Bryden, G.	Durham.
Bryson, V. H.	Tynemouth.
Bubb, L. G.	Finsbury, etc.
Buchan, —.	St. Helens.
*Buchan, C. M.	Sunderland.
Buchan, J.	Blaydon.
Buchan, J.	Stockton-on-Tees.
Buck, C. E.	Slough.
Buck, F. M.	Slough.
Buck, H. C.	Leyton.
Bucke, J. F.	Stroud.
Buckingham, C.	Croydon.
Buckland, A. E.	Manchester.
*Buckle, A. W.	London (N.W.).
Buckle, C.	Portsmouth.
Buckle, F.	Spennymoor.
Buckle, J. F.	Moreton-in-Marsh.
Buckler, A. R.	Torridge.
Buckler, J.	Birmingham.
Buckley, E.	Kidderminster.
Buckley, F. J.	East Lambeth.
Buckley, G. A.	Sheffield.
Buckley, H. L.	Staffordshire (N.).
*Buckley, J.	Chadderton.
*Buckley, J. C.	London (E.).
*Buckley, J. W.	Rotherham.
Buckley, M.	Wigan.
Buckley, W.	Liverpool.
Budd, H. J.	Portsmouth.
Buddery, H. M.	Croydon.
Buddery, S. J.	Ilford.
Budge, R. C.	Romford, etc.
Budge, W. T.	Portsmouth.

Name.	Association.
Buesnel, E. C.	London (W.).
Buffham, H. A.	Chester-le-Street.
Bugler, A. T.	Romford, etc.
Bull, A. E.	Reigate.
Bull, A. G.	Aldershot.
Bull, A. H.	Southwark.
Bull, C. E. A.	Woolwich.
Bull, G.	Woolwich.
Bull, W. A.	Portsmouth.
Bull, W. H.	London (E.).
Bull, W. J.	London (W.).
Bullard, —.	Deptford and Greenwich.
Bulled, —.	Devon (N.).
Bulled, A. J.	Devon (N.).
Bulley, J. H.	Plymouth.
Bulliment, W. S.	Hull.
Bullin, J. L.	Croydon.
Bullock, P.	Staffordshire (N.).
Bullock, W. I.	Swindon.
Bullock, W. P.	Swindon.
Bullough, —.	Bingley.
Bullough, F. W.	Lancaster
Bulman, R.	Crook.
Bulmer, C.	Newcastle-on-Tyne.
Bulmer, E.	York.
Bulmer, J.	Chester-le-Street.
Bulmer, R.	Gateshead.
Bunce, H.	Northwich.
Bunch, A. J.	Chiswick.
Bunch, H. W.	Tottenham, etc.
Bunney, D. S.	Cornwall (W.).
Bunting, E.	Leicester.
Burbridge, —.	Eastleigh, etc.
Burbridge, H.	East Lambeth.
Burch, A. J. W.	Surrey (N.W.).
Burch, W. F. T.	Southwark.
Burchell, H. E.	Nuneaton.
Burchell, H. E.	Worcester City.
Burdas, H. W.	Staffordshire (N.).
Burden, H. C.	Bristol.
Burden, W. H.	Brighton, etc.
Burdett, F. B.	Hackney.
Burdett, H. C.	East Ham.
Burdett, H. P.	Wellingborough.
Burdon, —.	Kingston and Surbiton.
Burdon, J. A.	Deptford and Greenwich.
Burdon, J. B. D.	Stockton-on-Tees.
Burfitt, —.	Willesden.
Burford, W.	Llanidloes.
Burge, —.	Somerset (N.).
Burge, E. W.	Portsmouth.
Burgess, A.	Leicester.
Burgess, C. V.	Ampthill, etc.
Burgess, G. G.	Leicester.
Burgess, H. A.	Finsbury, etc.
Burgess, J. W.	Bristol.
Burgess, R.	Hinckley.
Burgess, R.	East Lambeth.
Burgess, R. C.	Staffordshire (N.).
Burgess, W.	Great Yarmouth.
Burgess, W. J.	Dorset (S.).
Burgoyne, W. A.	Norfolk (W.).
Burke, E. H.	Newcastle-on-Tyne.
Burke, N.	Manchester.
Burke, P.	Bromley.
Burke, W. W.	Blackburn.
*Burkett, G. P. W.	East Lambeth.
Burley, E. A.	Derby (E.).
Burling, L.	Smethwick.

N.U.T. WAR RECORD

Name.	Association.
Burn, J.	Newcastle-on-Tyne.
Burn, J. P.	Norwich.
Burn, J. W.	Smethwick.
Burn, R. G.	Easington.
Burnell, E. B.	Hackney.
*Burnett, A. W. K.	Woolwich.
Burnett, E. S.	Woolwich.
Burnett, J.	Chester-le-Street.
Burnett, J. C.	Tynemouth.
Burnett, J. H.	Bristol.
Burnett, S. J.	Acton.
Burnham, W.	Northumberland (E.).
Burnip, W. L.	Crook.
Burniston, R. A.	Darlington.
Burnitt, A.	Goole.
Burns, —.	Ealing.
Burns, A.	Cumberland (W.).
Burns, A. J.	Barrow-in-Furness.
Burns, R.	Durham.
Burras, T.	Bristol.
Burraston, R. G.	Birmingham.
Burrell, G. O.	Nidderdale.
Burrell, H. T.	Chiswick.
Burridge, J.	Exeter City.
Burridge, J.	West Stanley.
Burrow, F. J.	Plymouth.
Burrow, T.	Workington.
Burrow, W. H.	Launceston.
Burrows, —.	Derby.
Burrows, A. G.	Portsmouth.
Burrows, A. W.	Barking.
Burrows, C.	Liverpool.
Burrows, F. A.	Wimbledon.
*Burrows, H. R.	Hull.
Burrows, H. W.	Norwich City.
Burrows, J.	Furness District.
Burrows, J.	Dudley.
Burrows, T. J.	Rhondda, etc.
Burrows, W. A.	Deptford and Greenwich.
Bursell, L.	East Ham.
Burt, C. G.	Southampton.
Burt, C. S.	Twickenham.
Burt, F.	Bristol.
Burt, G. A.	Plymouth.
Burt, G. H.	Gillingham.
Burt, L. F.	Dorset (S.).
Burt, R.	West Lambeth.
Burt, W.	Finsbury, etc.
Burtenshaw, A. C.	Lewisham.
Burton, —.	Nottingham.
Burton, C. A.	Norwich.
Burton, C. W.	Dorset (E.).
Burton, E. R.	Nottingham.
Burton, G.	Richmond (Yorks.).
Burton, H.	Barnsley.
Burton, H.	Kettering.
Burton, J. A.	Hackney.
Burton, W.	Southend-on-Sea.
Burton, W.	Tottenham, etc.
Burton, W. D.	East Cleveland.
Burton, W. H.	Nottingham
Burton, W. J.	Norfolk (W.).
Burton, W. J.	West Lambeth.
Burtt, R. E.	Warrington.
Bury, J. O.	Darwen.
Busby, A. R.	Yoxford.
Busby, J.	Salisbury.
Busby, R. G. C.	Sheffield.
Bush, —.	Gravesend, etc.
Bush, J. A.	Teddington.
Bush, L. H.	Norwich City.
Bushby, —.	Stourbridge.
Bushby, J.	Skipton.
Bushell, S.	Abercarn.
Bushell, W.	Ashton-under-Lyne
Bussey, G.	Norwich City.
*Butcher, A. G.	Brentford.
Butcher, (Miss) D.E.	Tynemouth.
Butcher, E.	Hackney.
Butcher, G.	Tonbridge.
Butcher, G. F.	Croydon.
Butcher, J. V.	Canterbury.
Butcher, R. N.	Ashford.
Butland, T. A.	Sheffield.
Butler (Miss)	West Ham.
Butler, —.	Sittingbourne, etc.
Butler, —.	Derby.
Butler, C.	London (W.).
Butler, C. C. F.	Uxbridge.
Butler, C. G.	Uxbridge.
*Butler, E. H.	Birmingham.
Butler, F.	East Lambeth.
Butler, F. C.	Surrey (N.W.).
Butler, G. T.	Nottingham.
Butler, J. C. W.	Dorset (E.).
Butler, R. W.	Birkenhead.
Butler, W.	Hackney.
Butler, W.	Goole.
Butt, (Miss) V. C.	Pontypool.
Butt, W. F. R.	Somerset (S.E.).
Butt, W. W.	Portsmouth.
Buttell, J.	Croydon.
Butter, W. S.	Hull.
Butterfield, —.	Chorley.
Butterfield, C. W.	Penrith.
Butters, W. H.	Salford.
Butterwick, S.	Sunderland.
Butterworth, —.	Heywood.
Butterworth, F.	Rossendale.
Buttery, A.	Cambridgeshire.
Buttery, B. F.	Worsley, etc.
Buttery, W. A.	West Bromwich, etc.
Button, J. W.	Northwich.
Buxton, F.	Ilkeston.
Buxton, H.	Ealing.
Buxton, H.	Ilkeston.
Buxton, J.	Staffordshire (N.).
Buxton, R. P.	West Lambeth.
Buxton, S.	Leicester.
Buxton, W. F.	Hull.
Bye, M. C.	Gloucester.
Byrne, —.	Bridgwater.
Byrne, A. M.	Croydon.
Byrne, E.	Croydon.
Byrne, E.	Bradford.
Byrne, J. F.	Manchester.
Bytheway, (Miss) G.	Walsall.
Bywell, E. P.	Liverpool.
Cabell, H. F.	Banbury.
Cabourne, —.	Lincoln.
Caddy, H.	Sheffield.
Cade, F.	Birmingham.
Cade, W.	Crewe.
Cadman, —.	Lincoln.
Cadman, J. J.	Sunderland.
Cadman, L.	Tottenham, etc.
Cadman, T. F.	East Lambeth.

TEACHERS WHO JOINED THE FORCES

Name.	Association.	Name.	Association.
Cadwallader, H.	Warwick.	Carbutt, H.	Spen Valley.
Cady, A. G. V.	Dorset (E.).	Card, A. W. D.	Hackney.
Cæsar, H. J.	West Lambeth.	Card, E.	Liverpool.
*Caiger, A. C.	Uxbridge.	Carden, W. A.	Guildford.
Cain, C. D.	Northwich.	**Cardell, E. J.**	Edmonton.
Cain, R. W.	Isle of Man.	Cardnell, H. E.	Southend-on-Sea.
Cain, W.	Isle of Man.	Cardwell, N.	Ormskirk.
Cain, W. G.	Barnes and Mortlake.	Cardwell, N.	Shirebrook.
Cainey, A.	Surrey (N.W.).	Care, P. M.	Maidenhead.
*Cairns, J. C.	East Lambeth.	Care, W. W. J.	Plymouth.
Calder, E. G.	Leeds.	Carey, A. F.	Hackney.
*Calder, J. S.	Leyton.	Carlin, —.	Hartlepools.
Calderbank, J.	Makerfield.	Carling, R. W.	Sheffield.
Calderwood, H.	Merthyr Tydfil.	**Carlisle, T.**	Salford.
*Caldwell, T. J.	Ebbw Vale.	**Carne, J. R.**	Hackney.
Calkin, P. H.	Southgate.	Carnegie, A.	Wallsend.
Callaghan, J.	Hartlepools.	Carpenter, B. C.	Birmingham.
Callaghan, J. A.	Leicester.	**Carpenter, E. S.**	Finsbury, etc.
Callaghan, T	Manchester.	Carpenter, G. F.	Hackney.
Callan, H.	Middlesbrough.	**Carpenter, H. A. S.**	Sheffield.
Calland, R.	Widnes.	**Carpenter, H. W.**	Dorking.
Callard, (Miss) T. A.	Watford.	Carpenter, S.	Northampton.
Callear, W. P.	Coalville.	Carr, —.	Ealing.
Callingham, J. S.	Faversham.	Carr, E.	Deptford and Greenwich.
Callister, H. J.	Sheffield.	Carr, E.	West Lambeth.
Calverley, —.	Birmingham.	Carr, F.	Erewash Valley, etc.
Calverley, A. H.	West Lambeth.	Carr, G. A.	Gateshead.
Calverley, B.	Leeds.	Carr, G. R.	Burnley.
Calvert, J. W.	Leeds.	Carr, H. G.	London (N.W.).
Cambourn, F.	Finsbury, etc.	**Carr, J. S.**	Liverpool.
Camburn, C.	Watford.	*Carr, J. V.	Widnes.
Cameron, H. S.	London (E.).	Carr, J. W.	Runcorn.
Cameron, J. W.	Sheffield.	Carr, K.	South Shields.
Cameron, T. L.	West Ham.	**Carr, L.**	Romford, etc.
Camidge, H. B.	York.	Carr, T.	Hackney.
Cammack, C.	Grimsby.	Carr, T. W. F.	Finsbury, etc.
Campbell, C.	London (N.W.).	Carr, W.	Blackpool.
Campbell, E. N.	London (W.).	Carr, W. T.	London (W.).
Campbell, J. D.	Liverpool.	Carrack, F.	Birmingham.
Campbell, J. W.	Leyton.	Carrick, A.	Teddington.
Campbell, R. K.	Liverpool.	Carrigan, A. S.	Grimsby.
Campbell, W. J.	Houghton-le-Spring.	Carrington, J. V.	Wellingborough.
*Campion, E.	London (W.).	Carrington, J. W.	Lewisham.
Campion, W. F.	Berks (N.).	Carroll, —.	St. Helens.
*Campion, W. J.	Hackney.	Carroll, G.	Cardiff.
Campling, A. C.	Epsom, etc.	Carroll, J.	Salford.
Camps, J. W.	Hackney.	Carruthers, —.	Liverpool.
Canby, T. B.	Hornsey.	*Carruthers, A. J.	Middlesbrough.
Candlin, W. C.	Smethwick.	**Carruthers, G.**	Salford.
Canham, R.	Middlesbrough.	**Carruthers, G.**	Skipton.
Cann, W. B.	Hornsey.	Carruthers, J.	Cumberland (W.).
Cannan, T. F.	Manchester.	Carruthers, J. R.	Ludlow.
Cannell, A.	Liverpool.	**Carson, F. M.**	London (N.W.).
Cannell, A. E.	Wallasey.	Carter, —.	London (N.W.).
Cannell, A. T.	Norwich City.	Carter, —.	London (W.).
Cannell, C. E.	Wallasey.	Carter, A.	Rochdale.
Cannell, E. A.	Warrington.	Carter, F.	Exeter City.
Canning, F.	Epsom, etc.	Carter, F.	Norfolk (N.E.).
Cannon, S.	Cambridge Borough.	Carter, F. G.	Huddersfield.
Cant, T.	Waterloo, etc.	Carter, F. N.	Salisbury.
Cant, T. H.	Liverpool.	**Carter, G.**	Willenhall.
Canton, J.	Mountain Ash.	Carter, G.	Hartlepools.
Capern, H. H.	Somerset (S.W.).	Carter, G. E.	Finsbury, etc.
Capper, F. C.	Northwich.	Carter, H.	Croydon.
Capper, S. H.	Sheffield.	*Carter, H. W.	Bradford.
Capps, H. J.	Deal, etc.	**Carter, I. G.**	Tottenham, etc.
Capsey, W. L.	Birmingham.	*Carter, J. A.	Liverpool.
Capstick, J. D.	Barnard Castle.	Carter, J. P.	Birmingham.
Carah, R.	Cornwall (W.).	Carter, J. S.	East Ham.

N.U.T. WAR RECORD

Name.	Association.
Carter, P. M.	West Lambeth.
Carter, R.	Westminster.
Carter, T.	West Bromwich, etc.
Carter, T. L.	Sheffield.
Carter, W. J.	Barking.
Carter, W. J. C.	Devon (N.).
Carter, W. K.	Sunderland.
Carter, W. L.	Finchley.
Carter, W. T.	Dorset (N.).
Cartledge, A.	Stafford.
Cartledge, A. E.	Retford.
Cartledge, H.	Staffordshire (N.).
Cartledge, J.	Sunderland.
Cartledge, M.	Sunderland.
Cartwright, B.	Lewisham.
Cartwright, C.	West Ham.
Cartwright, D.	Wakefield.
Cartwright, H.	Plymouth.
Cartwright, H.	Edmonton.
Cartrwright, H.	Finsbury, etc.
Cartwright, H. C.	Walsall.
Cartwright, H. H.	Dudley.
Cartwright, J.	Manchester.
Cartwright, J. H.	Bolton District.
Cartwright, W.	Bilston.
Case, C.	London (W.).
Caseley, W. W.	Gravesend, etc.
Casement, —.	Brighouse.
Cash, —.	Salford.
Cash, G. A.	Woolwich.
Cash, P.	Salford.
Cashman, J.	Newcastle-on-Tyne.
Cass, E.	Woolwich.
Cassady, H.	Acton.
Cassidy, J.	London (W.).
Cassidy, J.	Gateshead.
Casson, J. W.	Hull.
Casson, W. B.	East Cleveland.
Castle, J. A.	Blaydon.
Castle, L. J.	Teign and Dart.
Caswell, S.	Kidderminster.
Catchpole, D.	Durham.
Catchpole, W. J.	Leigh.
Catchside, C. E.	West Lambeth.
Catell, S. B.	Barnsley.
Cater, G. G.	Colchester, etc.
Catesby, P. J.	London (W.).
Catley, A.	Rotherham.
Catlin, B.	Gainsborough.
Caton, C. E.	East Ham.
Caton, C. E.	Stockport.
Caton, H. J.	Barking.
Caton, (Miss) I.	Carlisle.
Caton, J. L.	Hendon.
Catt, W. R.	Maidstone.
Cattanach, A. B.	Pembrokeshire (Mid.).
Cattell, A. G.	Southgate.
Cattell, D. E.	Sheffield.
Catterall, J.	Windermere.
Catterall, T.	Bury.
Cattermole, —.	Dover.
Catterwell, J. A. F.	Lowestoft.
Cattliff, J. E.	Newcastle-on-Tyne.
Caukhill, —.	London (W.).
Caukill, F.	Southwark.
Caukwell, H.	Walthamstow.
Cave, S. J.	East Lambeth.
Cave, W. W. J.	Plymouth.
Cavell, W. H.	Deal, etc.

Name.	Association
Cavill, C.	Sheffield.
Cawley, H.	Hertford.
Cawley, W.	Runcorn.
Cawley, W. F.	Leeds.
Cawthorne, A.	Ilkeston.
Cawthorne, F. S.	Leeds.
Cawthra, A.	Hull.
Chadder, F. A.	Birmingham.
Chadwick, —.	Denton, etc.
Chadwick, A. C.	Tamworth.
Chadwick, C. R.	London (E.).
Chadwick, G.	Manchester.
Chadwick, W.	Easington.
Chadwick, W.	Staffordshire (N.).
Chafen, W. B.	Southampton.
Chalk, C. P.	Southend-on-Sea.
Chalk, H.	Finchley.
Chalk, J.	West Ham.
Challinor, F. W.	Staffordshire (N.).
Challis, C.	Deptford and Greenwich.
Challis, S. W.	Brighton, etc.
Challis, V.	Manchester.
Chalmers, F.	Newbury.
Chaloner, —.	Crewe.
Chaloner, J.	Leigh.
Chamberlain, C. J.	West Lambeth.
Chamberlain, H.R.M.	Tunbridge Wells.
Chamberlin, E.	Leicester.
Chambers, H.	Waveney Valley.
Chambers, J. R. O.	Middlesbrough.
Chambers, N. W.	Barnard Castle.
Chambers, R. P.	Colwyn Bay.
Chambers, W. C.	Nottingham.
Chambers, W. T.	Faversham.
Chamings, R.	West Lambeth.
Champion, —.	Willesden.
Champion, H. B.	East Lambeth.
Champion, N.	Birkenhead.
Champion, W. A.	Leicester (Mid.).
Chance, A.	Nottingham.
Chance, C.	Birmingham.
Chance, J.	Birmingham.
Chandler, (Miss)	Canterbury.
Chandler, —.	Ealing.
Chandler, A. P.	Wallasey.
Chandler, E. A. B.	London (E.).
*Chandler, F. E.	Manchester.
Chandler, H. R.	Manchester.
Chandler, W. F.	Finsbury, etc.
Chanin, W.	Hackney.
Channing, P.	Bristol.
Channon, G. E.	East Lambeth.
Chant, —.	Taunton, etc.
Chaplin, —.	Ipswich.
Chaplin, J. J.	Workington.
Chaplin, P. J.	East Lambeth.
Chapman, —.	Doncaster.
Chapman, —.	Epsom, etc.
Chapman, —.	Ipswich.
Chapman, —.	Luton.
Chapman, A. S.	Plymouth.
Chapman, C. H. V.	Surrey (N.W.).
Chapman, E.	Dartford.
Chapman, E.	West Ham.
Chapman, F.	Finsbury, etc.
Chapman, F.	Birmingham.
Chapman, F. B.	Carnarvon.
Chapman, G. L.	Finsbury, etc.
Chapman, H.	Lancaster.

TEACHERS WHO JOINED THE FORCES

Name.	Association.
Chapman, H. L.	Hackney.
Chapman, J.	Northumberland (E.).
Chapman, J.	West Lambeth.
Chapman, J.	Wellingborough.
*Chapman, R. C.	East Ham.
Chapman, W.	Barking.
Chappel, J.	Sunderland.
Chappell, —.	West Ham.
Chappell, E.	Enfield.
Chappell, L.	Barnsley.
Chapple, J. N.	Tottenham, etc.
Chard, T. F.	Shrewsbury, etc.
Chard, T. N.	Brighton, etc.
Charles, A.	Widnes.
Charles, A. J.	Hackney.
Charles, B. J.	Flint County.
Charles, J. H.	Wrexham.
Charles, M.	Rhondda, etc.
Charles, T.	Rhondda, etc.
Charles, W. L.	Swansea.
Charleston, E.	Plymouth.
Charlesworth, F.	Sheffield.
Charlton, A. W.	Durham.
Charlton, F.	Erewash Valley, etc.
Charlton, G.	Northumberland (S.).
Charlton, G.	Blyth.
Charlton, H. J.	Ilford.
Charlton, J.	Manchester.
Charlton, (Miss) M. J.	Northumberland (E.).
Charlton, W.	South Shields.
Charlton, W.	Sunderland.
*Charlton, W. R.	Tynemouth.
Charnock, J.	Burnley.
Charters, T. B.	Carlisle.
Chatters, —.	Bury St. Edmunds.
Chatterton, —.	Altrincham.
Chatterton, J.	Northallerton.
Chatwin, C. F.	Leicester.
*Chaytor, R. G.	Vale of Derwent.
Cheeseman, G. W.	Kingston and Surbiton.
Cheesman, F. H.	Plymouth.
Cheetham, C. A.	Barrow-in-Furness.
Chell, J. B.	Bristol.
Cheney, J.	Loughborough.
Chesham, H. W.	Birmingham.
Cheshire, —.	Willesden.
Cheshire, A. H.	Birkenhead.
Cheshire, F. T. G.	London (N.W.).
Cheshire, H. B. G.	Bletchley.
Chester, J. M.	Croydon.
Chesterfield, —.	Huntingdonshire.
Chesterfield, H.	Rowley Regis.
Chesterfield, H. W.	Plymouth.
Chesworth, F. W.	Staffordshire (N.).
Chew, —.	Clitheroe.
Chick, A. G.	Hendon.
Chick, A. J.	Rhondda, etc.
Chick, E.	Exeter City.
Chick, (Miss) E. M.	Cardiff.
Chick, E. R.	West Lambeth.
Chick, H. G.	Westminster.
Chick, W.	Portsmouth.
Chicken, J.	Gateshead.
Chilcott, O. C.	Teddington.
Child, E.	Walsall.
Child, J.	Leeds.
Child, R.	Malton.
Child, S.	Leeds.
Childe, C.	Finsbury, etc.
Chillcott, A.	Bristol.
Chillington, W. E.	Rhondda, etc.
Chilton, P.	London (W.).
Ching, W. J.	Exeter District.
Chipchase, H.	Durham.
Chipperfield, G. F.	London (W.).
Chippington, J. R.	Romford, etc.
Chirgwin, E.	Cornwall (W.).
Chirgwin, J. O.	Rugby.
Chisman, —.	Willesden.
Chittenden, H. R.	Spennymoor.
Chitty, A. G.	Hackney.
Chivers, A. C.	Southgate.
Chivers, G. A. T.	Caerphilly.
Chivers, H. A.	Bristol.
Chivers, N. C.	Devizes.
*Chivers, S. N.	Caerphilly.
Chivers, W. H.	Bristol.
Choate, A. H.	Tottenham, etc.
Choules, W. A.	Plymouth.
Choyce, A.	Coalville.
Chrisp, T.	Durham.
Christall, W.	Liverpool.
Christian, G.	Middlesbrough.
Christian, J. C.	Whitehaven.
Christiansen, S.	Wallasey.
Christie, H. W.	Bradford.
Christie, R. A.	Liverpool.
Christmas, —.	Kingston and Surbiton.
Chubb, A. C.	Erith.
Chubb, J.	Westminster.
Chugg, —.	Devon (N.).
Chunn, A. O.	Southwark.
Chunn, J. W.	West Lambeth.
Church, —.	Ipswich.
Church, A. B.	Dartford.
Church, A. E.	Birmingham.
Church, A. E.	Harrow.
*Church, A. G.	London (E.).
Church, A. S.	Plymouth.
Church, O.	West Ham.
Church, G.	Dudley.
Church, R. V.	Finsbury, etc.
Church, S.	Enfield.
Church, W.	Luton.
Churcher, E.	West Lambeth.
Churchill, E. C.	East Ham.
Churm, H.	Walsall.
Chuter, —.	Farnham.
Chynoweth, J. H.	Liverpool.
Ciapassoni, F. L.	Middlesbrough.
Civil, G.	Portsmouth.
Clabburn, W. F.	Norwich City.
Clague, C.	Manchester.
Clamp, L. P.	Peterborough.
Clancey, J.	Finsbury, etc.
Clapham, W. S. R.	Croydon.
Clare, F. C.	Birmingham.
Clare, H.	Farnworth.
Clare, J. F.	Liverpool.
Clare, J. W.	Staffordshire (N.).
Clare, T.	Makerfield.
Clare, W. H.	Lewisham.
Claridge, F. E.	Coventry.
Clark, —.	Newbury.
Clark, A.	Louth.
Clark, A. G.	West Bromwich.
Clark, A. J.	East Lambeth.
Clark, C.	Dartford.

N.U.T. WAR RECORD

Name.	Association.
Clark, C. W.	London (N.W.).
Clark, E. S.	Plymouth.
Clark, F.	Leeds.
*Clark, F. C. C.	Halifax.
Clark, F. H.	Dorset (S.).
Clark, G.	East Lambeth.
Clark, G. M.	Maidstone.
*Clark, H. A.	Wolverhampton.
Clark, H. V.	Liverpool.
Clark, J. G.	Chester-le-Street.
Clark, J. L.	Blyth.
Clark, P.	Vale of Derwent.
Clark, P. W.	London (W.).
Clark, R. F.	Folkestone.
Clark, R. W.	Northumberland (S.).
Clark, S. H.	Ilford.
Clark, T.	Workington.
Clark, W.	Birmingham.
Clark, W.	Blackburn.
Clark, W.	Manchester.
Clark, W.	Swindon.
Clark, W. A.	Ilford.
Clark, W. H.	Bridgwater.
Clark, W. M.	Sunderland.
Clarke, —.	Burton-on-Trent.
Clarke, —.	Guildford.
Clarke, A.	Bury.
Clarke, A.	Erith.
*Clarke, A. E.	Ilford.
Clarke, A. E.	Altrincham.
Clarke, A. F.	Gillingham.
Clarke, C. F.	Reigate.
Clarke, C. G.	Aylesbury.
Clarke, C. W.	Farnham.
Clarke, E.	Hackney.
Clarke, E. R.	Cambridge Borough.
Clarke, E. W.	London (E.).
Clarke, E. W.	Southampton.
Clarke, F. C.	Leicester (Mid).
Clarke, F. W.	St. Helens.
Clarke, G.	Nottingham.
Clarke, H.	Calder Valley.
Clarke, H.	Birmingham.
Clarke, H.	Worthing.
Clarke, H.	Derby (E.).
Clarke, H. B.	Hackney.
*Clarke, H. C.	Mansfield Borough.
Clarke, H. G.	Uxbridge.
Clarke, J.	Manchester.
Clarke, J. E.	East Ham.
Clarke, P. O.	Leicester.
Clarke, P. V.	Lincoln.
Clarke, R. E.	Derby (E.).
*Clarke, V. C.	Faversham.
Clarke, W.	Birmingham.
Clarke, W. O.	Leicester.
Clarkson, B.	Preston Borough.
Clarkson, E.	Manchester.
Clarkson, F.	Manchester.
Clarkson, F.	Bishop Auckland.
*Claughton, W.	Oldham.
Clavell, H. D.	Hertford.
Claxton, A.	Great Yarmouth.
*Claxton, E.	Hunts.
Claxton, S. H.	Chatham, etc.
Clay, H. G.	Leicester.
Clay, W.	Folkestone.
Clayson, E. W.	London (W.).
Clayton, —.	Birmingham.

Name.	Association.
Clayton, C. F.	Clitheroe.
Clayton (Miss) E...	Sunderland.
Clayton, E. A.	Tottenham, etc.
Clayton, J. A.	Manchester.
Clayton, J. M.	Birmingham.
Clayton, P. W.	Barnsley.
Clayton, S.	Hull.
Clayton, W.	Liverpool.
Cleall, C. P.	Finsbury, etc.
Clear, C. A.	West Lambeth.
Cleary, D. A.	Southampton.
Cleary, F. B.	Deptford and Greenwich
Cleary, J.	Manchester.
Cleary, T. F.	Plymouth.
Cleator, A. E.	Fleetwood.
Cleaver, C. H.	Ealing.
Cleaver, G. W.	Ampthill, etc.
Cleaver, J.	Castleford, etc.
Cleaver, W. B.	Newport.
Clee, L. J.	Glamorgan (W.).
Clee, W. D.	Glamorgan (W.).
Clegg, A.	Huddersfield.
*Clegg, A. B.	Vale of Derwent.
Clegg, A. H.	Skipton.
Clegg, F.	Northumberland (E.).
Clegg, G.	Leeds.
Clegg, G. J.	Leyton.
Clegg, H.	Birmingham.
Clegg, J.	Driffield, etc.
Clegg, J.	Rochdale.
Clegg, R.	Rochdale.
*Cleghorn, R.	Gateshead.
Clemas, G. W.	Surrey (N.W.).
Clemenson, J.	Bishop Auckland.
Clement, A. G.	Dartford.
Clement, J.	Llanelly.
Clement, W. T.	Bristol.
Clements, R. C.	Northumberland (N.
Clementson, G.	Carlisle.
Cleminson, J.	Bishop Auckland.
Clennel, G.	Romford, etc.
Clennett, —.	Hastings.
Clennett, A. P.	Moreton-in-Marsh.
Clennett, F.	Thirsk.
Cleory, S. P.	Chatham, etc.
Cleveley, R.	Cheltenham.
Cleverley, G.	Ilford.
Cleverley, W. R.	Barnsley.
Clewly, H.	London (W.).
Cliff, A. W.	Wimbledon.
Cliff, F.	East Lambeth.
Cliffe, R. P.	Wolverhampton.
Clifford, D. J.	Birmingham.
Clifford, E.	York.
Clifford, F. J.	Stourbridge.
Clifford, T.	Widnes.
Clift, —.	Grimsby.
Clift, T. W.	Middlesbrough.
Clifton, C.	Norwich City.
Climo, R. S.	Cornwall (Mid).
Clinton, H.	Wolverhampton.
Clish, W. B.	Sunderland.
*Clist, L. F.	Brighton, etc.
Clitheroe, L.	Nelson, Colne, etc.
Cloake, —.	Deptford and Greenwich
Clode, H. G.	Teign and Dart.
Cloke, T.	Lewisham.
Close, G.	Plymouth.
Close, G. L.	Chester-le-Street.

TEACHERS WHO JOINED THE FORCES

Name.	Association.
Close, H.	Makerfield.
Close, J.	Abergavenny.
Clothier, H. W.	Northumberland (S.).
Clough, A.	Staffordshire (N.).
Clough, G.	Sheffield.
Clough, G. W.	Hendon.
*Clough, T.	Spennymoor.
Clough, W.	Hendon.
Clowes, R. G.	Staffordshire (N.).
Clubb, E. A.	Hackney.
Clucas, F.	Isle of Man.
Clucas, J. H.	Isle of Man.
Cluff, —.	Maidenhead.
Clynick, J.	Plymouth.
Coakley, F. J.	Warrington.
Coakley, N. F.	West Ham.
Coates, B.	Liverpool.
Coates, H.	Grimsby.
Coates, H. J.	Gloucester (N.).
Coates, J. T.	Manchester.
Coates, M.	Gateshead.
Coates, S.	Maidstone.
Coates, W.	Darlington.
Coates, W. H.	Newcastle-on-Tyne.
Cobb, A. B.	Hendon.
Cobb, H. J.	West Stanley.
Cobb, S. W.	Nottingham.
Cobbing, W. E.	Hackney.
Cobley, A. B.	York.
Cobley, J.	Willesden.
Cock, (Miss) D. M. S.	Barrow-in-Furness.
Cock, (Miss) E. A.	Barrow-in-Furness.
Cockburn, A. M.	West Lambeth.
Cockburn, D.	Crook.
Cockburn, W.	Tynemouth.
Cocker, W. K.	Darwen.
Cockersole, —.	Derby.
Cockersole, H.	Durham.
Cockerville, R.	Romford, etc.
Cockrem, W. J. C.	Kent (W.).
Cocks, C. J.	Southend-on-Sea.
Cocks, G.	West Lambeth.
Cocks, J. H.	West Lambeth.
Cocks, W.	Woolwich.
Cody, V. M. W.	Leyton.
Coe, —.	Deptford and Greenwich.
Coe, A.	Nottingham.
*Coe, A.	Rock and Tenbury.
Coe, E.	Faversham.
Coe, H.	Nottingham.
Coe, H. W.	Norfolk (W.).
Coe, R. H.	Isle of Thanet.
Coffin, —.	Crewe.
Coffin, P.	East Lambeth.
*Cogan, A.	Leeds.
Coghlan, H. G.	Birmingham.
Coghlan, J.	Cardiff.
Coghlan, J. C.	Eccles.
Coging, S.	Newark.
Cohen, —.	West Ham.
Cohen, B.	Leeds.
Cohen, E.	London (E.).
Cohen, J.	Southwark.
Cohen, M.	Walthamstow.
*Cohen, P.	Stockton-on-Tees.
Cohen, S.	London (E.).
Cohn, F.	West Ham.
Coker, E. C.	Romford, etc.
Colbeck, H.	Hackney.
Colbert, T. H.	Hull.
Colborne, F.	Swindon.
Cole, —.	Luton.
Cole, —.	Croydon.
Cole, —.	Sittingbourne.
Cole, (Miss) A. B.	Wimbledon.
Cole, A. F.	Isle of Axholme.
Cole, A. P.	Uxbridge.
Cole, A. W.	Ogmore, etc.
Cole, E. J.	Hackney.
Cole, G. L.	Ogmore, etc.
Cole, H.	Ilford.
Cole, H. C.	Chichester, etc.
Cole, J.	Easington.
Cole, T.	Lincoln.
Cole, W.	Northumberland (E.).
Cole, W. H.	Hull.
Cole, W. W.	Cardiff.
Coleman, A.	Sunderland.
Coleman, A. B.	Hornsey.
Coleman, A. E.	Shrewsbury.
Coleman, F. H.	Bedford Borough.
Coleman, G.	Wallasey.
Coleman, H.	Finsbury, etc.
Coleman, H.	East Lambeth.
Coleman, J. C.	Sunderland.
Coleman, P. M.	West Lambeth.
Coleman, W. H.	London (N.W.).
Coles, A. J.	Teign and Dart.
Coles, E. A.	Hornsey.
Coles, H. J.	Hornsey.
Coles, W.	Banbury.
Coley, J.	Birmingham.
Collar, E. J.	Acton.
Collar, A. W.	Oldham.
Collett, —.	Bodmin.
Collett, —.	Cheltenham.
Collett, (Miss)	Brierley Hill, etc.
Collett, C. H.	Hull.
Collett, F. G.	Finsbury, etc,
*Collett, H. F.	Leyton.
Collett, W. F.	Leyton.
Collier, C.	Southgate.
Collier, F. J.	Coventry.
Collier, (Miss) J.	Leicester.
Collier, J. F.	Lewisham.
Collin, R.	Newcastle-on-Tyne.
Collin, W. E.	Durham.
Colling, T.	Sunderland.
Collinge, J. F.	Maidstone.
Collings, H. C.	Wiltshire (W.).
Collings, H. J.	Southwark.
Collington, E.	Leicester.
Collingwood, I. C.	Stockton-on-Tees.
Collingwood, N. M.	Sunderland.
Collins, —.	Shrewsbury.
Collins, —.	Derby.
Collins, A. J.	Moreton-in-Marsh.
Collins, D. L.	Enfield.
Collins, E.	Plymouth.
Collins, E. G.	Dartford.
Collins, F.	Birmingham.
Collins, F. F.	Surrey (N.W.).
Collins, H.	Belper, etc.
Collins, H.	Kidderminster.
Collins, H. T.	Staines.
Collins, J. H.	Chichester.
Collins, J. W. H.	Surrey (N.W.).
Collins, J. T.	Isle of Wight.

N.U.T. WAR RECORD

NAME.	ASSOCIATION.
Collins, L. V.	Southend-on-Sea.
*Collins, S. H.	Southampton.
Co lins, T.	Birmingham.
Collins, T.	Mansfield Borough.
Collins, W. H.	Bath
Collins, W. H.	Plymouth.
Collins, W. J.	London (E).
Collinson, H. M.	Fondon (N.W.).
Collinson, J.	Manchester.
Collinson, J.	Furness District.
Collinson, J. A.	Fylde.
Collis, A. D.	Watford.
Collop, W. J.	Tottenham, etc.
Colman, J. R.	Durham.
Colman, W.	Durham.
Colquhoun, A.	Newcastle-on-Tyne.
Colthorpe, A. W.	Norwich.
Colwill, A. B.	Plymouth.
Colyer, F. T.	Erith.
Comean, A. J.	Southwark.
Comer, T.	Boston.
Compton, A. S.	East Lambeth.
Compton, S. H.	Deptford and Greenwich.
Concannon, J. H.	Birkenhead.
Conduct, E. W.	Chipping Norton.
Conelly, H. P.	East Lambeth.
Coney, —.	West Ham.
Conlan, R.	Easington.
Connell, J. W.	Sheffield.
*Connell, J. W.	Flint County.
Connelly, T.	Stockton.
Connelly, D.	Merthyr Tydfil.
Conner, J. O.	Bootle.
Connor, W. C.	Hackney.
Connors, A. H.	Chester.
Connors, J. A.	Newcastle-on-Tyne.
Conway, J. W.	Hackney.
Conway, L. O. D.	London (E.).
Conybere, H. A. G.	Bristol.
Cook, —.	Wallsend.
Cook, A.	Finsbury, etc.
Cook, A.	Itchen.
Cook, A. J.	West Lambeth.
Cook, E.	Abertillery.
Cook, E. G.	Finsbury, etc.
Cook, F. W.	Canterbury.
Cook, G. M.	Bristol.
Cook, J. E.	Durham.
Cook, J. H.	Dudley.
Cook, J. W. P.	Bristol.
Cook, P.	Doncaster.
Cook, P.	Durham.
Cook, R. V.	Lewisham.
Cook, S.	East Lambeth.
Cook, S.	Leicester.
Cook, (Miss) S. C.	Ebbw Vale.
Cook, V. D.	Finsbury, etc.
Cook, W.	Southend-on-Sea.
Cook, W. H.	Coventry.
Cooke (Miss)	Derby.
Cooke, —.	Blackpool.
Cooke, —.	Liverpool.
Cooke, —.	Tonbridge.
Cooke, A.	Derby.
Cooke, A. B.	Isle cf Wight.
Cooke, B. O.	Hull.
Cooke, C.	Nantwich.
Cooke, (Miss) C. A.	Derbyshire (E.).
Cooke, E. H.	Bristol.

NAME.	ASSOCIATION.
Cooke, E. J.	Dartford.
Cooke, G.	West Ham.
*Cooke, H. A.	Liverpool.
Cooke, H. J.	St. Helens.
Cooke, H. S.	Manchester.
Cooke, J.	Leyton.
Cooke, J. E.	Hull.
Cooke, J. J. O.	Finsbury, etc.
Cooke, T.	Manchester.
Cooke, T.	East Cleveland.
Cooke, T. G.	Plymouth.
Cooke, T. J.	London (W.).
Cooke, W.	Bridgnorth.
Cooke, W. A.	East Lambeth.
Cooke, W. A.	Teddington.
Cookson, G. C.	Castleford.
Cookson, L.	Manchester.
Cookson, S.	Chorley.
Cooling, R. T.	Teign and Dart.
Coombe, E. C. S.	Hackney.
Coombe, L. N.	Southwark.
Coombe, P. L.	Portsmouth.
Coombe, R. H.	Peterborough.
Coombes, H. H. P.	Taunton.
Coombes, J.	Exeter City.
Coombes, J. H.	Mountain Ash.
Coombes, W. J.	Westminster.
Coombs, T. J.	Plymouth.
Coombs, W. T.	East Lambeth.
Cooney, P.	Bootle.
Coop, A. E.	Manchester.
Cooper, —.	Leyton.
Cooper, A.	Brierley Hill, etc.
Cooper, A. C.	Wakefield.
Cooper, A. E.	Epsom, etc.
*Cooper, A. G.	Somerset (N.).
Cooper, B.	Cannock.
Cooper, B.	Doncaster.
Cooper, B. S.	Doncaster.
Cooper, C.	Gateshead.
Cooper, C.	Leyton.
Cooper, C. W.	Manchester.
Cooper, D. T.	Birmingham.
Cooper, F.	London (W.)
Cooper, F.	Doncaster.
Cooper, F. L.	Walsall.
Cooper, F. L.	Dorset (N.).
Cooper, F. T.	Finsbury, etc.
Cooper, G. J.	Hackney.
Cooper, H.	Sheffield.
Cooper, H. M.	Twickenham.
Cooper, J.	Gloucestershire (S.).
Cooper, J.	Birmingham.
Cooper, J. A.	Widnes.
Cooper, J. F.	Ormskirk.
Cooper, J. G.	Wakefield.
Cooper, M. A.	Surrey (N.W.).
Cooper, R.	Hertford.
Cooper, S. J.	Gravesend, etc.
Cooper-Smith, —.	Bishop's Stortford.
*Cooper, T. B.	Ealing.
Cooper, W.	Sheffield.
Cooper, W.	Manchester.
Cooper, W.	Gillingham.
Cooper, W.	Bolton Borough.
Cooper, W. F.	Woolwich.
Cope, J.	Staffordshire (N.).
Cope, W.	Birmingham.
Copeland, —.	Wallsend.
Copeland, A.	Hartlepools.

TEACHERS WHO JOINED THE FORCES

Name.	Association.	Name.	Association.
Copeland, J.	Castleford, etc.	Coulter, —.	Birmingham.
Copley, S.	Doncaster.	Coulter, A.	Leeds.
Copley, W.	Rotherham.	Coulthane, T. T.	Bishop Auckland
Copley, W.	Sheffield.	Coulthard, J.	Sunderland.
Copp, R.	Newport (Mon.).	Coulthard, J. R.	Hornsey.
Coppack, E.	Derby (E.).	Coulthard, W.	Blyth.
Coppin, A.	Coventry.	Coumbe, E. W.	London (W.).
Copping, W. E.	Bromley.	Counter, C.	Stockton-on-Tees.
Copplestone, —.	Cambridge Borough.	Coupman, A. J.	Tottenham, etc.
Coppock, B.	Birmingham.	Cousens, F. C.	Richmond (Surrey).
Copps, A. J.	Driffield, etc.	Cousens, R. E.	Romford, etc.
Corbett, —.	Ipswich.	Cousin, F. J.	Swindon.
Corbett, J.	Northumberland (S.).	Cousins, F.	London (W.).
Corby, W. O.	Ealing.	Court, A. B.	Birmingham.
Corderey, F. A.	Erith.	Coutanche, —.	West Ham.
Cordery, F. A.	Woolwich.	Coutts, A.	Jarrow
Corfe, H. A.	Tottenham, etc.	Couzens, B.	Chatham, etc.
Corfield, M.	Sandbach.	Couzens, R. C.	West Lambeth.
Corfield, W. E.	Coventry.	Cove, W. G.	Rhondda, etc.
Corfield, W. H.	Swansea.	Cowan, G.	South Shields.
Cork, J. C.	Canterbury.	Cowans, D. M.	East Lambeth.
Corke, G. D.	Surrey (N.W.).	Coward, —.	Eastleigh, etc.
Corker, R.	East Lambeth.	Cowdell, E. C.	Leicester.
Corker, R. R.	Durham.	Cowell, E.	Blaydon.
Corker, R. W.	Woolwich.	Cowell, J. J.	Staffordshire (N.).
Corkhill, A.	Sheffield.	Cowell, W. H.	Gravesend, etc.
Corless, A. J.	London (W.).	Cowen, E.	Hornsey.
Corlett, —.	Salford.	Cowen, H.	Newcastle-on-Tyne.
Corlett, A.	Great Yarmouth.	**Cowen, J.**	Whitehaven.
Corlett, J. F.	Isle of Man.	Cowen, S.	Burnley.
Corlett, W. H.	Darlington.	Cowen, W.	Sunderland.
Cormack, W.	Salford.	Cowgill, F.	Acton.
Cornall, —.	Warrington.	**Cowherd, T.**	Tottenham, etc.
Cornell, N.	Ealing.	Cowland, A. G.	Southwark.
Cornell, P. R.	Hackney.	**Cowles, R. P.**	Reading.
Corner, A. H.	Spennymoor.	Cowley, F. E.	Manchester.
Corner, G. C.	South Shields.	**Cowley, H. W.**	Ealing.
Corney, E.	Manchester.	Cowling, C.	Teign and Dart.
Cornish, A. J.	Liverpool.	Cowling, F.	Derbyshire (E.).
Cornish, H. D.	Stockport.	Cowling, J. C.	Sudbury.
Cornwell, P.	West Lambeth.	*Cowls, J. M.	Cornwall, (W.).
Corrall, C. W.	Braintree.	Cowls, P.	Cornwall (W.).
Corrie, —.	Kendal.	Cowmeadow, F. M.	Surrey (N.W.)
Corrie, E.	Eccles.	Cowper, E. T.	West Lambeth.
Corry, F.	Petersfield.	Cowper, W.	Carlisle.
Corry, T. H.	Sunderland.	Cox, —.	Radstock.
Cory, W. C.	East Lambeth.	Cox, —.	Exeter City.
Cosgrove, A. B.	Durham.	Cox, —.	Buxton.
Cosslett, E. T.	Bristol.	Cox, (Miss) A. E.	Manchester.
Costard, R. P.	East Lambeth.	Cox, A. F.	Bristol.
Costick, W. L.	Birmingham.	Cox, A. N.	Rock and Tenbury
Costigan, H. A.	Waterloo.	Cox, A. V.	Finsbury, etc.
Cotter, C. J.;	Finsbury, etc.	Cox, C. A.	East Lambeth.
Cotterall, A.	Manchester.	**Cox, E.**	Blackburn.
Cotterell, W. E.	West Lambeth.	Cox, F. J.	Romford. etc,
Cotton, —.	Derby.	Cox, F. V.	Tottenham, etc.
Cotton, —.	Deptford and Greenwich.	Cox, F. W. J.	Hastings.
Cotton, P. G.	Southampton.	Cox, G. J.	West Lambeth.
Cottrell, —.	Stourbridge.	Cox, G. W.	Worcester City.
Cottrell, F. O.	Cardiff.	Cox, H.	Leicester.
Cottrell, L. S. J.	Blyth.	Cox, H. E.	Bishop Auckland.
Cottrell, W. H.	East Lambeth.	Cox, H. J.	Great Yarmouth.
Couch, —.	Teign and Dart.	Cox, J.	Leeds.
Couldwell, H. C.	Hull.	Cox, J. P.	Oldham.
Couldwell, S. H.	Hull.	Cox, J. W.	Hackney.
Coulson, A.	Stokesley.	Cox, P.	Ilkeston.
Coulson, A. J.	Sunderland.	**Cox, P. E.**	Newcastle-on-Tyne.
Coulson, J. W.	Middlesbrough.	Cox, S.	Chesham.
Coultas, S.	Leeds.	Cox, S.	Slough.

115

N.U.T. WAR RECORD

Name.	Association.	Name.	Association.
Cox, T. H.	Somerset (E.C.).	**Crocker, H. H.**	West Ham.
Cox, V. J. W.	West Lambeth.	Crocker, W. J. S.	Plymouth.
Cox, W.	Leicester.	Crocombe, S. H.	Swansea.
Coxe, F.	Tottenham etc.	Croft, A.	Wakefield.
Coxhead, J.	Castleford, etc.	Croft, E.	Blackburn.
Coxon, G. R.	Northumberland (E.).	Croft, H. A.	Sheffield.
Coxwell,—.	Exeter City.	Croft, H. A.	Hull.
Crabbe, C. H.	Newcastle-on-Tyne.	Croft, J. H.	Easington.
Crabbe, H. C.	Isle of Ely.	Croft, W. H.	Nottingham.
Crabtree, E. J.	Lewisham.	Croften, A. R.	Chichester.
Crabtree, J.	Nelson, Colne, etc.	Crofts, —.	Nottingham.
Crabtree, J. A.	Todmorden.	**Crofts, W.**	Manchester.
*Crabtree, P.	Nelson, Colne, etc.	Crofts, W. A. J.	Derbyshire (E.).
Cracknell, G. H.	Twickenham.	Croker, —.	West Ham.
Cracknell, S. H.	Deptford and Greenwich.	Cronin, D.	Portsmouth.
Cragg, W. H.	Dewsbury, etc.	Crook, —.	Newbury.
Craggs, T. G.	Sunderland.	Crook, H. G.	Birmingham.
Craig, D.	East Lambeth.	Crook, W. G. S.	Buckingham.
Craig, H.	Darlington.	Crookall, R.	Barrow-in-Furness.
*Craig, J.	Newcastle-on-Tyne.	*Crookes, R. B.	Sheffield.
Craighill, G.	Darlington.	Crookes, W.	Sheffield.
Craine, T.	Hackney.	Croomes, —.	Petworth.
Cramp, G. H.	Leicester.	Croot, F. G.	Romford, etc.
Crampton, —.	Ealing.	Cropper, J.	Manchester.
*Crandon, G. L.	Bristol.	Crosby, B. C.	Spennymoor.
Crane, H. O.	Waveney Valley.	Crosby, H. E.	Kingston and Surbiton.
Crang, R. H.	Plymouth.	**Crosby, T.**	Blyth.
Cranswick, J.	Castleford, etc.	Crosland, C. E.	Barnsley.
Crapper, —.	East Lambeth.	Crosland, L. A.	Bradford.
Crapper, W.	Sheffield.	Cross, A.	East Lambeth.
Crates, A. E.	Ipswich.	Cross, A. H.	Lancaster.
Craven, A.	Keighley.	Cross, A. J.	Woolwich.
Craven, H.	Salford.	Cross, E. C.	Cornwall (E.).
Craven, H.	Gateshead.	Cross, E. W.	Manchester.
Craven, T.	Stroud.	**Cross, F.**	Thornaby-on-Tees.
Crawford, —.	Buxton.	**Cross, G.**	London (N.W.).
Crawford, A. E.	Rotherham.	Cross, G. H.	Birkenhead.
Crawford, G.	Houghton-le-Spring.	Crossfield, H. D.	Wakefield.
Crawford, G.	West Bromwich, etc.	Crossland, J. R.	Dewsbury, etc.
Crawford, J.	Woolwich.	Crossland, L.	Manchester.
Crawley, D. V.	Leicester.	Crossland, R.	Nottingham.
Crawshaw, A. E.	Gillingham.	Crossman, R. J.	Cardiff.
Crease, J. C.	Somerset (N.).	Crouch, C. N.	Worthing.
Creeggan, D.	York.	Crow, A.	Sunderland.
Creek, A. H.	Cornwall (W.).	*Crowder, A. E.	Grantham.
Creek, E.	Yoxford.	Crowe, E. E.	Finsbury, etc.
Creek, S. A.	Croydon.	Crowe, G. C.	Finchley.
Crellin, —.	London (N.W.).	Crowhurst, F. J.	Tottenham, etc.
Cresswell, A. W.	Northumberland (S.).	Crowhurst, H. G.	Brighton, etc.
Cresswell, G.	Durham.	Crowley, M.	West Ham.
Cresswell, J.	Sheffield.	Crowson, T.	Kingston and Surbiton.
Cresswell, J. J.	Durham.	Crowson, W. A.	Tottenham, etc.
Creswell, F. G.	Manchester.	Crowte, W. J.	Teign and Dart.
Cretney, W. G.	Manchester.	Crowther, —.	East Lambeth.
Crew, S. F.	Bath.	Crowther, A.	Cardiff.
Crewe, F.	Lancaster.	Crowther, C. W.	Rotherham.
Crewe, P.	Manchester.	Crowther, F.	Barnsley.
Crick, —.	West Ham.	Crowther, G. F.	Manchester
Crick, D. W.	Manchester.	Crowther, H.	Elland.
Crickmore, P. J.	Southampton.	Crowther, H.	Huddersfield.
Cridland, C. H.	Staines.	**Crowther, J.**	Bingley.
Cripps, E. C.	East Lambeth.	**Crowther, J.**	Mexborough.
Critchley, C. V.	Hyde.	Croxford, —.	Hackney.
Critchley, G. P.	Birmingham.	***Crozier, H. C.**	Sheffield.
Critchlow, J.	Nottingham.	Crumbie, E.	Plymouth.
Critten, P. G.	Ilford.	Crump, —.	East Lambeth.
Critten, S. H.	Tottenham, etc.	Crutchley, A.	Birmingham.
Crittenden, F.	Croydon.	Crutchley, J. A.	Abergavenny.
Croasdell, A. L.	Manchester.	Crutchley, W. L.	East Lambeth.

TEACHERS WHO JOINED THE FORCES

NAME.	ASSOCIATION.	NAME.	ASSOCIATION.
Cubbin, P.	Liverpool.	Dainow, M.	Westminster.
Cubey, H.	Hartlepools.	Dainty, C. H.	Birmingham.
Cude, C.	Brighton, etc.	Dakin, —.	Luton.
Cull, F. A.	Lewes.	Dakin, F.	Bradford.
Culliford, W. C.	London (E.).	Dakin, W. R.	Walsall.
Culling, —.	Devizes.	Dalby, D.	West Ham.
Culling, P. A.	Willesden.	Dalby, G. E.	Southwark.
Culmer, A. G.	Hendon.	Dalby, G. V.	Harrogate.
Culmer, M. H.	Walthamstow.	*Dalby, J.	Huddersfield.
Culpan, A. W.	Calder Valley.	Dale, A. L.	West Ham.
Culshaw, B. A.	Liverpool.	Dale, F.	Staffordshire (N.).
Culshaw, J.	Wigan.	Dale, H. A.	Wensleydale.
Cumberledge, J. A.	Cornwall (Mid).	Dale, J. A.	Macclesfield District.
Cumming, L. S.	Hackney.	*Dale, P.	Staffordshire (N.).
Cumming,(Miss)M.E.	Leicester.	Dale, R. A.	Warrington.
Cummins, J. R.	York.	Dale, W.	Crewe.
Cumper, C. V.	Bromley.	Dale, W.	Swindon.
Cundall, L. B.	Spennymoor.	Dales, H. L.	Vale of Derwent.
Cundell, T.	Northumberland (S.).	**Dalgoutte, G. O.**	Barnsley.
Cundliffe, O.	Rotherham.	Dall, C.	Surrey (N.W.).
Cunliffe, B.	Roch Valley.	Dalley, A. W.	Bishop's Stortford.
Cunningham, A. W.	Woolwich.	Dalley, J.	Bedford.
Cunningham, C. A.	Woolwich.	Daly, F.	London (E.).
Cunningham, H.	Birmingham.	*Dalziel, J.	Cumberland (W.).
Cunningham, S. H.	Liverpool.	**Damms, H.**	Rotherham.
Cunningham, J.	Bellingham.	Dance, A. J.	Andover.
Cunningham, J.	Liverpool.	*Dancer, A. C.	West Lambeth.
Cunningham, J.	Northumberland (E.).	Dane, —.	Crewe.
Cunningham, J.	Swadlincote.	Daniel, E. B.	Rhondda, etc.
Cunningham, J.	Liverpool.	Daniel, J. B.	Canterbury.
Curling, E. T.	Faversham.	Daniels, —.	Cambridgeshire
Curling, G.	Faversham.	**Daniels, A. V.**	South Shields.
Currie, G. H. N.	Nottingham.	Daniels, C. H.	Southgate.
Curry, L.	Chester-le-Street.	Daniels, D. J.	Glamorgan (W.).
Curry, N. G.	Holsworthy.	*Daniels, F.	Birmingham.
Curry, W.	Chester-le-Street.	**Daniels, G.**	Manchester.
Curry, W. J.	Vale of Derwent.	Daniels, J. H.	Birmingham.
Curryer, A. N.	Leyton.	Danielson, —.	Liverpool.
Curtis, A. E.	Brighton, etc.	Dann, —.	Grantham.
Curtis, A. P.	West Lambeth.	Dann, —.	Derby.
Curtis, H. A.	Southend-on-Sea.	Dann, E. J.	Manchester.
Curtis, H. F.	Plymouth.	Dann, J. H.	Southampton.
Curtis, J. H.	Gelligaer.	**Dann, S.**	Ilkeston.
Curtis, R. H.	Tottenham, etc.	Danson, C.	Birkenhead.
Curtis, S. J.	Reading.	Danson, G.	Preston District.
Curtis, S. S.	Birmingham.	Danson, W.	West Lambeth.
Curtis, W. H.	Isle of Thanet.	Darbey, A.	Bilston.
Curtis, W. S.	Hackney.	Darby, R.	Croydon.
Curwen, D.	Tottenham, etc.	*Dare, E. C.	London (E.).
Cushen, E. E.	Portsmouth.	D'Authreau, W.	Jersey.
Cushworth, J. W.	Bolton Borough.	Dargavel, T.	Preston District.
*Cuss, F. E.	Bromley.	**Dark, M. V.**	Brentford.
Cusworth, H.	London (W.).	Darke, C.	Coventry.
Cutchee, —.	Epsom, etc.	Darlington, L.	Runcorn.
Cuthbert, J. R.	North Cleveland.	Darlow, D. J.	Chippenham.
Cuthbertson, W. U.	Chester-le-Street.	Darrycott, E. J.	Durham.
Cutland, E.	Mexborough.	Darvell, W. G.	Nuneaton.
Cutland, J. W.	Birkenhead.	Date, W. E.	Leicester.
Cutland, W.	Bournemouth.	Datson, A.	London (E.).
Cutler, H.	Stourbridge.	Daulton, A.	Hull.
Cutter, E. O.	Wallsend.	Davenport, A.	Staffordshire (N.).
Cutteridge, J. O.	Liverpool.	Davenport, F.	Chester.
Cuttle, E.	West Ham.	**Davenport, H.**	Oldham.
Cutts, P.	Woolwich.	Davey, H. R.	Liverpool.
		Davey, J. W.	Liverpool.
*Dagg, T.	Burnley.	David, A. E.	Cowbridge, etc.
Daggett, E. C.	Norfolk (N.W.).	David, A. E.	Pembrokeshire (S.).
Dagnall, W.	Ormskirk.	David, J.	Wolverhampton.
Dagwell, F. S.	Plymouth.	David, P.	Swansea.

117

N.U.T. WAR RECORD

Name.	Association.
David, W. J.	Barry.
Davidson, —.	Sale.
Davidson, G. D.	Gateshead.
Davidson, G. G.	Sunderland.
Davidson, J.	Durham.
Davidson, W.	Gateshead.
Davie, J.	Finchley.
Davies, —.	Willesden.
Davies, A.	Abertillery.
Davies, (Miss) A.	Cardiff.
Davies, A. I.	Abertillery.
Davies, A. R.	Glamorgan (W.).
Davies, A. W.	Shropshire (E.).
Davies, B.	Glamorgan (Mid).
Davies, B.	Mountain Ash.
Davies, B.	Liverpool.
Davies, B.	Gelligaer.
Davies, B. E.	Caerphilly.
Davies, B. J.	Birmingham.
Davies, C.	Bridgend.
Davies, C.	Rhondda, etc.
Davies, C.	Swansea.
Davies, C.	Newport (Mon.).
Davies, C.	Ogmore, etc.
Davies, C. A.	Gillingham.
Davies, C. F.	Cardiff.
Davies, C. H.	Cardiff.
Davies, D.	Bridgend.
*Davies, D.	Aberdare.
Davies, D.	Gelligaer.
Davies, D.	Mountain Ash.
Davies, D. A.	Mountain Ash.
Davies, D. B.	Mountain Ash.
Davies, D. D.	Mountain Ash.
Davies, D. E.	Cowbridge, etc.
Davies, D. E.	Aberdare.
Davies, D. E.	Northwich.
Davies, D. E.	Maesteg.
Davies, D. G.	Pembrokeshire (Mid.).
Davies, D. G.	Aberdare.
Davies, D. H.	Mountain Ash.
Davies, D. J.	Rhondda, etc.
*Davies, D. J.	West Lambeth.
Davies, D. P.	Merthyr Tydfil.
Davies, D. R.	Cardiff.
Davies, D. R.	Cardiff.
Davies, D. S.	Rhondda, etc.
Davies, D. T.	Aberdare.
Davies, D. T.	Ebbw Vale.
Davies, E.	Rhondda, etc.
Davies, E.	Newport (Mon.).
Davies, E.	Portmadoc.
Davies, E.	Tredegar.
Davies, E.	Radnorshire.
Davies, E.	Aberdare.
Davies, E.	Swansea.
Davies, E.	Swansea.
Davies, E.	Festiniog.
Davies, E. A. M.	Aberdare.
*Davies, E. L.	Reading.
Davies, E. R.	Merthyr Tydfil.
Davies, E. S.	West Lambeth.
Davies, E. S.	Ogmore, etc.
Davies, E. T.	Gelligaer.
Davies, E. T.	Rhondda, etc.
Davies, E. W.	Liverpool.
Davies, F.	Mansfield.
Davies, F.	Rhondda, etc.
Davies, F.	Sale.
Davies, F.	Portsmouth.
Davies, F. W.	West Lambeth.
Davies, G.	Gelligaer.
Davies, G.	Rhondda, etc.
Davies, G. A.	Merthyr Tydfil.
Davies, G. B.	Barry.
Davies, G. F.	Ogmore, etc.
Davies, G. P.	Pembrokeshire (S.).
Davies, (Miss) H. C.	West Ham.
Davies, H. L.	Mountain Ash.
Davies, H. L. H.	Cardiff.
Davies, H. M.	Barry.
*Davies, H. R.	Newport (Mon.).
Davies, H. S.	Liverpool.
Davies, I.	Finsbury, etc.
Davies, I. D.	Rhondda, etc.
Davies, J.	Harrow.
Davies, J.	West Lambeth.
Davies, J.	Glamorgan (W.).
Davies, J.	Rhondda, etc.
Davies, J.	Northwich.
Davies, J.	Lampeter.
*Davies, J. E.	Aberdare.
Davies, J. E.	Pembrokeshire (Mid.).
Davies, J. I.	Llanfair.
Davies, J. J.	Deptford and Greenwich.
Davies, J. Ll.	Cambridge Borough.
Davies, J. P.	Abercarn.
Davies, J. R.	Wirral.
Davies, J. R.	Rhondda, etc.
Davies, J. S.	Newport (Mon.).
Davies, J. W.	Manchester.
Davies, L. F.	Festiniog.
Davies, L. H.	Wirral.
Davies, N.	Pembrokeshire (N.).
Davies, O.	Bourne.
Davies, O. E.	Rhondda, etc.
Davies, P.	Liverpool.
Davies, P.	Wrexham.
Davies, P.	Mountain Ash.
Davies, P. D.	Aberdare.
Davies, P. W.	Finsbury, etc.
Davies, Rees	Glamorgan (Mid).
Davies, R.	Tredegar.
Davies, R.	Cowbridge, etc.
Davies, R. E.	Mountain Ash.
Davies, R. J.	Glamorgan (W.).
Davies, R. R.	Merthyr Tydfil.
Davies, R. R.	Rhondda, etc.
Davies, S.	Lampeter.
Davies, T.	Mountain Ash.
*Davies, T.	Newport (Mon.).
Davies, T.	Aberdare.
Davies, T.	Rhondda, etc.
Davies, T.	Hackney.
Davies, T. A.	Tredegar.
Davies, T. C.	Cowbridge, etc.
Davies, T. D.	Aberdare.
Davies, T. G.	Glamorgan (W.)
Davies, T. H.	Brentford.
Davies, T. I.	Caerphilly.
Davies, T. M.	Rhondda, etc.
Davies, T. O. Y.	Lewisham.
Davies, W.	Hackney.
Davies, W.	Cardiff.
Davies, W.	Merthyr Tydfil.
Davies, W.	Rhondda, etc.
Davies, W. A.	Leeds.
Davies, W. A.	Glamorgan (W.).

TEACHERS WHO JOINED THE FORCES

Name.	Association.
Davies, W. E.	Llanelly.
Davies, W. E.	Ludlow.
Davies, W. H.	Mountain Ash.
Davies, W. H.	Hackney.
Davies, W. H.	Colchester, etc.
Davies, W. H.	Swansea.
Davies, W. J.	Mountain Ash.
Davies, W. J.	Glamorgan (Mid.).
Davies, W. J.	Glamorgan (W.).
Davies, W. J.	Merthyr Tydfil.
Davies, W. N.	Pembrokeshire (S.).
Davies, W. T.	Cardiff.
Davies, W. T.	Rowley Regis.
Davis, —.	Ealing.
Davis, —.	London (N.W.).
Davis, A.	Barrow-in-Furness.
Davis, A.	Cornwall (W.).
Davis, A. E.	Tottenham, etc.
Davis, A. J. R.	Cirencester.
Davis, A. L.	Bristol.
Davis, A. W.	Portsmouth.
Davis, C.	Northampton.
Davis, C. L.	Crook.
Davis, D.	Brierley Hill, etc.
Davis, E.	Hackney.
Davis, E. G.	Woolwich.
Davis, E. G.	West Lambeth.
Davis, F. A.	Hendon.
Davis, F. T.	Sheffield.
*Davis, G. H.	Bexhill.
Davis, H.	Swindon.
Davis, H.	Bolton Borough.
Davis, H. C.	Surrey (S.E.).
Davis, H. S.	Plymouth.
Davis, J.	Hereford.
Davis, J. J.	South Shields.
Davis, L. W.	Walsall.
Davis, M.	Tredegar.
Davis, O. W.	West Lambeth.
Davis, P. J.	Bristol.
Davis, R. J.	Twickenham.
Davis, S. C.	Portsmouth.
Davis, S. J.	Walsall.
Davis, S, W.	Southampton.
Davis, T.	Waveney Valley.
Davis, W.	Ilford.
Davis, W.	Woolwich.
Davis, W. H.	West Lambeth.
Davis, W. H. P.	East Lambeth.
Davis, W. N.	North Cleveland.
Davison, —.	Vale of Derwent.
Davison, A.	Liverpool.
Davison, E. R.	West Bromwich.
Davison, F.	Scarborough.
Davison, H. T.	Kidderminster.
Davison, J.	Newcastle-on-Tyne.
Davison, J. E.	Chester-le-Street.
Davison, L. E.	Manchester.
Davison M.	Sunderland.
Davison, O. L.	Norfolk (W.).
Davison, R. C.	Nottingham.
Davison, W.	Burnley.
Davison, W.	Sunderland.
Davison, W. M.	Alnwick.
*Davison, W. R.	South Shields.
Davonport, A. R.	Liverpool.
Davy, A. G.	Southgate.
Davy, D.	Kingston and Surbiton.
Dawber, A.	Wigan.
Dawe, H. C.	Isle of Thanet.
Dawers, E. H.	Retford.
Dawes, A. E.	Barry.
Dawes, A. E.	London (W.)
*Dawes, A. E.	Brentford.
Dawes, C. E.	Manchester.
Dawes, C. H.	Glamorgan (Mid.).
Dawes, E. J.	Birmingham.
Dawkins, D. J.	London (N.W.).
Dawkins, W. H.	Leominster.
Dawson, E. E.	Rochdale.
Dawson, F.	Sheffield.
Dawson, H.	Wimbledon.
*Dawson, J.	Manchester.
Dawson, J.	Sheffield.
Dawson, J. H.	Bolton Borough.
Dawson, L. E.	Bradford.
Dawson, R.	Crook.
Dawson, R.	Manchester.
Dawson, S.	Great Yarmouth.
Dawson, T. H.	Bristol.
Day, —.	Canterbury.
Day, A. H.	West Ham.
Day, B. G.	Somerset (N.).
Day, C. S.	West Lambeth.
Day, F.	Hackney.
Day, F.	Scarborough.
Day, G. E.	London (N.W.).
Day, H.	Ilford.
Day, H.	Wakefield.
Day, H. P.	Norfolk (S.).
Day, J. H.	West Lambeth.
Day, L. H.	Newport Pagnell.
Day, L. W.	Worksop.
Day, P. R.	Taunton. etc.
Day, R.	Gloucester.
Day, S.	Spen Valley.
Deacon, F. N.	Manchester.
Deacon, H. J.	Derby, (E.).
Deacon, M.	West Ham.
Deakin, E.	Gravesend.
Deakin, J.	Birmingham.
*Deal, W. J.	Southend-on-Sea.
Dean, F.	Buxton.
Dean, G.	High Wycombe.
Dean, H. E.	Hull.
Dean, J.	Chichester.
Dean, J. E.	Huddersfield.
Dean, J. H.	Hull.
Deane, A. E.	Enfield.
Deans, H.	Edmonton.
Deans, J. J.	Rowley Regis.
Dear, S.	Manchester.
Dear, A. J.	London (N.W.).
Dear. W. F.	Hinckley.
Dearden, J. Y.	Wilmslow.
*Dearing, C.	London (N.W.).
Dearnley, E.	Huddersfield.
Death, —.	Ipswich.
De Bierre, E. T.	Howden.
de Caux, H.	Stockton-on-Tees.
Deeson, L. A.	Wood Green.
de Grouchy, S.	Southampton.
Deighton, —.	Lincoln.
Deighton, H.	Manchester.
Deighton, H. W.	West Ham.
Delaney, B.	Finsbury, etc.
Dell, W.	Lancaster.
Delves, T.	Norwich District.

N.U.T. WAR RECORD

Name.	Association.
Demer, H.	Moreton-in-Marsh.
Demmery, J.	Harrow.
Dempsey, G.	Middleton.
Dempster, F.	Cornwall (Mid.).
Dendy, —.	Warrington.
Denham, H. E.	Plymouth.
Denly, A. H.	Croydon.
Denly, O. J.	London (W.).
Denness, R. B.	Southampton.
Dennett, —.	St. Helens.
Dennett, W. A. H.	Folkestone.
*Denney, A. W.	East Ham.
Dennie, W. J.	East Lambeth.
Denning, C. E.	Radstock.
Denning, C. W.	Dorking.
*Dennis, C. C.	Ludlow.
Dennis, G.	Lichfield.
Dennis, H. J.	Glamorgan (W.).
Dennis, W. T.	Epping and Ongar.
Dennison, R.	Gateshead.
Denniss, —.	Hitchin.
Denniss, E. A.	Sittingbourne.
Denny, E.	Redditch.
Denny, W. J.	Finsbury, etc.
Denoon, W. N.	Woolwich.
Dent, —.	Bromley.
Dent, G. C.	Leeds.
Dent, H. L.	Grimsby.
Dent, W. B.	Newcastle-on-Tyne.
Denton, H.	Dewsbury, etc.
Derbyshire, E.	Worsley, etc.
Derbyshire, J.	Stretford.
Derbyshire, J.	Manchester.
Derbyshire, S. W.	Birmingham.
Derrick, R. F.	East Lambeth.
Derrington, A. E.	Willenhall.
Desmond, S. M.	East Lambeth.
Despicht, T. L.	Westminster.
Deudney, F.	West Ham.
Devany, J.	Manchester.
Devereux, J. H.	Staffordshire (N.).
Devis, J. D.	Haslingden.
Devonshire, J.	Walthamstow.
Dewey, D.	Manchester.
Dewey, G. A.	Chichester.
Dewey, H.	Warminster.
Dewhurst, L.	West Stanley.
Dewhurst, W.	West Stanley.
Dexter, W. E.	Surrey (N.W.).
Dibb, —.	Doncaster.
Dibb, H. W.	Manchester.
Dibb, W. E.	Manchester.
Dibble, T. H.	Hackney.
*Dick, H. W.	Hull.
Dickens, A.	Wigan.
Dickens, C. E.	Hull.
Dickens, E. A.	Birkenhead.
Dickenson, —.	Accrington.
Dickenson, —.	Somerset (S.E.).
Dickenson, (Miss)	Spen Valley.
Dickenson, S.	Hackney.
Dickenson, W. H.	Hull.
Dickeson, A.	Sunderland.
Dickins, A. T.	Dudley.
Dickinson, (Miss)	Spen Valley.
Dickinson, A. E.	West Lambeth.
Dickinson, C.	Skipton.
Dickinson, H.	Hull.
Dickinson, J.	Wigan.
Dickinson, J. R.	Bootle.
Dickinson, R.	Durham.
Dickinson, S.	Nottingham.
Dickinson, T.	Denton, etc.
Dickinson, T.	Watford.
Dickinson, T.	Blaydon.
Dickinson, T. E.	Northumberland.(S.)
Dickinson, W. J.	Gateshead.
Dickison, W. H.	London (W.)
Dickson, J.	Somerset (N.).
Dier, F.	Gillingham.
Digby, —.	Dover.
Digby, A. E.	Deptford and Greenwich.
Dillon-Smith, W.	Barrow-in-Furness.
Dilrew, H. J.	Gravesend.
Dilworth, J.	Castleford, etc.
Dilworth, T.	Rossendale.
Dimmick, —.	Itchen.
Dimond, S.	Woolwich.
Dines, J.	Ilford.
Dinham, J.	Portsmouth.
Dinmore, H. D.	Hackney.
Dinmore, S. S.	Tottenham, etc.
Dinn, R. E.	West Ham.
Dinnin, J.	Northumberland (E.).
Dinsdale, D. H.	Bishop Auckland.
Dinsdale, E.	Fleetwood.
Dinsdale, T. E. C.	Grantham.
Dinwoodie, —.	Portsmouth.
*Diplock, F. H.	Flint County.
Dirkin, —.	Salford.
Diss, P.	Surrey (S.E.).
Divall, —.	Hastings.
Divine, A. J.	Leyton.
Divine, W.	Leyton.
Dix, H. H.	Derby.
Dix, J. H.	Derby.
Dix, R. T.	Derby.
Dix, W. A.	Norwich.
Dixon, —.	Salford.
Dixon, (Miss) A.	Liverpool.
Dixon, A.	Walsall.
Dixon, A.	Durham.
Dixon, A.	Gateshead.
Dixon, A.	Blackburn.
Dixon, (Miss) A. M.	Barry.
Dixon, C. G.	Darlington.
Dixon, D. T. G.	London (N.W.).
Dixon, F.	Carlisle.
Dixon, G.	Liverpool.
Dixon, H. G.	East Ham.
Dixon, H. N.	Durham (N.E.)
Dixon, J.	South Shields.
Dixon, J.	Bootle.
Dixon, J.	Tottenham, etc.
Dixon, J. P.	Blaydon.
Dixon, J. W.	Alnwick.
Dixon, L. F.	Essex (Mid.).
Dixon, O.	Birmingham.
Dixon, R.	Northumberland (E.).
Dixon, R. J.	Darlington.
Dixon, T.	Northumberland (E.).
Dixon, T.	Maryport.
Dixon, T. W.	Durham.
Dobb, W. E.	Croydon.
Dobbie, B.	Spennymoor.
Dobbin, S. A.	Northwich.
Dobbins, W. F.	Redditch.
Dobbs, T. E.	Hull.

TEACHERS WHO JOINED THE FORCES

Name.	Association.
Dobie, —.	East Lambeth.
Dobie, D. J.	Hebburn.
Dobing, H.	Stockton-on-Tees.
Dobson, —.	Salford.
Dobson, G.	Staffordshire (N.).
Dobson, G. B.	Sheffield.
Dobson, J. W.	Blackburn.
Dobson, N. S.	Bishop Auckland.
Dobson, P. H.	Canterbury.
Dobson, W. G.	Birmingham.
Dobson, W. J.	Hull.
Dodd, —.	Crewe.
Dodd, C. B.	Hackney.
Dodd, H. S.	Birmingham.
Dodd, J. W.	Makerfield.
Dodd, R. A.	Liverpool.
Dodd, S. J. A.	Chesham.
Dodd, W.	West Ham.
Dodd, W. R.	Newcastle-on-Tyne.
Dodderidge, R. W.	Enfield.
Dodds, —.	Blaydon.
Dodds, C. F.	Hull.
Dodds, R.	Sunderland.
Dodds, T. G.	Northumberland (S.).
Dodds, W.	Jarrow.
Dodge, S.	Somerset (S.W.).
Dodge, W. G.	Wellingborough.
Dodge, S. C.	East Lambeth.
Dodson, T.	Skipton.
Dodson, W. A.	Slough.
Dodson, W. A. B.	Castleford, etc.
Dodwell, G. E.	High Wycombe.
Dofort, —.	West Ham.
Doggart, —.	Salford.
Doggart, W. E.	Macclesfield Borough.
Dollery, P. J.	Plymouth.
Dolman, W. F.	Hartlepools.
Dolphin, F. G.	Birmingham.
Dolton, W. N.	Plymouth.
Dommett, R. P.	Portsmouth.
Donaghy, J. J.	West Stanley.
Donaghy, M.	West Lambeth.
Donbavand, T. E.	West Lambeth.
Donaldson, A.	Liverpool.
Donaldson, A. G.	Coventry.
Donaldson, S.	Bootle.
Donell. F.	Spalding, etc.
Donellan, T.	Tamworth.
Donnelly, —.	Middlesbrough.
Doolan, E.	St. Helens.
Doole, B.	Essex (Mid.).
Dooley, M.	Walthamstow.
Dooley, P. J.	East Lambeth.
Dootson, A.	Manchester.
Dootson, P.	Liverpool.
Doran, T. H.	Slough.
Dorey, J. A.	Birmingham.
Dormer, C. W.	Romford, etc.
Dormer, H. F.	Isle of Thanet.
Dorrance, B.	Wolverhampton.
Double, J.	Ipswich.
Dougherty, H. S.	Workington.
Doughty, H. J.	London (E.).
Douglas, G.	Itchen.
Douglas, H. J.	Wimbledon.
Douglas, H. J.	Surrey (N.W.).
Douglas, R. R.	Mexborough.
Dowden, L. F.	Yoxford.
Dowding, E. J.	Southampton.
*Dow, F. W.	Birmingham.
Dowell, W.	Windsor.
Dowling, A. E.	Leyton.
Dowman, —.	Lincoln.
Downend, G. F.	Leeds.
Downend, J. M.	Barnsley.
Downes, A. S.	Birmingham.
Downes, B.	Finsbury, etc.
Downes, D. W.	East Ham.
Downes, E.	Driffield, etc.
Downes, F. S.	Hackney.
Downham, F.	Birkenhead.
Downham, L. F.	London (W.).
Downie, A. E.	Manchester.
Downing, C. E.	Macclesfield Borough.
Downing, H. A.	Cornwall (W.).
Downing, H. H.	Newport (Mon.).
Downing, H. J.	Cornwall (W.).
Downing, J.	Chester.
*Downing, R.	Staffordshire (N.).
Downs, —.	Ealing.
Downs, J.	Abertillery.
Downs, R.	Abertillery.
Downsborough, E.	Bradford.
Dowsett, G. W.	East Lambeth.
Dowsing, J. B.	Houghton-le-Spring.
Doxford, A.	Newcastle-on-Tyne.
Doyle, F.	Carlisle.
Doyle, F. J.	Manchester.
Doyle, J. J.	Liverpool.
Doyle, J. J.	London (E.).
Doyne, W. L.	Oldham.
Drage, W. M.	London (E.).
Drake, A. C.	Devon (E.).
Drake, F.	Scarborough.
Drake, F. W.:	Northampton.
Drake, H.	Bradford.
Drake, H. J.	Plymouth.
Drake, W. J.	London (N.W.).
Drake, W. W.	Reading.
Dransfield, J. W.	York.
Draper, —.	Doncaster.
Draper, F. T.	Isle of Axholme.
Draper, S. H.	St. Albans.
Drayton, F. J.	London (E.).
Drennan, J.	Teign and Dart.
Drew, A. J.	Berkeley Vale.
Drew, F. H.	Devon (N.).
Drew, F. W.	Nottingham.
Drew, O.	Bath.
Drew, O. W.	Chippenham.
Drewett, G. J.	Slough.
Drinkwater, J.	Sheffield.
Drinkwater, (Miss) M. E.	Acton.
Driver, —.	Leicester.
Druery, J.	Workington.
Druitt, H. W.	Salisbury.
Drummond, —.	London (W.).
Drummond, J. J.	West Stanley.
Drummond, R. F.	Bootle.
Drury, —.	West Ham.
Drury, A.	Derby (E.).
Drury, O. W.	Rotherham.
Drury, H. E.	Grimsby.
Drury, M. W.	London (W.).
*Drury, S. C.	Barnes and Mortlake.
Drysdale, H.	Newcastle-on-Tyne.
Du Bois, J.	East Lambeth.

121

N.U.T. WAR RECORD

Name.	Association.	Name.	Association.
Dubois, J. H.	Birkenhead.	Duprès, E. C.	Westminster.
Duce, F. R.	Finsbury, etc.	**Durban, A. E.**	London (N.W.).
Duce, H. W.	Finsbury, etc.	Durbin, J.	London (N.W.).
Duckam, —.	East Ham.	Durdle, A.	Harrow.
Ducker, G.	Nottingham.	Durnford, A. C.	Walthamstow.
Duckett, J. E.	Leeds.	Du Rose, R.	Stockport.
*Duckworth, E. E.	Bolton Borough.	Durrans, W. E.	North Cleveland.
Duckworth, J. H.	Matlock, etc.	Durrant, A. S.	Sunderland.
Duckworth, W.	Accrington.	**Durrant, J.**	Derby (E.).
Duckworth, W. H.	Burnley.	Durrant, W. J.	Bradford.
Duddle, W. K.	Manchester.	Durston, G. O.	Cornwall (N.).
Dudley, —.	London (N.W.).	Durston, K.	Cornwall (N.).
Dudley, C. R.	Birkenhead.	**Dusting, J.**	Plymouth.
Dudley, C. W.	Lewes.	Duthy, —.	Willesden.
Dudley, F.	Dudley.	Dutton, W. A.	Sandbach.
Dudley, G. H.	Sheffield.	Dyball, C.	East Lambeth.
Duerdon, A. J.	Swadlincote.	Dye, A. G.	West Ham.
Duff, H.	Liverpool.	Dyer, —.	Cheltenham.
Duffy, C.	Newcastle-on-Tyne.	Dyer, C. E.	Southwark.
Duffy, E. A.	Liverpool.	**Dyer, F. P.**	Basingstoke.
Duffy, H. P.	Salop (E.).	Dyer, F. T.	Isle of Thanet.
Duffy, W.	Liverpool.	**Dyer, H.**	Hartlepools.
Dugard, P. W.	Birmingham.	*Dyer, P. T.	Leyton.
Du Heaume, G.	Jersey.	Dyer, S.	Barry.
Duke, F.	Barnsley.	Dyer, T. E.	East Lambeth.
Duke, J.	Houghton-le-Spring.	Dyer, W.	West Ham.
Duke, S. G.	Stockport.	Dyer, W. H.	Portsmouth.
Duke, W.	Willesden.	Dyke, J. J.	Brentford.
Duke, W. W.	Hull.	Dyke, J. T.	Warrington.
Dukes, G.	Worthing.	Dykes, H.	East Grinstead.
Duley, J. A.	London (W.).	Dykes, (Miss) M.	Manchester.
Dumore, F.	Northampton.	Dymond, L. A.	Tiverton.
Dunbar, J.	Northampton.	Dyson, A. E.	Sheffield.
Duncan, D.	Liverpool.	Dyson, B.	Halifax.
Duncan, H. L.	Hull.	Dyson, F.	Kingston and Surbiton.
Duncan, J.	Staffordshire (N.).	Dyson, F.	Huddersfield.
Duncan, W. A.	Sunderland.	**Dyson, J.**	Manchester.
Dunford, —.	Leicester.	**Dyson, S. G.**	Cambridge Borough.
Dunford, H. J.	London (E.).	**Dyson, W.**	Nottingham.
Dunger, —.	Deptford and Greenwich.	Dywien, E.	London (E.).
Dunham, A. C.	Hull.	Eade, (Miss) J. E.	Dorking.
Dunkerley, J. B.	Finsbury, etc.	Eaden, J. J.	Farnworth.
Dunlop, E.	Retford.	Eades, F. D.	Leicester.
Dunlop, R.	Bolton Borough.	Eagers, E.	Sheffield.
Dunlop, T.	Retford.	Eagers, W. A.	Maidenhead.
Dunn, —.	Derbyshire (E.).	Earb, (Miss) A.	Middlesbrough.
Dunn, F. C.	Wallasey.	Earl, R. J.	Bury St. Edmunds.
Dunn, C.	Cardiff.	Earle, W. G.	Enfield.
Dunn, D.	East Ham.	Earney, H. J.	Andover.
Dunn, E.	Leeds.	Earnshaw, H. A.	Huddersfield.
Dunn, F. J.	Plymouth.	Earnshaw, P. H.	London (N.W.).
Dunn, H. R.	Leeds.	Earwaker, G.	West Ham.
Dunn, H. R.	York.	Easey, S.	Waveney Valley.
Dunn, J.	Walthamstow.	Easom, A. T.	Nottingham.
Dunn, N.	Banbury.	East, A. W.	St. Albans.
Dunn, O. H.	Falmouth, etc.	Easter, H. W.	Lewisham.
Dunn, R.	Cheltenham.	Easterby, W.	Tottenham, etc.
Dunn, R.	Falmouth and Truro.	Eastham, F.	Bury.
Dunn, R. C.	Chester-le-Street.	Eastman, F. H.	Leicester (Mid).
Dunn, R. C.	Barnard Castle.	Easto, A. W.	Waveney Valley.
Dunn, W.	Hornsey.	Easton, E. G.	Finsbury, etc.
Dunn, W. A.	Deal, etc.	Easton, S. W.	Epsom, etc.
Dunning, J. E.	Manchester.	Eastwood, W. E.	Dewsbury, etc.
Dunning, M.	Bradford.	Eatherington, W. H.	Nottingham.
Dunphy, F.	Bradford.	Eaton, B. J. H.	Bournemouth.
Dunstan, —.	Portsmouth.	Eaton, R. M.	Southwark.
Dunstan, (Miss) M.	Cardiff.	**Eaves, A. T.**	Dover.
Dunster, (Miss) M.F.	Carlisle.	*Ebbetts, R. F.	Acton.
Dunton, D. F.	West Lambeth.		

122

TEACHERS WHO JOINED THE FORCES

Name.	Association.
Ebden, C.	Newcastle-on-Tyne.
Ebdon, C.	Houghton-le-Spring.
Ebdon, W. A.	London (W.).
Ebery, J.	Sutton Coldfield.
Eccles, G.	Manchester.
Eccles, J. S.	Dudley.
Ecclestone, A.	Wolverhampton.
Eckersley, W.	Manchester.
Edden, H. P.	London (N.W.).
Ede, C. P.	Whitehaven.
Ede, J. Chuter	Barnes and Mortlake.
Eden, H. E.	Hackney.
Eden, J. A. I.	Hackney.
*Edgar, J. G.	South Shields.
*Edgar, W. G.	South Shields.
Edge, H.	Flint County.
Edge, H. A.	Staffordshire (N.).
Edge, T.	Wellingborough.
Edmands, T. E.	
Edminston, —.	Sale.
Edmonds, —.	Birmingham.
Edmonds, —.	Exeter District.
Edmonds, A. J.	Birmingham.
Edmonds, H. J.	Croydon.
Edmonds, R.	Croydon.
Edmonds, R. L.	East Ham.
Edmonds, W. B.	Tottenham, etc.
Edmondson, —.	Derby.
Edmondson, E.	Barnard Castle.
Edmonston, J. S.	Birmingham.
Edmunds, D. J.	Rhondda, etc.
Edney, H. G.	Richmond (Surrey).
Edward, P. D.	Croydon.
Edwards, —.	Burton-on-Trent.
Edwards, A. E.	Croydon.
Edwards, A. G.	Bristol.
Edwards, A. L.	Birmingham.
Edwards, C. J.	Gelligaer.
Edwards, D. L.	West Lambeth.
Edwards, D. M.	Swansea.
Edwards, D. T.	Lampeter.
Edwards, E.	Hendon.
Edwards, E. A.	Tredegar.
Edwards, E. J.	Liverpool.
Edwards, F.	Manchester.
Edwards, G. V.	East Lambeth.
Edwards, H. C.	London (W.).
Edwards, I.	Aberdare.
Edwards, I. L.	Manchester.
Edwards, J.	Rhondda, etc.
Edwards, J.	Merthyr Tydfil.
Edwards, J.	Ogmore, etc.
Edwards, J.	Liverpool.
*Edwards, J.	Aberdare.
Edwards, J.	Northwich.
Edwards, J. E.	Hackney.
Edwards, J. H.	West Ham.
Edwards, J. H.	Flint County.
Edwards, J. M.	Cornwall (Mid).
Edwards, J. P.	Rhondda, etc.
Edwards, J. W. E.	Southampton.
Edwards, L.	Merthyr Tydfil.
Edwards, O. B.	Liverpool.
Edwards, P.	Macclesfield.
Edwards, R.	East Lambeth.
Edwards, R.	Builth Wells.
Edwards, R. J.	Southend-on-Sea.
Edwards, T.	Nottingham.
*Edwards, T. A.	East Lambeth.
Edwards, T. D.	Aberdare.
Edwards, W. C.	Hertford.
Edwards, W. J.	Wrexham.
Edwards, W. J.	Penarth.
Edwards, W. M.	Erith.
Edwards, W. S.	Newport (Mon.).
Edwards, W. W.	Launceston.
Edwardson, W.	Willesden.
*Eeles, F. T.	Stokesley.
Egan, (Miss) L.	Barrow-in-Furness.
Egerton, (Miss)	Burton-on-Trent.
Egerton, P. R.	Bootle.
Egerton, R.	Willesden.
Eggleshaw, H. W.	Mansfield Borough.
Eggleston, H. B.	West Stanley.
Egglestone, H.	Rotherham.
Egleton, W. H.	Bristol.
Eglin, R.	Manchester.
Eite, W.	Birmingham.
Ekendahl, T.	Wimbledon.
Eland, J. E.	Spennymoor.
Elborn, E. J.	Cambridge Borough.
Elcombe, E. E.	Nottingham.
Eldred, C.	Sudbury.
Eldridge, J. E.	Faversham.
Eldridge, J. T.	Birmingham.
Elford, A. J.	Cornwall (W.).
Elias, M. R.	Merthyr Tydfil.
Eling, A.	Southampton.
Elkington, E.	Leicester.
Elkington, O.	Bristol.
Eller, O.	Ashton-under-Lyne.
Elliot, P. A.	Erith.
Elliot, R. H.	South Shields.
Elliot, T. E.	Carlisle.
Elliott, A.	West Lambeth.
Elliott, A. W.	Salford.
Elliott, B.	London (W.).
Elliott, C. W.	Newcastle-on-Tyne.
Elliott, E.	Crook.
Elliott, E.	Mexborough.
Elliott, E. D.	Carlisle.
Elliott, H.	East Lambeth.
Elliott, H.	Portsmouth.
Elliott, H. V.	Croydon.
Elliott, J.	Alnwick.
Elliott, P.	Mexborough.
Elliott, R. E.	St. Albans.
Elliott, S. G.	West Lambeth.
Elliott, T. J.	Bromley.
Elliott, V. M.	West Lambeth.
Elliott, W. F.	Brighton, etc.
Elliott, W. J.	Dartford.
Elliott, W. L.	London (W.).
Ellis, —.	Folkestone.
Ellis, A.	Bradford.
Ellis, A. C.	Teign and Dart.
*Ellis, A. G.	Teign and Dart.
Ellis, A. P.	Coalville.
Ellis, A. W.	West Ham.
Ellis, B. T.	Dartford.
Ellis, C.	Dewsbury, etc.
Ellis, F. A.	Hull.
Ellis, F. F.	East Ham.
Ellis, J.	Woolwich.
Ellis, J.	Huddersfield.
Ellis, J. E.	Cornwall (W.).
Ellis, J. E.	Liverpool.
Ellis, J. W.	Barnsley.

N.U.T. WAR RECORD

Name.	Association.	Name.	Association.
Ellis, J. W.	West Ham.	Entwistle, H.	Nelson, Colne, etc.
Ellis, J. W.	London (W.).	Entwistle, H. L.	Bolton Borough.
Ellis, L.	Huddersfield.	Ephgrave, E. J.	Acton.
Ellis, O. C. de C.	Manchester.	Eppley, S. C.	Birmingham.
Ellis, P.	Norwich.	**Erwood, C. M. W.**	Woolwich.
Ellis, S.	Finsbury, etc.	Esmond, A. J.	Glamorgan (Mid).
Ellis, U.	Bishop's Stortford.	Espley, T. H.	Barkston Ash.
Ellison, C.	Kiveton Park.	Espley, T. H.	West Bromwich, etc.
Ellison, E. G.	Bradford.	*Essam, W.	Warwick.
Ellison, G. J.	East Lambeth.	**Essex, J.**	Malton.
Ellison, S.	Spen Valley.	Estill, J. E.	Hull.
Ellison, S.	Crook.	Etherington, —.	Romford, etc.
Ellison, S. G.	Swindon.	Etherington, H. M.	Lewisham.
Ellman, H. S.	Avon Valley.	*Eva, W. H.	Bolton Borough.
Ellson, —.	Doncaster.	Evans, —.	Dover.
Ellson, P.	Willesden.	Evans, —.	St. Helens.
Ellway, S.	Forest of Dean.	Evans, —.	Newbury.
*Ellwood, A.	Manchester.	Evans, —.	Boston.
Ellwood, A.	Bishop Auckland.	Evans, —.	Birmingham.
Ellwood, A. W.	Bishop Auckland.	Evans, —.	Shrewsbury.
Elsom, J. A.	East Lambeth.	**Evans, A. W.**	Birmingham.
Elson, A.	Petersfield, etc.	Evans, A.	Ogmore, etc.
Elson, A. S.	Alton.	Evans, A.	Sunderland.
Elton, L. G.	Walsall.	Evans, A. C.	Liverpool.
Elvin, —.	Lincoln.	Evans, A. E.	Woolwich.
Elwen, T.	Carlisle.	Evans, A. E.	Southport.
Ely, J. J.	Brighton, etc.	Evans, A. E.	London (W.).
Emanuel, S. M.	Swansea.	Evans, A. J.	Nuneaton.
Embleton, B. H.	Middlesbrough.	Evans, A. L.	Flint County.
Embleton, F.	Middlesbrough.	Evans, A. S.	Brighton, etc.
Emerson, H.	Grimsby.	Evans, A. T.	Jarrow.
Emerson, J.	Middlesbrough.	Evans, A. W.	Merthyr Tydfil.
Emerson, R.	Blaydon.	Evans, A. W.	Birmingham.
Emerton, T.	Makerfield.	Evans, B. E.	Gloucester.
Emery, —.	Forest of Dean.	Evans, B. S.	Glamorgan (W.).
Emery, T.	Abercarn.	Evans, B. T. C.	Erewash Valley, etc.
*Emery, W. J.	Luton.	Evans, C.	Gainsborough.
Emmerson, F.	Croydon.	Evans, C.	Oswestry.
Emmett, H.	Blackburn.	Evans, C. F.	Maesteg.
Emmott, R.	Litherland, etc.	Evans, C. H.	Aberdare.
Empringham, C. E.	Lincoln.	Evans, C. G.	Surrey (N.W.).
Endean, F. G.	West Lambeth.	Evans, C. J.	Cardiff.
England, F. G.	Uxbridge.	Evans, D.	Cardiganshire (N.).
England, H. A.	London (E.).	Evans, D.	Aberdare.
England, L.	Bath.	Evans, D. E.	Rhondda, etc.
England, R.	Teign and Dart.	Evans, D. F.	Pontypool.
England, R. E.	Birmingham.	Evans, D. G.	Petworth.
England, W.	Liverpool.	Evans, D. J.	Ogmore, etc.
England, W. S.	Liverpool.	Evans, D. N.	Tredegar.
England, W. W.	Southwark.	Evans, D. R.	Rhondda, etc.
Engledow, A. E.	East Ham.	Evans, D. T.	Ebbw Vale.
Engledow, F. W.	London (E.).	Evans, D. T.	Cardiff.
English, —.	Downham.	Evans, D. T.	Abertillery.
English, —.	Boston.	**Evans, E.**	Abertillery.
English, C.	Durham.	Evans, E.	Newport (Mon.).
English, C. E.	Woolwich.	Evans, E.	Maesteg.
English, C. T.	South Shields.	Evans, E.	Swansea.
English, J. G.	South Shields.	Evans, E.	Swansea.
English, S.	Grantham.	*Evans, E.	Sunderland.
English, W.	Chester-le-Street.	Evans, E.	Manchester.
Enoch, D.	Ogmore, etc.	Evans, E. B.	East Lambeth.
Enoch, G.	Hull.	Evans, E. C.	Birmingham.
Enoch, W. W.	Coventry.	Evans, E. H.	Pontypool.
*Ensell, E. E. B.	Gateshead.	Evans, E. T.	Ogmore, etc.
Ensoll, (Miss) G.	Middlesbrough.	Evans, E. V.	Maidenhead.
Ensor, R. N.	Manchester.	Evans, F.	Dudley.
*Enstone, A.	Banbury.	Evans, F.	Maesteg.
Entwistle, —.	Warrington.	Evans, F. G.	West Ham.
Entwistle, E.	Bolton District.	Evans, F. S.	Birmingham.

124

TEACHERS WHO JOINED THE FORCES

Name.	Association.	Name.	Association.
Evans, G.	Rhondda, etc.	Evans, W. E.	Rhondda, etc.
Evans, G.	Rhondda, etc.	Evans, W. G.	Pontypool.
Evans, G. H.	Walsall.	Evans, W. H.	Gelligaer.
Evans, G. R.	Barry.	Evans, W. H.	Liverpool.
Evans, G. R.	Ogmore, etc.	Evans, W. J.	Pontypool.
Evans, H.	Nottinghamshire (W.).	Evans, W. J.	Rhondda, etc.
Evans, H.	Rhondda, etc.	Evans, W. J.	Aberdare.
Evans, H.	Sheffield.	Evanson, A. C.	Birkenhead.
Evans, H.	Birkenhead.	Evatt, H.	Leicester (Mid).
Evans, H. B. Q.	Finsbury, etc.	Everard, T. B.	Lowestoft.
Evans, H. J.	Rhondda, etc.	**Everest, H. R.**	Winchester.
Evans, H. J.	Mountain Ash.	Everett, W. E.	Tottenham, etc.
Evans, I.	Exeter City.	Everett, W. H.	London (E.).
Evans, I.	Nuneaton.	*Everitt, W. A.	Birmingham.
Evans, I.	Rhondda, etc.	Everingham, J. B.	Bristol.
Evans, I. W.	Swansea.	Everitt, —.	East Lambeth.
Evans, J.	Bridgnorth.	Eveson, T. B.	East Lambeth.
Evans, J.	Gelligaer.	Evington, G.	Hull.
Evans, J.	Glamorgan (W.).	Evison, C. W.	West Lambeth.
Evans, J.	Rhondda, etc.	Ewan, J.	Lancaster.
Evans, J.	Glamorgan (W.).	Ewan, R. F.	Lancaster.
Evans, J.	Rhondda, etc.	Ewels, J.	Birmingham.
Evans, J.	Rhondda, etc.	Ewen, J. T.	Hebburn.
Evans, J.	Rhondda, etc.	Ewing, W. P.	Manchester.
Evans, J.	Mountain Ash.	*Exton, W.	Folkestone.
Evans, J.	Rhondda, etc.	Eyles, A. H.	Brentford.
Evans, J.	Wrexham.	Eyles, F. G.	Reading.
Evans, J. D.	Merthyr Tydfil.	Eyles, S. F.	Portsmouth.
Evans, J. H.	Merthyr Tydfil.	Eyres, A.	Folkestone.
Evans, J. L.	Gelligaer.		
Evans, J. M.	Swindon.	Facer, H. H.	Sunderland.
Evans, J. O.	Ebbw Vale.	Facey, W. J.	Liverpool.
Evans, J. T. R.	Glamorgan (Mid).	Faill, —.	Derby.
Evans, K. S.	West Lambeth.	Fairey, A. J. R.	Stockton-on-Tees.
*Evans, Llew.	Maesteg.	Fairey, A. M.	Tynemouth.
Evans, L. J.	London (N.W.).	Fairbrother, G.	Swadlincote.
Evans, M.	Lewisham.	Fairburn, H.	Woolwich.
*Evans, M.	Rhondda, etc.	**Fairchild, E. S.**	Somerset (N.).
Evans, O.	Penygroes.	Faircloth, W. D.	Hertfordshire (W.)
Evans, O. L.	Finsbury, etc.	Fairclough, F.	West Lambeth.
Evans, O. R.	Rhondda, etc.	Fairclough, F. M.	Liverpool.
Evans, P. L.	Southgate.	Fairfax, J.	Leyton.
Evans, R.	Sunderland.	Fairfoull, J. S.	Walthamstow.
Evans, R. D.	Merthyr Tydfil.	Fairham, (Miss)	Erith.
Evans, R. D.	Merthyr Tydfil.	Fairhurst, H.	Eccles.
Evans, R. G.	Rhondda, etc.	Fairhurst, H. E.	Liverpool.
Evans, R. P.	Menai.	**Fairless, E.**	Spennymoor.
Evans, R. S.	Tredegar.	*Fairley, R. E.	London (W.).
Evans, R. W.	Leominster.	Fairman, M.	Middlesbrough.
Evans, S.	Oldbury.	Fairmie, E. G. J.	Oldham.
Evans, S.	Erewash Valley, etc.	Fairs, E. J.	Ealing.
Evans, S. D.	Maesteg.	Fairweather, —.	Itchen.
Evans, T.	Mountain Ash.	Falcon, R. J.	Hindley.
Evans, T. F.	Llandudno.	**Falla, M. B.**	Dorset (N.).
Evans, T. J.	Pembrokeshire (N.).	Fallows, —.	Ipswich.
Evans, T. J.	Gelligaer.	Fance, C. W.	Southend-on-Sea.
Evans, T. J. F.	Rhondda, etc.	Fancort, H.	Peterborough.
Evans, T. M.	Barry.	Fancourt, W. L.	Kingston and Surbiton.
Evans, T. R.	Merthyr Tydfil.	Fanstone, G.	Tynemouth.
Evans, W.	Wrexham.	Fanthorpe, (Miss) F.	Eccles.
Evans, W.	Glamorgan (W.).	Faram, G. L.	Northampton.
Evans, W.	Glamorgan (Mid).	Faram, H.	Staffordshire (N.).
Evans, W.	Finsbury, etc.	Fargher, R. H.	Isle of Man.
Evans, W.	London (W.).	Farman, F. R.	Wimbledon.
Evans, W.	Swansea.	Farmer, A. E.	Northampton.
Evans, W. A.	Northampton.	*Farmer, F.	Leamington.
Evans, W. B.	West Lambeth.	**Farmer, G. H.**	Birmingham.
Evans, W. E.	Barking.	**Farmer, G. H.**	Tamworth.
Evans, W. E.	Devon (N.).	Farmer, L.	Loughborough.

N.U.T. WAR RECORD

Name.	Association.
Farminer, W. J.	Portsmouth.
Farnham, R.	Tottenham, etc.
Farnhill, F.	Roch Valley.
*Farnish, J.	Bradford.
Farnworth, J. W.	Blackburn.
Farr, F.	Somerset (N.).
Farr, F. J.	Plymouth.
Farr, H. C.	Dorking.
Farran, C. R.	Colchester, etc.
Farrand, J.	Hyde.
Farrant, J. W.	Great Yarmouth.
Farrants, M. C.	West Lambeth.
Farrar, A. E.	Huddersfield.
Farrar, C. C.	Durham.
Farrar, E.	Todmorden.
Farrar, J.	Bristol.
Farrar, S.	Chorley.
Farrell, M. J.	West Ham.
Farren, J. C.	Coventry.
Farrer, L. W.	West Lambeth.
*Farrer, W.	Durham.
Farrow, A. E.	Colchester, etc.
Farrow, E. S.	Portsmouth.
Farrow, F.	Lancaster.
Farrow, R. R.	London (W.).
Farthing, J.	Nottingham.
Fathers, (Mrs.) C.	Norwich City.
Faughan, W. P.	Bradford.
Faulder, T.	Erith.
Faulkner, E. F.	Woolwich.
Faulkner, F.	Surrey (S.E.).
Faux, J.	Kingston and Surbiton.
Fawbert, R.	Castleford, etc.
Fawcett, F.	Grimsby.
Fawcett, J.	York.
Fawcett, J. R.	Leicester (Mid).
Fawcett, (Miss) M.	London (E).
Fawcett, R.	Durham.
*Fawkes, —.	Burton-on-Trent.
Fay, —.	London (N.W.).
Fay, A. F.	Finsbury, etc.
Fay, F.	Bristol.
Fazakerley, —.	Rugby.
Fazakerley, —.	St. Helens.
Fear, E.	Wigan.
Fear, W. G.	Southwark.
Fearn, W. A. C.	Birmingham.
Feather, F. J.	Gelligaer.
Featherstone, F.	York.
Featherstone, T. R.	Stockton-on-Tees.
Featherstone, W.	Gateshead.
Fee, B. W.	Manchester.
Feest, E. L.	Brighton, etc.
Feigenbaum, I.	London (E.).
Fell, —.	Doncaster.
Fell, C.	Swindon.
Fell, E.	Nelson, Colne, etc.
Fell, T. I.	Liverpool.
Fell, W. J.	Deptford and Greenwich.
Fellgett, F. C.	London (W.).
Fellows, H.	Oldbury.
Fellows, H. A.	Bilston.
Fellows, H. E.	Coseley.
Feltham, —.	Reading.
Fenemore, W. E.	Brighton, etc.
Fenn, H. C.	West Lambeth.
Fennell, H. G.	Lewisham.
Fennell, L. W.	Gloucester.
Fennessy, E. P.	West Ham.

Name.	Association.
Fenney, N.	Sunderland.
Fenning, W.	Cheltenham.
Fenton, W.	Oldham.
Fenwick, —.	Thirsk.
Fenwick, A. S.	Leeds.
Fenwick, G. H.	Leeds.
Fenwick, J. M.	Hull.
Fergurson, T.	Spennymoor.
Ferguson, —.	London (N.W.).
Ferguson, A. G.	Cardiff.
Ferguson, H. H. E.	Finsbury, etc.
Ferguson, J. F. C.	Bridgwater.
Ferguson, W. R.	Hebburn.
Ferguson, W. V.	Finsbury, etc.
Ferley, A. D.	Forest of Dean.
Ferrell, T.	Blyth.
Ferrer, W. J.	Swansea.
Ferrier, —.	South Shields.
Ferrington, (Miss) M.	Leicester.
Ferry, (Miss) S. K.	East Ham.
Fettes, J. M.	Durham.
Fettes, J. P.	West Ham.
Fewster, R. J.	Birmingham.
Fickling, W.	Easington.
Fidler, W. E. G.	Richmond (Surrey).
Field, —.	Boston.
Field, H.	Hertfordshire (W.).
Field, J.	Gloucester.
Field, S. K.	Birmingham.
*Field, W.	Wakefield.
Field, W. J.	West Lambeth.
Fielden, H.	Workington.
Fielder, C.	Swansea.
Fieldhouse, —.	Nelson, Colne, etc.
Fielding, H.	Leeds.
*Fielding, J. W. S.	Glossop.
Fielding, R.	Leeds.
Fields, J. W.	Birmingham.
Figg, H. H.	Richmond (Surrey).
Figgins, R. J.	Brighton, etc.
Filby, J. E.	Birmingham.
Filmer, G. L.	Eastbourne.
Filmer, S. W.	Faversham.
Finch, A.	Erewash Valley, etc.
Finch, D.	Colchester, etc.
*Finch, R. A.	Liverpool.
Fincher, E. F.	Kingston and Surbiton.
Finerman, L.	London (E.).
Finlay, (Miss)	Cumberland (W.)
Finlay, D. C.	Liverpool.
Finlayson, A.	Shropshire.
Finlayson, J. G.	Blaydon.
Finn, D. F.	Birkenhead.
Finney, —.	St. Helens.
Finnie, W. S.	London (W.).
Finnigan, J. B.	Manchester.
Firbank, W.	Hartlepools.
Firman, G. J.	Barking.
Firth, —.	Penistone.
Firth, A.	Barkston Ash.
Firth, A.	Huddersfield.
Firth, A. E.	Chatham, etc.
Firth, G. H.	Rotherham.
Firth, J. B.	Bellingham.
Firth, S.	Spen Valley.
Firth, S.	Howden.
Fish, G. W.	Lancaster.
Fish, J.	Northumberland (N.).
Fish, P.	Blackburn.

126

TEACHERS WHO JOINED THE FORCES

Name.	Association.	Name.	Association.
Fisher, (Miss)	Northumberland (E.).	Flood, —.	Erith.
Fisher, —.	Salford.	Flook, G.	Rhondda, etc.
Fishe., A.	Bromsgrove.	Floyd, A. H.	Tottenham, etc.
Fisher, A.	Dewsbury, etc.	Floyd, A. J.	Cannock.
Fisher, A. R.	Walthamstow.	Flynn, F.	Lewes.
Fisher, A. W.	Durham.	Foden, I. J.	Pendle Forest.
Fisher, D.	Stockton-on-Tees.	Foden, O. C.	Southwark.
Fisher, E.	Leeds.	Foers, H.	Sheffield.
Fisher, F.	Bolton Borough.	Fogden, F.	Croydon.
Fisher, F.	Bolton District.	Foley, G. E.	Hackney.
*Fisher, G. H.	London (E.).	**Foley, J.**	London (W.).
*Fisher, H. W.	East Lambeth.	Foot, E. J.	Portsmouth.
Fisher, H. W.	Harwich.	**Foot, F. W.**	Ilford.
Fisher, J.	Pembrokeshire (S.).	Foot, G.	Northampton.
Fisher, J.	Finsbury, etc.	Forbes, —.	Barnsley.
Fisher, R.	Burton-on-Trent.	Forbes, H.	East Lambeth.
Fisher, T. W.	Leicester (Mid).	Forbes, J. T.	Folkestone.
Fisher, W. H.	Knutsford.	Forcer, F.	Hartlepools.
Fisher, W. J.	Stockton-on-Tees.	Ford, —.	Salisbury.
Fishpool, S. G.	Lewes.	Ford, —.	West Ham.
Fishwick, A.	Leeds.	Ford, A. J.	East Ham.
Fiske, C. E.	Waveney Valley.	**Ford, B.**	Vale of Derwent.
Fitt, J.	Maidenhead.	Ford, C.	Kent (W.).
Fitt, J. A.	Winchester.	Ford, E.	Yoxford.
Fitton, H.	Manchester.	Ford, G. W.	East Lambeth.
Fitton, T.	Epsom, etc.	Ford, H.	St. Helens.
FitzGeorge, W.	Lichfield.	*Ford, H. C.	East Lambeth.
Fitzjohn, H.	Peterborough.	Ford, J. F.	Stourbridge.
Flack, W. S.	Birmingham.	Ford, M.	Woolwich.
Flanders, A. H.	Tottenham, etc.	Ford, T. F.	Bolton District.
Flavin, P. C.	Watford.	Ford, T. H.	Norfolk. (N.E.).
Flear, T. E.	Sheffield.	Ford, W. J.	Dorking.
Fleetcroft, J. S.	London (N.W.)	Forder, P. S.	Waveney Valley.
Fleet, H.	Nottingham.	Fordham, C. H.	Hackney.
Fleming, G.	Durham.	Fordham, R. R.	Ampthill, etc.
Fleming, H.	West Stanley.	**Foreman, D. J.**	East Ham.
Fleming, J.	Birkenhead.	Foreman, T. F.	Isle of Axholme.
Fleming, R.	Fleetwood.	Forrest, B. G.	Birmingham.
Fleming, R.	Hartlepools.	Forrest, E. M.	London (W.).
Fleming, R.	Aylesbury.	Forrest, H. G.	Worthing.
Fleming, R. J.	Stourbridge.	**Forrest, W.**	Durham.
*Fleming, W. A. J.	Oldham.	Forrester, C. R.	Malvern, etc.
Fleming, W. E.	Darwen.	Forrester, H.	Staffordshire (N.).
Flemons, D. G.	Coventry.	Forrester, L. C.	London (E.).
Fletcher, A.	Stockport.	**Forryan, W. O.**	Bradford.
Fletcher, B. F.	Derby (E.).	**Forse, C. R.**	Staffordshire (N.).
Fletcher, C. H.	Coventry.	Forsey, S. R.	Kent (W.).
Fletcher, E.	West Lambeth.	Forsey, W.	Lewisham.
Fletcher, E. B.	Leeds.	Forshaw, E. J.	Durham.
Fletcher, E.	East Lambeth.	Forster, —.	Willesden.
Fletcher, F.	Hackney.	Forster, —.	St. Helens.
Fletcher, G. S.	Witney.	Forster, A.	Leeds.
Fletcher, H.	Sheffield.	Forster, A.	South Shields.
Fletcher, J.	Nottingham.	Forster, G. L.	Liverpool.
Fletcher, J. H.	Bolton Borough.	Forster, G. M.	Felling.
Fletcher, J. T.	New Forest.	Forster, H. H.	Wiltshire (W.).
Fletcher, J. T. M.	Spalding.	Forster, J. M.	Dudley.
Fletcher, L.	Brierley Hill, etc.	Forster, W. B.	Durham.
Fletcher, R.	Gloucester.	**Forsyth, R.**	Tynemouth.
Fletcher, W.	Bury.	Forsyth, W.	Barnard Castle.
Fletcher, W. W.	Sheffield.	Forsyth, W. J.	Finsbury, etc.
Fleury, W. F.	Jersey.	Fortescue, H.	Canterbury.
Flew, A. E.	London (W.).	Fosberry, F. H.	Alton.
Flewker, G. W.	Hartlepools.	Fosbrooke, F.	Dudley.
Flinks, A.	Birmingham.	Foskett, H. W.	Southwark.
Flint, C.	Sittingbourne.	Foss, J. K.	Gloucester.
*Flint, H. H.	West Lambeth.	Foster, —.	Doncaster.
Float, (Miss) A.	Leicester.	Foster, —.	Shrewsbury.
Float, (Miss) J.	Leicester.	Foster, A. D.	Tunbridge Wells.

N.U.T. WAR RECORD

Name.	Association.
Foster, C.	Sunderland.
Foster, (Miss) C.	Pembrokeshire (Mid.).
Foster, C. H.	Middlesbrough.
Foster, C. W.	Kingston and Surbiton.
*Foster, D.	West Lambeth.
Foster, F. E.	Staines.
Foster, G. O.	Croydon.
Foster, H. S.	Makerfield.
Foster, J.	Carlisle, etc.
Foster, J.	Rotherham.
Foster, J.	Jarrow.
Foster, J.	Bradford.
Foster, J. C.	Gateshead.
Foster, J. H.	Hull.
Foster, P.	Cannock.
Foster, T. M.	Crook.
Foster, W. J.	South Shields.
Foulds, F.	Manchester.
Foulds, F.	Halifax.
Foulger, E. C. J.	Coventry.
Foulger, F. J.	Norwich.
Foulger, W.	Finsbury, etc.
*Foulkes, J.	Warrington.
Foulkes, J. H.	Warrington.
Foulkes, S. J.	Birkenhead.
Fountain, H. C.	Lewisham.
Fourt, F.	Bromsgrove.
Fowler, —.	Cannock.
Fowler, A. R.	Leicester.
Fowler, C. E.	Portsmouth.
Fowler, E.	West Stanley.
Fowler, (Miss) E. A.	Bury St. Edmunds.
Fowler, H. E.	East Lambeth.
Fowler, J.	Hull.
Fowler, J.	East Lambeth.
Fowler, J. G.	London (E.)
Fowler, J. W. D.	Sunderland.
Fowler, W. F.	Dartford.
Fowles, G.	London (W.).
Fowles, J.	Shropshire.
Fowles, W.	Runcorn.
Fox, —.	Ealing.
Fox, C. J.	Deptford and Greenwich
Fox, G. F. B.	Twickenham.
Fox, H.	Eastleigh, etc.
Fox, H.	Derbyshire (E.).
Fox, H. E.	Sheffield.
Fox, H. G.	Peterborough.
Fox, H. J.	East Lambeth.
Fox, J.	London (E.).
*Fox, J.	Roch Valley.
Fox, J. G.	London (W.).
Fox, L. F.	Chatham, etc.
Fox, M. S.	Liverpool.
Fox, R.	Saddleworth.
Fox, R. J.	Southend-on-Sea.
Fox, S.	London (E.).
Fox, S. T.	Wellingborough.
Fox, T.	Jarrow.
Fox, T. F.	West Lambeth.
Foxcroft, J. G.	London (W.).
Foxon, A. H.	Leicester.
Foy, L.	Guernsey.
Foyle, W. H.	Northampton.
France, H.	Stalybridge.
France, R.	Finsbury, etc.
Franceers, E. T.	Rhondda, etc.
Francis, —.	Kettering.
Francis, —.	Salford.

Name.	Association.
Francis, A. E.	East Ham.
Francis, G. V.	Widnes.
Francis, H. L.	Cardiff.
*Francis, H. W.	Chatham, etc.
Francis, J. P.	Dover.
Francis, O. J.	Portsmouth.
Francis, P. W.	West Lambeth.
Francis, R. G.	Cardiff.
Francis, S. G.	Lowestoft.
Francis, T.	Houghton-le-Spring.
Francis, W. A. G.	London (E.).
Francis, W. J.	Stockport.
Frankis, P.	Hackney.
Frankish, G.	Driffield, etc.
Frankish, W.	Howden.
Frankland, C. D.	Leeds.
Frankland, J. H.	Burnley.
Frankland, N.	Eccles.
Franklin, H.	Brighton, etc.
Franklin, W. S.	Bishop Auckland.
*Franks, E.	Middlesbrough.
Franks, L. L.	London (E.).
Frape, H. W.	Leeds.
Fraser, H. D.	Southgate.
Fraser, J.	Rhondda, etc.
*Fraser, J.	Ipswich.
Fraser, R.	London. (W.)
Frayn, W. B.	Cornwall (W.).
Freckleton, S.	Derby.
Frederick, W.	Cowbridge, etc.
Free, E. R.	Deptford and Greenwich.
Freeborough, C.	London (E.).
Freegard, S. E. L.	Swindon.
Freeland, H. W.	London (W.).
Freeling, W. C.	Tynemouth.
Freeman, A. E.	Hitchen.
Freeman, A. J.	Hackney.
Freeman, A. M.	Southwark.
Freeman, A. W.	Waveney Valley.
Freeman, B. H. J.	Tottenham, etc.
Freeman, C. W.	Llanfair.
Freeman, E.	Norwich.
Freeman, F.	Chester.
Freeman, G. J.	West Lambeth.
Freeman, J.	Dudley.
Freeman, J.	Bolton District
Freeman, W.	Deptford and Greenwich.
Freemantle, —.	Great Yarmouth.
Freer, G. H.	Malton.
Freer, T. D.	Hull.
French, A. E.	Hackney.
French, E. J.	Lewisham.
French, J. L.	Wellingborough.
French, S.	Southwark.
*French, W. E.	London (W.).
Frendemacher, S. G.	Deptford and Greenwich.
Freshwater, T.	Willenhall.
*Fretwell, C. N.	Leeds.
Fretwell, O. N.	Peterborough.
Fretwell, W. A.	Leeds.
Frewing, P.	Warwick.
Fricker, A. C.	Swindon.
Friday, —.	Erith.
Frisby, F.	Bexhill.
Frith, —.	Doncaster.
Frith, F. H.	Mansfield.
Frith, J.	Sheffield.
Frodsham, S.	Macclesfield District.
Froehlich, W.	Manchester.

128

TEACHERS WHO JOINED THE FORCES

Name.	Association.
Froggatt, A.	Kiveton Park.
Froom, E, W. M.	Chorley.
Froome, A. J.	Windsor.
*Froome, G. W.	London (W.).
Frost, H. R.	Cornwall (E.).
Frost, H. R.	Cornwall (W.).
Frost, J. W.	Leicester.
Frost, O.	Barnsley.
Froude, E.	Chester.
Fry, (Miss)	Erith.
Fry, —.	Dorset (E.).
Fry, E. W.	Moreton-in-Marsh.
Fry, R. G.	Bristol.
Fryer, A.	Walsall.
Fryer, A. W.	East Ham.
*Fryer, G.	Mountain Ash.
Fuge, F. H.	Southgate.
Fugler, R. G.	Northwich.
Fulbeck, G. E.	Hornsey.
Fulford, —.	Willesden.
Fulford, F. E.	London (E.).
Fulford, R. A.	Eastleigh.
Fullbrook, F.	Brighton, etc.
Fuller, A. J.	Birmingham.
Fuller, R. H.	Manchester.
Fuller, W. H.	West Ham.
Fullerton, M.	Chester-le-Street.
Fullford, E. F.	London (E.).
Furling, W. J.	Brentford.
Furnass, S.	Stretford.
Furner, J. R.	East Lambeth.
Furness, W. S.	Warrington.
Furniss, W. V.	West Lambeth.
Furnival, J. H.	Birmingham.
Furze, R. J.	Woolwich.
Fyles, H.	Nantwich.
Gabe, G. T.	Faversham.
Gabe, R. T.	Cardiff.
Gachet, W. R.	Walthamstow.
Gaffney, T.	Liverpool.
Gagan, J. E.	Sheffield.
Gage, J. A. L.	Norfolk (W.).
Gahan, R.	Manchester.
Gair, G.	West Stanley.
Galbraith, C. T.	Warwickshire (N.).
Gale, F.	Croydon.
Gale, L.	Jersey.
Gall, J.	Liverpool.
Gall, W. H.	Liverpool.
Gallagher, A. G.	Plymouth.
Gallery, G.	London (N.W.).
Galley, R.	Barking.
Gallister, G. A.	Tottenham, etc.
Gallon, J. R.	Northumberland (E.).
Galton, L.	Willesden.
Gamson, G.	Tipton.
Gamson, G. C.	Dudley.
Ganderton, (Miss) M.G.	Cardiff.
Gandy, A. E.	Manchester.
Gane, H. O.	Kingston and Surbiton.
Gane, J. T.	Southampton.
Gapp, E. J.	East Ham.
Garbett, W.	Wakefield.
Gardam, H.	Skipton.
Gardener, J.	Chatham, etc.
Gardener, L. G.	Hull.
Gardiner, —.	Guildford.
Gardiner, G. S.	Sunderland.
Gardiner, S.	Bristol.
Gardiner, S. V.	Beverley.
Gardner, —.	Northampton.
Gardner, A. F.	Swindon.
Gardner, E. H.	Colchester, etc.
Gardner, H.	Newport (Mon.).
Gardner, H.	Deptford and Greenwich.
Gardner, H. G.	Walsall.
Gardner, J. T.	Finsbury, etc.
Garfield-Walters, J.	Rhondda, etc.
Garforth, J. H.	Spen Valley.
Garforth, P.	Alnwick.
Garland, —.	Bodmin.
Garland, —.	West Ham.
Garland, T. L.	Plymouth.
Garland, W. R.	East Ham.
Garlick, —.	Eastleigh, etc.
Garlick, J.	Huddersfield.
Garlick, J. P.	Castleford, etc.
Garner, C.	Runcorn.
Garner, F. A.	Surrey (N.W.).
*Garner, F. B.	Wimbledon.
Garner, F. H.	Leeds.
Garner, J. H.	Cambridgeshire.
Garner, P.	Ampthill, etc.
Garner, R.	Manchester.
Garner, R. L.	Farnham.
Garner, W.	Makerfield.
Garnett, G.	Whitehaven.
Garnett, J. H.	Gelligaer.
Garnier, F. T.	Jersey.
Garratt, F.	Dudley.
Garratt, J.	Coalville.
Garraway, —.	Bath.
Garrett, (Miss) D.	Erith.
Garrett, E.	East Lambeth.
Garrett, J. N.	Brackley, etc.
Garside, —.	Willesden.
Garside, J. W.	Houghton-le-Spring.
Garside, M.	Halifax.
Garton, —.	Deptford and Greenwich.
Garton, A. M.	Staffordshire (N.).
Garton, F. G.	Derbyshire (E.).
Garton, P.	Horsham, etc.
Gartside, —.	Sale.
Garwood, C.	Mexborough.
Gascoigne, A. E.	Southend-on-Sea.
Gascoigne, E.	London (N.W.).
Gascoyne, C.	Derby (E.).
Gaskarth, T. H.	Maryport.
Gaskell, C. H.	Chiswick.
Gaskin, —.	East Lambeth.
Gasser, J. G.	East Lambeth.
Gassick, M.	Staffordshire (N.).
Gasson, A. J.	Dartford.
Gastall, H. W.	Menai.
*Gastall, W. H.	Blackpool.
Gate, E.	Blaydon.
Gatehouse, H. O.	East Lambeth.
Gates, A. H.	Brighton, etc.
Gates, A. T.	Chatham, etc.
Gatford, H.	East Lambeth.
Gatter, F.	London (E.).
Gavin, L. J.	Bradford.
Gawthorpe, J.	Mexborough.
Gawthorpe, J.	Castleford, etc.
Gawthrop, S. R.	Maidenhead.
Gay, J. V.	Bristol.
Gay, W.	Bristol.

N.U.T. WAR RECORD

Name.	Association.
Gayfer, —.	Grimsby.
Gazzard, H.	Bristol.
Geary, —.	Hastings.
Geater, S.	Sittingbourne.
Geddes, J.	Plymouth.
Geddes, N.	Newcastle-on-Tyne.
Geddes, S.	Manchester.
Gedling, T. A.	South Shields.
Gee, J. H.	Makerfield.
Gee, W.	Sheffield.
Geen, A. L. S.	East Lambeth.
Gelsthorpe, A. H.	Mansfield Borough.
*Gempton, A. G.	Teign and Dart.
Gent, C. E.	Mansfield.
Gent, C. R.	Newcastle-on-Tyne.
Gentle, M. W.	Tonbridge.
Gentle, O.	Watford.
Gentry, A. V.	Romford, etc.
George, —.	Birmingham.
George, B.	Swansea.
George, B. J.	Southwark.
George, D. O.	Merthyr Tydfil.
George, H. G.	Swansea.
George, H. H.	Pontypool.
George, J. P.	Croydon.
George, R. L.	Bury.
George, S. O.	Deal, etc.
George, T.	West Lambeth.
George, V. A. S.	Basingstoke.
George, W.	Fishguard.
George, W.	Forest of Dean.
George, W. E.	Hackney.
George, W. F.	Croydon.
Germain, —.	Portsmouth.
*Germaney, W. T.	Westminster.
Gerrard, T.	Manchester.
Gerrard, T.	Manchester.
Gerrard, T.	Wigan.
Gerrey, C. F.	Bournemouth.
Gerrish, G. E.	Enfield.
Gess, A. P.	Gravesend.
Gethin, H. S.	Wolverhampton.
Gibbins, W. A.	Romford, etc.
Gibbins, W. J.	Spennymoor.
Gibbon, A.	Mountain Ash.
Gibbon, E. W.	Cardiff.
Gibbons, J.	Sunderland.
Gibbons, J. H.	Felling.
Gibbons, W. T.	Waveney Valley.
Gibbs, —.	Wimbledon.
Gibbs, A. E.	London (W.).
Gibbs, A. E. T.	Somerset (E.C.).
Gibbs, A. G.	Edmonton.
Gibbs, E.	Barnes and Mortlake.
Gibbs, E. W.	Plymouth.
Gibbs, F. A.	Southwark.
*Gibbs, F. J.	Birmingham.
Gibbs, G.	Penistone.
Gibbs, H.	Liverpool.
Gibbs, W. H.	Rugby.
Gibbs, W. H.	Staffordshire (N.).
Gibbs, W. H.	Brighton, etc.
Gibby, V.	Rhymney Valley.
Giblin, —.	St. Helens.
Gibson, —.	Hyndburn.
Gibson, —.	Leeds.
Gibson, —.	Newport (Mon.).
Gibson, A.	Hull.
Gibson, (Miss) B.	Sunderland.
Gibson, C.	Wimbledon.
Gibson, C. L.	Dewsbury, etc.
Gibson, E. J.	Liverpool.
*Gibson, E. S.	Sunderland.
Gibson, F.	Bolton District.
Gibson, H.	Liverpool.
Gibson, J.	Loughborough.
Gibson, J.	Halifax.
Gibson, J.	Northumberland (S.).
Gibson, J.	West Lambeth.
Gibson, J. H.	Liverpool.
Gibson, J. R.	London (E.).
Gibson, J. S.	York.
Gibson, M.	Durham.
Gibson, P. G. H.	Bishop's Waltham.
*Gibson, S.	Bishop Auckland.
Gibson, T.	London (W.).
Gibson, T. S.	Liverpool.
Gibson, T. W.	Northumberland (E.).
Gibson, W.	Leeds.
Gibson, W. E.	Northumberland (E.).
Gibson, W. J.	Warwickshire (N.).
Gibson, W. R.	Plymouth.
Giddings, A. J.	Manchester.
Giddins, —.	Alton.
Gidney, —.	Kettering.
Gidney, H.	Norfolk (N.W.).
Gilbart, J. H. W.	Tavistock.
Gilbert, —.	London (W.).
Gilbert, H. C.	Finsbury, etc.
Gilbert, H. J.	West Ham.
Gilbert, J. S. M.	Plymouth.
Gilbert, L. W.	Hornsey.
Gilbert, R.	Ealing.
Gilbert, R.	Millom.
Gilbert, S. F.	Kingsbridge.
Gilbert, T. A.	West Lambeth.
Gilby, H. J.	Ilford.
Gilbey, W. T.	Walsall.
Gilchrist, J. H.	Ingleborough.
Gilder, T.	Woolwich.
Gilderdale, S. P.	Birkenhead.
Giles, —.	Erith.
Giles, E. E.	Hackney.
Giles, F. C.	West Lambeth.
Giles, F. C.	Jarrow.
Giles, F. J.	Plymouth.
Giles, T.	West Ham.
Gilgrass, P. H.	Hull.
Gilhespy, J.	Gateshead.
Gill, A.	Willesden.
Gill, A. J.	Gillingham.
Gill, C.	Stockton on Tees.
Gill, D. C.	London (W.).
Gill, E.	Taunton, etc.
Gill, E.	Whitehaven.
Gill, E. F.	Watford.
Gill, E. J.	Sheffield.
Gill, F. H.	Sutton Coldfield.
Gill, H.	Leeds.
Gill, H.	Liverpool.
Gill, H.	Bath.
Gill, H. H.	Leyton.
Gill, H. H.	East Ham.
Gill, J. W.	Colchester, etc.
*Gill, N.	Somerset (N.).
Gill, S. F.	London (W.).
Gill, T. J.	Falmouth and Truro.
Gill, W.	Bury.

TEACHERS WHO JOINED THE FORCES

Name.	Association.
Gill, W. C.	Worthing.
Gill, W. J.	Deptford and Greenwich.
Gilliam, J. G.	Bletchley.
Gillard, E. A.	Hackney.
Gillard, L. P.	Exeter City.
Gillard, P. C. S.	Bristol.
Gillard, W.	Chipping Norton, etc.
Gillard, W. J.	Plymouth.
Gillender, A. W.	South Shields.
Gillett, A.	Chorley.
Gilley, J. C.	Sheffield.
Gilliam, A. V. G.	Warwick.
Gilliat, F.	Stockport.
Gillison, A. H.	Middlesbrough.
Gilliver, H.	Coalville.
Gillon, C. A.	Westminster.
Gilpin, M.	Exeter City.
Gilpin, R. J.	Gillingham.
Gimber, G. W.	Sheffield.
Gimson, P. J.	Woolwich.
Gingell, L. V.	Woolwich.
Gittings, F. J.	Wimbledon.
Gladden, —.	Crewe.
Gladden, W.	Crewe.
Gladwell, A. M.	Walthamstow.
Gladwell, J. H.	Worcester.
Gladwin, P.	Leeds.
Glanville, F. R.	Plymouth.
Glass, A.	Bristol.
Glass, H. D.	Finsbury, etc.
Glass, W. D.	Winchester.
Glasson, A. L.	Berkshire (N.).
Glasson, W.	Cornwall (W.).
Glastonbury, —.	Newbury.
Glaves, A.	Hull.
Gleadall, J.	East Lambeth.
Gleadhill, E.	Middlesbrough.
Gleave, —.	Reading.
Gleaves, J. T.	Staffordshire (N.).
Gledhill, E.	Bradford.
Gledhill, J.	Bradford.
Gledhill, (Miss) S.	Castleford, etc.
Gledhill, W.	Penistone.
Gleeson, D.	Wigan.
Glendon, E. T.	Birmingham.
Glenister, G. E.	Brighton, etc.
Glenn, —.	Salford.
Glickman, D.	Manchester.
Glockler, S. A.	Tottenham, etc.
Glossop, H. G.	Goole.
Glover, B.	South Shields.
Glover, C. E.	Liverpool.
Glover, C. R.	Southend-on-Sea.
Glover, J. W. E.	Isle of Wight.
Glover, M. J.	Warrington.
*Goacher, F.	Willesden.
Goater, B.	Portsmouth.
Goates, G. E.	Hendon.
Godber, —.	Petworth.
Goddard, —.	Huntingdonshire.
Goddard, A. E.	Leicester.
Goddard, A. E.	Barnes and Mortlake.
Goddard, B. R.	Winchester.
Goddard, F. W.	Walthamstow.
Goddard, S. B.	Walthamstow.
Godden, E. W.	Southend-on-Sea.
Godfrey, E. A.	West Lambeth.
Godfrey, F.	Makerfield.
Godfrey, H.	Sheffield.

Name.	Association.
Godfrey, M.	Hull.
Godfrey, N.	Dover.
Godfrey, W. E.	Derby (E.).
Godley, J. L.	Shirebrook.
Godley, P. C.	Tonbridge.
Godman, A.	London (E.).
Godward, P.	Skipton.
*Godwin, J.	Chester.
Goer, E. C.	Kidderminster.
Goffin, C. W.	Norwich.
Going, P. J.	Southampton.
Golafarb, M.	London (E.).
Gold, H.	Bristol.
Goldbeck, M. S.	Sunderland.
Goldberg, M.	Leeds.
Golder, E. A.	West Ham.
Goldfinch, A.	Bristol.
Goldman, P.	Leeds.
Goldring, —.	Willesden.
Goldring, H.	Brighton, etc.
Golds, A.	Macclesfield Borough.
Goldsbrough, E. C.	Stockton-on-Tees.
Goldspink, C.	Melton Mowbray.
Goldstone, F. W.	Sheffield.
Golightly, A.	Leyton.
Golightly, W.	Vale of Derwent.
*Golland, A. R.	Darlington.
Golledge, E. J.	Ealing.
Gomm, A. G.	Aylesbury.
Gomme, C.	Maidstone.
Gooch, S.	Liverpool.
Goodall, —.	Nottingham.
Goodband, —.	Derby.
Goodchild, R. J.	Chiswick.
Goode, —.	Birmingham.
Goode, F. W.	Pontypool.
Goodey, A. N.	Hertford.
Goodfellow, G.	Maidstone.
Goodfellow, G. H.	Leyton.
Goodger, P.	Woolwich.
Goodhall, C. J.	Leeds.
Goodhall, J.	Chatham, etc.
Goodhead, F. H.	Westminster.
Goodhill, W.	Leeds.
Goodhind, —.	Derby.
Goodier, T.	Stockport.
Gooding, J. S.	Peterborough.
Goodison, A. L.	Finsbury, etc.
*Goodland, P. H. E.	East Lambeth.
Goodman, G. W. H.	Chipping Norton, etc.
*Goodman, S. F.	Wallasey.
Goodsell, A.	Maidstone.
Goodwill, —.	Heywood.
Goodwin, —.	Chadderton.
Goodwin, A.	Richmond (Surrey).
Goodwin, A. E.	Gloucester.
Goodwin, A. J.	London (E.).
Goodwin, F. O. P.	Eastbourne.
Goodwin, F. R.	Shrewsbury.
Goodwin, H.	West Ham.
Goodwin, R. J.	Hackney.
*Goodwin, J. T.	Bishop Auckland.
Goodwins, R. E.	Norwich.
Goodyear, C. A.	Ormskirk.
Goodyer, H. S.	Birmingham.
Goodyear, H. S.	Wakefield.
Goose, B. A.	Cambridgeshire.
Goose, T. H.	Deptford and Greenwich.
Gorden, H.	Manchester.

N.U.T. WAR RECORD

Name.	Association.
Gordon, A.	East Lambeth.
Gordon, G.	Leicester.
Gordon, G. H.	Hackney.
Gordon, G. J.	Gillingham.
Gordon, G. N.	Newcastle-on-Tyne.
Gordon, G. V.	London (E.).
Gordon, G. W.	Bolton Borough.
Gordon, H.	South Shields.
Gore, A. E.	Liverpool.
Gore, A. L.	Uxbridge.
Gorton, J.	Wigan.
Gorton, W.	Workington.
Gorvett, A.	Wiltshire (W.).
Gorvett, H.	Rhondda, etc.
Gosham, E. W.	Southampton.
Gosling, —.	West Ham.
Gosling, C. F.	Southwark.
Gosling, (Miss) L.	Dewsbury, etc.
Gosling, (Miss) L.	Leeds.
Goss, C. L.	Taunton, etc.
Goss, F.	West Stanley.
Gosse, M.	Hull.
Gott, —.	Doncaster.
Goudie, T.	Chester-le-Street.
Gough, H. T.	Worcester City.
Gough, J. S.	Liverpool.
Gough, W. P.	Gelligaer.
Gould, F.	Birmingham.
Gould, J. W.	Sheffield.
Goulden, R.	Doncaster.
Gourvitch, I.	Hackney.
Gover, C. H.	Gloucester (S.).
Govier, W. T.	Plymouth.
Gowar, —.	Somerset (N.).
Gowar, F. W.	Southgate.
Gowdie, T.	Chester-le-Street.
Gower, A. E.	Dewsbury, etc.
Gower, A. E.	Spen Valley.
Gower, G.	Mountain Ash
Gowers, E. A.	Sudbury.
Gowing, —.	Luton.
Gowing, F.	Norfolk (S.).
*Gowland, S. J.	Roch Valley.
Grabois, L.	Liverpool.
Grace, L.	Dewsbury, etc.
Grace, T.	Gateshead.
Gracey, H.	Walthamstow.
Graebe, H. F.	Horsham, etc.
Graham, —.	St. Helens.
Graham, —.	Tottenham, etc.
Graham, A. E.	Hartlepools.
Graham, D.	Crompton and Royton.
Graham, H.	Finsbury, etc.
Graham, J. W.	Sunderland.
*Graham, M.	Carlisle.
Graham, O.	Darwen.
Graham, T.	London (N.W.)
Graham, T. G.	Staffordshire (N.).
Graham, T. W.	Blaydon.
Graham-Vevers, J.	Skipton.
Graham, W.	Newcastle-on-Tyne.
Graham, W. G.	Wallsend.
Graham, W. T.	East Ham.
Grain, A.	Nuneaton.
Grainger, F. T.	Birmingham.
Grainger, W.	Durham.
Grainger, W.	Guildford.
Grainger, W. R.	Nottingham.
Granger, E. R.	Nottingham.
Grant, —.	Kingston and Surbiton.
Grant, A. H.	Cardiff.
Grant, A. S.	Sunderland.
Grant, C.	Mexborough.
Grant, G.	Birkenhead.
Grant, G. A.	Dorset (E.).
Grant, G. F.	Wallsend
Grant, H. R.	Plymouth.
Grant, P.	Tynemouth.
Grant, R.	Wallsend.
Grant, R. C.	Cardiff.
*Grant, W. P.	Dartford.
Gratton, G. H.	West Ham.
Gratton, G. H. L.	Romford, etc.
*Grattridge, A. W.	Leicester.
Graveling, A. E.	Norwich.
*Gravelle, H. L.	Cardiff.
Graver, G. F.	Loughborough.
Graves, —.	West Ham.
Graves, A.	Manchester.
Graves, C.	Wimbledon.
Gravestock, W. J.	West Lambeth.
Graville, W. W.	Darlington.
Gray, —.	Blaydon.
Gray, —.	Hinckley.
Gray, A.	West Stanley.
Gray, E.	West Stanley.
Gray, E.	East Lambeth.
Gray, F. H.	Cardiff.
Gray, H.	Leeds.
Gray, H. C.	Northumberland (E.).
Gray, H. S.	West Ham.
Gray, J.	Nottingham.
Gray, W.	Bexhill.
Gray, W.	Wigan.
Grayson, A.	Salford.
Grayston, S. E.	Loughborough.
Greasley, E.	Leicester.
Greaves, H.	Birmingham.
Greaves, H.	Birmingham.
Greaves, H.	Dudley.
Greaves, T.	Sunderland.
Gredley, L.	Southend-on-Sea.
Green, —.	Edmonton.
Green, —.	Birmingham.
Green, A.	Birmingham.
Green, A. A.	Hackney.
Green, A. B.	Finchley.
Green, A. J.	Doncaster.
Green, C.	Leek.
Green, C. F.	Tynemouth.
Green, C. H.	Great Yarmouth.
Green, C. H.	Finsbury, etc.
Green, E.	Liverpool.
*Green, E.	Leeds.
Green, E. L.	Hackney.
Green, F. C.	East Ham.
Green, (Miss) G.	Leeds.
Green, H.	West Ham.
Green, H.	London (E.).
Green, H.	Cambridge Borough.
Green, H.	Loughborough.
Green, H.	Birmingham.
Green, H. A.	London (E.).
Green, H. A.	Bilston.
Green, H. C.	Tamworth.
Green, H. E.	Wimbledon.
Green, H. M.	Birmingham.
Green, H. W.	Eastbourne.

TEACHERS WHO JOINED THE FORCES

Name.	Association.
Green, J.	Gloucester.
Green, J.	Manchester.
Green, J. L.	Preston District.
Green, L.	London (N.W.).
Green, L.	Gainsborough.
Green, L. H.	Birmingham.
Green, L. N.	Birmingham.
Green, M.	Sheffield.
Green, P.	Barnet.
Green, R.	Skipton.
Green, R.	Portsmouth.
Green, T.	Birmingham.
Green, T.	Crook.
Green, T. H.	Chester-le-Street.
Green, W.	Durham.
Green, W. G.	London (E.).
Green, W. W.	Middlesbrough.
Greenan, F.	London (E.).
Greene, W.	Liverpool.
Greene, W.	Manchester.
Greener, H. P.	Northumberland (S.).
Greengrass, F.	Woolwich.
Greenhalf, A. O.	Edmonton.
Greenhalgh, A. C.	Sunderland.
Greenhalgh, A. G.	West Ham.
Greenhalgh, H. F.	Chatham, etc.
Greenhalgh, J. T.	London (E.).
Greenhalgh, J. W.	Erewash Valley, etc.
Greenhill, E. O.	Staffordshire (N.).
Greening, G. W.	Dorset (W.).
Greenshields, J.	Woolwich.
Greenslade, F. C.	Bristol.
Greenslade, P. G.	Brentford.
*Greensmith, E. B.	East Lambeth.
Greenstreet, P.	Folkestone.
Greenwell, J. J.	Newcastle-on-Tyne.
Greenwood, —.	Hyndburn.
Greenwood, —.	Accrington.
Greenwood, —.	London (W.).
Greenwood, A.	Birkenhead.
Greenwood, A.	Liverpool.
Greenwood, A. G.	Hackney.
Greenwood, E.	Burnley.
Greenwood, E. B.	Ripon.
Greenwood, F.	Furness.
Greenwood, F.	Todmorden.
Greenwood, H.	London (W.).
Greenwood, J.	Rugby.
Greenwood, N.	Keighley.
Greenwood, N.	Brighouse.
Greenwood, R.	Doncaster.
Greenwood, W. H.	Leeds.
Greenyer, L. V.	West Lambeth.
Gregory, —.	Ogmore, etc.
Gregory, A.	Staffordshire (N.).
Gregory, A. E.	Reading.
Gregory, A. J.	Woolwich.
Gregory, C.	East Lambeth.
Gregory, E. W.	Bristol.
Gregory, H.	Staffordshire (N.).
Gregory, H.	Macclesfield District.
Gregory, J. H.	Dudley.
Gregory, L.	Hindley.
Gregory, W.	Bath.
Gregory, W. J. S.	Cornwall (E.).
Gregson, W. H.	Makerfield.
Grensille, J. W.	Tipton.
Greville, S. Eden	Hastings.
Grey, J.	Cardiff.

Name.	Association.
Grey, R. E.	Bishop Auckland.
Grey, W. A.	Brighton, etc.
Gribben, W. F.	Bishop's Waltham.
Gribbin, H.	Stockton.
Grice, P. S.	West Ham.
Grice, W.	Liverpool.
Gridley, G. C.	St. Albans.
Griffin, G. E.	Southwark.
Griffin, G. H.	Ealing.
Griffin, H. H.	Cornwall (W.).
Griffin, J. T.	Essex (N.).
Griffin, L.	Cardiff.
Griffin, L.	Manchester.
Griffin, T.	Birmingham.
Griffin, W. J.	Birmingham.
Griffith, A.	Southend-on-Sea.
Griffith, D. J.	Rhondda, etc.
Griffith, D. R.	Carnarvon.
Griffith, F. Y.	Vale of Clwyd
Griffith, G. D.	Gloucester (S.).
Griffith, R.	Cwmtawe.
Griffith, R. E.	Carnarvon (S.).
Griffiths, —.	Gravesend.
Griffiths, A.	Stockton-on-Tees.
Griffiths, A.	Deptford and Greenwich.
Griffiths, A. E.	East Lambeth.
Griffiths, A. E.	Staffordshire (N.).
Griffiths, A. G.	Maesteg.
Griffiths, D.	Glamorgan (Mid.).
Griffiths, D.	Aberdare.
Griffiths, D. F.	Llanelly.
Griffiths, D. F.	Ogmore, etc.
Griffiths, D. J.	Newcastle.
Griffiths, E.	Caerphilly.
Griffiths, E. J.	Liverpool.
Griffiths, E. T.	Mountain Ash.
Griffiths, H.	Northwich.
Griffiths, H. C.	West Bromwich, etc.
Griffiths, H. D.	Swansea.
Griffiths, H. J.	Sheffield.
Griffiths, J.	Tottenham, etc.
Griffiths, J.	Glamorgan (W.).
Griffiths, J.	Cardiff.
Griffiths, J. B.	Swansea.
Griffiths, J. E.	Maesteg.
Griffiths, J. E.	Glamorgan (Mid.).
Griffiths, J. E.	Wrexham.
Griffiths, L.	Birmingham.
Griffiths, L. R.	Maesteg.
Griffiths, O.	Southend-on-Sea.
Griffiths, R.	Farnworth.
Griffiths, R. E.	Easington.
Griffiths, R. H.	Pontypool.
Griffiths, R. T.	Pembrokeshire (Mid.).
Griffiths, T.	Birkenhead.
Griffiths, T.	Chorley.
Griffiths, T. D.	Nantyglo.
Griffiths, T. S.	Monmouth.
Griffiths, W.	Glamorgan (Mid.).
Griffiths, W. E.	Glamorgan (Mid.).
Griffiths, W. F.	Pembrokeshire (Mid.).
Griffiths, W. T.	Caerphilly.
Grigg, —.	Reading.
Griggs, A.	Barnsley.
Grime, A.	Grantham.
Grime, G.	Atherton, etc.
Grimes, H. W.	Ipswich.
Grimshaw, J.	Darwen.
Grindle, H. J.	Newport (Mon.).

N.U.T. WAR RECORD

Name.	Association.
Grisdale, W.	Bolton Borough.
Groark, T.	Rochdale.
Groarke, —.	Warrington.
Groarke, —.	Salford.
Groom, A. G.	Finsbury, etc.
Groom, A. L.	Folkestone.
Groom, C. H.	Maidstone.
Groom, G. S.	Croydon.
Groom, H. S.	Chesham.
Groome, (Miss)	Kettering.
Gross, A.	West Lambeth.
Gross, W. H. B.	Barrow-in-Furness.
Gross, W. V.	Ilford.
Grosse, —.	Dorset (E.).
Grossmith, G.	Deal, etc.
Grout, W. J.	Southend-on-Sea.
Grove, G.	Birmingham.
Grove, G.	Nottingham.
Groves, K.	Glamorgan (Mid.).
Groves, L.	Hackney.
Groves, R. L.	Crook.
Growtage, A.	Hertford.
Gruar, W. J.	Rhondda, etc.
Grubb, J. D.	Blackpool.
Grube, J. G.	Durham.
Gruchy, C.	Harrow.
Grudgings, L.	Leicester.
Grudgings, W.	Leicester.
Grundy, J.	Portsmouth.
Guest, C. E.	Barnsley.
*Guest, G.	Haslingden.
Guest, H.	Preston Borough.
Guest, (Miss) J.	Barnsley.
Guest, (Miss) J.	Barnsley.
Guest, J. J.	Wolverhampton.
Guest, W.	Wakefield.
Guffick, R. S.	York.
Gulliver, P. A.	Finsbury, etc,
Gulliver, W. J.	Leicester.
Gummerson, W.	Bradford.
Gundry, —.	Doncaster.
Gunn, H. J.	Staffordshire (N.).
Gunn, R.	Easington.
Gunner, —.	Bromley.
Gunning, W. T.	Bath.
Gunter, T. J.	London (E.).
Guppy, S. J.	Andover.
Gurney, J.	Warwick.
Gurney, W.	Liverpool.
Gurr, B. T.	Brighton, etc.
Guscatt, —.	Ealing.
Gush, A. M.	Tiverton.
Gussin, F. G.	Ilford.
Gutsell, V.	Dover.
Gutteridge, G. P.	Wellingborough.
Gutteridge, E. N.	Croydon.
Gutteridge, T. F.	Southwark.
Guy, —.	Somerset (S.W.).
Guy, C.	Houghton-le-Spring.
Gwilliam, R.	Farnham.
*Gwynne, G. D.	Rhymney Valley.
Gwynne, W. E.	Cardiff.
Gwyther, —.	West Ham.
Habakuk, E. G. H.	Barry.
Habgood, F.	Bolton Borough.
Hack, R.	Croydon.
Hack, W. H.	Hackney.
Hacker, W.	Hull.

Name.	Association.
Hackett, A. E.	Rowley Regis.
Hackett, E.	Stourbridge.
Hackett, E. F.	Itchen.
*Hacking, W. T.	Darwen.
*Hacon, C. R.	Ipswich.
Hadden, A. L.	Woolwich.
Hadden, E. O.	Gateshead.
Hadden, J. G.	Gateshead.
Haddocks, W. B.	Eccles.
Haddon, C. T.	Hornsey.
Haddon, L.	Mexborough.
Haddow, A.	Carlisle.
Haddy, A. J.	London (E.).
Hadley, T. W.	Dudley.
Hadfield, J. H.	Louth.
Hadida, J.	Finsbury, etc.
Hadingham, B. G.	Norwich.
Hadman, A. G.	Southgate.
Hagan, A. P.	Bootle.
Haggar, A.	Southwark.
Haggar, L. W.	Leyton.
Hagger, —.	Ealing.
Hagstrom, T.	Pontypool.
Hague, C. H.	West Lambeth.
Hague, F.	Woolwich.
Hague, H.	Sheffield.
Hague, J. H.	Liverpool.
Haig, E. R.	West Ward, Westmorland.
Haig, F.	Chatham, etc.
Haigh, A.	Leeds.
Haigh, G. E.	Halifax.
Haigh, P. M.	Watford.
Haigh, R.	Grimsby,
Haile, A. M.	Hartlepools.
Hailey, E. D.	Croydon.
Haines, R.	Somerset (S.W.).
Haining, W.	Wilmslow.
Hair, F.	Chester-le-Street.
Haire, E. H.	Birkenhead.
Hale, F. E.	Gloucester (N.).
Hale, G. L.	London (W.).
*Hales, B. C.	East Lambeth.
Hales, H. B.	Leeds.
Hales, H. S. D.	Gloucestershire (S.).
Haley, E. S.	West Lambeth.
Haley, H. P.	West Lambeth.
Haley, U.	Crook.
Haliburton, C. W.	Staffordshire (N.).
Hall, —.	Warrington.
Hall, A. E.	West Ham.
Hall, A. H.	Tottenham, etc.
Hall, C. H.	Bristol.
*Hall, C. W.	Birkenhead.
Hall, C. W.	Leeds.
Hall, E.	Northampton.
Hall, F.	East Ham.
Hall, F.	Portsmouth.
Hall, F. H.	Walthamstow.
Hall, F. R.	Tottenham, etc.
Hall, G. B.	Hull.
Hall, H.	Sheffield.
Hall, H.	Chadderton.
Hall, H.	Leeds.
Hall, H. H.	Tamworth.
Hall, H. W.	Bromley.
Hall, J.	Rutland.
? Hall, J.	Norwich.
Hall, J.	Preston Borough.

TEACHERS WHO JOINED THE FORCES

Name.	Association.
Hall, J.	Manchester.
Hall, J.	Maryport.
Hall, J. A.	Chester-le-Street.
Hall, J. K.	Houghton-le-Spring.
Hall, J. M.	Portsmouth.
Hall, J. M.	Durham.
Hall, J. W.	Durham.
Hall, J. W.	Barnsley.
Hall, M. A.	Leeds.
Hall, P.	Norwich City.
Hall, P. C.	East Lambeth.
Hall, P. H.	Barking.
Hall, R.	West Stanley.
Hall, S.	Norwich.
Hall, S.	Doncaster.
Hall, S. R.	Tynemouth.
Hall, T.	Dorset (S.).
Hall, W.	Doncaster.
Hall, W.	Wallsend.
Hall, W.	West Stanley.
Hall, W. D.	Ilkeston.
Hall, W. H.	Leominster.
Hallam, A.	Leeds.
Hallam, E.	Derby.
Hallam, H.	Llanelly.
Hallam, H.	Buxton.
Hallam, H. C.	Dorset (S.).
Hallam, J.	East Lambeth.
Hallam, W.	Matlock, etc.
Hallas, J.	Manchester.
*Hallett, H. H. L.	Falmouth and Truro.
*Halliday, B. J.	Boston.
Halliday, E.	Willesden.
Halliday, H.	Liverpool.
Halliday, J.	East Ham.
Halliday, W. H.	Liverpool.
Halliwell, C.	Nuneaton.
Halliwell, G. A.	Southwark.
Halliwell, T.	Nuneaton.
***Hallum, H. G.**	Southampton.
Hallworth, T.	Manchester.
Hallworth, T. H.	Derbyshire (E.).
Halman, H. E.	Coventry.
Halpin, L.	Liverpool.
Halsall, —.	Salford.
Halstead, —.	Nelson, Colne. etc.
Halton, H.	Ormskirk.
Hamblin, —.	Ealing.
Hambly, R.	Cornwall (Mid)
Hambrey, R.	Stourbridge.
*Hamby, A.	Penistone.
Hamer, W. H.	London (W.).
Hames, —.	Doncaster.
Hamilton, F. W.	London (W.).
Hamilton, J. K.	Northumberland (S.).
Hamilton, R.	Birkenhead.
Hamilton, W.	Stockton-on-Tees.
Hamilton, W. G.	Nottingham.
Hamilton, W. R.	Hartlepools.
Hamlyn, W. B.	Plymouth.
Hammans, H.	Gillingham.
Hammett, E. J.	Newport (Mon.).
Hammond, —.	Sittingbourne, etc.
Hammond, A. E.	Plymouth.
Hammond, A. J.	Finsbury, etc.
Hammond, B.	Chatham, etc.
*Hammond, S. H.	London (N.W.).
Hammond, W. H.	Portsmouth.
Hamnett, E.	Leeds.

Name.	Association.
Hampshire, —.	Preston District.
Hampshire, C. W.	Sheffield.
Hampson, J.	Stockport.
Hampton, E. J.	Tamworth.
*Hampton, R.	Mexborough.
Hampton, F.	Hackney.
Hampton, S.	Chatham, etc.
Hanby, D.	York.
Hanby, H.	Bristol.
Hancock, —.	Ilkeston.
Hancock, A.	Birmingham.
Hancock, E. J.	Leeds.
Hancock, (Miss)E. J.	Newport (Mon.).
Hancock, F.	St. Albans.
Hancock, F.	Leicester.
Hancock, F. R.	Knutsford.
Hancock, G.	Bristol.
Hancock, G. E.	Ealing.
Hancock, H.	Leicester (Mid)
Hancock, H.	Wimbledon.
Hancock, J.	Walsall.
Hancock, J. E.	Leeds.
Hancock, J. L.	Finsbury, etc.
Hancock, N.	Staffordshire (N.).
Hancock, P. H.	Berkshire (N.).
Hancock, R. H.	Staffordshire (N.).
Hancock, T.	Market Rasen.
Hancock, T. W.	Sandbach.
Hancock, W.	Newcastle-on-Tyne.
Hancock, W.	Liverpool.
Hancox, —.	Buxton.
Hand, F. E.	Southwark.
Hand, G. C.	Birmingham.
Hand, L.	Aldershot.
Hand, W. C.	Cannock.
Handcock, R.	Blaydon.
Handcock, W. A.	Grantham.
Handford, C. C.	Derbyshire (E.).
Handford, J.	Leicester (Mid).
Hands, F.	Newport (Mon.).
Handy, J.	Portsmouth.
*Haney, F. J.	Liverpool.
Hanford, H. S.	Sheffield.
Hanger, J. H.	Middlesbrough.
Hankins, J. F.	Uxbridge.
*Hankins, J. W.	Derby (E.).
Hanley, A.	Manchester.
Hanley, J. A.	Manchester.
Hanley, T.	Castleford, etc.
Hanmer, P.	Wrexham.
Hann, E. M.	Teign and Dart.
Hanna, —.	Salford.
Hanna, W.	Swansea.
Hannaby, H.	Wrexham.
Hannah, J.	West Ham.
Hansen, H.	London (N.W.).
Hansford, J. S.	Bristol.
Hanson, D. H.	Chichester.
Hanson, F. W.	Birmingham.
Hanson, H.	Swindon.
Hanson, R. D.	Maesteg.
Hanson, T. W.	Swadlincote.
Hanson, W. E.	Derby.
Harber, L. G.	West Ham.
Harbott, L.	Leyton.
Harbron, R.	Blyth.
Harcombe, —.	Rhondda, etc.
Harcourt, W.	Birmingham.
Hard, J.	Teign and Dart.

N.U.T. WAR RECORD

Name.	Association.
Hard, W. T.	East Lambeth.
Hardcastle, E.	Hull.
Hardcastle, F.	Sheffield.
Hardcastle, W.	Denton, etc.
Harden, W. F.	Heathfield, etc.
Harden, W. F.	East Lambeth.
Harding, —.	Cornwall (Mid).
Harding, —.	Forest of Dean.
Harding, —.	Dartford.
Harding, —.	Eastleigh, etc.
Harding, —.	Salford.
Harding, A.	Tottenham, etc.
*Harding, C.	Birmingham.
Harding, F. A.	Birmingham.
Harding, F. A.	Worsley, etc.
Harding, G. A.	Wrexham.
Harding, W. E.	Wallasey.
Harding, O. J.	Bradford.
Harding, R. F.	Liverpool.
Harding, W. E.	West Lambeth.
Harding, W. E.	Birmingham.
Harding, W. E.	Wallasey.
Harding, W. V.	Southwark.
Hardisty, G.	Bury.
Hardman, W. P.	Worksop.
Hardwick, A. G.	Leeds.
*Hardwick, R.	Birmingham.
Hardy, A. W.	Walthamstow.
Hardy, B. H.	Norwich.
Hardy, (Miss) E.	Cardiff.
Hardy, F. R.	Durham.
Hardy, H.	Derbyshire (E.).
Hardy, P. J.	Liverpool.
Hardy, R. T.	Darlington.
Hare, A.	Surrey (S.E.).
Hare, T. O.	Northumberland (S.).
*Hares, J.	Cardiff.
Hares, H. G.	Stroud.
Hargreaves, —.	Nottingham.
Hargreaves, F. B.	Chatham, etc.
Hargreaves, H.	Eccles.
Hargreaves, J.	Deptford and Greenwich.
Hargreaves, J. H....	Derbyshire (E.).
Hargreaves, P.	Huddersfield.
Hargreaves, W.	Pendle Forest.
Hargreaves, W.	Blackburn.
Hargreaves, W.	Whitehaven.
*Harker, T. R.	Chester-le-Street.
Harland, T. M.	Bradford.
Harland, W. H.	Scarborough.
Harle, F.	Leicester.
Harle, W.	Newcastle-on-Tyne.
Harling, —.	Hyndburn.
Harman, T. A.	Hackney.
Harman, W.	Oxford.
*Harmsworth, H. J.	Banbury.
Harper, C.	Manchester.
Harper, F. R.	Bradford.
Harper, F. S.	Birmingham.
Harper, G.	Hackney.
Harper, H.	Coalville.
Harper, H. S.	Bedford Borough.
Harper, J. E.	Nottingham.
*Harper, J. R.	Dudley.
Harper, W. F.	Chiswick.
Harratt, J. H.	Coalville.
Harrby, T. A.	Rhondda, etc.
Harries, E. C.	Cardiff.
Harries, J. S.	Pembrokeshire (Mid.

Name.	Association.
Harries, T.	Rhondda, etc.
*Harriman, H. W.	Walsall.
Harris, —.	West Ham.
Harris, —.	Devonshire (N.).
Harris, —.	Maidstone.
Harris, A. E.	Worcester City.
Harris, B. D.	Cardiff.
Harris, B. H.	Nuneaton.
Harris, C.	Liverpool.
Harris, C.	Maidstone.
Harris, C. W.	Birmingham.
Harris, D.	Hereford.
Harris, D. D.	Cardiff.
Harris, D. J.	Barry.
Harris, E.	Bristol.
Harris, E.	Mountain Ash.
Harris, E.	Swindon.
Harris, E. C.	Cardiff.
Harris, E. G.	Birmingham.
Harris, F.	East Lambeth.
Harris, F.	Grantham.
Harris, G. F.	Gloucester.
Harris, H.	London (N.W.).
Harris, H. B.	West Lambeth.
Harris, H. G.	London (N.W.).
Harris, H. J.	Northampton.
Harris, H. J.	Bristol.
Harris, H. T.	Finsbury, etc.
Harris, H. V.	Birmingham.
Harris, H. V. W.	Bournemouth.
Harris, J.	Rhondda, etc.
Harris, J. F.	Derbyshire (E.).
Harris, J. F. H.	Plymouth.
Harris, J. H.	Derbyshire (E.).
Harris, J. W. T.	Hornsey.
Harris, L.	Swindon.
*Harris, L.	Wrexham.
Harris, L.	Reading.
Harris, L. H.	Manchester.
Harris, L. I.	Croydon.
Harris, P.	London (E.).
Harris, P. G.	Wrexham.
Harris, P. G.	West Lambeth.
Harris, P. H.	Birmingham.
Harris, P. U.	West Ham.
Harris, R. C.	Tottenham, etc.
Harris, R. W. J.	Worcester City.
Harris, T.	Glamorgan (Mid).
Harris, T.	Derby.
Harris, T. A.	Pembrokeshire (Mid).
Harris, W. A.	Exeter City.
Harris, W. E. R.	Bristol.
Harris, W. C.	Cornwall (W.).
Harris, W. H.	Liverpool.
Harris, W. H.	Abercarn and District.
Harris, W. N.	Harrow.
Harris, W. W.	Finsbury, etc.
Harrison, —.	Keighley.
Harrison, —.	Salford.
Harrison, A.	Uxbridge.
Harrison, A. F.	Birmingham.
Harrison, A. H.	Southampton.
Harrison, A. K.	West Ham.
Harrison, D.	Northumberland (E.).
Harrison, D.	Watford.
Harrison, E.	Leeds.
Harrison, E.	Leeds.
Harrison, E.	Northumberland (E.).
Harrison, E. A.	Cowbridge.

TEACHERS WHO JOINED THE FORCES

Name.	Association.	Name.	Association.
Harrison, E. A.	Doncaster.	Hartley, J.	Cockermouth.
Harrison, E. H.	Worsley.	Hartley, J.	Leeds.
Harrison, E. J.	Castleford, etc.	Hartley, W.	Wakefield.
Harrison, E. M.	Cambridge Borough.	Hartshorn, J.	Finsbury, etc.
Harrison, F.	Northampton.	Hartshorn, (Miss) L.	Leicester.
Harrison, F. C.	Easington.	Hartshorne, A.	Sunderland.
Harrison, F. C.	Ilkeston.	Harvey, A.	Brighton, etc.
Harrison, F. H.	Leeds.	Harvey, A. F.	Birmingham.
Harrison, F. S.	Grimsby.	Harvey, C. E.	Chatham, etc.
Harrison, G.	Grimsby.	*Harvey, E. A.	Banbury.
Harrison, G. M.	Great Yarmouth.	Harvey, E. B.	Rotherham.
Harrison, H.	Middlesbrough.	*Harvey, E. C.	Portsmouth.
Harrison, H.	Cumberland (W.).	Harvey, F. G.	Durham.
Harrison, H. P.	Gloucestershire (S.).	Harvey, H.	Cornwall (E.).
Harrison, J.	Workington.	Harvey, J.	Cornwall (W.).
Harrison, J.	Hornsey.	Harvey, J. P.	Leyton.
*Harrison, J.	Hull.	Harvey, S.	Falmouth and Truro.
Harrison, J.	Leeds.	Harvey, S.	Southend-on-Sea.
Harrison, L. P.	Louth, etc.	Harwood, H. T.	Manchester.
Harrison, (Miss) M.	Scarborough.	Harwood, J.	Sheffield.
Harrison, R.	Liverpool.	Haselden, E. A.	Finsbury, etc.
Harrison, R.	Stockton-on-Tees.	Haselden, H. E.	Makerfield.
Harrison, R.	Huntingdonshire.	Haslam, —.	Derby.
*Harrison, R. F.	Waveney Valley.	Haslam, F.	East Ham.
Harrison, R. S.	Berkshire (N.).	Haslam, J.	Bury.
Harrison, S. P.	Birmingham.	Haslam, W.	Chadderton.
Harrison, T. R. S.	Barnard Castle.	Hasler, —.	East Lambeth.
Harrison, W.	Doncaster.	Haslock, —.	West Ham.
Harrison, W.	Flint County.	Hassall, C.	Staffordshire (N.).
Harrison, W.	Crook.	Hastilow, A.	Tipton.
Harrold, A.	Staffordshire (N.).	Hastings, C.	Norwich.
Harrold, W. L.	Leicester.	Hastings, P.	Birmingham.
Harrop, B. C.	Dewsbury, etc.	Haswell, W. R.	Newcastle-on-Tyne.
Harrop, (Miss) I.	Manchester.	Hatcher, E. W.	Westminster.
Harrop, W.	Darwen.	Hatcher, H. H.	Plymouth.
Harrow, P. A.	Hackney.	Hatfield, W.	Nottingham (W.).
Harroway, E. T.	Bristol.	Hathaway, J. L.	London (W.).
Harrup, W. D.	Southampton.	Hattam, H. C.	East Lambeth.
Harrup, W. D.	Dorset (S.).	Hatten, E.	West Lambeth.
Harry, E. J.	Glamorgan (W.).	Hattersley, W. A.	Willesden.
Harry, G. W.	Bridgend.	Hatton, —.	Berkeley Vale.
Harry, H.	Cornwall (Mid)	Hatton, F. J.	East Lambeth.
Harry, T.	Swansea.	Hatton, S. F.	London (N.W.).
Hart, —.	East Lambeth.	Haughton, —.	Knutsford.
Hart, A. K.	West Lambeth.	Haughton, W. G.	Bury.
Hart, A. R.	Isle of Wight.	Haunton, R.	West Ham.
Hart, C.	Sheffield.	Hauxwell, G. W.	Durham.
Hart, E.	Kent (W.).	Havelock, (Miss)V.G.	Doncaster.
Hart, E.	London (E.).	Haver, W.	Houghton-le-Spring.
Hart, E. F. C.	Dorset (E.).	Haward, A. E.	London (N.W.).
Hart, F. D.	Woolwich.	Haward, N. P.	Tottenham, etc.
Hart, G. J.	Horsham.	Haward, R. A.	Hackney.
Hart, G. P.	Hendon.	Hawbrook, G. L.	Runcorn.
Hart, J. W.	Halifax.	Hawes, A. G.	Deptford and Greenwich.
Hart, L. S.	Hitchin.	Hawker, —.	Teign and Dart.
Hart, P.	Croydon.	Hawker, G. E.	Bristol.
Hart, S. W.	Leeds.	Hawker, P.	Cheltenham.
Hart, T. J.	Cornwall (W.).	Hawkes, E. W.	Southwark.
Hart, W.	Bury St. Edmunds.	Hawkes, J. C.	Romford, etc.
Hart, W. S.	Hackney.	Hawkes, W. G. W.	Hackney.
Hartland, G. H.	Cardiff.	Hawkesworth, —.	Nantwich.
Hartland, L. C.	Abercarn.	Hawkesworth, E.	Warrington.
Hartles, W. E.	Brighton, etc.	Hawkesworth, H.	West Ham.
Hartley, B.	Leeds.	Hawkey, F. V.	West Ham.
Hartley, C.	Warwickshire (N.).	Hawkhead, J. F.	Gateshead.
Hartley, E.	Nelson, Colne, etc.	Hawkins, —.	Folkestone.
Hartley, E. S.	Sheffield.	Hawkins, D. C.	Brighton, etc.
Hartley, H.	Wigan.	Hawkins, D. E.	London (N.W.).
Hartley, H. G.	Spen Valley.	Hawkins, F.	Deptford and Greenwich.

N.U.T. WAR RECORD

Name.	Association.
Hawkins, F. P.	Northampton.
Hawkins, H.	Wellingborough.
Hawkins, H.	Wakefield.
Hawkins, H. H.	Cornwall (W.).
Hawkins, H. R.	Cardiff.
Hawkins, J.	Blackburn.
Hawkins, J. H.	Sheffield.
Hawkins, J. T.	Slough.
Hawkins, L.	Taunton, etc.
Hawkins, L. C.	Kingston and Surbiton.
Hawkins, R. H.	Southwark.
Hawkins, W.	Willesden.
Hawkins, W. C. G.	Willesden.
Hawksworth, J.	Deptford and Greenwich.
Hawley, C. J.	Tottenham, etc.
Hawley, J.	Leeds.
Haworth, C.	Manchester.
Haworth, H.	Blackpool.
Haworth, H.	Blackpool.
*Haworth, J. B.	Denton, etc.
Haworth, J. T.	Haslingden.
Hawthorne, E.	York.
Hay, —.	Cheltenham.
Hay, C. R.	Stokesley.
Hay, W. G.	Isle of Ely.
Haycock, —.	Northants.
Haycock, H.	Newcastle-on-Tyne.
Hayden, J.	Croydon.
Hayes, —.	Warrington.
Hayes, C.	East Dereham.
Hayes, F.	Manchester.
*Hayes, F.	Accrington.
Hayes, F. T.	Sheffield.
Hayes, G. W.	Manchester.
Hayes, H. H.	West Lambeth.
Hayes, J. J.	Nottingham.
Hayes, L.	Leeds.
Hayes, M.	Horsham, etc.
Hayler, E. A.	Brighton, etc.
Haynes, A. E.	Dorset (N.).
Haynes, C. R.	West Lambeth.
Haynes, O. S.	Barnsley.
Haynes, E. B.	Northwich.
Haynes, H. M.	Dorset (S.).
*Haynes, J. W.	Tynemouth.
Haynes, R. L.	Erewash Valley, etc.
Haynes, T.	Barnet.
Haysom, A. J.	Canterbury.
Hayston, T.	Cockermouth.
Hayter, H.	Guildford.
Hayton, F.	Edmonton.
Hayward, A. H. D.	London (W.).
Hayward, A. W.	Taunton, etc.
Hayward, C.	Cardiff.
Hayward, G.	Cheltenham.
Hayward, H.	Pontypool.
Hayward, H. E.	Moreton-in-Marsh.
Hayward, H. H.	Portsmouth.
Hayward, J. R.	Hull.
Hayward, W.	Glamorgan (Mid).
*Hayward, W. H.	Birmingham.
Haywood, —.	Salford.
Haywood, A. V.	Ashbourne, etc.
Haywood, F. S.	Tottenham, etc.
Haywood, J.	Wallsend.
Hazelden, H. W. G.	Dartford.
Head, J.	West Bromwich, etc.
Head, P. T.	Tottenham, etc.
Head, W. E.	Wimbledon.
Head, W. H.	Tottenham, etc.
Headford, H. R.	West Stanley.
Headford, J.	Vale of Derwent.
Heafield, S.	Leeds.
Heal, —.	Preston Borough.
Heal, W. R.	Dorking.
Heald, E. J.	Manchester.
Heald, T. H.	Manchester.
Healey, F.	Rugby.
Healey, H. A.	Spalding, etc.
Healey, R.	Darlington.
Heap, A. T.	Leeds.
Heap, F.	Leeds.
Heap, F. W.	Blackpool.
Heap, H.	Worthing.
Heap, R.	Bury.
Heap, S. V.	Skipton.
Heard, E.	Southwark.
Heard, H. W.	Bristol.
Heard, J.	Somerset (S.E.).
Heard, J. G.	London (E.).
Heard, P. A.	West Lambeth.
Heard, T. H.	Plymouth.
Hearmon, L.	Tunbridge Wells.
Hearn, F. W.	Finsbury, etc.
Heasman, B. R.	Southwark.
Heath, (Miss)	West Ham.
Heath, F.	Aldershot.
Heath, F.	Worcester City.
Heath, J.	Warwick.
Heath, J.	Staffordshire (N.).
Heath, J.	Warwick.
Heath, T.	Staffordshire (N.).
*Heath, W. L.	West Ham.
Heathcote, A.	Barnsley.
Heathcote, C. J.	Wigan.
Heathcote, H. R.	Manchester.
Heathcote, W. T.	Stockport.
Heather, W.	Brighton, etc.
Heatherington, T.	West Stanley.
Heatley, T. S.	Liverpool.
Heaton, F. V.	Wigan.
Heaton, R. W.	Blackpool.
Heaton, W. G.	Worthing.
Hebden, J. L.	Rossendale.
Hebdon, J. A.	Darlington.
Hedderwick, A.	Watford.
Hedger, A.	Surrey (S.E.).
Hedger, L.	Kingston and Surbiton.
Hedger, W. S.	Easington.
Hedley, G. F.	Wrexham.
Hedgeland, G. S.	Staines.
Heeley, A.	Huddersfield.
Heeley, E.	Barnsley.
Heeps, F. B.	Bedford Borough.
Hegan, J. J.	Preston Borough.
Height, W.	Leyton.
Hellicar, G. H.	Hackney.
Helliwell, B. I.	Harrow.
Helliwell, R. A.	Bradford.
Helm, —.	Birmingham.
*Helmer, B.	Birmingham.
Helsdon, P. J.	Tottenham, etc.
Hemingway, —.	Doncaster.
Hemingway, C.	Wakefield.
Hemingway, H.	Wakefield.
Hemingway, J.	Darlington.
Hemingway, P.	Twickenham.
Hemingway, W. M.	Leeds.

TEACHERS WHO JOINED THE FORCES

Name.	Association.	Name.	Association.
Hemming, A. H.	Birmingham.	Hewitson, J.	Derbyshire (E.).
Hemphill, J.	Liverpool.	Hewitson, S. R.	East Lambeth.
Hemphill, R.	Liverpool.	Hewitt, —.	Warwickshire (N.).
Hemsley, M.	Gravesend.	Hewitt, A.	Hendon.
Henderson, —.	St. Helens.	Hewitt, A.	Wallasey.
Henderson, E.	Great Yarmouth.	Hewitt, F.	Chester.
Henderson, G. F.	Tottenham, etc.	Hewitt, G.	Walsall.
Henderson, J. H.	Croydon.	**Hewitt, G. S.**	Southampton.
Henderson, J. L.	Newcastle-on-Tyne.	Hewitt, H. J.	Manchester.
Henderson, J. R.	Dartford.	Hewitt, M.	Hitchin.
Henderson, J. T.	Cannock.	*Hewitt, R. G.	Huddersfield.
Henderson, R. F. G.	Lewisham.	Hewitt, T. J.	Tottenham, etc.
Henderson, T.	Northumberland (E.).	**Hewitt, W.**	Reigate.
Henderson, W.	Carlisle.	Hewitt, W. H.	Finsbury, etc.
Hennessey, E.	Westminster.	Hewlett, A. H.	London (E.).
Hennessey, E. T.	Westminster.	Hewlett, E. J.	Essex (N.).
Hennig, C. W.	West Lambeth.	Hewlett, W. C.	Plymouth.
Henning, H. F.	West Lambeth.	Hewson, A. J.	Birmingham.
Henretty, W.	Liverpool.	Hewson, E.	Romford, etc.
Henry, —.	Doncaster.	Hewson, G. A.	Hackney.
Henry, G. C.	Barnsley.	Hey, A. C.	Durham.
Hensby, F.	Hertford.	Hey, T.	Brighouse.
Henshall, —.	Crewe.	Hey, W.	Edmonton.
Henshaw, A. H.	Kiveton Park.	Heywood, J. H.	East Ham.
Henshaw, R. L.	Bolton Borough.	**Heywood, T.**	Manchester.
Henshaw, T.	Wrexham.	Heyworth, —.	Wigan.
Henshawe, S.	Matlock, etc.	Heyworth, J.	Pendle Forest.
Hensley, J. P.	Cornwall (W.).	Heyworth, T.	Accrington.
Henstridge, C. L.	London (N.W.).	Hibbard, W.	Mansfield Borough.
Henwood, R. J.	Dorset (N.).	Hibbert, C.	West Lambeth.
Hepburn, —.	Willesden.	Hibbert, S.	Manchester.
Hepple, —.	Hebburn.	Hibbs, —.	Teign and Dart.
Hepple, J. W.	Newcastle-on-Tyne.	**Hickey, R.**	Cardiff.
Hepworth, F.	Manchester.	Hickford, H. A.	London (E.).
Hepworth, J. H.	Castleford, etc.	Hickford, J.	Enfield.
Hepworth, J. S.	Barkston Ash.	Hickley, F.	Coventry.
Hepworth, T. E.	Sheffield.	Hickling, —.	East Ham.
Herbert, —.	Ipswich.	**Hickling, A. E.**	Liverpool.
Herbert, —.	West Ham.	Hickman, F. C.	Stourbridge.
Herbert, E. G.	Smethwick.	Hickman, J. W.	Boston.
Herbert, H. D.	Mansfield.	Hicks, —.	Devon (N.).
Herbert, H. O. M.	Surrey (N.W.).	Hicks, A.	London (E.).
Herbert, J. H.	Pontypool.	Hicks, F.	Reigate.
Herbert, J. W.	Enfield.	Hicks, G.	Mountain Ash.
Herbert, T. E.	West Lambeth.	Hicks, H.	Brentford.
Herbert, W. F.	West Lambeth.	**Hicks, H.**	Hull.
Heritage, A.	Tipton.	Hicks, J. C.	Portsmouth.
Hermiston, F.	North Cleveland.	Hicks, J. S.	Sheffield.
*Hermiston, R. N.	Middlesbrough.	Hicks, R. F.	Acton.
Herries, G. R.	Wolverhampton.	**Hicks, W. G.**	Kent (W.).
Herring, C. K.	Stretford.	Higgie, J. W.	Rugby.
Herring, R. V.	London (N.W.).	Higgins, A. C.	Fairford, etc.
Herschman, P.	West Lambeth.	Higgins, E. J.	Liverpool.
Hervey, W. H.	Plymouth.	Higgins, E. J.	Staffordshire (N.).
Heseltine, J. S.	East Cleveland.	Higgins, F. J. T.	Marlborough.
Hesketh, R. O.	Hyndburn.	Higgins, F. K.	Sheffield.
Hesketh, T.	Wigan.	Higgins, J.	Birkenhead.
Heslop, F.	Northumberland (S.).	Higgins, J.	Coalville.
Heslop, J. G.	Chester-le-Street.	Higgins, L. J.	Ogmore.
Heslop, N.	Wallsend.	**Higgins, L. T.**	Manchester.
Heslop, W.	Darlington.	Higgins, T.	Widnes.
Heslop, W. A.	Vale of Derwent.	Higgins, W.	Stourbridge.
Hetherington, A.	Stockton-on-Tees.	**Higginson, F.**	Dudley.
Hetherington, C. C.	Southend-on-Sea.	Higginson, W.	West Ham.
Hetherington, W.	Manchester.	Higgs, P. E.	Rutland.
Hewett, —.	Ealing.	Higgs, W. E.	Leeds.
Hewett, J.	Walthamstow.	Higgs, W. J.	West Lambeth.
Hewit, T.	Northumberland (E.).	High, E. H.	Finsbury, etc.
Hewitson, J.	Chester-le-Street.	High, (Miss) M.	Bishop Auckland.

N.U.T. WAR RECORD

Name.	Association.
High, P.	Tottenham, etc.
High, R.	West Ham.
Higham, C. H.	Hinckley.
*Higham, E.	Denton, etc.
Higham, S.	Hinckley.
Highfield, W.	Rotherham.
Hignell, F. W.	Norfolk (W.).
Hilditch, N. S.	London (N.W.).
Hildred, E. V.	West Ham.
Hiles, E.	Stockport.
Hiley, H.	Abercarn.
Hill, —.	Leeds.
Hill, —.	Lincoln.
Hill, —.	Gravesend.
Hill, A. E.	Nottingham.
Hill, A. E.	Wimbledon.
Hill, A. R.	Liverpool.
Hill, C.	Fairford, etc.
Hill, C. S.	Bath.
Hill, E.	Grimsby.
Hill, (Miss) E.	Leicester.
Hill, F.	Hartlepools.
Hill, F.	Heywood.
Hill, F.	Durham.
Hill, F.	Preston Borough.
Hill, F. C.	East Lambeth.
Hill, F. W. G.	Surrey (N.W.).
Hill, G. J.	Glamorgan (Mid).
Hill, H.	Manchester.
Hill, H.	Scarborough.
Hill, H.	Woolwich.
Hill, H. W.	London (E.).
Hill, J.	Westminster.
Hill, J.	Bristol.
Hill, J. A.	Manchester.
Hill, J. E.	Newcastle-on-Tyne.
Hill, J. G.	Newcastle-on-Tyne.
Hill, J. R.	Chipping Norton.
Hill, J. T.	Newcastle-on-Tyne.
Hill, R.	Gloucester.
Hill, R.	Willesden.
Hill, R. H.	Sheffield.
Hill, S. J.	East Ham.
Hill, S. T.	Hitchin, etc.
Hill, T.	Wolverhampton.
Hill, T. O.	Newcastle-on-Tyne.
Hill, W.	Bristol.
Hill, W.	Somerset (S.W.).
Hill, W. H.	Workington.
Hill, W. J.	Portsmouth.
Hillary, —.	Nelson, Colne, etc.
Hillary, A.	Bishop Auckland.
Hillcoat, T.	Leeds.
Hilliar, H. J.	Bishop's Waltham.
Hillier, C.	West Lambeth.
Hillier, J.	Tottenham, etc.
Hillier, L. R.	Dartford.
Hillier, W. H.	Edmonton.
Hilling, —.	Epsom, etc.
Hillman, P. W.	West Lambeth.
Hills, A. J.	London (W.).
Hills, J. T.	Southwark.
Hills, R. E.	Hailsham.
Hilton, A.	Oldham.
Hilton, E.	Sheffield.
Hilton, H.	Oldham.
Hilton, H. A.	Birmingham.
Hilyer, J.	Manchester.
Hince, T. H.	Northumberland (E.).

Name.	Association.
Hinchliffe, —.	Somerset (N.).
Hinchliffe, F. B.	Dewsbury, etc.
Hinchliffe, J. H.	Sheffield.
Hinchliffe, J. R.	Dewsbury, etc.
Hind, —.	St. Helens.
Hind, C. W.	Nottingham.
Hind, (Miss) M.	Newark.
Hinde, —.	Newport Pagnell.
Hinde, F. W.	Walthamstow.
Hinde, G. H.	Manchester.
Hindell, W. A.	East Lambeth.
Hinder, R. J.	Reading.
Hindle, J.	Accrington.
Hindle, T. B.	Haslingden.
Hindshaw, —.	Salford.
Hindman, H. E.	Plymouth.
Hindson, J. C.	London (W.).
Hine, H.	Leek, etc.
Hindshaw, —.	Salford.
Hingley, E. T.	Tynemouth.
Hinton, L.	Salisbury.
Hinton, S. E.	New Forest.
Hipkins, N.	Smethwick.
Hipkiss, J.	Rowley Regis.
Hird, H.	Enfield.
Hird, R. W.	Sunderland.
Hirons, H.	Worcester City.
Hirst, E. P. K.	Huddersfield.
Hirst, H.	Huddersfield.
Hirst, J.	Barnsley.
Hirst, J.	Rotherham.
Hirst, J. E.	Rotherham.
Hirst, N.	Birmingham.
Hirst, R.	Huddersfield.
Hirst, R. B.	Derbyshire (E.).
Hirst, W. H.	Ingleborough.
Hirst, W.	Hyde.
Hiscock, J.	Deptford and Greenwich.
Hitch, W.	West Ham.
Hitchcock, T. C. B.	Enfield.
Hitchcock, W. J.	West Lambeth.
Hitchens, A. E.	Portsmouth.
Hitchens, J. H.	Falmouth and Truro.
Hitchens, W. J.	Cornwall (W.).
Hitchin, R.	Hyde.
Hitchin, W.	Rotherham.
Hitchings, C.	Hackney.
Hoare, —.	Reading.
Hoare, E. G.	Chippenham.
Hoare, E. T. R.	Southampton.
Hoare, H. M.	Watford.
Hoare, W. B.	Guildford.
Hobbs, A.	Teign and Dart.
Hobbs, J.	Gloucester.
Hobbs, J. T.	Rowley Regis.
Hobbs, R. A.	Cardiff.
Hobbs, R. G.	Southend-on-Sea.
Hobbs, W. F.	Gloucester.
Hobday, W. H.	Sheffield.
Hobley, A. J.	Bradford.
Hobson, A. J.	Birmingham.
Hobson, F.	Leeds.
Hobson, J. E.	Sheffield.
Hockaday, G. B.	Middleton.
Hocken, W. A.	Hackney.
Hockey, C. L.	Barrow-in-Furness.
Hocking, G. W.	Castleford, etc.
*Hockridge, J. R.	Plymouth.
Hodder, P. C.	Portsmouth.

TEACHERS WHO JOINED THE FORCES

Name.	Association.
Hodge, F. A.	Gillingham.
Hodge, J. H.	Hendon.
Hodge, W.	West Ham.
Hodges, A.	Swindon.
Hodges, H. P.	Cambridgeshire.
Hodges, R...	Gloucester.
Hodges, W. R.	Nottingham.
Hodges, W. S.	Abertillery.
Hodgetts, J.	Birmingham.
Hodgetts, R. H.	Smethwick.
Hodgetts, V. R.	Rowley Regis.
Hodgkins, R.	Wakefield.
Hodgkinson, A.	Lancaster.
Hodgkinson, R.	Barrow-in-Furness.
Hodgkinson, W.	Nottingham.
Hodgson, E. R.	Burnley.
Hodgson, F.	Hartlepools.
Hodgson, (Miss) G.	Hartlepools.
Hodgson, G.	Preston Borough.
Hodgson, J.	Bradford.
Hodgson, J. R.	Surrey (N.W.).
Hodgson, J. W.	Furness.
Hodgson, T. E.	Sale.
Hodgson, W.	Bradford.
Hodson, C.	Huddersfield.
Hodson, G. P.	Sunderland.
Hodson, W. F.	Hull.
Hoff, E.	Crewe.
Hogan, W. I.	Tredegar.
Hogarth, E. H.	Newcastle-on-Tyne.
*Hogg, G. E.	Tynemouth.
*Hogg, J. C.	Derby (E.).
Hogg, R.	South Shields.
Hogg, W.	Gillingham.
Hoggins, —.	Shrewsbury.
Holbrook, H.	Newport (Mon.).
Holbrook, H. S.	Birmingham.
Holdcroft, A. F.	Daventry.
Holden, —.	Preston Borough.
Holden, —.	Hindley.
Holden, C.	Bolton Borough.
Holden, F. T.	St. Helens.
Holden, H. C. K.	Manchester.
Holden, M. L.	Finchley.
*Holder, A. E.	Birmingham.
Holder, C. S.	Croydon.
Holdich, K.	Deptford and Greenwich.
Holdsworth, B.	Queensbury.
Hole, M.	Reading.
Hole, W. C.	Coventry
Holgate, J. W.	Haslingden.
Holker, H. O.	Bury.
Holland, —.	St. Helens.
Holland, —.	Kingston and Surbiton.
Holland, A.	Manchester.
Holland, E. T.	Blaydon.
Holland, F.	East Lambeth.
Holland, F. H.	Lewisham.
Holland, G. F.	Westminster.
Holland, H. E.	Lewisham.
Holland, J. C.	Blackburn.
Holland, J. H.	East Cleveland.
Holland, W.	Sheffield.
Holland, W. O.	Sheffield.
Hollands, W. H.	East Lambeth.
Hollas, F.	Elland.
Hollick, B. G.	Birmingham.
Holliman, C. S.	West Lambeth.
Hollinghurst, A.	Bootle.
Hollings, H.	Bradford.
Hollings, P.	Keighley.
Hollingsworth, S. L.	Birmingham.
Hollingum, (Miss) M.	London (E.).
Hollinshead, O.	Manchester.
Hollis, C.	Norfolk (W.).
Hollis, F. A.	Hertford.
Hollis, S.	Sheffield.
Hollis, W. J.	Derbyshire (E.).
Hollman, P.	Cambridgeshire.
Holloway, F.	London (N.W.).
Holloway, F. H.	Finsbury etc.
Holloway, H. E.	Gloucester.
Holloway, R.	Willesden.
Holloway, R. J.	West Lambeth.
Hollyoak, H. H.	Staines.
Holman, V.	Forest of Dean.
Holmberg, F.	London (W.).
Holme, L.	Derby.
Holmes, —.	Worksop.
Holmes, —.	Hinckley.
Holmes, (A.	Dover.
Holmes (Miss) A.	Waterloo, etc.
Holmes, A. T.	Braintree.
Holmes, C.	Derbyshire (E.).
Holmes, E...	Calder Valley.
Holmes, E. F.	Ilford.
Holmes, G. T.	Bishop Auckland.
Holmes, H.	Leeds.
*Holmes, H...	Doncaster.
Holmes, H.	Castleford, etc.
Holmes, H.	Grantham.
Holmes, J. F.	Hull.
Holmes, J. W.	East Lambeth.
Holmes, R.	Leeds.
Holmes, S.	Newcastle-on-Tyne.
Holmes, W.	Liverpool.
Holmes, W.	Crook.
Holt, —.	Willesden.
Holt, A.	East Ham.
Holt, A.	Manchester.
Holt, B.	Coventry.
*Holt, G.	Rossendale.
Holt, G.	Leeds.
Holt, H.	Rochdale.
Holt, H.	Rossendale.
Holt, J.	Warrington.
Holt, J.	St. Helens.
Holt, L. E.	Burnley.
Holt, R.	West Stanley.
Holt, R. O.	Manchester.
Holt, T.	West Ham.
Holt, T. A.	Southampton.
Holt, W.	Rochdale.
Holt, W. J.	Walthamstow.
Holton, A. W.	Watford.
Holway, E.	Finsbury, etc.
Holyoak, F. A.	Wimbledon.
Homer, E.	West Lambeth.
Honderwood, R.	Makerfield, etc.
Hone (Miss)	Kettering.
Honey, —.	Reading.
Honey, W. J.	Harrow.
Honeyball, H.	Spennymoor.
Honeysett, J. S.	West Lambeth.
Honeywood, —.	London (W.).
Honicke, C. H.	Twickenham.
Honner, A. J.	Finsbury, etc.
Hood, —.	Aldershot.

N.U.T. WAR RECORD

Name.	Association.
Hook, E.	London (N.W.).
Hook, F. W.	Aylesbury.
Hook, S. D.	Bridgwater.
Hoole, W. D.	Sunderland.
Hooley, —.	Derby.
Hooley, H.	Ilkeston.
Hoolihan, N. J.	Liverpool.
Hooper, C.	Plymouth.
Hooper, H. C.	Penarth.
*Hooper, J. W.	Southwark.
Hooper, R. J.	Kingsbridge.
Hooper, V C.	Torridge.
*Hooson, H. B.	Hackney.
Hooton, C. W.	Lincoln.
Hopcroft, H.	Swindon.
Hope, E. H.	Cheltenham.
Hope, H.	Manchester.
Hope, J. P.	Brentford.
Hope, R.	Carlisle.
Hope, R. P.	Spennymoor.
Hopkin, J. R.	Glamorgan (W.).
Hopkins, D.	Gelligear.
Hopkins, D. O.	Rhondda, etc.
Hopkins, D. M.	Birmingham.
*Hopkins, F.	Edmonton.
Hopkins, F.	East Lambeth.
Hopkins, G. L.	Barry.
Hopkins, R.	Rhondda, etc.
Hopkins, S. C.	Swansea.
Hopkins, T.	Merthyr Tydfil.
Hopkins, W. G.	Manchester.
*Hopkinson, E.	Nottinghamshire (W.).
*Hopkinson, O.	Crewe.
Hopkinson, S.	Hackney.
Hopkinson, W. E.	Spen Valley.
Hopkinson, W. E.	Richmond (Surrey).
Hopley, W. A.	Finsbury, etc.
Hopper, M.	West Stanley.
Hopping, S.	Exeter City.
Hopson, A. J.	Dover.
Hopton, G. H. W.	Bristol.
Hordley, W. H.	West Lambeth.
Hore, C.	Portsmouth.
Hore, G. J.	Portsmouth.
Hore, W. E.	Maldon, etc.
Hore, W. J. B.	Plymouth.
Horler, E.	Hereford.
Horn, A. D.	Hull.
Horn, C. B.	London (E.).
Horn, F.	Shipley.
*Horn, H.	Grimsby.
Horn, J. H.	Weardale.
Horn, J. W.	Manchester.
Hornblower, P. B.	Shropshire (E.).
Hornbuckle, T. A.	Witney.
Horne, E.	Croydon.
Horne, F. A.	Woolwich.
Horne, F. G.	Bristol.
Horne, G. G.	Dorset (S.).
Horne, W.	Todmorden.
Horne, W. J.	West Ham.
Horne, W. P. J.	Macclesfield District.
Horner, W. H.	Ingleborough.
Horniblow, —.	London (W.).
Hornsby, H. G.	Liverpool.
Hornsby, W.	Finsbury, etc.
Horrocks, W.	Exeter District.
Horobin, F. A. E.	Deptford and Greenwich.
Horseley, E. J.	Birmingham.
Horseman, W. M.	Darlington.
Horsfall, G.	Manchester.
Horsfall, H. T.	Hull.
Horsfall, J. B.	Newport Pagnell, etc.
Horsfield, E.	Penistone.
Horsfield, J. H.	Doncaster.
Horsfield, R.	Blaydon.
Horsford, A.	London (N.W.).
Horsley, A.	Barnsley.
Horsley, F.	Finsbury, etc.
Horsley, R.	Tottenham, etc.
Horsman, S. B.	Scarborough.
Horswill, A. S.	Coventry.
Horton, A.	Tynemouth.
Horton, H.	London (E.).
Horton, H. O.	Birmingham.
Horton, J. C.	Wolverhampton.
Horton, O.	West Bromwich.
Horton, W.	Kidderminster.
Horwood, A. K.	London (W.).
Hosegood, G. F.	Hornsey.
Hosegood, H. H.	Torridge.
Hoskin, W. A.	Deptford and Greenwich.
Hosking, J. P.	Bodmin.
Hosking, L.	West Ham.
Hostler, A. C.	Birmingham.
Hotten, H. J.	West Ham.
Houderwood, R.	Makerfield.
Hough, H.	Bolton Borough.
Hough, J. W.	Manchester.
Houghton, C. B.	Croydon.
Houghton, E. H.	Basingstoke.
Houghton, H.	Chorley.
Houghton, T. W.	Knutsford.
Houghton, W. H.	Warrington.
Houlden, —.	Doncaster.
Houldey, W. G.	Birmingham.
Houlding, F.	Barking.
Houlding, H. S.	Barking.
Houlton, —.	Derby.
Hounsell, A.	Leyton.
Hounsell, D. R.	Barking.
Hounsell, F. W.	Leyton.
Hounsell, H.	Walthamstow.
Hourahane, F.	Cardiff.
Hourahane, J. P.	Cardiff.
Hourie, W.	Middlesbrough.
House, S.	Chester-le-Street.
Houseley, E. E.	West Lambeth.
*Houseley, P. B.	Derbyshire (E.).
Houslop, L.	Tottenham, etc.
How, M. J. V.	Cambridgeshire.
How, W.	West Ham.
Howard, A.	East Ham.
Howard, A. A.	Birmingham.
Howard, A. C.	Plymouth.
Howard, C.	Birmingham.
Howard, C. T.	Lewisham.
Howard, C. V.	Hartlepools.
*Howard, G. R.	Great Yarmouth.
Howard, H.	Hartlepools.
Howard, H. B.	Newcastle-on-Tyne.
Howard, J.	Swansea.
Howard, J. G.	Hull.
Howard, J. H.	Farnworth.
Howard, R.	Cambridge Borough.
Howard, R. D.	Nottingham.
Howard, T.	Widnes.
Howarth, A.	Roch Valley.

TEACHERS WHO JOINED THE FORCES

Name.	Association.	Name.	Association.
Howarth, B.	Rochdale.	Huggins, C.	Hackney.
Howarth, C.	Rochdale.	Hughes, —.	Sale.
Howarth, E.	Halifax.	Hughes, A. G.	West Lambeth.
Howarth, F.	Doncaster.	Hughes, A. J.	Llanelly.
Howarth, H.	Preston Borough.	Hughes, A. R.	Liverpool.
Howarth, R.	Dorset (W.).	**Hughes, B. T.**	Rhondda, etc.
Howarth, R.	Sheffield.	Hughes, C.	Finsbury, etc.
Howarth, S.	Ormskirk.	Hughes, D.	Leicester.
Howarth, W. H.	Rochdale.	Hughes, E...	Wrexham.
Howcroft, A. S.	Oldham.	Hughes, E...	Yoxford.
Howe, A. W.	Hackney.	Hughes, E...	Swindon.
Howell, —.	Devon (N.).	Hughes, E...	Rhondda, etc.
Howell, A.	Darlington.	*Hughes, E. J.	Flint County.
Howell, C. E.	East Ham.	Hughes, E. T.	Welshpool.
Howell, D. R.	Pontypool.	Hughes, F.	Chester.
Howell, H. H.	Llanelly.	Hughes, F.	Carlisle.
Howell, J. ..	Llanelly.	*Hughes, G.	Mountain Ash.
Howell, J. ..	Northwich.	Hughes, G. L.	Llandudno.
Howell, J. ..	Rhondda, etc.	Hughes, H.	Croydon.
Howell, L. C.	London (W.).	Hughes, H. A.	Llanidloes.
Howell, S. H.	Rhondda, etc.	Hughes, (Miss) H. D.	Llandudno.
Howell, S. P.	Derby.	Hughes, H. E.	Llandudno.
Howell, T. ..	Rhondda, etc.	Hughes, H. G.	Bristol.
Howell, W.	Staffordshire (N.).	Hughes, H. G.	Wirral.
Howell, W. H.	Tottenham, etc.	Hughes, H. N.	Abercarn.
Howells, D. W.	Mountain Ash.	Hughes, I.	Crewe.
Howells, F. J.	Castleford, etc.	Hughes, J.	Gelligear.
Howells, H. E.	Easingwold.	**Hughes, J.** ..	Newcastle-on-Tyne.
Howells, J...	Mountain Ash.	Hughes, J.	Carnarvon.
Howells, J...	Aberdare.	Hughes, J. D.	Llandudno.
Howells, J. A.	Oxford.	**Hughes, J. E.**	Llandudno.
Howells, J. E.	Aberdare.	Hughes, J. H.	Colwyn Bay.
Howells, T. H.	Ilford.	Hughes, J. Ll.	Llandudno.
Howells, W. L.	Rhondda, etc.	Hughes, J. O.	Menai.
Howes, A. ..	Hendon.	Hughes, J. S.	Brighton, etc.
Howes, A. ..	Wakefield.	Hughes, J. W.	Newcastle-on-Tyne.
Howes, A. ..	Portsmouth.	Hughes, L.	Downham.
Howie, C. W.	Newcastle-on-Tyne.	Hughes, L. G.	Portsmouth.
Howitt, G.	Carlisle.	Hughes, L. S.	Newcastle-on-Tyne.
Howitt, J. E.	London (E.).	Hughes, O...	London (W.).
Howley, J.	Liverpool.	Hughes, P. G.	Rhondda, etc.
Howley, W. J.	Liverpool.	Hughes, P. J.	Liverpool.
Howship, (Miss)	West Ham.	Hughes, R.	Harrogate.
Hoyle, A. ..	Rochdale.	Hughes, R. E.	Carnarvon (S.).
Hoyle, W. F.	Manchester.	Hughes, R. H. R.	Southport.
Hub, W. W. F.	South Shields.	Hughes, R. O.	Glamorgan (W.).
Huband, F. P.	Birmingham.	Hughes, S.	Sheffield.
Hubball, E.	Wolverhampton.	Hughes, S. C.	Tottenham, etc.
Hubble, W.	Wednesbury.	Hughes, S. P.	Flint County.
Hubert, —.	London (N.W.).	Hughes, T.	Newport (Mon.)
Huck, —. ..	Isle of Wight.	Hughes, T. E.	Colchester, etc.
Huck, W. S.	Kendal.	Hughes, T. L.	Liverpool.
Huddart, A.	East Lambeth.	**Hughes, W.**	Sheffield.
Huddy, L. ..	Watford.	Hughes, W. H.	Birkenhead.
Hudson, A.	Spennymoor.	Hughes, W. J.	London (N.W.).
Hudson, A. W. C.	Manchester.	Hugill, T. W.	Plymouth.
Hudson, C. B.	Epsom, etc.	Huitt, H. ..	Woolwich.
*Hudson, F. M.	South Shields.	Huitt, T. H.	Derbyshire (E.).
Hudson, G. H.	Grimsby.	Huke, E. T.	Wellingborough.
Hudson,(Miss) G. M.	Litherland, etc.	Hulbert, H.	Swindon.
Hudson, H. E.	Leyton.	Hull, A. J.	Forest of Dean.
Hudson, H. W.	Kingston and Surbiton.	**Hull, H. B.**	Wimbledon.
Hudson, J.	Durham.	Hull, H. J. P.	Tottenham, etc.
Hudson, J. A.	Derby (E.).	Hull, T. ..	Bishop Auckland.
Hudson, J. H.	Salford.	Hull, T. H...	Bishop Auckland.
Hudson, V.	Staffordshire (N.).	Hull, V. G.	Portsmouth.
Hudson, W.	Birmingham.	Hullah, M. C.	Glossop.
Hudson, W. L.	Southend-on-Sea.	Hulland, W. E.	Blaydon.
Hudspith, A.	Newcastle-on-Tyne.	Hullcoop, R. W.	Oxfordshire (S.).

143   K

N.U.T. WAR RECORD

Name.	Association.
Hulme, A.	Macclesfield District.
Hulme, C.	Hull.
Hulme, H.	York.
Hulme, S.	Radcliffe.
Huls, H.	Grimsby.
Hulse, H.	Chester.
Humble, A. T.	Darlington.
Humbles, T.	Stockport.
Hume, W. L.	Tottenham, etc.
Humphrey, H.	Reading.
Humphreys, A.	Manchester.
Humphreys, (Miss) A.	Leicester.
Humphreys, A. G.	London (E.).
Humphreys, D.	Idris.
Humphreys, (Miss) D.	Newcastle-on-Tyne.
Humphreys, E. A.	Croydon.
Humphreys, E. D.	Aberdare.
*Humphreys, E. W.	East Ham.
Humphreys, F. W.	Chatham, etc.
Humphreys, G. F.	Deptford and Greenwich.
Humphreys, G. V.	Llanfair.
Humphreys, J.	Wrexham.
Humphreys, J. R.	Menai.
Humphreys, J. S.	Merthyr Tydfil.
Humphreys, P.	Staffordshire (N.).
Humphreys, R.	Llandudno.
Humphreys, T. A.	West Lambeth.
Humphreys, W.	Barry.
Humphreys, W.	Flint County.
*Humphreys, W. A.	Hackney.
Humphries, (Mrs.)	Gloucestershire (S.).
Humphries, F. W.	Gloucestershire (S.).
Humphries, L.	Woolwich.
Humphries, W. J.	Barry.
Humphris, E. G.	Bath.
Humphris, H. W.	East Ward, Westmorland.
Humphryes, G.	Hornsey.
Hunkin, F.	Cornwall (Mid.).
Hunnam, H.	Sunderland.
Hunnam, R.	Sunderland.
Hunneyball, T. W.	West Lambeth.
Hunsley, F.	York.
Hunsworth, H.	Rochdale.
Hunt, A. E.	Leicester (Mid.).
Hunt, A. J.	Lewisham.
Hunt, A. L.	Brighton, etc.
Hunt, A. M.	Walthamstow.
Hunt, B.	Wolverhampton.
Hunt, F.	Manchester.
Hunt, G. L.	Southwark.
Hunt, G. N.	Bolton Borough.
Hunt, H.	Sale.
Hunt, J.	Middlesbrough.
Hunt, J. J.	Dover.
*Hunt, J. S.	East Ham.
Hunt, R.	Preston District.
Hunt, R.	London (W.).
Hunt, R.	West Lambeth.
Hunt, S. S.	Lewisham.
Hunt, W. A.	Oxford.
Hunt, W. B.	Wimbledon.
Hunt, W. W.	West Lambeth.
Hunter, A. T.	Tavistock.
Hunter, B. O.	Crook.
Hunter, C.	Worsley.

Name,	Association.
Hunter, H. C.	Hartlepools.
Hunter, J. K.	Newcastle-on-Tyne.
Hunter, N.	Castleford, etc.
*Hunter, R. E.	South Shields.
Hunter, R. H.	Northumberland (N.).
Hunter, S. H.	Spennymoor.
Hunter, W.	South Shields.
Hunter, W. M.	South Shields.
Huntley, A.	Vale of Derwent.
Hurd, A.	Taunton, etc.
Hurd, H. W.	Hornsey.
Hurd, W.	London (N.W.).
Hurdle, W. C.	West Ham.
Hurdman, A. S.	Sunderland.
Hurdman, J.	Sunderland.
Hurley, —.	Bridgwater.
Hurley, F.	Finsbury, etc.
Hurley, J.	Birkenhead.
Hurley, W. E.	Dorset (N.).
Hurlstone, W.	Stourbridge.
*Hurrell, H. R. W.	Staines.
Hurren, H. M.	Yoxford.
Hurren, S. A.	London (N.W.).
Hurst, E. F.	Uxbridge.
Hurst, G. T.	East Lambeth.
Hurst, H. R.	Sheffield.
Hurst, J. G.	Swindon.
Hurst, W. H.	Watford.
Husband, A. L.	Cornwall (Mid.).
Husband, G.	Middlesbrough.
Husband, G. F.	Middlesbrough.
Huskins, T.	Finsbury, etc.
Huson, E. A.	Norwich.
Hussey, T. A.	Woolwich.
Hussey, W. H.	Woolwich.
Hutchens, F.	Plymouth.
Hutchings, —.	London (N.W.).
Hutchings, J. W.	Plymouth.
Hutchings, S. L.	Plymouth.
Hutchins, S. L.	Plymouth.
Hutchins, W.	Hendon.
Hutchinson, A. W.	York.
Hutchinson, E. O.	Hull.
Hutchinson, G. K. M.	Finsbury, etc.
Hutchinson, H. W.	Lewisham.
Hutchinson, M. O.	London (E.).
Hutchinson, W.	East Lambeth.
Hutchinson, W.	Spennymoor.
Hutchinson, W. J.	Birmingham.
Hutchison, D.	Gateshead.
Hutson, F. W.	Southwark.
Hutt, L. R.	West Lambeth.
Hutton, —.	Crewe.
Hutton, C. B.	Warrington.
Hutton, E. J.	Middlesbrough.
Hutton, J.	Southwark.
Hutton, J.	Middlesbrough.
Huyton, W.	Willesden.
Hyde, —.	Farnham.
Hyde, B.	Sheffield.
Hyde, C.	Kettering.
Hyde, H.	Jarrow.
Hyde, H. W.	Southampton.
Hylton, J. C.	Sunderland.
Hymans, A.	London (E.).
Hymans, L. H.	Finsbury, etc.
Hynes, J.	Dewsbury, etc.
Hyslop, H.	West Lambeth.
*Hyslop, M.	Newcastle-on-Tyne.

TEACHERS WHO JOINED THE FORCES

Name.	Association.	Name.	Association.
I Anson, H. H.	Hull.	Jackson, —.	Salford.
I'Anson, J...	Birmingham.	Jackson, —.	Hinckley.
Ibberson, C. S.	Saddleworth.	Jackson, —.	Hyndburn.
Ibbett, T. P.	Bedford.	**Jackson, A. F.**	Hendon.
Ibbotson, —.	Boston.	**Jackson, A. S.**	Nottingham.
Ibbotson, C.	Sheffield.	Jackson, B.	Easington.
Ibbotson, F.	Walsall.	Jackson, C.	Gloucester.
Ibbotson, P.	Heathfield, etc.	**Jackson, O. E.**	Oldham.
Iden, —.	Deptford and Greenwich.	Jackson, E.	Crook.
Iddon, D.	Makerfield.	Jackson, F.	Easington.
Iddon, H.	Preston District.	Jackson, F.	Durham.
Idle, G. W...	Harrogate.	Jackson, G.	Portsmouth.
Idle, L.	Wakefield.	Jackson, H.	Rochdale.
Iggleden, J. H. F...	Portsmouth.	**Jackson, H.**	Wakefield.
Iles, J. C.	Bristol.	Jackson, H.	Wolverhampton.
Iles, T. H.	East Cleveland.	Jackson, H. K.	Bootle.
Iles, W.	Luton.	Jackson, H. L.	Leeds.
*Iliffe, J.	Hornsey.	Jackson, H. L.	Leeds.
Illingworth, —.	Wallasey.	Jackson, I.	Stretford.
Illingworth, E. A.	Ripon.	Jackson, J.	Darwen.
Illingworth, L.	Halifax.	Jackson, J.	Barrow-in-Furness.
Inchley, H.	Mexborough.	Jackson, J.	Enfield.
Ing, W.	Oxford.	Jackson, J. A.	Widnes.
Ingell, A. H.	Sheffield.	Jackson, J. R.	Worcester City.
Ingham, E.	Rotherham.	Jackson, J. R.	Surrey (N.W.).
Ingham, H.	Cambridge, Borough.	Jackson, J. W.	Coalville.
Ingham, J. W.	Isle of Axholme.	Jackson, (Miss) L. R.	Newport Pagnell.
Ingham, W.	Nelson, Colne, etc.	Jackson, N.	Blyth.
Ingle, H. J.	Kiveton Park.	Jackson, R.	Anglesey.
Inglis, (Miss) A. K.	West Ham.	Jackson, R. A.	Doncaster.
Ingram, J. O.	Tredegar.	*Jackson, R. G.	Hendon.
Innes, A. H.	Hackney.	Jackson, R. O.	Leeds.
Instrell, A. W.	Southwark.	Jackson, R. W.	Doncaster.
Iredale, J. T.	Staines.	Jackson, S.	Wakefield.
Ireland, A.	Widnes.	Jackson, S. D.	Hackney.
Ireland, F. S.	Cumberland (W.).	Jackson, T.	Erewash Valley, etc.
Ireland, F. W.	Farnworth.	Jackson, T.	Liverpool.
Ireland, H...	Widnes.	Jackson, T. H.	Liverpool.
Ireland, J. H.	Liverpool.	Jackson, T. V.	Sheffield.
Ireland, P.	Portsmouth.	Jackson, T. W.	Lewisham.
Ireland, R.	Liverpool.	Jackson, W.	Sheffield.
Ireland, W.	Surrey, (S.E.).	Jackson, W. E.	Winchester.
Ireland, W. G.	Hackney.	**Jackson, W. J.**	Hull.
Irish, W. E.	Plymouth.	Jacob, J. H.	Pontypool.
Irlam, L. J.	Salford.	Jacobs, —.	Kidderminster.
Irvin, J. G.	Hackney.	Jacobs, C.	South Shields.
Irving, E.	Coventry.	Jacobs, J.	Tottenham, etc.
Irving, R.	Lancaster.	Jacobs, W. J.	Woolwich.
Irwin, H.	Workington.	Jacobsen, C.	Grimsby.
*Irwin, J. E.	Birmingham.	Jacques, —.	Chester.
Isaac, A. J.	Exeter City.	**Jacques, F.**..	Bridgend.
Isaac, G. W.	Liverpool.	Jacques, J. C.	Driffield, etc.
Isaac, I.	Rhondda, etc.	Jacques, (Miss) S.	Oldbury.
Isaac, J. P.	Gelligaer.	Jacquest, J. W.	Shirebrook.
Isaac, L.	Gelligaer.	*Jaggard, F. W.	Hornsey.
Isaac, T.	Birmingham.	Jagger, F.	Barnsley.
Isaac, W. G.	Plymouth.	Jagger, W. H.	Leeds.
Isaacs, A. H.	Southgate.	James, A.	Cambridge Borough.
Isherwood, A.	Lancaster.	James, A. A.	Rotherham.
Isherwood, R.	Knutsford.	James, A. E.	Birmingham.
Isom, —.	Bury St. Edmunds.	James, (Miss) A. G.	Colchester.
Ithell, R. G.	Liverpool.	James, A. H.	Gloucester.
Ivamy, E.	Twickenham.	James, A. H.	West Lambeth.
Ives, G. A. S.	Ilford.	James, A. J.	Merthyr Tydfil.
Ivory, W. W.	Watford.	James, D.	Pontypool.
Izon, E. W.	Birmingham.	James, D. C.	Willesden.
Izzard, —.	Northampton.	James, D. M.	Warrington.
		James, E.	Carmarthen.
Jack, R. H.	Hackney.	James, E.	Leicester.

N.U.T. WAR RECORD

NAME.	ASSOCIATION.
James, E.	Brighton, etc.
James, E. B.	Smethwick.
James, E. G.	Liverpool.
James, E. P.	Cowbridge, etc.
James, F. A.	Plymouth.
James, F. J.	West Lambeth.
James, F. W.	Maesteg.
James, G. H.	Forest of Dean.
James, G. T.	Glamorgan (Mid.).
James, H. A.	Leominster.
James, H. G.	West Lambeth.
James, J.	Abertillery.
James, J. E.	East Lambeth.
James, J. E.	Rhondda, etc.
James, J. M. S.	Aberdare.
James, J. N.	Birmingham.
James, J. P.	Cwmtawe.
James, J. S.	Pontypool.
James, J. T.	Aberdare.
James, J. T.	Glamorgan (Mid.).
James, L. W.	Reading.
James, O.	Bridgend.
James, P. G.	Leeds.
James, P. G.	West Lambeth.
James, S. H.	Willesden.
James, T. J.	Swansea.
James, T. W.	Rhondda, etc.
James, V. G.	Cornwall (E.).
James, V. G.	Glamorgan (Mid.).
James, W.	Llanelly.
James, W.	Birmingham.
James, W.	Aberdare.
James, W. F.	Pembrokeshire (Mid.).
James, W. H.	Dorset (S.).
James, W. H.	Manchester.
James, W. H.	Exeter District.
James, W. P.	Rhondda, etc.
James, W. T.	Folkestone.
James, W. T.	Leeds.
Jane, W. J.	Rhondda, etc.
Janes, —.	Willesden.
Janes, —.	Surrey (S.E.).
Janes, A. E.	Brentford.
Janes, G.	Coventry.
Jaques, W. L.	Scarborough.
Jardine, R.	Carlisle.
Jarman, —.	Reading.
Jarman, F.	Norfolk (S.).
Jarman, H. W.	Winchester.
Jarman, J. S.	Hartlepools.
Jarman, R.	Leeds.
Jarmin, F.	Ross.
Jarrett, E. J.	Chatham, etc.
Jarvis, A. J.	Hackney.
Jarvis, A. J.	Tottenham, etc.
Jarvis, C. H.	Leeds.
Jarvis, F.	Finsbury, etc.
Jarvis, J.	Vale of Derwent.
Jarvis, P. W.	Peterborough.
Jarvis, W. C. L.	Oxford.
Jasper, H.	East Lambeth.
Jauncey, J.	Manchester.
*Jay, A.	Willenhall.
Jay, H. E.	East Lambeth.
Jeal, W. P.	Kingston and Surbiton.
Jeary, G. H.	Erith.
Jeavens, H.	Birmingham.
Jetcoate, F.	West Lambeth.
Jefferies, E. E.	Liverpool.
Jefferies, H.	Taunton, etc.
Jefferies, J. E.	Stroud.
Jefferson, S. C.	Surrey (N.W.).
Jeffery, A.	Southgate.
Jeffery, S.	Barnes and Mortlake.
Jeffery, W.	Cheltenham.
Jefferys, (Miss)	Erith.
Jefford, G. R.	Eastbourne.
Jefford, T.	Dorset (N.).
Jeffrey, A.	Tynemouth.
Jeffreys, —.	Ipswich.
Jeffreys, —.	Aldershot.
Jeffreys, C. W.	Tottenham, etc.
Jeffreys, D.	Cwmtawe.
Jeffreys, H. P.	Finsbury, etc.
Jeffreys, J.	Nantyglo.
Jeffreys, R.	Cwmtawe.
Jeffreys, W. J.	Glamorgan (W.).
Jeffries, L. V.	Colchester, etc.
Jeffry, —.	Devon (N.).
Jeffs, C. A.	Lewisham.
Jehu, F. C.	London (E.).
Jelbart, —.	Hackney.
Jelleyman, H. W.	Birmingham.
Jemmison, R.	Howden.
Jenken, H. E.	Southwark.
Jenkin, A. W.	Cornwall (Mid.).
Jenkin, E. P.	Cornwall (W.).
Jenkin, W. O.	Walthamstow.
Jenkin, W. P.	Birmingham.
Jenkins, —.	Ogmore, etc.
Jenkins, A.	Caerphilly.
Jenkins, A.	Tamworth.
Jenkins, A.	Tredegar.
Jenkins, A. E.	Swansea.
Jenkins, A. J.	Cardiff.
Jenkins, C.	Epsom, etc.
Jenkins, D.	Glamorgan (W.).
Jenkins, E. C.	Glamorgan (Mid.).
Jenkins, E. C.	Hackney.
Jenkins, E. I.	Woolwich.
Jenkins, E. P.	Aylesbury.
Jenkins, E. R.	East Lambeth.
Jenkins, F.	Glamorgan (W.).
Jenkins, F. C.	Cardiff.
Jenkins, F. E.	East Ham.
Jenkins, F. J.	Swansea.
Jenkins, H.	Rhondda, etc.
Jenkins, J.	Sheffield.
Jenkins, J. C.	Hackney.
Jenkins, J. H.	Glamorgan (Mid.).
Jenkins, J. J.	St. Davids, etc.
Jenkins, L.	Rhondda, etc.
Jenkins, M.	Llanelly.
Jenkins, (Miss) M.	Cardiff.
Jenkins, S.	Dudley.
Jenkins, S.	London (W.).
Jenkins, S. O.	Swansea.
Jenkins, T.	Marlborough.
Jenkins, T. F.	Cardiff.
Jenkins, T. G.	Glamorgan (Mid.).
Jenkins, W. A.	Bristol.
Jenkins, W. E.	Rhondda, etc.
*Jenkins, W. E.	Tredegar.
Jenkins, W. I.	Pontypool.
Jenkinson, E.	Sheffield.
Jenkinson, F.	Liverpool.
Jenkinson, J.	Hindley.
Jenkinson, J. A.	Wirral.

TEACHERS WHO JOINED THE FORCES

Name.	Association.
*Jenkinson, S. R.	Whitehaven.
*Jenks, F. A.	Barking.
Jenman, C. J.	West Lambeth.
Jenn, —.	East Lambeth.
Jenner, E. L.	Southend-on-Sea.
Jennings, A. J.	Coventry.
Jennings, A. W.	Walthamstow.
Jennings, D.	Castleford, etc.
Jennings, H.	Staffordshire (N.).
Jennings, H.	Dudley.
Jennings, H. G.	Swindon.
Jennings, J.	Taunton, etc.
Jennings, P.	Hornsey.
Jennings, R. J.	Harrow.
Jennings, W.	Crook.
Jennings, W.	Bristol.
Jennings, W. A.	Dudley.
Jennings, W. E.	Leicester.
Jennison, J. W.	Leeds.
Jenrick, G. B.	Southwark.
Jephson, H.	Birmingham.
Jepson, J. A. W.	Darwen.
Jeremiah, P.	Woolwich.
Jeremiah, T. R.	London (E.).
Jervis, C. A.	Romford, etc.
Jervis, R. J.	Somerset (S.E.).
Jervis, S.	Leyton.
Jessop, A.	Sheffield.
Jessop, G. N.	Leeds.
Jessop, R.	West Lambeth.
Jeune, G.	Jersey.
Jewels, J. G.	Wallsend.
Jewels, T. H.	Wallsend.
Jewitt, E. W.	Sunderland.
Jewson, S.	West Bromwich.
Jex, E. H.	Coventry.
Jeynes, A. G. H.	Harrow.
Jeynes, T. G.	Hackney.
Joad, H.	Canterbury, etc.
Job, G. W.	Westminster.
Jobling, J. W.	Hartlepools.
Joel, J. G.	Chatham, etc.
John, A.	Caerphilly.
John, B.	Rhondda, etc.
John, I.	Cardiff.
John, (Miss) M. I.	Newport (Mon.).
John, T. E.	Ogmore, etc.
John, W.	Rhondda, etc.
John, W. G.	Glamorgan (W.).
John, W. G.	Pembrokeshire (S.).
John, W. H.	Glamorgan (W.).
John, W. H.	Knutsford.
John, W. H.	Cowbridge, etc.
John, W. T.	Cardiff.
Johncock, S. W.	Sittingbourne, etc.
Johns, D. S. O.	Cardiff.
Johns, F. J.	Plymouth.
*Johns, F. T.	Bedford Borough.
Johns, F. W.	Falmouth and Truro.
Johns, J. A.	Carmarthen.
Johns, J. E.	Plymouth.
Johns, R. S.	Llandovery.
Johnson, —.	Salford.
Johnson, —.	Buxton.
Johnson, —.	Deptford and Greenwich.
Johnson (Miss)	Nottingham.
Johnson, A.	Darlington.
Johnson, A.	West Stanley.
Johnson, A. E.	Bromley.
Johnson, B. O.	Huddersfield.
Johnson, C.	Halifax.
Johnson, C. A.	Northwich.
Johnson, C. H.	Driffield, etc.
Johnson, C. W.	Northampton.
Johnson, D.	Vale of Derwent.
Johnson, E.	West Lambeth.
Johnson, E. A.	Morley.
Johnson, F.	Hull.
Johnson, F. H.	Walthamstow.
Johnson, G. A.	Harrow.
Johnson, G. B.	East Lambeth.
Johnson, G. F.	Birmingham.
Johnson, G. J.	East Ham.
Johnson, G. W.	Easington.
Johnson, H. E.	Gravesend.
Johnson, H. E.	Chester-le-Street.
Johnson, H. H.	Bootle.
Johnson, H. O.	Liverpool.
Johnson, H. S.	Southwark.
Johnson, I.	West Lambeth.
Johnson, J.	Southgate.
Johnson, J.	Southend-on-Sea.
Johnson, J.	Bishop Auckland.
Johnson, J. A.	Hull.
Johnson, J. E. C.	Cannock.
Johnson, J. L.	Rowley Regis.
*Johnson, J. R.	Sunderland.
Johnson, J. W.	London (N.W.).
Johnson, L.	Peterborough.
Johnson, (Miss) M.	Bradford.
Johnson, P.	Sheffield.
Johnson, P. A.	Leicester.
Johnson, P. A.	Birkenhead.
Johnson, S.	Southport.
Johnson, T.	Rotherham. etc.
Johnson, T.	Spennymoor.
Johnson, T.	Chester-le-Street.
Johnson, V. R.	Reading.
Johnson, W.	Stafford.
Johnson, W. J.	Portsmouth.
Johnston, G. T.	Hull.
Johnston, H.	West Ham.
Johnston, H.	West Ham.
Johnston, I.	Durham.
Johnston, S. C.	Workington.
Johnston, T.	Melton Mowbray.
Johnston, V. B.	Birmingham.
Johnstone, (Miss) A. S.	Cardiff.
Jolley, —.	Belper and Crich.
Jolley, —.	Salford.
Jolley, H.	Barnsley.
Jolley, J.	Bolton Borough.
Jolley, V.	Eccles.
Jolly, F.	Chorley.
Jolly, F. W.	Coventry.
Jolly, J. A.	London (W.).
Jones, (Miss)	West Ham.
Jones, (Miss)	West Ham.
Jones, —.	Wimbledon.
Jones, A.	Oldham.
Jones, A.	Rhondda, etc.
Jones, A.	Edmonton.
Jones, A.	Newport (Mon.).
Jones, A.	Nottingham.
Jones, A.	Swansea.
Jones, A. B.	Swansea.
Jones, A. B.	Woolwich.

N.U.T. WAR RECORD

Name.	Association.	Name.	Association.
Jones, A. H.	Rhondda, etc.	Jones, F.	Sheffield.
Jones, A. H.	Surrey (N.W.).	Jones, F. A.	Rhondda, etc.
Jones, A. J.	Cannock.	Jones, F. D.	Preston District.
Jones, A. L.	East Lambeth.	Jones, F. H.	Birmingham.
Jones, A. O.	Lincoln.	**Jones, F. W.**	Mexborough.
Jones, B.	Southwark.	Jones, G.	Aberdare.
Jones, B.	Gelligaer.	**Jones, G.**	Rhondda, etc.
Jones, B. H.	Nantyglo.	Jones, G.	Portsmouth.
Jones, B. J.	Bridgend.	Jones, G. A.	Sittingbourne, etc.
Jones, B. L.	Ebbw Vale.	Jones, G. D.	Liverpool.
Jones, C.	Nantwich.	Jones, G. H.	Bristol.
Jones, C.	Liverpool.	*Jones, G. H.	Eastbourne.
Jones, C. A.	Birmingham.	**Jones, G. R.**	Pembrokeshire (Mid.).
Jones, C. A. W.	Liverpool.	Jones, G. S. W.	Birmingham.
Jones, C. E.	Wrexham.	**Jones, G. T.**	Rhondda, etc.
Jones, C. F.	Manchester.	Jones, H.	Glamorgan (W.).
Jones, C. H.	Liverpool.	Jones, H.	West Bromwich.
Jones, O. O.	Menai.	Jones, H.	Dudley.
Jones, D.	Llandovery.	Jones, H.	Abercarn.
Jones, D.	Barry.	Jones, H.	Forest of Dean.
Jones, D.	Brierley Hill.	**Jones, H.**	Wood Green.
Jones, D.	Pembrokeshire (Mid.).	Jones, H. A.	Reading.
Jones, D.	Newport (Mon.).	Jones, H. A.	Flint County.
Jones, D. A.	Wrexham.	Jones, H. B.	Willenhall.
Jones, D. B.	Aberdare.	Jones, H. B.	Wolverhampton.
Jones, D. E.	Llandyssul, etc.	Jones, H. D.	Finsbury, etc.
Jones, D. E.	Merthyr Tydfil.	**Jones, H. F. C.**	Southwark.
Jones, D. E.	Aberdare.	Jones, H. F.	Tottenham, etc.
Jones, D. E.	Carmarthen.	Jones, H. H.	Wilmslow.
Jones, D. J.	Newport (Mon.).	Jones, H. M.	Birmingham.
Jones, D. J.	Pontypool.	Jones, H. N.	Flint.
Jones, D. J.	Glamorgan (Mid.).	Jones, H. R.	Forest of Dean.
Jones, D. J.	Swansea.	Jones, H. T.	Merthyr Tydfil.
Jones, D. J.	Rhondda, etc.	Jones, H. T.	Abercarn.
*Jones, D. J.	Gelligaer.	**Jones, H. V.**	Builth Wells.
Jones, D. J.	Southwark.	Jones, H. W.	Warwickshire (N.).
Jones, D. L.	Barry.	Jones, H. W.	Carnarvon.
Jones, D. P.	Liverpool.	Jones, I.	Ogmore, etc.
Jones, D. P.	Southend-on-Sea.	Jones, I.	Bridgend.
Jones, D. S. E.	Liverpool.	Jones, I. A.	Radnor County.
Jones, D. W.	Epsom, etc.	Jones, I. G.	Hackney.
Jones, E.	Merthyr Tydfil.	Jones, I. T.	Rhondda, etc.
Jones, E.	Brynmawr.	Jones, J.	Rhondda, etc.
Jones, E.	Lampeter.	Jones, J.	Wakefield.
Jones, E.	Exeter City.	Jones, J.	Bridgend.
Jones, E.	Carmarthen.	Jones, J.	Wrexham.
Jones, E.	Epsom, etc.	Jones, J.	Barry.
Jones, E.	Ealing.	Jones, J.	Liverpool.
Jones, E.	Sheffield.	Jones, J.	Manchester.
Jones, E. C.	Durham.	Jones, J.	Manchester.
Jones, E. D.	Rhondda, etc.	Jones, J.	Glamorgan (W.).
Jones, E. D.	Southend-on-Sea.	Jones, J.	Bilston.
Jones, E. H.	Ebbw Vale.	Jones, J. A.	Southend-on-Sea.
Jones, E. J.	London (N.W.).	**Jones, J. B.**	Wigan.
Jones, E. L.	Merthyr Tydfil.	Jones, J. B.	Rhondda, etc.
Jones, (Miss) E. M.	West Ham.	Jones, J. B.	Chadderton.
Jones, E. M.	Birmingham.	Jones, J. D.	Lampeter.
Jones, E. N.	Wrexham.	Jones, J. D.	Merthyr Tydfil.
Jones, E. O.	Walsall.	Jones, J. E.	Glamorgan (Mid.).
Jones, E. P.	Swindon.	Jones, J. E.	Llanidloes.
Jones, E. R.	Rhondda, etc.	Jones, J. E.	Nantyglo.
Jones, F.	Exeter District.	Jones, J. E.	Birkenhead.
Jones, F.	Rotherham.	Jones, J. E.	London (E.).
Jones, F.	Staffordshire (N.).	Jones, J. E.	Hackney.
Jones, F.	Teign and Dart.	Jones, J. E. H.	Nantyglo.
Jones, F.	Manchester.	*Jones, J. Glynne.	Stafford.
Jones, F.	Ashton-under-Lyne.	Jones, J. H.	Abertillery.
Jones, F.	Warwick.	Jones, J. H.	Machynlleth.
Jones, F.	London (E.).	Jones, J. H.	Wrexham.

TEACHERS WHO JOINED THE FORCES

NAME.	ASSOCIATION.	NAME.	ASSOCIATION.
Jones, J. H.	Wrexham.	**Jones, T.**	Hartlepools.
Jones, J. H.	Liverpool.	Jones, T.	Merthyr Tydfil.
Jones, J. I...	Cardiff.	Jones, T.	Northwich.
Jones, J. I. C.	Gelligaer.	Jones, T.	Cowbridge, etc.
Jones, J. J.	Isle of Thanet.	Jones, T. ...	Llandudno.
Jones, J. J.	Bury.	Jones, T. E.	Ogmore, etc.
Jones, J. L.	Jarrow.	Jones, T. J.	Ogmore, etc.
Jones, J. L.	London (N.W.).	Jones, T. J.	Cardiff.
Jones, J. M.	Ebbw Vale.	Jones, T. J.	Glamorgan (W.).
Jones, J. M.	Blaydon.	Jones, T. J.	Hackney.
Jones, J. R.	Glamorgan (Mid.).	Jones, T. J.	Gelligaer.
Jones, J. R. D.	Bootle.	Jones, T. L.	Northwich.
Jones, J. S.	East Lambeth.	Jones, T. M.	Rhondda, etc.
Jones, J. S.	Finsbury, etc.	Jones, T. P.	Wrexham.
Jones, J. T.	Anglesey.	Jones, T. R.	Merthyr Tydfil.
Jones, J. T.	Aberdare.	Jones, T. W.	Wem.
Jones, J. T.	Bootle.	Jones, T. W. G.	Birkenhead.
Jones, J. T.	Rhondda, etc.	Jones, W. ..	Halstead.
Jones, J. T.	Vale of Clwyd.	Jones, W. ..	Leyton.
Jones, J. T.	Abergavenny.	Jones, W. ..	Llandovery.
Jones, J. W.	Merthyr Tydfil.	Jones, W. ..	Rhondda, etc.
Jones, J. W.	Glamorgan (Mid.).	Jones, W. ..	Hyde.
Jones, J. W.	St. Davids, etc.	Jones, W. ..	Stroud.
Jones, L. ..	Runcorn.	Jones, W. ..	Caerphilly.
Jones, L. ..	Newport (Mon.).	**Jones, W. ..**	Carnarvon (S./.
Jones, L. ..	Abercarn and District.	Jones, W. A.	Chester.
Jones, L. A.	Leeds.	Jones, W. A.	Tredegar.
Jones, L. A.	Newcastle-on-Tyne.	Jones, W. A.	Menai.
Jones, L. B.	Huddersfield.	Jones, W. D.	Carnarvon.
Jones, L. H.	West Lambeth.	Jones, W. G.	Merthyr Tydfil.
Jones, L. M.	Carnarvon.	Jones, W. G.	Carnarvon.
Jones, L. S.	Sheffield.	**Jones, W. H.**	Birkenhead.
Jones, L. T.	Maesteg.	Jones, W. H.	Flint County.
Jones, M. ..	Merthyr Tydfil.	Jones, W. H. L.	Westminster.
Jones, M. ..	Isle of Wight	Jones, W. J.	Llandudno.
Jones, M. D.	Glamorgan (Mid.).	Jones, W. J. E.	Birkenhead.
Jones, M. D.	Leicester.	Jones, W. L.:	Doncaster.
Jones (Miss) M. W.	Llandudno.	Jones, W. M.	Flint County.
Jones, O. ..	Anglesey.	Jones, W. M.	Mountain Ash.
Jones, O. C.	West Ham.	Jones, W. M.	Cardiff.
Jones, O. G.	Ebbw Vale.	Jones, W. O.	Penygroes.
Jones, O. I.	Mountain Ash.	Jones, W. S.	Mountain Ash.
Jones, O. T.	Anglesey.	Jones, W. T.	Rhondda, etc.
Jones, P. C.	Oldham.	Jones, W. W.	Cardiff.
Jones, P. S.	Salford.	**Jope, R.** ..	Enfield.
Jones, P. W.	St. Albans.	Jopling, J.	Tottenham, etc.
Jones, P. W.	East Lambeth.	Jordan, —.	Kingston and Surbiton.
Jones, P. W. K.	Hereford.	Jordan, H.	Bridgnorth.
Jones, (Miss) Rhys.	Newport (Mon.).	Jordan, H. A.	Uxbridge.
Jones, R. ..	Preston Borough.	Jordan, P. ...	Birmingham.
Jones, R. ..	Carnarvon.	Jordan, R.	Acton.
Jones, R. ..	Nantyglo.	Jordan, S. B.	Manchester.
Jones, R. A.	Runcorn.	Jordon, A.	Birmingham.
Jones, R. E.	Hackney.	Josephs, A.	South Shields.
Jones, R. E.	Liverpool.	Josephs, B.	South Shields.
Jones, R. J.	Newport (Mon.).	Josephs, I.	South Shields.
Jones, R. O.	Bootle.	Joshua, G. L.	Cardiff.
Jones, R. P.	Hull.	Joshua, T. ...	Rhondda, etc.
Jones, R. T.	Bournemouth.	Joslin, J. J.	Barry.
Jones, R. W.	Derby.	*Joss, E. J.	Houghton-le-Spring.
*Jones, R. W.	Liverpool.	Jourd, W. T.	Erith.
Jones, S. ..	Ogmore, etc.	Journeaux, I. A.	Jersey.
Jones, S. ..	Mountain Ash.	Joy, A. E. ..	Staffordshire (N.).
Jones, S. ..	Tredegar.	**Joy, D.** ..	York.
Jones, S. M.	Pontypool.	Joy, F. ..	Finsbury, etc.
Jones, T. ..	West Lambeth.	Joy, H. ..	Leeds.
Jones, T. ..	Merthyr Tydfil.	Joy, L. ..	Leeds.
Jones, T. ..	Hackney.	Joy, P. ..	Portsmouth.
Jones, T. ..	Newport (Mon.).	Joy, W. ..	Howden.

N.U.T. WAR RECORD

Name.	Association.
Joyce, A.	Crook.
Joyce, A. J.	Bristol.
Joyce, E.	Manchester.
Joyce, T.	Lincoln.
Joynson, —.	Salford.
Joynson, W.	Manchester.
Jubb, A. B.	Dewsbury, etc.
Jubb, J. B.	Manchester.
Jubb, J. E.	Brentford.
Jubb, W.	Lincoln.
Judd, F. G. H.	Watford.
Judd, H. C.	Southampton.
Judd, H. R.	Gelligaer.
Jude, —.	London (N.W.).
Jude, C. W.	Southwark.
Jukes, F.	Stroud.
Jukes, R. W.	Cannock.
Juliff, —.	Cheltenham.
Julyan, W. L.	Devizes.
Jupp, E. J.	Itchen.
Jurd, R. H. A.	Hackney.
Kadwill, H. J.	Dartford.
Kaighin, G. H.	Birmingham.
Kane, D. L. P.	Birmingham.
Kane, L.	St. Helens.
Katon, F. C. H.	Attleborough, etc.
Kay, A. L.	Walthamstow.
Kay, C. F.	Birmingham.
Kay, G.	Southwark.
Kay, H.	Darwen.
Kay, J.	Staffordshire (N.).
Kay, J.	Leeds.
Kay, J. B.	Alton.
Kay, J. H.	Sandbach.
*Kay, S. T.	Liverpool.
Kay, W.	Darwen.
Kaye, A. E.	Birmingham.
Kaye, E.	Castleford, etc.
Kaye, P.	Spen Valley.
Keal, R.	Hull.
Kealey, F.	Lincoln.
Kear, B. M.	Forest of Dean.
Kear, I.	Forest of Dean.
Kearney, B.	Manchester.
Kearney, P. L.	Liverpool.
Kearns, B.	Waveney Valley.
Keast, F.	Barrow-in-Furness.
Keast, H.	Cornwall (E.).
Keast, H. W.	Plymouth.
Keast, R. H.	Falmouth.
Keay, E. J.	West Lambeth.
Keeble, A. F.	Nottingham.
Keeble, R. C.	St. Albans.
Keedy, E. N.	South Shields.
Keeley, A. E.	London (E.).
Keeling, A. E.	London (W.).
Keeling, W. J.	Bournemouth.
Keen, —.	Newbury.
Keen, B. A.	Swadlincote.
Keen, (Miss) G. W.	East Ham.
Keen, I. S.	Lancaster.
Keen, J.	Easington.
*Keen, J. W.	Harrow
Keene, A.	West Ham.
Keene, J. F.	Staffordshire (N.).
*Keevil, F. G.	Reigate.
Keith, H. W.	Newcastle-on-Tyne.
Kelbrick, T. V.	Manchester.

Name.	Association.
Kellaway, B.	Cornwall (Mid.).
Kellaway, W. H.	Plymouth.
Kellett, G. W.	Barnsley.
Kellow, T.	Plymouth.
Kelly, —.	St. Helens.
Kelly, A. C. P.	Liverpool.
Kelly, B. J.	Manchester.
Kelly, F.	Gateshead.
Kelly, F. C.	Newcastle-on-Tyne.
Kelly, J.	London (E.).
Kelly, J.	Manchester.
Kelly, J. H.	Isle of Man.
Kelly, J. J.	Cumberland (W.).
Kelly, L.	Middlesbrough.
Kelly, M. J.	London (N.W.)
Kelly, P. E.	Brentford.
Kelly, R.	Blackburn.
Kelly, R. T.	Hackney.
Kelsall, J.	Workington.
*Kelsey, L. J.	Coventry.
Kemble, W.	Plymouth.
Kemp, —.	Epsom, etc.
Kemp, —.	Willesden.
Kemp, —.	Ipswich.
Kemp, —.	Leicester.
Kemp, P. H.	Finsbury, etc.
Kemp, S.	Finsbury, etc.
Kemp, S.	Hull.
Kemp, W.	Manchester.
Kemp, W. H.	Uxbridge.
Kemp, W. S.	London (W.).
Kempster, A. W.	Kingston and Surbiton.
Kemsley, W.	Finsbury, etc.
Kendall, —.	Grimsby.
Kendrick, L. W.	Melton Mowbray.
Kendrick, W.	Wimbledon.
Kennard, W. T.	Brighton, etc.
Kennedy, I.	Workington.
Kennedy, J.	Manchester.
*Kennedy, J. L.	South Shields.
Kennedy, R.	Durham.
Kennett, F. T. F.	Plymouth.
Kennett, R. J.	Tottenham, etc.
Kennett, W. M.	Barnsley.
Kenningham, C. E.	Hull.
Kenny, M.	Woolwich.
Kenshole, (Miss) I.	Merthyr Tydfil.
Kent, A. L.	London (N.W.).
Kent, E. W.	Hackney.
Kent, F. N.	Sheffield.
Kent, G.	Blackburn.
*Kent, H. G.	Brighton, etc.
Kent, P. J.	Nottingham.
Kent, T. R.	Slough.
Kent, W. E.	Portsmouth.
Kentfield, F.	West Lambeth.
Kenworthy, T. B.	Pocklington, etc.
Kenwright, F.	St. Helens.
Kenyon, C.	Durham.
Kenyon, E.	Litherland, etc.
Kenyon, J. E.	Makerfield.
Ker, A. J.	Ealing.
Kerby, —.	Liverpool.
Kerby, W.	London (W.).
Kermode, G. D.	Birkenhead.
Kernick, J. C.	Rutland.
Kerr, R.	Leeds.
Kerridge, —.	Ipswich.
Kerridge, J. B. D.	Eastbourne.

TEACHERS WHO JOINED THE FORCES

NAME.	ASSOCIATION.	NAME.	ASSOCIATION.
Kerridge, T.	Essex (Mid.).	Kinghorn, W. G.	Newcastle-on-Tyne.
Kerrison, H. W.	West Lambeth.	Kingsland, —.	Deal.
Kerry, A. H.	Mexborough.	Kingston, H. P.	Willenhall.
Kershaw, E.	Bishop Auckland.	Kinman, H. B.	Sheffield.
Kershaw, J.	Surrey (N.W.).	Kinnaird, J.	Gateshead.
Kerslake, J.	Willesden.	Kinns, P. C.	Liverpool.
Kerwood, H. C.	Forest of Dean.	Kipling, W. A.	Stockton.
Kesting, E. C.	Newcastle-on-Tyne.	Kippen, J.	Wallsend.
Ketcher, P. T.	Teddington.	Kirby, C. G.	Leyton.
Kew, H.	Grimsby.	Kirby, A. J.	York.
Kew, R. G.	York.	Kirby, E.	Barnsley.
Key, A. E.	Oldbury.	Kirby, G.	Finsbury, etc.
Key, C. W.	London (E.).	Kirby, H.	Barnsley.
Keys, E.	Gloucester.	Kirby, T.	Malvern, etc.
Keys, W. H.	West Lambeth.	Kirby, W. T.	Reading.
Kidd, A.	Staffordshire (N.).	Kirk, —.	Boston.
Kidd, D. L.	Birmingham.	Kirk, C. H.	Leicester.
Kiernan, O.	Leeds.	Kirk, C. J.	Middlesbrough.
Kift, H.	Somerset (N.).	Kirk, J. L.	Nottingham.
*Kilburn, P.	Mexborough.	Kirk, W. T.	Bishop Auckland.
Kilcross, A.	Liverpool.	**Kirkbride, R. W.**	Lancaster.
Killeck, E.	Yoxford.	Kirkby, A.	Castleford, etc.
Killeen, J. F.	Jarrow.	Kirkby, A.	Leeds.
Killick, H. P.	Pontypool.	Kirkham, H. H.	Birmingham.
Killington, F. J.	Dorset (S.).	Kirkham, T. H.	Staffordshire (N.).
Killip, E.	Liverpool.	Kirkham, W. G. W.	Haslingden.
Killip, R. L.	Sheffield.	Kirkman, R. A.	Shirebrook.
Kilner, C. A.	Hackney.	**Kirkpatrick, J.**	Manchester.
Kilvington, B. P.	Bletchley.	Kirkup, G. R.	Durham.
Kimber, A. R.	West Lambeth.	**Kirkwood, J.**	Hackney.
Kimber, V. G. W.	Southampton.	*Kirtley, R. W.	South Shields.
Kimberley, B.	Stourbridge.	Kitchen, A. E.	Woolwich.
Kimberley, J.	Spalding.	Kitchen, E. D.	Keighley.
King, —.	Stourbridge.	Kitchen, J.	Stockport.
King, —.	Eastleigh.	Kitchen, J. J.	Spennymoor.
King, A.	Dorset (E.).	Kitchen, (Miss) L.	Barrow-in-Furness.
King, A. E.	Essex (Mid.).	Kitchen, W. H.	Leeds.
King, C.	Deptford and Greenwich.	Kitchener, P.	London (N.W.).
King, E. W.	West Ham.	Kitcher, —.	East Lambeth.
King, E. W.	Brentford.	Kitching, J.	Bishop Auckland.
King, F.	West Lambeth.	Kitching, W.	Birmingham.
*King, F.	Liverpool.	Kite, F.	Eastbourne.
King, F.	Bootle.	Kitson, D. A.	Dewsbury, etc.
King, F. W.	East Lambeth.	**Kitson, T. A. B.**	Dewsbury, etc.
King, G.	Southwark.	Kitt, A. J.	Plymouth.
King, G.	London (E.).	Kitto, J. D.	Plymouth.
King, G.	North Cleveland.	Kitto, T. E.	Manchester.
King, H.	Bishop Auckland.	Kitts, —.	St. Helens.
King, A. H.	London (W.).	**Klein, F.**	Ealing.
King, H. S.	Shirebrook.	Knaggs, H.	Leeds.
King, I.	West Ham.	Knaggs, J. H.	Darlington.
King, J.	Wolverhampton.	Knapman, E.	Teign and Dart.
King, J.	Leeds.	Knapp, W. C.	Harrow.
King, L.	Ripon.	Knapton, J. D.	Nelson, Colne, etc.
King, L. A.	London (W.).	Knee, E. S.	Sheffield.
*King, M. P.	London (W.).	Kneebone, —.	Ealing.
King, P. W.	London (W.).	Knief, C. A.	West Ham.
King, S.	Surrey (N.W.).	Knight, (Miss)	Northampton.
King, (Mrs.) N.	Wakefield.	Knight, —.	Matlock, etc.
King, N. J.	Nottinghamshire (W.)	Knight, —.	Eastleigh, etc.
King, P.	Swindon.	Knight, A.	Kidderminster.
King, T. A.	Shipley.	Knight, A. G.	Willenhall.
King, W.	Liverpool.	Knight, A. T.	Dudley.
King, W. E. T.	Southampton.	**Knight, O. E.**	Worksop.
King, W. J.	Tottenham, etc.	Knight, E. F.	West Lambeth.
King, W. L.	South Shields.	Knight, F. H. P.	Crook.
Kingcome, G. W.	Plymouth.	Knight, G. A.	Leicester (Mid.).
Kingdon, A. W.	Plymouth.	Knight, G. F.	Wellingborough.
Kingham, E. P.	Eastbourne.	**Knight, J.**	Bodmin.

N.U.T. WAR RECORD

Name.	Association.
Knight, H. A. W.	London (N.W.).
Knight, H. J.	Worcester City.
Knight, H. L.	East Lambeth.
Knight, J. V.	Portsmouth.
Knight, J. W.	Chichester.
Knight, S.	Finsbury, etc.
Knight, W.	Driffield, etc.
Knightbridge, B. A.	London (E.).
Knighton, A. E.	Nottingham.
Knighton, J. B.	Sheffield.
Knights, E. H. T.	Sudbury.
Knights, G. W.	Birmingham.
Knott, L. C.	Ampthill, etc.
Knott, W. A. P.	Crompton, etc.
Knowles, —.	Blaydon.
Knowles, —.	Warrington.
Knowles, F. W.	Clitheroe.
Knowles, H. F.	Glamorgan (Mid.).
Knowles, H. F. W.	Gravesend.
Knowles, J.	Huntingdonshire.
Knowles, J. C.	Epsom, etc.
Knowles, M. P.	Mexborough.
Knowles, T.	Leeds.
Knowles, T.	Leeds.
Knowlson, E.	Liverpool.
Knox, H.	Newcastle-on-Tyne.
Knox, J. W.	Northumberland (S.).
Knuckey, J. J.	Willesden.
Koppack, C.	Stroud.
Kyd, C. S.	Penarth.
Kydd, W. J.	Bromley.
Kynaston, P. T.	Chiswick.
Lacey, E. A.	Hull.
Lacey, H. C.	Gloucester.
Lacy, H.	Leeds.
Lacy, W. B.	Kingston and Surbiton.
Ladkin, W.	Wakefield.
Laflin, O. H.	Worcester City.
Laidler, G. H.	Liverpool.
Laidler, J.	Easington.
Laidlow, W.	Leeds.
Laister, H.	Rowley Regis.
Lake, W. E. R.	Plymouth.
Lake, W. L.	Lewisham.
Lakeman, H. B.	London (W.).
Lally, J.	Manchester.
Lamacraft, G. H.	Teign and Dart.
Lamacraft, W. H.	Portsmouth.
*Lamb, C. W.	West Lambeth.
Lamb, D.	Durham.
Lamb, F. A.	Runcorn.
Lamb, G.	Hertford.
Lamb, H.	Dudley.
Lamb, N. W.	Plymouth.
Lamb, R. R.	South Shields.
Lamb, T. W.	Bishop Auckland.
Lambert, —.	Leeds.
Lambert, A.	Woolwich.
Lambert, A. A.	Fishguard.
Lambert, G. W.	Brecon.
Lambert, H.	Wimbledon.
Lambert, J. W.	Leicester.
Lambert, L.	Northwich.
Lambert, R. N.	Sheffield.
Lambourne, F.	Chiswick.
Lambton, C. S.	Durham.
Lampard, O. C. H.	Stockport.
Lamplugh, S.	Croydon.

Name.	Association.
Lancaster, C. A.	Liverpool.
Lancaster, F.	Woolwich.
Lancaster, G. E.	Westminster.
Lancaster, L. J.	Woolwich.
Lancaster, W.	Burnley.
Lancaster, W.	Blackburn.
Lance, F.	Ilford.
*Lanceley, T.	Chester.
Landels, —.	Bromley.
Lander, E. C. M.	Newport Pagnell, etc.
Landon, H.	Staffordshire (N.).
*Landon, L. A.	Staffordshire (N.).
Landrey, A.	Plymouth.
Lane, —.	Sittingbourne.
Lane, A.	Oldham.
Lane, A.	Stockport.
Lane, A. C.	Brighouse.
Lane, A. W.	Evesham.
Lane, C. J. W.	Leicester.
Lane, F. L.	West Ham.
Lane, G.	London (W.).
Lane, H. C.	Lewisham.
Lane, R. S.	Hebburn.
Lane, S.	Bristol.
Lane, W.	Tredegar.
Lang, —.	London (W.).
Lang, (Miss) E.	Clitheroe.
Lang, R. W.	London (W.).
Lang, S. D.	Southwark.
Langdon, —.	West Ham.
Langdon, R.	Warminster.
Langford, (Miss) A.	Vale of Derwent.
Langford, A. G.	West Lambeth.
Langford, A. H.	Newport (Mon.).
Langford, E. A.	Oxford (S.).
Langford, G.	Newport (Mon.).
Langford, G. W.	Hackney.
Langford, W.	Tipton.
Langler, H. W.	West Ham.
Langley, —.	Grimsby.
Langley, G. H.	Romford, etc.
Langston, G.	Gloucester.
Langton, J. T.	Leicester.
Langwell, B. H.	Birmingham.
Lansdale, A.	Blackburn.
Lansdall, P. G.	Hackney.
Lansdell, C. A.	Norwich City.
Lansdell, W. A.	Great Yarmouth.
Lansdowne, L. R.	Colchester, etc.
Lantsberry, G. E. T.	Manchester.
Lapes, J. E.	Manchester.
Lapierre, G. R. L.	Oldham.
Lapping, G.	Wallsend.
Lapwood, E.	Birmingham.
Lapworth, W.	Hendon.
Larber, W. B.	West Ham.
Larcombe, H. J.	Gloucester.
Larcombe, W. J.	Tottenham, etc.
Large, —.	London (N.W.).
Large, E. O.	Penistone.
Large, H.	Bootle.
Large, R. P.	West Lambeth.
Larking, S. H.	West Ham.
Larking, S. L.	West Ham.
Larter, J.	Lowestoft.
Lascelles, R. G.	Liverpool.
Lassey, J.	Dewsbury, etc.
Last, H.	Wimbledon.
Last, H. G.	East Ham.

TEACHERS WHO JOINED THE FORCES

Name.	Association.
Latham, D. E.	Birmingham.
Latham, E. F.	Widnes.
Latham, F. C. J.	Woolwich.
Latham, G.	Southwark.
Latham, W.	Manchester.
Latter, W. W.	Southwark.
Lattimer, —.	Epsom, etc.
Lattimer, F. H.	Sunderland.
Laughton, H. T.	Nottingham.
Launder, W. G.	London (N.W.).
Laurence, A. H.	Warwickshire (N.).
Lavender, E.	Hendon.
Laver, C. H.	Sheffield.
Laverick, R.	Bishop Auckland.
Lavers, —.	Kidderminster.
Lavers, —.	Teign and Dart.
Laverty, T.	London (W.).
Law, —.	Kettering.
Law, E.	Isle of Ely.
Lawes, A. J.	Bristol.
Lawler, W...	Liverpool.
Lawless, B.	West Lambeth.
Lawley, H...	Walsall.
Lawrence, C. W.	Nottingham.
Lawrence, E. E.	St. David's, etc.
Lawrence, S. A.	Birmingham.
Lawrie, J.	Wirral.
Laws, B. O.	Nottingham.
Lawson, G. D.	Alnwick.
Lawson, R. O.	Bolton Borough.
Lawson, W. D.	Manchester.
Lawton, A.	Staffordshire (N.).
Lawton, F...	Staffordshire (N.).
Lawton, H.	Crewe.
Lawton, R. H.	Barrow-in-Furness.
Lawton, S. C.	Barrow-in-Furness.
Lax, A. E.	Stockton-on-Tees.
Lax, H.	Barnsley.
Lay, A. G.	Dorking.
Laycock, T.	Scarborough.
Laycock, W. S.	Devizes.
Layton, P. M.	Bishop Auckland.
Lazonby, C.	Durham.
Lea, —.	Petworth.
Lea, H.	Manchester.
Leach, —.	Northampton.
Leach, —.	Salford.
Leach, C. H.	Finsbury, etc.
Leach, F. J.	London (E.).
Leach, H.	Warrington.
Leach, L.	Willesden.
Leach, W.	Sale.
Leach, W. F.	Winchester.
Leadbeater, —.	Northampton.
Leafe, A.	Leicester.
Leak, A. T.	Sheffield.
*__Leake, G. E. A.__	Reading.
Leake, H.	Uxbridge.
Leaky, P.	Barry.
Lean, W. L.	Cornwall (E.).
Leaney, F. J.	Brighton, etc.
Leaning, C. W.	Nottingham.
Leaper, W.	Finsbury, etc.
Leaphard, E. P.	London (N.W.).
Leat, E. J.	Slough.
Leathard, J.	Northumberland (E.).
Leatherdale, —.	Kettering.
Leatt, H. J.	Exeter City.
Leaver, —.	East Lambeth.
Leaver, P.	Wimbledon.
*Leavis, T.	Bolton Borough.
Le Blancq, F. C.	Jersey.
Leckie, J.	Spennymoor.
Ledger, T. W.	Hull.
Ledgerwood, H.	Barrow-in-Furness.
Lee, A.	Manchester.
Lee, A. J.	Staines.
Lee, D.	Hebburn.
Lee, F.	Chippenham.
Lee, F. H.	Hornsey.
Lee, H.	Liverpool.
Lee, H. S.	London (N.W.).
Lee, J.	Bishop Auckland.
Lee, J. H.	East Ham.
Lee, J. P.	Finsbury, etc.
Lee, L. G. H.	Wellingborough.
Lee, L. P.	Rhondda, etc.
Leech, T.	Enfield.
Leedam, W. D.	Willenhall.
*Leeds, G. J.	Southend-on-Sea.
Leek, G. J.	Worcester City.
Leeming, A. T.	Jarrow.
Lees, C.	Walsall.
Lees, F.	Oldham.
Lees, J.	Newport (Mon.).
Lees, L.	Wakefield.
Lees, R.	Ashton, etc.
Leese, E.	Staffordshire (N.).
Leese, W. H.	East Lambeth.
Leeson, F.	Grantham.
Leeson, L. G.	Sittingbourne, etc.
Leeson, T. G. M.	Southampton.
Le Feuvre, M.	Jersey.
Legerton, C. W. S.	West Lambeth.
Legg, H. G.	Woolwich.
Legg, W. A.	Deptford and Greenwich.
Legg, W. R.	Chester-le-Street.
Legge, C. R.	Buckinghamshire.
Leggett, E. G.	Southampton.
Leggett, H. R.	Eastleigh.
Leggett, S. J.	Deptford and Greenwich.
Leggott, W.	Goole.
Le Grice, S.	Great Yarmouth.
Le Gros, C. L.	Teddington.
Leigh, E.	Lewisham.
Leigh, F.	Manchester.
Leigh, P. C. J.	Southampton.
Leigh, R.	Manchester.
Leigh, W. B.	Maidstone.
Leighton, J. W.	Deptford and Greenwich.
Leighton, (Miss) L.	Walsall.
Leivers, D.	Nottingham.
Leivers, S.	Coalville.
Lello, H.	Calder Valley.
Lello, W. P.	London (E.).
Lemmon, E. T.	York.
Lemmon, W.	Barnard Castle.
Lemon, T. V.	Stratford-on-Avon.
Lennox, J.	Gateshead.
Lenthall, C.	Sheffield.
Lenton, —.	Bishop's Stortford.
Lenz, W. A. P.	West Ham.
Leonard, A. G.	West Ham.
Leonard, G.	Birmingham.
Leonard, J. A.	Rhondda, etc.
Leonard, J. P.	Birkenhead.
Leonard, S. B.	Huddersfield.
Leonard, V. C. H.	London (E..

N.U.T. WAR RECORD

Name.	Association.
Leonard, W. C.	Darlington.
Leopold, W. A.	Glamorganshire (W.).
Le Powell, J.	Stourbridge.
Le Quesne, —.	Coventry.
Lerry, F. H.	Finsbury, etc.
Leslie, —.	Bath.
Leslie, H.	Scarborough.
Leslie, O. T.	Brentford.
Leslie, W.	Sunderland.
Lester, G. H.	Birmingham.
Lethbridge, (Miss) A.	Plymouth.
Lethbridge, E. H.	Brighton, etc.
Letherby, A.	Plymouth.
Letkey (Miss)	East Ham.
Letts, H.	Leicester.
Levene, S.	London (E).
Levens, A.	Burnley.
Levers, H. L.	Portsmouth.
Levine, A. E.	Birmingham.
Levitt, E.	Wakefield.
*Levy, J.	London (E.).
Lewcock, O.	Portsmouth.
Lewendon, H. T.	Oxford District.
Lewin, C. O. H.	Liverpool.
Lewin, H. G.	Finsbury, etc.
Lewington, F. J.	Southampton.
Lewis, —.	Birmingham.
Lewis, —.	Liverpool.
Lewis, A.	Manchester.
Lewis, A.	Eccles.
Lewis, A.	Glamorganshire (W.).
Lewis, A.	Rhondda, etc.
Lewis, A. D.	Plymouth.
Lewis, A. H. T.	Gloucester.
Lewis, A. S.	Worcester City.
Lewis, B.	Cambridgeshire.
Lewis, B. T.	Bridgend.
Lewis, C.	Tredegar.
Lewis, C. L.	London (W.).
Lewis, D.	Cardiff.
Lewis, D. J.	Tredegar.
Lewis, D. L.	Pembrokeshire (S.).
Lewis, D. R.	Newport (Mon.).
Lewis, E.	East Lambeth.
Lewis, E. R.	Hornsey.
Lewis, F.	Gloucester.
Lewis, G.	Swansea.
Lewis, G. A.	Rhondda, etc.
Lewis, G. F.	Bristol.
Lewis, G. H.	Birkenhead.
Lewis, G. P.	Llanelly.
Lewis, G. W.	Birmingham.
Lewis, H.	Swadlincote.
Lewis, H. C.	Tottenham, etc.
Lewis, H. L.	Northampton.
Lewis, H. V. W.	Ebbw Vale.
Lewis, I.	Rhondda, etc.
Lewis, J.	Tottenham, etc.
Lewis, J. A.	Merthyr Tydfil.
Lewis, J. A.	Pembrokeshire (Mid.).
Lewis, J. D.	Rhondda, etc.
Lewis, J. H.	Rhondda, etc.
Lewis, J. H.	Rhondda, etc.
Lewis, J. L.	Aberayron.
Lewis, J. O.	Aberdare.
Lewis, J. T.	Portsmouth.
Lewis, Mrs. K. M.	Rhondda, etc.
Lewis, L.	Merthyr Tydfil.
Lewis, L. C.	London (W.).
Lewis, L. M.	Birkenhead.
Lewis, L. W.	Liverpool.
Lewis, P.	Rhondda, etc.
Lewis, P. D.	Rhondda, etc.
Lewis, P. M.	Abercarn.
Lewis, R. O.	Evesham.
Lewis, R. H.	Rhondda, etc.
Lewis, R. L.	Abertillery.
Lewis, S.	Gloucestershire (S.).
Lewis, S. H.	Finsbury, etc.
Lewis, S. J.	Tredegar.
Lewis, T.	West Ham.
Lewis, T.	Rhondda, etc.
Lewis, T.	Cardiff.
Lewis, T. A.	Rhondda, etc.
Lewis, T. B.	Rhondda, etc.
Lewis, T. C.	Litherland, etc.
Lewis, T. J.	Mountain Ash.
Lewis, T. J.	Aberdare.
Lewis, T. J.	Barry.
Lewis, T. L.	Swansea.
Lewis, T. S.	Glamorgan (Mid.).
Lewis, W.	Pontypool.
Lewis, W.	Bath.
Lewis, W.	Sheffield.
Lewis, W. Bowen	Fishguard.
Lewis, W. H.	Swansea.
Lewis, W. S.	Falmouth and Truro.
Leyden, D. M.	South Shields.
Leyden, J. L.	South Shields.
Leyland, H.	Wharfedale.
Leyshon, S.	Swansea.
Licence, R. C.	Finsbury, etc.
Lickess, H.	Finsbury, etc.
Liddell, A.	Blaydon.
Liddicott, G.	Swansea.
Liddle, G.	Darlington.
Liddle, J.	Stockton-on-Tees.
Lidington, E. L.	West Lambeth.
Liedtke, —.	Ogmore, etc.
Light, G.	Liverpool.
Light, S. T.	Enfield.
Lightfoot, (Miss)	Northallerton.
Lightfoot, B. S.	Bristol.
Lightfoot, H.	Bishop's Stortford.
Lightfoot, W.	Willesden.
Lightley, E.	Harrow.
Lilley, A.	Wakefield.
Lilley, E. G.	London (N.W.).
Lilley, F.	Kettering.
Lilley, G.	Cambridge Borough.
Lilley, P.	Middlesbrough.
Lilliman, A.	Watford.
Liming, L. H.	Finsbury, etc.
Linch, C. R.	Portsmouth.
Lindley, F.	Wolverhampton.
Lindley, S.	Huddersfield.
Lindley, S. H.	Hyde.
Lindop, —.	Ealing.
Lindow, J.	Spen Valley.
*Lindsay, D.	Worcester City.
Lindsay, H.	Worthing.
Lindsay, J.	Easington.
Lineham, E.	Portsmouth.
Lineham, W.	Gravesend.
Ling, M.	Hull.
Ling, R. W.	Leyton.
Lingard, F.	Hull.
Linge, H.	Hackney.

TEACHERS WHO JOINED THE FORCES

NAME.	ASSOCIATION.
Linley, G. W.	Birmingham.
Linn, —.	East Lambeth.
*Lintern, E. C.	Luton.
Lintott, E.	Bradford.
Liptrott, A. T.	Bolton District.
Lishman, A. V.	Bradford.
Lishman, F. P.	Houghton-le-Spring.
*Lishman, T. B.	Bolton District.
Lisle, C.	Nottingham.
*Lisle, J. R.	Blyth.
Lissimore, E.	West Bromwich, etc.
Lister, A. S.	Croydon.
Lister, E.	Derby (E.).
*Lister, Rhodes	Spen Valley.
Little, A. J.	London (E.).
Little, E. R.	Vale of Derwent.
Little, J. C. H.	Chatham, etc.
Little, (Miss) L. M.	Cardiff.
Little, T. G.	Chester-le-Street.
Little, W. B.	Brackley, etc.
Little, W. P.	Harrow.
Littlefair, A.	Middlesbrough.
Littlejohn, J.	Tottenham, etc.
Littler, J.	London (E.).
Littler, J. H.	Manchester.
Littlewood, F.	Elland.
Liversedge, A. E.	Leeds.
Livesey, —.	Preston Borough.
Livesey, E. L.	Doncaster.
Livesey, E. N.	Preston District.
Livesey, L.	Manchester.
Livingstone, H.	Newcastle-on-Tyne.
Llewellyn, B. S.	Abercarn.
Llewellyn, D. G.	Caerphilly.
Llewellyn, E.	Cardiff.
Llewellyn, G. H.	Birmingham.
*Llewellyn, T.	Rhondda, etc.
Llewellyn, T. J.	Cardiff.
Llewellyn, W.	Pembrokeshire (S.).
Llewhellin, G. E.	London (W.).
Lloyd, —.	West Ham.
Lloyd, —.	Hereford.
Lloyd, A.	Knutsford.
Lloyd, A.	Wolverhampton.
Lloyd, A. E.	Abertillery.
Lloyd, A. G.	West Stanley.
Lloyd, A. L.	Newport Pagnell.
Lloyd, A. R.	Rhondda, etc.
Lloyd, E.	Tredegar.
Lloyd, E.	Wallesay.
*Lloyd, E. A.	West Lambeth.
*Lloyd, E. E.	Leeds.
Lloyd, E. J.	Rhondda, etc.
Lloyd, F.	Norfolk (N.W.).
Lloyd, H. C.	Llandudno.
Lloyd, H. J.	East Lambeth.
Lloyd, I.	Mountain Ash.
Lloyd, I.	Rhondda, etc.
Lloyd, R. G.	Gillingham.
Lloyd, W.	Rotherham.
Lloyd, W. A.	Rhondda, etc.
*Lloyd, W. H.	Harrow.
Lloyd, W. J.	Edmonton.
Lloyd, W. J.	Llandovery.
Lloyd, W. R.	Rhondda, etc.
Loader, H. C.	Winchester.
Loam, M.	Chester.
Lobb, W. H.	Birkenhead.
Lock, A.	Birmingham.
Lock, W. H.	Rhondda, etc.
Locke, A.	Northumberland (E.).
Locke, J.	Northumberland (E.).
*Locker, A. C.	Birmingham.
Locker, H.	Teddington.
Lockett, —.	Hyndburn.
Lockett, —.	Hyndburn.
Lockett, W. C.	Birmingham.
Lockeyear, J. H.	Finsbury, etc.
Lockley, F. W.	Wolverhampton.
Lockley, P.	Melton Mowbray.
Lockwood, —.	Penistone.
Lockwood, A.	Huddersfield.
Lockwood, A.	Wharfedale.
Lockwood, A.	Wakefield.
Lockwood, H.	Darlington.
Lodge, A.	West Lambeth.
Lodge, A. H.	Stockport.
Lodge, C. J.	Woolwich.
Lofthouse, A. E.	Newcastle-on-Tyne.
*Lofthouse, L. F.	Manchester.
Lofthouse, R. L.	Hackney.
Lofting, J. H.	Portsmouth.
Loftus, J.	Birkenhead.
Logan, (Miss) A.	Newcastle-on-Tyne.
Logan, A.	Darlington.
Logan, R. B.	Felling.
Loman, F. T.	Plymouth.
Lomas, —.	Derby.
Lomas, H.	Manchester.
Lomax, F.	Huddersfield.
Lomer, J.	Cornwall (Mid.).
London, R. H.	Barnes and Mortlake.
Long, —.	Bromley.
Long, —.	Reading.
Long, E. W.	Birmingham.
Long, F. P.	Nelson, Colne, etc.
Long, G. A.	Sheffield.
Long, H. W. M.	Leyton.
Long, S. E.	Southampton.
Long, S. F.	Bristol.
Long, W. B. A.	Isle of Ely.
Long, W. E.	East Lambeth.
Long, W. J.	Leighton Buzzard.
*Longbottom, E.	Birmingham.
Longden, C.	Hull.
Longdon, D.	Nottingham.
Longhurst, D. F.	Willesden.
Longman, H. B.	Norfolk (W.).
Longmore, R. A.	Kidderminster.
Longworth, (Miss) E.	Bolton District.
Lonsdale, —.	Deptford and Greenwich.
Lonsdale, F.	Stockton-on-Tees.
Lonsdale, S. J.	Lewisham.
Looms, W. R. D.	Nuneaton.
Loosemore, E.	Teign and Dart.
Loosemore, P.	London (N.W.).
Lord, —.	Wigan.
*Lord, A.	Halifax.
Lord, A. M.	Nottingham.
Lord, B.	Keighley.
Lord, E. W.	West Lambeth.
Lord, J. A.	Barnsley.
Lord, L. H.	Rossendale.
Lord, (Miss) M.	Bradford.
Lord, S. H.	Nottingham.
Lord, T. N.	Kingston and Surbiton.
Lord, W. C.	Hackney.
Lorimier, W. J. L.	London (E.).

N.U.T. WAR RECORD

Name.	Association.
Lorriman, J.	Tynemouth.
Loryman, P. W.	Bradford.
Lough, G.	Plymouth.
Loughborough, —.	West Ham.
Loughlin, A. J.	Teign and Dart.
Loughlin, J. O.	Wigan.
Lovatt, A. G.	Marlborough.
Lovatt, H.	Whitchurch.
Lovatt, W. G.	Newport (Mon.).
Love, —.	Ealing.
Loveless, R. B.	Farnham.
Loveless, T. G.	Easington.
Lovell, E. R.	Dorset (E.).
Lovell, A.	Nelson, Colne, etc.
Lovell, E. R.	Dorset (S.).
Lovelock, F. J.	Swindon.
Loveridge, F. W.	Southport.
*Lovering, P. W.	Chatham, etc.
Lovern, J.	Liverpool.
Lovesey, G.	London (W.).
Lovett, C.	Romford, etc.
Lovett, R. F.	Chiswick.
Lovett, W. C.	Castleford, etc.
Lovitt, A.	Northampton.
Low, D.	Newcastle-on-Tyne.
Low, G. F.	Bristol.
Low, J.	West Stanley.
Lowbridge, —.	Ipswich.
Lowe, —.	Ingleborough.
Lowe, A. W.	Aylesbury.
Lowe, C.	Shropshire (E.).
Lowe, F.	Nottingham.
Lowe, H.	West Bromwich, etc.
Lowe, J. F.	Penrith.
Lowe, R. C.	Bury.
Lowe, T.	Staffordshire (N.).
Lowe, W. H.	Stockport.
*Lowery, H. E. S.	Whitehaven.
Lowery, J. H.	Cannock.
Lowing, L. L.	Bromley.
Lowley, F.	Sunderland.
Lowndes, C. A.	Ampthill, etc.
Lowndes, G. B.	Romford, etc.
Lowry, (Miss)	Manchester.
Lowry, A. P.	London (W.).
Lowry, C. H.	Macclesfield District.
Lowther, C.	Manchester.
Lucas, A. G.	Merthyr Tydfil.
Lucas, A. J.	Kidderminster.
Lucas, C.	Newcastle-on-Tyne.
Lucas, E.	Hornsey.
Lucas, E.	Staffordshire (N.).
Lucas, E. W.	Walthamstow.
Lucas, F.	West Lambeth.
Lucas, F. C.	Colchester.
Lucas, M. T.	West Lambeth.
Lucas, R. C.	Witney.
Lucas, W. G.	Sheffield.
Luck, C. F.	Ipswich.
Ludbrook, F.	Yoxford.
Luddon, J.	Hartlepools.
Ludford, C. H.	Banbury.
Ludgrove, —.	Nottingham.
Ludlam, E. B.	Bristol.
Ludlam, T. R.	Sheffield.
Ludlow, E. R.	Birmingham.
Ludlow, H. G.	Slough.
Luen, S. A.	Barry.
Luery, A. E.	East Ham.
Lugg, J.	Tottenham, etc.
Lugg, W. H.	Richmond (Surrey).
Luke, F.	Hackney.
Luke, G.	Preston Borough.
Luke, L. P.	Leeds.
Lumb, —.	Grimsby.
Lumb, W. P.	Dorset N.).
Lumsden, T. A.	Southwark.
Lund, B.	Gravesend.
Lunn, H.	Buckingham.
Lunn, H. J.	Ebbw Vale.
Lunn, R. H.	London (E.).
Lunt, H.	Liverpool.
Lunt, J.	Ormskirk.
Lupson, F. W.	Barnard Castle.
Lupton, C.	Halstead.
Lupton, F. W.	Berkshire (N.).
Lupton, H.	Harrogate.
Lupton, T.	Spen Valley.
Lupton, T.	Radnor.
Luscombe, J.	West Lambeth.
Lush, —.	Eastleigh.
Lush, E. B.	Croydon.
Lusher, T. H.	South Shields.
Luton, —.	West Ham.
Luxton, F.	Exeter District.
Lyall, G. M. A.	Croydon.
Lyall, J. E.	Spennymoor.
Lydamore, W. F.	Leyton.
Lydford, H. O.	Dorset (E.).
Lynch, E. R.	Hull.
Lynch, J.	Portsmouth.
Lynch, W. H.	Bradford.
Lynes, F.	Norwich.
Lynes, N.	Swindon.
Lyon, F. W.	Woolwich.
Lyon, G. F.	Norfolk (W.).
Lythall, F. H.	Leicester.
Mably, H.	Exeter City.
Mabley, W.	Exeter District.
Mabon, R.	Jarrow.
Macauley, D.	West Lambeth.
MacCormack, P. J.	Manchester.
MacCormick, E. M.	Gillingham.
Macdonald. —.	London (W.).
MacDonald, F.	Northumberland (S.).
Macdonald, J. G.	East Lambeth.
Macdonald, P. T.	Makerfield.
Mace, A. H.	Cardiff.
Macey, W. S.	Enfield.
MacFarlane, W. K.	Leeds.
MacGeorge, D.	Richmond (Surrey).
MacGowan, H.	Edmonton.
Machett, —.	Bath.
Machin, G.	West Lambeth.
Machin, J. S.	Hull.
Macintyre, A.	Sheffield.
Mack, J.	Portsmouth.
Mackenzie, A. H.	Carlisle.
Mackenzie, J. E.	Brentford.
Mackenzie, W. S.	Spen Valley.
Mackerell, F.	Easington.
Mackinlay, A. J.	Bedford Borough.
Mackintosh, C. M.	Cumberland (W.).
Mackintosh, J. C.	London (N.W.).
Mackintosh, W.	Aberdare.
Mackness, F. C.	Castleford, etc.
Macleod, N. M.	Hull.

TEACHERS WHO JOINED THE FORCES

Name.	Association.
Macpherson, G.	Spennymoor.
Maddick, J.	Twickenham.
Maddison, E. R.	West Stanley.
Maddison, R.	Northumberland (E.).
Maddock, F. E.	Plymouth.
Maddock, J. W.	Huddersfield.
Maddocks, W. A.	Chester.
Maddocks, W. A.	Wirral.
Maddox, E.	Bala.
Maddrell, J. K.	Liverpool.
Maddrick, H. R.	Bristol.
Madge, M. H. A.	West Lambeth.
Madge, S. J.	Hornsey.
Madge, W. T.	Cowbridge, etc.
Maggs, —.	Bath.
Magill, W. J.	Hull.
Maguire, D. S.	Gillingham.
Mahon, J.	Mexborough.
Mahon, S.	North Cleveland.
Mahon, T. E.	Heywood.
Mahoney, B. J.	Plymouth.
Mahony, —.	Blackpool.
Maidment, D. J.	Rhondda, etc.
Maidment, E. A.	London (W.).
Maile, B. O.	Abercarn and District.
Main, T.	Northumberland (E.).
Mais, W.	Darlington.
Maishment, S.	Sheffield.
Major, E. H. R.	Brighton, etc.
Malby, R.	Sheffield.
Malcolm, A.	Warrington.
Malcolm, E. G.	Plymouth.
Malcolm, R. G.	Worcester City.
Malden, J. W.	Tunbridge Wells.
Male, H. H.	Cornwall (E.).
Malein, H. A.	Ilford.
Maley, R. J. H.	London (W.).
Malins, T. H.	Coventry.
Maller, A. G.	Brighton, etc.
Malley, W. G.	Birkenhead.
Mallinson, —.	St. Helens.
Mallinson, S.	Harrogate.
Mallpress, H.	Spen Valley.
Mallpress, V. K.	East Lambeth.
Maloney, D.	Brynmawr.
Malt, S.	Norwich.
Maltby, A. P.	Biggleswade.
Mandell, W.	West Lambeth.
Mander, A. J.	Luton.
Mandover, A. C. P.	Ealing.
Mangham, S.	West Lambeth.
Mangles, B. S.	Gillingham.
Mangold, C. F.	East Lambeth.
Manifold, R.	Chester.
Manley, J.	Durham.
Manley, J. J.	Somerset (N.).
Manley, W.	Bradford.
Mann, A. F.	Norwich City.
Mann, F. D.	Dudley.
Mann, G. W.	Pudsey.
Mann, M. H.	Finsbury, etc.
Mann, T.	Reigate.
Mann, W. A.	Swindon.
Manners, W. A.	Northwich.
Manning, A. F.	Reading.
Manning, E. R.	Southampton.
*Manning, J.	Liverpool.
Manning, M. J.	Bristol.
Mansbridge, F. W.	Surrey (N.W.).
*Mansell, C. J.	Birmingham.
Mansell, W. C.	Staffordshire (N.).
Mansfield, C.	Coventry.
Mansfield, J. A.	Maidstone.
Manwaring, G. V.	Norfolk (N.E.).
*Mapham, N.	London (W.).
Mapp, R. C.	Leicester.
March, F.	Colchester, etc.
March, F. E.	Portsmouth.
March, R. E.	York.
Marchant, G. C.	Rhondda, etc.
Marchant, J. A.	Finsbury, etc.
Marchant, P. J.	Maldon.
Marchant, S. H.	Deptford and Greenwich.
Margerison, L.	Blackpool.
Margetto, C. E.	West Lambeth.
Margham, F.	Surrey (N.W.).
Margrett, —.	Southwark.
Markall, E. C.	Hackney.
Markham, —.	Cambridge Borough.
Markham, —.	Ipswich.
Markham, E.	Manchester.
Markham, P.	Hackney.
Markless, D.	Walsall.
Marks, —.	Dover.
Marks, —.	Ealing.
Marks, A. G.	Newcastle-on-Tyne.
Marks, A. P.	London (W.).
Marks, A. T.	Farnham.
Marks, F. C.	Plymouth.
Marks, H. T.	Doncaster.
Marks, L. C.	Hackney.
Markwick, H.	Lewes.
Marland, J.	Eccles.
Marlborough, —.	Doncaster.
Marle, H.	Gloucestershire (S.).
Marley, F. G.	Tynemouth.
Marlow, A. A.	West Lambeth.
Marlow, F. G.	London (W.).
Marlow, F. J.	Leicester.
Marlow, G.	Salford.
*Marples, H.	Sheffield.
Marra, H.	Accrington.
Marren, —.	Grimsby.
Marrington, R.	West Lambeth.
Marriott, J.	Sheffield.
Marriott, J. W.	Ilford.
Marriott, S. J.	Leyton.
Marriott, T. P.	Chesham.
Marrow, P.	Sale.
Marsden, A.	Brighouse.
Marsden, D.	Stretford.
*Marsden, F. K.	Brighouse.
Marsden, H.	Calder Valley.
Marsden, H.	Oldham.
Marsden, H. L.	Manchester.
Marsden, J. B.	Blackburn.
Marsden, J. W.	Manchester.
Marsden, R.	Crook.
Marsh, —.	Nottingham.
Marsh, —.	Reading.
Marsh, A. J.	Abercarn.
Marsh, E. V.	Daventry.
Marsh, E. W.	Plymouth.
Marsh, F. F.	Surrey (N.W.).
Marsh, F. J.	Bristol.
Marsh, J.	Liverpool.
Marsh, J.	Nottingham.
Marsh, R. A.	Mexborough.

N.U.T. WAR RECORD

Name.	Association.	Name.	Association.
Marsh, S.	Birmingham.	Mason, F. E. W.	South Shields.
Marsh, W. J.	Hackney.	Mason, G.	Wakefield.
Marshall, —.	Ipswich.	Mason, J.	Nottingham.
Marshall, A.	Hull.	Mason, J. A.	Manchester.
Marshall, C. S.	Croydon.	Mason, J. G.	Manchester.
Marshall, (Miss) E. M.	Halifax.	Mason, J. G.	Manchester.
Marshall, F. J.	West Lambeth.	Mason, J. W.	West Stanley.
*Marshall, F. J.	London (W.).	Mason, P. A.	Birmingham.
Marshall, F. R.	Northallerton.	**Mason, R.**	Manchester.
Marshall, F. S.	Dorset (E.).	Mason, R.	Hebburn.
Marshall, H.	Manchester.	Mason, W. G.	Aberdare.
Marshall, J.	Plymouth.	Mason, W. H.	Manchester.
Marshall, J. F.	Blyth.	Massey, E.	Manchester.
Marshall, L. E.	Southampton.	Massey, J. J.	Liverpool.
Marshall, P.	Loughborough.	Massing, G. E.	Norwich.
Marshall, R. R.	Blyth.	Masterman, A. W.	Hartlepools.
Marshall, R. W.	London (E.).	Masters, S. P.	Deal, etc.
Marshall, W. E.	Northumberland (E.).	**Masters, T.**	Mountain Ash.
Marshall, W. T.	Walsall.	Maston, A. S.	Wharfedale.
Marsland, —.	East Lambeth.	Mather, E.	Manchester.
Marsland, W. L.	Manchester.	Mather, J. H.	East Lambeth.
Marston, F.	Wolverhampton.	Mathew, M.	Wimbledon.
Marston, R. F.	Hackney.	Mathews, W. H.	Brentford.
Martel, E.	Hackney.	**Mathieu, J.**	Manchester.
Martin, —.	Tottenham, etc.	Mattey, S. B.	Woolwich.
Martin, —.	Ipswich.	Matthew, E. F. W.	Durham.
Martin, A.	Gloucestershire (S.).	Matthew, J. W.	Durham.
Martin, A. A.	Swindon.	Matthewman, A. S.	Louth, etc.
Martin, A. E. W.	Colchester, etc.	Matthews, —.	Deptford and Greenwich.
*Martin, A. F.	Peterborough.	Matthews, —.	Ealing.
Martin, A. R.	Ripon.	Matthews, —.	Hastings.
Martin, B.	Coventry.	Matthews, A. W. H.	London (N.W.).
Martin, B.	West Bromwich, etc.	Matthews, C. C.	Bishop Auckland.
Martin, C. H.	Tottenham, etc.	**Matthews, E. S.**	Wood Green.
*Martin, D. G.	Liverpool.	Matthews, F.	Hackney.
Martin, E. W.	Tottenham, etc.	Matthews, F. J.	Bath.
Martin, E. W.	East Lambeth.	Matthews, F. W.	London (W.).
Martin, F.	Maidstone.	Matthews, H.	Cardiff.
Martin, F.	Wallsend.	Matthews, H.	Tottenham, etc.
Martin, F.	Plymouth.	Matthews, L.	Barking.
Martin, F.	Crewe.	Matthews, P.	Radstock.
Martin, G. L.	Norwich.	Matthews, R.	Dorset (E.).
Martin, H.	Kettering.	Matthews, R. C.	Eastbourne.
Martin, J.	West Ham.	Matthews, R. J.	Portsmouth.
Martin, J. A. W.	Maidstone.	Matthews, T. F. G.	Cornwall (W.).
Martin, J. R.	Crook.	Matthews, W. E.	London (W.).
Martin, J. R. F.	Weardale.	Matthews, W. H.	Teign and Dart.
Martin, P. H.	Tottenham, etc.	Matthews, W. R. C.	London (W.).
*Martin, R. R. S.	Alnwick.	Mattingly, G. E.	Swindon.
*Martin, S.	Teign and Dart.	Mattinson, H. B.	Whitehaven.
Martin, T. G.	Cornwall (E.).	Mattock, N. H.	Peterborough.
Martin, W.	Birmingham.	Maude, G. W.	Manchester.
Martin, W. A.	Plymouth.	Maughan, N.	Newcastle-on-Tyne.
Martin, W. E.	Hackney.	Maughan, W.	Blaydon.
Martin, W. H.	Carnarvon.	Maunder, A.	Exeter City.
Martindale, S.	Durham.	Maunder, C. P.	Dorset (E.).
Martyn, R. O. F.	Birmingham.	Maunder, G. C.	Finsbury, etc.
Marven, F. H.	Romford, etc.	Maunder, G. H. S.	Liverpool.
Mascord, A. E.	Coventry.	Maw, W. F.	Leicester.
Mashiter, E.	Blackburn.	Mawer, A. L.	Nidderdale.
Maskelyne, F.	Wirral.	Mawson, A. W.	Gainsborough.
Mason, (Miss)	West Ham.	Mawson, J.	Kettering.
Mason, —.	Crewe.	Mawson, P. G.	Crook.
Mason, —.	Sale.	Mawson, W. E.	Leeds.
Mason, —.	Salisbury.	*Maxey, H. R.	Blyth.
Mason, C.	Liverpool.	Maxey, W. S.	Peterborough.
Mason, C. F.	Chiswick.	Maxted, F. J.	Deal, etc.
Mason, C. J.	Plymouth.	Maxwell, J. H.	Manchester.
Mason, E.	Sunderland.	May, A.	Leominster.

TEACHERS WHO JOINED THE FORCES

Name.	Association.	Name.	Association.
May, A. C.	Southend-on-Sea.	McGrath, F.	Finsbury, etc.
May, E. N. H.	Norfolk (N.W.).	**McGrath, W. E.**	Wigan.
May, F.	Bishop's Stortford.	McGreal, T.	West Ham.
May, F.	Exeter District.	McGuiness, J.	Bootle.
May, H.	Reading.	McGuinness, —.	Liverpool.
May, J. R.	Kingston and Surbiton.	**McGuinness, G.**	Birkenhead.
May, O.	Gateshead.	McGuinness, T.	Blaydon.
May, W.	Wolverhampton.	McGuire, J. C.	Finsbury, etc.
May, W. J.	Hertford.	McHaffie, A. E.	London (E.).
Maycock, W.	Manchester.	McHaffie, W. H.	West Lambeth.
Mayhew, —.	South Shields.	McHarrie, W. C.	London (E.).
Mayhew, H. W.	Croydon.	*McHugh, R.	South Shields.
Mayhew, O.	Gateshead.	McInley, —.	Reading.
Maynard, H. C.	Ashford.	McInley, E. S.	London (W.).
Maynard, H. M.	Smethwick.	McInnes, L.	Lewisham.
Maynard, S. M.	Tonbridge.	**McIntosh, —.**	Warwickshire (N.).
Mayne, T. R.	Willesden.	McIntyre, C. C.	Manchester.
Maynes, W.	Erith.	**McIntyre, D.**	Manchester.
Mayo, F. J.	East Ham.	McIntyre, D.	Blackburn.
McAdam, A. C.	Stalybridge, etc.	McIsaac, —.	Bromley.
McAlister, H. P.	London (N.W.).	McIver, J.	Manchester.
McAllister, —.	Surrey (N.W.).	McIvor, R.	West Lambeth.
McAndrews, J. W.	Northumberland (S.).	McKaig, P. C.	Manchester.
McArthur, C.	Southampton.	McKay, G. T.	Hartlepools.
McAuley, J. H.	Brentford.	McKelvey, —.	Hyndburn.
McCagney, A.	Barrow.	McKenna, B.	Liverpool.
McCaig, H.	Nottingham.	McKenzie, C.	Liverpool.
McCall, —.	Lincoln.	McKenzie, D.	South Shields.
McCall, T. V.	Finsbury, etc.	McKeon, R. F. J.	London (N.W.).
McCallum, J. H.	South Shields.	McKibbin, W.	Chatham, etc.
McCalvey, C.	South Shields.	**McKimmie, A. J.**	Southwark.
McCann, J.	Bolton Borough.	McKimmie, J. R.	Lewisham.
McCann, T.	Manchester.	McKinnon, D.	West Ham.
McCarthy, D.	Merthyr Tydfil.	McKinsey, H.	Mexborough.
McCarthy, J.	Cardiff.	McKno, J.	Liverpool.
McCarthy, J. C.	Liverpool.	McKowen, (Miss) H.	Lancaster.
McCarthy, J. W.	West Lambeth.	McLachlan, N.	Liverpool.
McCauley, V.	Woolwich.	McLaughlin, —.	Woolwich.
McCleary, E.	South Shields.	McLaughlin, J. A.	Oldham.
McClelland, J.	Birkenhead.	McLean, J.	Southport.
McCluskey, J.	Liverpool.	McLeed, —.	Epping, etc.
McConnell, J.	Wallsend.	McLeish, J.	London (W.).
McConway, H. J.	Hebburn.	McLoughlin, —.	Liverpool.
McCormack, M.	West Ham.	McMahon, F. J.	Newcastle.
McCormick, C. F.	West Ham.	McMahon, J.	Burnley.
McCormick, J. H.	Hornsey.	McManners, S.	Spennymoor.
McCourt, J. F.	Westminster.	McManus, A.	Birmingham.
McCoy, R. L.	Liverpool.	McMath, W.	Reading.
McCready, W. H.	Bolton Borough.	McMillan, A.	West Lambeth.
McCubbin, P. G.	Leeds.	McMullen, J. H.	Carlisle.
McCullagh, M.	Tynemouth.	McMullin, D.	Surrey (N.W.).
McCulloch, H. M.	Sunderland.	*McNamara, P.	Manchester.
McCullogh, R.	Gateshead.	**McNamee, G.**	Plymouth.
McDonald, A.	Liverpool.	**McNaught, T.**	Birkenhead.
McDonald, E.	Blaydon.	McNeil, G. W.	Alnwick.
McDonald, W. J.	Woolwich.	McNeill, W.	Barrow-in-Furness.
McDowall, W.	Liverpool.	McNicholas, H.	Stockton-on-Tees.
McElroy, G. H.	Bootle.	McNulty, J.	Nelson, Colne, etc.
McEnery, —.	Jarrow.	McPeake, E.	Jarrow.
McFarlane, —.	Deptford and Greenwich	McQuarrie, A. D.	Waterloo, etc.
McGann, —.	Salford.	McQue, J.	Swansea.
McGarty, B.	Sittingbourne, etc.	McQuire, J.	Hyndburn.
McGibbon, —.	London (N.W.).	McVey, J.	Woolwich.
McGinn, J. F.	Crook.	McWilliams, —.	West Stanley.
McGough, J.	Carlisle.	Mead, C.	Devizes.
McGough, M.	Stockton-on-Tees.	Mead, L. J. W.	Bournemouth.
McGoldrich, —.	Wigan.	Meadows, G.	Retford.
McGovern, J. B.	Southampton	Meadows, J.	Durham (N.E.).
McGowan, W. J.	Hartlepools	Meadows, R. L.	Nottingham.

N.U.T. WAR RECORD

Name.	Association.
Meadows-Taylor, H. T.	Farnham.
Meads, C.	Southwark.
Meakin, H.	Luton.
*Meakin, H. M.	Worksop.
Meakins, A. T.	Somerset (E.C.).
Mear, E.	Sheffield.
Mears, G. F.	Portsmouth.
Mears, G. H. R.	West Lambeth.
Measures, J. V.	Leicester (Mid).
Meaton, C.	London (E.).
Meaton, H. J.	Brighton, etc.
Meaton, S.	Brighton, etc.
Medland, W. G.	St. Albans.
Medley, A. F.	West Ham.
Medley, J. S.	Spen Valley.
Mee, E. J.	Warrington.
Meecham, D. J.	Swansea.
Meehan, J.	Liverpool.
Meek, —.	Ipswich.
Meek, A. W.	Southwark.
Meek, H.	Finsbury, etc.
Meek, H. G.	Plymouth.
Meeks, E.	Leeds.
Meeten, M.	Dorking.
Meggett, J. C.	Birmingham.
Meir, T. S.	Middlesbrough.
Melem, E.	Manchester.
Melhuish, —.	Taunton, etc.
Mellers, P.	Leamington.
*Mellers, W.	Rotherham.
Melles, E. M.	London (W.).
Mellett, G.	Brighton, etc.
Mellis, E.	London (W.).
Mellor, —.	Nottingham.
Mellor, A.	Staffordshire (N.).
Mellor, F.	Chester-le-Street.
Mellor, F. R.	Wakefield.
Mellor, G. R.	Finchley.
Mellor, H.	Huddersfield.
Mellor, J.	Derby (E.).
Mellor, J. Q.	Crompton, etc.
Mellor, J. P.	Bournemouth.
Mellor, S.	Sheffield.
Melton, F. E.	Bletchley.
Mennear, J. M.	Chester-le-Street.
Mepham, W. A.	West Ham.
Mercer, A.	Alton.
Mercer, A.	Hyde.
Mercer, A. G.	St. Helens.
Mercer, B.	Tottenham, etc.
Mercer, F.	Leicester.
Mercer, J. L.	Burnley.
Mercer, R.	Woolwich.
Mercer, S.	Elland.
Merck, S. H.	London (W.).
Meredith, —.	Crewe.
Merrett, A.	Surrey, (S.E.).
Merrick, T. F.	Birmingham.
Merrifield, A.	Portsmouth.
Merrill, A. E. N.	Blackburn.
Merrill, (Miss) E.	East Ham.
Merriman, —.	Croydon.
Merriman, A. W.	London (E.).
Merritt, —.	Willesden.
Merritt, F. W.	Dartford.
*Merry, T. A.	Erewash Valley, etc.
Mersch, L. J.	West Lambeth.
Merser, F.	Northampton.

Name.	Association.
Messenger, F. P.	Maesteg.
Messenger, H.	Leicester.
Metcalf, F. A.	East Ham.
Metcalf, S. G.	Nottingham.
Metcalf, (Miss) M.	Cardiff.
Metcalf, W. J.	Bradford.
Metcalfe, A.	Leeds.
Metcalfe, A. J.	Chester-le-Street.
Metcalfe, F. E.	Manchester.
Metcalfe, R.	Chester-le-Street.
Mettrick, C.	Huddersfield.
Mew, J.	Portsmouth.
Mew, P. C.	Swindon.
Mewis, N. C.	Woolwich.
Meyrick, B.	Hackney.
Meyrick, E. D.	Hackney.
Michell, F. C.	Plymouth.
Michell, J.	Ealing.
Middlehurst, —.	Warrington.
Middlemas, D. L.	Woolwich.
Middleton, A. B.	Hartlepools.
Middleton, (Miss) M.	Leicester.
Midgley, —.	West Ham.
Midgley, L. V.	Bishop's Waltham.
Midgley, R.	Manchester.
Midwood, H.	Morley.
Midwood, J. T.	Dewsbury, etc.
Milbourne, J.	Scarborough.
Miles, —.	Gravesend.
Miles, B.	Isle of Ely.
Miles, C. F.	London (W.).
Miles, F. J.	Woolwich.
Miles, H.	Oxford.
*Miles, R. W.	Woolwich.
Miles, W. H.	Walthamstow.
Milford, C. A.	Ingleborough.
Milk, E. E.	Cambridge Borough.
Millar, E.	West Ham.
Millar, J.	Glamorgan (Mid.).
Millar, J.	Wigan.
Millard, E. L.	Bridgwater.
Millard, F. S.	Bristol.
Millard, J.	Woolwich.
Millard, J.	Tipton.
Millard, P.	Swansea.
Millard, R. A.	Portsmouth.
Millard, T. P.	Hull.
Milledge, G.	West Lambeth.
Miller, —.	Taunton, etc.
Miller, —.	Northumberland (E.).
Miller, A.	Northampton.
Miller, B. J.	Uxbridge.
Miller, C. E.	Liverpool.
Miller, C. J.	Staffordshire (N.).
Miller, E. P.	East Ham.
Miller, F. J.	Kiveton Park.
*Miller, F. J.	Southport.
Miller, G.	East Dereham.
Miller, G. G. I.	South Shields.
Miller, J.	Northumberland (S.).
Miller, R. O.	Hackney.
Miller, T.	Whitehaven.
Miller, W. L.	Hull.
Miller, W. R.	Gateshead.
Miller, W. W.	Aldershot.
Millerchip, D.	Walsall.
Millett, A. S.	London (W.).
*Millett, F.	Bromley.
Millican, P. C.	Bristol.

160

TEACHERS WHO JOINED THE FORCES

Name.	Association.
Millie, W. H.	Hackney.
Milligan, R. O.	Northwich.
Millman, (Miss) K. A.	London (W.).
Millner, F. F.	Driffield, etc.
Millner, G. H.	Manchester.
Mills, —.	East Lambeth.
Mills, —.	East Lambeth.
Mills, A.	Bootle.
Mills, A. W.	Plymouth.
Mills, B.	Exeter City.
Mills, C.	Portsmouth.
Mills, C. J.	Bristol.
Mills, H.	Crook.
Mills, J. T.	Carlisle.
Mills, R.	Berkshire (N.).
Mills, R.	Tynemouth.
Mills, R. R.	Avon Valley.
Mills, S. J.	Birmingham.
Mills, W.	Itchen.
Mills, W. H.	St. Helens.
Mills, W. R.	Finsbury, etc.
Milne, G.	Manchester.
Milne, J.	South Shields.
Milne, J.	Walthamstow.
Milne, W. J.	Tynemouth.
Milner, F.	Hull.
*Milner, F.	Bolton Borough.
Milner, F.	London (W.).
Milner, H.	Bournemouth.
Milner, J.	Bradford.
Milner, J. C.	Barnsley.
Milner, L.	Croydon.
Milner, S.	Leeds.
Milnthorpe, G. T.	Darlington.
Milton, E. A.	Romford, etc.
Milton, E. A.	Sheffield.
Minards, W.	Warrington.
Mincher, S. G.	Birmingham.
Minhinnick, —.	Maidenhead.
Minihan, A.	Newcastle-on-Tyne.
Minks, T.	Blaydon.
Minns, W.	Durham.
Minshall, F.	Runcorn.
Minton, C. V.	Llanfyllin.
Mirrington, T. W.	Colchester, etc.
Mitchell, —.	East Lambeth.
Mitchell, —.	East Lambeth.
Mitchell, —.	Deptford and Greenwich.
Mitchell, A.	Birmingham.
Mitchell, A. A.	Birmingham.
Mitchell, A. E.	Bradford.
Mitchell, B.	Oldham.
Mitchell, C. J.	Dartford.
Mitchell, E.	Northampton.
Mitchell, E. H.	West Ham.
Mitchell, E. J. T.	Windsor.
Mitchell, F. D.	Spennymoor.
Mitchell, F. J.	Woolwich.
Mitchell, F. M.	Gloucester (S.).
Mitchell, G. H.	Halifax.
Mitchell, G. P.	Birmingham.
Mitchell, H.	High Wycombe.
Mitchell, H.	Vale of Derwent.
Mitchell, H. E.	West Bromwich.
Mitchell, H. T.	
Mitchell, H. W.	Liverpool.
Mitchell, J.	Litherland.
Mitchell, J.	London (E.).
Mitchell, J.	West Lambeth.
Mitchell, J. H.	Falmouth and Truro.
Mitchell, J. M. G.	Oxford District.
Mitchell, M.	Hendon.
Mitchell, P.	Bradford.
*Mitchell, R.	Bradford.
Mitchell, S. C.	Southwark.
Mitchell, T. J.	Bexhill.
Mitchell, W.	Blyth.
Mitchell, W. H.	Halifax.
Mitchell, W. H.	Swansea.
Mitchelmore, J. F.	Kettering.
Mitchley, S.	Harrow.
Mitchley, T. A.	Harrow.
Mizen, H.	Bristol
*Moakler, R. J.	Staffordshire (N.).
Moan, J.	Finsbury, etc.
Mobbs, E. C.	Sittingbourne, etc.
Mockett, T. H.	Chorley, etc.
Moffat, T.	Wallsend.
Moffat, J.	Alnwick.
Moffatt, J.	Blaydon.
Moffatt, J. H.	Burnley.
Moffatt, W. R.	South Shields.
Mogford, A. T.	Edmonton.
Mogford, C. J.	Bristol.
Mogg, —.	West Ham.
Mogridge, L.	Liverpool.
Moir, D. McN.	Itchen.
Mold, J. H.	Harrow.
Mole, —.	Nelson, Colne, etc.
Mole, D.	Rowley Regis.
Mole, T.	Newcastle-on-Tyne.
Mollard, T. H.	Wirral.
*Mollett, E. B.	Croydon.
Moloney, T.	Manchester.
Molteno, L. O.	Guernsey.
Molyneaux, C.	Chester.
Molyneaux, O.	York.
Molyneaux, J.	Warrington.
Monaghan, J. C.	London (E.).
Money, J. W.	West Lambeth.
Monk, F. V.	Tottenham, etc.
Monkhouse, J. A.	West Lambeth.
Monks, S.	St. Helens.
Monteith, J.	St. Helens.
Montgomery, W. E.	Manchester.
Moody, (Miss)	Isle of Wight.
Moody, A.	London (W.).
Moody, H.	Castleford, etc.
Moody, (Miss) M. C.	Cardiff.
Moody, W.	Gloucester.
Moon, A. B.	Newport (Mon.).
Moon, B.	West Bromwich, etc.
Moon, F. P.	Teign and Dart.
Moon, H. J.	Manchester.
Moon, S. H.	Birmingham.
Mooney, R.	Liverpool.
Moore, —.	Canterbury.
Moore, —.	West Ham.
Moore, A. H.	Cardiff.
Moore, A. T.	Wimbledon.
Moore, A. W.	London (W.).
Moore, E. R.	Wakefield.
Moore, E. W.	Leicester.
Moore, F.	Dorset (N.).
Moore, F.	Farnworth.
Moore, F. G.	Plymouth.
Moore, F. G.	Manchester.
Moore, G.	Gloucester.

Name.	Association.
Moore, G. S.	Loughborough.
Moore, H.	Spennymoor.
Moore, H.	Wrexham.
Moore, H.	Birmingham.
Moore, H.	Swansea.
*Moore, H.	Vale of Derwent.
Moore, H. H.	Walsall.
Moore, J.	Durham.
Moore, J.	Lewisham.
Moore, M. W.	Grantham.
Moore, P.	West Lambeth.
Moore, S.	West Ham.
Moore, T.	Barrow-in-Furness.
Moore, V. W.	Birmingham.
Moore, W.	Maidstone.
Moore, W. E.	Birmingham.
Moore, W. P.	Sheffield.
Moores, H.	Salford.
Moores, R. J.	Plymouth.
Moores, W.	Bury.
Moorhouse, (Miss) E.	Stretford.
Moorhouse, W. E.	Gillingham.
Mooring, L.	Colchester, etc.
Moorman, (Miss) E.	Plymouth.
Morgan, —.	Northampton.
Morgan, —.	West Ham.
Morgan, A.	Wrexham.
Morgan, A.	Barry.
*Morgan, A. L.	Rhondda, etc.
Morgan, A. O.	Finsbury, etc.
Morgan, A. W. P.	Birmingham.
Morgan, (Miss) B.	Rhondda, etc.
Morgan, B.	Glamorgan (Mid.).
Morgan, C.	Merthyr Tydfil.
Morgan, C. D.	Glamorgan (W.).
Morgan, C. J.	Newcastle-on-Tyne.
Morgan, D.	Caerphilly.
Morgan, D. E.	Merthyr Tydfil.
Morgan, D. J	Lampeter.
Morgan, D. W.	Fishguard.
Morgan, E. J.	Caerphilly.
Morgan, E. M.	Lewisham.
Morgan, E. S.	Swansea.
Morgan, E. T.	Finsbury, etc.
Morgan, F.	Deptford and Greenwich.
Morgan, F.	Derbyshire (E.).
Morgan, F. R.	Cardiff.
Morgan, G.	Rhondda, etc.
Morgan, (Miss) G. G.	Bridgend.
Morgan, G. P.	Tredegar.
Morgan, H. R.	Swansea.
Morgan, J.	Rhondda, etc.
Morgan, J.	Ogmore, etc.
Morgan, J.	Cardiff.
Morgan, J.	Swansea.
Morgan, J.	Glamorgan (W.).
Morgan, J.	Nantyglo.
Morgan, J. D	Rhondda, etc.
Morgan, J. H.	Birmingham.
Morgan, J. J.	Carnarvon.
Morgan-Jones, W.	Flint County.
Morgan, J. T.	London (E.).
Morgan-Lewis, J. W.	Manchester.
Morgan, M.	Llandovery.
Morgan, M. T.	Cardiff.
Morgan, P. A.	Surrey (S.E.).
Morgan-Richards, W.	Caerphilly.
Morgan, R.	Ogmore, etc.
Morgan, R.	Maidstone.
Morgan, R. C.	East Ham.
Morgan, R. H.	Dudley.
Morgan, R. S.	Tredegar.
Morgan, R. W.	Brynmawr.
Morgan, S. O.	Swansea.
Morgan, S. W.	Southampton.
*Morgan, T.	Ebbw Vale.
Morgan, T. H.	Cowbridge, etc.
Morgan, T. J.	Swansea.
Morgan, T. J.	Rhondda, etc.
Morgan, T. V.	Cowbridge, etc.
Morgan, W.	Middlesbrough.
Morgan, W.	Manchester.
Morgan, W. C.	Glamorgan (Mid.).
Morgan, W. C. S.	Mountain Ash.
Morgan, W. P.	Birmingham.
Morgan, W. R.	Rhondda, etc.
Morgenroth, —.	Barry.
Morland, E. R.	Manchester.
Morley, E.	Leeds.
Morley, J. D.	Sheffield.
Morley, R.	Southampton.
Morley, R. A.	Northampton.
Morley, W. A.	West Bromwich, etc.
Morling, —.	Deptford and Greenwich.
Morrell, —.	Birmingham.
Morrell, A.	Birmingham.
Morrell, E. G.	Coventry.
Morrell, E. P.	Birmingham.
Morrell, H.	Huddersfield.
Morris, —.	Llandudno.
Morris, —.	Willesden.
Morris, A.	Birkenhead.
Morris, A.	Sheffield.
Morris, A.	Dewsbury, etc.
Morris, A. E.	London (E.).
Morris, A. G.	Castleford, etc.
Morris, B. R.	Dudley.
Morris, D.	Rhondda, etc.
Morris, D.	Idris.
Morris, D. J.	Llandudno.
Morris, D, T.	Rhondda, etc.
Morris, E.	Chorley, etc.
Morris, E.	Llanelly.
Morris, E. L.	Maesteg.
Morris, F.	Sittingbourne, etc.
Morris, F.	Flint County.
Morris, F. H.	Glossop.
Morris, G.	Rhondda, etc.
Morris, H.	Bromley.
Morris, H.	Hull.
Morris, H. D.	Southgate.
Morris, H. E.	Walsall.
Morris, H. H.	Aberdare.
Morris, H. H.	Willenhall.
Morris, H. T.	Pontypool.
Morris, J.	Marlborough.
Morris, J.	Cheltenham.
Morris, J.	Manchester.
Morris, J. F.	Cardiff.
Morris, J. O.	Maesteg.
Morris, M.	Edmonton.
Morris, N. A.	Wolverhampton.
Morris, P. M.	London (E.).
Morris, R.	Liverpool.
Morris, R. H.	Gelligaer.
Morris, R. W.	Enfield.
Morris, S. H.	Wood Green.
Morris, T.	Bolton District.
Morris, T.	Flint County.

TEACHERS WHO JOINED THE FORCES

Name.	Association.	Name.	Association.
Morris, T. S.	Bolton Borough.	Moule, —.	Kettering.
Morris, W.	Leicester.	Moulton, W. R.	Kent (W.).
Morris, W.	Sheffield.	Mounsey, —.	Derby.
*Morris, W.	Reading.	**Mountain, J. W.**	Leeds.
Morris, W. A.	Rhondda, etc.	Mountain, W. H. S.	Reigate.
Morris, W. A. D.	Barrow-in-Furness.	Mountford, —.	Birmingham.
Morris, W. C.	Abertillery.	**Mountford, E. H.**	Cambridge Borough.
Morris, W. G.	Wallasey.	Mountford, E. J. W.	London (E.).
Morris, W. G. S.	Deal, etc.	Mountford, H.	Sheffield.
Morris, W. I.	Ebbw Vale.	Mountford, H. R.	Warwickshire (N.).
Morris, W. J.		**Mountford, T.**	Sheffield.
Morris, W. J.	Mountain Ash.	Mountford, W.	Staffordshire (N.).
Morris, W. P.	West Lambeth.	Mowle, H. W.	Manchester.
Morrison, —.	London (N.W.).	Moyce, H. S.	Kingston and Surbiton.
Morrison, A.	Jarrow.	Moyer, —.	Birkenhead.
Morrison, J.	Darlington.	Moyes, —.	West Ham.
Morrison, J.	West Lambeth.	Moyle, —.	Crewe.
Morrison, T.	Middlesbrough.	Muckley, W. E.	Birmingham.
Morse, S. C.	Rhondda, etc.	Mucklow, F.	Rowley Regis.
Morsley, H. V.	Slough.	Mudd, W.	Sheffield.
Morson, A.	West Stanley.	**Muddiman, J. E.**	Daventry.
Morson, C.	West Stanley.	Mudge, C. P.	Ipswich.
Mortimer, —.	Petersfield, etc.	Mudge, G. W.	Windermere.
Mortimer, E. C.	Bristol.	Muggleton, (Miss)	Birmingham.
Mortimer, R. E.	Forest of Dean.	*Muir, A. W.	Northumberland (E.).
Mortimore, P. A.	Coventry.	Mullens, —.	Portsmouth.
Morton, C.	East Lambeth.	**Mulligan, P.**	Portsmouth.
Morton, E.	London (W.).	Mullinger, L. H.	Northampton.
Morton, F.	Leeds.	Mumford, F. A. E.	Finsbury, etc.
Morton, H.	Blackburn.	Mumford, H. L.	Surrey (N.W.).
Morton, H.	Darlington.	Muncaster, R. A.	Southgate.
Morton, J.	London (W.).	Munday, A. W.	Harrow.
Morton, S.	Halifax.	Munday, J. T.	Blaydon.
Morton, W. L.	Stockport.	Munday, W.	West Lambeth.
Moscrop, W.	Deptford and Greenwich.	Munden, H. G.	Finsbury, etc.
Moseley, C. L.	Acton.	*Mundy, F. G.	Warminster.
Moseley, D.	Caerphilly.	Munn, (Miss) L.	Shipley.
Moses, B.	Manchester.	*Munnings, H.	Hendon.
Mosley, —.	Ilkeston.	Munnings, R. J.	Hackney.
*Mosley, E.	Salisbury.	Munro, —.	Salford.
Mosley, S.	Derby.	Munro, F. W.	Avon Valley.
Moss, —.	Stafford.	Munro, J. M.	Blaydon.
Moss, A. L.	Stretford.	Munroe, J.	Glamorgan (Mid.).
Moss, E.	Leyton.	Munsch, A. F.	Brighton, etc.
Moss, F.	West Ham.	Munt, F.	London (W.).
Moss, H.	Dewsbury, etc.	Munton, F. T. N.	Birmingham.
Moss, H. C.	East Lambeth.	Murch, F. W.	Hackney.
Moss, H. S.	Tottenham, etc.	*Murch, T. A.	East Lambeth.
Moss, J.	Crewe.	**Murdock, F. A.**	Eccles.
Moss, J.	Fylde.	Murfitt, B. W. H.	Finsbury, etc.
Moss, J. H.	West Ham.	Murfitt, G.	Tottenham, etc.
Moss, S. F.	Makerfield.	Murgitroyd, —.	West Ham.
Moss, S. H.	London (N.W.).	Murgitroyd, (Miss) L.	West Ham.
Moss, T.	Preston District.	Murney, J. J.	Manchester.
Moss, T. R.	Stockton-on-Tees.	Murphy, A.	Plymouth.
Moss, W.	Preston District.	**Murphy, C.**	Swansea.
Moss, W. J.	Shropshire (E.).	Murphy, D.	Brynmawr.
Mosscrop, E.	Southport.	Murphy, E.	Widnes.
Mossman, —.	Gateshead.	Murphy, M.	Leeds.
Mossman, A. L.	Stroud.	Murray, A.	Blackburn.
Mossop, M. H.	Leeds.	Murray, A. C.	Lewisham.
Mostyn, J.	Llanfyllin.	Murray, D. G.	Castleford, etc.
Motts, E.	Teign and Dart.	Murray, H.	Crook.
Mouboussin, V.	Newcastle-on-Tyne.	Murray, J.	Northumberland (S.).
Mould, C.	Cardiff.	Murray, J.	South Shields.
Mould, W.	Rutland.	Murray, J. C.	Liverpool.
Moulding, L. A.	Surrey (N.W.).	Murray, J. J.	Ludlow.
Moulding, S. D.	Surrey (N.W.).	Murray, P. J. V.	Newcastle-on-Tyne.
Moulding, T.	Blackburn.	*Murray, R.	Bootle.

N.U.T. WAR RECORD

NAME.	ASSOCIATION.
Murray, W.	Gloucester.
Murrell, —.	London (N.W.).
Murrell, G. A.	Deptford and Greenwich.
Murrell, P. A.	Chiswick.
Musgrove, —.	Sale.
Musgrove, C. H. B.	Coventry.
Musgrove, J. W.	Sale.
Muspratt, —.	Warminster.
Musselwhite, B. G.	Isle of Wight.
Musson, —.	Derby.
Mutton, R...	Cornwall (Mid.).
Mycock, C. G.	Bristol.
Myers, C.	Barnet.
Myers, F.	Hull.
Myers, F.	Nelson Colne, etc.
Myers, G.	Sunderland.
Myers, J. N. C.	Leeds.
Myers, M. A.	Bradford.
Myers, R.	Tynemouth.
Myers, R. W.	Middlesbrough.
Myers, S.	East Lambeth.
Myers, W.	Leamington.
Myland, C.	Southampton.
Mynn, C. W.	Hornsey.
Naish, A. E.	Tonbridge.
Naish, H. C.	Tottenham, etc.
Nait, R.	South Shields.
Nancarrow, S.	Cornwall. (Mid.)
Nancarrow, S. H.	Cornwall (E.).
Nangle, J. J.	Wakefield.
Nankiwell, F. M.	Cornwall (E.).
Nanson, J.	Cockermouth.
Naphtali, J. S.	Eccles.
Napier, J. O.	South Shields.
Napper, E.	London (E.).
Nappin, A.	Accrington.
Napthine, —.	Yoxford.
Nasby, S. C.	Stockton-on-Tees.
Nash, C. —.	Reading.
Nash, A. A.	Reading.
Nash, A. E.	Liverpool.
Nash, W.	West Lambeth.
*Nash, W. H.	East Lambeth.
Nathan, D.	London (E.).
Nathan, R. S.	Liverpool.
Naylor, A. G.	Halifax.
Naylor, G.	Rotherham.
Naylor, G. G.	Norfolk (W.).
Naylor, H.	Wigan.
Naylor, H.	Norfolk (N.W.).
Naylor, J. E. P.	Cardiff.
Naylor, T. W.	Bishop Auckland.
Naylor, W. H.	Wigan.
Neal, A. B.	Wakefield.
Neal, A. R.	Coventry.
Neal, C. B.	Watford.
Neal, F. J.	West Lambeth.
Neal, J. N.	Lewisham.
Neal, R.	Lowestoft.
Neal, W.	Luton.
Neale, —.	Shrewsbury.
Neale, E. G.	Bournemouth.
Neale, H.	Birmingham.
Neale, J. H.	Leicester (Mid)
Neale, R. A.	Kettering.
Neasham, G. W.	Darlington.
Neat, M. L.	West Lambeth.
Neat, W. W.	Nantyglo.

NAME.	ASSOCIATION.
*Neave, J. R.	Twickenham.
Nebel, L. G.	Woolwich.
Needham, C.	Dewsbury, etc.
Needham, F. E.	Coalville.
Neilson, T.	Manchester.
Nelder, G. O. A.	Cambridge Borough.
Nelson, A.	Finsbury, etc.
Nelson, A. H.	Croydon.
Nelson, F.	Durham.
Nelson, G.	London (E.).
Nelson, G. A.	Manchester.
Nelson, G. F.	Hackney.
Nelson, J. B.	Windermere.
Nelson, M.	Sunderland.
Nelson, O.	Liverpool.
Nelson, S. R.	Walthamstow.
Nerney, J.	Tottenham, etc.
Nesbit, —.	West Stanley.
Nesbitt, G. K.	Manchester.
Nesbitt, R.	South Shields.
Ness, F.	Liverpool.
Ness, L.	Darlington.
Nethercot, P. P.	Maidstone.
Nevaro, W. B.	Colchester, etc.
Neve, G. E.	Hull.
Nevey, F.	Deptford and Greenwich.
Neville, —.	Kingston and Surbiton.
Neville, O.	Itchen.
Neville, G. C. L.	Tottenham, etc.
*Neville, L.	Teddington.
*Nevitt, A.	Llandudno.
New, S. C.	Bristol.
Newberry, C.	Cardiff.
Newbold, H.	Manchester.
Newbold, H. G.	Shrewsbury.
Newbold, R. H.	London (W.).
Newborn, W. E.	Oundle, etc.
Newbound, J. F.	Stockton-on-Tees.
Newburn, —.	Warrington.
Newbury, C.	Cardiff.
Newbury, L. H.	Coventry.
Newby, T.	South Shields.
*Newcombe, F.	Stockton-on-Tees.
Newcombe, J. P.	Plymouth.
Newey, —.	Reading.
Newham, E. C.	Acton.
Newham, J. D.	London (E.).
Newell, W.	Todmorden.
Newill, F. C.	Coseley.
Newing, W.	Edmonton.
*Newis, H. T.	Manchester.
Newitt, A.	Birkenhead.
Newitt, W. J.	West Ham.
Newling, C. P.	Essex (N.).
Newman, —.	New Forest.
Newman, —.	Reading.
Newman, A. E.	Bristol.
Newman, A. V.	Bristol.
Newman, A. W.	London (W.).
Newman, F. E.	Chippenham.
Newman, F. E.	Wiltshire (W.).
Newman, H. T.	Hornsey.
Newman, P. H.	Devon (Mid).
Newman, P. R.	Deptford and Greenwich.
Newman, R. C.	Liverpool.
Newman, W. E.	Blackpool.
Newnes, W. G.	Bolton Borough.
Newnham, A. E.	Birmingham.
Newnham, J. W. F.	Birmingham.

TEACHERS WHO JOINED THE FORCES

Name.	Association.	Name.	Association.
Newport, —.	West Ham.	Nightingale, B.	Oldbury.
Newport, G.	Northwich.	Niman, N.	Leeds.
Newport, P.	Lewisham.	Ninnis, D. A.	Merthyr Tydfil.
Newport, R.	Runcorn.	**Ninnis, J.**	Exeter District.
Newsam, H.	Jarrow.	Nisbet, W. H.	London (E.).
Newsham, —.	St. Helens.	Nisbett, P. F.	London (E.).
Newsham, P.	York.	Nisbett, T.	West Lambeth.
Newsome, H. F.	Sheffield.	Nixon, E. S.	Carlisle.
Newstead, B.	Malton.	Nixon, F.	Northwich.
Newton, E.	Halstead.	Nixon, G.	East Lambeth.
Newton, F.	Walthamstow.	Nixon, G. O.	West Ham.
Newton, (Miss) G.	Sunderland.	Nixon, S. J.	Wigan.
Newton, G.	Hertford.	Nixon, W. C. P.	Middlesbrough.
Newton, H. H.	Sheffield.	Nixon, W. J.	Tottenham, etc.
Newton, J. E.	Oldham.	Noake-Mooring, L.	Tottenham, etc.
Newton-Jones, H.	Flint County.	Noakes, E. J.	East Lambeth.
Newton, P.	Denton, etc.	Noall, A.	Sunderland.
Newton, P. D.	Stockport.	Nobbs, A. L.	Hackney.
Newton, T.	Keighley.	Noble, —.	Southport.
Newton, T.	Tottenham, etc.	Noble, A.	Stockton-on-Tees.
Newton, T. A.	Southampton.	Noble, A. E.	Liverpool.
Nichol, W.	Northumberland (S.).	**Noble, B.**	Wakefield.
Nicholas, B. M.	Rhondda, etc.	Noble, C. F.	Ilford.
Nicholas, E. O.	Wrexham.	Noble, G. B.	Sunderland.
Nicholas, E. R.	London (N.W.).	Noble, H. A.	Cardiff.
Nicholas, J. A.	Glamorgan (Mid).	Noble, H. B.	Cockermouth.
Nicholas, J. R.	Wrexham.	Noble, W.	Ilford.
Nicholas, S.	Rhondda, etc.	Noblett, J.	Blackburn.
Nicholas, W. A.	East Ham.	**Nock, F. T.**	Sheffield.
Nicholas, W. I.	Glamorgan (Mid).	Nodder, E.	Gillingham.
Nicholl, H.	Bradford.	**Noon, G.**	Blaydon.
Nicholl, L. M.	Castleford, etc.	Noonan, J.	Hindley.
Nicholls, A. P.	Bishop's Stortford.	**Noone, J.**	Halifax.
Nicholls, D.	Kidderminster.	Noot, W. S.	Pembroke (Mid).
Nicholls, F. C.	West Lambeth.	Norburn, A. H.	Mansfield Borough.
Nicholls, F. W. T.	Exeter District.	**Norcross, W. H.**	West Ham.
Nicholls, H.	Penistone.	Norgrove, J. C.	Birkenhead.
*Nicholls, L.	East Lambeth.	Norman, A. C.	Jarrow.
Nicholls, L. H.	Salford.	Norman, A. S.	Dover.
Nicholls, S. W.	Cornwall (Mid).	Norman, G. A.	Finsbury, etc.
Nicholls, T. C.	Falmouth and Truro.	Norman, H. W.	Cornwall (E.).
Nicholls, T. W.	Hackney.	Norman, W. L.	Ilford.
Nicholls, W.	Willesden.	**Norman, W. S.**	Brighton, etc.
Nicholls, W.	Windsor.	Normanton, H. W.	Leeds.
Nichols, A. W.	Gillingham.	Norminton, —.	Grimsby.
Nichols, J. A.	Middlesbrough.	Norminton, J. S.	Stockport.
Nicholson, —.	Southend-on-Sea.	Norris, A.	Plymouth.
Nicholson, —.	Blaydon.	Norris, C. J.	Chichester.
Nicholson, A.	Chester.	Norris, E. C.	London (E.).
Nicholson, D. N.	Gloucestershire (S.).	Norris, H. B.	Hackney.
Nicholson, E.	West Stanley.	Norris, H. S.	Birmingham.
Nicholson, E.	Gateshead.	Norris, H. W. C.	Southampton.
Nicholson, E.	Avon Valley.	**Norris, J. H.**	Manchester.
Nicholson, E. P.	Wrexham.	Norris, L. C.	Portsmouth.
Nicholson, F.	Thornaby-on-Tees.	Norris, P. C.	Finsbury, etc.
Nicholson, F. E. A.	Bedford.	North, B. B.	Durham.
Nicholson, F. H.	Hackney.	North, E. L. G.	Bristol.
Nicholson, H.	Stockton.	North, E. T.	Darlington.
Nicholson, J. H.	Barnard Castle.	*North, H.	Worksop.
Nicholson, L. S.	Hull.	North, H. J.	Birmingham.
Nicholson, R. J.	Northumberland (E.).	North, R. J.	East Ham.
*Nicholson, W. P.	Chester-le-Street.	**North, S. F.**	Eastbourne.
Nicol, (Miss)	West Ham.	Northeast, S.	Brighton, etc.
Nicol, P.	West Lambeth.	Northedge, J. A.	Hull.
Nicolls, F.	Kent (W.).	Northern, T.	Bedford Borough
Nicolson, F.	Barnsley.	Northmore, J. L.	Furness.
Nickalls, J. W.	Ashford.	Norton, F.	Cirencester.
Nicklin, C. E.	Staffordshire (N.).	Norton, F.	Kettering.
Nickson, F.	Wallasey.	Norton, F. R.	Devon (N.).

165

N.U.T. WAR RECORD

Name.	Association.
Norton, G.	Nottingham.
Norton, N.	Tottenham, etc.
*Norton, P. O.	London (N.W.).
Norton, W.	Swindon.
Norwell, F. A.	Leicester.
Norwell, H.	Birmingham.
Norwood, G. A. H.	Oxford.
Notzing, E.	Salford.
Nowell, W. N.	Shropshire (E.).
Noyce, L. C.	East Ham.
Nudds, H. R.	Tottenham, etc.
Nugent, S.	London (W.).
Nunn, C. S.	Radnorshire.
Nunn, F. L.	Hackney.
Nunn, H. W.	Lewisham.
Nunn, W.	Spennymoor.
Nunney, P. H.	Chester-le-Street.
Nurse, A.	West Ham.
Nurse, W.	Finsbury, etc.
Nutman, —.	West Ham.
Nuttall, —.	Middlesbrough.
Nuttall, F.	Darwen.
Nuttall, J. W.	Manchester.
Nuttall, R.	Leeds.
Nutter, A. L.	Nelson, Colne, etc.
Nutter, H.	Burnley.
Nutter, J. E. C.	Somerset (E.C.).
Nutter, J. H.	Bishop Auckland.
Nutton, H.	Halifax.
Nyland, T.	Hackney.
Oakey, A. H.	West Lambeth.
Oakley, F.	Nottinghamshire (W.).
Oaks, T.	Gainsborough.
Oakshette, H. M.	East Lambeth.
Oaten, A. G.	Bristol.
Oates, E. H.	Cornwall (W.).
Oates, J. P.	Plymouth.
Oates, J. S.	Cornwall (W.).
Obee, L. E.	Woolwich.
Obee, P. H.	Woolwich.
Obery, E.	West Ham.
O'Brien, —.	Salford.
O'Byrne, W.	Liverpool.
O'Connell, J.	West Ham.
O'Connor, J.	Widnes.
Odam, N. J.	East Lambeth.
Odam, W.	Peterborough.
*Odams, F.	Willesden.
Oddy, G.	Dartford.
Odell, F.	Luton.
Odell, T. M.	Erith.
Odgers, J. R.	Cornwall (W.).
Odle, G.	East Lambeth.
Odling, A. J.	Walthamstow.
O'Donnell, J. J.	Newcastle-on-Tyne.
O'Fee, S.	Plymouth.
Offord, R.	Lewisham.
Ofield, J. W.	Leicester.
*Ogden, B. D.	Wimbledon.
Ogden, E. H.	Liverpool.
Ogden, F.	Southend-on-Sea.
Ogden, G.	Manchester.
Ogden, G. W. E.	Manchester.
Ogden, S.	Birmingham.
Ogden, T.	Hindley.
Ogden, W.	Liverpool.
Ogg, Miss K. E.	Newcastle-on-Tyne.
Ogle, A. F.	Isle of Axholme.
*Ogle, H.	Redditch.
Ogle, P. D.	Deptford and Greenwich.
Ogle, T. W.	Southwark.
Oglethorpe, G.	Cockermouth.
Ogley, G. Y.	Doncaster.
Ogston, (Miss) M.	Gateshead.
O'Hara, C.	Stockton-on-Tees.
O'Hara, S. V.	Hackney.
O'Hare, J.	Liverpool.
Ohlson, A.	South Shields.
Oke, W.	West Lambeth.
Oldfield, —.	Walthamstow.
Oldfield, A. E.	Leeds.
Oldland, W. S.	Tottenham, etc.
Oldham, G.	Hyde.
Oldman, F. J.	Liverpool.
Oldroyd, C.	Hull.
Oldroyd, J. H.	Dewsbury, etc.
Oldroyd, J. R.	Birmingham.
Olds, W.	Cornwall (W.).
*Oliphant, L.	Maryport.
Olive, R.	Stretford.
Oliver, A. E.	Croydon.
Oliver, A. C.	West Ham.
Oliver, B. H.	Hertford.
Oliver, C.	Durham.
Oliver, H. V.	Wimbledon.
Oliver, J.	Aberdare.
Oliver, J.	Oldham.
Oliver, L. F.	Birmingham.
*Oliver, M. F.	Bishop Auckland.
Oliver, R.	Spennymoor.
Ollif, W.	Bath.
Olorenshaw, N.	Derbyshire (E.).
O'Mara, F. W.	Birkenhead.
O'May, (Miss) L.	Huddersfield.
Ong, O. S. B.	Norwich.
Onions, (Miss) H.	Tredegar.
*O'Nions, R.	Barnes and Mortlake
Onions, W.	Tredegar.
Openshaw, T. W.	Burnley.
Oram, F. C.	Cardiff.
Oram, W. R.	Bristol.
Orchard, A.	Portsmouth.
Orchard, C.	Waveney Valley.
Orchard, C.	Yoxford.
Orchard, M.	Faversham.
Orchardson, T.	Manchester.
Ord, W. A.	Northumberland (E.).
Ore, J.	Finsbury, etc.
Ore, J. F.	Finsbury, etc.
O'Reilly, E. J.	Hartlepools.
O'Reilly, J.	East Lambeth.
Orford, A. H.	Stourbridge.
Orgill, —.	Devon (N.).
Orill, R. J.	Rhondda, etc.
Orme, A. H.	Knutsford.
Orme, H.	Northwich.
Ormerod, J.	Manchester.
Ormerod, T.	Westminster.
Ormiston, A.	Norwich.
Ormond, T. E.	Attleborough, etc.
Orr, F.	Sunderland.
Orrell, N. G.	Southport.
Orrell, W. W.	Rochdale.
Orton, G. H.	Teddington.
Osborn, A. G.	Birmingham.
Osborne, A.	Grimsby.
Osborne, C. G.	Birmingham.

TEACHERS WHO JOINED THE FORCES

Name.	Association.	Name.	Association.
Osborne, E. J.	Dudley.	Paddick, T. H.	Rhondda, etc.
Osborne, E. T.	Falmouth and Truro.	Paddy, J. H.	Staines.
Osborne, F.	Cornwall (W.).	Padfield, W. J.	Tredegar.
Osborne, F. W.	Bournemouth.	Padget, J. J.	Swindon.
Osborne, H.	Birmingham.	Page, A. G.	St. Albans.
Osborne, J.	Vale of Derwent.	*Page, C. A.	Leicester.
Osborne, W.	Crook.	Page, C. B.	West Lambeth.
Osborne, W. E. C.	Swindon.	*Page, F. G.	Hull.
Osborne, W. J.	Hitchin.	Page, F. W.	Birmingham.
Osman, E.	London (N.W.).	Page, G. H.	Nottingham.
Osman, F.	Dartford.	Page, G. W.	Newport Pagnell.
Osman, L.	Romford, etc.	Page, I. W.	Doncaster.
Ostick, G. F.	Watford.	Page, R. W.	Watford.
Ostick, H.	Harrogate.	Page, W.	Deptford and Greenwich.
O'Sullivan, —.	Grimsby.	**Paget, O.**	Devizes.
Otter, W. H.	Chippenham.	**Paget, O.**	Reading.
Ottewill, J.	Gillingham.	Pagett, R. P.	Lewisham.
Oulton, L.	Northwich.	Paice, T. C. F.	Marlborough.
Outlaw, O. T.	Lowestoft.	Pain, A. F.	East Ham.
Over, A.	Bishop Auckland.	Pain, E. F. W.	West Lambeth.
Overfield, —.	Ipswich.	Paine, A. H.	Plymouth.
Overton, R. J.	Barnet.	Painter, A. E.	Exeter District.
Owen, A.	St. Helens.	Painter, G. C.	Smethwick.
Owen, D.	Rhondda, etc.	*Painting, A. A.	Worcester City.
Owen, D.	Cardiff.	Palin, A.	Bradford.
Owen, D.	Rhondda, etc.	Palin, F.	Westminster.
Owen, E.	Festiniog.	Palk, F. A.	East Lambeth.
Owen, E. E.	Glamorgan (Mid.).	Palk, H. F.	Staines.
Owen, E. T.	Caerphilly.	Palliser, J. H.	York.
Owen, F. P.	Hackney.	Pallister, R.	Northumberland (E.).
Owen, G.	Bromley.	Palmer, —.	Eastleigh.
Owen, G.	Spennymoor.	Palmer, A.	Woolwich.
Owen, H.	Anglesey.	Palmer, C. N.	Chippenham.
Owen, H. M.	Swansea.	Palmer, E. E. L.	Southwark.
Owen, H. O.	Rossendale.	Palmer, F.	Staines.
Owen, J.	Barry.	*Palmer, F.	Croydon.
Owen, J.	Pontypool.	**Palmer, F. A.**	Bury St. Edmunds.
Owen, J. J.	Glamorgan (W.).	**Palmer, F. R.**	Dorset (N.).
Owen, J. M.	Welshpool.	Palmer, G.	Gloucester (S.).
Owen, L. P.	Hackney.	Palmer, G.	Ampthill, etc.
Owen, M.	Mountain Ash.	Palmer, G. G.	Portsmouth.
Owen, M. J.	Chester.	**Palmer, G. R.**	West Lambeth.
Owen, R.	Chorley.	Palmer, H.	London (W.).
Owen, R.	Finsbury, etc.	Palmer, H.	Tottenham, etc.
Owen, R. A.	Cardiff.	**Palmer, H.**	Birkenhead.
Owen, R. E.	Newtown.	Palmer, H. E.	Bristol.
Owen, T.	Isle of Axholme.	**Palmer, H. J.**	Ealing.
Owen, T. E.	Ilford.	Palmer, J.	Rhondda, etc.
Owen, T. G.	Taunton, etc.	Palmer, J. G.	Woolwich.
Owen, W. A.	Leek.	Palmer, J. H.	Bridgwater.
Owen, W. H.	Flint County.	Palmer, L.	Norwich.
Owen, W. H.	Dartford.	**Palmer, L.**	Deptford and Greenwich.
Owen, W. H.	Harrow.	Palmer, R. E.	Tottenham, etc.
Owen, W. H.	Liverpool.	Palmer, S. A.	Fleetwood.
Owen, W. J.	Swansea.	Palmer, W. W.	South Shields.
Owens, J.	Abercarn.	Palphramand, H.	Northallerton.
Owens, J.	Newcastle-on-Tyne.	Pamely, C. D.	Bristol.
Owens, J.	Basingstoke.	Pannett, C. W.	Brighton, etc.
Oxford, G.	East Lambeth.	Panniers, (Miss) M.	Ebbw Vale.
Oxley, E.	Wallsend.	Panton, H.	Hull.
		Pape, R. H.	Beverley.
Pace, A.	West Ham.	Papineau, O.	Leyton.
Pace, M.	West Stanley.	Papworth, —.	Kingston and Surbiton.
Packer, B. F.	East Ham.	**Parbery, W.**	Crewe.
Packer, E. V.	East Ham.	Pardoe, H. H.	London (W.).
Packer, H. S.	London (N.W.).	Pardoe, S. J.	Dudley.
Packer, W. G.	West Lambeth.	Pargeter, E. W.	Stokesley.
Packman, F.	Aylesbury.	Pargeter, J. P.	Dartford.
Padden, G.	Easington.	Paris, J. G.	Southend-on-Sea.

N.U.T. WAR RECORD

Name.	Association.	Name.	Association.
Parish, F.	Kettering.	Parr, Randall	Huntingdonshire.
Parish, W. J.	Tottenham, etc.	Parr, R.	Leigh.
Park, J. G.	Hexham, etc.	Parr, T.	Mexborough.
*Parke, E. A.	Newcastle-on-Tyne.	Parrack, J.	Alnwick.
*Parke, J.	Newcastle-on-Tyne.	Parratt, A. H.	Sheffield.
Parker, —.	Cheltenham.	Parrington, F. W.	Bury.
Parker, —.	Bath.	Parrington, S.	Dewsbury, etc.
Parker, —.	Spen Valley.	Parritt, P.	West Bromwich, etc.
Parker, —.	Glossop.	Parry, D. H.	Aberdare.
Parker, A.	Leeds.	Parry, E. O.	Bradford.
Parker, A. E. L.	Sunderland.	Parry, F.	Southampton.
Parker, A. V.	Hackney.	Parry, G. J.	Aberdare.
Parker, E. A.	Hackney.	Parry, H. D.	Wrexham.
Parker, E. J.	East Lambeth.	Parry, J. E.	Cardiganshire (N.).
Parker, F.	Romford, etc.	Parry, R. E.	London (W.).
Parker, F. J. H.	London (N.W.).	**Parry, T. E.**	London (E.).
Parker, G. W.	Eccles.	Parry, W. E.	Pembrokeshire (S.).
Parker, H.	Leigh.	Parry, W. L.	Warwickshire (N.).
Parker, H. W.	Cannock.	Parry, W. T.	Buckingham.
Parker, J.	Nuneaton.	Parsons, —.	Kettering.
Parker, J.	Blaydon.	Parsons, A.	Watford.
Parker, J.	Manchester.	Parsons, A. C.	Bishop's Waltham.
Parker, J.	Burnley.	Parsons, A. H.	West Lambeth.
Parker, J. A.	Chester-le-Street.	Parsons, (Miss) B. A.	Bristol.
Parker, J. F.	Westminster.	Parsons, A. H.	Leyton.
Parker, J. H.	Liverpool.	*Parsons, E. H.	Liverpool.
Parker, J. H.	Barkston Ash.	**Parsons, E. O.**	Bedford Borough.
Parker, L.	Tottenham, etc.	Parsons, H. B.	Gravesend.
Parker, (Miss) M.	Doncaster.	Parsons, H. E.	Berkshire (N.).
Parker, (Miss) M. E.	Manchester.	**Parsons, M. J.**	East Cleveland.
Parker, N. L.	East Lambeth.	Parsons, R.	Smethwick.
Parker, R. H.	Leeds.	Parsons, W.	Launceston.
Parker, R. J.	Halifax.	Partington, G.	Bolton District.
Parker, R. L.	Finsbury, etc.	Partington, H.	Nottinghamshire (W.).
Parker, S.	Weardale.	Partington, M.	Atherton, etc.
Parker, T.	Barrow-in-Furness.	Partridge, —.	Kettering.
Parker, W. E.	Blaydon.	**Partridge, A. F.**	Uxbridge.
Parker, W. H.	West Lambeth.	Partridge, J.	Birmingham.
Parker, W. J.	Barking.	Partridge, W. J.	Harrow.
Parker, W. T.	Cardiff.	Pasfield, H.	Dudley.
*Parkes, C. H.	Bradford.	Paskin, S. R.	Wolverhampton.
Parkes, L. J.	Rowley Regis.	Patchett, J. L.	Manchester.
Parkes, T.	Birmingham.	Patchin, H. V.	Brighton, etc.
Parkes, W.	Deptford and Greenwich.	Paternoster, A. F.	Leyton.
Parkhouse, H.	Hackney.	Paterson, J.	York.
Parkin, —.	Derby.	Pates, R. C.	Staines.
Parkin, —.	Doncaster.	Patten, C. J.	London (W.).
Parkin, B. D.	Stroud.	Patterson, F.	Litherland, etc.
Parkin, G. E.	East Lambeth.	**Patterson, J.**	Northumberland (E.).
Parkin, J. L.	Spen Valley.	Patterson, R. A.	Walsall.
Parkington, J. A.	Liverpool.	Patterson, (Miss) S.	Sunderland.
Parkinson, —.	Kettering.	*Patterson, S. B.	Walsall.
Parkinson, E.	Driffield, etc.	Pattinson, H.	Darlington.
Parkinson, E.	Bradford.	**Pattinson, W.**	Maryport.
Parkinson, F. W.	Blackburn.	Pattison, A.	Blyth.
Parkinson, G.	Leicester.	**Pattison, C. L.**	Sunderland.
*Parkinson, G. H.	Bootle.	Pattison, P. C.	Spennymoor.
Parkinson, J. C.	Furness.	Pattrick, J.	Hartlepools.
Parkinson, R.	Gateshead.	Paul, W. J.	Liverpool.
Parkinson, W.	Scarborough.	Pawson, G. A.	Hull.
Parks, M. J.	Ashford.	Pawson, H.	Tottenham, etc.
Parmee, C.	Eastbourne.	Paxton, J.	Darlington.
Parminter, J. B. V.	Leeds.	Payne, —.	Exeter City.
Parnell, J.	Cornwall (Mid.).	**Payne, A. C.**	East Dereham.
Parnum, J. H.	West Ham.	Payne, A. F.	East Lambeth.
Parr, E.	Woolwich.	Payne, C. J.	Birmingham.
Parr, F. T.	Staffordshire (N.).	*Payne, E. G.	Cheltenham.
Parr, G. F.	Widnes.	Payne, (Miss) F. W.	Leicester.
Parr, G. H.	Barnard Castle.	Payne, G. J.	Finsbury, etc.

TEACHERS WHO JOINED THE FORCES

Name.	Association.	Name.	Association.
Payne, H.	Sheffield.	**Pearson, G. P.**	Finsbury, etc.
*Payne, H.	Sheffield.	Pearson, H. A.	Southwark.
Payne, H. F.	Hackney.	Pearson, H. E.	Somerset (S.E.).
Payne, J.	Brentford.	Pearson, J...	Preston Borough.
Payne, J. A.	Manchester.	Pearson, J...	Brierley Hill, etc.
Payne, S. T.	Chatham, etc.	**Pearson, J. A.**	West Lambeth.
Payne, W.	London (W.).	Pearson, J. B.	Ashton.
Paynter, E. V.	Plymouth.	Pearson, J. F.	Rotherham.
Paynter, G. A.	Ealing.	Pearson, J. H.	Sunderland.
Payton, B. G.	East Ham.	Pearson, J. T.	Manchester.
Peach, —.	East Leigh.	Pearson, L.	Coseley.
Peach, J. R...	Liverpool.	Pearson, P.	Teign and Dart.
Peach, S. A.	Brighton, etc.	Pearson, R. H.	Hartlepools.
Peach, W. S.	Birmingham.	Pearson, V.	Witney. etc.
Peach, W. S.	Derby.	**Pearson, W.**	Finsbury, etc.
Peachment, C.	Bury.	Pearson, W. H.	Bilston.
Peacock, D. B.	Cornwall (Mid).	Peart, A.	Gloucester.
Peacock, E.	East Lambeth.	Peart, E. F.	Crook.
Peacock, F. G.	Southampton.	Peat, R. C.	Hull.
Peacock, J. A.	Newcastle-on-Tyne.	Peberdy, R.	Sittingbourne, etc.
Peacock, L.	Hull.	Peck, F.	Colchester, etc.
Peacock, R H.	Hackney.	Peck, F.	London (E.).
Peacock, R. M.	Teddington.	Peck, R. H.	Barking.
Peacock, T.	Gloucester (N.).	Pedelty, J. E.	Castleford, etc.
Peacock, W.	West Stanley.	Pedlar, V. T.	Plymouth.
Peadon, H.	West Stanley.	Pedler, F. J.	Merthyr Tydfil.
Peak, E. E.	Hull.	Pedley, E.	Shirebrook.
Peak, T. G.	Blaydon.	Pedley, J. R.	Willenhall.
Peake, E. H.	Portsmouth.	Peebles, J.	Sunderland.
*Peake, F.	Harrow.	**Peek, T. A.**	Nottingham.
Peake, H.	Nottingham.	Peel, C. C. W.	Hertford.
Peake, W. E.	Manchester.	Peel, J. H.	Burnley.
Peake, W. H.	Leighton Buzzard.	Peel, R. L.	Middlesbrough.
Peaker, A.	Warrington.	**Peet, J. T.**	Hornsey.
Peal, E. F.	Bromley.	Pegg, H. W.	London (E.).
Peal, E. G.	West Lambeth.	Pegler, W.	Dudley.
Peal, F. C.	East Lambeth.	Pegram, F...	Finsbury, etc.
Pearce, A. E.	Walthamstow.	Pell, C. H. B.	Brighton, etc.
Pearce, A. J.	Plymouth.	Pell, W. J.	Brighton, etc.
Pearce, D. R.	Leeds.	Pellow, E. C.	Southwark.
Pearce, G. F.	Wakefield.	Pells, F. G...	Leyton.
Pearce, H.	Stockton-on-Tees.	Pemberton, A. S.	Leicester.
*Pearce, H.	Erewash Valley, etc.	**Pemberton, W.**	Blackburn.
Pearce, H.	Southwark.	Pemberton, J. F.	Staffordshire (N.).
Pearce, H. G.	Birmingham.	Penaluna, W.	Cornwall (W.).
Pearce, H. M.	Liverpool.	Pender, C.	Birmingham.
Pearce, J. W.	Sunderland.	Pender, H. H.	Plymouth.
Pearce, M. G.	Edmonton.	**Pendlebury, R.**	Bradford.
Pearce, S.	Brynmawr.	Pendlebury, R.	Bolton Borough.
Pearce, T.	Cornwall (Mid).	Pendleton, H.	Nottingham.
*Pearce, W.	Teign and Dart.	Pengelley, —.	Bodmin.
Pearce, W. S.	Lincoln.	Pengelly, —.	Rotherham.
Pearn, —.	Richmond (Surrey).	Pengelly, B. E.	West Ham.
Pearse, O. G.	Woolwich.	Pengelly, E. J.	Bootle.
Pearse, J. M.	Moreton-in-Marsh.	Pengelly, W. C.	Kingsbridge.
Pearsc, R. C.	Woolwich.	Pengelly, W. L.	Worthing.
Pearson, —.	Colchester, etc.	Penlington, B.	Barnsley.
Pearson, —.	Wiltshire (W.).	Penlington, H. N.	Barnsley.
*Pearson, A.	Durham.	Penn, W.	Daventry.
Pearson, A.	Merthyr Tydfil.	Pennington, —.	St. Helens.
Pearson, A.	Liverpool.	Pennington, D.	Bury.
Pearson, C. K.	Harrow.	Penney, —.	Kettering.
Pearson, O. T.	Birkenhead.	**Penney, F. G.**	Itchen.
Pearson, C. T.	Castleford, etc.	Pennington, H. S.	Bristol.
Pearson, F.	Hexham, etc.	**Penny, H. E.**	Jersey.
Pearson, F. A.	Kingston and Surbiton.	Penny, J.	Birkenhead.
Pearson, F. E.	Southwark.	Penson, C. H.	Staffordshire (N.).
Pearson, F. H.	Pudsey.	Penrice, J.	Solihull.
Pearson, F. J.	Hackney.	Penrose, C. F.	St. Helens.

N.U.T. WAR RECORD

Name.	Association.	Name.	Association.
Pentney, C. H.	Harrow.	*Pewtress, A. W.	Rossendale.
Penwill, A.	Reading.	Peyton, —.	Reading.
Penzer, W. W.	Dudley.	Pflanz, F. W.	West Ham.
Pepler, —.	Willesden.	Phair, J.	Liverpool.
*Pepler, F. C.	London (E.).	Phalp, G.	Easington.
Peplow, H.	West Lambeth.	Phelps, W.	Gloucester.
Pepper, B.	Loughborough.	Phennah, W.	Wrexham.
Pepper, F. J.	Leicestershire (Mid).	Phibbs, R. L.	Manchester.
Pepper, G.	Driffield, etc.	**Philbey, G.**	Sheffield.
Pepper, J. W.	Willesden.	Philipps, —.	Warrington.
Pepperell, F. W.	Cardiff.	Philipps, R.	Derbyshire (E.).
Pepperell, W.	Halifax.	Philips, R. J.	Tunbridge Wells.
Percival, A.	Leamington.	Philipson, S.	Hartlepools.
Percival, G.	Grantham.	*Philipson, T.	Spennymoor.
Percival, H.	Stockport.	Phillimore, P. H.	West Lambeth.
Percival, T. B.	Rochdale.	Phillips, —.	Deptford and Greenwich.
Percy, G. B.	Lichfield.	Phillips, A.	Wakefield.
Perdue, E. K.	Bristol.	Phillips, A.	Walthamstow.
Perfect, S.	Manchester.	**Phillips, A.**	Barry.
Perfrement, J.	Blaydon.	*Phillips, A. J.	West Lambeth.
Perkin, F.	West Lambeth.	Phillips, A. J.	East Lambeth.
Perkins, A. E.	Birmingham.	Phillips, A. L.	Retford.
Perkins, G.	West Bromwich.	Phillips, B.	Wimbledon.
Perkins, G. W.	Hull.	*Phillips, C. A.	Waterloo, etc.
Perkins, H. S.	Ashton-under-Lyne.	Phillips, D. A.	Rhondda, etc.
Perkins, J. H.	East Lambeth.	Phillips, D. D.	Swansea.
Perkins, L.	Wellingborough.	Phillips, E.	West Lambeth.
Perkins, L. C.	Plymouth.	Phillips, E. F.	Leyton.
*Perkins, W.	Leicester.	Phillips, E. J.	Ogmore, etc.
Perkins, W. E.	Kidderminster.	**Phillips, E. J.**	Farnham.
Perks, F.	Redditch.	*Phillips, E. M.	Burton-on-Trent.
Perks, H.	Cannock.	Phillips, E. N.	Finsbury, etc.
Permain, F.	London (W.).	Phillips, E. R.	Brighton, etc.
Perriam (Miss)	East Ham.	Phillips, F. E. W.	Romford, etc.
Perrier, W. S.	Leyton.	Phillips, F. J.	Brighton, etc.
Perrin, —.	Sutton Coldfield.	Phillips, G. A.	Mexborough.
Perrin, E. E.	London (W.).	Phillips, H.	Luton.
Perrin, H. E.	Kingston and Surbiton.	Phillips, I.	Barry.
Perrin, J.	Thornaby-on-Tees.	Phillips, J.	Chester-le-Street.
Perring, A. J.	Finsbury, etc.	Phillips, J.	Rhondda, etc.
Perry, —.	East Lambeth.	Phillips, J.	West Bromwich.
Perry, —.	Penistone.	Phillips, J. G.	Cardiff.
Perry, E. J.	Cornwall (W.).	**Phillips, J. J.**	Coseley.
Perry, E. J.	Hackney.	Phillips, J. J.	Rhondda, etc.
Perry, J. G.	Chiswick.	Phillips, J. V.	Staffordshire (N.).
Perry, P.	Shropshire.	Phillips, O.	Cowbridge, etc.
Perry, R.	Leeds.	Phillips, P.	Barry.
*Perry, R. C.	Cirencester, etc.	**Phillips, R.**	Grimsby.
Perry, S.	Woolwich.	Phillips, R. E.	Tiverton, etc.
Perry, T. L.	Dudley.	Phillips, R. G.	Stourbridge.
Perry, T. L.	Somerset (S.E.).	Phillips, T. A.	Braintree.
Perry, V. E.	Birmingham.	Phillips, T. B.	Llanelly.
Perry, W. J. H.	Swindon.	Phillips, T. T.	Exeter District.
Perryman, F. M.	West Lambeth.	Phillips, W.	Rhondda, etc.
Pert, L. H.	Deptford and Greenwich.	Phillips, W. C.	North Cleveland.
Pescod, W. F.	Southampton.	Phillips, W. E.	Flint County.
Peters, —.	Gravesend, etc.	Phillips, W. G.	Abercarn.
Peters, H.	Cornwall (W.).	*Phillips, W. H.	Southend-on-Sea.
Pethrick, P. J.	Plymouth.	Phillips, W. J.	Cornwall (W.).
Petsch, R.	Hull.	Phillips, W. J.	Birmingham.
Pett, —.	Doncaster.	Phillips, W. J. G.	Pontypool.
Pett, C. H.	Plymouth.	Phillips, W. T.	Rhondda, etc.
Pett, J.	West Ham.	Philpott, —.	Birmingham.
Petterson, —.	Leyton.	Philpott, H.	Dover.
Pettet, H. F.	Brentford.	Philpott, S. A.	Westminster.
Pettitt, P. J.	West Ham.	*Philpotts, S. J.	East Lambeth.
Pettitt, V. S.	Bury St. Edmunds.	Phipps, J. H.	East Lambeth.
Petty, B.	Bishop Auckland.	Phipps, S. J.	West Lambeth.
Petty, W. E.	Hull.	Pichard, —.	Hyndburn.

170

TEACHERS WHO JOINED THE FORCES

Name.	Association.
Pickard, —.	London (N.W.).
Pickard, E. E.	Leeds.
Pickard, F. R.	Staines.
Pickard, J. C.	Nottingham.
Pickard, W. A.	Cardiff.
Pickbourne, L.	London (W.).
Pickerill, J.	Nantwich.
Pickering, A. W.	North Cleveland.
Pickering, C.	Middlesbrough.
Pickering, F. S.	Birmingham.
Pickering, H.	Hackney.
Pickering, J. R.	Leeds.
Pickering, R.	Newcastle-on-Tyne.
Pickersgill, R. M.	Sheffield.
Pickett, J.	Makerfield.
Pickett, J.	Aldershot.
Pickles, —.	East Lambeth.
Pickles, H.	Bingley.
Pickles, T.	Nottingham.
Pickles, W.	London (W.).
Pickstone, J.	Knutsford.
Pickup, A.	Worsley.
Pickup, H.	Manchester.
Pickworth (Miss)	Leicester.
Pidcock, —.	Salford.
Pidd, S.	Isle of Axholme.
Pidsley, C.	London (N.W.).
Pierce, G. W.	Winchester.
Pierce, J. M.	Rugby.
Pierce, L.	London (E.).
Pierce-Jones, J. D.	Carnarvon.
Pierce, H. Lloyd	Menai.
Pierce, T. O.	Llandudno.
Pigg, W. S.	Jarrow.
Piggott, P. W.	Portsmouth.
Pike, C. R.	Warwickshire (N.).
Pike, G.	Newbury.
Pike, P. H.	Southend-on-Sea.
Pilbin, J.	South Shields.
Pile, E. H.	Brighton, etc.
Pilkington, A. G.	Exeter District.
Pilling, —.	Lincoln.
Pilling, J. W.	Durham.
Pinch, W.	Lancaster.
Pinches, G. V.	Wirral.
Pincombe, W. J.	London (N.W.).
Pinder, J.	Middlesbrough.
Pine, H. H.	Brighton, etc.
Pink, W.	Ashford.
*Pinkney, M. R.	Blaydon.
Pinkney, R.	Aldershot.
Pinkney, W. W.	Colchester, etc.
Pinnington, —.	St. Helens.
Pinnock, A. J.	Enfield.
Pipe, J.	West Lambeth.
Pipe, P. D.	Willesden.
Pipe, R. H.	Ipswich.
Piper, A. B.	West Lambeth.
Piper, A. G.	Tottenham, etc.
Piper, H.	Birmingham.
Piper, H. C.	Southend-on-Sea.
Piper, R. C.	Wolverhampton.
Piper, R. W.	Wolverhampton.
Pirie, J.	Colchester, etc.
*Pitcher, W. H.	Chatham, etc.
Pitchers, G.	Portsmouth.
Pitchford, A. C.	Shropshire (E.).
Pitchford, H. H.	Willenhall.
Pitman, A. H.	Eastleigh.

Name.	Association.
Pitman, R. D.	London (W.).
Pitt, S.	Runcorn.
Pitt, W.	Exeter City.
Pitts, G. W.	London (N.W.).
Pitts, H. B.	Leyton.
Pitts, T. J.	Dorset (S.)
Pittuck, B.	East Lambeth.
Pizzey, W. A.	Deptford and Greenwich.
Place, H.	Accrington.
Place, H.	Hinckley.
Plane, J. E.	Leicester.
Plant, A.	Spilsby.
Plascott, R. H. C.	Southampton.
Plater, G. W.	South Shields.
Platt, A. J.	Eastbourne.
Platt, E. H.	Northwich.
Platt, F.	Leicester.
Platt, J.	Manchester.
Plattin, E. W.	Norfolk (N.W.).
Platts, E.	Manchester.
Platts, J. W.	Liverpool.
Player, J. L.	Hackney.
Player, S. S.	Coventry.
Playle, W. E. G.	Erith.
Pleasants, W. C.	Waveney Valley.
Pledger, G.	
Plenty, A. H. S.	Southend-on-Sea.
Pleydell, —.	Wimbledon.
Pleydell, R. W.	East Lambeth.
Ploughman, (Miss) M.	Southampton.
Plowright, C.	Surrey (S.E.).
Plowright, F.	London (N.W.).
Plumb, H. E.	Norfolk (W.).
Plumbley, (Miss) E. L.	Leyton.
Plumley, E.	Swindon.
Plummer, F.	Colchester, etc.
Plummer, S.	Abertillery.
Poad, F.	Bridgwater.
Pocock, A. V.	East Lambeth.
Pogmore, R.	Nottingham.
Poingdestre, F.	Jersey.
Points, W. G.	Cambridge Borough.
Poll, A.	Leeds.
Pollard, H.	Brighton, etc.
Pollard, J.	Stockport.
Pollard, O. J. Y.	Bridgwater.
*Pollard, P. J.	Woolwich.
Polley, F. H.	Tottenham, etc.
Pollitt, G. A.	Liverpool.
Pollock, W.	West Ham.
Pomeroy, P. S.	Finchley.
Ponsford, E. H.	Wimbledon.
Ponting, D.	Stroud.
Ponton, G. L.	Watford.
Poole, A.	Hastings.
Poole, C. E.	Swansea.
Poole, G.	St. Helens.
Poole, G. W.	Dorset (E.).
Poole, P.	East Lambeth.
Pooler, J.	Nottingham.
Pooley, C. H.	Norfolk (W.).
Pooley, H.	Erith.
Pope, A.	London (N.W.).
Pope, A. E.	Dorset (S.).
Pope, A. R.	Bristol.
Pope, H. J.	Hendon.
Pope, T. C.	London (E.).
Pople, —.	Berkeley Vale.
Poplett, J. E.	Kingston, etc.

N.U.T. WAR RECORD

Name.	Association.
Popleton, A.	Wakefield.
Popple, W...	Mexborough.
Porter, —.	Bromley.
Porter, —.	Salford.
Porter, B.	Liverpool.
Porter, B. A.	London (W.).
Porter, D.	Staffordshire (N.).
*Porter, G. E.	East Lambeth.
Porter, H.	Manchester.
Porter, J. J.	Spalding.
Porter, L. V.	Downham.
Porter, P.	Bolton Borough.
Porter, P. G.	Southwark.
Porter, R. P.	Lancaster.
Porter, S.	Ilford.
Porter, W.	Liverpool.
Portman, L.	Stourbridge.
Portnell, T. F.	Kendal.
Portsmouth, —.	Reading.
Postle, F. W.	East Lambeth.
Potbury, M.	West Lambeth.
*Potter, A. C.	Romford, etc.
Potter, F. G.	Oxfordshire (S.).
Potter, G. E.	Gillingham.
Potter, O.	Norfolk (N.W.)
Potter, T.	Nottingham.
Potter, W...	Tynemouth.
Potter, W. H. J.	Bristol.
Potter, W. J.	Hackney.
Potter, W. S.	East Lambeth.
Potts, —.	Burton-on-Trent.
Potts, E.	Newcastle-on-Tyne.
Potts, J.	Easington.
Potts, J. T. S.	Barkston Ash.
Potts, L.	Barnsley.
Pougher, G. A.	Northumberland (E).
Poulain, H. R.	West Ham.
Poulter, —	Tottenham, etc.
Poulter, R. A.	Tottenham, etc.
Poulton, —	Cheltenham.
Poulton, A. W.	Northampton.
Pound, J. T.	Portsmouth.
Pountney, E. B.	Birmingham.
Powditch, —	Ipswich.
Powe, W.	Willesden.
Powell, —.	Crewe.
Powell, A. L.	Manchester.
*Powell, A. T.	Nantwich.
Powell, A. V.	Southwark.
Powell, C. H.	Watford.
Powell, D.	Cwmtawe.
Powell, E.	Pontypool.
Powell, E. C.	Tredegar.
Powell, E. E.	Westminster.
Powell, E. G.	Birmingham.
Powell, E. N.	Swindon.
Powell, G.	Swansea.
Powell, H. W.	Hertford.
Powell, J.	Birmingham.
Powell, J. E.	Isle of Thanet.
Powell, J. H.	Enfield.
Powell, J. R.	Stockport.
Powell, J. R.	Ludlow.
Powell, L.	Glamorgan (Mid).
Powell, M. L.	Cardiff.
*Powell, P. W.	Hinckley.
Powell, T. A.	Hull.
Powell, W.	Tredegar.
Powell, W. G.	Stamford.

Name.	Association.
Powley, —.	Sleaford.
Powley, G. P.	Epsom, etc.
Powley, E. W.	West Lambeth.
Pownall, R.	Makerfield.
Powner, F.	Stockport.
Poynter, W. J.	Leeds.
Poyser, W.	Rotherham.
Pragnell, A. G.	Hackney.
Prall, W.	Portsmouth.
Pratt, —.	Cambridgeshire.
Pratt, A. T.	Chichester.
*Pratt, B.	Birmingham.
Pratt, B.	Loughborough.
Pratt, C.	Alnwick.
Pratt, F.	Hull.
Pratt, G.	Ilford.
Pratt, J. H.	Cardiff.
Pratt, N. J. B.	Kingston and Surbiton.
*Precious, H. P.	Leyton.
*Prentice, A.	West Lambeth.
Prentice, J. F.	Gelligaer.
Prescott, A.	Southwark.
Prescott, E. R.	Bristol.
Press, A.	Woolwich.
Pressdee, A.	Cardiff.
Pressey, G...	London (W.).
Preston, A. J.	Oxford.
Preston, E.	Stockport.
Preston, E.	Bootle.
Preston, E.	Spennymoor.
Preston, H. J.	Leicester.
Preston, J. C.	Driffield, etc.
*Preston, J. T.	London (E.).
Preston, W. J.	Oxfordshire (S.).
Price, A. B.	Birmingham.
Price, A. J.	Newport (Mon.).
Price, A. J.	Cheltenham.
Price, C. A.	Bournemouth.
Price, D.	Merthyr Tydfil.
Price, D. C.	Merthyr Tydfil.
Price, D. E.	Rotherham.
Price, D. E.	Ogmore, etc.
Price, D. J.	Merthyr Tydfil.
Price, E. W.	Bristol.
Price, F. E.	Somerset (E.C.).
Price, G. J.	East Lambeth.
Price, J.	Rotherham.
Price, J.	Llandovery.
Price, J. H.	Ludlow.
Price, J. O.	Wrexham.
Price, L. D.	Liverpool.
Price, O.	Merthyr Tydfil.
Price, P. P.	Ainwick.
Price, R. D.	Merthyr Tydfil.
Price, S. J.	Warrington.
*Price, W. J.	Southwark.
Price, W. J.	Staffordshire (N.).
Prickett, J. E.	Durham.
Prideaux, E. A.	Sheffield.
Prideaux, J. H.	Plymouth.
Priddy, H. W.	Blaydon.
Priest, F. D.	Coventry.
Priest, H. B.	Tottenham, etc.
Priest, W. G.	Norwich.
Priestley, —.	Doncaster.
Primmer, C.	Portsmouth.
Prince, A.	London (W.).
Prince, A.	Hackney.
Prince, A.	Barnsley.

TEACHERS WHO JOINED THE FORCES

Name.	Association.
Prince, A.	Stafford.
Prince, H.	Warwick.
Prince, H. V.	Preston Borough.
Prince, T.	Sunderland.
*Pring, B. V.	Croydon.
*Pringle, L.	Newcastle-on-Tyne.
Pringle, M.	Newcastle-on-Tyne.
Pringle, T.	Newcastle-on-Tyne.
Prior, A. E.	Isle of Thanet.
Pritchard, —.	London (N.W.).
Pritchard, —.	Birmingham.
Pritchard, A.	Woolwich.
Pritchard, A.	Tredegar.
Pritchard, C.	Southampton.
Pritchard, F. J.	Wrexham.
Pritchard, J. S.	East Lambeth.
Pritchard, S. G.	Northumberland (S.).
Pritchard, (Miss) W.	Birkenhead.
Pritchard, W. H.	Leeds.
Pritchett, R.	Leicester.
Probert, —.	Crewe.
Probert, A.	Wrexham.
Probert, G.	Hereford.
Probert, W. T. O.	East Lambeth.
Procter, A. D. G.	London (E.).
Procter, A. E.	Doncaster.
Procter, W.	Newtown.
Proctor, H.	Staffordshire (N.).
Proctor, L.	Hull.
Proctor, P.	Bradford.
Protheroe, E.	Pontypool.
Protheroe, J.	Rhondda, etc.
Prout, G.	Stroud.
Prudent, E. G.	Barnet.
Prudham, T. P.	Blaydon.
Pryce, M.	Warwick.
Pryce, R. E.	Merthyr Tydfil.
Puddephot, W.	Birmingham.
Puddicombe, L.	East Lambeth.
Pudney, H. W.	Canterbury.
Pudney, L. S.	Southwark.
Pugh (Miss)	East Ham.
Pugh, —.	Isle of Wight.
Pugh, —.	St. Helens.
Pugh, A.	Mountain Ash.
Pugh, C.	Coseley.
Pugh, D. H.	Rhondda, etc.
Pugh, D. W.	Cardiff.
*Pugh, G. H.	Bristol.
Pugh, H. G.	East Lambeth.
Pugh, H. W. J.	Oxford District.
Pugh, J. M.	Idris.
Pugh, R.	Liverpool.
*Pugh, R. H.	Rhondda, etc.
Pugh, W. J. F.	Westminster.
Pughe, H.	Tredegar.
Pughe, M. J.	Merthyr Tydfil.
Pullan, J. W.	Hull.
Pullen, E. H.	Somerset (E.C.).
Pullen, E. H.	Redditch.
Pullen, J. W.	Hackney.
Pullen, S. F. D. J.	Hackney.
Pullen, W.	Walsall.
Pulleyn, H. C.	Portsmouth.
Pulman, F.	Watford.
Pulpher, L.	Nottingham.
Punchard, F. M.	London (W.).
Punter, C. E.	Southwark.
Purcell, F.	Salford.

Name.	Association.
Purcell, W. F.	Leyton.
Purdey, S. H.	London (E.).
Purkis, H. S.	Jersey.
Purnell, A. J.	West Lambeth.
Purnell, C. C.	Radstock.
Purnell, H. M.	Leicester.
Purnell, R. S.	Bristol.
Purser, A. H.	Acton.
Purser, S. J.	West Ham.
Purssord, P.	Surrey (S.E.).
Purtill, J. H.	London (W.).
Purvis, A.	Finsbury, etc.
Putt, J.	Falmouth and Truro.
Pyburn, T. B.	Houghton-le-Spring.
Pyburn, W.	Sunderland.
Pybus, F.	Ripon.
Pybus, R.	Bishop Auckland.
Pycock, G.	Sheffield.
Pye, J.	Bootle.
Pye, J.	Ingleborough.
Pye, R.	Clitheroe.
Pyne, A. J.	Tiverton.
Pyrah, J. W.	Dewsbury, etc.
Quance, S. J.	Birmingham.
Quarrelle, B.	Leyton.
Quartermaine, —.	Walthamstow.
Quayle, J.	North Cleveland.
Quayle, J.	Southgate.
Quayle, J. G.	Finsbury, etc.
Quennell, E. A.	West Lambeth.
Quick, E. J.	Huntingdonshire.
Quick, E. L.	Kidderminster.
Quick, (Miss) H.	East Ham.
Quick, N.	Tottenham, etc.
Quick, (Miss) O.	West Ham.
Quick, R. H. P.	Horsham, etc.
Quinn, L. T.	Manchester.
Rabbitt, C.	Ashford.
Rabjohns, D.	Worcester City.
Rabson, A. R.	Walthamstow.
Rackham, W.	Surrey (S.E.).
Radcliefe, (Miss) M.	Manchester.
Radcliffe, I. T.	Market Drayton.
Radcliffe, J. H.	Stalybridge, etc.
Radcliffe, W.	Mexborough.
Radeske, W. H.	Hull.
Radford, A.	West Lambeth.
*Radford, C. G.	Mansfield.
Radford, G. L.	Southend-on-Sea.
Radford, E. J.	Makerfield.
Radford, G. E.	Somerset (N.).
Radford, W. T.	Sheffield.
Radmore, R.	Cleobury Mortimer.
Radway, E. J.	Swindon.
Raine, T. R.	Chester-le-Street.
Raines, W. H.	Harrow.
Raisbeck, G.	Brighton, etc.
Raistrick, J. W.	Belper, etc.
Raitt, W.	Northumberland (E.).
Ralph, E. W.	Bournemouth.
Ralph, G.	Brighton, etc.
Rambow, E.	Middlesbrough.
Rampton, A.	West Lambeth.
Ramsbottom, —.	Salford.
Ramsbottom, R. E.	Dorset (E.).
Ramsbottom, W.	Blackburn.
Ramsden, A.	Accrington.
*Ramsden, T. V.	Bradford.

173

N.U.T. WAR RECORD

Name.	Association.
Ramsey, C. E.	Surrey (S.E.).
Ramsey, E. S.	Guildford.
Ramsey, J. G.	Castleford, etc.
Ramshaw, A. R.	Durham.
Rand, P. A.	Birmingham.
Randall, —.	East Lambeth.
Randall, A.	Reading.
Randall, G. H.	Stroud.
Randall, H. A.	Birmingham.
Randell, J. B.	Bridgwater.
Randell, W. F.	Derby.
Randle, G. H. W.	Birmingham.
Randle, W. M.	Birmingham.
Raney, A.	York.
Rankin, C.	Rhondda, etc.
Rankine, W. F.	Farnham.
*Ranner, C. E.	Liverpool.
Ransby, R.	Yoxford.
Ransom, H. J.	Hastings.
Ransome, H.	Stockton-on-Tees.
*Raper, D. A.	Stockton-on-Tees.
Raper, E. B.	Morley.
Ratcliff, F. W.	Faversham.
Ratcliffe, —.	Crewe.
Ratcliffe, G. W.	Belper and Crich.
Ratcliffe, R.	Makerfield.
*Rathbone, H. L.	West Bromwich, etc.
Rattenbury, W. A.	Harrow.
Raven, E.	Brighton, etc.
Raven, W. A.	Romford, etc.
Ravenhill, F.	Ealing.
Ravenscroft, S.	Manchester.
Ravenscroft, T.	Manchester.
Raw, R. V.	Durham.
Raw, T. E.	Gateshead.
Rawbon, V. W. W.	Rochdale.
Rawes, L. N.	Barnes and Mortlake.
Rawling, G.	Cumberland (W.).
Rawlings, A. P.	Norfolk (N.W.).
Rawlings, F.	Swindon.
Rawlings, P. E.	Twickenham.
Rawlings, W.	Abercarn.
Rawlings, W.	Teign and Dart.
Rawlins, C.	Stockport.
Rawlins, F. Z.	Abergavenny.
Rawlinson, C. S.	Barkston Ash.
Rawnsley, E.	Bradford.
Rawson, J. W.	Sheffield.
Ray, A. N.	Durham.
Ray, C. B.	East Lambeth.
Ray, E. W. D.	Maidstone.
Ray, F. C.	West Lambeth.
Ray, G. F.	Hull.
Ray, W.	Hackney.
Raybould, G. H.	Dudley.
*Rayment, F.	Hertford.
Raymond, H.	Grantham.
Rayner, C.	Southend-on-Sea.
Rayner, C. L. G.	East Lambeth.
Rayner, E.	Harrow.
Rayner, P.	Sudbury.
Raynes, J. A.	Wharfedale.
Rayns, F. W.	Hackney.
Raynor, D.	Basingstoke.
Raynor, S.	Vale of Derwent.
Rayson, H. G.	Sheffield.
Rayson, R. B.	York.
Rayson, W. D.	York.
Razzall, H.	Scarborough.
Rea, G. L.	York.
*Read, —.	Hastings.
Read, C. E.	West Lambeth.
Read, (Miss) E. V.	Sunderland.
*Read, H. S.	Croydon.
Read, H. T. O.	Hackney.
Read, R.	Norwich.
*Reade, A.	Monmouth.
Reading, C.	St. Albans.
Reading, W. H.	Portsmouth.
Ready, F. C.	Cardiff.
Reaney, J. W.	Sheffield.
Reason, C. A. V.	Portsmouth.
Reay, J.	Cockermouth.
Reay, J. B.	Derbyshire (E.).
*Reay, T.	Northumberland (E.).
Reay, T.	Carlisle.
Rebensdorf, H.	Brynmawr.
Reddish, —.	Warrington.
Redfearn, C. J. N.	London (N.W.).
Redfern, R.	Manchester.
Redfern, S.	Lewisham.
Redfern, T.	Manchester.
Redford, A. C.	West Lambeth.
Redford, R. P.	Blyth.
Redhouse, H. E.	Twickenham.
Redler, H.	Worcester City.
Redpath, —.	Redditch.
Reed, O. S.	Abertillery.
Reed, F.	Wellingborough.
Reed, G. H.	Dorset (E.).
Reed, H.	Surrey (N.W.).
Reed, J.	Huddersfield.
Reed, J. W.	Cornwall (W.).
Reed, (Miss) M.	Wolverhampton.
Reed, R. J. A.	Deptford and Greenwich.
Reed, S. J.	Pembrokeshire (Mid.).
Reed, T.	Blaydon.
Reed, T.	Spennymoor.
Reed, W.	Huddersfield.
Reed, W.	Roch Valley.
Reed, W. D.	Bellingham.
Reed, W. E.	Woolwich.
Reed, W. J.	Lewisham.
Reed, W. O.	Stockton-on-Tees.
Reeder, —.	Brentford.
Reeder, E. E	Hull.
Reeder, J.	Hull.
Reeks, F. A.	Westminster.
Reely, —.	Reading.
Reeman, L.	Sheffield.
Rees, —.	East Lambeth.
Rees, —.	Ogmore, etc.
Rees, A.	Aberdare.
Rees, C. S.	Northwich.
Rees, D.	Tredegar.
Rees, D.	Bridgend.
Rees, D. A.	Cwmtawe.
Rees, D. H.	Merthyr Tydfil.
Rees, D. J.	Carmarthen.
Rees, D. L.	Glamorgan (W.).
Rees, D. R.	Rhondda, etc.
Rees, D. S.	Cardiff.
Rees, E. B.	Barry.
Rees, E. J.	Newport (Mon.).
*Rees, E. T.	Barry.
Rees, E. T.	Chatham, etc.
Rees, E. W.	Mountain Ash.
Rees, F. S.	Llanelly.

TEACHERS WHO JOINED THE FORCES

Name.	Association.	Name.	Association.
Rees, G. T.	Aberdare.	Reverson, W.	Dartford.
Rees, H. G.	East Lambeth.	Rewcastle, J. J.	Newcastle-on-Tyne.
Rees, H. J. M.	Kingsbridge.	Rewell, R. H.	East Lambeth.
Rees, H. T.	Swansea.	Reynolds, —.	Reading.
Rees, I.	Aberdare.	Reynolds, —.	West Ham.
Rees, I.	Rhondda, etc.	Reynolds, A. J.	London (W.).
Rees, J.	Braintree.	Reynolds, B.	Brynmawr.
Rees, J.	Swansea.	Reynolds, C.	Glamorgan (Mid).
Rees, J. D.	Pontypool.	Reynolds, F. H.	Wellingborough.
Rees, J. E.	Llanelly.	**Reynolds, F. L.**	Reading.
Rees, J. L. B.	Barry.	Reynolds, H. A.	Nantwich.
Rees, M.	Rhondda, etc.	Reynolds, H. O.	East Lambeth.
Rees, R.	Newport.	Reynolds, J.	Dartford.
Rees, S. J.	Rhondda, etc.	Reynolds, J.	Newport (Mon.).
Rees, T. B.	Rhondda, etc.	Reynolds, J.	Sale.
Rees, T. C.	Rhondda, etc.	Reynolds, J. W.	Wellingborough.
Rees, T. W. E.	Liverpool.	**Reynolds, N. J.**	Bridgwater.
Rees, V. H.	Finsbury, etc.	Reynolds, R.	Birkenhead.
Rees, W.	Llanelly.	Reynolds, T. C.	Leicester.
Rees, W.	Carmarthen.	Reynolds, W.	Cornwall (E.).
Rees, W. C.	Cardiff.	Reynolds, W. E.	East Lambeth.
Rees, W. C.	Mountain Ash.	Reynolds, W. F.	Southwark.
Rees, W. H.	Southwark.	Reynolds, W. O.	Plymouth.
Rees, W. J.	Glamorgan (Mid).	Rhoderick, E. O.	Rhondda, etc.
Rees, W. M.	Mountain Ash.	Rhoderick, T. A.	Rhondda, etc.
Rees, W. S.	Rhondda, etc.	Rhodes, A.	Shropshire (E.).
Reese, T. H.	Ebbw Vale.	Rhodes, A. M.	Wilmslow.
Reeve, E. R.	Nelson, Colne, etc.	Rhodes, J. W.	Hexham, etc.
Reeve, L. R.	East Lambeth.	Rhodes, N.	Birmingham.
Reeve, S. R.	Brentford.	Rhodes, R. C.	Birmingham.
Reeve, W. A.	South Shields.	Rhodes, T.	Leeds.
Reeve, W. R.	London (W.).	Rhodes, W.	Macclesfield Borough.
Reeves, —.	Radstock.	Rhodes, W. E.	Staffordshire (N.).
Reeves, C.	Epsom, etc.	Rhodes, W. J.	Wolverhampton.
Reeves, F.	Brentford.	Rhymes, W. S.	Hackney.
Reeves, H.	Staffordshire (N.).	Rhys, L.	West Stanley.
Reeves, J. E.	Birmingham.	Rice, —.	Kingston and Surbiton.
Reeves, L. G.	Reading.	Rice, —.	Warrington.
Reeves, S.	Epsom, etc.	Rice, G.	Leeds.
Regan, A.	Portsmouth.	Rice, H. J.	Portsmouth.
Regan, A.	Willesden.	Rice, H. T.	Portsmouth.
Regan, F.	Wigan.	Rice, J. A.	Hull.
Regan, H.	West Lambeth.	Rice, R. P.	Coalville.
Regan, W. A.	Skipton.	Rice, R. W.	Wimbledon.
Regis, L.	Lowestoft.	Rich, J. S.	London (E.).
Register, B. J.	Sheffield.	Rich, P.	London (N.W.).
Reid, A.	North Cleveland.	Richards, A.	Hackney.
Reid, D. W.	Tottenham, etc.	Richards, A.	Pembrokeshire (S.).
Reid, G. H. S.	Gillingham.	Richards, A. C.	Finsbury, etc.
*Reid, J.	Huddersfield District.	Richards, A. E.	Wallasey.
Reid, R.	West Ham.	Richards, A. E.	Tredegar.
Reid, T. H.	Liverpool.	Richards, A. J.	Glamorgan (Mid).
Reid, W. T.	West Ham.	Richards, C.	Walsall.
Reidy, M. J.	Hackney.	Richards, C. A.	Edmonton.
Reinstadtler, A. J.	Tottenham, etc.	Richards, C. J.	Coventry.
Relf, E. W.	Westminster.	Richards, C. W. D.	Oxford, etc.
Rendall, H. W.	Dorset (S.).	Richards, D. C.	Pontypool.
Rendall, L. A.	Castleford, etc.	Richards, D. H.	Ogmore, etc.
Rendell, R. H.	Eastleigh, etc.	Richards, E. O.	Swansea.
Rennie, —.	St. Helens.	Richards, F.	Devon (Mid).
Rennie, J. H.	Finsbury, etc.	Richards, H.	Cornwall (W.).
Renouf, A. E.	Bristol.	Richards, H.	Stourbridge.
Renshaw, C. S.	Manchester.	**Richards, H.**	Middlesbrough.
Renton, A.	Northumberland (S.).	Richards, H. E.	Llanelly.
Renton, H. W.	Swadlincote.	Richards, I.	Merthyr Tydfil.
Renwick, W.	Chorley.	Richards, I.	Mountain Ash.
Rest, T.	Nottingham.	Richards, J.	Warwickshire (N.).
Revell, F. G.	Isle of Ely.	Richards, J.	Swansea.
Revell, L.	Brentford.	Richards, J.	Ebbw Vale.

N.U.T. WAR RECORD

Name.	Association.
Richards, J. D.	Cardiff.
Richards, J. F.	Cornwall (W.).
Richards, J. H.	Vale of Clwyd.
Richards, J. R.	Rhondda, etc.
Richards, J. S.	Cardiff.
Richards, J. S.	Isle of Thanet.
Richards, L. J.	Willenhall.
Richards, L. Ll.	Cowbridge, etc.
Richards, R. D.	Mountain Ash.
Richards, S.	Basingstoke.
Richards, T. A.	Bishop's Waltham.
Richards, T. J.	Mountain Ash.
Richards, W. Morgan	Caerphilly.
Richards, T. R.	Glamorgan (Mid).
Richards, T. W.	Mountain Ash.
Richards, W. L.	Gelligaer.
Richards, W. P.	East Lambeth.
Richards, W. T.	Nottingham.
Richardson, —.	Blaydon.
Richardson, —.	Dover.
Richardson, —.	Hindley.
Richardson, A. L.	Chester-le-Street.
Richardson, C. T.	Canterbury.
Richardson, F.	Boston.
Richardson, G. D.	Leicester.
Richardson, (Miss) H.	Rochdale.
Richardson, H.	Penrith.
Richardson, H.	Middlesbrough.
Richardson, H. B.	East Lambeth.
Richardson, H. B.	Sunderland.
Richardson, H. W.	Barnsley.
Richardson, J.	Hyndburn.
Richardson, J.	Bishop Auckland.
Richardson, J.	Crook.
Richardson, J.	Durham.
Richardson, J. H.	Runcorn.
Richardson, J. J.	Finsbury, etc.
Richardson, J. R.	Mexborough.
Richardson, J. S.	South Shields.
Richardson, J. W.	Hexham.
Richardson, J. W.	Wimbledon.
Richardson, N.	Sunderland.
Richardson, O. G.	Doncaster.
Richardson, R.	Barnet.
Richardson, R.	Manchester.
Richardson, R. E.	Doncaster.
Richardson, R. G.	Brighton, etc.
Richardson, R. W.	Hull.
Richardson, T.	Northallerton.
Richardson, T. J.	Birmingham.
Richardson, T. W.	Northumberland (S.).
Richardson, W. R.	Darlington.
Richens, —.	Ipswich.
Richens, W. E.	Swindon.
Riches, P. G.	Stockport.
Richman, A. E.	Leyton.
Richmond, R.	Grimsby.
Richold, R. P.	Colchester.
Richter, A. D.	Liverpool.
Richter, A. G.	East Lambeth.
*Rickaby, J. D.	Newcastle-on-Tyne.
Rickard, —...	Cornwall (E.).
Rickard, A.	Exeter City.
Rickard, B. C. J.	Plymouth.
Rickard, G. P.	Plymouth.
Rickatson, L. A.	Southwark.
Rickatts, —.	Ealing.
Rickerby, E.	Carlisle.
Ricketts, E.	Surrey (N.W.).

Name.	Association.
Ricketts, G. H.	Stroud.
Ricketts, J.	Deptford and Greenwich.
Riddle, J.	Sunderland.
Riddlesworth, —.	Shrewsbury.
Ride, E.	Sheffield.
Ridel, A. T.	Bexhill.
Riden, W. G.	Cardiff.
Ridge, H. G.	Nottingham.
Ridge, W. J.	Westminster.
Ridges, A. P.	Southampton.
Ridgeway, G.	Staffordshire (N.).
Ridgeway, W.	Rotherham.
Ridgwell, H.	Walthamstow.
Ridley, —.	St. Helens.
Ridley, T. G.	Plymouth.
Ridout, C. J.	Ilford.
Ridout, F.-S.	Barnes and Mortlake.
Ridsdale, H.	Mansfield Borough.
Ries, —.	Deptford and Greenwich.
Rigby, H.	Rugby.
Rigby, R.	Southgate.
Rigby, S.	Hackney.
Rigbye, R.	Lancaster.
Rigg, L. A.	London (N.W.).
Rigg, R. E.	Tynemouth.
Rigg, T.	Crook.
Riggall, F. S.	Chester.
Riggs, R. F.	London (W.).
Rignall, J. R.	West Lambeth.
Riley, —.	Stafford.
Riley, A.	Manchester.
Riley, E.	Hyndburn.
Riley, H. S.	West Bromwich.
*Riley, W. H.	Sale.
Riley, F.	Manchester.
Riley, F. P.	Sheffield.
Riley, H. C.	Calder Valley.
Riley, H. R.	Derby.
Riley, J. L.	Manchester.
Riley, R.	Blackburn.
Riley, W. H.	Hull.
Rilstone, R. R.	Finsbury, etc.
Rimington, C. T.	Hull.
*Rimington, E.	Hull.
Rimmer, G.	Hereford.
Rimmer, E. T.	Liverpool.
Rimmer, I. H.	Radnor County.
Rimmer, L.	Runcorn.
Ring, F.	Bromley.
Ringland, E. C.	Finsbury, etc.
Ringrose, E. B.	Liverpool.
Rintoul, E. R.	West Lambeth.
Ripper, S. C.	Dorking.
Rippin, R. A.	Hackney.
Rippon, —.	Doncaster.
Risby, H.	Dewsbury, etc.
Riseborough, L.	Chester-le-Street.
Rising, T. C.	Lowestoft.
Ritchie, —.	Salford.
Ritchie, G. A.	Hackney.
Ritson, J. R.	Sheffield.
Ritzema, J. R.	South Shields.
Rivers, A. J.	Teddington.
Rivers, F. R.	Somerset (S.E.).
Rivers, G. C.	West Ham.
Rivers, G. S.	Chester-le-Street.
Rix, F. E.	Staines.
Rixham, (Mrs.) W. M.	Newcastle-on-Tyne.
Roach, P. A.	Lowestoft.

176

TEACHERS WHO JOINED THE FORCES

Name.	Association.	Name.	Association.
Readley, T.	Nottingham.	Roberts, P. W.	Portsmouth.
Roake, A.	Woolwich.	Roberts, R. H.	Penygroes.
Rean, W. T.	Newcastle-on-Tyne.	Roberts, S. H.	London (E.).
Robbins, G. N.	Birmingham.	Roberts, S. W.	Burnley.
Robbins, H. G.	London (E.).	Roberts, T.	Barking.
Robbins, J. R.	Bexhill.	**Roberts, T.**	West Lambeth.
*Roberton, W. H.	Willesden.	*Roberts, T.	Flint County.
Roberts, —.	Buxton.	Roberts, T. A.	Ogmore, etc.
Roberts, —.	Northants.	Roberts, T. H.	Birmingham.
Roberts, —.	Derby.	Roberts, T. L.	Llandudno.
Roberts, —.	Portsmouth.	Roberts, T. O.	Oswestry.
Roberts, —.	Portsmouth.	Roberts, V. H.	Flint County.
Roberts, —.	London (N.W.).	**Roberts, W.**	West Bromwich, etc.
Roberts, —.	West Ham.	Roberts, W.	Durham.
Roberts, —.	Liverpool.	**Roberts, W.**	Vale of Clwyd.
Roberts, A.	Liverpool.	Roberts, W. A.	Leyton.
Roberts, A.	Mountain Ash.	Roberts, W. A.	Anglesey.
Roberts, A.	Brierley Hill, etc.	Roberts, W. A.	Northampton.
Roberts, A. J.	Bristol.	Roberts, W. D.	Maesteg.
Roberts, A. W. J.	Gloucestershire (S.).	Roberts, W. E.	Flint County.
Roberts, C. A.	Birmingham.	Roberts, W. E.	Caerphilly.
Roberts, C. A.	Worksop.	Roberts, W. F.	Teign and Dart.
*Roberts, C. H. H.	West Lambeth.	Roberts, W. H.	Anglesey.
Roberts, C. S.	Barry.	Roberts, W. L.	Liverpool.
Roberts, D. E.	Somerset (N.).	Roberts, W. M.	Tottenham, etc.
Roberts, D. O.	Aberdare.	Roberts, W. N.	Hackney.
Roberts, D. S.	Caerphilly.	Roberts, W. S.	Anglesey.
Roberts, E.	Anglesey.	**Robertson, A. H.**	Blaydon.
Roberts, E.	Manchester.	Robertson, D. B.	West Lambeth.
Roberts, E.	Spennymoor.	Robertson, J.	Gateshead.
Roberts, E.	Gelligaer.	Robertson, P. W.	Tynemouth.
Roberts, E. J.	Welshpool.	Robertson, R.	Birmingham.
Roberts, F.	Bala.	Robertson, R. J.	Staines.
Roberts, F.	Ashton-under-Lyne.	Robertson, W. G.	East Ham.
Roberts, F.	Ealing.	Robin, N. O.	Finsbury, etc.
Roberts, F. S.	London (W.).	Robins, H. T.	West Ham.
Roberts, F. W.	Twickenham.	Robinson, —.	Lincoln.
Roberts, F. W.	Loughborough.	Robinson, —.	Salford.
Roberts, G.	Leeds.	Robinson, —.	Bury St. Edmunds.
Roberts, G.	Rutland.	Robinson, —.	Canterbury.
Roberts, G.	Norfolk (N.W.).	Robinson, —.	Shrewsbury.
Roberts, G. D.	Chester-le-Street.	Robinson, A.	London (W.).
Roberts, G. F.	Penygroes.	Robinson, A.	Sheffield.
Roberts, G. H.	Hull.	**Robinson, A. G.**	Birmingham.
Roberts, G. J.	Merthyr Tydfil.	Robinson, A. T.	Darwen.
Roberts, H.	Manchester.	Robinson, B. C.	Cannock.
Roberts, H.	Heywood.	Robinson, C. E.	Bury.
Roberts, H.	Leeds.	Robinson, C. L.	Coventry.
Roberts, H.	Flint County.	Robinson, C. T.	Liverpool.
Roberts, H.	Rhondda, etc.	Robinson, D.	Nantwich.
Roberts, H.	East Lambeth.	Robinson, E.	Vale of Derwent.
Roberts, H. F.	Huddersfield.	Robinson, E.	Erewash Valley, etc.
Roberts, H. K.	West Bromwich.	Robinson, E. C.	Barnard Castle.
Roberts, H. O.	Abergavenny.	Robinson, E. J.	Leeds.
Roberts, H. S.	Northwich.	**Robinson, F.**	Spennymoor.
Roberts, I. O.	Ogmore, etc.	Robinson, F. W. H.	Hartlepools.
Roberts, J.	Llandudno.	Robinson, G. L.	York.
*Roberts, J. A.	Caerphilly.	Robinson, G. L.	Liverpool.
Roberts, J. D.	Tredegar.	Robinson, G. T.	Northumberland (S.).
Roberts, J. J.	Festiniog.	Robinson, H.	Birkenhead.
Roberts, J. L.	Ebbw Vale.	Robinson, H.	Darwen.
Roberts, J. M.	Cowbridge, etc.	Robinson, H.	Manchester.
Roberts, Jones M.	Colwyn Bay.	Robinson, H. B.	Salford.
Roberts, J. R.	Walsall.	Robinson, H. E.	Walthamstow.
Roberts, J. W.	Manchester.	Robinson, H. L.	Rotherham.
Roberts, L.	Tipton.	Robinson, H. S.	Tottenham, etc.
Roberts, M.	Manchester.	Robinson, H. T.	Newcastle-on-Tyne.
Roberts, O.	Wallasey.	**Robinson, J.**	Sale.
Roberts, O. E.	Wrexham.	Robinson, J.	Sheffield.

N.U.T. WAR RECORD

Name.	Association.	Name.	Association.
Robinson, J.	Rhondda, etc.	Roe, C. P.	Bristol.
Robinson, J. A.	Ormskirk.	Roe, D.	Leeds.
Robinson, J. C.	Windermere.	Roe, F. H.	Derby.
Robinson, J. E.	Manchester.	Roe, W.	Willesden.
Robinson, J. E.	Whitehaven.	Rogers, —.	Deptford and Greenwich.
Robinson, J. F.	Sunderland.	**Rogers, A. H.**	Nuneaton.
Robinson, J. N.	Stretford.	Rogers, A. R. J.	Surrey (N.W.).
Robinson, J. R.	West Lambeth.	Rogers, A. T.	Willenhall.
Robinson, K.	Chadderton.	Rogers, E.	Tunbridge Wells.
Robinson, N.	Chippenham.	Rogers, F. G.	Eastbourne.
Robinson, R. R.	Kidderminster.	Rogers, G. T.	Swadlincote.
Robinson, R. T.	Bootle.	Rogers, H. E. G.	Southampton.
Robinson, S.	Castleford, etc.	Rogers, H. N.	Stockport.
Robinson, S.	Sheffield.	Rogers, J. E.	Hackney.
Robinson, S.	Hartlepools.	Rogers, J. P.	Wrexham.
Robinson, S.	Birmingham.	Rogers, J. T.	Blyth.
Robinson, S. C.	Bingley.	Rogers, (Miss) L.	Leicester.
Robinson, S. C.	Chiswick.	Rogers, (Miss) M. E.	Barrow-in-Furness.
Robinson, V.	Birkenhead.	Rogers, R. L.	Southgate.
Robinson, W.	Hull.	**Rogers, T.**	Mountain Ash.
Robinson, W.	Middleton.	Rogers, T. H.	Cornwall (W.).
Robinson, W. H.	Brentford.	Rogers, T. J. A.	Bristol.
Robinson, W. J.	Shipley.	Rogers, W.	Tredegar.
Roblin, W.	Carmarthen.	Rogers, W. A.	West Lambeth.
Robson, (Miss) A.	Alnwick.	Rogers, W. E.	Wallasey.
Robson, A.	Durham.	Rogerson, R.	Maryport.
Robson, A.	Durham.	Roles, J. H.	Romford, etc.
Robson, D.	Tottenham, etc.	Rolfe, O. C.	Romford, etc.
Robson, F.	Spennymoor.	Rollason, E.	Croydon.
Robson, F.	Stockton-on-Tees.	**Rollason, H.**	Ilkeston.
Robson, H.	Tynemouth.	Rollason, M. H.	Chester-le-Street.
Robson, H.	Darlington.	Rollinson, B.	West Lambeth.
Robson, H. L.	Durham.	Rollinson, F.	Manchester.
Robson, J. A.	Walsall.	Rood, W. J.	West Lambeth.
Robson, J. G.	Finsbury, etc.	Rook, G.	Great Yarmouth.
Robson, W.	London (E.).	Rooke, —.	Wimbledon.
Robson, J. E.	Northumberland (E.).	Rooksby, A. R. N.	Grantham.
Robson, J. G.	Northumberland (N.).	Roper, H.	Portsmouth.
Robson, J. T.	Sunderland.	**Roper, W. L.**	Wakefield.
Robson, J. W.	Houghton-le-Spring.	Rosborough, S. M.	Southend-on-Sea.
Robson, J. W.	Jarrow.	Roscoe, E.	Manchester.
Robson, R. R.	Barnard Castle.	**Rose, —.**	Newbury.
Robson, T.	Chester-le-Street.	**Rose, A. G.**	East Lambeth.
Robson, T.	Durham.	Rose, C. H.	Birmingham.
Robson, T. W.	Blyth.	Rose, C. J.	London (N.W.).
Robson, W.	Vale of Derwent.	Rose, C. V.	Dudley.
Robson, W. P.	Manchester.	Rose, E.	West Lambeth.
Roche, J. W.	Ebbw Vale.	Rose, H.	Epping, etc.
Rochester, W.	Liverpool.	Rose, H. A.	East Ham.
Rockley, D.	Finsbury, etc.	Rose, H. A.	Hull.
Rockliff, (Miss)	Liverpool.	Rose, J. G.	Isle of Thanet.
Rodd, E. W.	Isle of Wight.	**Rose, T.**	East Lambeth.
Rodda, —.	Taunton, etc.	Rose, T.	Nottingham.
Rodda, W. J.	Northampton.	Rose, W. W.	West Stanley.
Roddam, —.	Blaydon.	Rosewarne, V. S.	Lewisham.
Roden, H.	Surrey (N.W.).	Roskrow, R.	Cornwall (W.).
Roderick, F.	Bilston.	**Ross, A.**	Northumberland (E.).
Roderick, F.	Llanelly.	Ross, C. R.	Wakefield.
Roderick, P.	Edmonton.	**Ross, D.**	Aldershot.
Rodger, W. M.	Blaydon.	Ross, J. W.	Bootle.
Rodgers, R. J.	West Lambeth.	Ross, R.	Willesden.
Rodges, —.	Willesden.	Ross, S. A.	Leicester (Mid).
Rodham, W. L.	Weardale.	Rossell, T.	Tottenham, etc.
Rodnight, W. B.	London (N.W.).	Rosser, F. T.	Hackney.
Rodway, —.	Isle of Wight.	Rossi, B. P.	Harrow.
Rodwell, O. A.	Surrey (N.W.).	Rostron, A.	Heywood.
*Rodwell, E.	West Lambeth.	Rostron, J.	Hackney.
Roe, —.	Romford, etc.	**Rothen, F.**	Croydon.
Roe, A.	Willesden.	Rotherham, J.	Durham.

178

TEACHERS WHO JOINED THE FORCES

NAME.	ASSOCIATION.	NAME.	ASSOCIATION.
Rothery, J.	Cockermouth.	Rundell, A. A.	Castleford, etc.
*Rothfield, A.	West Lambeth.	Rundell, D. W.	Portsmouth.
Rothwell, —.	Bromley.	Rundle, C.	Portsmouth.
Rothwell, G.	Calder Valley.	**Rundle, J. G.**	Bristol.
Roughan, E.	Staffordshire (N.).	Runge, G.	Aberdare.
Roughan, T.	Staffordshire (N.).	Rush, H. H.	Ealing.
Roughsedge, R. L.	Worsley.	Rushforth, R.	Surrey (S.E.).
Round, A.	Smethwick.	Rushmore, F. M.	Colchester, etc.
Rouse, A. W.	Bradford.	Rushton, (Miss)	London (W.).
Rouse, H.	Willesden.	Rushton, A.	Staffordshire (N.).
Rousseau, A.	East Lambeth.	Rushton, C.	Halifax.
Routledge, J. A.	Carlisle.	**Rushton, G.**	Derby (E.).
Routledge, J. T.	Newcastle-on-Tyne.	Rushton, G. H.	Crompton, etc.
Routley, P. C.	Bristol.	Rushworth, C.	Goole.
Routley, W. S.	West Lambeth.	**Rushworth, H.**	Accrington.
Rowberry, C.	Stourbridge.	Rushworth, J. E.	Huddersfield.
Rowbotham, A.	Staffordshire (N.).	Russell, A.	Weardale.
Rowden, J. H.	Calder Valley.	**Russell, A. O.**	Gloucester.
Rowe, —.	Portsmouth.	Russell, C. F.	Newark.
Rowe, A. V.	London (W.).	Russell, E. G.	Dartford.
Rowe, C.	Liverpool.	Russell, F.	Erith.
Rowe, C. A.	Mexborough.	**Russell, F.**	Watford.
Rowe, E.	West Stanley.	Russell, G. J.	East Ham.
Rowe, E. J.	Cumberland (W.).	Russell, H.	Southampton.
Rowe, F. W.	Wallasey.	Russell, J.	Liverpool.
Rowe, G. A.	Bristol.	Russell, J. C. K.	Moreton-in-Marsh.
Rowe, H. H.	Weardale.	Russell, J. D.	Brighton, etc.
Rowe, J. A.	Plymouth.	**Russell, R.**	Gateshead.
Rowe, J. C.	Hull.	Russell, T. E. B.	Newcastle-on-Tyne.
Rowe, J. H.	Liverpool.	Russell, W.	Finsbury, etc.
Rowe, S. D.	Finsbury, etc.	Russell, W. A.	Southwark.
Rowe, T. G.	Cornwall (W.).	Russett, W. F.	Bristol.
Rowe, W.	Mexborough.	Rust, A. W.	East Ham.
Rowe, W.	Northumberland (E.).	Rust, G.	Gloucester.
Rowell, J. F.	Sunderland.	Rutherford, J. W.	Wallsend.
Rowell, J. W.	Newcastle-on-Tyne.	**Rutherford, N. E.**	Barrow-in-Furness.
Rowell, P.	Northampton.	**Rutherford, R.**	Northumberland (E.).
Rowland, A.	Derbyshire (E.).	Rutledge, C.	Blaydon.
Rowland, A. I.	Bootle.	Rutledge, W.	London (W.).
Rowland, E. O.	Newcastle-on-Tyne.	Rutt, B. G.	Uxbridge.
Rowland, F.	Erith.	Rutter, A.	Downham.
Rowland, T. H.	Swansea.	Rutter, J. A. P.	Norfolk (N.W.).
Rowland, W. E.	East Ham.	Rutter, S.	Preston Borough.
Rowlands, —.	Ogmore, etc.	Ryall, E. G.	Exeter District.
Rowlands, G. W.	Peterborough.	Ryall, W. J.	Winchester.
*Rowlands, H.	Carnarvonshire (S.).	Ryan, —.	St. Helens.
Rowlands, H. J.	Winchester.	Ryan, C.	Bootle.
Rowlands, J. C.	Menai.	Ryan, G.	Portsmouth.
Rowlands, S.	Rhondda, etc.	Ryan, J.	Lewisham.
Rowlands, W.	Llandudno.	Ryde, W. H.	Faversham.
Rowlands, W.	Pontypool.	Ryder, E. W.	Chatham, etc.
Rowlandson, R.	Salford.	Ryder, F.	West Bromwich, etc.
Rowlatt, J. J.	Tottenham, etc.	Ryder, F.	Eccles.
Rowley, —.	Hereford.	Rydings, H.	Blackburn.
Rowley, P.	Birmingham.	Rylatt, H.	West Lambeth.
Rowse, C. M.	Plymouth.	Rymer, R.	Ormskirk.
Rowse, J. Y.	Rugby.		
Rowson, E.	Chipping Norton.	Sabey, L.	Northampton.
Rowson, J. W.	Hackney.	Sackfield, J. C.	Hull.
Royce, W. V.	Edmonton.	Sadler, (Miss) B.	East Ham.
Royston, G.	Cambridgeshire.	**Sadler, G**	Ipswich.
Rubery, P.	Doncaster.	Sadler, H. W.	Bromsgrove.
Rudd, (Miss)	Birmingham.	**Sadler, J. J.**	Oldbury.
Rudd, F. J.	Portsmouth.	**Sadler, W. H.**	Cambridgeshire.
Rudman, C. E.	Tottenham, etc.	Saer, C.	Fleetwood.
Rudman, F. C.	Tottenham, etc.	Saer, W. R.	Llanelly.
Ruffell, S. R.	Southampton.	**Sagar, F.**	Hyndburn.
Rule, —.	Blaydon.	Sage, G.	Bristol.
Rumsey, O. G.	Abertillery.	Sager, J. T.	London (E.).

N.U.T. WAR RECORD

Name.	Association.
Sainsbury, H. G.	Salisbury.
Saint, —.	Northumberland (S.).
Saint, T. G.	Alnwick.
St. Quentin, E.	Waveney Valley.
Sainty, F. B.	Eccles.
*Sainty, J. E.	Norwich City.
Sainty, J. S.	East Lambeth.
Salisbury, —.	Shrewsbury.
Sale, E. W.	Deptford and Greenwich.
Sale, F.	Hornsey.
Salmon, —.	Wood Green.
Salmon, F.	Hackney.
Salmon, H.	Stockton-on-Tees.
Salmon, T.	Castleford, etc.
Salmon, V. E. T.	Hackney.
Salmon, W.	East Cleveland.
*Salt, A.	Widnes.
Salt, A. E.	Manchester.
Salt, L.	Gillingham.
Salter, —.	Guildford.
Salter, C. W.	Bedford.
Salter, H. B.	Bridgwater.
Salter, H. W.	Bristol.
Salter, W. H.	Leicester.
Salvage, G.	Brighton, etc.
Sambrook, A. W.	Cannock.
*Sampson, R. W. K.	Falmouth and Truro.
Samson, G. C.	Dudley.
Samuel, B.	London (E.).
Samuel, D...	Llanelly.
Samuel, D...	Llanelly.
Samuel, J. P.	Hornsey.
Samuel, W. J.	Caerphilly.
Samuels, A. P.	Kettering.
Sanbrook, F.	Walsall.
Sandars, F.	Birmingham.
Sanders, A. J.	Sheffield.
Sanders, B.	Isle of Wight.
Sanders, C.	Devon (N.).
Sanders, C. E.	Lowestoft.
Sanders, F. A.	Nottingham.
Sanders, F. G.	West Lambeth.
Sanders, F. P.	Northampton.
Sanders, H. A.	Ilford.
Sanders, H. J.	Willesden.
Sanders, H. S.	Walsall.
Sanders, P. J.	Glamorgan (W.).
Sanders, W. F.	Willesden.
Sanders, W. R.	Worcester District.
Sanderson, A.	Hartlepools.
Sanderson, A. R.	Bradford.
Sanderson, C.	Barkston Ash.
*Sanderson, C.	Spennymoor.
Sanderson, G.	Carlisle.
Sanderson, G.	Blyth.
Sanderson, G. G.	Chester.
Sanderson, J. B.	Gateshead.
Sanderson, J. J.	Houghton-le-Spring.
Sandland, —.	Doncaster.
Sands, P.	Woolwich.
Sandwith, G.	Whitehaven.
Sanford, W. H.	Romford, etc.
Sanger, R.	Walsall.
Sargent, J. W.	Tipton.
Sargent, O. A.	Cornwall (E.).
Sargent, S. R.	Manchester.
Sargesson, R. M.	Birmingham.
Sarginson, R.	Wallasey.
Sarginson, W.	Carlisle.

Name.	Association.
Sarson, G. H.	Sheffield.
Satterthwaite, F.	Walsall.
Saul, —.	Reading.
Saul-Brown, G. M.	Dorset (S.).
Saunders, —.	Ogmore, etc.
Saunders, —.	Bromley.
Saunders, —.	Ealing.
Saunders, A.	East Lambeth.
Saunders, C. H.	Brighton, etc.
Saunders, D. H.	Somerset (S.W.).
Saunders, E. G.	Edmonton.
Saunders, F. J. B.	East Lambeth.
Saunders, J.	Derby (E.).
Saunders, P. A.	Kingston and Surbiton.
Saunders, R. H. B.	Plymouth.
Saunders, R. J.	Lowestoft.
Saunderson, F.	Sheffield.
Sauvain, A.	Blackburn.
Savage, H. G.	East Lambeth.
Savage, H. W.	Surrey (S.E.).
Savage, T. C. P.	Liverpool.
Savage, T. M.	Warrington.
Savage, W.	Maidstone.
Savill, E. S.	Hackney.
Saville, —.	London (N.W.).
Sawdy, H. E.	East Lambeth.
Sawford, A. D. C.	Norwich.
Sawrey, K. S.	Barrow-in-Furness.
Sawtell, H. M.	Swindon.
Sawyer, A.	East Lambeth.
Saxby, G. W.	Dorset, (S.).
Saxby, (Miss) L.	Newcastle-on-Tyne.
Saxby, W. E.	Finsbury, etc.
Saxon, E. W.	West Lambeth.
Sayer, A. H.	Ilford.
Sayer, C.	Leeds.
Sayer, G.	Great Yarmouth.
Sayer, P.	Leeds.
Sayle, J. D.	East Lambeth.
Sayle, R.	Oxford, etc.
Scace, G. W.	Stockton-on-Tees.
Scace, J. H.	Stockton-on-Tees.
Scaddan, C. E.	Portsmouth.
Scaife, F. W.	York.
Scale, W. F.	Norfolk (W.).
Scales, C. W.	Chichester.
Scales, J.	Carlisle.
Scanlan, W.	Bristol.
Scarborough, H.	Sheffield.
Scarborough, H. T.	Portsmouth.
Scarisbrick, E.	Devon (E.).
Scarisbrick, J. M.	Liverpool.
Scarlett, E. J.	Norwich.
Scarth, A. E.	Sunderland.
Schafran, M.	London (E.).
Schmidt, —.	Doncaster.
Schofield, —.	Blaydon.
Schofield, E. B.	Huddersfield.
Schofield, H.	Bradford.
Schofield, H.	Worsley, etc.
Schofield, J.	Sheffield.
Scholes, B.	Manchester.
Scholfield, J. R.	Bilston.
Schwartz, G. L.	West Lambeth.
Scoltock, B.	Shropshire (E.).
Scoltock, P.	Birmingham.
Schonhut, F. A.	Rotherham.
Scorar, T.	Bury.
Score, W.	Enfield.

180

TEACHERS WHO JOINED THE FORCES

Name.	Association.
Scorer, J.	Wallsend.
Scorer, J.	Blaydon.
Scothorne, J. P.	Nottinghamshire (W.).
Scott, A.	Willesden.
Scott, A.	Leeds.
Scott, A. C.	Lewisham.
Scott, B. T.	Slough.
Scott, C.	Stafford.
Scott, E. C.	Salisbury.
Scott, F. E.	Felling.
Scott, G.	Wimbledon.
Scott, G.	Carlisle.
Scott, G.	Liverpool.
Scott, (Miss) G. M.	Cardiff.
Scott, H.	Stockton-on-Tees.
Scott, H.	Gateshead.
Scott, H.	Barking.
Scott, H.	Weald of Kent.
Scott, J.	Mexborough.
Scott, J.	Sheffield.
Scott, J. F.	Bolton Borough.
Scott, J. G.	Sunderland.
Scott, W. A.	Huddersfield.
Scott, W. D.	Finsbury, etc.
Scott, W. D.	London (W.).
Scott, W. E.	Portsmouth.
Scott, W. T.	Staines.
Scragg, W.	Maidenhead.
Screech, S. A.	Plymouth.
Screeton, N. H.	Southwark.
Scriven, R. H.	Brierley Hill, etc.
Scrivens, —.	Deptford and Greenwich.
Scully, B.	Manchester.
Scully, R. W.	Glamorgan (W.).
Scutcheon, A. C.	Norwich City.
Scutt, E. V.	London (W.).
Scutt, H.	North Cleveland.
Scutt, W. J.	London (W.).
Seabrook, S. E.	Finsbury, etc.
Seager, E.	Harrow.
Seal, J. R.	Maidstone.
Seal, W. M.	Hertford.
Seals, B. W.	Isle of Ely.
Seaman, A.	Finsbury, etc.
Seanor, W. A.	Wakefield.
Searl, A. A. F.	Farnham.
Searle, E. J.	Pembrokeshire (S.).
Searle, F.	Bury St. Edmunds.
Searle, J. C.	London (N.W.).
Searle, L.	East Ham.
Searle, W. G.	Enfield.
Searle, W. J.	Bristol.
Searls, O.	Southgate.
Sears, C.	Tottenham, etc.
Secker, E.	Croydon.
Secker, E.	Dewsbury, etc.
Seddon, —.	Salford.
Seddon, A.	Manchester.
Seddon, G.	Durham.
Seddon, J. W.	Bolton Borough.
Seddon, T. F.	Makerfield.
Seddon, W.	Manchester.
Sedgley, J. P.	Birmingham.
Sedgwick, J.	Manchester.
Sedwell, S.	Hackney.
Seed, A.	Barnsley.
Seed, F.	West Stanley.
Seed, H. A.	West Stanley.
Seed, J.	Preston Borough.
Seed, J. R.	Taunton, etc.
Seedhouse, J.	Luton.
Seeley, H.	Barnsley.
*****Seeviour, S. H.**	Winchester.
Sefton, P.	Sheffield.
Segal, S.	Leyton.
Selby, —.	Worksop.
Selby, A. E.	Hackney.
Selby, P.	West Ham.
Seldon, W. J.	St. Helens.
Self, W. T.	Croydon.
Selkirk, A.	Chester-le-Street.
Selkirk, W. O.	Middlesbrough.
Seller, F. C.	Hull.
Selley, W. H.	West Lambeth.
Sells, W.	Leyton.
Selman, A. J.	Bristol.
Selwood, —.	Redditch.
Semmons, W. W.	Tottenham, etc.
Semple, P.	Hendon.
Sendall, W.	Malvern, etc.
Senior, A.	Queensbury.
Senior, J. A, C.	Sheffield.
Senior, R. L.	Blackburn.
Senior, W. T.	Wakefield.
Senogles, T. H.	Cumberland (W.).
Sentance, —.	Boston.
Senton, R.	Ipswich.
Sephton, R. T.	Derby.
Serginson, J.	North Cleveland.
Settle, N.	Huddersfield.
Sever, G.	Doncaster.
Sevier, T. J.	West Lambeth.
Sewell, R. E.	Sheffield.
Sexton, R.	Edmonton.
Seymour, W. J.	East Ham.
Shackell, R.	Swindon.
Shacklady, —.	St. Helens.
Shackleton, W.	Manchester.
Shackleton, W.	Walthamstow.
Shacklock, W. E.	Nottingham.
Shafto, H. V.	Dorking.
Shakespeare, F.	Wolverhampton.
*Shambrook, R. J.	East Lambeth.
Shand, (Miss) E. J.	Chester.
Shandley, R. N.	West Ham.
Shanks, O. W.	Aldershot.
Shapcott, W.	Enfield.
Shapland, —.	Devon (N.).
Shapley, (Miss) A. M.	Newcastle-on-Tyne.
Shardlow, H.	Sheffield.
Shardlow, J. F.	Whitehaven.
Share, A.	Coseley.
Sharman, H. L.	Gillingham.
Sharman, J.	Brighton, etc.
Sharman, J.	Nottingham.
Sharp, B.	Mansfield.
Sharp, E. T.	Maryport.
Sharp, F. E.	Hexham, etc.
Sharp, J.	Burnley.
Sharp, J. F.	West Ham.
Sharp, R. A.	Canterbury.
Sharp, T. B.	Nottingham.
Sharpe, F.	East Ham.
Sharpe, H.	Surrey (N.W.).
Sharpe, H. E.	Bourne.
Sharpe, J. W.	Hull.
Sharpe, O. J.	Hertford.
Sharples, J.	Eccles.

N.U.T. WAR RECORD

Name.	Association.
Sharples, T. C.	Ingleborough.
Shattock, S. C.	Taunton, etc.
Shatwell, H. G.	Manchester.
Shaw, —.	Northampton.
Shaw, A.	Leeds.
Shaw, A. J.	Leyton.
Shaw, A. J.	Southend-on-Sea.
Shaw, B.	Rotherham.
Shaw, C.	Accrington.
Shaw, O. G.	Ilkeston.
Shaw, C. J.	Ilford.
Shaw, D.	Erith.
Shaw, E. B.	Croydon.
Shaw, E. E.	Ashton-under-Lyne.
Shaw, F.	Dudley.
Shaw, F. S.	Liverpool.
Shaw, F. W.	Tipton.
Shaw, G. L.	Lancaster.
Shaw, H. C.	Huddersfield.
Shaw, H. H.	Nottingham.
Shaw, H. L.	Manchester.
Shaw, H. S.	Flint County.
Shaw, J.	Hull.
Shaw, J.	Portsmouth.
Shaw, J. R.	Manchester.
*****Shaw, J. W.**	Northampton.
Shaw, L.	Macclesfield.
Shaw, L. F.	Finsbury, etc.
Shaw, N. C.	Dartford.
Shaw, O. W.	West Ham.
Shaw, P.	Wakefield.
Shaw, R.	Salford.
Shaw, R. S.	Dartford.
Shaw, T.	Manchester.
Shaw, T. H.	Bradford.
Shaw, W.	Ilford.
Shaw, W. B.	Liverpool.
Shaw, W. T.	West Ham.
Shawcross, W.	Manchester.
Shea, W. D.	West Lambeth.
Shean, P. C.	West Ham.
Shearer, E. J.	Southampton.
Shearman, W. R.	Leyton.
Shears, M. C.	London (W.).
Sheather, H.	Hackney.
Shee, N.	Liverpool.
Sheedy, D. A.	Long Eaton.
Sheffield, —.	Crewe.
Sheldon, F. G.	Reading.
Sheldon, J.	Nottingham.
Sheldon, R. G.	East Ham.
Sheldrake, —.	Deptford and Greenwich.
*Sheldrik, H. L.	Chatham, etc.
Shelley, H...	Southwark.
Shennan, T. P.	London (E.).
Shenton, A.	Bristol.
Shenton, F. G.	Staffordshire (N.).
Shepherd, —.	Derby.
Shepherd, —.	Southwark.
Shepherd, A. L.	Brierley Hill, etc.
Shepherd, E.	Rochdale.
Shepherd, E. R.	Bradford.
Shepherd, R. H.	Swadlincote.
Shepherd, T.	Carlisle.
Shepherd, W.	Carlisle.
Shepherd, W.	Grimsby.
Shepherd W.	Erewash Valley, etc.
Shepherd, W.	Leigh.
Shepherd, W. J.	East Cleveland.

Name.	Association.
Shepherdson, A. J.	Sheffield.
Sheppard, A. R.	Flint County.
Sheppard, —.	Redditch.
Sheppard, A.	Finsbury, etc.
Sheppard, G.	Hull.
Sheppard, T. H.	Rugby.
Sheppard, W. J.	Somerset (N.).
Sheraton, H. A.	Tottenham, etc.
Shere, —.	Exeter City.
Sheridan, —.	Salford.
Sherrington, P.	Manchester.
*Sherry, L. R.	Swindon.
Sherwin, E.	Derby.
Sherwood, W.	Tipton.
Sherwood, W. A. E.	Wellingborough.
Sheward, —.	Warrington.
Shiack, J.	Sunderland.
Shiel, B. R.	Birmingham.
Shield, E. H.	Bristol.
Shield, F. J.	Leicester.
Shields, J. A.	Tredegar.
Shields, W. M.	Hartlepools.
Shiell, A. W.	Sheffield.
Shilston, H. H.	Cornwall (W.).
Shilvock, A. C.	East Lambeth.
Shimmin, E. C.	Isle of Man.
Shimmin, W. A.	Deptford and Greenwich.
Shiner, G. E.	Bristol.
Shingler, J.	Staffordshire (N.).
Shingler, R.	Barnet.
Shipton, W. B.	Birmingham.
Shipley, T.	Tynemouth.
Shipley, T.	Sheffield.
Shipman, W.	Birkenhead.
Shippam, S. P.	Wakefield.
Shippen, J. F.	Newcastle-on-Tyne.
Shippen, J. G.	Spennymoor.
Shipton, W. B.	Birmingham.
Shirley, S. J.	Acton.
Shoebridge, E. W.	Newport Pagnell.
Shoesmith, A.	Folkestone.
Shoobridge, H. J. A.	Tonbridge.
Shooter, C. W.	Sheffield.
*Shooter, J. H.	Sheffield.
Shore, E.	Oldham.
Shorrock, P.	Birmingham.
Short, E. H.	Plymouth.
Short, H. F.	Newark.
Short, J. T.	Rhondda, etc.
Shorter, F. S.	Reigate.
Shorthouse, B.	Birmingham.
Shorthouse, F. J.	Woolwich.
Shortridge, L.	Durham.
Shortridge, W.	Chatham, etc.
Shotton, —.	Wolverhampton.
Shrewsbury, —.	Grimsby.
Shrewsbury, J.	Deptford and Greenwich.
Shrive, G. A.	Wimbledon.
Shuard, R. W.	London (N.W.).
Shufflebotham, H.	Bolton District.
Shuker, F. J.	Birmingham.
Shurmer, H. H.	Gloucester.
Shuttlewood, —.	Leicester.
Shuttlewood, T.	Gravesend.
Shuttleworth, —.	Birmingham.
Shuttleworth, A.	West Lambeth.
Shuttleworth, A.	Liverpool.
Shuttleworth, F.	Bolton Borough.
Sibbit, G. B.	Newcastle-on-Tyne.
Sibbit, H.	Newcastle-on-Tyne.

TEACHERS WHO JOINED THE FORCES

Name.	Association.
Sibley, D. W.	Swadlincote.
Sibley, F. W.	Radnor.
Sidaway, B.	Stourbridge.
Sidaway, J. N.	Cheltenham.
Siddall, A.	Sheffield.
Siddorn, —.	Willesden.
Sidebottom, E.	Bellingham.
Sidebottom, J. W.	South Shields.
Sidebottom, N.	Sunderland.
Sidwell, W. T.	Rugby.
Siebert, S. P.	Hackney.
Silk, E.	Nantyglo.
Silk, G.	Birmingham.
Silley, F. S.	Teign and Dart.
Sillitoe, G.	Dudley.
Sills, G.	Nottingham.
Sills, (Miss) G. K.	Nottingham.
Sills, W. W.	Sudbury.
Silver, —.	Reading.
Silverstone, J.	London (E.).
Silvester, F.	Chichester.
*Simcock, F. W.	Warrington.
Simcock, H.	Staffordshire (N.).
Simcoe, H. G.	Brackley, etc.
Simcox, A. W.	Willenhall.
Simcox, L.	West Bromwich, etc.
Simester, B. J.	Southampton.
Simkin, W. J.	Cannock.
Simmonds, A. E.	Hackney.
Simmonds, D. W.	Tavistock.
Simmonds, J. W.	East Cleveland.
Simmonds, O. W.	Hartlepools.
Simmonds, P. W.	Brighton, etc.
Simmons, A.	Birmingham.
Simmons, A. J.	Chatham, etc.
Simmons, H. B.	Barkston Ash.
Simmons, H. V.	Durham.
Simon, R.	Carlisle.
Simon, R. T.	Idris.
Simons, B.	London (E.).
Simons, E. A.	Sheffield.
Simons, H. J.	Nottingham.
*Simons, L.	Deptford and Greenwich.
Simmons, R. E.	London (E.).
Simmons, W. R.	Southwark.
Simpson (Miss)	Southgate.
Simpson, A. A.	Birmingham.
Simpson, C. P.	Hull.
Simpson, H.	Manchester.
Simpson, H. A.	Nottinghamshire (W.).
Simpson, L.	Castleford, etc.
Simpson, R.	Manchester.
Simpson, R. A.	Easington.
Simpson, R. W.	Liverpool.
Simpson, S.	Biggleswade.
Simpson, S. B.	Dudley.
Simpson, W. A.	Folkestone.
Simpson, W. O.	Willesden.
Sims, C.	Gloucester.
Sims, S. G.	Forest of Dean.
Sinclair, —.	Warrington.
Sinclair, A. J.	Portsmouth.
Sinclair, J.	Liverpool.
Sinclair, J.	Barnard Castle.
Sinclair, W. E.	Deptford and Greenwich.
Sinden, A. H.	Southgate.
Singleton, E.	Preston Borough.
Singleton, F.	Birmingham.
Singleton, W.	Blackpool.
Sinkinson, T. V.	Wigan.
Sirett, C. F.	Staffordshire (N.).
Sizeland, O.	London (E.).
*Sizeland, R.	London, (N.W.).
Sizer, E. J.	Norwich.
Skeates, A. R.	Bristol.
Skellern, H.	Staffordshire (N.).
Skelly, —.	Wallsend.
Skelton, C.	Penrith.
Skelton, C. S.	Hull.
Skelton, E. C.	Rotherham.
Skelton, F. S.	Hull.
Skelton, H. A.	Rotherham.
Skenfield, F. J.	Merthyr Tydfil.
Skerrett, H. A. D.	Staffordshire (N.).
Skerry, (Miss) A.	Newcastle-on-Tyne.
Skey, —.	Cheltenham.
Skilbeck, H.	Whitby.
Skillicorn, J.	Isle of Man.
Skimpton, —.	Northampton.
Skinner, A.	Hackney.
Skinner, E. H. J.	Southgate.
Skinner, G. S.	Stockport.
Skinner, H. H.	Great Yarmouth.
Skinner, L. T.	Hackney.
Skinner, P. A.	Bilston.
Skinner, R. H.	Birkenhead.
Skinner, V.	Ogmore, etc.
Skinner, W. J.	Durham.
Skipp, —.	Hereford.
Skipsey, W.	East Ham.
Skirrow, H. W.	Newark.
Skone, W. H.	Pembrokeshire (Mid).
Skull, L.	Erewash Valley, etc.
Skurr, W.	Chester-le-Street.
*Skuse, S. C.	Tredegar.
Skyrme, —.	Gravesend.
Slack, A. J.	Leek.
Slack, O. A.	Doncaster.
Slack, H. M.	Barnsley.
Sladden, W. F.	Walthamstow.
Sladdin, E. A.	Brighouse.
Slade, E. M.	Bristol.
Slade, W. J.	Birmingham.
Slaney, J. W.	Dewsbury, etc.
Slater, A.	Doncaster.
Slater, G. W.	Tynemouth.
*Slater, H. A.	Nottingham.
Slater, J. H.	Oldham.
Slater, R.	Preston District.
Slater, R. A.	Newcastle-on-Tyne.
Slater, R. J.	Burton-on-Trent.
*Slater, T.	Northumberland (E.).
Slattery, G. M.	Walthamstow.
Slavin, H. B.	Sheffield.
Slaughter, H.	Coventry.
*Sleath, C. G.	Wolverhampton.
Sleath, T. W.	Coventry.
Slee, H.	Luton.
Slee, J.	Leyton.
Sleep, R. C.	Cornwall (E.).
Sleight, —.	Nottinghamshire (W.).
Sleight, R.	Leicestershire (Mid).
Slidel, S. R.	Eastbourne.
Slimming, J. L.	Hull.
Sloane, J.	Darwen.
Sloman, C. S.	West Lambeth.
Sloman, H.	Brighton, etc.
Sloman, H. F.	Tunbridge Wells.

N.U.T. WAR RECORD

Name.	Association.	Name.	Association.
Smailes, J. R.	Hexham, etc.	Smith, E.	Nottingham.
Small, F.	Portsmouth.	Smith, E.	Grimsby.
Small, F. G.	East Lambeth.	Smith, E.	Norfolk (N.W.).
Smallcombe, A. G.	Bristol.	Smith, E.	Ipswich.
Smalley, J. N.	Doncaster.	Smith, E. A.	Berkeley Vale.
Smalley, O. H.	Manchester.	Smith, E. A.	Brighouse.
Smallman, W.	Birmingham.	Smith, E. A.	Portsmouth.
Smallshaw, W.	Dorset (W.).	Smith, E. C.	Birmingham.
Smallwood, R.	Vale of Derwent.	Smith, E. G.	West Ham.
Smart, —.	Bath.	Smith, E. H.	Willesden.
Smart, —.	Derby.	Smith, E. H.	Chatham, etc.
Smart, —.	West Ham.	**Smith, E. J.**	Bridgwater.
*Smart, J. E.	Makerfield.	Smith, E. J.	Dover.
Smart, W.	Driffield, etc.	Smith, E. S.	Woolwich.
Smart, W. O.	Leeds.	Smith, E. S.	Reading.
Smart, W. R.	Harrow.	**Smith, E. W.**	Mexborough.
Smeardon, W. S.	Willesden.	Smith, E. W.	Forest of Dean.
Smedley, —.	Birmingham.	Smith, E. W.	Isle of Ely.
Smedley, A.	Macclesfield District.	Smith, E. W.	Harrow.
Smedley, J. H.	Birmingham.	Smith, F.	Workington.
Smee, P. G. F.	Willesden.	Smith, F.	Leigh.
Smeeton, E.	Nottingham.	Smith, F.	Rotherham.
Smethurst, H. C.	Gillingham.	*Smith, F.	Halifax.
Smethurst, J. S.	Hull.	Smith, F.	Crewe.
Smethurst, R.	Manchester.	Smith, (Miss) F. A.	Waterloo.
Smith, —.	St. Helens.	*Smith, F. C.	Hackney.
Smith, A.	Devon (N.).	Smith, F. D.	Gillingham.
Smith, A.	Ilkeston.	**Smith, F. G.**	Gloucester.
Smith, A.	Leeds.	Smith, F. G.	Nottingham.
Smith, A.	Blackburn.	**Smith, F. G.**	Gateshead.
Smith, A.	Birmingham.	Smith, F. H.	Brighton, etc.
*Smith, A. E.	Kingston and Surbiton.	**Smith, F. H.**	Croydon.
Smith, A. E.	Leicester.	Smith, F. H.	Lancaster.
Smith, A. E.	Manchester.	Smith, F. J.	Sheffield.
Smith, A. E.	Finchley.	Smith, F. J.	Goole.
Smith, A. G.	Gloucester.	Smith, F. K.	Walsall.
Smith, A. Gower	Manchester.	Smith, F. M.	West Lambeth.
Smith, A. J.	Portsmouth.	Smith, F. R.	St. Albans.
Smith, A. J.	Birmingham.	**Smith, F. W.**	West Lambeth.
Smith, A. J.	Liverpool.	**Smith, F. W.**	Swindon.
Smith, A. J.	Liverpool.	Smith, G.	Ilford.
Smith, A. L.	Southgate.	Smith, G.	Deal.
Smith, A. L.	Watford.	Smith, G. A.	London (W.).
Smith, A. M.	Hackney.	Smith, G. C.	Mexborough.
Smith, A. R.	Kettering.	Smith, G. C. L.	Walthamstow.
Smith, A. R.	Birmingham.	Smith, G. E.	Portsmouth.
Smith, A. T.	Watford.	Smith, G. S.	Tottenham, etc.
Smith, B.	Birmingham.	Smith, G. S.	Driffield, etc.
Smith, B. O.	Brierley Hill, etc.	Smith, G. Y.	Barry.
Smith, C.	Gloucester.	**Smith, H.**	Leeds.
Smith, C.	Northumberland (S.).	*Smith, H.	Leyton.
*Smith, C.	Teddington.	Smith, H.	Cambridge Borough.
Smith, C. G. H.	Reading.	Smith, H.	Manchester.
*Smith, C. H.	Cardiff.	Smith, H.	Burnley.
Smith, C. H.	Teign and Dart.	Smith, H.	Leeds.
Smith, C. H.	Shropshire (E).	Smith, H.	Kingston and Surbiton.
Smith, C. L.	Acton.	Smith, H.	Keighley.
Smith, C. R.	Sunderland.	Smith, H.	Wakefield.
Smith, C. V.	Leicester.	**Smith, H.**	Wallsend.
Smith, C. V.	Makerfield.	Smith, H.	Birmingham.
Smith, D.	Barry.	Smith, H.	Leeds.
Smith, D.	Romford, etc.	Smith, H. A.	Northampton.
Smith, D. I. C.	Plymouth.	Smith, H. A.	Guildford.
Smith, D. J.	Dartford.	Smith, H. B.	Leeds.
Smith, D. P.	Bradford.	Smith, H. B.	Wirral.
Smith, D. W.	Coventry.	Smith, H. F.	Birmingham.
Smith, E.	Skipton.	Smith, H. G.	Wakefield.
Smith, E.	Manchester.	Smith, H. J.	Kingston and Surbiton.

TEACHERS WHO JOINED THE FORCES

NAME.	ASSOCIATION.
Smith, H. M.	East Ham.
Smith, H. P.	Portsmouth.
Smith, H. P.	Leamington.
Smith, H. S.	Northwich.
Smith, H. T.	Derbyshire (E.).
Smith, J.	Market Drayton.
Smith, J.	Preston Borough.
Smith, J.	Coventry.
Smith, J.	Liverpool.
Smith, J. A.	Barking.
Smith, J. A.	Hereford.
Smith, J. A.	Swansea.
Smith, J. C.	Oldham.
Smith, J. E.	Berkeley Vale.
Smith, J. E.	Harrogate.
Smith, J. H.	Nottingham.
Smith, J. H.	Nidderdale.
Smith, J. H.	Leeds.
Smith, J. H. T.	Watford.
Smith, J. R.	Spennymoor.
Smith, J. R.	Durham.
Smith, J. R.	Wirral.
Smith, J. T.	Surrey (N.W.).
Smith, J. W.	Liverpool.
Smith, (Miss) L.	Barnsley.
Smith, L.	Warwickshire (N.).
Smith, L. E.	Surrey (N.W.).
Smith, L. S.	Colchester, etc.
Smith, L. W.	Barnsley.
Smith, M.	Woolwich.
Smith, M.	Surrey (S.E.).
Smith, M.	Devizes.
Smith, M. D.	Cockermouth.
Smith, M. D.	Wallsend.
Smith, N.	Blaydon.
Smith, N.	Wigan.
Smith, N.	Castleford, etc.
Smith, O. W.	Barnsley.
Smith, P.	Blaydon.
*Smith, P. J.	East Lambeth.
Smith, P. R.	Dewsbury, etc.
Smith, R.	Swindon.
Smith, R. C.	Ipswich.
Smith, R. F.	Manchester.
Smith, R. G.	Sheffield.
Smith, R. H.	London (E.).
Smith, R. H.	Chester-le-Street.
Smith, R. M.	Coalville.
Smith, R. W.	Lincoln.
Smith, S.	Hendon.
Smith, S.	Pocklington.
Smith, S.	West Ham.
Smith, S.	Dewsbury, etc.
Smith, S.	St. Albans.
Smith, S.	Hartlepools.
Smith, S.	Ashbourne.
Smith, S.	Birmingham.
Smith, S.	Norfolk (N.W.).
Smith, S.	Staffordshire (N.).
Smith, S.	Gravesend.
Smith, S. C.	Nottinghamshire (W.).
Smith, S. D.	Burnley.
Smith, S. E.	Wharfedale.
Smith, S. F.	London (E.).
Smith, S. R.	Liverpool.
Smith, S. W.	Manchester.
Smith, S. W.	Pembrokeshire (S.).
*Smith, S. W.	Vale of Derwent.
Smith, T.	Darwen.
Smith, T.	Bolton Borough.
Smith, T.	Staffordshire (N.).
Smith, T.	North Cleveland.
Smith, T. E.	Pembrokeshire (S.).
Smith, T. H.	Vale of Derwent.
Smith, T. M. C.	Halstead.
Smith, T. W.	Doncaster.
Smith, T. W.	Penarth.
Smith, V.	Tottenham, etc.
Smith, W.	Manchester.
Smith, W.	Portsmouth.
Smith, W.	Wolverhampton.
Smith, W.	South Shields.
Smith, W.	Derby.
Smith, W. A.	York.
Smith, W. A.	Durham.
Smith, W. A.	Southwark.
Smith, W. C. T.	Liverpool.
Smith, W. D.	Northumberland (E.).
Smith, W. H.	Abercarn and District.
Smith, W. H.	Derby.
Smith, W. H.	London (W.).
Smith, W. H.	Walthamstow.
Smith, W. H.	South Shields.
Smith, W. H.	Rutland.
Smith, W. H.	Spennymoor.
Smith, W. H.	Hull.
Smith, W. I.	Winchester.
Smith, W. J.	West Lambeth.
Smith, W. J.	Deptford and Greenwich.
Smith, W. J.	London (W.).
Smith, W. J.	Winchester.
Smith, W. J.	Portsmouth.
Smith, W. J.	Staffordshire (N.).
Smith, W. J.	Dartford.
Smith, W. Phipps	Walsall.
Smith, W. T.	London (W.).
Smith, W. T.	Woolwich.
Smith, W. W.	East Ham.
Smitham, W.	Cornwall (W.).
Smoldon, W. L.	West Ham.
Smout, R.	Coseley.
Smout, S.	Coseley.
Smyth, P. C.	Finsbury, etc.
Smyth, T.	Northumberland (E.).
Smythem, G. F.	Wellingborough.
Snalam, F.	Preston District.
Snape, R.	Hyde.
Snee, E. A.	Deptford and Greenwich.
Snell, A. C.	Brecon.
Snell, D. H.	West Lambeth.
*Snell, J. E.	Coventry.
Snell, L.	Ipswich.
Snelling, H.	Norwich.
*Snook, A. G.	Barry.
Snow, G. H.	Liverpool.
Snow, W. R.	Nottingham.
Snowden, J.	Hartlepools.
Soames, B. C.	Deptford and Greenwich.
Soar, W. H.	Colchester, etc.
*Sockett, J. W.	Birmingham.
Soko, A. S.	London (E.).
Solomons, S.	London (E.).
Solloway, T.	Manchester.
Somerset, A.	Whitby.
Sommer, F.	Southgate.
Sommerton, H.	London (W.).
Soons, S. E.	Tottenham, etc.
Soper, J. E.	Windsor.

N.U.T. WAR RECORD

Name.	Association.
Soper, S. L.	Enfield.
Soper, S. R.	Exeter City.
Sopwith, R. E.	Tynemouth.
Sorton, H.	Manchester.
Souch, —.	Reading.
Soul, C. F.	Barking.
South, H. J.	Woolwich.
Southall, A. C.	Kingston and Surbiton.
Southall, S. R.	Newport (Mon.).
Southam, G. G.	Barking.
Southan, —.	Stourbridge.
Southcomb, G.	Liverpool.
Southcombe, S. P.	Bristol.
Southern, —.	Chester.
Southern, M.	Hexham, etc.
Southern, E.	Northwich.
Southern, J.	Northwich.
Southerst, J. R.	Finsbury, etc.
Southgate, A. C. J.	Aldershot.
Southgate, R. W.	Birmingham.
Southgate, H. E.	Cornwall (E.).
Southgate, S. C.	Enfield.
Southron, W.	Willesden.
Southwell, J.	Queensbury.
Southwick, C. T.	Richmond (Surrey).
Sowerbutts, F.	Nelson, Colne, etc.
Sowerbutts, T.	Manchester.
Sowerby, I.	Penrith.
Sowerby, J.	Blaydon.
Sowerby, W.	Leeds.
Sowter, S. J.	North Cleveland.
Spall, H.	Tynemouth.
Spanner, J. G. C.	Deptford and Greenwich.
Spanswick, E. F.	Watford.
Sparey, H.	Bath.
Spargo, S. J.	Stretford.
Sparham, E.	Derbyshire (E.).
Spark, J. W.	Stockton-on-Tees.
Sparke, C. H.	Canterbury.
Sparke, J. F.	Weardale.
Sparkes, H. B.	Coventry.
Sparkes, H. H.	Cockermouth.
Sparkes, H. W.	Brighton, etc.
Sparkes, R. H.	Darlington.
Sparks, J. F.	Gloucester.
Sparrow, F.	Hackney.
Sparrow, G. W.	Crewe.
Sparrow, R.	Gloucester.
Sparshott, E.	Acton.
Spary, C. H.	London (N.W.).
Spary, H. B.	London (N.W.).
Spaven, F. W.	Lewisham.
Spawls, W. E.	Hartlepools.
Speake, H. E.	Ebbw Vale.
Spearing, G. T.	Rotherham.
Speight, B.	Hackney.
Speight, J. C. L.	Wakefield.
Speight, S.	Bishop Auckland.
Spencer, —.	Isle of Wight.
Spencer, A.	Burnley.
*Spencer, A.	Bradford.
Spencer, A. G.	Dorset (W.).
Spencer, (Miss) C.	Norwich.
Spencer, C.	Nottingham.
Spencer, F.	Leigh.
Spencer, F.	Great Yarmouth.
Spencer, G.	Nelson, Colne, etc.
Spencer, G. W.	Doncaster.
Spencer, H. N.	Bridgend.
Spencer, J.	Jarrow.
*Spencer, L. K.	Hackney.
Spencer, P.	Sunderland.
Spencer, R. B.	Burnley.
Spencer, S.	Nottinghamshire (W.).
Spencer, V. L.	Burnley.
Spencer, W. E.	Leeds.
Spencer, W. J.	Brentford.
Spendlove, —.	Derby.
Spendlow, E.	Barnsley.
*Sperring, A. H.	Portsmouth.
Spicer, B.	London (E.).
Spicer, B. F.	Hackney.
Spickernell, D. L.	Birmingham.
Spikins, H. C.	Hull.
Spilman, G.	Darlington.
Spilman, J. H.	Isle of Wight.
Spilsbury, B.	East Lambeth.
*Spink, H. M.	Liverpool.
Spinks, —.	West Ham.
Spinks, J. T.	Pontypool.
Spinks, L. C.	West Ham.
Spinner, C. W.	Essex (Mid).
Sporne, —.	Ealing.
Sporne, R. W.	Northampton.
Spraggon, C. R.	Newcastle-on-Tyne.
Sprague, J.	Dartford.
Spreadbury, W. H.	West Lambeth.
Springbett, (Miss) A.	Barking.
Springbett, G. T.	Southwark.
Sproxton, A.	Stokesley.
Spruce, —.	Wallasey.
Spurgeon, T. G.	Enfield.
Squier, G. E.	Walthamstow.
Squire, A. R. G.	Leominster.
Squire, H. A.	Birmingham.
Squire, J.	Norfolk (S.).
Squire, J. P.	East Lambeth.
Squire, W. D.	London (W.).
Squire, M.	Great Yarmouth.
Stace, A. W.	Hornsey.
Stacey, A. F.	Devon (N.).
Stacey, G. W.	Bath.
Stacey, R. L.	East Lambeth.
Stacey, W.	Bristol.
Stacey, W. F.	Eastbourne.
Stacey, W. H.	Woolwich.
*Stackhouse, P. C.	Birmingham.
Stadden, T. C.	Finsbury, etc.
Stafford, G.	Bolton District.
Stafford, H.	Birmingham.
Stafford, L.	Rutland.
Stafford, R. H.	Sunderland.
Stafford, T. A.	Peterborough.
Stagg, C. E.	Glossop.
Stagg, E. A.	Somerset (S.E.).
Stainer, G. A.	Chiswick.
Stainer, J.	Portsmouth.
Staines, A.	Ilford.
Stainforth, G.	Hull.
Staley, B.	Matlock, etc.
Staley, W.	London (E.).
Stallard, G.	Walthamstow.
Stalley, O. G.	Bury St. Edmunds.
Stamford, F. O.	Enfield.
Stamp, H.	Retford.
Stampe, A. W.	Bristol.
Stampen, J. R.	Easington.
Stanbridge, J.	Willesden.

TEACHERS WHO JOINED THE FORCES

Name.	Association.
Stanbridge, W. J.	Willenhall.
Stanbury, H.	Westminster.
*Stancliffe, W.	Huddersfield.
Standen, J. W.	Tynemouth.
Standen, W.	Manchester.
Standish, F.	Belper and Crich.
Standley, A. T.	North Cleveland.
Standley, F. W.	East Ham.
Stanfield, P. E.	London (E.).
*Stanfield, T. W.	Crook.
Stanfield, W. A.	West Lambeth.
Stanger, J. H.	Tynemouth.
Staniforth, J. E.	Great Yarmouth.
Stanley, —.	West Ham.
Stanley, —.	Salford.
Stanley, A.	Southend-on-Sea.
Stanley, A. E.	West Ham.
Stanley, A. H.	Walsall.
Stanley, E...	Cannock.
Stanley, H. C.	Worksop.
Stanley, P. E.	Isle of Thanet.
Stanley, W.	Birmingham.
Stannard, A. M.	Tottenham, etc.
Stannard, G. W.	East Lambeth.
*Stanners, H.	Brentford.
Stansfield, H.	Manchester.
Stanton, J. B.	Birmingham.
Stanton, R. M.	London (W.).
Stanton, R. W.	Evesham.
Stanway, A. G.	Birmingham.
Stanway, G. E.	Worcester City.
Stanway, H. G.	Gillingham.
Stanworth, P.	Burnley.
Staples, A. G.	Daventry.
Staples S. A.	Doncaster.
Stapleton, C. G.	Surrey (N.W.).
Starkey, —.	Warwickshire (N.).
Starkie, T. A.	Pendle Forest.
Starling, —.	Hastings.
Staton, S.	Sheffield.
Staton, T. V.	Nottinghamshire (W.).
Staveley, F.	Wigan.
Stead, T.	Newcastle-on-Tyne.
Steadman, A.	Leicestershire (Mid).
Steains, L.	Sale.
Steane, F...	Coventry.
Steane, V.	Kent (W.).
Stears, F. R.	Isle of Wight.
Stebbings, J. W.	Hull.
Stedman, E.	Makerfield.
Stedman, J.	Tottenham etc.
Steeds, J. A.	Dorking.
Steel, H. H.	Bourne.
Steel, J.	Slough.
Steel, J. H.	Felling.
Steele, —.	Mexborough.
Steele, —.	Crewe.
*Steele, A.	South Shields.
Steele, A. E.	Spilsby.
Steele, D.	Staffordshire (N.).
Steele, F. A.	Surrey (N.W.).
Steele, J. R.	Chatham, etc.
Steen, J. H.	Chester.
Steeper, P. H.	Liverpool.
Steer, —.	Warminster.
Steer, H.	Rotherham.
Steger, J.	Bristol.
Stein, S. A.	London (E.).
Stembridge, R.	Bromley.
Stenhouse, W.	Bradford.
Stent, E. O.	Jersey.
Stephen, N.	Isle of Man.
Stephens, D. G.	Newport (Mon.).
Stephens, F. B.	Ilford.
Stephens, F. R.	East Lambeth.
Stephens, L.	Ogmore, etc.
Stephens, R. H.	Westminster.
Stephens, T.	Castleford, etc.
Stephens, W. A.	North Cleveland.
Stephens, W. H.	Nantyglo.
Stephens, W. T.	Rhymney Valley.
Stephenson, A.	Gateshead.
Stephenson, G.	Barnsley.
Stephenson, H. W.	Stourbridge.
Stephenson, J.	Makerfield.
Stephenson, J. C.	Crook.
Stephenson, J. L.	Leicester.
Stephenson, J. R.	South Shields.
Stephenson, W.	Crook.
Stephenson, W. G.	Hexham, etc.
Sternberg, V.	Leeds.
Sternwhite, W.	Darlington.
Steven, A...	West Ham.
Steven, A.	Hackney.
Stevens, —.	Ealing.
Stevens, —.	Reading.
Stevens, —.	Birmingham.
Stevens, (Miss) A.	Cornwall (Mid).
Stevens, A. G.	Teign and Dart.
Stevens, C. A.	London (N.W.).
Stevens, C. R.	Finsbury, etc.
Stevens, G. A.	Gillingham.
Stevens, H.	Birmingham.
Stevens, H. F.	Berkeley Vale.
Stevens, H. R.	Hull.
Stevens, H. W.	Southwark.
Stevens, J. H.	Norfolk (W.).
Stevens, J. L.	Hackney.
Stevens, W.	Brierley Hill, etc.
Stevens, W. H.	Isle of Thanet.
Stevens, W. T.	West Lambeth.
Stevenson (Miss)	West Ham.
Stevenson, A.	Nottingham.
Stevenson, A. L.	Southampton.
Stevenson, C.	Newark.
Stevenson, (Miss) D.	Grimsby.
Stevenson, F. N.	Nottingham.
Stevenson, F. S. D.	Liverpool.
Stevenson, G.	Sheffield.
*Stevenson, J. C.	Hackney.
Stevenson, J. F.	Kingston and Surbiton.
*Stevenson, W.	Makerfield.
Stevenson, W. F.	Isle of Man.
Steventon, C.	Surrey (N.W.).
Steventon, E. K.	Birmingham.
Steventon, G.	Surrey (N.W.).
Steventon, R. W.	Birmingham.
Stew, F. G.	Leek.
Stewardson, J. H.	Kettering.
Stewardson, S. C.	Liverpool.
Stewart, A.	Carlisle.
Stewart, J.	Romford, etc.
Stewart, J.	Hornsey.
Stewart, J.	Salford.
Stewart, M. C. K.	Bootle.
Stewart, W.	Liverpool.
Stewart, W.	Houghton-le-Spring.
Stewart, W.	Nottingham.

N.U.T. WAR RECORD

Name.	Association.	Name.	Association.
Stibbard, H. J.	Newark.	Strange, T.	East Lambeth.
Stickland, H. E.	Somerset (S.W.).	Strangeways, J. W.	Lancaster.
Stiff, F. E.	Birmingham.	Stratford, G.	Falmouth and Truro.
Stiff, S. T.	Birmingham.	Stratton, P. G.	Smethwick.
Stillman, P. H.	Maidstone.	Straughan, W. P.	Alnwick.
Stilwell, A. P.	Portsmouth.	Straw, A. G.	East Lambeth.
Stimson, H. F.	Peterborough.	Straw, J.	Ilkeston.
Stinson, C.	Birmingham.	*Straw, J. W.	Chester-le-Street.
Stirlands, —.	Birmingham.	Strawbridge, —.	Deptford and Greenwich.
Stirling, M.	Sunderland.	Strawston, C. W.	Finsbury, etc.
Stirrup, R.	Birkenhead.	Stream, E.	Grimsby.
Stirrup, T.	Warrington.	Streather, J. H.	West Lambeth.
Stirrup, W.	Northwich.	Street, —.	Portsmouth
Stoakes, W. E.	Portsmouth.	**Street, A.**	Doncaster.
Stobbs, H.	Chester-le-Street.	Street. H. W.	Castleford, etc.
Stock, E. J.	Birmingham.	*Streets, A. H.	Harrow.
Stock, W.	St. Helens.	Strelini, J. P.	Tottenham, etc.
Stockdale, W. H.	Blaydon.	**Stribling, L. J.**	Plymouth.
Stocker, W. J.	Hackney.	Strickland, H. W. H.	Tottenham, etc.
*Stockley, P. H.	Sheffield.	**Strickley, W.**	Birmingham.
Stockley, W. J.	Barking.	Stringer, —.	Petworth.
Stocks, A. E.	West Ham.	**Stringer, A. E.**	Ashton-under-Lyne.
Stocks, W.	York.	**Stringer, A. O.**	Atherton, etc.
Stockton, W. B.	Wilmslow.	Stringer, E. B.	Nottingham.
Stockwell, A. E.	Leeds.	Stringer, W.	Guernsey.
Stokeld, R. H.	Durham.	Strong, A. E.	London (E.).
Stokes, —.	East Dereham.	**Strong, G.**	Bath.
Stokes, A. R.	Colchester, etc.	Stroud, J. E. C.	Wimbledon.
Stokes, I.	Cannock.	Strudwick, A. E. V.	Birmingham.
Stokes, R. B.	Hackney.	Strudwick, E. A. V.	Bristol.
Stokoe, E.	Kingston and Surbiton.	Strutt, H. F.	Finsbury, etc.
Stone, —.	Ogmore, etc.	Stuart, C. W.	West Lambeth.
Stone, A. R.	Wallasey.	Stubbington, A. R.	Avon Valley.
Stone, B.	Surrey (N.W.).	**Stubbs, A. J.**	Tunbridge Wells.
Stone, E.	Southend-on-Sea.	*Stubbs, F. W. A.	Matlock and Bakewell.
Stone, E. G.	Hackney.	Stubbs, J.	Wellingborough.
Stone, F.	Alnwick.	Stubbs, J. A.	Southwark.
Stone, F. N.	West Lambeth.	Stubington, R. J.	Birmingham.
Stone, G.	West Lambeth.	Stuffins, A.	Hull.
Stone, H.	Plymouth.	Sturdy, A.	Finchley.
Stone, J. A.	Heathfield.	*Sturdy, O.	Cardiff.
Stone, J. C.	London (E.).	Sturgess, A. W.	Southwark.
Stone, J. H.	Birmingham.	Sturgis, C. R.	Bristol.
Stone, R. A.	Oxford District.	Sturton, C. F.	East Ham.
Stone, R. W. S.	Gloucestershire (S.).	**Sturtridge, F.**	Hackney.
Stone, W. B.	Worthing.	Stutchbury, C. R.	Guernsey.
Stone, W. F. E.	Plymouth.	**Styler, F. W.**	Birmingham.
Stones, J.	Leeds.	Styles, A. E.	Avon Valley.
Stones, J.	Leeds.	Styles, T. A.	Malvern.
Storer, H.	Tynemouth.	**Suddens, A. J.**	Coventry.
Storey, J.	Hull.	Suddens, H. T. s	Coventry.
*Storey, S. O.	Stockton-on-Tees.	Sudren, R.	Manchester.
Storrow, B.	Northumberland (E.).	Sudworth, J. B.	Blackburn.
Stotesbury, E.	Lewisham.	Suffield, W. L.	Sunderland.
Stott, E.	Nottingham.	Suffling, A. J.	Maidenhead.
Stott, G. D.	Hartlepools.	Sugden, —.	Bath.
Stott, J.	Bath.	Sugden, H.	Leeds.
Stott, J. E.	Manchester.	Sugden, J. D.	Huddersfield.
Stott, J. P.	Kent (W.).	**Sugden, T.**	Rotherham.
*Stott, L. R.	Morley.	Sugden, W.	Stockton on-Tees.
*Stott, S.	Huddersfield.	Suley, W. D.	Harrogate.
Stott, S. F.	Liverpool.	Sullivan, D.	Rhondda, etc.
Stow, E.	Bradford.	Sullivan, F.	Hackney.
Stow, F.	Deptford and Greenwich.	Sullivan, H.	Blackburn.
Stowell, F.	Nottingham.	*Sullivan, W. E.	Rhondda, etc.
Stowell, M. Q.	Isle of Man.	Summerbell, A.	Durham.
St. Paer, B. de	Leeds.	Summerlin, F. D.	Wellingborough.
Stradwick, —.	Birmingham.	**Summers, E. H.**	Portsmouth.
Strang, E. P.	Westminster.	Summers, H. E.	Rhondda, etc.

TEACHERS WHO JOINED THE FORCES

Name.	Association.	Name.	Association.
*Summers, O.	Birmingham.	Swinburne, E. M.	Nottingham.
Summers, O. A.	Solihull.	Swindale, J.	East Lambeth.
Summers, W.	Wakefield.	Swindale, R.	Birmingham.
Summersby, W.	East Lambeth.	Swindells, S.	Leeds.
Summerscales, —.	Swadlincote.	Swinden, B. C.	Huddersfield.
Summersgill, J.	Manchester.	Swithinbank, J. M.	Liverpool.
Summerton, L. H.	Smethwick.	*Swithinbank, W.	Liverpool.
Summerton, W.	Leamington.	Syddall, J.	Kendal.
Sumner, —.	Kidderminster.	Sykes, E. T.	Selby.
*Sumner, R.	Liverpool.	Sykes, F.	Willesden.
Sumner, W.	Chester.	Sykes, G. M.	Huddersfield.
Sunderland, H. H.	Bradford.	*Sykes, H. C.	Bradford.
Sunderland, P.	Halifax.	Sykes, P.	Dartford.
Surman, L. P.	Gloucester.	Sykes, P. E.	Norfolk (N.E.).
Surtees, W.	Vale of Derwent.	Sykes, R.	Manchester.
Sutcliffe, C. E. T.	Birmingham.	Sykes, V. H.	Hornsey.
Sutcliffe, F.	Roch Valley.	Sykes, W. E.	Mexborough.
Sutcliffe, F.	Halifax.	Symes, L. C.	Walthamstow.
Sutcliffe, F. M.	Huddersfield.	Symon, —.	Deptford and Greenwich.
Sutcliffe, G.	Blaydon.	Symonds, C. J.	Wolverhampton.
Sutcliffe, H.	Burnley.	Symonds, W. J.	Shrewsbury.
Sutcliffe, J.	Bradford.	Symons, W. P.	Cornwall (W.).
Sutcliffe, O.	Oldham.	Syson, W. B.	Nottingham.
Sutcliffe, R. H.	West Ham.		
Sutherland, C. C.	Sunderland.	Taberner, S.	Leicester.
Sutherst, —.	Heywood.	Taft, J. G.	Huntingdonshire.
Sutton, (Miss)	Erith.	Tait, F.	Newcastle-on-Tyne.
Sutton, A. J.	Teddington.	**Tait, H.**	Northumberland (E.).
Sutton, B. H.	Hull.	Tait, J. A.	Hackney.
Sutton, B. P.	Birmingham.	Tait, W.	Bradford.
Sutton, G. H.	Birmingham.	Talbot, A.	Derbyshire (E.).
Sutton, H. G.	Portsmouth.	Talbot, E. C.	Southwark.
Sutton, H. T.	Manchester.	**Talbot, R. S.**	Kidderminster.
Sutton, J. F.	Birmingham.	Talbot, W.	Birmingham.
Sutton, J. W.	Hull.	Talbutt, —.	Kettering.
Sutton, J. W.	Staffordshire (N.).	Talbutt, P. J.	Birmingham.
Sutton, P. E.	Northampton.	Tall, G. A.	Plymouth.
Sutton, R.	Sandbach.	Tallantire, J.	Manchester.
Sutton, W.	Liverpool.	Tallboys, H.	Romford, etc.
Sutton, W. H.	Evesham.	Tamblyn, H. C.	Cornwall (Mid).
Sutton, W. H.	Erewash Valley, etc.	Tams, A.	Staffordshire (N.).
Swaffer, J.	London (E.).	Tams, E. T.	London (E.).
Swaffield, W.	Dorset (W.).	Tandy, H.	Dorset (E.).
Swainson, F.	Sheffield.	Tanfield, C. R.	London (W.).
Swainson, H.	Sheffield.	Tangye, C. H. W.	East Lambeth.
Swainson, R.	Furness.	**Tanner, D. T.**	Rhondda, etc.
Swallow, E. L.	Huddersfield.	Tanner, F.	Gloucester.
Swallow, G. H.	Eccles.	*Tanner, O. B.	Rhymney Valley.
Swallow, H.	Surrey (N.W.)	Tanner, W. C.	East Lambeth.
Swallow, W.	Surrey (N.W.)	Taplin, F. H.	Birmingham.
Swalwell, E.	Uxbridge.	Tapp, F. C.	Hastings.
Swan, D.	Swindon.	Tapp, W. B.	Bradford.
Swan, S. H.	Tottenham, etc.	**Tarlton, R. T.**	West Ham.
Swancot, J.	Southend-on-Sea.	Tarn, W.	Crook.
Swann, —.	Cambridge Borough.	Tarran, J.	East Ham.
Swannack, F.	Worksop.	Tarrant, A.	Portsmouth.
Swanson, J. H.	Plymouth.	Tarrant, F. N.	Eastbourne.
Swash, L. A.	Cardiff.	Tasker, —.	Southport.
Swayne, A. B.	Swansea.	Tate, G. E.	Castleford, etc.
Sweeney, D.	Derby.	**Tate, J. M.**	Northumberland (N.).
*Sweeting, E.	Newport (Mon.).	Tathan, H.	Ilkeston.
Swift, A.	Wigan.	Tattersall, H. N.	Manchester.
Swift, A. C.	Mexborough.	Taunt, H. J.	East Ham.
Swift, E.	Croydon.	Taverner, D. T.	Wrexham.
Swift, H.	Manchester.	Taylerson, S. W.	Chester-le-Street.
Swift, H.	Sheffield.	**Taylforth, W.**	Manchester.
Swift, J. A.	Birmingham.	Taylor, —.	St. Helens.
Swift, W.	Peterborough.	Taylor, A.	Furness.
Swinbank, J.	Castleford, etc.	Taylor, A.	Ashton-under-Lyne.

N.U.T. WAR RECORD

Name.	Association.	Name.	Association.
Taylor, A.	Ilkeston.	Taylor, R.	Stroud.
Taylor, A.	Bristol.	*Taylor, R. A.	Manchester.
Taylor, A.	Walsall.	Taylor, R. B.	Wem.
Taylor, A.	Manchester.	Taylor, R. W.	Jersey.
Taylor, A.	Tipton.	Taylor, S.	Walsall.
Taylor, A.	Surrey (N.W.).	Taylor, S.	Preston Borough.
Taylor, A. G.	Southampton.	Taylor, S.	Newcastle-on-Tyne.
Taylor, A. J.	Hackney.	Taylor, S.	Gloucester.
Taylor, B. A.	Spalding, etc.	Taylor, S. F.	Gloucester.
Taylor, B. B.	Ipswich.	Taylor, S. S.	Coventry.
Taylor, B. G. A.	St. Albans.	Taylor, T. T.	Dorset (E.).
Taylor, B. W.	Staffordshire (N.).	Taylor, W.	Darlington.
Taylor, C.	Liverpool.	Taylor, W.	New Forest.
Taylor, C. A.	Stockport.	Taylor, W.	Spennymoor.
Taylor, C. B.	Wigan.	Taylor, W.	Preston Borough.
Taylor, C. E.	Surrey (N.W.).	Taylor, W. E.	Manchester.
Taylor, C. E.	Staines.	**Taylor, W. F.**	Lewisham.
Taylor, C. H.	London (W.).	Taylor, W. S.	Leeds.
Taylor, C. V.	Walsall.	Taylorson, T.	West Ham.
Taylor, C. W.	Hornsey.	**Tayton, W. E.**	Nuneaton.
Taylor, C. W. R.	West Lambeth.	Teager, W.	Yoxford.
Taylor, D.	West Ham.	Teagle, H. C.	London (E.).
Taylor, E.	Wimbledon.	Teague, —.	London (W.).
Taylor, E. G.	Harrow.	Teague, H. W.	Rowley Regis.
Taylor, F.	Durham.	Teale, A.	Rotherham.
Taylor, F. A.	Enfield.	**Teale, J. A.**	Wakefield.
Taylor, F. C.	Lewes.	**Teale, N. D.**	Leeds.
Taylor, F. C. W.	Blackpool.	Teall, A.	Hull.
Taylor, F. E.	Birmingham.	Teare, —.	Salford.
Taylor, F. E.	Hornsey.	Teare, H.	Worcester District.
Taylor, F. G.	Finsbury, etc.	Teare, J. G.	Liverpool.
Taylor, F. J.	Southwark.	Teasdale, E. A.	Middlesbrough.
Taylor, F. H. H.	Hackney.	Teasdale, G.	Blaydon.
Taylor, F. W.	Wolverhampton.	Teasdale, J. C.	Darlington.
Taylor, G. A.	Manchester.	Teasdale, J. H.	Sunderland.
Taylor, G. C.	Knutsford.	Teasel, H. W.	London (E.).
Taylor, G. E.	Cardiff.	Tebbutt, W.	East Dereham.
*Taylor, G. J.	West Ham.	Tee, H. E.	Romford, etc.
Taylor, H.	Ormskirk.	Teece, R.	Barnet.
Taylor, H.	Worsley.	Teesdale, (Miss)	Felling.
Taylor, H.	Leeds.	Teesdale, S.	York.
Taylor, H.	Hyndburn.	Telford, —.	Bromley.
Taylor, H.	Cardiff.	Telford, F.	Wallsend.
Taylor, H.	Wakefield.	*Telford, W. T.	Slough.
Taylor, H.	West Lambeth.	Telling, F. W.	Marlborough.
Taylor, H.	Hackney.	Telling, W.	Wimbledon.
Taylor, H. E.	Portsmouth.	Templar, E. A.	Brentford.
*Taylor, H. G.	Plymouth.	Temple, —.	Northumberland (E.).
Taylor, H. T. Meadows	Farnham.	Temple, H.	Ipswich.
Taylor, J.	Sittingbourne.	Templeton, —.	West Stanley.
Taylor, J.	Manchester.	**Temperton, B. S.**	Brighouse.
Taylor, J.	Hyndburn.	Tench, R. J.	Walsall.
Taylor, J.	Gainsborough.	Tennant, W. J.	Somerset (S.E.).
Taylor, J. G.	Carlisle.	**Terrell, V. J.**	Southwark.
Taylor, J. H.	Liverpool.	Terry, A.	Nottingham.
Taylor, J. H. W.	Leicester.	Terry, F.	Grimsby.
Taylor, J. J.	Blaydon.	Terry, H. G.	Maidstone.
Taylor, J. R. M.	Bournemouth.	Terry, J. C.	Blackpool.
*Taylor, J. W. A.	Liverpool.	Tewkesbury, G. E.	Rhondda, etc.
Taylor, (Miss) L.	West Ham.	**Thacker, A. C.**	Nuneaton.
Taylor, L.	London (W.).	Thacker, C. I.	Lowestoft.
Taylor, L.	Hertford.	Thackray, A. J.	Sunderland.
Taylor, L. R.	Grimsby.	Thackray, C.	Spen Valley.
Taylor, L. S.	Nottingham.	Theakston, A. E.	Beverley.
Taylor, M. J.	Walsall.	Thew, A.	West Lambeth.
Taylor, O. A.	London (W.).	Thewlis, (Miss) K.	Huddersfield.
Taylor, O. E.	Finsbury, etc.	Thexton, (Miss)	Derby.
Taylor, P.	Spennymoor.	Thexton, (Miss) B.	Barrow-in-Furness.
		Thexton, (Miss) H.M.	Barrow-in-Furness.

TEACHERS WHO JOINED THE FORCES

Name.	Association.	Name.	Association.
Third, H. M.	East Lambeth.	Thomas, J.	Rhondda, etc.
Thirkettle, A.	Brighton, etc.	Thomas, J. A.	Penygroes.
Thirsk, H. O.	Swadlincote.	Thomas, J. H.	Cwmtawe.
Thirlwall, H. A.	Finsbury, etc.	Thomas, J. G.	East Lambeth.
Thirtle, H. G.	West Lambeth.	**Thomas, J. G.**	London (E.).
Thoburn, W. D.	Nantyglo.	Thomas, J. G.	Cornwall (Mid).
Thoday, W. H.	West Lambeth.	Thomas, J. L.	Glamorgan (W.).
Thomas, —.	Bromley.	Thomas, J. P.	Lewisham.
Thomas, —.	London (N.W.).	Thomas, J. S.	Oxford.
Thomas, —.	Reading.	Thomas, J. W.	Swindon.
Thomas, —.	Birmingham.	Thomas, J. W.	Westminster.
Thomas, A.	Cardiganshire (N.).	Thomas, J. W.	Festiniog.
Thomas, A. A.	Staines.	Thomas, J. W.	Hackney.
Thomas, A. C.	Portsmouth.	Thomas, L.	Rhondda, etc.
Thomas, A. D.	Birmingham.	Thomas, L.	Merthyr Tydfil.
Thomas, A. E.	Smethwick.	Thomas, L. J.	Hackney.
Thomas, A. H.	Brighton, etc.	**Thomas, L. J.**	Glamorgan (W.).
Thomas, A. R.	Nottinghamshire (W.).	Thomas, L. M.	Nantyglo.
Thomas, A. S.	Bristol.	**Thomas, Morgan**	Glamorgan (Mid).
Thomas, A. V.	Gelligaer.	Thomas, M.	Nantyglo, etc.
Thomas, A. W.	Croydon.	Thomas, O.	Worthing.
Thomas, B.	Glamorgan (Mid).	Thomas, R.	London (E.).
Thomas, B.	Bristol.	Thomas, R. E.	Penarth.
*Thomas, B.	Mountain Ash.	Thomas, R. G.	Manchester.
Thomas, B.	Penarth.	Thomas, R. H.	Pembrokeshire (Mid).
*Thomas, B. S. B.	Pembrokeshire (S.)	*Thomas, S.	Todmorden.
Thomas, C.	Hackney.	Thomas, S. H.	Mountain Ash.
Thomas, C. J.	Pembrokeshire (Mid).	Thomas, S. M.	Oldham.
Thomas, D.	Rhondda, etc.	Thomas, S. O.	Merthyr Tydfil.
Thomas, D.	Colwyn Bay.	Thomas, S. R.	Cardiff.
Thomas, D. G.	Epsom, etc.	Thomas, S. W.	Portsmouth.
Thomas, D. H.	Glamorgan (W.).	*Thomas, T.	Aberdare.
Thomas, D. H.	Llanelly.	Thomas, T.	Rhondda, etc.
Thomas, D. O.	Barry.	Thomas, T. C.	Hertford.
Thomas, D. T.	West Lambeth.	Thomas, T. H.	Tottenham, etc.
Thomas, D. W.	Swansea.	**Thomas, T. J.**	Plymouth.
Thomas, E.	Carmarthen.	Thomas, T. M.	Cardiff.
Thomas, E.	Newport (Mon.).	Thomas, T. S.	Barry.
Thomas, E.	Penygroes.	Thomas, U.	Rhondda, etc.
*Thomas, E. B.	Mountain Ash.	Thomas, W.	Swansea.
Thomas, E. H.	Merthyr Tydfil.	Thomas, W.	Hartlepools.
Thomas, E. H.	Newport (Mon.).	**Thomas, W.**	Pembrokeshire (Mid).
Thomas, E. H.	Walthamstow.	Thomas, W.	Liverpool.
Thomas, E. T.	Abercarn.	Thomas, W.	Liverpool.
Thomas, E. W.	Aberdare.	Thomas, W.	West Lambeth.
Thomas, F.	Nottingham.	Thomas, W.	Forest of Dean.
Thomas, F. J.	Bodmin.	Thomas, W. A.	Rhondda, etc.
Thomas, F. L.	London (W.).	Thomas, W. C.	Bridgwater.
Thomas, F. W. J...	Woolwich.	Thomas, W. D.	Glamorgan (Mid).
Thomas, G.	Liverpool.	Thomas, W. D.	Rhondda, etc.
Thomas, G.	Westminster.	Thomas, W. E.	Ogmore, etc.
Thomas, G. A.	Anglesey.	Thomas, W. G.	Tredegar.
Thomas, G. B.	Portsmouth.	*Thomas, W. I.	Aberdare.
Thomas, G. R.	Glamorgan (W.).	Thomas, W. J.	Caerphilly.
Thomas, H.	Finsbury, etc.	Thomas, W. J.	Portsmouth.
Thomas, H.	Llanfair.	Thomas, W. K.	Launceston.
Thomas, H.	Mountain Ash.	Thomas, W. P.	Caerphilly.
*Thomas, H. E.	Bootle.	Thomas, W. R.	Rhondda, etc.
Thomas, H. H.	Millom.	Thomas, W. S.	Caerphilly.
Thomas, H. R.	Abertillery.	Thomason, G.	Chester.
Thomas, H. W.	Liverpool.	Thomason, J.	Gloucestershire (S.).
Thomas, I.	Mountain Ash.	Thomlinson, —.	St. Helens.
Thomas, I. G.	Mountain Ash.	Thompson, —.	Middlesbrough.
Thomas, I. J.	Rhondda, etc.	Thompson, —.	Doncaster.
Thomas, I. P.	Glamorgan (Mid).	Thompson, A.	Maldon.
Thomas, J.	Cornwall (W.).	Thompson, A. A.	Harrogate.
Thomas, J.	Llanelly.	Thompson, A. A.	Hackney.
Thomas, J.	Glamorgan (Mid).	Thompson, A. E.	Birmingham.
Thomas, J.	Lewes.	**Thompson, A. M.**	Derby.

N.U.T. WAR RECORD

Name.	Association.	Name.	Association.
Thompson, C.	Norfolk (N.W.).	Thorpe, B.	Leicester.
Thompson, C.	Eccles.	Thorpe, H.	Ipswich.
Thompson, C.	Wirral.	Thorpe, J.	Liverpool.
Thompson, E.	Gateshead.	Thorpe, T.	Barrow-in-Furness.
Thompson, E. F.	Portsmouth.	Thorpe, W. D.	Norwich.
Thompson, E. S.	Driffield, etc.	Threapleton, H.	Pudsey.
Thompson, E. Y.	Norfolk (N.W.).	Thrippleton,	
Thompson, F.	Burton-on-Trent.	(Miss) V.	Harrogate.
Thompson, F. A.	Wellingborough.	Thrower, J.	Norwich.
Thompson, F. C.	Lewisham.	Thrutchley, J. R. G.	Manchester.
Thompson, F. H.	Deptford and Greenwich.	Thurlow, B.	Sittingbourne, etc.
Thompson, O. H.	Smethwick.	Thurlow, F.	Colchester, etc.
Thompson, H.	West Stanley.	Thwaites, R.	Southgate.
Thompson, H.	Barrow-in-Furness.	**Thwaites, R.**	Carlisle.
Thompson, H.	Dewsbury, etc.	Ticehurst, A. G.	Southwark.
*Thompson, J.	Oldham.	**Tickle, A. B.**	Liverpool.
Thompson, J.	Manchester.	Tickle, A. P.	Bootle.
Thompson, J.	Hull.	Tickle, J. D.	Scarborough.
Thompson, J.	Liverpool.	Tickle, T. S.	Workington.
Thompson, J. A.	Kingston and Surbiton.	Tickner, —.	Bromley.
Thompson, J. G.	Newcastle-on-Tyne.	Tickner, H. J.	Willesden.
Thompson, J. R.	Durham.	*Tidswell, S.	Halifax.
Thompson, J. R.	Newcastle-on-Tyne.	Tidyman, P.	Cumberland (W.).
Thompson, J. S.	Birmingham.	Tiffin, J. J.	Sheffield.
Thompson, J. W.	Hull.	Tiley, —.	Gravesend.
Thompson, J. W.	Rhondda, etc.	Tillen, C. E. L.	Salisbury.
Thompson, L.	Chester.	Tilley, J.	Durham.
Thompson, L.	Birmingham.	Tillotson, G.	Nelson, Colne, etc.
Thompson, N.	Derby.	Tillson, W. H.	Stamford.
Thompson, N.	Spennymoor.	Tilney, H. G.	Pontypool.
Thompson, O.	Nottingham	Tilson, H. R.	Surrey (N.W.).
Thompson, P.	Castleford.	*Tilson, J. H.	Romford etc.
Thompson, P.	Blackburn.	Timbury, H.	Liverpool.
Thompson, R.	Northumberland (E.).	Timmins, A.	Birmingham.
Thompson, R. A.	Willesden.	Timmis, F.	Staffordshire (N.).
Thompson, R. M.	Spennymoor.	Timmons, T.	Manchester.
Thompson, T.	North Cleveland.	Timmons, T.	Wigan.
Thompson, T.	Northumberland (E.).	Timms, B.	Birmingham.
Thompson, T. N.	Doncaster.	Timms, B. P.	Birmingham.
Thompson, W.	Northumberland (E.).	Timms, W.	Evesham.
Thompson, W.	London (W.).	**Timpson, W. M.**	London (E.).
Thompson, W.	Liverpool.	**Tindale, E.**	West Ham.
Thompson, W.	Sunderland.	Tindall, (Miss) E. M.	Huddersfield.
Thompson, W. J.	Hackney.	Tindle, G.	Vale of Derwent.
Thompson, W. W.	Hackney.	Tindle, G. D.	Bournemouth.
Thomson, (Miss)	Erith.	**Tindle, J. W.**	Bradford.
Thomson, J.	Coalville.	Tingle, J. A.	Sheffield.
Thomson, (Miss) M.	Liverpool.	Tingle, R. L. A.	Hackney.
Thomson, W.	Finsbury, etc.	Tingle, T.	Ilkeston.
Thorn, H.	Lowestoft.	Tinker, (Miss) N.	Manchester.
Thorn, H. B.	Fairford.	Tinnswood, L. B.	London (N.W.).
Thorne, G.	Penistone.	Tipler, A. J.	Willesden.
Thorneloe, H. P.	Smethwick.	Tipler, W.	Watford.
Thornhill, F.	Liverpool.	Tipney, F.	Bristol.
Thornley, M.	Roch Valley.	Tipper, L. M.	West Lambeth.
Thornton, —.	Leyton.	Tippett, P. J.	Plymouth.
Thornton, —.	Doncaster.	Tipping, (Miss) A.	Worcester City.
Thornton, C. A.	Chester-le-Street.	Tipping, S.	Heywood.
Thornton, D. C.	Grimsby.	Tipping, S. L.	Liverpool.
Thornton, F. H.	St. Helens.	Tipton, C. H.	Gloucestershire (S.).
Thornton, H.	Great Yarmouth.	Tissington, —.	Finsbury, etc.
Thornton, H. D.	Huddersfield.	**Tite, K. G. W.**	Nuneaton.
Thornton, H. T.	London (N.W.).	Titheradge, J. W.	Lewes.
Thornton, H. V.	London (E.).	*Titley, W.	Newcastle-on-Tyne.
Thornton, R.	Bradford.	Titmous, H.	Surrey (N.W.).
Thornton, S.	Castleford.	Titmus, C.	Leyton.
Thornton, W.	Westminster.	Todd, A.	Hartlepools.
Thorp, A.	Hull.	Todd, A.	Leeds.
Thorp, H. J.	East Lambeth.	Todd, C. W. E.	Lowestoft.

TEACHERS WHO JOINED THE FORCES

Name.	Association.
Todd, E.	Sunderland.
Todd, E. H.	Enfield.
Todd, E. T.	Hull.
Todd, F. W.	Barnsley.
Todd, H. C.	Manchester.
Todd, R. M.	Hartlepools.
Todds, W.	East Lambeth.
Todman, G. V.	London (N.W.).
Toft, J.	Salford.
Tolfree, W. N.	Edmonton.
Toll, J. E.	Bellingham.
Toll, P. E. S.	Harrow.
Tolson, E.	Bradford.
Tolson, H.	Liverpool.
Tom, T. H.	Falmouth and Truro.
Tomalin, W. C.	Northampton.
Tomkin, W. E.	Finsbury, etc.
Tomkins, E.	Hull.
Tomkins, T. F.	Stretford.
Tomkins, W. F.	Litherland, etc.
Tomkinson, W. I.	St. Helens.
Tomlin, E.	Ealing.
Tomlinson, —.	Birmingham.
Tomlinson, —.	Doncaster.
*Tomlinson, A.	Willesden.
Tomlinson, H.	Derbyshire (E.).
Tomlinson, J. L.	Malton.
Tomlinson, P.	Liverpool.
Tomlinson, T. P.	Goole.
Tompkins, A. G.	Edmonton.
Tompkins, P. E.	Northants.
Tompkinson, P. A.	Bedford Borough.
Tompkinson, P. J.	Middleton.
Tompson, (Miss) D.	Leicester.
Tompson, S.	Portsmouth.
Toms, P. H.	Northampton.
Toms, W.	Coventry.
Tonge, H.	Bolton Borough.
Tongue, A. L.	Kingston and Surbiton.
Tongue, J. W. C.	Birmingham.
Tongue, W.	Horsham, etc.
Tonkin, A. O.	Isle of Man.
Tonkin, C. B.	Plymouth.
Tonkin, E. R.	Plymouth.
Tonkin, W.	Woolwich.
Tonkins, A.	Cirencester, etc.
Tonkinson, (Miss) E.	Sunderland.
Tonks, —.	Salford.
Toolan, J.	Bootle.
Toole, O.	Bromley.
Toombs, A. E.	Twickenham.
Toomer, W.	Southampton.
Toomey, A. L.	North Cleveland.
Toon, A.	Nottingham.
Toon, H. R.	Nottingham.
Toop, S. A.	Aldershot.
Tootill, W. H.	Bolton District.
Topham, B.	Sheffield.
Topley, S. M.	Maryport.
Topliss, B.	Sheffield.
Topp, J.	Salford.
Topping, R. B.	Hull.
Topsfield, F. T.	Southend-on-Sea.
Torr, R. E.	Isle of Man.
Torrance, —.	St. Helens.
Torrance, S.	Coventry.
*Tossell, I. G.	St. Davids.
Tottle, B.	Hornsey.
Tottman, R. R.	East Ham.
Tovey, W. J.	Watford.
Towers, J.	London (E.).
Towers, J.	Durham.
Towler, —.	East Dereham.
Towler, E. W. J.	Bridgwater.
Towler, F.	Finsbury, etc.
Towning, J. R.	Bourne.
Townley, J. M.	Chatham, etc.
Townsend, —.	Gravesend.
Townsend, A. G. C.	Tottenham, etc.
Townsend, E.	Spalding, etc.
Townsend, F. G.	Pendle Forest.
*Townsend, H. E. R.	Sutton Coldfield.
Townsend, H. S.	Dorset (E.).
Townsend, J. E.	West Lambeth.
Townsend, J. W	Sheffield.
Townsend, R.	Fleetwood.
Townson, F.	London (W.).
Toyer, A. M.	Whitby.
Toyer, V. O.	East Cleveland.
Toyer, W. B.	Chester-le-Street.
Toyne, J. E.	Derbyshire (E.).
Tozer, E. V.	Worcester City.
Tozer, V.	Teign and Dart.
Trace, R.	Hackney.
Trahearn, W.	Kidderminster.
Traice, A.	Birmingham.
Train, G. P.	Ilford.
Train, H.	Leominster.
Trainer, W. L.	Northumberland (N.).
Tranter, H. H.	Wolverhampton.
Tranter, J. H.	Deal, etc.
Trask, S. R.	Deptford and Greenwich.
Trasler, G. P.	Hackney.
Travers, G.	Manchester.
Travers, R. G.	West Lambeth.
Treble, R. J.	Petersfield.
Tregonning, C.	Cornwall (Mid).
Treloar, A. B.	Cornwall (Mid).
Treloar, L.	Cornwall (W.).
Tremain, J. L.	Walthamstow.
Tremeer, F. H.	London (N.W.).
Tremeer, S. C.	London (W.).
Tremlett, E.	Chester.
Tremlett, G.	Chester.
Treneer, H.	Exeter City.
Treneer, H. E.	Cornwall (W.).
Trenholme, J.	Wakefield.
Trent, —.	Ipswich.
Trerise, W. T. L.	Cornwall (Mid).
Tressider, J.	Falmouth and Truro.
Trethewey, —.	Doncaster.
Trevaskis, J.	West Bromwich, etc.
Trevenen, G. H.	Westminster.
Trevor, —.	Stafford.
Trevor, A.	Crook.
Trevor, B. G.	Northumberland (S.).
Trevor, J.	Birmingham.
Trew, H.	Bath.
Trewick, R.	Barnard Castle.
Trewn, F. W.	Birmingham.
Trezise, J. E.	Hackney.
Trickett, W. E.	Flint County.
Triffin, J. J.	Sheffield.
Trigg (Miss)	Northumberland (E.).
*Trigg, G.	Barkston Ash.
Trigg, W. S.	Caerphilly.
Triggs, F. T.	Portsmouth.
Trim, H. W.	Dorking.

N.U.T. WAR RECORD

Name.	Association.	Name.	Association.
Trinick, W.	Plymouth.	Turner, E.	Walthamstow.
Tripp, E.	Luton.	Turner, E. E.	Cardiff.
Tripp, H.	Southgate.	Turner, E. J.	Cornwall (Mid).
Tripp, R. H.	Liverpool.	Turner, F.	Bedford.
Trivett, A.	Lewisham.	Turner, F.	Plymouth.
Troakes, W. J.	Newport (Mon.).	Turner, F.	Barnsley.
Trodd, J. W.	Isle of Wight.	Turner, F. H.	Manchester.
Troke, P. A.	Worcester City.	Turner, G.	Derby (E.).
Trollope, —.	Willesden.	Turner, G. F.	Lincoln.
Tromans, H.	Rowley Regis.	Turner, G. H.	Berkeley Vale.
Trotter, W. J. B.	Chichester.	Turner, G. H.	Plymouth.
Trowell, A. A.	Lincoln.	Turner, H.	Cannock.
Trubody, R.	Bristol.	Turner, H.	Enfield.
Truelove, C. W.	West Ham.	Turner, H.	Hornsey.
Trueman, C. T.	Newcastle-on-Tyne.	Turner, H. J.	Nottingham.
Truman, T. C.	Hackney.	Turner, J.	Hackney.
Truman, W. C.	West Lambeth.	Turner, J.	Rossendale.
Trump, C. H.	Bristol.	*Turner, J.	Manchester.
*Trump, R. W.	Birmingham.	Turner, J. T.	Southend-on-Sea.
Truscott, R.	Falmouth and Truro.	Turner, L.	Coventry.
Trussell, T.	Ilford.	Turner, L.	Leeds.
Trustram, W. P.	Brighton, etc.	Turner, L.	Derby.
Tubb, C.	Deptford and Greenwich.	Turner, L. B.	Tottenham, etc.
Tubb, C.	Surrey (N.W.).	Turner, R.	Barnsley.
Tubby, P. E.	Newport Pagnell.	Turner, S. A.	Blackpool.
Tuck, —.	Dover.	*Turner, T.	Finchley.
Tucker, —.	East Lambeth.	Turner, T. G.	Lincoln.
Tucker, —.	Deptford and Greenwich.	Turner, T. H.	Kendal.
Tucker, A.	Gillingham.	Turner, T. W.	Tottenham, etc.
Tucker, A. J.	Newark.	Turner, W.	Stratford-on-Avon.
Tucker, E. W.	Itchen.	Turner, W.	Hartlepools.
Tucker, H. E.	Bristol.	Turner, W. E.	Swadlincote.
Tucker, J. F.	Walthamstow.	Turner, W. H.	Willenhall.
Tucker, L.	Liverpool.	Turner, W. J.	West Lambeth.
Tucker, L. W.	Enfield.	Turner, W. J.	Teign and Dart.
Tucker, P.	Wimbledon.	Turner, W. L. T.	West Ham.
Tucker, W. A.	London (E.).	Turney, W.	West Ham.
Tue, G. A.	Oxford.	Turpin, C.	Sunderland.
Tuer, R. S.	Woolwich.	Turpin, S.	Jersey.
Tuffin, —.	Newport (Mon.).	Tustin, H.	Northumberland (S.).
Tuffin, E. A.	Teddington.	Tutt, H. R.	Croydon.
Tufnell, —.	Wimbledon.	Tuttell, A. G.	Birmingham.
Tuite, P.	Portsmouth.	Tweddle, J.	Crook.
Tuite, W.	Portsmouth.	Tweddle, J. H.	Newcastle-on-Tyne.
Tuke, L. A.	Liverpool.	Tweddle, R.	Blaydon.
Tuke, S. W.	Peterborough.	Tweedale, —.	Salford.
Tully, F.	Bishop Auckland.	*Tweedie, D. S.	Sunderland.
Tully, W. J.	Oxfordshire (S.).	Tweedie, J.	Sunderland.
Tunnicliffe, A.	Birmingham.	Twigg, —.	Wilmslow.
Tunnicliffe, B.	Swadlincote.	Twigg, G. A.	Harrogate.
Tunnicliffe, H.	Nidderdale.	Twigg, S.	Ashbourne.
Tunstall, J.	Yoxford.	Twine, W.	Portsmouth.
Turk, J. W.	Chester-le-Street.	Twiney, W. O.	Rhondda, etc.
Turnage, R. G.	Hackney.	Twiselton, C. H.	Leicester.
Turnbull, C. H.	Wimbledon.	Twyman, A.	Dover.
Turnbull, E.	Blaydon.	Twyman, F. J.	Colchester, etc.
Turnbull, J. J.	Bellingham.	Tyas, F. P.	Sheffield.
Turner, —.	Sale.	Tyas, W. N.	Rotherham.
Turner, —.	Warwick.	Tye, W.	Rochdale.
Turner, —.	Ipswich.	Tyldesley, W.	Atherton, etc.
Turner, —.	Reading.	Tyler, C.	Liverpool.
Turner, A.	Spennymoor.	Tyler, C. E.	Plymouth.
Turner, A. E.	Durham.	Tyler, E. C.	Bristol.
Turner, A. E.	Gloucestershire (S.).	**Tyler, H. J.**	Swansea.
Turner, A. L.	Penistone.	Tyler, J.	Gelligaer.
*Turner, A. T.	West Ham.	Tyler, J. T. W.	Leicester.
Turner, (Miss) B. C.	Cardiff.	Tyler, V.	Surrey (N.W.).
Turner, C.	Reading.	Tymms, S. W.	Spennymoor.
Turner, D.	Forest of Dean.	Tyrrell, —.	Buxton.

TEACHERS WHO JOINED THE FORCES

Name.	Association.
Tyson, E.	Nantwich.
Tyson, J. J.	Staffordshire (N.).
Tyson, R.	Bournemouth.
Tyson, W. H.	Easington.
Tyzzer, A.	Bodmin.
Udall, M. V.	Staffordshire (N.).
Uden, W.	Southwark.
Uglow, H.	Woolwich.
Uglow, S.	Gloucestershire (S.).
Umbers, J. L.	Birmingham.
Umpley, O.	Sheffield.
Underhay, C. J.	Portsmouth.
Underhill, R. A.	Exeter District.
Underwood, A. J.	Teddington.
Underwood, F.	Ilkeston.
Underwood, P. A.	Manchester.
Unwin, A.	Nottingham.
Unwin, G. E.	Sheffield.
Unwin, M.	Derby (E.).
Upham, W. L.	London (W.).
Upton, —.	Reading.
Upton, E. A.	St. Albans.
Upton, F. R.	Hull.
Upton, J. S.	Manchester.
Ure, W.	Gateshead.
Urquhart, G. S.	Hackney.
Urwin, C. P.	West Stanley.
Urwin, H.	Northumberland (S.).
Usher, R. E.	Westminster.
Utting, A. V.	Birmingham.
Uttley, C. H.	Sheffield.
Vagg, E. G.	Swansea.
Valentine, O. K.	Manchester.
Valentine, W. H.	Farnworth.
Vallow, P.	Grimsby.
Vallance, R. H.	Birmingham.
Vandenbergh, J. T.	Tottenham, etc.
Vanderhook, S.	London (W.).
Van Derplank, —.	Newport (Mon.).
Vanes, E. A.	Birmingham.
Vann, H.	Leicester.
Vanner, F.	London (W.).
Vanstone, —.	Teign and Dart.
Vanstone, E.	Devon (Mid.).
Vanstone, H. W.	Bath.
Vardy, T.	Penistone.
*Vardy, W. H.	Mansfield.
Varley, —.	Hitchin.
Varley, A. H.	Sunderland.
Varley, F.	Leeds.
*Varley, W.	York.
Varley, W. H.	Leeds.
Varney, —.	Derby.
Varney, W. R.	Sheffield.
Varney, W. V.	East Lambeth.
Vasey, H. D.	East Ham.
Vasey, W. W.	Hartlepools.
*Vassiere, H. J.	Walthamstow.
Vaughan, —.	Rotherham.
Vaughan, G.	Tredegar.
Vaughan, H.	Birmingham.
Vaughan, J.	Worsley, etc.
*Vaughan, J. D.	Bradford.
Vaughan, S.	Glamorgan (Mid).
Vaughan, S. P.	East Lambeth.
Vaughan, W. G.	Bradford.
Vavey, H.	Blackburn.
Veale, —.	Bath.
Veasey, K. F.	Folkestone.
Veater, H. J.	Pocklington.
Veevers, W.	Northumberland (N.).
Veitch, E.	Carlisle.
Veitch, R. W.	Castleford, etc.
Venables, (Miss)	Mansfield Borough.
Venn, —.	Reading.
Venner, B.	Staines.
Venner, T. E.	Sunderland.
Venness, E.	West Lambeth.
Venning, H.	East Lambeth.
Vernon, G. C.	Hackney.
Vernon, N.	Manchester.
Verney, S. H.	Gloucestershire (N.).
Verrall, A.	East Lambeth.
Verrall, H. G.	West Lambeth.
Verrier, F. G.	Finsbury, etc.
Verroll, —.	Newbury.
Veysey, S.	Hertford.
Vicarage, F.	Tredegar.
Vicars, C. R.	Nottingham.
Viccars, H. W.	Leicester.
Vickers, A. D. L.	Hartlepools.
Vickers, F. F.	Shropshire (E.)
Vickers, H. J.	Reading.
Vickery, L. E.	Birmingham.
*Vincent, H. C.	Bootle.
Vincent, P.	Woolwich.
Vincent, R.	Leyton.
Vincett, —.	Hastings.
Vine, A. M.	Portsmouth.
Vine, H.	Lewisham.
Vinen, G.	Leek.
*Viner, H.	Liverpool.
Viney, J.	Dorking.
Vint, T.	Chester-le-Street.
Virgo, S. O.	Tottenham, etc.
Vivash, J. B.	Bromley.
Vivey, F.	Southampton.
Voice, —.	Reading.
Voisin, A. J.	Woolwich.
Vokes, B.	Surrey (N.W.).
Vollum, L.	Scarborough.
Waddington, G.	Spen Valley.
Waddington, G. E.	Carlisle.
Waddington, J. W.	Spennymoor.
Waddington, R. J.	Liverpool.
Wade, A. A.	Bishop Auckland.
Wade, E. G.	Woolwich.
Wade, W.	Northumberland (S.).
Wade, W.	West Lambeth.
Wade, W. A.	Birmingham.
Wade, W. C.	Eccles.
Wadge, H.	Launceston.
Wadham, J. B.	Tottenham, etc.
Wadsworth, —.	West Ham.
Wadsworth, J. H.	Barkston Ash.
Wadsworth, R. A. J.	Bedford Borough.
Wadsworth, T.	Howden.
Wager, B. E. S.	Portsmouth.
Wager, C. H.	Sunderland.
Wager, H. W.	Gloucester.
Wagborn, —.	Tottenham, etc.
Wagstaffe, F.	Barnsley.
Wagstaffe, W. J.	West Lambeth.
Wagland, F.	Bristol.
Waidson, —.	Walsall.
Waight, R.	Bexhill.

N.U.T. WAR RECORD

Name.	Association.	Name.	Association.
Wailing, C. G.	Gillingham.	Walker, H.	Northampton.
Wain, (Miss) B.	Leicester.	Walker, H. T.	West Ham.
Wain, C. J.	Staffordshire (N.).	Walker, J.	Bradford.
Wain, H. D.	Rotherham.	Walker, J. A.	London (E.).
Waine, H.	Tynemouth.	**Walker, J. A.**	London (W.).
Waine, S. C.	Dartford.	**Walker, J. C.**	Leeds.
Wainwright, —.	Redditch.	Walker, J. H.	East Lambeth.
Wainwright, —.	Hinckley.	Walker, L.	Erewash Valley, etc.
Wainwright, E.	Lincoln.	Walker, P.	Durham.
Wainwright, F.	Bromsgrove.	Walker, P. R.	Solihull.
Wait, A. T.	Wirral.	Walker, R.	Barrow-in-Furness.
Waite, A. O.	East Lambeth.	Walker, R.	London (N.W.).
Waite, A. W.	Birmingham.	Walker, R.	Spennymoor.
Waite, E.	Barry.	Walker, R.	Ashton and District.
Waite, F. C.	Dorset (S.).	Walker, S.	Manchester.
Waite, H. H.	Manchester.	Walker, W. E.	Sunderland.
Waite, T. C.	Bellingham.	Walker, W. H.	Skipton.
Waites, R.	Middlesbrough.	**Walker, W. H.**	Epsom, etc.
Wake, R.	Castleford, etc.	Wall, C. E.	West Lambeth.
*Wake, T. H.	Newcastle-on-Tyne.	Wall, (Miss) F.	London (N.W.).
Wakefield, E.	Mansfield Borough.	Wall, J. A.	West Lambeth.
Wakefield, H.	Manchester.	Wall, R.	Buxton.
Wakefield, W. R.	Gloucester.	Wall, T. D.	Newcastle-on-Tyne.
Wakeley, J.	Faversham.	Wallace, C. D.	Rotherham.
Wakeley, H. E.	Plymouth.	**Wallace, D. S.**	Tynemouth.
Wakerley, H.	Birmingham.	Wallace, J. T.	Bishop's Stortford.
Walden, A.	Knutsford.	Wallace, S. H.	Workington.
Walden, H.	Norfolk (W.).	*Wallace, T.	Northumberland (S.).
Waldrom, J.	Leicestershire (Mid)	Wallace, W. J.	East Cleveland.
Waldron, E.	Leominster.	Waller, J.	Durham.
Waldron, H.	Portsmouth.	**Waller, J. G.**	Surrey (N.W.).
Waldron, P.	Finsbury, etc.	Waller, S. H.	Sheffield.
Waldron, R. L.	Ashford.	Walling, L. E.	Woolwich.
Wale, R. R.	Woolwich.	Walling, S. A.	Plymouth.
Wale, S. J.	Hackney.	Wallington, —.	Tottenham, etc.
Wales, F. L.	Lowestoft.	Wallington, F.	High Wycombe.
Walford, E. R.	Romford, etc.	Wallington, F. G.	West Lambeth.
Walford, H.	Southend-on-Sea.	Wallis, A. W.	Tottenham, etc.
Walkden, —.	Birmingham.	Wallis, C. F.	Weald of Kent.
Walkem, C.	Woolwich.	Wallis, J.	Liverpool.
Walker, —.	Liverpool.	Wallis, J.	Woolwich.
Walker, —.	Leicester.	Wallis, L. F.	Finchley.
Walker, A.	Buxton.	Walls, A. G.	Woolwich.
Walker, A.	Leeds.	Walls, E. W.	East Lambeth.
Walker, A.	West Ham.	Wallwork, J. H.	Worsley, etc.
Walker, A. F.	Newark.	Wallwork, R. E.	Manchester.
Walker, A. J. N.	Southend-on-Sea.	Walmsley, —.	Boston.
Walker, B. G.	Wolverhampton.	**Walmsley, E. L.**	Oldham.
Walker, C.	Bury.	Walmsley, G. H.	Worsley.
Walker, C.	Hull.	Walmsley, W.	Manchester.
Walker, E.	Crewe.	Walpole, D. W.	Great Yarmouth.
Walker, E.	Northants.	Walsh, —.	St. Helens.
Walker, E. G.	Manchester.	*Walsh, A.	Nelson, Colne, etc.
Walker, E. J.	Twickenham.	Walsh, C. E.	East Lambeth.
Walker, F.	Lincoln.	*Walsh, E.	South Shields.
Walker, F.	Hull.	*Walsh, F.	South Shields.
Walker, F.	Darlington.	Walsh, G.	Manchester.
Walker, F. B.	Carlisle.	Walsh, H.	Castleford, etc.
Walker, F. J.	London (N.W.).	Walsh, J. E.	Middlesbrough.
Walker, F. K.	Staffordshire (N.).	Walsh, M.	London (E.).
Walker, G.	Carlisle.	Walsh, M.	East Lambeth.
Walker, G. F.	Twickenham.	Walsh, P. J.	Plymouth.
Walker, G. H.	West Lambeth.	Walsh, T. F.	Easington.
Walker, G. S.	Spilsby.	Walsham, C. H.	Hackney.
Walker, H.	Bolton Borough.	Walshe, C.	London (N.W.).
Walker, H.	Hinckley.	Walter, A. C.	Buckingham.
Walker, H.	London (E.).	Walter, H. J. C.	Maryport.
Walker, H.	Willesden.	Walter, W. E.	Brighton, etc.
Walker, H.	Darlington.	Walter, W. G.	London (E.).

TEACHERS WHO JOINED THE FORCES

Name.	Association.	Name.	Association.
Walter, W. H. S.	Eastbourne.	Warden, A. J.	Leicester.
Walters, —.	Itchen.	Wardle, C. R.	Nottinghamshire (W.).
Walters, F.	London (W.).	**Wardle, J. G.**	Hull.
Walters, H.	West Bromwich, etc.	**Wardley, M. E.**	East Lambeth.
Walters, J.	Caerphilly.	Wardman, O.	London (W.).
Walters, J. G.	London (N.W.).	Ware, —.	Canterbury.
Walters, J. V.	Chester.	Ware, E. A.	Bristol.
Walters, T.	Wolverhampton.	Ware, J. H.	West Lambeth.
Walters, T. H.	Wolverhampton.	Wareham, C. J.	Coventry.
Walters, T. W.	Rhondda, etc.	**Wareham, F. W.**	Westminster.
Walters, V. T.	Uxbridge.	Wareham, T. W.	Birmingham.
Walters, W. E.	Glamorgan (W.).	Waring, —.	Salford.
Walton, A.	Durham.	Waring, F.	Windermere.
Walton, A. E.	Colchester, etc.	Waring, F. G.	London (E.).
Walton, G.	Stockton-on-Tees.	**Waring, G.**	York.
Walton, G. A.	Easington.	Warne, —.	Willesden.
Walton, H.	Vale of Derwent.	**Warne, A. H.**	Brighton, etc.
Walton, J.	Bingley.	Warner, A. C.	Grantham.
Walton, J.	West Ham.	Warner, E. F.	West Lambeth.
Walton, J. T.	Portsmouth.	Warner, H.	Finsbury, etc.
Walton, R.	Southport.	**Warner, P. S.**	Exeter City.
Walton, S.	Durham.	Warner, W.	Coventry.
Walton, S.	Bishop Auckland.	Warr, —.	Wimbledon.
Walton, T.	Kiveton Park.	Warr, H. F.	Leighton Buzzard.
Walton, W.	Stockport.	Warrell, C.	Flint County.
Wanless, C. O. E.	Durham (N.E.).	Warren, —.	Kingston and Surbiton.
Warburton, H.	Manchester.	Warren, —.	Ipswich.
Warburton, W. H.	Staffordshire (N.).	**Warren, A. F.**	London (E.).
Warby, A. S.	Norwich.	**Warren, A. J. T.**	Worcester District.
Ward, —.	Salford.	Warren, A. R.	Portsmouth.
Ward, A.	Nottingham.	Warren, F.	Castleford, etc.
Ward, A.	Portsmouth.	Warren, F. C.	West Lambeth.
Ward, A. B.	Leeds.	**Warren, H.**	London (W.).
Ward, A. J.	East Lambeth.	Warren, M. W.	Chipping Norton.
Ward, A. J.	Plymouth.	Warren, T. A.	Westminster.
Ward, B.	Liverpool.	*Warren, W. N.	Barry.
Ward, E.	Birmingham.	**Warren, W. S.**	Kiveton Park.
Ward, E.	Huddersfield.	**Warriner, T. A. L.**	Birmingham.
Ward, E.	West Ham.	Warring, S. J.	Slough.
Ward, E.	Walthamstow.	Warrington, L. H.	Nottingham.
Ward, E. J.	Tottenham, etc.	Warwick, —.	Hebburn.
Ward, E. M. (Miss)	South Shields.	Warwick, J. A.	Newcastle-on-Tyne.
Ward, E. S.	Birmingham.	Wash, W.	Barnard Castle.
Ward, F.	Barnsley.	Washington, S. B.	Manchester.
Ward, F.	Ealing.	Wasson, C.	Easington.
Ward, F.	Hull.	Waterer, G.	West Lambeth.
Ward, G.	Somerset (N.).	Waterhouse, H.	Leeds.
Ward, G.	Loughborough.	Waterhouse, J. L.	Makerfield.
Ward (Miss) H.	Hartlepools.	**Waterland, D.**	West Lambeth.
Ward, H. B.	Norwich.	Waterman, W. C.	Hackney.
Ward, H. J.	Norwich.	Waters, —.	West Ham.
Ward, J. S.	Huddersfield.	Waters, A. J.	East Ham.
Ward, (Miss) M.	Southend-on-Sea.	*Waters, H. G.	York.
Ward, M.	Derbyshire (E.).	Waters, L.	Maidstone.
Ward, P. W.	Oldbury.	Waterworth, J. N.	Wigan.
Ward, R.	Bolton Borough.	Waterworth, T. P.	West Lambeth.
Ward, R.	West Ham.	**Watkin, A. C.**	Birmingham.
Ward, R. H. V.	Staffordshire (N.).	Watkin, N.	Newtown.
Ward R. T.	Birmingham.	Watkin, W.	Durham.
Ward, T.	South Shields.	Watkins, A. E.	Bristol.
Ward, T.	Darlington.	Watkins, C.	Birkenhead.
Ward, T.	Hexham, etc.	Watkins, D. J.	Llandovery, etc.
Ward, T.	Huddersfield.	Watkins, F.	Birmingham.
Ward, W.	Ingleborough.	Watkins, H.	East Lambeth.
Ward, W.	Hull.	Watkins, J. E.	Glamorgan (W.).
*Ward, W. C. J.	Finchley.	**Watkins, T. G.**	Leeds.
*Ward, W. P.	Birmingham.	Watkins, W. A.	London (W.).
Ward, W. R.	Birmingham.	Watkins, W. L.	Rock and Tenbury.
*Ward, W. W.	Swansea.	Watkins, W. M.	Makerfield.

N.U.T. WAR RECORD

Name.	Association.
Watkins, W. M.	Aberdare.
Watkinson, L. E.	Leeds.
Watkis, E. P.	Wolverhampton.
Watkis, F. B.	Waveney Valley.
Watling, H.	Sheffield.
Watling, W. T.	Norwich.
Watmough, F. T.	Hull.
Watmough, H. C.	Hindley.
Watmough, J. C.	South Shields.
Watmough, L.	Hull.
Watson, —.	Derby.
Watson, —.	London (W.).
Watson, A.	Wallsend.
Watson, A.	Southwark.
Watson, A. E.	Swadlincote.
Watson, A. N.	East Cleveland.
Watson, C.	Manchester.
Watson, C.	Itchen.
Watson, C. E.	East Cleveland.
Watson, C. H.	Leicester.
Watson, E.	Manchester.
Watson, E. G.	Newcastle-on-Tyne.
Watson, E. M.	Teign and Dart.
Watson, F...	Halifax.
Watson, F. F.	Tynemouth.
Watson, F. J.	Doncaster.
Watson, G.	Watford.
Watson, G.	Manchester.
Watson, G.	Kingston and Surbiton.
Watson, G. E.	Chatham, etc.
Watson, G. F.	Easington.
Watson, G. P.	Chester-le-Street.
Watson, H.	Liverpool.
*Watson, H.	Liverpool.
Watson, H.	Rotherham.
Watson, (Miss) I.	Hexham, etc.
Watson, J.	Manchester.
Watson, (Miss) J. A.	West Ham.
Watson, J. E.	Hull.
Watson, J. K.	Manchester.
Watson, J. P.	Castleford, etc.
Watson, J. W.	Swindon.
Watson, L. G.	Cumberland (W.).
Watson, M.	Hull.
Watson, (Miss) N.	East Ham.
Watson, N.	Nelson, Colne, etc.
Watson, R.	Market Rasen.
*Watson, R.	Cambridge Borough.
Watson, R. E.	Bradford.
Watson, R. W.	Hackney.
Watson, S. J.	Hackney.
Watson, S. T.	London (W.).
Watson, T...	Hexham, etc.
Watson, T. C.	Liverpool.
Watson, V. J.	Chiswick.
Watson, W.	Durham.
Watson, W. F.	Canterbury.
Watson, W. P.	West Lambeth.
*Watt, G. R.	Woolwich.
Watterson, H. R.	Anglesey.
Watterson, J.	Manchester.
Wattison, D.	Staffordshire (N.).
Watton, W.	Horsham, etc.
Watts, —.	London (N.W.).
Watts, —.	West Ham.
Watts, B. J.	West Lambeth.
Watts, C.	Gillingham.
Watts, P. F.	London (W.).
Watts, P. H.	Portsmouth.
Watts, R. K.	Llanelly.
Watts, W. J.	Llanelly.
Waud, E. H.	Chester-le-Street.
Way, F. S.	Caerphilly.
Way, H. E.	West Lambeth.
Wayles, J.	Walsall.
Waymark, —.	Willesden.
Waymouth, G. J.	Horncastle.
Waywell, F.	Altrincham.
Wealthall, —.	Castleford, etc.
Wear, W.	Liverpool.
Wearn, C. J.	Isle of Wight.
Weatherby, C. A.	London (N.W.)
Weatherdon, H. B.	Walthamstow.
Weatherill, G. A.	Market Rasen.
Weatherley, F. H.	Harrow.
Weatherley, W. J.	Blaydon.
Weatherstone, B.	Cockermouth.
*Weaver, A. A.	Barnes and Mortlake.
Weaver, F...	Barnes and Mortlake.
Weaver, F. E.	Staffordshire (N.).
Weaver, J. E.	Dartford.
Weaver, J. R.	Kiveton Park.
Weaver, W. G.	Plymouth.
Weaver, W. R.	Teign and Dart.
Weaving, —.	Cheltenham.
Webb, —.	Bury St. Edmunds.
Webb, —.	East Lambeth.
Webb, —.	Salford.
Webb, A. E.	Bristol.
Webb, A. C.	Hackney.
Webb, A. H.	Birmingham.
Webb, A. H. W.	West Ham.
Webb, B. S.	Glamorgan (Mid).
*Webb, C.	Newbury.
Webb, C. S.	Harrow.
Webb, F.	Birmingham.
Webb, H.	East Ham.
Webb, J.	Coseley.
Webb, J. E.	Leyton.
Webb, J. G.	Pembrokeshire (Mid).
Webb, J. T. P.	Bristol.
Webb, J. W.	Bristol.
Webb, L.	Dudley.
Webb, P. C.	Stretford.
Webb, R. P.	Brighouse.
Webb, S. C.	Pembrokeshire (S.).
Webb, T. W.	Derbyshire (E.).
Webb, W.	Dudley.
Webb, W. A. B.	Banbury.
Webbe, W...	West Ham.
Webber, C. J.	Surrey (N.W.).
Webber, E. C.	East Lambeth.
Webber, J.	Bromley.
Webber, J.	Hartlepools.
Webber, P.	London (W.).
Webber, P. E.	Hackney.
Webber, T.	Norwich.
Weber, W. C.	London (E.).
Webley, C. E.	Erith.
Webster, —.	Preston Borough.
Webster, —.	Doncaster.
Webster, A. E.	Reading.
Webster, E.	Bootle.
Webster, F. H.	Sheffield.
Webster, H. G.	Deptford and Greenwich.
Webster, J.	Mexborough.
Webster, J. H.	Makerfield.
Wedd, W. F.	Birmingham.

TEACHERS WHO JOINED THE FORCES

Name.	Association.
Weddall, H. W.	Norfolk (W.).
Weder, C.	Surrey (S.E.).
Wedge, J. L.	Finsbury etc.
*Wedgwood, J.	Cumberland (W.).
Wedlake, F. H.	Liverpool.
Weedon, E.	Middlesbrough.
Weedy, W. T.	Southampton.
Weeks, —.	Reading.
Weightman, A.	Leicester.
Weights, J. H.	Liverpool.
Welch, A. F. C.	London (E.).
Welch, G. H.	Sunderland.
Welch, J.	Gateshead.
Welch, J.	Sunderland.
Welch, J. G.	Folkestone.
*Welch, T.	Spennymoor.
Welchman, N. T.	Wiltshire (W.).
Welford, A. A.	Surrey (N.W.).
Welling, L. G.	Dewsbury etc.
Wellington, J.	Gloucester.
Wells, F.	Dartford.
Wells, G. H.	Southwark.
Wells, G. J.	Tottenham etc.
Welsh, —.	West Stanley.
Welsh, E.	Stockton-on-Tees.
Welsh, J. S.	Liverpool.
Welton, C. H.	Ealing.
Welton, (Miss) L.	Sunderland.
Welton, W. N.	Maidstone.
Wenham, F. C.	Barrow-in-Furness.
Went, A. G.	Walthamstow.
Werner, F. O.	Hull.
Werry, H. S.	Vale of Derwent.
Wesché, H. C.	East Lambeth.
Wescombe, W. F.	Somerset (N.).
West, —.	Leyton.
West, A.	Bridgwater.
West, C. E.	West Lambeth.
West, F. E.	Teddington.
West, F. R. McC.	Worcester City.
West, G.	Brentford.
West, G. A.	Hull.
West, H.	East Lambeth.
West, H. D.	Leicestershire (Mid).
West, J.	Scarborough.
West, J. W.	Lewisham.
West, R. P. H.	Stroud.
West, W.	Brentford.
West, W.	Southampton.
West, W. J.	Swansea.
West, W. N.	Erith.
Westaway, L. J.	London (N.W.).
Westcott, S. H.	Plymouth.
Westcott, W. H.	London (N.W.).
Western, (Miss) H.	Birmingham.
Western, R.	Halifax.
Westgate, F.	Great Yarmouth.
Westmore, W.	Guildford.
Westoby, E.	Goole.
Weston, —.	East Lambeth.
Weston, C. E.	London (E.).
Weston, C. R.	Leicestershire (Mid).
Weston, E. P.	Newcastle-on-Tyne.
Weston, G. M.	Northampton.
Weston, H. E.	Birmingham.
Weston, L. C.	West Lambeth.
Weston, T.	Middlesbrough.
Weston, W.	Willesden.
Weston, W. J.	Waterloo.
Weston, W. P.	Erewash Valley, etc.
Westwell, (Miss)	Warrington.
Westwell, —.	Warrington.
Westwood, —.	Derby.
Westwood, G.	Worcester City.
Westwood, T.	Barrow-in-Furness.
Westwood, W. A.	Malvern, etc.
Westwood, W. I.	Birmingham.
Weth, W. D.	Kent (W.).
Wevell, —.	Bridgwater.
Weymouth, P. E.	Isle of Thanet.
Whale, E.	Cornwall (Mid).
Whale, G.	Kent (W.).
Whalley, G.	Chorley.
Whalley, H.	Darlington.
Whatley, A.	East Lambeth.
Whatley, F. G.	Bishop's Waltham.
Whatmore, L. W.	Birmingham.
Wharton, —.	Buxton.
Whattler, A. G.	Chatham, etc.
Wheale, T.	Wolverhampton.
Whealing, D.	Manchester.
Wheatcroft, F. G.	West Lambeth.
Wheatley, H.	Dewsbury, etc.
Wheatley, H.	Grimsby.
Wheatley, T.	Bradford.
Wheatley, T. P.	Driffield, etc.
Wheeldon, A.	Barnsley.
Wheeldon, T.	Leicestershire (Mid).
Wheeldon, T.	Barnsley.
Wheeler, —.	Luton.
Wheeler, A.	Lewisham.
Wheeler, A. T.	Plymouth.
Wheeler, E. J.	Oxford.
Wheeler, F. G.	Deptford and Greenwich.
Wheeler, G.	Cheltenham.
Wheeler, H. G.	Twickenham, etc.
Wheeler, H. H.	Maidstone.
Wheeler, J.	Surrey (N.W.).
Wheeler, L. E.	Glamorgan (Mid).
Wheeler, W.	Woolwich.
Wheeler, W. S.	Coventry.
Wheelhouse, T. W.	Leeds.
Whelan, J.	Woolwich.
Wheldon, R.	Bishop Auckland.
Whetton, —.	Hereford.
While, A. C.	South Shields.
While, T. S.	Newcastle-on-Tyne.
Whipp, W. H.	Manchester.
Whitbourn, W. H.	Brighton, etc.
Whitbread, H.	West Lambeth.
Whitby, —.	Peterborough.
White, —.	Hebburn.
White, A.	Hackney.
White, A.	Nottingham.
White, A.	Sheffield.
White, A. T.	Plymouth.
White, B. C.	Rotherham.
White, C.	Deptford and Greenwich.
White, C.	Ipswich.
White, C.	Manchester.
White, C. T.	Walsall.
White, E.	Cornwall (E.).
White, E.	London N.W.).
White, F.	Isle of Thanet.
White, F. R.	Wellingborough.
White, F. W.	Staines.
White, G. H. S.	Isle of Wight.
White, G. W.	Melton Mowbray.

N.U.T. WAR RECORD

Name.	Association.
White, H.	Blackpool.
White, H. B.	Wirral.
White, H. C.	East Ham.
*White, H. C.	Hastings.
White, H. G.	Ludlow.
White, J.	Furness.
White, J.	Derbyshire (E.).
White, J. A. C.	Avon Valley.
White, J. D.	Chester-le-Street.
White, J. F.	Deptford and Greenwich.
White, J. H.	Reading.
White, L. J. B.	Rhondda, etc.
White, M.	Newcastle-on-Tyne.
White, N. E.	Walsall.
White, O.	Woolwich.
White, O.	Erith.
White, P.	Reading.
White, R.	Easington, etc.
*White, R. H.	Carnarvonshire (S.).
White, R. L.	Bishop Auckland.
White, S. H.	Erith.
White, W.	Richmond (Surrey).
White, W.	Belper and Crich.
White, W. C.	Basingstoke.
White, W. E.	Nottingham.
White, W. F.	Staines.
White, W. G.	Liverpool.
White, W. G.	Kingston and Surbiton.
White, W. G. F.	Staines.
White, W. H. S.	Stroud.
White, W. S. G.	Southampton.
Whitear, J. C.	Teign and Dart.
Whitehead, C. A.	Oldham.
Whitehead, D. H.	Bootle.
Whitehead, F.	Northwich.
Whitehead, G.	Knutsford.
Whitehead, H.	Bolton Borough.
Whitehead, H.	Rotherham.
Whitehead, J. G.	South Shields.
Whitehead, N.	West Lambeth.
Whitehead, J. T.	Sheffield.
Whitehead, T. W.	Bradford.
Whitehead, W. L.	Bolton District.
Whitehorn, E.	Finsbury, etc.
Whitehouse, —.	St. Helens.
Whitehouse, A. C.	Winchester.
Whitehouse, H.	Tipton.
*Whitehouse, J.	Warrington.
Whitehouse, J. C.	Dudley.
Whitehouse, W. S.	Hartlepools.
Whitehurst, A. P.	Staffordshire N.).
Whitelegg, H.	Smethwick.
Whiteley, F. J.	Hackney.
Whiteley, H. P.	Elland.
Whiteley, L. G.	Blackburn.
Whiteley, W. L.	Canterbury.
Whiteman, H.	East Lambeth.
Whiteside, H.	St. Helens.
Whitfield, F.	Portsmouth.
Whitfield, G. A.	Warrington.
Whitfield, R.	South Shields.
Whitfield, T.	Widnes.
Witham, W.	Carlisle.
Whiting, C. E.	Birmingham.
Whiting, W. E.	Ampthill, etc.
Whitley, C. L.	Wimbledon.
Whitlock, A. E.	London (W.).
*Whitmarsh, A. J.	Weald of Kent.
Whitmarsh, P. H.	Plymouth.

Name.	Association.
Whitmore, —.	Ipswich.
Whitmore. A.	Redditch.
Whitnall, E. J.	Manchester.
Whitney, A.	Burnley.
Whitney, C. W.	Brentford.
Whitney, G. R.	Wellingborough.
Whitney, T.	Merthyr Tydfil.
Whittaker, —.	Nelson, Colne, etc.
Whittaker, A.	Todmorden.
Whittaker, B.	Birmingham.
Whittaker, G.	Manchester.
Whittaker, G. E.	Hull.
Whittaker, H.	Vale of Derwent.
Whittaker, H.	Northumberland (S.).
Whittaker, J.	Bradford.
Whittaker, J. H.	Birmingham.
Whittaker, L. T.	Hull.
Whittaker, R. C.	Swansea.
Whittaker, T.	Tottenham, etc.
Whittaker, W.	Worsley, etc.
Whittaker, W. H.	Middlesbrough.
Whittaker, W. S.	Launceston.
Whittemore, —.	Birmingham.
Whittey, E. W. M.	Ilford.
Whitting, S. L.	Chichester.
Whittingham, A. W.	Reading.
Whittingham, F.	Birmingham.
Whittingham, J. F.	Hendon.
Whittingham, S. H. B.	Manchester.
Whittingstall, J.	Sheffield.
Whittle, A.	St. Helens.
Whittle, E. T.	Liverpool.
Whittles, J. S.	Bristol.
*Whittles, W.	Birmingham.
Whittlesey, A.	Harwich.
Whittlestone, H.	Canterbury.
Whitwam, H.	Huddersfield.
Whitwam, J. H.	Huddersfield.
Whitwell, H.	Leicester.
Whitworth, E. C.	Hornsey.
Whitworth, F. W.	Birmingham.
Wholey, F.	Finsbury, etc.
Wholley, C. M. G.	Sheffield.
Whone, C.	Keighley.
Whyman, J. W.	Bolton Borough.
Wibberley, —.	Derby.
Wibley, T. J.	Doncaster.
Wickens, G.	West Ham.
Wickes, A.	Surrey (N.W.).
Wicks, J. D.	Coventry.
Wicks, W. J.	Finsbury, etc.
Widdess, D. C.	Bradford.
Widdicombe. H. W.	Hackney.
Widgery, S. W.	Canterbury.
Widman, G. A.	Bristol.
Wiener, L.	South Shields.
Wigg, F. S.	Norfolk (N.W.).
Wiggans, R.	Manchester.
Wiggins, —.	East Ham.
Wigglesworth, G.	Barnsley.
Wigham, W. S.	Blaydon.
Wight, H. R.	Newcastle-on-Tyne.
Wightman, —.	East Lambeth.
Wightman, C. N.	Bridgnorth.
Wightman, E. W.	London (E.).
*Wightman, J.	Merthyr Tydfil.
Wightman, W. J.	Jarrow.
Wigley, D. E.	Aberdare.

TEACHERS WHO JOINED THE FORCES

NAME	ASSOCIATION	NAME	ASSOCIATION
Wigley, H. J.	Stafford.	**Wilkinson, W. A.**	Hackney.
*Wignall, A.	Hyde.	Wilkinson, W. D.	Essex (N.).
Wigston, J.	Carlisle.	**Wilks, O.**	Walsall.
Wilbraham, G. W.	Beverley.	Wilman, S.	Sheffield.
Wilcock, —.	St. Helens.	Willdig, H. W.	Willenhall.
Wilcock, F. W.	Burnley.	Willdig, J. H. M.	Saddleworth.
Wilcock, H. A.	Manchester.	Wille, —.	Deptford and Greenwich.
Wilcock, J. E.	Manchester.	Willes, —.	Warwick.
Wilcock, T.	Lancaster.	Willett, C. W.	Staffordshire (N.).
Wilcox, —.	Northampton.	Willett, R.	East Lambeth.
Wilcox, B.	Deptford and Greenwich.	Willetts, T. J.	Birmingham.
Wilcox, D. W.	Radstock.	Williams, A.	Carnarvon.
Wilcox, H.	Bristol.	Williams, A.	Portsmouth.
Wilcox, R. H.	London (N.W.).	Williams, A.	Worsley, etc.
Wild, F.	Burnley.	Williams, A.	Devon (N.).
Wild, F.	Forest of Dean.	**Williams, A.**	Ogmore, etc.
Wild, H.	Ashton-under-Lyne.	Williams, A.	Ogmore, etc.
Wild, (Miss) J. M.	Liverpool.	Williams, A.	Abertillery.
Wild, L.	London (N.W.).	Williams, A. C.	Glamorgan (Mid).
Wilde, F. E.	Southampton.	Williams, A. G.	Pembrokeshire (S.).
Wilde, T.	Gateshead.	Williams, A. H.	Stourbridge.
Wilde, W. J.	Leeds.	Williams, A. T.	Tregedar.
Wilding, T. W.	Birmingham.	Williams, B. E.	Welshpool.
Wildman, P. H.	Leicester.	Williams, B. G.	Carmarthen.
Wilford, A. E.	Kettering.	Williams, C.	London (W.).
Wilford, C.	Hereford.	Williams, C. E.	Acton.
Wilford, G.	Sheffield.	Williams, C. J. M.	Isle of Wight.
Wilford, C. W.	Carmarthen.	Williams, C. R.	London (N.W.).
Wilkes, A. H.	Birmingham.	Williams, C. S.	Westminster.
Wilkes, L.	Bury.	Williams, C. T.	Rhondda, etc.
Wilkins, —.	Luton.	Williams, D.	Caerphilly.
Wilkins, B. H.	West Lambeth.	Williams, D.	Rhondda, etc.
Wilkins, G. A.	Liverpool.	Williams, D.	Aberdare.
Wilkins, H.	Hackney.	Williams, D.	Merthyr Tydfil.
Wilkins, L. G.	Birmingham.	Williams, D.	Llandudno.
Wilkins, W. A.	St. Albans.	Williams, D.	Glamorgan (Mid).
Wilkinson, —.	Birmingham.	**Williams, D. J.**	Brynmawr.
Wilkinson, —.	Bromley.	Williams, D. J.	Rhondda, etc.
Wilkinson, A.	Gateshead.	**Williams, D. J.**	East Lambeth.
Wilkinson, A.	Hull.	Williams, D. J.	Glamorgan (W.).
Wilkinson, A.	Liverpool.	Williams, D. S.	Rhondda etc.
Wilkinson, A. C.	Stockport.	Williams, D. T.	Merthyr Tydfil.
Wilkinson, A. L.	Dewsbury, etc.	Williams, D. V.	Cwmtawe.
Wilkinson, B.	Birmingham.	**Williams, E.**	Rhondda, etc.
Wilkinson, E.	Preston District.	Williams, E.	Gelligaer.
Wilkinson, F.	Bishop Auckland.	Williams, E.	Portsmouth.
Wilkinson, F.	Nottingham.	Williams, E.	Llandudno.
Wilkinson, G. A.	Sunderland.	Williams, E.	Bexhill.
Wilkinson, G. E.	Leeds.	Williams, E.	Stretford.
Wilkinson, H.	Hull.	**Williams, E. D.**	Tredegar.
Wilkinson, H.	Blackburn.	Williams, E. C.	Barnes and Mortlake.
Wilkinson, H. R.	Spennymoor.	Williams, E. D.	Tredegar.
Wilkinson, J.	Durham.	Williams, E. E.	Richmond (Surrey).
Wilkinson, J.	Blackpool.	Williams, E. G.	Nantwich.
Wilkinson, J.	Mexborough.	Williams, E. H.	Hendon.
Wilkinson, J. H.	Hull.	Williams, E. J. H.	Flint County.
Wilkinson, J. H.	Sunderland.	**Williams, E. R.**	Festiniog.
Wilkinson, J. J.	Birmingham.	Williams, E. T.	Birkenhead.
Wilkinson, J. P.	Maidstone.	Williams, E. W.	Rhondda, etc.
Wilkinson, J. W.	Chester-le-Street.	Williams, E. W.	Malton.
Wilkinson, O. G.	Wakefield.	Williams, F.	Portsmouth.
Wilkinson, P.	Huddersfield.	Williams, F.	Carnarvon.
Wilkinson, R.	North Cleveland.	Williams, F. G.	Yoxford.
Wilkinson, R.	East Lambeth.	Williams, F. H.	Sheffield.
Wilkinson, R. E.	Walthamstow.	Williams, F. J.	Deptford and Greenwich.
Wilkinson, R. J.	Newcastle-on-Tyne.	Williams, F. J.	Manchester.
Wilkinson, T.	Cockermouth.	Williams, Glyn	Flint County.
Wilkinson, V. A. S.	Keighley.	Williams, G.	Bolton District.
Wilkinson, W.	Leeds.	Williams, G.	Manchester.

201

N.U.T. WAR RECORD

Name.	Association.
Williams, G.	Maesteg.
Williams, Gomer	Flint County.
Williams, G. O.	Menai.
Williams, G. R. S.	Leamington.
Williams, H.	Festiniog.
Williams, H.	Finsbury, etc.
Williams, H.	Aberdare.
Williams, H.	Anglesey.
Williams, H.	Chesham.
Williams, H.	Northwich.
Williams, H.	Birmingham.
*Williams, H.	Erith.
Williams, H.	Festiniog.
Williams, H. A.	Bristol.
Williams, H. H.	Swindon.
Williams, H. H.	London (N.W.).
Williams, H. J.	Pontypool.
*Williams, H. T.	Dover.
Williams, I.	Ogmore, etc.
Williams, J.	Ogmore, etc.
Williams, J.	Swansea.
Williams, J.	Finsbury, etc.
Williams, J.	Bootle.
Williams, J.	Rhondda, etc.
Williams, J. A.	Glamorgan (W.).
Williams, J. A.	Rhondda, etc.
Williams, J. C.	Gelligaer.
Williams, J. E.	Caerphilly.
Williams, J. E.	Merthyr Tydfil.
Williams, J. E.	Gelligaer.
Williams, J. E.	Rhondda, etc.
Williams, J. G.	Cardiganshire (N.).
Williams, J. G.	Liverpool.
Williams, J. H.	Newport (Mon.).
Williams, J. H.	Wrexham.
Williams, J. H.	Blaydon.
Williams, J. L.	Liverpool.
Williams, J. M.	Barry.
Williams, J. P.	Chepstow.
Williams, J. P.	East Ham.
Williams, J. R.	Caerphilly.
Williams, J. S.	Liverpool.
Williams, J. T.	Rhondda, etc.
Williams, J. T.	Willenhall.
Williams, J. W. H.	Dartford.
Williams, L.	Portsmouth.
Williams, L.	Merthyr Tydfil.
Williams, L.	Colwyn Bay.
Williams, L. J.	Hereford.
Williams, M. P.	Festiniog.
Williams, M. T.	Llangollen.
Williams, N.	Tipton.
Williams, N. R.	Willesden.
Williams, O.	Cardiff.
Williams, O. G.	Birmingham.
Williams, R.	Tredegar.
Williams, R.	Surrey (N.W.).
Williams, R.	Cowbridge, etc.
Williams, R.	Norwich.
Williams, R. A.	West Lambeth.
Williams, R. C.	Hyde.
Williams, R. H.	Manchester.
Williams, R. T.	Glamorgan (Mid).
Williams, S.	Ilford.
Williams, S.	Rhondda, etc.
Williams, S.	Surrey (N.W.).
Williams, S. A.	London (W.).
Williams, S. M.	East Lambeth.
Williams, T.	Finsbury, etc.
Williams, T.	Bromley.
Williams, T.	Glamorgan (W.).
Williams, T.	Cardiff.
Williams, T.	Maesteg.
Williams, T.	Birkenhead.
Williams, T. D.	Merthyr Tydfil.
Williams, T. G.	Bootle.
Williams, T. H.	Cornwall (W.).
Williams, T. H.	Isle of Ely.
Williams, T. J.	Rhondda, etc.
Williams, T. J.	Merthyr Tydfil.
Williams, T. J.	Portsmouth.
Williams, T. J.	Aberdare.
Williams, T. R.	Gelligaer.
Williams, T. S.	Tredegar.
Williams, T. S.	Maldon.
Williams, T. T.	Nantyglo.
Williams, W.	Festiniog.
Williams, W.	Ebbw Vale.
Williams, W.	Aberdare.
Williams, W.	Glamorgan (Mid).
Williams, W. A.	Woolwich.
Williams, W. E.	Swansea.
Williams, W. G.	Nottingham.
Williams, W. I.	Rhondda, etc.
Williams, W. J.	Carnarvon.
Williams, W. J.	Rhondda, etc.
Williams, W. J.	Rhondda, etc.
Williams, W. J.	Merthyr Tydfil.
Williams, W. J.	Sunderland.
Williams, W. L.	Maesteg.
Williams, W. P.	Lowestoft.
Williams, W. R.	Flint County.
Williams, W. T.	Llandudno.
Williams, W. W.	Rossendale.
Williams, Y.	Ogmore, etc.
Williamson, A.	Liverpool.
Williamson, A.	Woolwich.
Williamson, F. H.	Portsmouth.
Williamson, G.	Macclesfield District.
Williamson, H.	Sheffield.
Williamson, J.	Sheffield.
Williamson, J. V.	Leeds.
Williamson, R.	Dewsbury, etc.
Willimont, H. E.	Hackney.
Willing, E. J.	Exeter City.
Willingham, W.	Birmingham.
Willings, V.	Scarborough.
Wilington, H. S.	Walsall.
Willis, (Miss)	West Ham.
Willis, —.	Hastings.
Willis, —.	London (W.).
Willis, —.	West Ham.
Willis, A. W.	East Lambeth.
Willis, (Miss) D.	London (W.).
Willis, E. H.	Portsmouth.
Willis, H. F.	Leicester.
Willis, H. L.	Brentford.
Willis, O. P.	Birmingham.
Willis, R. G.	London (E.).
Willis, R. W.	Hendon.
Willis, T. W.	Tottenham, etc.
Willis, W. F. B.	West Lambeth.
Willmer, E.	Hornsey.
Willmer, R. A. P.	Hackney.
Willmore, E.	Gillingham.
Willott, H.	Manchester.
Willoughby, —.	Folkestone.
Wilis, W.	Willesden.

TEACHERS WHO JOINED THE FORCES

Name.	Association.
Willis, W. T.	Portsmouth.
Willshire, R.	Portsmouth.
Wilmut, F. S.	Southampton.
Wilsden, H.	Tunbridge Wells.
Wilson, —.	Darlington.
Wilson, A.	Sunderland.
Wilson, A.	Northumberland (E.).
Wilson, A. O.	Leeds.
Wilson, A. P.	Norwich.
Wilson, C.	Merthyr Tydfil.
Wilson, C. F.	West Lambeth.
Wilson, G. L.	Nottingham.
Wilson, C. O.	Sale.
Wilson, C. W.	Manchester.
Wilson, D.	Belper, etc.
*Wilson, D.	Sunderland.
Wilson, E.	Grimsby.
Wilson, F.	Nottingham.
Wilson, F.	Bradford.
Wilson, F. E.	East Ham.
Wilson, F. J.	Rochdale.
Wilson, G.	Newcastle-on-Tyne.
Wilson, G. E.	Walthamstow.
Wilson, G. F.	Manchester.
Wilson, G. H.	Sheffield.
Wilson, G. H.	Cumberland (W.).
Wilson, G. P.	Castleford, etc.
Wilson, G. R. A.	Caerphilly.
Wilson, G. T.	Manchester.
Wilson, G. V.	Birmingham.
Wilson, H.	Durham.
Wilson, H	Birmingham.
Wilson, H.	Walsall.
Wilson, H. B.	Doncaster.
Wilson, H. D.	Rotherham.
Wilson, H. M.	Mexborough.
Wilson, I. D.	Stockton-on-Tees.
Wilson, I. S.	Doncaster.
Wilson, J.	Northumberland (E.).
*Wilson, J.	Shipley.
*Wilson, J.	South Shields.
Wilson J.	Durham.
Wilson, J.	Guernsey.
Wilson, J. D.	Sunderland.
Wilson, J. H.	London (E.).
Wilson, J. S.	Durham.
Wilson, J. W.	Halifax.
Wilson, J. W. B.	Shipley.
Wilson, P. S.	Wallasey.
Wilson, P. T.	Swindon.
Wilson, R. E.	Liverpool.
Wilson, R. H.	Chester-le-Street.
Wilson, R. W.	East Ham.
Wilson, S.	Halifax.
Wilson, S.	Sunderland.
Wilson, S. C.	Tottenham, etc.
*Wilson, S. J.	Hyde.
Wilson, S. J.	Stockton-on-Tees.
Wilson, T. E. B.	Grimsby.
Wilson, T. F.	Preston Borough.
Wilson, T. N.	Carlisle.
Wilson, W.	Bishop Auckland.
Wilson, W.	Cockermouth.
Wilson, W.	Durham.
Wilson, W. J.	Whitehaven.
Wilton, B.	Mountain Ash.
Wilton, E. W.	Leeds.
Wilton, H.	West Lambeth.
Wiltshire, C. J.	Cardiff.
Wiltshire, G. H.	Aylesbury.
Wimbury, H.	Walsall.
Wimbush, B. G.	Willesden.
Wimpey, —.	Exeter City.
Winbury, W. W.	Pembrokeshire (S.).
Winbush, E T	Hackney.
Winch, J. A.	Enfield.
*Winchester, C. F.	Dartford.
Wind, F.	Gateshead.
Windass, A.	Nottingham.
Winder, H.	London (E.).
Windebank, V. N. J.	Horsham, etc.
*Windmill, J. W.	Brierley Hill, etc.
Windsor, E.	Burton-on-Trent.
Windsor, F. V.	Staffordshire (N.).
Windust, —.	Salisbury.
Winfield, T. K.	Leeds.
Wing, T. A.	New Forest.
Wingfield, H.	West Ham.
Wingrave, E. H.	Brighton, etc.
Winham, R. W.	Beverley.
Winn, G. E.	London (E.).
Winn, H. W.	Southwark.
Winn, J.	Barnard Castle.
Winn, L.	Southwark.
Winn, L. T.	Stockton-on-Tees.
Winn, N.	Stockton-on-Tees.
Winn, R.	Grimsby.
Winn, T.	Whitby.
Winnall, H.	Spalding, etc.
Wins, W. E.	Swansea.
Winspear, H.	Scarborough.
Winstanley, R. H.	Sunderland.
Winstanley, W.	Mexborough.
Winston, E.	Furness.
Winter, —.	Cheltenham.
Winter, J. O.	South Shields.
Winter, J. T.	Stockton-on-Tees.
Winter, S. B.	Liverpool.
Winter, T. R.	Portsmouth.
Winter, W.	Tynemouth.
Winterbotham, J.	Nottingham.
Winterburn, J. F.	Selby.
Winters, R.	Brighton, etc.
Winters, R. F. E.	Brighton, etc.
Winterton, J. M.	Brentford.
*Wintle, G. H.	Forest of Dean.
Winton, G.	Abercarn and District
Wisdom, A.	London (W.).
Wisdom, S. J.	Coventry.
Wise, E. L.	Dorset (W.).
Wise, F.	Walsall.
Wise, F. V.	Surrey (N.W.).
Wise, H. C.	Birmingham.
Wise, P. A.	Darlington.
Wiseman, —.	Birmingham.
Wiseman, A.	Barking.
Wiseman, A. J.	Uxbridge.
Wiseman, G. A.	Sunderland.
Wiseman, S.	Easington.
Wiseman, T. L.	Birmingham.
Witcomb, A.	Staffordshire (N.).
Witcombe, H. G.	Chipping Norton, etc.
Witcombe, S. F.	Deptford and Greenwich.
Witham, H.	Middlesbrough.
Witham, H.	Manchester.
Wittrick, H. D.	Hertford.
Witts, E. G.	Hornsey.
Witts, W.	West Lambeth.

N.U.T. WAR RECORD

Name.	Association.
Witty, E.	Hull.
Witty, H. W.	East Lambeth.
Witty, J. G.	Hull.
Woffenden, H.	Rothwell.
Wolfe, S. G.	Rugby.
Wolfendale, F.	Wigan.
Wolfenden, F.	Oldham.
Wolfenden, F.	Blackpool.
Wolfson, —.	East Lambeth.
Wolstencroft, J.	Bolton District.
Wolstenholme, L.	Manchester.
Wolton, F. W. G.	Doncaster.
Womack, F. W.	Manchester.
Womersley, Rev. W. E.	Wakefield.
Wood, —.	St. Helens.
Wood, A. E.	Woolwich.
Wood, A. G. J.	Sheffield.
Wood, A. H.	Southampton.
Wood, A. H. E.	East Ham.
Wood, A. J.	Walthamstow.
Wood, A. J.	London (E.).
Wood, B.	London (W.).
Wood, B.	East Lambeth.
Wood, C.	Huntingdonshire.
Wood, C. C.	Sheffield.
Wood, C. H.	Lincoln.
Wood, C. P.	Manchester.
Wood, C. W.	Middlesbrough.
*Wood, E.	Sheffield.
Wood, E. B.	Rochdale.
Wood, E. J.	Birmingham.
Wood, F.	Easington.
Wood, F.	London (N.W.)
Wood, F.	Oldham.
Wood, F. D.	Chippenham.
Wood, G.	York.
Wood, G. H.	West Lambeth.
Wood, H.	London (E.).
Wood, H.	Staffordshire (N.).
Wood, I.	Manchester.
Wood, J.	Bolton Borough.
Wood, J.	Teddington.
Wood, J.	Manchester.
Wood, J.	Liverpool.
Wood, J.	Dewsbury, etc.
Wood, J. M.	Cumberland (W.).
Wood, J. R.	Nottingham.
Wood, J. S.	Isle of Axholme.
Wood, M. J.	Worcester City.
Wood, R.	Rotherham.
Wood, R. F.	Doncaster.
Wood, R. G.	Chippenham.
Wood, R. J.	Bolton Borough.
Wood, R. J.	Stockport.
Wood, S.	Walsall.
Wood, S. A.	London (W.).
Wood, T. G.	Huddersfield.
Wood, W.	Hull.
Wood, W.	Nottingham.
Wood, W. J.	Acton.
Wood, W. T.	Woolwich.
Woodall, J. H.	Walthamstow.
Woodcock, —.	Preston Borough.
Woodcock, E. F.	Manchester.
*Woodcock, T.	Doncaster.
Woodgate, G.	Hackney.
Woodhall, H.	Smethwick.
Woodhead, A.	Huddersfield.

Name.	Association.
Woodhead, E. W.	Stourbridge.
Woodhead, H. G.	Sheffield.
Woodhead, J.	Bury.
Woodhouse, —.	Devon (N.).
Woodhouse, —.	Ealing.
Woodhouse, F. C.	East Lambeth.
Woodhouse, (Miss) M.	Wharfedale.
Woodhouse, M. L.	Manchester.
Woodhouse, S. J.	Walsall.
Woodin, —.	Ealing.
Wooding, A. E.	Lichfield.
Woodington, H. J.	Bristol.
Woodland, —.	Radstock.
Woodley, —.	Sittingbourne, etc.
Woodman, —.	West Ham.
Woodman, —.	Willesden.
Woodman, W. O.	Liverpool.
Woodroffe, W.	East Lambeth.
Woodrow, H.	Bournemouth.
Woods, B. J.	Nottinghamshire (W.).
Woods, C.	Lewisham.
Woods, E.	Hyndburn.
Woods, E. C.	Deptford and **Greenwich**.
Woods, E. J.	Finsbury, etc.
Woods, F. H.	Portsmouth.
Woods, F. H.	West Lambeth.
Woods, G.	Manchester.
Woods, J. H.	Leyton.
***Woods, J. W.**	Barnet.
Woods, P.	Norwich.
*Woods, Mrs. R.	Heathfield, etc.
Woods, T. E.	Bolton Borough.
Woods, W.	Wigan.
Woodward, A. H.	Doncaster.
Woodward, F.	Oxfordshire (W.).
Woodward, F. C.	Deptford and Greenwich.
Woodward, G. H.	West Bromwich.
Woodward, H.	Nottinghamshire (W.).
Woodward, J.	Bridgwater.
Woodward, J. L.	Hull.
Woodward, P.	West Bromwich, etc.
Woodward, W.	East Lambeth.
Woodward, W. R.	Isle of Ely.
Woolcock, H.	Brighton, etc.
Woolcock, H. G. R.	Plymouth.
Wooldridge, F.	Stourbridge.
Wooldridge, T. C.	Nelson, Colne, etc.
Wooley, G.	Birmingham.
Woolf, S.	Walthamstow.
Wolff, A. H.	London (E.).
Woollett, J. C.	East Lambeth.
Woolley (Miss)	Barry.
Woolley, S.	Woolwich.
Woollam, H. E.	Chester.
Woollen, S.	Bristol.
Woolmer, —.	Leicester.
Woolridge, J. C.	Watford.
Woolridge, W. H.	Birmingham.
Woolstencroft, J.	Wirral.
Woolven, D.	Liverpool.
Wootton, A. H.	Aylesbury.
Wootton, B. M.	Ampthill, etc.
Wootton, C.	Leicestershire (Mid).
Wootton, D.	Tipton.
Wootton, G. N.	Surrey (N.W.).
Wootton, R. W.	Gloucestershire (S.).
Wordingham, V. R.	Isle of Ely.

TEACHERS WHO JOINED THE FORCES

Name.	Association.
Wordsworth, (Miss) A. E.	Wrexham.
Workman, E.	Southgate.
Workman, G. J.	London (E.).
Worley, E. G.	Brentford.
Worner, P.	Finsbury, etc.
Worsley, A.	Manchester.
Worsley, E. F.	Enfield.
Worswick, J. E. J.	Manchester.
Worth, A. E.	Ludlow.
Worthing, R. C.	Birmingham.
Worthington, J. B.	Willesden.
Worthy, W. H.	Teign and Dart.
Wotton, A. E.	Finsbury, etc.
Wragg, C. W.	Sheffield.
Wragg, J. W.	Sheffield.
Wraith, H. J.	East Lambeth.
Wray, C. R.	Birmingham.
Wray, H.	Bishop Auckland.
Wray, W.	Chichester.
Wren, E. J.	Chippenham.
Wren, F.	West Lambeth.
Wren, H.	West Lambeth.
Wrenn, W. A. E.	Southampton.
Wriggleworth, F.	Dorking.
Wright, —.	Belper and Crich.
Wright, —.	Derby.
Wright, A.	Bury.
Wright, A.	Rotherham.
Wright, A. E.	Sunderland.
Wright, A. E.	Darlington.
Wright, C.	Wakefield.
Wright, C.	Finsbury, etc.
Wright, C. E.	Cornwall, (W.).
Wright, C. H.	Maidstone.
Wright, F.	Sheffield.
Wright, F.	York.
Wright, F. H.	Ashbourne, etc.
Wright, F. H.	Newcastle-on-Tyne.
Wright, F. W.	Birmingham.
Wright, G. H.	Brighton, etc.
Wright, G. H.	Nottingham.
Wright, G. W.	Birmingham.
Wright, H.	East Lambeth.
Wright, H.	Skipton.
Wright, H. G.	Hackney.
Wright, H. S.	Stockton-on-Tees.
Wright, H. W.	Chester.
Wright, J.	Newcastle-on-Tyne.
Wright, J.	Berkshire (N.).
Wright, J.	Southport.
Wright, J. C.	Liverpool.
Wright, J. H.	Aldershot.
Wright, J. H.	Birkenhead.
Wright, J. R.	Sheffield.
Wright, J. W.	Huddersfield.
Wright, J. W.	Leigh.
Wright, R. A.	Cambridge.
Wright, R. T.	Derbyshire (E.).
Wright, S.	Willenhall.
Wright, S.	Staffordshire (N.).
Wright, S.	Cheltenham.
Wright, S. A.	Northumberland (E.).
Wright, S. C.	Westminster.
Wright, S. H.	Huddersfield.
Wright, T.	Birmingham.
Wright, T.	Northumberland (E.).
Wright, T. B.	Sheffield.
*Wright, W.	Hartlepools.

Name.	Association.
Wright, W.	Northumberland (S.).
Wright, W.	Great Yarmouth.
Wright, W.	Gateshead.
Wright, W. C.	Radstock.
Wright, W. O.	Scarborough.
Wright, W. H.	Carnarvon.
Wright, W. J.	West Ham.
Wrightson, G.	Grimsby.
Wrigley, H. B.	York.
Wrigley, J.	Westminster.
Wrigley, R.	Crompton, etc.
Wroe, W. D.	Lincoln.
Wroot, E.	Hackney.
Wyatt, A.	Portsmouth.
Wyatt, J. C.	Teign and Dart.
Wyatt, W. J.	East Lambeth.
Wybrow, —.	Oxfordshire (S.).
Wych, J.	Manchester.
Wyles, S.	London (E.).
Wylie, W. S.	South Shields.
Wyness, W. G.	East Ham.
Wynn, F.	Beverley.
Wynn, H.	Spennymoor.
Wynn, P.	Shrewsbury.
Wynne, A. G.	Oldham.
Wynne, G. T. M.	Flint County.
Wynne, H.	Leeds.
Wynne, H.	Pocklington.
Wynne, J. A.	London (N.W.).
Wyse, J. W.	Teign and Dart.
Wyse, W. J.	West Lambeth.
Yabsley, R.	Cheltenham.
Yabsley, W. H.	Wimbledon.
Yalden, E. C.	Finsbury, etc.
Yale, F.	Liverpool.
Yarde, J. C.	Birmingham.
Yardy, E. G.	Isle of Ely.
Yardley, F.	Coventry.
Yardley, B. W.	Melton Mowbray.
Yarham, E. M.	West Lambeth.
Yarker, —.	Grantham.
Yarwood, —.	Willesden.
Yarwood, J.	Chester.
Yates, B.	Shrewsbury.
Yates, E.	Darwen.
Yates, J. H.	Chorley.
Yates, J. L.	Wolverhampton.
*Yates, W.	Ingleborough.
Yates, W. S.	Bodmin.
Yeadon, J.	Wharfedale.
Veal, R.	Hartlepools.
Yearsley, H. A.	Runcorn.
Yeaxlee, A. H.	Southgate.
Yelland, —.	Bromley.
Yendall, T. E.	Abercarn.
Yeoman, G.	Exeter City.
Yeoman, W. G.	East Cleveland.
Yeomans, —.	Spalding, etc.
Yeomans, R. J.	Stockton-on-Tees.
Yeomaus, S. C.	Loughborough.
York, A.	Walsall.
York, C.	Northampton.
Yorke, —.	Chester.
Yorke, A. G.	Lewisham.
Youd, F.	Runcorn.
Youhill, J. C.	Leeds.
Young, A.	Aylesbury.
Young, A.	New Forest.

N.U.T. WAR RECORD

Name.	Association.	Name.	Association.
Young, A. D.	Worthing.	Young, T.	Bromley.
Young, A. H.	Tottenham, etc.	Young, T. C.	Sunderland.
Young, C.	Woolwich.	Young, W.	Chadderton.
Young, D.	Jarrow.	Young, W. J.	Ilford.
Young, E.	Reigate.	*Youngs, A. L.	Tottenham, etc.
Young, F.	London (E.).	Youngs, C. W.	Preston District.
Young, F.	Hackney.	Youngs, P. R.	Basingstoke.
Young, F. B.	Bristol.	Youngs, W. H.	Peterborough.
Young, G. C.	Hackney.	Youngson, E.	Jarrow.
Young, G. W.	Hartlepools.		
Young, J.	Southampton.	Zaktrager, M.	London (E.).
*Young, J. W.	Northumberland (E.).	Zeffert, A.	London (E.).
Young, Miss M.A.E.	Cardiff.	Zetterstrom, J. N.	Merthyr Tydfil.
Young, S.	Aylesbury.		

NOTE.—With regard to the lists which are given in this book, one of the greatest difficulties in compiling them has been that of ascertaining which teachers were honoured for gallant services, and if in the records any names are omitted it is, we believe, due not to lack of inquiry and research, but to reluctance on the part of those honoured to give any details unless actually confronted with a definite request.

MEMBERS OF THE STAFF OF HAMILTON HOUSE WHO SERVED WITH THE FORCES.

NOTE.—The names of those killed in the war are printed in this type.

NATIONAL UNION OF TEACHERS.

NAME.	RANK.	REGIMENT.
Aird, A. W.	L.-Cpl.	London.
Allen, A. E.	Bombardier	R.G.A.
Barr, H. B.	Pte.	R. Fusiliers.
Bright, F.	Pte.	Northamptonshire.
Bull, F. E.	Cpl.	R.A.V.C.
Burns, A.	Cpl.	R. Fusiliers.
Clark, G. F.	Sgt.	Q.V.R.
Darvill, W. H.	Sgt.	R.F.A.
Dean, J. A.	Sgnlr.	R.N.V.R.
Fairbairn, T. F.	L.-Cpl.	Queen's Westminsters.
Goldstone, F. W.	Capt.	R.A.S.C. and General Staff.
Green, G. C.	Stoker	H.M.S. *Shannon*.
Heslop, S. F.	Cpl.	Middlesex.
Hunt, R.	Pte.	R. Fusiliers.
Kinch, A. T.	Cpl.	R. W. Yorks.
King, C. W.	Trooper	Herts Yeomanry.
Palmer, A.	Cpl.	Middlesex.
Payne, H. J.	Act. C.S.M.	W. Kent.
Powell, P. S.	Pte.	A.P.C.
Struebig, A. V.	Rifleman	London.
Tate, R. G.	Sgt.	The Rangers (T.).
Wardle, R. G.	Sgnlr.	H.M.S. *Mars*.
Young, E. D.	Pte.	B.R.C., attd. R.A.M.C.

TEACHERS' PROVIDENT SOCIETY.

Anderson, A. C.	Pte.	London Scottish.
Bailey, J.	Driver	R.A.S.C.
Byrne, C. (Roumanian Cross of Military Virtue).	Sgt.	Herts Yeomanry.
Bower, L. G.	C.Q.M.S.	Q.V.R.
Congdon, C. J.	Sgt.	B.R.C., attd. French Army.
Grieveson, L. W.	Pte.	R. W. Kent.
Gruner, A. H. C.	Cpl.	Middlesex.
Harvey, W. F.	Bombardier	R.F.A.
Hermitage, E.	Driver	R.F.A.
Johnson, W.	Sgt.	London.
Pointer, A. J.	2nd Lieut.	Middlesex.
Pope, A.	Sgt.	R. W. Kent.
Purton, F.	Cpl.	E. Surrey.
Robins, A. J.	Lieut.	City of London Yeomanry.
Sterling, H. H.	2nd Lieut.	M.G.C.
Talbot, W.	Pte.	S. Staffs.
Thomas, J. C.	Driver	R.A.S.C.
Whieldon, T.	Gnr.	R.G.A.
Williams, P. P. H.	Gnr.	R.F.A.
Wreford, J.	Pte.	Trench Mortar Battery.

BENEVOLENT AND ORPHAN COUNCIL.

Bennett, P.	Cpl.	London.
Giles, W. T.	Cpl.	Herts Yeomanry.
Hodgskin, A. E.	Pte.	Gloucester Hussars.
Keen, F.	Pte.	Middlesex.
Pritchard, F.	Rifleman	Queen's Westminster Rifles.